INTERVENTION WITH CHILDREN AND ADOLESCENTS

An Interdisciplinary Perspective

PAULA ALLEN-MEARES

University of Michigan

MARK W. FRASER

University of North Carolina at Chapel Hill

Boston   New York   San Francisco
Mexico City   Montreal   Toronto   London   Madrid   Munich   Paris
Hong Kong   Singapore   Tokyo   Cape Town   Sydney

Series Editor: *Patricia Quinlin*
Editor in Chief: *Karen Hanson*
Editorial Assistant: *Annemarie Kennedy*
Marketing Manager: *Taryn Wahlquist*
Editorial Production Service: *TKM Productions*
Manufacturing Buyer: *JoAnne Sweeney*
Cover Administrator: *Kristina Mose-Libon*
Electronic Composition: *Omegatype Typography, Inc.*

For related titles and support materials, visit our online catalog at www.ablongman.com.

Between the time Website information is gathered and published, some sites may have closed. Also, the transcription of URLs can result in typographical errors. The publisher would appreciate notification where these occur so that they may be corrected in subsequent editions.

Library of Congress Cataloging-in-Publication Data

Intervention with children and adolescents : an interdisciplinary perspective / [edited by]
   Paula Allen-Meares, Mark W. Fraser.
      p. cm.
   Includes bibliographical references and index.
   ISBN 0-205-34196-9
   1. Social work with children–United States. 2. Social work with teenagers–United
States. I. Allen-Meares, Paula. II. Fraser, Mark W.

   HV741.I64 2004
   362.7'0973–dc21

                                                                                                 2002043724

Printed in the United States of America

10 9 8 7 6   13 12 11 10 09

CONTENTS

ACKNOWLEDGMENTS

I would like to thank my colleagues at the University of Michigan for their invaluable assistance with this text. In the mid-90s, I published a text entitled *Social Work with Children and Adolescents*. The book was reviewed extensively by practitioners and researchers around the country. Due to the extensive feedback from these experts, as well as many of our colleagues at Michigan—representing psychology, social work, child development, education, and psychiatry—the book was reconceptualized to incorporate an interdisciplinary perspective. Given Mark Fraser's experise and knowledge on intervention with children and youth, I invited him to collaborate with me. Together, we worked on an outline for this new book, and distributed it to a broad group of scholars for their feedback. *Intervention with Children and Adolescents* draws its strength from the diverse group of scholars who lent their time and expertise to its review in the early stages.

FOREWORD

J. DAVID HAWKINS
University of Washington

In 1980, in research commissioned by the Office of Juvenile Justice and Delinquency Prevention, William Berleman (1980) reviewed all the delinquency prevention experiments that had been conducted in the United States to that point. He found 10 adequately controlled prevention experiments. Not one produced significant reductions in delinquency. At that time, we did not know how to prevent delinquency. We did not know how to prevent adolescent drug abuse. We did not know how to prevent unwanted teen pregnancies. We did not know how to prevent many of the health and behavior problems addressed in this book.

In the intervening two decades, prevention science has come of age. Founded on the basic premises of public health, many of the advances in prevention science in recent years have focused on reducing health and behavior problems in children and adolescents. In the past few years, the Substance Abuse and Mental Health Services Administration (SAMHSA), the U.S. Department of Education, the U.S. Surgeon General, the Center for the Study and Prevention of Violence, the Collaborative for Academic Social and Emotional Learning (CASEL), the Channing Bete Company, the National Institute on Drug Abuse, and others (CASEL, in press; Elliott, 1998; National Institute on Drug Abuse, National Institutes of Health, 1997; Posey, Wong, Catalano, Hawkins, & Dusenbury, 2000; Safe and Drug-Free Schools Program, 2001; SAMHSA, 2002; Surgeon General, 2001) have published lists of tested effective prevention and youth development policies, programs, and actions. These lists contain anywhere from 10 to 90 preventive interventions—interventions that have been tested and that work. This sea of change in knowledge regarding how to promote positive youth development and prevent health and behavior problems in young people has been built on our growing understanding of risk and protective factors for these problems and how they operate. As understanding of the predictors of youth outcomes has grown, it has been put to use in the design of interventions that have succeeded. Prevention scientists have proven that problems such as substance abuse, bullying, violence, and teen pregnancy can be prevented. Positive youth development has been empirically validated (Catalano, Berglund, Ryan, Lonczak, & Hawkins, 1999; National Research Council, Institute of Medicine, 2002).

Nevertheless, across the country, untested approaches are the norm in many education, juvenile justice, and human service organizations. The effectiveness of programs in actually preventing the problems they were designed to prevent has not been a standard by which we have judged our public expenditures or philanthropic contributions. As a result, preventive services are often first cut, viewed as a soft expense, rather than as a sound investment in the future.

This book will help to change this. It is a near encyclopedia of the current state of knowledge in prevention science applied to children and adolescents. It begins with reviews of cross-cutting issues affecting child development: risk and reduction exposure, gender similarities and differences, and poverty.

Later chapters of the book are organized by specific outcomes: schizophrenia, depression, suicide, school dropout, drug abuse, AIDS/STD, bullying, youth violence, and more. Each is of value in itself as a statement of the current state of scientific advance as related to that specific outcome. As such, individual chapters will be of utility for practitioners and policymakers in addition to researchers. Each chapter identifies the empirically validated risk and protective factors for a focal problem, and summarizes current knowledge regarding the effective prevention and/or treatment of the problem. Because of recent dramatic advances in knowledge in areas such as substance abuse and violence prevention, many of these chapters provide a strong scientific foundation for shifts in public and philanthropic investments toward effective preventive actions even before symptoms of problems emerge. In other areas, such as schizophrenia, knowledge of risk factors has advanced to the point that research-based approaches to prevention now appear plausible, though rigorous trials focused on preventing schizophrenia remain to be conducted. Thus, these chapters will help guide research, policy, and practice to promote healthy child and adolescent development and to prevent health, mental health, behavior, and achievement problems.

Clearly, unique predictors contribute to specific problems. Nevertheless, what is striking, as one reads the individual chapters here, is the degree to which many of the same risk and protective factors emerge again and again as predictors of diverse future problems. The contribution of poverty to a wide range of problems in child and adolescent development is an example so noteworthy that Chapter 6 is devoted entirely to this important risk factor. What is important about this chapter is that it focuses on a common shared risk factor for many negative outcomes and it investigates a range of interventions that could reduce the negative effects of poverty on all these outcomes and, ultimately, raise future generations out of poverty. We should increasingly organize our thinking and prevention policies this way. As a society, we need to consider how shared risk factors for a wide range of problems—factors such as poor family management practices or low commitment to schooling, sometimes called *engagement* or *connectedness*—can be addressed by effective developmental and preventive policies, programs, and actions. We should assess the effects of these interventions on a wide range of outcomes for which they are likely to have preventive benefits, given their shared predictors.

This book underscores the growing understanding that none of the child and adolescent problems addressed in this book is likely to be solved by individual professionals working alone, whether in education, mental health, public health, or juvenile justice. Chapter 2 demonstrates the fact that exposure to multiple risks, not some single noxious risk factor, dramatically increases the likelihood of a range of negative outcomes. This means that multiple risk factors must be addressed to reduce the likelihood of problems among those most likely to develop them. Multiple protective factors must be strengthened. These predictors exist in neighborhood, school, family, and peer contexts as well as in individuals, and have varying predictive strength at different developmental periods. Effective prevention and youth development systems ultimately will bring together all those concerned with the healthy development of children: parents, neighborhood residents, educators, public health workers, mental health workers, social service workers, law enforcement and justice workers, and civic, business, and religious leaders. They will collaborate to identify elevated risks and protection gaps faced by their young people. They will address these with effective interventions implemented by those in the best position to do so with the participation of those needed to ensure success. They will monitor risk and protection levels as well as outcomes over time, in the youth population, to ensure that their work is producing the desired outcomes for children. This book provides the foundation to guide such efforts.

Although primarily focused on the prevention of a range of health, mental health, behavior, and achievement problems, the chapters of this text demonstrate that building strengths and protective factors in neighborhoods, families, schools, and individuals is an important part of creating public health. Both the reduction of risk and the promotion of strengths and protective factors are necessary to ensure the healthy development of children.

REFERENCES

Berleman, W. C. (1980). *Reports of the National Juvenile Justice Assessment Centers. Juvenile delinquency prevention experiments: A review and analysis.* Washington, DC: U.S. Department of Justice, Law Enforcement Assistance Administration, Office of Juvenile Justice and Delinquency Prevention.

Catalano, R. F., Berglund, M. L., Ryan, J. A. M., Lonczak, H. S., & Hawkins, J. D. (1999). *Positive youth development in the United States. Research findings on evaluations of the positive youth development programs.* Report to the U.S. Department of Health and Human Services, Office of the Assistant Secretary for Planning and Evaluation and National Institute for Child Health and Human Development. Seattle: Social Development Research Group, University of Washington School of Social Work.

Collaborative for Academic Social and Emotional Learning (CASEL). (in press). *Safe and sound. An educational leader's guide to evidence-based social and emotional learning programs.* Chicago: Department of Psychology, University of Illinois at Chicago.

Elliott, D. S. (1998). *Blueprints for violence prevention.* Boulder: Center for the Study and Prevention of Violence, Institute of Behavioral Science, University of Colorado at Boulder.

National Institute on Drug Abuse, National Institutes of Health. (1997). *Preventing drug use among children and adolescents: A research-based guide.* (National Institutes of Health Publication Number 97-4212). Bethesda, MD: National Institutes of Health.

National Research Council, Institute of Medicine. (2002). *Community programs to promote youth development.* Committee on Community-Level Programs for Youth. Jacquelynne Eccles & Jennifer Gootman (Eds.). Board on Children Youth and Families, Division of Behavioral and Social Sciences and Education. Washington, DC: National Academy Press.

Posey, R., Wong, S., Catalano, R. F., Hawkins, J. D., & Dusenbury, L. (2000). *Communities That Care prevention strategies: A research guide to what works.* Seattle: Developmental Research and Programs.

Safe and Drug-Free Schools Program. (2001). *Safe, disciplined, and drug free schools expert panel.* U.S. Department of Education. Retrieved September 17, 2002, from the World Wide Web: http://www.ed.gov/offices/OERI/ORAD/KAD/expert_panel/drug-free.html.

Substance Abuse and Mental Health Services Administration. (2002). *SAMSHA model programs. Effective substance abuse and mental health programs for every community.* U.S. Department of Health and Human Services, Substance Abuse and Mental Health Services Administration, Center for Substance Abuse Prevention. Retrieved September 17, 2002, from the World Wide Web: http://www.samhsa.gov/center/csap/modelprograms/default.cfm.

Surgeon General. (2001). *Youth violence: A report of the surgeon general.* Washington, DC: Department of Health and Human Services, U.S. Public Health Service.

EDITORS

Paula Allen-Meares is Dean and Norma Radin Collegiate Professor of Social Work at the University of Michigan School of Social Work. Her research interests include the tasks and functions of social workers employed in educational settings; psychopathology in children, adolescents, and families; adolescent sexuality; premature parenthood; and various aspects of social work practice. She is a University of Michigan Fellow and principal investigator of numerous grants/projects.

Mark W. Fraser is the John A. Tate Distinguished Professor for Children in Need at the University of North Carolina School of Social Work. His professional interests include children and families at risk; substance abuse and other forms of antisocial behavior; and research methods and training. The principal investigator of a number of research projects, his work has focused on developing family- and school-based interventions for children at risk of drug abuse and delinquency.

Ron Avi Astor is an Associate Professor of Social Work and Education at the University of Michigan. His work centers on children's understanding of violence and school violence interventions. He has won numerous awards, including a Senior Scholar Fulbright Fellowship, National Academy of Education/Spencer Fellowship, and a H. F. Guggenheim Fellowship.

Tamara Atkinson received her M.S.W. from the University of North Carolina at Chapel Hill. She is currently working on a research project at the Center for Child and Family Health investigating the effects of community violence on children who have already sustained trauma from physical and/or sexual abuse.

Oscar A. Barbarin is Distinguished Professor in the University of North Carolina's School of Social Work and a Fellow of the Frank Porter Graham Child Development Center. He is involved in a longitudinal study of the social and emotional development of South African children, and has recently published a book entitled *Mandela's Children* that describes the effects of poverty, violence, and family life on South African children from birth to age 5.

Rami Benbenishty is a Professor of Social Work at Hebrew University of Jerusalem. He is a leading international expert on issues of school violence. He is currently the principal investigator of one of the largest school violence studies conducted in any country to date, exploring how different forms of violence are manifested in different cultures and in different school contexts.

Roslyn B. Binford is a doctoral candidate in the Clinical Science and Psychopathology Research Training Program at the University of Minnesota. She provides individual and group psychotherapy to adolescents and adults at The Emily Program, an outpatient eating disorders treatment facility in St. Paul, Minnesota.

Gilbert J. Botvin is a Professor in both the Department of Public Health and the Department of Psychiatry at Cornell University Medical College, and is the Director of Cornell's Institute for Prevention Research. He is widely recognized as an expert in the field of tobacco, alcohol, and drug abuse prevention.

Jeanne Brooks-Gunn is a Professor of Child Development and Education at Teachers College, Columbia University. She is the first Director of the Center for Children and Family at Teachers College. Brooks-Gunn specializes in policy-oriented research focusing on family and community influences on the development of children, youth, and families.

Richard F. Catalano is a Professor in the School of Social Work and Associate Director of the Social Development Research Group at the University of Washington. For more than 20 years, he has led research and program development to promote positive youth development and prevent problem behavior.

Ick-Joong Chung is an Assistant Professor in the Department of Social Welfare, Duksung Women's University in Seoul, Korea. He has worked primarily to understand the relationship between poverty and children's development—specifically, how children develop and how families function in disadvantaged social environments.

Cheri Coleman received her M.S.W. from the University of North Carolina at Chapel Hill. She is currently working at Frank Porter Graham Child Development Institute on research examining the family and social environments of prekindergarten children of various ethnic and socioeconomic backgrounds.

Jacqueline Corcoran has been an Assistant Professor at Virginia Commonwealth University School of Social Work since 2000. She teaches courses in direct social work practice and human behavior in the social environment, and has published numerous articles in the areas of family practice, solution-focused therapy, crisis intervention, and adolescent pregnancy.

Richard A. Embry is an Assistant Professor at the Columbia University School of Social Work where he teaches advanced clinical practice with families and children. His research interests address the areas of child maltreatment prevention and treatment, child welfare system reform, and family violence and people with disabilities.

William S. Etnyre is a clinical social worker at Hall Health Mental Health Clinic at the University of Washington and also has a private practice. He received his M.S.W. in 1975 and is completing his doctoral studies at Smith College, School of Social Work. He is interested in pathways to gay identity as influenced by diverse social and cultural factors.

Cynthia Franklin is a Professor at the University of Texas at Austin, School of Social Work, where she teaches courses on clinical practice, family therapy, and research methods. Franklin specializes in clinical practice, and is especially known for her expertise in school social work and practice-research integration.

Allison Sidle Fuligni has been a Research Scientist at the Center for Children and Families at Teachers College, Columbia University, since 1996. She has recently joined the Center for the Improvement of Child Care Quality at UCLA. Current research topics include child care, the transition to parenthood, and the patterns of shared caregiving in two-parent families.

Mary Rogers Gillmore is a Professor and the Associate Dean for Research at the University of Washington, School of Social Work. Her research interests include alcohol and drug use, sexual risk-taking behaviors, adolescent problem behaviors, and empowerment of women and minorities.

Debbie Gioia-Hasick is an Assistant Professor at the University of Michigan, School of Social Work. The design of her NIMH-funded predoctoral study, *The Meaning of Work for Young Adults with Schizophrenia: A Mixed Method Study,* allowed her to create individual work trajectories based on in-depth interviews about employment before and after onset of schizophrenia.

Kenneth W. Griffin is an Assistant Professor in the Department of Public Health at Weill Medical College of Cornell University. He conducts research on adolescent risk behaviors, with a primary focus on the etiology and prevention of tobacco and alcohol use, illicit drug use, and violent and aggressive behaviors among youth.

Neil B. Guterman is an Associate Professor at the Columbia University School of Social Work. His research is concerned with intervention addressing children, victimization, and violence, with a particular focus on the early prevention of child abuse and neglect, and children's exposure to community violence.

Leslie Morrison Gutman is a Research Fellow at the Center for Human Growth and Development at the University of Michigan. She received her Ph.D. in Education and Psychology at the University of Michigan in 1998. Her research focuses on the factors that support the positive developmental outcomes of high-risk, minority youth.

Magdalena Hernandez is a Developmental Psychology doctoral student at Teacher's College, Columbia University. Her interests are in the areas of parenting and early intervention. Under the sponsorship of a Ford Foundation/National Academy of Sciences Fellowship, Hernandez is currently investigating the relationship between poverty, economic stress, parenting practices, and children's cognitive outcomes.

Todd I. Herrenkohl is an Assistant Professor of Social Work and Research Analyst with the Social Development Research Group at the University of Washington. His research interests include the consequences of child maltreatment and resilience in children, youth violence, and prevention.

Melissa L. Hoffmann is a clinical psychologist and Assistant Professor in the Department of Psychiatry at the University of Tennessee Health Science Center. She specializes in child and family therapy as well as working with adolescent sexual offenders.

Mark C. Holter is an Assistant Professor at the University of Michigan School of Social Work, and a Faculty Associate of the University's Center on Poverty, Risk, and Mental Health. Holter's research interests involve the structure, effectiveness, and costs of services for persons with psychiatric disabilities. He is the father of a son with autism.

James C. Howell worked at the federal Office of Juvenile Justice and Deliquency Prevention, U.S. Department of Justice, for 20 years, mostly as Director of Research and Program Development. He is currently an Adjunct Researcher with the National Youth Gang Center, Institute for Intergovernmental Research, in Tallahassee, Florida, where he conducts research on youth gangs.

Joy L. Johnson-Lind currently works at the University of Minnesota's Eating Disorders Research Program within the Department of Psychiatry where she conducts clinical assessments and coordinates various research studies. Johnson-Lind is also employed at St. Paul Children's Hospital where she serves as a crisis social worker.

Sandra J. Kaplan is the Vice-Chairman of the Department of Psychiatry for Child and Adolescent Psychiatry at North Shore University Hospital in Manhasset, New York, and Professor of Clinical Psychiatry at New York University School of Medicine. Her leadership on behalf of traumatized children has included the development of, and advocacy for, a wide array of mental health services, professional and public educational programs, and research efforts.

Miriam R. Linver is a research scientist at the Center for Children and Families at Teacher's College, Columbia University. Her research centers on understanding the processes through which income affects children, youth, and families. Linver is also interested in educational and occupational issues in the transition to adulthood.

John F. Longres is Professor Emeritus at the University of Washington, School of Social Work. He has published widely in the areas of mental health, race and ethnicity, and gay and lesbian issues. Longres's research interests also include service use and delivery, and troubled and delinquent adolescents.

Mark J. Macgowan is an Assistant Professor at the School of Social Work at Florida International University in Miami where he teaches direct practice. Macgowan's research centers on youth with problems with violence, substance abuse, and suicidal behaviors. His state and federally funded projects emphasize culturally sensitive interventions for Latinos, and the treatment of alcohol problems among violence-prone youth.

Michelle Marchant is an Assistant Professor in the Department of Counseling Psychology and Special Education at Brigham Young University. Her research interests are in the areas of emotional behavior disorders as they relate to children, youth, and families. Marchant has a public school teaching background as well as experience in coordinating programs for at-risk populations.

Terry McCandies is an Investigator at the Frank Porter Graham Child Development Institute and is the Project Director of the Multi-State Study of the Family and Social Environments of Pre-kindergarten Children. Her research interests include exploring the influence of gender, ethnicity, and socioeconomic status on children's school readiness and early childhood achievement gaps.

Heather Ann Meyer is an Assistant Professor of Psychology at Bridgewater College. She received a combined Ph.D. in Education and Psychology from the University of Michigan. Her work centers on teacher practices surrounding issues of school violence. Meyer has also researched the safety of children's routes to and from school and the issues of gender and school violence.

Kathryn B. Miller is a research associate at the Eating Disorders Research Program in the Department of Psychiatry at the University of Minnesota. She received her Ph.D. in Clinical Psychology from the University of Minnesota in 2000. Miller has authored scientific papers on eating disorders and has worked in a clinical capacity, assessing and treating individuals with eating disorders.

Carol T. Mowbray is a Professor and former Associate Dean for Research at the University of Michigan's School of Social Work. She also holds an appointment in Psychology. Mowbray's major focus is on mental health services research. She has written extensively on gender differences in mental health and is currently conducting an NIMH-funded, multiwave research study on women with a serious mental illness coping with parenthood.

William D. Murphy is a Professor in the Department of Psychiatry at the University of Tennessee Health Science Center. He is Director of the University of Tennessee Professional Psychology Internship Consortium, and is Director of the Special Problems Unit, a sex offender treatment program operated through the University of Tennessee Health Science Center. Murphy specializes in the treatment of adult and adolescent sex offenders.

Melissa Pederson Mussell is an Associate Professor at the Graduate School of Professional Psychology at the University of St. Thomas. Mussell has published numerous articles pertaining to eating disorders, particularly related to treatment efficacy. She maintains a private practice specializing in helping individuals overcome eating disorders.

Daphna Oyserman is an Associate Professor, School of Social Work, Associate Professor, Department of Psychology, and Associate Research Scientist, Institute for Social Research at the University of Michigan. She studies well-being in children and adolescents, with particular emphasis on race, ethnicity, and cultural contextual features.

I. Jacqueline Page is a clinical psychologist and an Assistant Professor in the Department of Psychiatry at the University of Tennessee Health Science Center. She specializes in working with adolescent male and female offenders, sexually reactive children, and sexual abuse victims.

Ronald O. Pitner is an Assistant Professor at George Warren Brown School of Social Work at Washington University. He received a joint Ph.D. from the University of Michigan in Social Psychology and Social Work. His work explores how culture and stereotypes impact children's approval of violence in different social contexts.

Cathryn C. Potter is an Associate Professor and the Executive Director of the Institute for Families at the Graduate School of Social Work, University of Denver. Her research focuses on effective interventions for children and families served in child welfare, children's mental health and juvenile justice programs.

Lisa Rogers is a psychologist at The Emily Program, an outpatient eating disorders program in St. Paul, Minnesota, where she conducts individual therapy and facilitates the adolescent group and the parent group. Rogers also has a private practice in the same city where she works primarily with children and adolescents.

Russell W. Rumberger has been a faculty member in the Graduate School of Education at the University of California, Santa Barbara, since 1987 and has served as the Director of the University of California Linguistic Minority Research Institute since October 1998. He has conducted academic and policy research in the areas of education and work and the schooling of disadvantaged students.

Arnold J. Sameroff, a developmental psychologist, is a Professor of Psychology and a Senior Research Scientist at the Center for Human Growth and Development at the University of Michigan, where he is director of the Center for Development and Mental Health. He is engaged in a number of longitudinal projects with infants, school-aged children, and adolescents, studying the effects of family, community, school, and peer group on social-emotional and academic success.

Kimberly A. Tyler is an Assistant Professor in Sociology at the University of Nebraska–Lincoln. Her research interests include sexual risk-taking behaviors, early childhood abuse, and sexual victimization among homeless and runaway adolescents. Tyler also specializes in the study of social support and intergenerational relations.

Les B. Whitbeck is a Professor of Sociology at the University of Nebraska–Lincoln. His research focus is adolescent risk and resilience. He is currently conducting a longitudinal study of homeless and runaway adolescents in four midwestern states. Whitbeck also is principal investigator for a longitudinal developmental study of 450 American Indian adolescents and their families in the upper Midwest.

Lynn K. Wilder is an Assistant Professor in the Department of Psychology and Special Education at Brigham Young University. She researches and publishes in the area of special education classification of and services for students with emotional/behavioral disorders from diverse cultures and low socioeconomic groups and in the area of strength-based behavioral assessment.

K. Richard Young is the Associate Dean for Research and Graduate Studies and a Professor of Counseling Psychology and Special Education at Brigham Young University. He is also a licensed psychologist. Young specializes in the treatment of children and youth with antisocial behavior and dysfunctional families.

CHAPTER 1

INTRODUCTION

PAULA ALLEN-MEARES

MARK W. FRASER

This book offers an interdisciplinary perspective on intervention with children and adolescents. Its primary purpose is to provide cutting-edge research and theory on interventions that promote the healthy development of children and adolescents and the environments in which they function. Each chapter is written by leading scholars and/or practitioners.

The first six chapters of the book focus on aspects of youth identity and development that are essential for practice regardless of one's field and/or discipline. They include:

- Risk and protective factors, including the construct of resilience and the relation of cumulative risk to child developmental outcomes
- Race, ethnicity, and culture, including cognitive frameworks on the influence of culture and the effects of racism and discrimination on developmental outcomes
- Gender, including overall differences in the incidence and prevalence of social and health problems, and research on such differences
- Gay, lesbian, bisexual, and transgender issues, including issues related to being an invisible minority group without basic legal protections and practice implications for working with adolescents who "come out"
- Poverty and its effects on achievement and developmental outcomes, including its impact on the functioning of families, schools, and neighborhoods

In most books on the topic of intervention with children and adolescents, the aforementioned themes are not prominent. However, they are foundational in understanding the individual characteristics and the interactions/dynamics of environments in which children and youth grow and develop into adulthood.

The remaining chapters address select topical issues in practice with children and adolescents. Each chapter follows a similar structure of defining a topic, reviewing epidemiological data related to the topic, and then discussing the latest findings regarding both etiology and intervention. The chapters contain a critical analysis of the problem or presenting condition; data on the incidence and prevalence of the problem/condition; and a review of the biopsychosocial factors related to the problem, with special attention to the following:

- Risk factors
- Protective factors
- Developmental differences in risk factors
- Differences of race, ethnicity, and culture
- Differences of gender and other variations in risk factors or etiology

Promising interventions, both preventive and rehabilitative (i.e., treatment and recovery as appropriate) are included, and in many instances practice guidelines are presented. The chapters are arranged developmentally, starting with issues related to younger children and concluding with issues germane to older children.

Most chapters of this book include case illustrations, additional reading lists that expand on content contained in the chapter, and questions for further discussion. Each author cites the most recent empirical research on the intervention. Psychologists, social workers, research scientists, educators, physicians, criminologists, sociologists, and public policy leaders have contributed to this book. Their different but related perspectives set this book apart from most others written on the topic. To understand the processes and procedures for the promotion of growth and rehabilitation fully, interdisciplinary perspectives are suggested. In other words, we need multiple lenses, research, and theories from a variety of disciplines to formulate a comprehensive view of functioning. We can no longer afford to ignore a holistic approach to serving children and adolescents.

Today, many of our children and adolescents experience major problems in functioning and are at risk of poor or problematic developmental outcomes. Such difficulties cut across racial and ethnic groups, socioeconomic status, gender, and sexual orientation. Complicated problems such as child abuse and neglect, sexual abuse, learning difficulties, schizophrenia and other serious mental disorders, depression, suicide, truancy, alcohol and drug abuse, promiscuity, premature parenthood, homelessness, and aggressive and violent behaviors confront practitioners who work with children and youths. Although entire books and journals are devoted to these topics, practitioners rarely have time to study in depth. This book is designed to summarize the latest research in each problem area.

Clearly, what readers will surmise or learn from the authors' unique contributions is that individual characteristics and environmental conditions interact to cause difficulty in functioning. In reviewing the risk and protective factor perspective, Sameroff and Gutman's discussion in Chapter 2 accentuates this point. Although the target of most interventions has been the child and adolescent, the social environment is an equally and probably more important determinant of youths' present and later mental health. Sameroff and Gutman's data suggest that the environment contributes more to developmental outcomes than individual factors and psychopathology. Identifying social and environmental risk factors—as difficult as it may be, given our knowledge about them—is an important preliminary task for effective intervention and prevention. It is the cumulative effect of risk—accruing at multiple levels of children's ecology—that potentiates serious social problems, ranging from academic failure to youth violence. Because no single pathway leads to social and health problems in childhood, no universal interventions apply to all of them. Designing successful interventions must consider the number and mix of both risk and protective factors. Although authors may use somewhat different terminology, nested versus overlapping models of influence, direct versus mediated models, and cumulative versus individual risk studies under the heading of ecological models of risk are discussed in each chapter.

In Chapter 3, Barbarin, McCandies, Coleman, and Atkinson explore achievement gaps affecting ethnic minority children and socioemotional development by drawing on analyses of data from the National Early Childhood Learning Study and other sources. They argue that the cultural group to which children belong, the neighborhood in which they live and its demographic compositioning, the school they attend, and the opportunities embedded within these developmental settings all have potential to affect developmental outcomes. They constitute sources of difficulty and challenge in the life span of ethnic and minority youths. In other words, health and well-being disparities begin in infancy and continue throughout the life span for these youths.

Although it is not possible in one chapter to fully explore the consequences of gender differences and their effects on child development, in Chapter 4 Potter examines gender from the perspective of individual characteristics that must be considered in practice. Clearly, gender affects us all and these effects exert influences at different system levels. But it is the intersection of gender in the understanding of self, peer relationships and experiences, school performance and life aspirations, and family relationships that is especially important in the provision of services. Potter concludes her chapter with a very special observation—that the professional literature does not provide clear guidelines about when and how we might best take gender into account when considering different interventions. If we are to intervene effectively with children and adolescents, it is extremely important to consider gender, along with race/ethnicity and socioeconomic status, as we design, implement, and evaluate interventions.

Equally important in the discussion of gender differences is sexual orientation. Too little, if any, attention is given to this very important topic. In Chapter 5, Longres and Etnyre discuss the social construction of sexual orientation. They review prevalence data and explore theories of sexual orientation in contemporary society and issues of cultural diversity. From these analyses, guidelines for practice that promote healthy youth development and self-determination regardless of sexual orientation are presented. These authors agree that an affirming practice is one that does not make sexual orientation problematic. The practitioner's role is to enable those who do "come out" as gay or lesbian to achieve a healthy sexual identity. Cultural values rooted in fear, hostility, and false beliefs place these youths at risk.

Besides cultural, gender, and sexual orientation differences that impact developmental outcomes and functioning, poverty is a contextual variable that affects even the best-conceived interventions. In Chapter 5, Linver, Fuligni, Hernandez, and Brooks-Gunn define poverty and its effects on health, physical development, socioemotional and behavioral functioning, as well as cognitive and academic achievement. Specifically, the authors locate poverty in the neighborhood and describe its interactions with ethnicity, age, and gender. Drawing on a risk and resilience perspective, the chapter articulates the direct and insidious indirect effects of poverty on child development. Children exposed to poverty are nested in overlapping structures that lack financial, formal, and informal resources required for positive developmental outcomes.

Although there is still considerable controversy as to what, precisely, constitutes physical child abuse and neglect, organized efforts to address the problem have been identified for more than a century in the United States. In Chapter 7, Guterman and Embry discuss the immediate and long-term outcomes of children and adolescents who experience physical abuse and neglect. Clearly, the younger the victim, the more devastating the consequences are likely to be. Although solid evidence is not available, recent advances in neurological assessment document that early childhood maltreatment holds disturbing implications for later life, including brain contusions, brain atrophy, and an alteration of the development of the limbic system of the brain linked with memory. Like other chapters, Chapter 7 adopts a transactional perspective/ecological framework for locating the child/adolescent in various systems—micro-system (representing the parent and the child and their interactions); the meso- and exo-system in which the parent/child dyad is embedded, including the settings/network of relationships and institutions; and the macro-system, comprised of social structural elements—the etiology of physical abuse and neglect, and the untangling of prevention and intervention/treatment strategies are discussed. Clearly, considerable research is needed in this area to guide the development of practice principles.

Related to physical abuse and neglect, sexual abuse has become a major social and health problem. In Chapter 8, Kaplan draws on three major sources of data on child maltreatment—the Third National Incidence Study, Reports from the States to the National Child Abuse Data and Neglect Data System, and population surveys—to describe the increased incidence of sexual abuse. Risk factors associated with sexual abuse, clinical aspects of assessment (i.e., physical examinations, mental health correlates, risk for mental disorders, and academic-behavioral problems), and biological studies that examine posttraumatic stress syndrome, dissociative identity disorder, multiple personality disorder, hormone level fluctuations, and earlier onset of menarche are discussed. Of particular importance in terms of practice and intervention is interviewing allegedly abused children and adolescents. Kaplan argues that although there has been considerable reliance on anatomically detailed dolls in the identification of sexual abuse, there is no reliable clinical strategy involving these dolls that has been found to provide evidence that a child has been sexually abused. Different mental health theories, medications, family intervention, and prevention are explored. Kaplan maintains that despite the high prevalence and the devastating mental health consequences, there are insufficient resources and empirically validated interventions to deal with the problem. The inherent complications in the development of this body of knowledge are also discussed.

In Chapter 9, Young, Marchant, and Wilder describe several interventions that target students with emotional, aggressive, and behavioral disorders. The chapter discusses the risk and protective factors that provide the foundation for the content, assessment, and interventions at all levels of the school program. It also provides information about the establishment of a comprehensive assessment system, the implementation of multiple levels of intervention, the design of interventions, and the involvement of parents and family in the intervention process. Prevalence data, gender, ethnic, and socioeconomic information are included. Practical guidelines are offered throughout the chapter.

Autism is a severe and lifelong developmental disorder identified in early childhood. It afflicts the core of socialization with a profound impact on communicative, cognitive, and emotional development. There is no known cure for the disorder. However, recent evidence has demonstrated that early intervention can improve outcomes significantly in a wide range of areas. In Chapter 10, Holter reviews recent work in diagnoses and assessment, as well as the common elements of effective programming for children with autism and autism-like disorders. The differences in theoretical orientation of the interventions explored in the chapter are debated, revolving around an applied behavioral analysis approach versus a developmental framework. A listing of assessment instruments and their respective reliability/validity properties provide the practitioner with useful tools and information.

Schizophrenia is usually considered to be an adult disorder, but it can have childhood onset and when it does, it is devastating. Research-based knowledge of early onset is even more limited than for adults who suffer from the disorder. Mowbray and Gioia-Hasick point out a number of interrelated issues that undermine the identification of the disorder and thus effective intervention. For example, there is low consensus on diagnostic criteria and/or core symptoms due to rapid change, growth, and development. There is also neurocognitive heterogeneity at the onset of the disorder that is not understood fully, and children's symptoms are not obvious because they may be masked with hallucinations and delusions. There appears to be a higher rate of childhood schizophrenia in males, and the risk of co-occurring substance abuse is particularly high among adolescent males. The chapter discusses theories, as well as risk factors—both individual and environmental—that contribute to the disorder. A number of interventions take into account what we know empirically about schizophrenia (e.g., pharmacology, social rehabilitation, vocational rehabilitation, assertive community treatment, and family psychoeducation). These interventions are reviewed. The authors also devote considerable discussion to prevention, early intervention, and recovery. Three novel treatments are posited: providing schizophrenia education to the family physician, developing interventions at school sites, and creating comprehensive programs provided through Early Psychosis Prevention and Intervention Centers.

Another disorder that is receiving considerable attention is depression in childhood and adolescence. Issues such as definitions of the disorder, criteria and methods for assessment, prevalence of depression and the likelihood that it will co-occur with other disorders, the antecedents and consequences of depression, and preventive interventions relevant to the promotion of healthy development and the reduction of risk are all explored in Chapter 12. Consistent with themes of the other chapters, such issues as gender, race/ethnicity, poverty, and sexual orientation are given particular emphasis. Oyserman discusses the myth that very young children are immune from depression. Furthermore, consideration is given to a number of contextual and antecedent variables—such as poverty, problematic neighborhoods, and family stress—that have been ignored in the discussions of this topic found elsewhere.

As depression in childhood and adolescence has gained the attention of practitioners and researchers, so has the increased suicide and death rate among 10- to 19-year-olds. In Chapter 13, Macgowan describes youth suicide from a public health perspective. He defines a four-stage problem-response continuum: defining the problem, identifying risk and protective factors, evaluating alternative interventions, and implementing intervention strategies. Gender differences, cultural variations, and evidence-based intervention and prevention strategies are discussed. Macgowan describes the considerable progress that has been made during the past decade in understanding the factors related to youth suicide and how to prevent this serious social problem.

Explanations for the increase in school dropout rates vary from psychological and social to economic contributors. During the last decade, rates of graduation from diploma-granting programs in the United States have actually declined, while rates of graduation from alternative programs (such as G.E.D. programs) have increased. Reviews of various theoretical and empirical research that attempts to explain why students drop out of high school are, at best, complex. Again, as the theoretical perspective undergirding this book suggests, there are individual characteristics and institutional contextual contributors found in students' families, schools, communities, and peers. In Chapter 14, Rumberger examines various programmatic and systemic strategies pertaining to dropout prevention.

As U.S. dropout rates have increased, so have the widespread use of and experimentation with alcohol, tobacco, and/or other drugs during the early teenage years. A subset of youth who experiment with tobacco and alcohol become heavy users and some will eventually use illicit drugs. Griffin and Botvin discuss in Chapter 15 the use of "club drugs," such as ecstasy, and their sharp increase among American teenagers. The chapter focuses on protective factors for adolescent substance use, ranging from individual and social influences, to the role of neighborhood factors and societal influences. Theories of etiology, the role of gender and acculturation, how risk factors change over the course of adolescent development, and empirically based prevention and treatment approaches are contrasted and critiqued. Although there are promising findings, the empirical validation undergirding many interventions is, at best, in the early stages of development. Replication over time and adaptations are needed before one can claim with any confidence that a specific approach is indeed effective.

Half of all new HIV infections are thought to occur among people under 25 years old; this represents about 20,000 new HIV infections each year. It appears that young women of color and young men who have sex with men have been hardest hit. In Chapter 16, Gillmore discusses the sexual activity of our nation's youth, the fact that our youth are relatively knowledgeable about AIDS and pregnancy prevention, and the general access to reproductive health care that includes contraceptives without parental consent. Gillmore reviews the empirical literature, addressing such questions as: What factors predict sexual initiation and unprotected sex among adolescents and how has this information been used to inform AIDS prevention and intervention?

In Chapter 17, Tyler and Whitbeck differentiate runaways, homeless, throw-aways, and street kids and provide the latest prevalence rates available and empirical studies that explore race/ethnicity, age, gender, and socioeconomic issues. Risk factors for running away and staying away (i.e., precocious adult behaviors, family risk factors, peer influences, school failure, other deviant behaviors, and lack of effective informal and formal alternatives to homes) are explored. A category of youth that is not widely discussed is "resilient runaways." Resilient factors include age at first run, presence of a caring relative who ties the child to some adult contact and supervision, academic success, employment, transitional living programs, and youth outreach programs. Traditional treatment programs, service continuums, and other practice guidelines are articulated. The authors conclude that runaway youths often go unnoticed, and thus advocacy on their behalf is desperately needed to reduce both the rate of occurrence and to prevent the devastating consequences.

Premature parenthood and parenting is not a new social problem. There is no dearth of research on the topic or of theories that link this social problem to individual characteristics and/or contextual/environmental contributors. In Chapter 18, Corcoran and Franklin maintain that even though the past decade has brought a decline in adolescent pregnancy, the U.S. rates are higher than rates in other developing countries. Empirically identified risk and protective factors at the bio-psycho-social levels, the individual level, the immediate social environment level, and the broad social environment levels are discussed in terms of primary and secondary prevention of pregnancy. Risk as well as resilience are explored. Clearly, other risk behaviors are associated with adolescent pregnancy and parenting (e.g., substance use, dropping out, running away, poor school achievement, and acting on impulses). Evidence-based prevention and treatment programs to reduce risk and increase crucial protective factors are discussed. Particular attention is given to Latinos and African American adolescents younger than age 15.

Though the literature and empirical evidence are only in the embryonic stage of development, bullying and violence in our nation's schools are under investigation by researchers affiliated with a number of different disciplines. Researchers in psychology, sociology, social work and education have been exploring:

- Epidemiological rates of bullies and victims at different ages
- Risk factors associated with bullying and victimization
- Individual child characteristics of bullies and victims
- Parenting styles that increase or decrease a child's chance of being a bully or a victim
- School setting characteristics associated with each
- Intervention strategies and programs that reduce the rates of bullying and victimization

In Chapter 19, Astor, Benbenishty, Pitner, and Meyer present innovative strategies for monitoring and mapping these problematic behaviors.

Whereas in Chapter 19, bullying and victimization are the targets of intervention, the issue of youth violence, and school-based and community-based intervention related to youth violence, are discussed in Chapter 20. Herrenkohl, Chung, and Catalano review current research and risk factors for youth violence. Special attention is given to gender and ethnic differences in the developmental etiology of violence. Also, the chapter reviews evidence on empirically based preventive interventions that seek to reduce risks and enhance protection among children and adolescents. Discussion centers on interventions that target high-risk children and youths, as well as change larger systems to support children's cognitive, social, and emotional development. Programs focused on reducing recidivism among court-involved and violent youth add to the distinctive contribution of the chapter. Consistent with a large number of chapters contained in this book, discussion of practice implications and directions for future research are offered.

Adolescent sex offenders account for a significant proportion of sexual physical assaults against children. In Chapter 21, Murphy, Page, and Hoffmann provide an overview of the literature, characteristics of those who assault sexually, and empirically supported interventions. In addition, the impact of societal attitudes and media are explored. Gender differences and those youth who are developmentally delayed sex offenders are considered in regard to their unique needs and life circumstances. In other words, individual factors, family factors, and social factors that contribute to this problematic behavior are outlined.

In a related chapter on youth antisocial behavior, the youth gang problem is described by Howell in Chapter 22. This country has seen a rapid proliferation of youth gangs. The number of cities and towns with youth gang problems continues to increase. Gangs threaten the safety of our schools and neighborhoods, and they contribute to major economic losses for those communities that are unable to control their proliferation. The long-term consequences of gang involvement are clear—loss of lives, educational attainment, and economic self-sufficiency. A developmental model is employed in the chapter to examine risk and protective factors in the individual, formal and informal groups, and neighborhood domains. The prevalence of gang membership, the effects of gang participation, and the latest interventions provide the reader with a rich resource to guide practice.

Anorexia nervosa, bulimia nervosa, and other eating disorders are potentially life-threatening conditions, affecting between 4 and 16 percent of the adolescent population. Largely experienced by girls, eating disorders can be successfully treated. New cognitive behavioral, psychodynamic, and family therapies used in community-based prevention and intervention are described by Binford, Mussell, Rogers, and Johnson-Lind in Chapter 23. Because severe eating disorders often require hospitalization, the authors also review inpatient or partial hospitalization programs and research on the effectiveness of psychoactive medication for eating problems. The book concludes with Chapter 24, written by Fraser and Allen-Meares. They discuss the hopes and enduring challenges of interdisciplinary intervention with children and adolescents.

Overall, this collection of chapters provides information on the design of more effective programs for children and youth. On balance, the book invokes a risk and resilience orientation in which, at the broadest level, interventions are conceptualized as reducing risk factors and promoting protective factors related to social and health problems. Advances in knowledge regarding the development of social and health problems are beginning to permit a level of precision in the design of services that has not previously been possible. This book chronicles this knowledge. It reviews the latest theories, summarizes findings on innovative interventions, and critically distills characterizations of individual, group, and contextual contributors to mental health, conduct, physical health, achievement, and general functioning in childhood and adolescence.

CHAPTER 2

CONTRIBUTIONS OF RISK RESEARCH TO THE DESIGN OF SUCCESSFUL INTERVENTIONS

ARNOLD J. SAMEROFF
University of Michigan

LESLIE MORRISON GUTMAN
University of Michigan

Intervening to improve child development has not been an easily accomplished task. Although the target for most interventions has been the behavior of the child, it may be that the child's social environment is an equal or possibly more important determinant of later mental health. Identifying such social risk factors is an important preliminary task for successful intervention programs, given the large number of troubled youth.

Mental health continues to be a major problem, with approximately 21 percent of 9- to 17-year-old children having diagnosable disorders (Shaffer et al., 1996). Although many of these disorders have minimal impairment, four million children, representing 11 percent of the population, have significant impairment, and another 4 percent have extreme impairment (Surgeon General, 1999). In an examination of how many children are at risk for mental disorders, the Centers for Disease Control and Prevention (2000) reported that 28 percent of high school children felt blue or hopeless, 19 percent had considered suicide, and 8 percent had made an attempt. Although the majority of youth do not have such problems, the number who do is substantial. Decreasing these numbers requires a clear understanding of the causes of these childhood problems. One of the clear correlates of increasing childhood problems is the declining quality of children's environments.

Concurrent with the high level of problems among children, family resources for coping with these problems have diminished. Almost a quarter of children live in families with incomes below the poverty line (Children's Defense Fund, 1992), and family behavior is also a major problem. The Children's Defense Fund (1995) estimates that between 3 and 10 million children experience domestic violence yearly.

Declines in family resources for supporting child development have been offset by social programs that offer compensatory professional or economic means. Unfortunately, these resources are in decline. The beneficial utilization of available intervention resources requires a comprehensive analysis of the etiology of problems in child development. A central requirement of successful interventions for children is the recognition that there are multiple contributors at multiple levels of children's ecology. Moreover, there is a different balance of contributors for each child such that there are no universal treatments applicable to all children.

In a critical appraisal of efforts to reduce children's psychosocial disorders published 20 years ago, Rutter (1982) was led to conclude that knowledge of the topic was limited and that there were few interventions of proven value. Rutter's assessment is still accurate in the interim, but it underestimates the field's full capability if current knowledge was fully utilized. The two greatest intervention myths identified by Rutter were that there are single causes for disorders and that these causes can be eliminated by treating the child as an individual. Whatever substance can be found in this area of research points to multiple, not single, causation as the rule and the need for intervening in the child-rearing context as of equal or greater importance than treating the child.

We will begin with an overview of concepts of risk focusing on the differences between deterministic causal factors and probabilistic risk factors. Then we will describe the assessment of typical risk factors and explore the predictive efficacy of single and multiple risk indices. Finally, we will try to identify social protective factors and individual resiliency that would allow the child to overcome adversity and achieve developmental competence.

ASSESSING RISKS

Where science is seen as the search for causes, a discussion of risk factors may appear to be a substitute for a more basic understanding of why individuals succeed or fail. Where risks represent only probabilities, causes would seem to represent truths. But the history of research into the etiology of all biological disorders has demonstrated that there are no single sufficient causes. The term *risk factors* itself arose from epidemiological research seeking the cause of heart disease (Costello & Angold, 2000). In the most comprehensive of these efforts, the Framingham Study, it was found that no one factor was either necessary or sufficient (Dawber, 1980). Hypertension, obesity, lack of exercise, and smoking all made significant contributions to heart disease at the population level, but for any single affected individual there was a different combination of these factors.

We will discuss a similar result in our search for the causes of developmental problems in children and adolescents. It will not be any single factor that causes such difficulties, but a set of factors that contribute to the outcome.

Representative Risk Factors

Let us turn for a moment to research aimed at identifying representative risk factors in the development of cognitive and socioemotional competence. Such child competencies have been found to be strongly related to family mental health and especially to social class. In an investigation of a sample of families with a high level of maternal psychopathology, children were followed from birth through high school in the Rochester Longitudinal

Study (RLS; Sameroff, Seifer, & Zax, 1982). In the RLS, socioeconomic status was the best single variable for predicting children's cognitive competence and an important predictor of socioemotional functioning, but the circumstances of families within the same social class differed quite markedly. Socioeconomic status (SES) has an impact on parenting, parental attitudes and beliefs, family interactions, and the availability of institutions in the surrounding community. From the data available in the RLS, we chose a set of variables that were related to economic circumstance but were not the same as SES (Sameroff, Seifer, Barocas, Zax, & Greenspan, 1987). We then tested whether poor cognitive and socioemotional development was related to the risk factors associated with low socioeconomic circumstances. The definitions of the 10 environmental risk variables were (1) a history of maternal mental illness; (2) high maternal anxiety; (3) parental perspectives that reflected rigidity in the attitudes, beliefs, and values that mothers had in regard to their child's development; (4) few positive maternal interactions with the child observed during infancy; (5) head of household in unskilled occupations; (6) minimal maternal education; (7) disadvantaged minority status; (8) single parenthood; (9) stressful life events; and (10) large family size. Each of these risk factors has a large literature documenting their potential for deleterious developmental effects (Cichetti & Cohen, 1995; Damon & Eisenberg, 1998; Sameroff, Lewis, & Miller, 2000). Each of these variables was a risk factor for preschool competence. For both cognitive and mental health outcomes, the high-risk group for each factor had worse scores than the low-risk group.

Cumulative versus Single Risk Studies

To take a broader perspective when examining the factors that may be targeted for intervention efforts, multiple settings and multiple systems must be examined (Bronfenbrenner, 1979) because risk factors tend to cluster in the same individuals. This new requirement is daunting to researchers trained primarily to focus on individual behavioral processes (Baldwin, Baldwin, Kasser, Zax, Sameroff, & Seifer, 1993). Many investigators who started out examining a single risk factor soon realized that risk rarely occurs alone (Kalil & Kunz, 1999; Masten & Coatsworth, 1998). Since children often experience many risks and recurring stressors, focusing on a single risk factor does not address the reality of most children's lives.

As a way of improving predictive power, Rutter (1979) argued that it was not any particular risk factor but the number of risk factors in a child's background that led to psychiatric disorder. Psychiatric risk for a sample of 10-year-olds rose from 2 percent in families with zero or one risk factor to 20 percent in families with four or more. Similarly, Williams, Anderson, McGee, and Silva (1990) related behavioral disorders in 11-year-olds to a cumulative disadvantage score. For the children with less than two disadvantages, only 7 percent had behavior problems, whereas for the children with eight or more disadvantages, the rate was 40 percent. Even more risk factors were used by Fergusson, Horwood, and Lynsky (1994) in a study of the effects of 39 measures of family problems on the adolescent mental health of a sample of New Zealand children. Again, the result was the more risk factors, the more behavioral problems.

In the RLS, there were statistically significant differences between high- and low-risk groups for each variable, although most children with only a single risk factor did not have a major developmental problem. But when we used the new strategy and created a multiple risk score that was the total number of risks for each individual family, major differences were found on mental health and intelligence measures between those children with few risks and those with many. On the intelligence test, children with no environmental risks scored more than 30 points higher than children with eight or nine risk factors. No preschoolers in the zero-risk group had IQs below 85; 26 percent of those in the high-risk group did. On average, each risk factor reduced the child's IQ score by 4 points. Four-year-olds in the high-risk group (five or more risk factors) were 12.3 times as likely to be rated as having clinical mental health symptoms.

An important question is whether these negative effects are the result of the accumulation of risk factors or the action of a specific risk factor. Data from the families that had a moderate multiple risk score (3 to 5 out of 10) were analyzed to determine which risk factors occurred together and whether specific combinations had worse effects than others. The families fell into five groups with different combinations of high-risk conditions. Despite these differences, developmental competencies were the same for children in the five groups. It seems that it is not any single risk but the combination of multiple risks that was associated with reduced competence. No single factor was regularly related to either poor or good outcomes. What this means is that it is unlikely that universal interventions can be found for the problems of children. For every family situation a unique combination of risk factors will require a unique set of intervention strategies embedded within a developmental model. Moreover, as in the Framingham study of heart disease (Dawber, 1980), no single variable was either a necessary or sufficient determinant of good or bad outcomes. Only in families with multiple risk factors was the child's competence placed in jeopardy.

Community Studies of Risk

In order to establish a normative base for the prevalence of risk factors and their association with mental health outcomes, a study is required with a large representative sample and a clearly conceptualized model of risk. Unfortunately, as yet there has not been such an epidemiological study of children's mental health. Moreover, most studies of the effects of risk on development have not applied an ecological perspective in their conceptualization. As a consequence, ecological analyses are post hoc rather than a priori.

An example of such a study is an analysis of the progress of several thousand young children, from kindergarten to third grade, using community samples from 30 sites (Peck, Sameroff, Ramey, & Ramey, 1999). From the data collected, 14 risk factors were chosen that tapped ecological levels from parent behavior to neighborhood characteristics. The number of risk factors were summed, and a linear relation was found between the multiple environmental risk score and school outcomes of academic achievement and social competence supporting the findings from the RLS. Although this study used a large sample in multiple sites, the children were not a representative sample of the community and the risk factors were selected from available data rather than planned in advance.

Another set of data on the effects of multiple environmental risks on child development was provided by a study of adolescents in a group of Philadelphia families (Furstenberg, Cook, Eccles, Elder, & Sameroff, 1999). Mothers, fathers, and offspring were interviewed in close to 500 families where there was a youth between the ages of 11 and 14.

Although not a representative sample, the families varied widely in socioeconomic status and racial composition.

An advantage of the Philadelphia project was that a more conceptual approach was taken in the design so that environmental measures were available at a number of ecological levels. For the analyses of environmental risk, variables were grouped and examined within subsystems that affected the adolescent, from those microsystems (Bronfenbrenner, 1979) in which the child was an active participant to those systems more distal to the child where any effect had to be mediated by more proximal variables.

To approximate an ecological model, six groupings of 20 environmental risk variables reflecting different relations to the adolescent were built into the design (see Table 2.1). The intention was to be able to have multiple factors in each of the six ecological subsystems. *Family Processes* was the first grouping and included variables in the family microsystem that were directly experienced by the child and that would fit into a category of parent-child interaction. These included support for autonomy, behavior control, parental involvement, and family climate. The second grouping was *Parent Characteristics,* which included mental health, sense of efficacy, resourcefulness, and level of education. The *Family Structure* grouping included the parents' marital status, as well as the socioeconomic indicators of household crowding and receiving welfare payments. The fourth grouping was *Management of Community* and was comprised of variables of institutional involvement, informal

TABLE 2.1   Risk Variables in Domains of the Social Ecology in the Philadelphia Study

DOMAIN	VARIABLE
Family Processes	Support for autonomy Discipline effectiveness Parental investment Family climate
Parent Characteristics	Education Efficacy Resourcefulness Mental health
Family Structure	Marital status Household crowding Welfare receipt
Management of Community	Institutional involvement Informal networks Social resources Economic adjustment
Peers	Prosocial Antisocial
Community	Neighborhood SES Neighborhood problems School climate

networks, social resources, and adjustments to economic pressure. The fifth grouping, *Peers,* included indicators of another microsystem of the child—the extent to which the youth was associated with prosocial and antisocial peers. *Community,* the sixth grouping, represented the ecological level most distal to the youth and the family. It included a census tract variable reflecting the average income and educational level of the neighborhood the family lived in, a parental report of the number of problems in the neighborhood, and the climate of the adolescent's school.

Many risk factors have been identified in previous research that used only a single adolescent outcome, such as delinquency (Stouthamer-Loeber, Loeber, Farrington, Zhang, van Kammen, & Maguin, 1993). To examine the generality of risk factors requires that there be multiple outcomes in the study. In the Philadelphia study, in addition to the larger number of ecological variables, we had a wider array of youth assessments for interpreting developmental competence. The five outcomes used to characterize successful adolescence were *Psychological Adjustment; Self-Competence; Problem Behaviors* based on youth reports of experiences with drugs, delinquency, and early sexual behavior; *Activity Involvement* based on combined youth and parent reports of participation in sports, religious, extracurricular, and community projects; and *Academic Performance* as reflected in grades.

To examine the effect of the accumulation of risks, scores were calculated for each adolescent. The resulting range was from a minimum of 0 to a maximum of 13 out of 20 possible risk factors. When the five normalized adolescent outcome scores were plotted against the number of risk factors, a very large decline in outcome was found with increasing risk for every outcome (see Figure 2.1) (Sameroff, Bartko, et al., 1999).

Whether cumulative risk scores meaningfully increase predictive efficiency can be demonstrated by an odds-ratio analysis, comparisons of the odds of having a bad outcome in a high-risk versus a low-risk environment. For the typical analysis of relative and attributable risk, the outcome variable is usually discrete, either succumbing to a disease or disorder or not. For children, there are few discrete negative outcomes. They are generally too young to have many pregnancies or arrests, and the rate of academic failure is not particularly high. In the Philadelphia study, bad outcomes were artificially created by identifying the 25 percent of adolescents who were doing the most poorly in terms of psychological adjustment, self-competence, problem behavior, activity involvement, or academic performance.

The relative risk in the high-risk group (eight or more risks) for each of the bad outcomes was substantially higher than in the low-risk group (three or fewer risks). The strongest effects were for *Academic Performance,* where the relative risk for a bad outcome increased from 7 percent in the low-risk group to 45 percent in the high-risk group, an odds ratio of 6.7 to 1. The odds ratios for *Psychological Adjustment, Problem Behavior, Self-Competence,* and *Activity Involvement* were 5.7, 4.5, 3.4, and 2.7, respectively. For the important cognitive and socioemotional outcomes of youth, there seem to be powerful negative effects of the accumulation of environmental risk factors.

From these studies one would hope that a standardized measure of ecological risk would have been developed. This is not yet the case. Each study used a slightly different set of variables sampling from various social domains. But what is compelling in the results of these studies is that whatever the set of variables used, the universal finding was that the more ecological risk factors, the worse the outcome for the child.

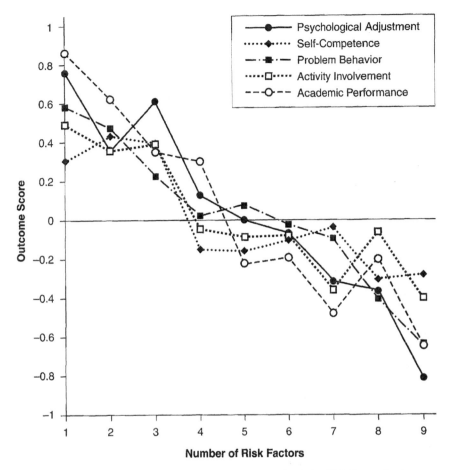

FIGURE 2.1   Relation of Five Youth Outcomes to Multiple Risk Score in the Philadelphia Study

RESILIENCE AND PROTECTIVE FACTORS

A major counterpoint to changing the social circumstances of children's lives is the idea of changing the characteristics of the children themselves. Resilience connotes positive adaptation by individuals despite severe adversity. Over the past three decades, studies of resilience have focused on individual variation in response to risky conditions such as stressful life events (Garmezy, Masten, & Tellegen, 1984; Weist, Freedman, Paskewitz, Proescher, et al., 1995), exposure to community violence (White, Bruce, Farrell, & Kliewer, 1998), maltreatment (Moran & Eckenrode, 1992), urban poverty (Luthar, 1999), and maternal mental illness (Sameroff et al., 1982).

These studies have brought sharper attention to the protective factors that influence stress resistance in children and adolescents. Although earlier studies focused primarily on personal attributes, such as high IQ, that were associated with manifestations of competence in children despite exposure to stressful events (Garmezy et al., 1984), later research incorporated protective factors in the social context. For example, Garmezy (1993) identified three broad sets of variables that have been found to operate as protective factors in stress-resistant children, including (1) characteristics of the child, such as temperament, cognitive skills, and positive responsiveness to others; (2) families that are marked by warmth, cohesion, and structure; and (3) the availability of external support systems.

Recently, however, there has been sharp criticism concerning the construct of resilience and the methods used by resilience researchers (see Luthar, Cicchetti, & Becker, 2000). One of the main criticisms concerns the absence of a unifying conceptual framework that encompasses its integration across disciplines and specialized areas. A scientific basis for intervention research necessitates precise terminology to build on earlier classifications and to ensure its continued vitality (Luthar et al., 2000).

Many current research reports use the phrase *protective factor* as synonymous with *competence-enhancing factor,* but early pioneers of resilience research restricted the use of the term to situations where there was an interaction with a risk variable. In this sense, the effect of a protective factor would be minimal in low-risk populations, but be magnified in the presence of one or more risk variables (Garmezy et al., 1984; Rutter, 1987). For example, in one of the earliest studies examining protective factors, Garmezy and colleagues (1984) found an interactive effect between stress and IQ that predicted Peabody Individual Achievement Test (PIAT) scores in a sample of elementary school-age children living in an urban community. High-IQ children maintained good achievement at both low and high levels of stress, but performance dropped off as a function of higher stress for the low-IQ children. More recent studies have also examined interactive effects models on a variety of outcomes, including mental health (Luthar, Cushing, Merikangas, & Rounsaville, 1998; Zimmerman, Ramirez-Valles, & Maton, 1998), cognitive competence (Gutman, Sameroff, & Eccles, in press; Luthar, 1991), and behavior problems (Weist, Freedman, Paskewitz, & Proescher, 1995).

However, many other researchers have been using the term *protective factors* to describe factors associated with desirable outcomes independent of the occurrence of social disadvantage or adverse circumstances. In the findings from the National Longitudinal Study on Adolescent Health, for example, protective factors were those associated with lower levels of emotional distress, susceptibility to suicide, involvement in violence, substance use, and sexual behaviors (Resnick, Bearman, Blum, Bauman, et al., 1997). In another large study of tenth-graders, social self-efficacy and social support were negatively associated with depression and therefore defined as "protective factors" (McFarlane, Bellissimo, & Norman, 1995). Although Rutter (1987) has argued that protective factors can only have meaning in the face of adversity, in these studies, protective factors were defined as simply the positive pole of risk factors (Stouthhamer-Loeber, Loeber, Farrington, Zhang, Van Kammen, & Maguin, 1993). In this sense, Sameroff (1999) proposed that a better term for the positive end of the risk dimension would be *promotive* rather than *protective factors*. A promotive factor would have a positive effect in both high- and low-risk populations, reserving the term *protective factor* for variables that only facilitated the development of high-risk children.

Promotive Factors

To examine the different effects of risk and promotive influences, we created a set of promotive factors by cutting each of our risk dimensions at the top quartile rather than at the bottom (Sameroff et al., 1999). So, for example, where a negative family climate had been a risk factor, a positive family climate now became a promotive factor, or where a parent's poor mental health was a risk factor, the parent's good mental health became promotive. We then summed these promotive factors and examined their relation to the five Philadelphia outcomes. There was a similar range of promotive factors, from families with none to families with 15 out of a possible 20. The effects of the multiple promotive factor score mirrored the effects of multiple risks. Families with many promotive factors did substantially better than families with few promotive factors. For the youth in the Philadelphia sample, there does not seem to be much difference between the influence of risk and promotive variables. The more risk factors, where the child is in the worst part of the distribution, the worse the outcomes; the more promotive factors, where the child is in the best part of the distribution, the better the outcomes. In short, when taken as part of a constellation of environmental influences on child development, most contextual variables in the parents, the family, the neighborhood, and the culture at large seem to be dimensional, aiding in general child development at one end and inhibiting it at the other. For intervention purposes, increasing promotive factors has the same effect as reducing risks, but these factors are the same for most children, most of the time.

Seeking Resilience

Although most family and social factors seem to have linear effects on child competence, for intervention purposes it is worthwhile to determine if there are some factors that would show an interactive effect. One approach is to determine if some environmental factor would buffer the effects of other risks. Another is to search for factors in the child that would serve such functions.

On the environmental side, we examined the effect of some single risk factors in the Philadelphia study about which economists and sociologists have been very concerned: income level and marital status (Sameroff et al. 1999). Although one would think that these factors should have powerful effects on the fate of children, we did not find such differences when these single variables were put into a broader ecological framework. Differences in effects on child competence disappeared when we controlled for the number of other environmental risk factors in each family. To test the effects of different amounts of financial resources, we split our sample of families into those with high-, middle-, and low-income levels. For the family structure comparison, we split the sample into groups of children living in two-parent versus single-parent families. In each case, there were no differences in the relation to child competence when we compared groups of children with the same number of risk factors raised in rich or poor families or families with one or two parents (Sameroff et al., 1999). There are many successful adults who were raised in poverty and there are many unsuccessful ones who were raised in affluence. There are many healthy and happy adults who come from broken homes, and there are many unhappy ones who were raised by two parents.

Again, what our analyses of these data reveal is that it is not a single environmental factor that makes a difference but the constellation of risks in each family's life. The reason that income and marital status seem to make major differences in child development is not because they are overarching variables in themselves, but because they are strongly associated with a combination of other risk factors. For example, where 39 percent of poor children lived in high-risk families with more than 7 risk factors, only 7 percent of affluent children did. Similarly, where 29 percent of single-parent families live in high-risk social conditions, only 15 percent of two-parent families do.

Protective Factors

In a more recent study, Gutman, Sameroff, and Eccles (2002) did find interactions. In many studies of resilience, there has been a confound between high-risk samples and ethnic differences (e.g., the high-risk groups have been primarily African American, whereas the low-risk groups have been primarily European American) (Baldwin et al., 1993). We examined the effects of multiple risk and protective factors on the academic outcomes of African American adolescents from families in a large county in Maryland that included a full range of SES (Eccles, Early, Frasier, Belansky, & McCarthy, 1997). A multiple risk score for each family was calculated based on factors shown to have deleterious effects on children and adolescents. These factors included maternal depression, family income, highest occupation in the household, maternal education, marital status, number of children living in the household, family stressful events, percent neighborhood poverty, percent neighborhood female-headed households, and percent neighborhood welfare recipients. We then defined parenting behavior and social support as positive variables to determine whether they had promotive (i.e., direct) and/or protective (i.e., interactive) effects.

Consistent with research described earlier (Rutter, 1979; Sameroff et al., 1987, 1993), we (Gutman et al., 2001) found that the more risk factors adolescents experienced, the worse their academic outcomes. As the number of risk factors increased, adolescents had lower grade point averages, more absences, and lower math achievement test scores. But different promotive and protective factors also emerged as significant contributors, depending on the nature of the achievement-related outcome that was assessed. Factors were identified that were promotive only, such as parental school involvement, that had positive influences on all youth, and those that had both promotive and protective effects, such as consistent discipline.

There were also factors that were protective only, such as peer support. In particular, peer support was associated with higher math achievement test scores for higher-risk adolescents, but did not affect the math achievement test scores of lower-risk adolescents (see Figure 2.2). Although peer support for academic success may be limited for African American adolescents (Steinberg, Dornbusch, & Brown, 1992), African American adolescents exposed to multiple risks who perceive that they can depend on their peers for help with their personal and school difficulties may be more likely to experience higher academic outcomes than their counterparts who perceive their peers as less supportive.

A surprise were the variables that were thought to be positive but showed negative effects instead, such as democratic decision making. We found that fewer opportunities for adolescent democratic decision making were associated with higher grade point averages and math achievement test scores for African American adolescents with more risks, whereas democratic decision making had little or no effect on the grade point averages and math achievement test scores of adolescents with fewer risks. Children and adolescents who live in more dangerous environments may benefit from high levels of parental control, whereas children living in less risky neighborhoods may experience negative effects of such restrictive control (Baumrind, 1972; Furstenberg et al., 1999).

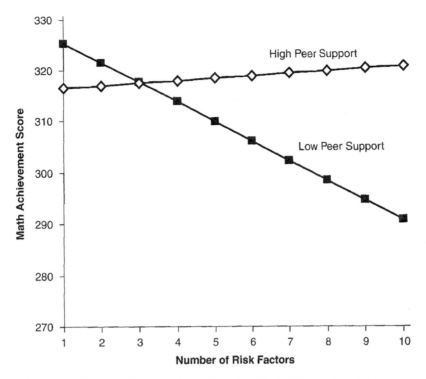

FIGURE 2.2   Effect of High and Low Levels of Social Support on Math Achievement in High- and Low-Risk Groups of Adolescents in the Maryland Study

We are presenting the details of such studies to demonstrate the complexity of deciding on appropriate interventions for children and adolescents. To maximize the efficacy of intervention efforts to foster development, comparing the positive and negative effects of social and individual factors is necessary to understand the processes that lead to more or less successful adolescent outcomes. For example, based on the results of the Maryland study, intervention efforts aimed at increasing parental school involvement are important for all African American students, a promotive effect, whereas African American youth exposed to multiple risks may especially benefit from efforts designed to enhance peer networks in early adolescence, such as peer mentoring or tutoring programs (a protective effect). Examples of intervention efforts that aim to change school climates with supportive, nurturing environments that emphasize parental involvement and high expectations for all students have been undertaken by researchers, including Comer (1980), as well as independent, private, and charter schools for African Americans.

The Resilient Child

Personal characteristics should be important ingredients in each child's development. To give some perspective on the individual contribution to the effects of risk, some child characteristics were included in the Philadelphia study (Furstenberg et al., 1999). Personal variables can be divided into *demographic* (e.g., gender and race) and *behavioral* domains (e.g., efficacy). The relation between risk scores and outcomes for separate groups of boys and girls and between African Americans and whites were examined and no differences were found. When the relation between our summary competence measure and risk factors was compared for gender and racial groups, the curves were essentially overlapping—the more risk factors, the worse the developmental outcomes.

Like the SES variable on the environmental side, race and gender are not behavioral variables. Therefore, it would be of greater interest to investigate the influence of variables with psychological content. A personality variable that is given great importance in discussions of successful development is resourcefulness. Is it possible that despite social adversity, those children with high levels of "human capital," such as intelligence and social competence (Coleman, 1988), are able to overcome minimal resources at home and in the community to reach levels of achievement comparable to children from more highly advantaged social strata?

In the Philadelphia study, we were able to measure this construct of resourcefulness with a set of questions asked of the parent and child about the youth's capacity to solve problems, overcome difficulties, and bounce back from setbacks. We divided the sample into high- and low-efficacy groups and looked at their adolescent outcomes. Indeed, high efficacious youth were more competent than those with low efficacy on our measures of adolescent competence.

But what happens to this effect when we take environmental adversity into account? When we matched high- and low-efficacy children for the number of environmental risk factors, the difference in general competence between youth in the high and low environmental risk conditions was far greater than that between high resourceful and low resourceful groups. High-efficacious adolescents in high-risk conditions did worse than low-efficacious youth in low-risk conditions (Sameroff et al., 1999). For some, it may be a surprise to learn that the ineffective offspring of advantaged families may have a much easier developmental path than more resourceful multirisk children.

One of the weaknesses in the Philadelphia study is that the data are cross-sectional. Finding causal factors is impossible unless one has longitudinal developmental data, and difficult even then. The Rochester study did have a series of developmental assessments that permitted a longitudinal view of the contribution of individual factors to developmental success. We could see how infant competence affected preschool competence, and then how preschool competence affected high school competence.

From the Rochester data collected during the first year of life, we created a multiple competence score for each child during infancy that included 12 factors. These were scores from newborn medical and behavioral tests, temperament assessments, and developmental scales. We then divided the sample into groups of high- and low-competent infants and examined as outcomes their 4-year-old IQ and socioemotional functioning scores. We found no relation between infant competence and 4-year-old IQ or socioemotional problems. We could not find infant protective factors (Sameroff et al., 1999).

However, infant developmental scales may be weak predictors because they assess different developmental functions than are captured by later cognitive and personality assessments. Perhaps if we move up the age scale we may find that characteristics of these children at 4 years of age may be protective for adolescent achievements at 18 years. We divided the 4-year-olds into high- and low-mental health groups and high- and low-IQ groups. We then compared these groups on how they did at 18 years of age on their mental health and measures of school achievement. More resourceful children did better, on average, than less resourceful children. But, as in the Philadelphia data, when we controlled for environmental risk, the differences between children with high and low levels of early competence paled when compared to the differences in performance between children in high- and low-risk social environments. In each case, we found again that high-competent children in high-risk environments did worse than low-competent children in low-risk environments.

If 4-year competence is still too ephemeral to resist the negative consequences of adverse social circumstance, would competent children at 13 years fare better than the 4-year-olds? At 13 years, we divided the adolescents into high- and low-mental health groups and high- and low-intelligence groups and examined their 18-year behavior. Again, in each case, 13-year-old youth with better mental health and intelligence did better within the same social risk conditions, but groups of children with high levels of competence living in conditions of high environmental risk did worse than competent groups in low-risk conditions, but more to our point, they did worse than low-competent children in low-risk environments (Sameroff et al., 1999). The negative effects of a disadvantaged environment seem to be more powerful contributors to child achievement at every age than the personality characteristics of the child (see Figure 2.3).

Income level and marital status on the family side, and gender, race, efficacy, mental health, and achievement on the personal side, taken alone may have statistically significant effects on adolescent behavior, but these differences pale in comparison with the accumulation of multiple negative influences that characterize our high-risk groups. The overlap in outcomes for low-income versus high-income families, families with one or two parents, boys versus girls, African Americans versus whites, and high-resourceful and low-resourceful youth is substantial for most psychological outcomes, but the overlap is far less in comparisons of groups of children reared in conditions of high versus low levels of multiple risk, where gender, race, resourcefulness, income, and number of parents in the home are only single factors. The important implication is that a focus on individual characteristics of individuals or families can never explain more than a tiny proportion of variance in behavioral development. To truly appreciate the determinants of competency requires attention being paid to a broad constellation of ecological factors in which these individuals and families are embedded. Moreover, the search for resilience in select groups may be less efficient than seeking promotive influences that produce everyday competence in all children (Masten, 2001). The concern with preventing developmental failures has often clouded the fact that the majority of children in every social class and ethnic group are not failures. They get jobs, have successful social relationships, and raise a new generation of children.

Prevention research can also be seen as true experiments in altering the course of development, thereby providing opportunities to test theories of development and resilience (Cicchetti & Toth, 1992; Coie, Watt, West, Hawkins, Asarnow, Markman, Ramey, Shure, & Long, 1993; Masten, 1999). In turn, research on risk and resilience can help practitioners design effective prevention and intervention programs. For example, as studies of resilience have shown that children typically experience multiple risks and resources in their lives, it is unlikely that a "magic bullet" for prevention or intervention will be found (Masten & Coatsworth, 1998). Prevention and intervention efforts emerging from this realization describe cumulative protection efforts to target multiple risks rather than single risk factors

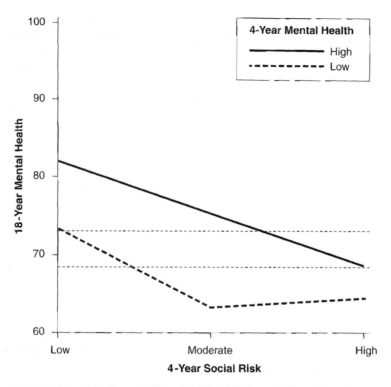

FIGURE 2.3   Relation of 4-Year Multiple Risk to 18-Year Mental Health Global Assessment Scores for Groups of Children in the Rochester Longitudinal Study

(Coie et al., 1993). Masten (2001) concludes that the most surprising result of risk studies is the ordinariness of resilience and that resilience is both common and usually arises from the normative functions of human adaptational systems.

IMPLICATIONS FOR INTERVENTION

We began this chapter with a discussion of models of prevention and the probabilistic nature of risk factors. Most children with a single social risk factor have a low probability of disorder. But as the number of risk factors accumulate, the probability increases. The conclusion for intervention strategies is that the more risk factors that can be eliminated, the lower the probability. Although it might appear that changing single factors would prevent bad things from happening—for example, taking away guns from children to prevent their involvement in serious crimes or encouraging the use of contraceptives to prevent infection with a sexually transmitted disease— the reality is that for most children most of the time, these risks are embedded in the context of many other risks. Therefore, to prevent such bad outcomes, other risk factors in the family and the community need to be addressed as well.

Similarly, if one wanted to target specific problems, such as eating disorders or sexual offending, the number of risks in the child's environment might be a better predictor of intervention outcome than the intervention itself. A guide to what may be expected to result from an intervention directed at specific problem behaviors is provided by the research on resilience. In general, these studies have found that such resilience is more a consequence of a low level of social adversity than of any enduring characteristic of the child. As a consequence, success for child-directed interventions would be found only for low-risk children, whereas high-risk children would be immune to these programs unless the scope of the intervention would address problems in the multiple levels of the child's social ecology, including the parents, family, peer group, school, and community. If a risk assessment determines that there are multiple risks, successful intervention will be beyond the scope of most community programs that are targeted at single factors. Indeed, there have been only a few research programs that have such high levels of comprehensiveness.

In summary, the utility of a multirisk assessment can be seen as twofold. First is the identification of youth who are truly at high risk for developmental problems. This may be important for programs with limited resources that want to serve the most troubled families. Second is an opposite goal of identifying low-risk children for whom limited interventions might have an effect. In the same vein, it provides an explanation for why limited interventions targeting single risks frequently fail. A classroom intervention in an inner-city school might achieve good results in the classroom, but whether it will have an effect on the later development of the child will be a function of the number of other problems in the child's life. Recognizing the complexity of influences on child and adolescent development is important for every professional service provider.

DISCUSSION QUESTIONS

1. Are risk factors that interfere with development the same as promotive factors that facilitate development (e.g., warm parents are good, cold parents are bad), or are they different (e.g., child abuse is different in kind from the disciplinary strategies that occur in all families)?

2. Is the negative effect of multiple risk factors different if they are all in one domain (e.g., the family), or if they are scattered across many domains (e.g., some in the school, some in the peer group, and some in the community)?

3. Are there certain factors that can be changed that will have a multiplicative effect by changing a number of other risk factors (e.g., higher income)?

SUGGESTED READINGS

Coie, J. D., Watt, N. F., West, S., Hawkins, J. D., Asarnow, J. R., Markman, H. J., Ramey, S. L., Shure, M. B., & Long, B. (1993). The science of prevention. *American Psychologist, 48,* 1013–1022.

Luthar, S. S., Cicchetti, D., & Becker, B. (2000). The construct of resilience: A critical evaluation and guidelines for future work. *Child Development, 71,* 543–562.

Masten, A. S. (2001). Ordinary magic: Resilience processes in development. *American Psychologist, 56(3),* 227–238.

REFERENCES

Baldwin, A. L., Baldwin, C., Kasser, T., Zax, M., Sameroff, A., & Seifer, R. (1993). Contextual risk and resiliency during late adolescence. *Development and Psychopathology, 5,* 741–761.

Baumrind, D. (1972). An exploratory study of socialization effects on black children: Some black-white comparisons. *Child Development, 43,* 261–267.

Bronfenbrenner, U. (1979). *The ecology of human development.* Cambridge, MA: Harvard University Press.

Carnegie Council on Adolescent Development. (1995). *Great transitions: Preparing adolescents for the new century.* New York: Carnegie.

Centers for Disease Control and Prevention. (2000, June 9). Youth Risk Behavior Surveillance—United States, 1999. *Morbidity & Mortality Weekly Report, 49(SS-5),* 1–96.

Children's Defense Fund. (1992). Child poverty hits 25-year high, growing by nearly 1 million children in 1991. *CDF Reports, 13(12),* 2.

Children's Defense Fund. (1995). *The state of America's children: 1995.* Washington, DC: Children's Defense Fund.

Cicchetti, D., & Cohen, D. (Eds.). (1995). *Developmental psychopathology, Vol. 2: Risk, disorder, and adaptation.* New York: Wiley.

Cicchetti, D., & Toth, S. L. (1995). Developmental psychopathology and disorders of affect. In D. Cicchetti & D. J. Cohen (Eds.), *Developmental psychopathology, Vol. 2* (pp. 369–420). New York: Wiley.

Coie, J. D., Watt, N. F., West, S., Hawkins, J. D., Asarnow, J. R., Markman, H. J., Ramey, S. L., Shure, M. B., & Long, B. (1993). The science of prevention. *American Psychologist, 48,* 1013–1022.

Coleman, J. (1988). Social capital in the creation of human capital. *American Journal of Sociology, 94,* S95–S120.

Comer, J. P. (1980). *School power.* New York: The Free Press.

Costello, E. J., & Angold, A. (2000). Developmental epidemiology: A framework for developmental psychopathology. In A. Sameroff, M. Lewis, & S. Miller (Eds.), *Handbook of developmental psychopathology.* New York: Plenum.

Damon, W., & Eisenberg, N. (Eds.). (1998). *Handbook of child psychology. Vol. 3: Social, emotional, and personality development* (5th ed.). New York: Wiley.

Dawber, T. R. (1980). *The Framingham Study: The epidemiology of coronary heart disease.* Cambridge, MA: Harvard University Press.

Eccles, J. S., Early, D., Frasier, K., Belansky, E., & McCarthy, K. (1997). The relation of connection, regulation, and support for autonomy to adolescents' functioning. *Journal of Adolescent Research, 12,* 263–286.

Fergusson, D. M., Horwood, L. J., & Lynsky, M. T. (1994). The childhoods of multiple problem adolescents: A 15-year longitudinal study. *Journal of Child Psychology and Psychiatry, 35,* 1123–1140.

Fischer, K. (1980). A theory of cognitive development: The control and construction of hierarchies of skills. *Psychological Review, 87,* 477–531.

Fischer, K., & Bidell, T. (1998). Dynamic development of psychological structures in action and thought. In R. Lerner (Ed.) & W. Damon (Series Ed.), *Handbook of child psychology* (5th ed., pp. 467–561). New York: Wiley.

Furstenberg, F. F., Jr., Cook, T., Eccles, J., Elder, G. H., & Sameroff, A. J. (1999). *Managing to make it: Urban families and adolescent success.* Chicago: University of Chicago Press.

Garmezy, N. (1993). Children in poverty: Resilience despite risk. *Psychiatry, 56,* 127–136.

Garmezy, N., Masten, A. S., & Tellegan, A. (1984). The study of stress and competence in children: A building block of developmental psychopathology. *Child Development, 55,* 97–111.

Gordon, R. (1983). An operational definition of prevention. *Public Health Reports, 98,* 107–109.

Gutman, L. M., Sameroff, A. S., & Eccles, J. S. (2002). The academic achievement of African-American students during early adolescence: An examination of multiple risk, promotive, and protective Factors. *American Journal of Community Psychology, 30,* 367–399.

Kalil, A., & Kunz, J. (1999). First births among unmarried adolescent girls: Risk and protective factors. *Social Work Research, 23(3),* 197–208.

Luthar, S. S. (1999). *Poverty and children's adjustment.* Newbury Park, CA: Sage.

Luthar, S. S., Cicchetti, D., & Becker, B. (2000). The construct of resilience: A critical evaluation and guidelines for future work. *Child Development, 71,* 543–562.

Luthar, S. S., Cushing, G., Merikangas, K. R., & Rounsaville, B. J. (1998). Multiple jeopardy: Risk/protective factors among addicted mothers' offspring. *Development and Psychopathology, 10,* 117–136.

Luthar, S. S., Doernberger, C. H., & Zigler, E. (1993). Resilience is not a unidimensional construct: Insights from a prospective study on inner-city adolescents. *Development and Psychopathology, 5,* 703–717.

Masten, A. S. (1999). Resilience comes of age: Reflections on the past and outlook for the next generation of research. In M. D. Glantz & J. L. Johnson (Eds.), *Resilience and development: Positive life adaptations* (pp. 281–296). New York: Kluwer Academic/Plenum.

Masten, A. S. (2001). Ordinary magic: Resilience processes in development. *American Psychologist, 56(3),* 227–238.

Masten, A. S., & Coatsworth, J. D. (1998). The development of competence in favorable and unfavorable environments: Lessons from research on successful children. *American Psychologist, 53,* 205–220.

McFarlane, A. H., Bellissimo, A., & Norman, G. R. (1995). The role of family and peers in social self-efficacy: Links to depression in adolescence. *American Journal of Orthopsychiatry, 65,* 402–410.

O'Dougherty-Wright, M., Masten, A. S., Northwood, A., & Hubbard, J. J. (1997). Long-term effects of massive trauma: Developmental and psychobiological perspectives. In D. Cicchetti & S. L. Toth (Eds.), *Rochester Symposium on Developmental Psychopathology, Vol. 8: Developmental perspectives on trauma* (pp. 181–225). Rochester, NY: University of Rochester Press.

Peck, S., Sameroff, A., Ramey, S., & Ramey, C. (1999, April). *Transition into school: Ecological risks for adaptation and achievement in a national sample.* Paper presented at the Biennial Meeting of the Society for Research and Development, Albuquerque.

Resnick, M., Bearman, P., Blum, R., Bauman, K., Harris, K., Jones, J., Tabor, J., et al. (1997). Protecting adolescents from harm: Findings from the longitudinal study on adolescent health. *Journal of the American Medical Association, 278(10),* 823–832.

Rutter, M. (1979). Protective factors in children's responses to stress and disadvantage. In M. W. Kent & J. E. Rolf (Eds.), *Primary prevention of psychopathology, Vol. 3: Social competence in children.* Hanover, NH: University Press of New England.

Rutter, M. (1982). Prevention of children's psychosocial disorders: Myths and substance. *Pediatrics, 70,* 883–894.

Rutter, M. (1987). Continuities and discontinuities from infancy. In J. Osofsky (Ed.), *Handbook of infant development* (2nd ed., pp. 1256–1296). New York: Wiley & Sons.

Sameroff, A. J. (1999). Ecological perspectives on developmental risk. In J. D. Osofsky & H. E. Fitzgerald (Eds.), *WAIMH handbook of infant mental health, Vol. 4: Infant mental health groups at risk* (pp. 223–248). New York: Wiley.

Sameroff, A. J., Bartko, W. T., Baldwin, A., Baldwin, C., & Seifer, R. (1999). Family and social influences on the development of child competence. In M. Lewis & C. Feiring (Eds.), *Families, risk, and competence.* Mahwah, NJ: Erlbaum.

Sameroff, A., Lewis, M., & Miller, S. (Eds.). (2000). *Handbook of developmental psychopathology.* New York: Plenum.

Sameroff, A. J., Seifer, R., Baldwin, A., & Baldwin, C. (1993). Stability of intelligence from preschool to adolescence: The influence of social and family risk factors. *Child Development, 64,* 80–97.

Sameroff, A. J., Seifer, R., Barocas, B., Zax, M., & Greenspan, S. (1987). IQ scores of 4-year-old children: Social-environmental risk factors. *Pediatrics, 79(3),* 343–350.

Sameroff, A. J., Seifer, R., & Zax, M. (1982). Early development of children at risk for emotional disorder. *Monographs of the Society for Research in Child Development, 47* (7, Serial No. 199).

Shaffer, D., Fisher, P., Dulcan, M. K., Davies, M., Piacentini, J., Schwab-Stone, M. E., Lahey, B. B., Bourdon, K., Jensen, P. S., Bird, H. R., Canino, G., & Regier, D. A. (1996). The NIMH Diagnostic Interview Schedule for Children Version 2.3 (DISC-2.3): Description, acceptability, prevalence rates, and performance in the MECA study. Methods for the epidemiology of child and adolescent mental disorders study. *Journal of the American Academy of Child and Adolescent Psychiatry, 35,* 865–877.

Steinberg, L., Dornbusch, S. M., & Brown, B. B. (1992). Ethnic differences in adolescent achievement: An ecological perspective. *American Psychologist, 47,* 723–729.

Stouthamer-Loeber, M., Loeber, R., Farrington, D. P., Zhang, Q., van Kammen, W., & Maguin, E. (1993). The double edge of protective and risk factors for delinquency: Interrelations and developmental patterns. *Development and Psychopathology, 5,* 683–701.

Surgeon General. (1999). *Mental health: A report of the surgeon general.* Washington, DC: Government Printing Office.

Weist, M., Freedman, A., Pakewitz, D., Proescher, E., & Flaherty, L. (1995). Urban youth under stress: Empirical identification of protective factors. *Journal of Youth and Adolescence, 24(6),* 705–721.

Williams, S., Anderson, J., McGee, R., & Silva, P. A. (1990). Risk factors for behavioral and emotional disorder in preadolescent children. *Journal of the American Academy of Child and Adolescent Psychiatry, 29,* 413–419.

Zeanah, C. H. (2000). *Handbook of infant mental health.* New York: Guilford.

Zimmerman, M., Ramirez-Valles, J., & Maton, K. (1998). Resilience among urban African American male adolescents: A study of the prospective effects of sociopolitical control on their mental health. *American Journal of Community Psychology, 27(6),* 733–751.

CHAPTER 3

ETHNICITY AND CULTURE

OSCAR BARBARIN
University of North Carolina at Chapel Hill

TERRY McCANDIES
University of North Carolina at Chapel Hill

CHERI COLEMAN
University of North Carolina at Chapel Hill

TAMARA ATKINSON
University of North Carolina at Chapel Hill

America of the twenty-first century will be markedly different in its ethnic composition from America of the past two centuries. As a consequence of immigration and differential ethnic birth rates, the United States is undergoing a remarkable transformation from a society whose majority is of European lineage to a more pluralistic society with considerable ethnic and cultural diversity. Even as the range of U.S. ethnic groups widens and non-Europeans move toward becoming a majority, the economic, social, psychological, and physical risks associated with non-European ethnicity have not diminished. Growing up in ethnic and cultural minority communities continues to be associated with lower probabilities of favorable developmental outcomes. This situation may worsen before it improves. The anticipated changes in the demographic makeup of this country may themselves exacerbate inter-ethnic tensions and conflict. A great deal of emotional ambivalence surrounds the use of ethnic and racial distinctions in a society that has struggled to experience itself as a single nation. In an attempt to overcome a historical legacy of legal inequality and racial prejudice, as well as current social and economic disparities, the United States is caught between viewing race and ethnic differences as a threat to national unity and as a source of national strength.

Partially as a consequence of this history and psychological ambivalence, conceptual confusion surrounds notions of race, ethnicity, and culture in the United States. The term *race* is commonly but imprecisely used to denote population group differences based presumably on skin color and other physical features assumed to mark biologically and genetically distinct groups. An alternative formulation of population group difference relies on the term *ethnicity,* which is based on psychological and social features and thus avoids the assumption of a genetic or biological underpinning as a basis of distinguishing one group from another. *Ethnicity,* then, is a self-designated category that defines a social group with a shared history, culture, language, or national origin. Through ethnic self-designations, individuals and families express an affinity for and affiliate socially with a group of people who have adopted a similar identity. Closely related to the concept of ethnicity is the notion of culture. *Culture* is a source of unity and cohesion of individuals who identify with an ethnic group. Whereas ethnicity exists at the psychological level within individuals and families, culture exists at the symbolic level. Culture is a dynamic and shared system of beliefs, mores, values, attitudes, practices, roles, artifacts, symbols, and language. Culture represents a group's collective wisdom and aspirations that surround and are reflected in routines of daily living. Culture guides how a group appraises strains and solves problems, how it approaches mundane tasks and how it addresses eschatological challenges such as the meaning of life and death. Thus, culture has many elements that combine like the strands of a rope that bind members of ethnic groups one to another. Culture is reflected in the structure of social relationships within and outside the group, and it defines obligations and rights among the individuals who share a common identity. Culture is a dynamic and high-order social construct that resides largely in the realm of imagination.

What is most intriguing in the United States and in many societies is how consistently health, income, and quality of life indicators are ordered and differentiated along ethnic lines. In effect, constructs that are essentially psychosocial and symbolic in nature become a means for assigning individuals to groups whose life prospects, resources, and general welfare come to differ so greatly. Efforts to overcome ethnic disparities in health, social, and academic outcomes of children and adolescents depend on understanding the processes by which culture and ethnicity are linked to compromised social, academic, behavioral, and emotional functioning. This chapter summarizes what is known about ethnic differences on indicators of well-being from birth through adolescence and proposes plausible risk and protective mechanisms that mediate the relationship between ethnicity and developmental outcomes. The chapter begins with a review of studies that have explored how ethnic and cultural group differences play out in the mental health and health status of children, adolescents, and their families.

THE CONFOUND OF ETHNICITY AND SOCIOECONOMIC STUDIES IN STUDIES OF DEVELOPMENT

Few would argue with the assertion that the cultural group children belong to, the neighborhood they live in, the demographic composition of the school they attend, and the opportunities and frustrations embedded within these developmental settings all have the potential to affect development. All of these contextual factors interact with children's biological and psychological dispositions, and collectively shape children's social, emotional, and behavioral adjustment (Barbarin, 1993). Yet, studies delineating specific influences of these social factors on children's development are unusual. This is true in part because constructs such as culture are very difficult to define and because ethnicity interacts with and is confounded with social class or socioeconomic status (SES; Hill & Bush, 2001). Thus, when researchers test for and find significant statistical effects of SES and ethnicity, the processes through which each construct exerts influence are unclear and often left unexplained. Much of the research on ethnic differences in developmental outcomes is designed in such a way that makes it impossible to refute arguments that these effects attributed to ethnicity are actually reducible to SES effects. Therefore, unless socioeconomic factors are well controlled, ethnicity may simply be a proxy for the uncontrolled economic and social inequities that are associated with children's ethnic minority status rather than a reflection of biological, genetic, or cultural differences.

ETHNICITY AND MENTAL HEALTH

We begin this section by examining differences in mental health for children of color. By our definition, children of color include those who are African American, Native American and American Indian, Asian American and Pacific Islander, and Latino American (Latino) and under the age of 18. Nearly all of the studies surveyed compared children of color to the dominant European American group, and thus we offer very little information on within-ethnic group differences.

African American Children and Youth

There is a substantially larger body of mental health epidemiological data on African American children collected with a wider array of research designs than on any other ethnic group. These data often give reason for concern about the mental health status of African American children from infancy through adolescence. For example, adaptation problems measured in terms of social competence, compliance, maturity, academic effort, and intellectual focus were observed in 68 percent of kindergarten children from an urban poor African American community (Kellam, Branch, Agrawal, & Ensminger, 1975). Although these data were collected in a single urban area in the Midwest and may not be entirely representative of African American children, there are data from national probability samples of African Americans suggesting rates of difficulty that are somewhat lower but worthy of concern nevertheless. For instance, using data from the Child Health Supplement to the National Health Interview Survey (1988), Barbarin and Soler (1993) report that 15.3 percent of African American children under the age of 12 were described as often unable to sit still, 10.6 percent as unable to concentrate, and 7.8 percent as often fearful or anxious.

The mental health status of African American children as a group may be difficult to discern from symptom rates without information on how other groups fare on the same dimensions. However, comparative data may be less informative than they appear because of the difficulty noted earlier in controlling adequately for the confounding effect of SES in ethnic comparisons, and the studies have produced inconsistent results. Divergences in the study designs and the methods used to collect these data may account in part for discrepancies among these studies whose conclusions range from no effect to significant effects of ethnicity on mental health symptoms. But the discrepancies do not stop there. Even studies finding significant ethnic effects diverge on whether African Americans or Euro-Americans have higher rates of mental health problems. For example, some studies show that African American children and adolescents have higher rates of certain anxiety disorders (Neal & Turner, 1991; Safren et al., 2000), depression (Roberts et al., 1997), conduct disorder (Costello et al., 1988), functional enuresis (Costello et al., 1996), and symptoms of attention deficit hyperactivity disorder (DuPaul, Power, Anstopoulous, Reid, McGoey, & Ikeda, 1997). Moreover, African Americans from preschool through adolescence score more frequently in the clinical range on the Child Behavior Checklist (CBCL), a dimensional measure of internalizing and externalizing symptoms, than the normative group consisting mostly of European American children and adolescents (e.g., see Leadbeater & Bishop, 1994). There have been arguments and counterarguments about whether these are true differences or if they reflect problems in the calibration of the measures themselves.

Some of the findings may be due to research artifacts such as sampling. Sampling biases may indeed account for some of the inconsistent findings, as it is often the case that only a small number of African American participants are included in the sample of epidemiological research when culture and ethnicity are considered. For example, Kashani and Orvaschel (1988) reported in their epidemiological study that African American subjects had a higher prevalence of anxiety disorders than European American subjects, but the sample included only eight African American children. Even when a sufficient number of African American children are included in the sample, they are usually compared to European American middle-class children and adolescents (Graham, 1992).

The overrepresentation of African American children in impoverished rural and urban areas in epidemiological surveys is another potential problem. Because poverty and stressful environmental conditions are related to children's mental health, confounding economic and community conditions with ethnicity is problematic to one's understanding of any differences that are detected between African American and European American children's mental health.

Another problem that adds to the complexity of understanding differences between African American and European American children's mental health is that of ethnic minority status. The minority experience has a psychological impact, which may include the experience of prejudice and discrimination (see Phinney, 1996). In this regard, ethnic minority children, particularly African American youth in more socioeconomically disadvantaged strata, may experience more stress than other American children. Therefore, life conditions (i.e., social and economic inequities) may be the common theme that ties together these inconsistent findings.

There is growing evidence that these ethnic differences in mental health status have their origins in SES. When socioeconomic status and residence are controlled, the differences disappear entirely or result in higher rates of psychiatric symptoms among European American children. For example, in a study examining the effects of poverty on the prevalence of psychiatric disorders in rural black and Euro-American children, Costello, Keeler, Gordon, and Angold (2001) found poor Euro-American children had significantly more emotional disorders, particularly depression, and more oppositional defiant and conduct disorders than did poor black children. Hill (2001) reports similar results when comparable SES samples of African American and Euro-American preschool children were examined. When the socioeconomic backgrounds were the same for a diverse sample of Euro-American and

African American children, Euro-American preschoolers reported more anxious symptoms than did African American children. When indicators of socioeconomic status are controlled in other studies (e.g., Neal, Lilly, & Zakis, 1993; Siegel et al., 1998), no differences in the prevalence of psychiatric disorders among African American and Euro-American children have been found, leading some researchers to conclude there are more similarities than differences between African American and Euro-American children. Collectively, these studies reinforce the importance of poverty as a risk factor in determining the mental health status of African American children. The same argument may be extended to other ethnic minority children in the United States.

Hispanic/Latino Children and Youth

As in the situation of African American children, epidemiological studies of Latino children and adolescents reveal a pattern of findings that give reason for alarm. Latino children and youth experience a significant number of mental health problems, and, in most cases, more problems than Euro-American youth (U.S. Department of Health and Human Services, 2001). For example, Lequerica and Hermosa (1995) found that about 13 percent of Latino preschool children from a pediatric clinic scored in the clinical range on the CBCL. These rates are similar to those reported for African American preschool children. Glover and colleagues (1999) found that anxiety-related symptoms were more common among Latino children in middle schools than among Euro-American students. This was particularly true for children of Mexican descent. Vaszonyi and Flannery (1997) also found a greater frequency of delinquency behaviors among sixth- and seventh-grade Latino children than among Euro-American students. Similarly, Achenbach and colleagues (1990) report that Puerto Rican youth had significantly higher total problem scores than Euro-Americans. The single exception to this trend is a study of Latino 10- to 16-year-old boys in Dade County, Florida. Here, Vega and colleagues (1995) compared the total problem scores on the CBCL of Latino, Euro-American, and African American boys and found no significant differences.

Nationwide, Latino children and adolescents report more depressive symptomatology (Roberts & Chen, 1995; Roberts & Sobhan, 1992) than do Euro-American students. Unlike the studies of African American children, even when controlling for sociodemographic influences, Mexican American youth have significantly higher rates of depression than do Euro-American youth (Roberts et al., 1997). Interestingly, however, when immigration status is considered, Latino children living in the United States appear to be at greater risk for mental health problems. For instance, when Swanson and his team (1992) compared Mexican American adolescents living in Texas to Mexican American adolescents living in Mexico, Texan youth (48 percent) reported more depressive symptoms than did Mexican youth (39 percent). Adolescents residing in Texas also reported more illicit drug use and more suicidal ideation than those residing in Mexico. This suggests that adapting to life in the United States and other stressors associated with acculturation may have a significant impact on the mental health of Latino youth. Taken together, these data suggest that Latino children and adolescents are at significant risk for mental health problems and, in many cases, are at greater risk than Euro-American children. Additional work examining acculturation stress among Latino youth is warranted, as Puerto Rican and Mexican American children living in the United States may be at significant risk.

Native American Children and Youth

One of the most consistent findings among Native American youth is the high rate of alcohol use and substance abuse or dependence. The Great Smoky Mountain Study assessed psychiatric disorders among 431 children and adolescents between the ages of 9 and 13 (Costello, Angold, Burns, et al., 1996). Children were defined as Native American if they were enrolled in a recognized tribe or were first- or second-generation descendants of an enrolled member. Overall, Native American children were found to have fairly similar rates of psychiatric disorder (17 percent) as did Euro-American children living in surrounding counties (19 percent). However, higher rates of substance abuse or dependence were found in Native American children in comparison to Euro-American children. The difference in substance abuse was almost totally accounted for by alcohol use among 13-year-old Native American children (Costello et al., 1997).

In a school-based epidemiological study of youths living in the Northern Plains, Beales and colleagues (1997) found the five most consistent psychiatric disorders among Native American children between the ages of 13 and 17 were alcohol dependence or abuse (11 percent), attention deficit with hyperactivity (11 percent), marijuana abuse (9 percent), major depression (5 percent), and abuse of other substances, such as inhalants (4 percent). Aoun and Gregory (1998) also found that alcohol use and inhalant use were the most common types of problems for which Eskimo children received mental health services. The routine practice of boarding school education for Native American students has been proposed as a major contributor to these significant mental health problems (Kunitz et al., 1999; Irwin & Roll, 1995). Accordingly, a compromised mental health status is the consequence of the practice of separating Native American children from family sources of attachment and support, and socializing them in settings that ignore or denigrate the cultural practices that might ground them as adults, strengthen their identity, and help them cope with stressful life events.

Asian American Children and Youth

According to the Surgeon General's Report (U.S. Department of Health and Human Services, 2001), very little is known about the mental health needs of the diverse population of Asian American children and adolescents. Of the studies that have been conducted, most find few differences between Asian American youth and Euro-American youth. For example, both Filipino and Hawaiian high school students were found to have similar rates of depressive symptoms to those of Euro-American youth (Edman et al., 1998; Nahulu et al., 1996). However, in comparison to other U.S. students, Chinese immigrant students have higher rates of anxiety (Sue & Zane, 1985). In fact, Pang (1991) investigated the possibility that Asian American youth may be more susceptible to test anxiety because of stronger cultural emphasis on academic achievement and parental respect. In this study, Asian American ($n = 25$) and Euro-American ($n = 66$) middle school children from an advanced math class were compared on measures of self-concept, perceptions of parental support and pressure, perceptions of the importance of pleasing one's parents, and math grades. Asian American children exhibited higher test anxiety scores and stronger efforts directed at pleasing their parents. However, student perceptions of the need to please parents and parental pressure significantly and uniquely predicted test anxiety, whereas ethnicity and gender did not. The fact that ethnicity was not a significant unique predictor when perceptions of the need to please parents and parental pressure were entered into the regression analysis raises the possibility that the effects of ethnicity on test anxiety may be mediated by perceptions of pleasing one's parents and parental pressure. To answer important questions with regard to ethnicity and children's mental health, increasing awareness of the complexities involved in conducting empirical research with multicultural youth is needed.

ETHNIC DIFFERENCES IN HEALTH, PHYSICAL DEVELOPMENT, AND RISKY BEHAVIOR

The indissoluble link of mind and body undergirds the argument that an analysis of the evidence on the effects of ethnicity and culture on mental health is incomplete without some understanding of what is known about how these factors are related to physical health. Reviewing the data on physical health reveals a pattern that is strikingly similar to the one observed for mental health. Very clear ethnic group disparities exist in the arena of physical health and development from birth through adolescence. For example, low birth weight (LBW) is an important early indicator of health and development. It is a precursor to other developmental disparities in children and can lead to an increase in infant morbidity. The rate of LBW among African Americans is almost twice that of Latinos and Euro-Americans. For example, in 1997, LBW occurred in 6.42 percent of Latino infants, 6.46 percent of Euro-American infants, and 13.01 percent of African American infants (Ventura, Martin, Curtin, & Mathews, 1999).

African American and Latino children are more likely to suffer from other debilitating conditions that have the potential for disrupting life and getting in the way of normal developmental tasks. For instance, respiratory illnesses such as asthma are much more prevalent among African American than Euro-American children. Children of color are also less likely to receive adequate care for the treatment of asthma. Ortega and colleagues (2002) found that African American and Latino children were less likely to receive the same care for asthma as Euro-American children, whether they were being seen in a public or private clinic. All of these health disparities can lead to higher rates of morbidity and mortality in children of color (Montgomery, Kiely, & Pappas, 1996). Differences in health status may be the result of restricted access to preventive and primary health care. Native American, African American, and Latino children all tended to be in poorer health than Euro-American children, even when income was controlled (Flores, Bauchner, Feinstein, & Nguyen, 1999). These health disparities begin in infancy and continue throughout the lifespan of children of color.

Ethnic disparities exist in other aspects of health. Obesity is a striking example. Overweight children are at higher risk for developing other physical health problems in adulthood, such as heart disease, diabetes, and hypertension. Parental attitudes about weight may play a critical role in the higher incidence of obesity among African American children. For example, Jain and associates (2001) conducted focus groups with low-income mothers of preschoolers who were all considered to be overweight based on their weight-for-height percentile and their body mass index. They found that the mothers (mostly African American) felt that as long as their children were physically active and ate well, they would not consider them to be overweight. This seems to suggest that the mothers of these children have different beliefs about what is considered healthy and what may be considered overweight. This is a significant problem because preadolescent (9- and 10-year-old) girls are greatly impacted by their mothers' opinions and were more likely to try to lose weight if their mothers said that they weighed too much (Schreiber et al., 1996). This held true for both Euro-American and African American girls in the study. Although the children may be eating well (meaning they are eating what is given to them), they may not be eating balanced meals or the right kinds of foods to maintain good health and nutrition. This can lead to the children being overweight or obese.

According to national health statistics, homicide, suicide, and accidental injury are responsible for three-quarters of all adolescent deaths (National Center for Health Statistics, 1999). Most causes of adolescent morbidity and mortality are thought to be preventable. Studies of adolescent morbidity and mortality—including sexual behavior, substance use, and injury-related behaviors—reveal prevalence rates of health problems, and the risky behaviors that precede them varied by social class, race/ethnicity, gender, and age (Millstein et al., 1992). Rates of cigarette smoking used to be highest in African American adolescents (68 percent), followed by Latinos (60 percent), Euro-Americans (51 percent), and Asian Americans (42 percent). However, more recent reports indicate that Euro-American and Latino youth have significantly higher rates of smoking than do black youth (Lewis, Harrell, Bradley, & Deng, 2000). In any case, studies consistently find cigarette smoking is more common among older adolescents, but the first experience with a cigarette is frequently reported to occur around the sixth grade. Ethnic minority and impoverished teens may be more prone to engage in high-risk activities as they develop more independence from parents and other adults (Jessor, 1992).

With regard to alcohol use, we have already noted the substantial problems this poses among Native Americans 13 years and older. Among the other ethnic groups, Latino and Euro-American adolescents reported the highest rates of drinking (82 and 81 percent, respectively). Asian American and African American adolescents reported the lowest rates (55 and 74 percent, respectively). After alcohol and nicotine, marijuana is the most widely used drug in the United States. Whereas Euro-American adolescents were significantly more likely to use marijuana in the 1980s, Latino and African American adolescents now use marijuana at virtually the same rate. These findings are striking because historically African American adolescent substance abuse rates have been lower than those of Euro-American and Latino adolescents (for reviews see De La Rosa, Vega, & Radisch, 2000; Best, Rawaf, Rowley, Floyd, Manning, & Strang, 2001). It is important to note that the sample was more highly representative of middle- to upper-middle class youth. It is not clear whether the higher rates of marijuana use apply to lower SES African American youth.

The onset and rates of sexual activity also varied as a function of race/ethnicity. African American adolescents were most likely to be sexually active (50 percent), followed by Latinos (23 percent), Euro-Americans (11 percent), and Asian Americans (8 percent). Sexual activity began early in these adolescents, with almost half the participants initiating coitus prior to 11 years of age.

Ethnic minority status has also been linked to homicide deaths. For example, rates of homicide death among minority youth are disproportionately high (Waller, Baker, & Szocka,

1989). In a study of homicide rates among newborn to 4-year-old children in the Los Angeles area, results indicated that African American children were at the greatest risk of homicide, with African American males being at extremely high risk. Latino boys had the next highest rate, and Euro-Americans had the lowest. The patterns of homicide risk by ethnic group for this group of young children parallels what is found for older children (Abel, 1986; Blaser, 1983; Christoffel, 1990).

DELINQUENCY

Risk-taking sometimes takes the form of delinquent behavior. Delinquent acts range in seriousness from shoplifting and vandalism to robbery, rape, and murder. Changes in the population growth by age and ethnicity have been accompanied by changes in crime rates. Since 1994, the number of homicides, violent crimes, robberies, and motor theft have declined and, by 2000, they reached the lowest level ever recorded. Although the number of crimes is at an all-time low, over the past six years or so, the number of gangs has grown dramatically, and most of the members are ethnic minority youths. For example, a 1992 national survey estimated the number of gangs at 4,881 gangs with a membership of 249,324 (Curry, Ball, & Fox, 1994). By 1996, estimates increased to 31,000 gangs with a membership of 846,000 (National Youth Gang Center, 1997). The results from these two surveys combined with the national arrest statistics (Federal Bureau of Investigation, 1996) show that nearly half of gang members are African American (48 percent) and just as many are Latino (43 percent) youths. This estimate is all the more alarming because it is likely to be conservatively low.

A distinction must be made between *gang involvement* and *gang delinquency* (Curry & Spergel, 1992; Walker-Barnes & Mason, 2001). Gang involvement can mean participating in nondelinquent activities, such as hanging out with a gang, wearing gang colors, and flashing gang hand signs on purpose. This may not be as grave a concern, short of the negative impact it may have on the maintenance of academic performance and other pro-social values. Gang delinquency is a different story. It involves selling drugs, breaking the law, violating social norms, and committing violent acts. The ability to draw conclusions about implications of the social functioning and development of African American and Latino youth who make up most gangs is weakened by the failure of much of the existing body of evidence to make this distinction. In two studies of high-risk youth living in Chicago, Curry and Spergel (1988) found the rate of gang-related violence in Chicago's Latino communities was more than twice the rate in African American communities. Interestingly, they also found that for males in the Latino community, associating with gang members led to gang membership less often than was true for males in the African American community (Curry & Spergel, 1992).

However, effectively involved parenting made more of a difference in curtailing gang membership in the African American community than among Latinos and Euro-Americans (Walker-Barnes & Mason, 2001). Specifically, high levels of behavioral control by parents (i.e., intense supervision and monitoring) and low levels of psychological control (i.e., lesser manipulative and guilt-based control) were related to low levels of involvement with gangs and gang delinquency among African American youth, but not for Latino and Euro-American youth. In fact, high levels of behavioral control were related to increases in both gang involvement and gang delinquency among Euro-American youth, and high levels of psychological control were related to decreases in gang involvement among Latino youth. Although gang-related behavior for youth from all ethnic backgrounds appears to be influenced, at least to some extent, by parenting behavior, these findings highlight the need for different treatment strategies for youth from different ethnic backgrounds.

ACADEMIC ACHIEVEMENT
AND CHILDREN OF COLOR

Educational success has been identified as an important protective factor against a host of adolescent difficulties such as gang membership, delinquency, substance use, and teen pregnancy. Success in school is influenced by many factors that are strongly related to SES, ethnicity, and culture. On the sociocultural side, McClelland (1955) argued that some children achieve more than others due to the values of the culture in which they are reared. After comparing several cultures during different periods of history, McCelland concluded that achievement motivation, or the persistence toward success and excellence, is an acquired, culturally based drive.

Socialization processes within family, peer groups, and school shape and mediate these orientations toward and aspirations for achievement. The literature linking socialization (i.e., parental expectations for and involvement in children's education) to achievement is extensive (for reviews, see Baker, 1996; Henderson & Berla, 1994; Thorkildsen & Stein, 1998; & U.S. Department of Education, 1994). Many different types of parenting behaviors and practices have been associated with positive student outcomes. Those include authoritative parenting practices (Baumrind, 1974; Clark, 1983; Fletcher, Darling, Steinberg, & Dornbusch, 1995); high expectations and aspirations (Astone & McLanahan, 1991; Griffith, 1996; Halle, Kurtz-Costes, & Mahoney, 1997; Luster & McAdoo, 1996); parent-teacher communications, participation in school events or activities, parental assistance at home, and participation in and discussion about learning activities (Baker & Stevenson, 1987; Comer, 1988; Eccles & Harold, 1993); and strong parent social networks or social capital (Coleman & Hoffer, 1987). Despite the vast amount of research relating different types of parenting to student achievement, we do not have a clear picture of whether and how parent involvement differs across racial/ethnic groups independent of income.

Socioeconomic status is strongly related to children's success in school. Children who are in poor health, do not get enough to eat, are preoccupied with problems at home, or have low self-esteem do not fare as well as other students. American education as a system does not afford children from low income and racial/ethnic minority backgrounds the same educational opportunities, on average, as middle-income nonminority children (Ogbu, 1978, 1987). Many poor children arrive at school well behind their more economically advantaged peers. Data from the Early Childhood Learning Study (ECLS-k) provide a rich account of the skills children come to school with and the extent to which they further develop skills over the initial kindergarten year (U.S. Department of Education, National Center for Educational Statistics, 1998). Overall, African American and Latino children enter school with fewer of the precursor skills needed for progress toward fluent reading. For example, fewer

African American children than Euro-American children demonstrated the proficiency standard for recognizing letters (55 versus 73 percent) and for distinguishing beginning sounds (19 versus 34 percent) and ending sounds (9 versus 20 percent).

Few American children, irrespective of ethnicity, enter kindergarten with the ability to read words. Barbarin (2002) examined data on the success of kindergarten instructional programs in reducing the ethnic gaps in the skills children need to make the transition to sight-reading. Over the kindergarten year, Euro-Americans who as a group entered with more pre-literacy skills were by the end of the year more likely to become proficient at reading words than African Americans. Among African Americans, females were slightly more likely to become proficient sight-readers in kindergarten than males. After a year in kindergarten, 7 percent of African American males, 9 percent of African American females, 13 percent of Euro-American males, and 17 percent of Euro-American females were able to read.

Although all groups of children improve, they do not improve equally nor do they improve enough to narrow the gap. The gaps between blacks and Euro-Americans that were evident at the beginning of the kindergarten year still existed at the end of the fourth- and fifth-grade years. Chronic school-based inequities, such as lower teacher expectations and unexamined ability-grouping practices, clearly exacerbate these differences (Fritzberg, 2001).

Early school failure establishes a developmental trajectory and pattern that strongly influences later performance in school (Alexander & Entwisle, 1988; Jimerson, Egeland, & Teo, 1999; Luster & McAdoo, 1996). As children mature, the consequences of early academic deficits accumulate. On most standardized measures of academic functioning, African American and Latino children score significantly lower than Euro-American and Asian American children. For example, Cosden, Zimmer, and Tuss (1993) found that significantly greater proportions of Latino students were identified as having academic problems in kindergarten and first grade when compared to their Euro-American counterparts. Latino children were more likely than Euro-Americans to be retained or socially promoted in kindergarten and first grade (Cosden et al., 1999).

By the fourth grade, ethnicity continues to be associated with marked differences in achievement. According to the NAEP assessment of reading and math (NAEP, 2000 website), Euro-American and Asian American fourth-graders achieved higher mean scores than their African American, Latino, and Native American peers. Ethnic minority groups are more likely to be retained or identified with early school problems (Barona & Garcia, 1990). Many school systems across the country have difficulty retaining African American and Latino students through high school, and, for those students who remain in school, a disproportionate number experience academic problems (Grossman & Shigaki, 1994; Cosden, Zimmer, Reyes, & Gutierrez, 1995). Kominski and Adams (1992) reported that in 1990, 58 percent of Latinos between the ages of 20 to 24 were high school graduates, compared to 80 percent of African Americans and 85 percent of non-Latino Euro-Americans. Put differently, there is also evidence that minority youth are at greater risk for poor academic performance and school dropout, with Latino youth at greater risk than either Euro-American or African American youth (Chavez, Oetting, & Swaim, 1994; Fernandez, Paulsen, & Hirano-Nakanishi, 1989; Ripple & Luthar, 1998).

The relationship between SES and academic achievement is strikingly similar to that observed for ethnicity. Some might argue that this is for good and easily understandable reasons due to the confound between SES and ethnicity. Among African American and Latino children it is not only the poor who fall behind. In fact, Barbarin (2001) found that ethnic achievement gaps in reading and numeracy were as great, if not greater, at high levels of SES than they were at low SES levels. Thus, the expected benefit of high SES in reducing ethnic disparities in achievement fails to materialize, as the gaps still exist rather than narrowing as the SES of the children increases (Barbarin, in press).

ETHNICITY AND CHILD WELFARE

Like the canary in the mine, the level of participation in the child welfare system is one sensitive indicator of the well-being of a group of children and the success of their families in managing the strains of daily living. On that score, children of color, particularly African American children, are not faring well. Historically, they have been and continue to be overrepresented in the child welfare system in this country. Children of color make up approximately 34 percent of the population of children in the United States, yet the percentage of children of color who had substantiated cases of abuse or neglect was a striking 47 percent in 1996 (U.S. Bureau of the Census, 1996, as cited in Kapp, McDonald, & Diamond, 2001). The difference in these statistics for African American children is even greater than in the general population of children of color. African American children comprise 15 percent of the U.S. child population, but they made up 27 percent of the substantiated cases of abuse and neglect in 1996 (Kapp, McDonald, & Diamond, 2001). In addition, African American children made up 41 percent of the population of children in the child welfare system in 1995 (Morton, 1999).

The disparities in substantiated cases of abuse and neglect and in the percentage of children in the child welfare system in general and the greater incidence of African American children in the child welfare system specifically are related to the greater likelihood of African American children to be in low-income families (Stehno, 1990; Morton, 1999; Kapp, McDonald, & Diamond, 2001). Morton (1999) has suggested, however, that the more likely explanations are that African American families are reported for child abuse and neglect more often than Euro-American families, that African American families are investigated at higher rates than are Euro-American families, and that there is inherent bias involved in deciding whether a case should be substantiated or not. These explanations seem more plausible given that Latino children are not overrepresented in the child welfare system but are just as or even more likely to be living in low-income households as African American children (Morton, 1999).

In addition to being disproportionately represented in the child welfare system, African American children are more likely to be placed in out-of-home care, have longer stays in foster care once they are placed there, and have their cases open longer than Euro-American children (Kapp, McDonald, & Diamond, 2001; Morton, 1999). Of those who are available for adoption, African American children are much more likely to have longer waits for adoptions to be legalized (Barth, Courtney, & Berry, 1994; Hogan & Siu, 1988). African American children are more likely to be involved in the child welfare system than Euro-American children and even other groups of children of color, and once involved are more likely to be involved for longer periods of time. This in turn can lead to a lack of stability for these children that can lead to poor outcomes in other areas of their development.

SOURCES OF RISK AND RESILIENCE
RELATED TO ETHNICITY

Data on ethnic and economic disparities in functioning are numerous and compelling. In contrast, efforts to account for these disparities are sparse and often tepid. Ethnic differences in outcomes are often presented without explanation and without attempts to identify the underlying sources of risks. Efforts to address the underlying risks focus most often on one of three mechanisms: economic inequality, culturally based socialization practices, and stigmatizing social processes. Presented in this section is an overview of these three sources of risk. Each section ends by highlighting recent studies of competence and resilience that are related to ethnicity.

ECONOMIC INEQUALITY

A long history of racism, ethnically based social stratification, and economic disadvantage makes it difficult to separate the risks associated with ethnicity as a cultural phenomenon from ethnicity as a socioeconomic phenomenon. The risks associated with ethnicity may be due to the disproportionate number of ethnic minorities who suffer economic disadvantage. For example, African American men earn 40 percent less than European Americans with comparable education. Furthermore, in 1998, the percent of African American households living below the poverty level stood at 26.5 percent, compared to less than 10 percent for European Americans.

Although the risk mechanisms associated with low SES are very complex, there is a strong and growing literature showing a clear relationship between SES and material hardship to adverse development of children (McLoyd, 1998). By itself, low SES is associated with a dearth of human and financial capital that has adverse consequences for family well-being and children's development. For example, low SES may lead some families to accept limited roles and aspirations for themselves and their children and to cast doubts on their own ability to change their living circumstances. Working in demanding and low-paying jobs places additional strains on the relationships between parents and their children. The distress associated with demanding jobs and making financial ends meet can increase parental irritability and depression, which may in turn reduce supportive involvement needed to spur children's language development, motivation, and effective coping strategies.

Constricted verbal exchanges between parent and children may contribute to more limited vocabularies, delays in phonological processing skills, and limited general knowledge that serves as the platform for subsequent knowledge development (Hart & Risley, 1995). Because of the restrictive discourse styles, diminished communication from parents, and low exposure to print media, children growing up in low-income households may not develop as much knowledge of language and of the world around them as children from economically advantaged backgrounds. Consequently, ethnic differences in outcomes may be a natural consequence that flows from the strains of and adaptations to economic disadvantage and material hardship attendant to low SES.

Although socioeconomic forces shape family life, family strengths such as close supportive relationships, high expectations, and fair and consistent discipline can sometimes compensate for the adverse effects of poverty on children's readiness for schooling and academic achievement (Myers & Taylor, 1998). For example, low SES is associated with academic deficiencies, but, when poor families provide supportive environments for their children, the children develop the social and cognitive skills necessary to succeed academically. Since SES is associated with material hardship that translates into a high rate of mundane stressors or daily hassles that affect morale and personal functioning, other cultural resources that seem to offer protection to children against adverse developmental outcomes include growing up in extended family structures, strong ethnic identity, high levels of family spirituality, and parental access to social support (Barbarin, 1993; McLoyd, 2001).

CULTURAL AND SOCIALIZATION PRACTICES

Culture and the distinctive approaches to child socialization that flow from it are plausible sources of ethnic differences in child outcomes. "Culture influences every aspect of human development and is reflected in child rearing beliefs and practices designed to promote healthy adaptation" (Shonkoff & Phillips, 2000, p. 25). Culture is embedded in domains that have high relevance for children's academic and socioemotional development: home language, socialization goals and methods, values about education, and views of children's development and what they need to acquire competencies. But how does it achieve that effect? What are the mechanisms through which culture leads to differential outcomes? Cultural practices—as expressed in language, values, behavioral norms, and distinct socialization practices— are among the important ways in which ethnicity influences development.

Since the family is the main conduit for disseminating culture (Garcia Coll & Magnuson, 2000), especially during the first several years of a child's life, the familial environment plays a large role in child development. Garcia Coll (1990) sums this up well when she states, "Because of their families' biological, social, economic, and cultural backgrounds, minority infants are exposed to a variety of early experiences that are unique and can potentially influence their developmental outcome" (p. 270). Not only is the family environment significant in how children learn to interact with their world but it is also important in determining the way that children are socialized. Wagenaar and Coates (1999) analyzed data from the National Household Education Survey of 1993 on children between the ages of 3 and 9 and found that family structures of African American children differed quite a bit from that of both Latino and Euro-American children. African American children were more likely to live in single-parent households, which can in turn lead to African American children experiencing greater rates of living in conditions of poverty. African American and Latino children are more likely than Euro-American children to live in family structures that include grandparents and/or other extended family members, and the activities and expectations for these children differ from those of Euro-American children (Wagenaar & Coates, 1999). These family constellations would suggest that African American and Latino children are more likely to have adults around to interact with; however, one must consider that the adults in these households may be very busy working outside of the home or trying to keep up with the things that need to be done inside the home in order to keep the household running smoothly. These distinctions in the family environments to which children are exposed lead to differences in their socialization, which in turn can lead to distinctions in children's attempts to self-regulate.

Brody, Flor, and Gibson (1999) described self-regulation as "a pivotal process that links parenting practices to child competencies. It focuses on individual differences in children's ability to set goals, to persist while working toward those goals, and to be aware of the contingencies operating in their environments" (p. 1199). They found that among African American single mothers living in a rural area, parental beliefs about whether they could affect their children's development played a significant role in the development of self-regulation in the children (Brody, Flor, & Gibson, 1999). Similarly, Murray and Brody (1999) have found that protective factors such as consistent discipline, community support, and daily routines, along with parental beliefs that they can affect their children's development, are equally important in the development of self-regulation of children in single-parent African American families. The development of self-regulation is an important step for children from all backgrounds, as it impacts on how children perceive and interact with the world.

Cultural differences arise out of the different challenges, opportunities, deprivations, and resources a group encounters. Cultural groups might assign different meanings and value to knowledge and might prioritize relationships differently depending on their history of privation and the current demands that fill their lives. Culturally distinct socialization practices could arise from conceptions of childhood and dependence, behavioral norms, and one's place and value in the larger society. These processes undergird the practices and values families use to nurture competence and guide development. Partially as a consequence of environmental demands and social conditions, families differ in socialization goals and practices that might be reflected, for example, in beliefs about how independent children should be and how early in life independence should be encouraged (Lambert & Weisz, 1992; Weisz & Sigman, 1993). Cultural demands, values, and worldviews determine how children's academic aspirations and social behaviors are expressed and interpreted. Academic strategies and emotional responses promoted as adaptive in one setting may be judged problematic in other cultural milieus. At the same time, differences in cultural conceptualizations of social relations may shape expectations of how children should behave or express their emotions. For example, Guerra, Huesmann, Tolan, Van Acker, and Eron (1995) demonstrated that specific cultural attitudes and beliefs underlie the high levels of conduct problems often observed in ethnic minority children. They tested the relationships of aggression to poverty-related stress and to the worldviews of Latino and African American children. Both stress and beliefs significantly predicted levels of aggression. Behavioral norms about aggression may differ because of being perceived as working well for the current circumstances and contributing to adaptation and some greater good.

The strain of negotiating the varied demands of culturally different worlds may itself undermine well-being. Being a part of some ethnic groups may impose a cost such as discrimination and carry social demands and psychological burdens not borne by other groups (Fisher, Wallace, & Fenton, 2000). Being a member of an ethnic minority group in the United States brings with it a degree of stress related to the strain of being different while trying to fit in. The recognition of one's differences from mainstream culture results in acculturation stress. Nervous tension involved in the process of acculturation (i.e., strains involved in how much to try to fit in and how much to retain or lose one's cultural origin) are related to higher levels of drug use and delinquency among Latino adolescents (Vega, Gil,

& Wagner, 1998). However, the relationship between acculturation and drug use is complex. Low acculturation is a risk factor for U.S.-born Latinos but a protective factor for immigrant-born Latinos. High rates of drug use are found among low acculturated U.S.-born Latinos presumably because they experience language problems, diminished employment prospects, discrimination, and acculturation conflicts (Vega, Gil, & Wagner, 1998).

Some ethnic groups that occupy a specific ecological niche with their own rules and resources related to work, sexuality, and criminal behavior may have their own codes about what is required to deserve respect and maintain honor and dignity. Some of these rules and codes of conduct may be at odds with expectations and behavior judged inappropriate by the larger society (Anderson, 2002). Adherence to what Anderson has termed *street codes* may be implicated in differential academic achievement, language use, employment, health, and academic outcomes experienced by ethnic minority youth.

As a consequence, the impact of ethnicity and culture on development most likely occurs through a process of differential socialization experiences of children. Members of cultural and ethnic groups may have differing views with respect to their own socialization goals and practices. In raising children, parents have the goal of preparing children for aspects of the adult life that they will face (Ogbu, 1981). To the extent that children are being raised to live in different worlds psychologically and socially, the requisite competencies parents seek to impart are also likely to differ. The process through which parents socialize their children on issues of language use, values, approaches to solving problems, worldviews, notions of morality and spirituality, and ethnic identity occurs either directly or indirectly. In other words, children learn through internalizing direct and implicit messages about how to view oneself, one's ethnicity and that of others, and how to cope with the possibility of racism (Hughes & Chen, 1999). Wittingly and unwittingly, families also teach important lessons that have a significant impact on children's academic motivation and achievement as well as their social and emotional competence.

> We saw all the children grow up to talk and behave like their families. Parents who said, "Move," and "Shut up" had children who did the same; parents who explained, "you hafta play by yourself, O.K, because I'm trying to make lunch and I hafta get the baby up" had children who also explained at length. We saw that language style was the best indicator of the culture being transmitted to children. The educated parents we observed, themselves children of educated parents, were transmitting to the next generation an upper-SES culture with its care for politeness and distinctions in status. (Hart & Risley, 1995, p. 58)

Another aspect of cultural socialization is the effort undertaken by family, peers, and schools to prepare children and adolescents for racist encounters. Through socialization, adults may train children to expect discrimination, racial profiling, intensive surveillance in stores, and the assumption by others that they are ignorant, dangerous, and lazy. Although this anticipatory socialization may help children by lowering disappointment when they are not valued and treated kindly, it may also have the impact of increasing anxiety and hyper-vigilance and lead them to be less trusting of persons not belonging to their ethnic group. Effective family functioning can be a potent source of protection against adverse outcomes. High levels of familism, family cohesion, and communication, and low levels of parent derogation of children are associated with low levels of delinquency and drug use among Latino adolescents (Vega, Gil, & Wagner, 1998).

STIGMATIZING SOCIAL PROCESSES

How others perceive members of an ethnic group represents another potential influence on outcome. Ethnicity and culture by their very nature permeate and shape personal identity and may reinforce perceived differences. Through language, customs, mores, behavioral norms, beliefs, rituals, and values, the sense of self is formed and boundaries are established that separate and distinguish one's own ethnic group from others. At the level of symbolic and concrete artifacts, culture and ethnicity strongly influence the construction of personal identity—how one views oneself and one's place in the world. These differences set the stage for discrimination of one ethnic group from another. On occasion, such discrimination may have negative consequences. Ethnic differences in developmental outcomes may also be influenced by how children come to view themselves when they encounter the negative view that others have about and communicate to them (Reyna, 2000; Steele, 1999). Through a process of prejudgment, discrimination, stigmatization, and social stratification, children belonging to one ethnic group may be valued, encouraged, and reinforced while those belonging to a different group are disparaged and provided with relatively fewer opportunities to grow and to develop. Stigma or the denigration of some groups involves the process of attributing to individuals characteristics, usually negative, principally on the basis of their membership in some readily identifiable and disparaged group (Goffman, 1986). The prejudgments or stereotypes are attributed to all members of the group and can have devastating effects on how well children are treated and afforded opportunities to develop their competencies (Becker, Ainlay, & Coleman, 1986).

For the stigmatization process to be effective in influencing developmental outcomes, the child must belong to an ethnic or cultural group that possesses distinguishing features that are easily recognized and marked. If the perceptions of others are a major influence, one should see these effects more markedly on groups that are easily identified by such perceptible features as skin color, language, and dress. In fact, adolescents who experience the highest level of discrimination distress come from easily identified and marginalized groups, such as African Americans and Latinos who perceive selective treatment in school, in stores, and by police, and Asian groups who are subjected to higher levels of peer discrimination (Fisher, Wallace, & Fenton, 2000).

Language, culture, skin color, and other physical features provide convenient and salient markers that are used consciously or subconsciously to distinguish and separate out children from ethnic groups and to position them for denigration. These physical markers may set children up for low expectations from teachers. For example, if African American and Latino youth felt that they were perceived as unintelligent and dangerous, they might display high levels of discrimination distress associated with low self-esteem (Fisher, Wallace, & Fenton, 2000). Differences in hair, skin tone and texture, and other physical features may make ethnic minority children a target for teasing by children who are in the majority. Thus, the process through which ethnicity acts as a risk factor can be conceptualized in two ways. First, African American and Latino children may stand out because of distinctive physical features. These distinctive physical features are inaccurately associated with intellectual inferiority. Second, when Standard English is not the preferred or predominant language to which children are exposed at home, low English proficiency may be interpreted as low cognitive ability. Black dialect and Spanish become ways of marking children not only as different but also as intellectually inferior. These differences may be associated with lower initial performance on academic tasks in pre-kindergarten and in kindergarten. Once the association of culture, physical appearance, and language is made to low performance, the basis for low expectations about future performance is established. For example, non-Latino American teachers often misinterpret a Latino parent or child's passivity as a lack of interest or intelligence. However, it is often the case that Latino children and parents are trying to be respectful or are encountering a language barrier. Ironically, teachers' low expectations may in time influence how parents come to see their children. This cascading of diminished expectations may result in both parents and teachers having limited views of what their children are capable of in school. In time, the evaluative perceptions of children by parents and teachers and the expectancy that they will not perform becomes a source of anxiety, which diminishes performance in certain settings.

For example, African American students' anticipation of racial stereotyping and low expectations of achievement seems to undermine their effort and success at difficult tasks (Steele, 1999). The term *stereotype threat* is used to portray how anticipation of being a target of prejudice creates a situation in which anxiety dampers academic performance. For example, in an academic setting where performance is important to the individual, the belief that one is negatively prejudged, irrespective of how true it is, increases anxiety and reduces morale and persistence in the effort to do difficult tasks (Steele, 1997). The stereotyped explanation that African American students cannot perform as well as Euro-American students academically may be internalized and in time affect achievement, particularly on those occasions in which negative prejudgments about one's abilities are thought to exist (Steele, 1997). In this case, it is not necessary that the individual internalize the negative prejudgments but that he or she anticipates that they will occur and operate in a given social situation.

Children whose parents emphasized a positive racial identity, who exposed children to cultural heritage, and who prepared them for discriminatory encounters have better problem-solving skills, fewer problem behaviors (O'Brien-Caughy, Randolph, & O'Campo, 2002) and higher self-esteem (Fisher, Wallace, & Fenton, 2000) than children with little exposure to ethnic identity and preparation for discrimination. A strong cultural identity appears to offer some protection against substance use. Latino adolescents who identify with some referent group—Latino, bicultural, or American—have much lower rates of alcohol and marijuana use than Latino adolescents who have weak or nonexistent cultural identities (Vega, Gil, & Wagner, 1998).

The academic and socioemotional functioning of children can be greatly impacted by several different factors, including strong efficacious communities, high-quality schools, and well-functioning families (Esposito, 1999). The existence of warm, emotionally supportive relationships and a cohesive family structure optimize parental functioning and in turn contribute to favorable academic outcomes for children (Jenkins, 1989). In the presence of a strong bond of attachment, what parents believe about their children's abilities exerts considerable influence over what they ultimately do to promote intellectual growth and socioemotional competence (Eccles, 1983). Bempechat (1998) adds to this by describing the academic support practices of parents and their contribution to the enhancement of children's motivation to learn.

The teacher-student relationship that results from the interactions between a teacher and a student can also significantly impact a student's achievement level and socioemotional development. In a study of more than 150 low-income mostly African American and Latino children, Esposito (1999) found that academic competence and teacher-student relationships were moderately related over the course of all three years that the children were studied. Salisbury, Rees, and Gorard (1999) pointed out that "the level, quality and tone of teacher-pupil interaction is a major factor in the teaching-learning process, with direct impacts on the achievement of both boys and girls" (p. 408). In citing Nieto (1996), Muller, Katz, and Dance (1999) suggested that "teacher caring [is] a key factor in the students' achievement of success" (p. 298). African American and Latino students, when asked about their favorite qualities in teachers, communicated that they felt most drawn to teachers who do whatever is necessary to encourage learning (Muller, Katz, & Dance, 1999). Teachers' attitudes and perceptions of students can play a significant role in the formation of student-teacher relationships, and these relationships can in turn have an impact on the students' learning and development.

Along with teachers' expectations and the teacher-student relationship, school climate can also affect children's achievement (Esposito, 1999). *School climate* is defined as "perceptions of the physical and psychological school environment, including relationships among and between administration, teachers, parents, students and the community at large; instructional and extracurricular management; the condition of the school building and grounds; and the encouragement of the development of academic and social values among students" (Esposito, 1999, p. 366). It encompasses the previous factors that have been discussed as well as other underlying factors that contribute to the whole of a child's academic and social development. Maintaining an overall positive school environment with good teacher-student relationships and high teacher expectations appears to be an essential way to encourage the academic, social, and emotional development of children.

CASE STUDY
PRESCHOOL PROGRAMS AND LANGUAGE ACQUISITION

As an example of how culture and family environment can have an impact on a child's development, think about a 5-year-old African American male named Jamaal who is just beginning kindergarten. Jamaal is the youngest of three boys from a low SES family. Jamaal's older brothers, Derek and James, are ages 9 and 7, respectively. The three boys play and watch television together, but none of them had significant opportunities to gain the prerequisite skills necessary to achieving initial success in the kindergarten classroom. More specifically, teachers considered Jamaal's ability to recognize shapes, colors, letters, and numbers to be well below grade level. Since Jamaal's parents both work outside the home, they were unable to spend significant time assisting Jamaal and his brothers with learning these skills, and none of the boys attended any formal preschool programs. The boys were cared for by their grandmother before they entered school and continue to be cared for by her after school and when school is not in session.

In addition, Jamaal's speech patterns are often incomprehensible, so he not only enters kindergarten with deficits in academic skills but he is also lagging in his language skills and vocabulary development. Since his family generally knows what he wants, Jamaal has not had to put much effort into learning the exact words for particular items or into making sure that his speech is clearly understood by those outside of his family. Jamaal is very likely to experience a great deal of frustration during his kindergarten year due to not knowing many of the same things that his age-mates already know. Not knowing the words for particular items or being misunderstood by his teachers is especially frustrating for Jamaal, and he gets quite upset when his peers laugh at him or leave him out of their activities because they see him as acting or speaking differently.

Suppose Jamaal decides to react to his frustration with his teachers by deciding not to attempt communicating verbally any longer. While this could exacerbate his frustration, it could also potentially be the source of what could be seen as a behavior problem. If Jamaal decides that, since he is unable to communicate his needs verbally, he will just get up and get what he wants when he wants it, and he may be seen by his teachers as disruptive and a conduct problem. These same teachers may already have lowered expectations for Jamaal because of the way that he has presented initially (lagging in academic and social skills). Jamaal might also decide to act out his frustration with his peers by hitting or kicking them or yelling at them. This would also be disruptive to the classroom and could lead to Jamaal being sent home frequently. Thus, what started out as a problem of not having the skills to be successful in the first weeks of school is compounded by behavioral problems and potential loss of classroom instruction time from being sent home. This may lead teachers and classmates to have more negative expectations for Jamaal and other children who may present like him. This then becomes a cycle by which the race and ethnicity (as reflected in speech patterns) of a child is viewed as a source of risk.

Suppose, however, that Jamaal's teacher and other school personnel are able to work closely with the family to encourage Jamaal's interest in academics and to assist them with increasing Jamaal's vocabulary. Perhaps then his behavioral problems can be averted entirely or at least ended quickly. If the school psychologist and social worker are aware of Jamaal's situation and are prepared adequately to deal with cases such as his, perhaps they can work with the teacher and Jamaal's family to improve the situation. If measures are put into place to allow school personnel the time and framework to contact Jamaal's parents for an in-depth discussion of the issues and what may work best for him in this situation, he will be able to gain more from the kindergarten classroom than he will otherwise. Ideally, Jamaal would have attended some preschool program that addressed these issues even earlier. This would have helped him in adjusting to the kindergarten classroom and helped to alleviate some of the frustration that he experienced.

PRACTICE PRINCIPLES

Socioeconomic Status and Academic Success

Poverty is a consistent and powerful risk factor for adversity in general and poor developmental outcomes in ethnic minority populations. Although economic empowerment is essential to moderate the effects of poverty, there is no substitute for educational attainment. Teachers, counselors, social workers, and psychologists can assist in the development of children's internal aspirations and attitudes by empowering parents and students. Many states have started to implement statewide systems of standardized testing to assess outcomes. This more easily allows researchers and public health workers to assist parents, providers, and advocates in building their knowledge on what is needed from schools and after-school programs to ensure that every child has access to an early education program that will allow him or her to reach his or her full potential.

Ethnicity and Cultural Socialization

Knowledge and appreciation of cultural differences is often stated but is axiomatic and key to success with ethnic minority populations. This is easier said than done. Culture is dynamic and changing. Constant gathering of knowledge and updating of existing understanding of different cultural practices and groups is essential. It is not enough to stop at knowledge and sensitivity. Competence in addressing the issue(s) of cultural variation brings to social work is as much about attitude as it is about knowledge of facts. But it is more than that. Attitudes must drive, direct, and inform social behavior and practices.

Assess and utilize cultural resources such as spirituality and extended family. Personal and family spiritual beliefs and practices along with attachment to a supportive religious community can foster competence. Encouraging and supporting these in social work programs can make a difference.

Value, Strengthen, and Support the Formation of a Positive Ethnic Identity

Raise consciousness about racism and oppression. Promote the use of paradoxical attributions related to appreciation of the reality of discrimination with the counterforce of personal efficacy in determining the outcome of one's life. That is, nurturing adults should reinforce the idea that no matter what the odds may be, personal effort can make a difference.

Parental efficacy can be a powerful moderator of risk, especially for African American children and youth. Support programs aimed at reducing stress can lower the effects of strain on the physical health and emotional well-being of parents. These social resources can also help foster and maintain high levels of parental warmth toward their children. They can empower parents in setting and monitoring of high behavioral and academic expectations. Social resources, caring adults, and community-bridging professionals—all are potent resources in promoting resilience of children and youth. Successful mentoring programs such as Big Brothers and Big Sisters underscore the importance of having warm, emotionally responsive relationships within a regime of high academic expectations and demanding standards of social behavior. Just as families provide a critical context for children's development, community organizations such as churches, schools, and neighborhood-sponsored recreational centers strongly influence children and family functioning.

Attacking racism in all its forms and supporting children to deal with its effects are essential. Social workers and other professionals can help by understanding and anticipating the effects of racial derogation and *stigma*. Inculcating children and adolescents in developing trusting relationships with people who are ethnically different, even when their reflex is to expect prejudice and stereotyping, is critical.

The purpose of this chapter was to provide an overview of the effects of ethnicity and culture on children's development. Overall, research in this area is lacking, and the research that has been conducted is often confounded with socioeconomics and community residence, making it difficult to discern the true effects of ethnicity and culture. The increasing multiculturalism of this nation represents both a challenge and an opportunity for developmental and social science to broaden its knowledge base. Interdisciplinary investigations and examining the following questions are encouraged to illuminate the environmental sources of strength, resilience, and hardiness that children and families show when coping with the task of belonging and adapting to an ever-increasing pluralistic and multicultural society.

DISCUSSION QUESTIONS

1. How do ethnicity and SES interact as risk factors for outcomes such as academic achievement? Explain the black/Euro-American achievement gap in high SES groups.

2. To what extent do socialization processes intended to strengthen ethnic and cultural identity serve as risk and protective factors for academic, social, and emotional functioning? Does an emphasis on ethnic and cultural difference drive a social wedge and increase ethnic tensions among adolescence? Explain. Does ethnic socialization prepare children and adolescences for stigmatizing situations and prejudice? Explain.

3. Discuss along what dimension might the home and school practices be compared.

4. How do SES and ethnicity interact to account for disparities in the health and well-being of African American and Latino children?

5. How do stigmatizing perceptions affect the psychological health and academic achievement of African American and Latino adolescents? Are the influences the same for young children and adolescents? Explain.

6. In what ways can family functioning and adult/child relationships be viewed as sources of resilience that protect African American and Latino children and promote health, behavioral self-regulation, social competence, and the acquisition of literacy and numeracy?

SUGGESTED READINGS

Barbarin, O., & Richter, L. (2001). *Mandela's children: Child development in post-apartheid South Africa.* New York: Routledge.

Barrera, M., Jr., Castro, F. G., & Biglan, A. (1999). Ethnicity, substance use, and development: Exemplars for exploring group differences and similarities. *Development and Psychopathology, 11,* 805–822.

Bempechat, J. (1998). *Against the odds: How "at-risk" children exceed expectations.* San Francisco: Jossey-Bass.

Clark, R. (1983). *Family life and school achievement: Why poor children succeed and fail.* Chicago: University of Chicago Press.

Pinderhughes, E. (1989). *Understanding race, ethnicity and power.* New York: The Free Press.

Reyna, C. (2000). Lazy, dumb, or industrious: When stereotypes convey attribution information in the classroom. *Educational Psychology Review, 12,* 85–110.

REFERENCES

Abel, E. L. (1986). Childhood homicide in Erie County, New York. *Pediatrics, 77,* 709–713.

Achenbach, T. M., Bird, H. R., Canino, G., & Phares, V. (1990). Epidemiological comparisons of Puerto Rican and U.S. mainland children: Parent, teacher, and self reports. *Journal of the American Academy of Child and Adolescent Psychiatry, 29*(1), 84–93.

Alexander, K. L., & Entwisle, D. R. (1988). Achievement in the first 2 years of school: Pattern and processes. *Monographs of the Society for Research in Child Development, 53*(2).

Anderson, E. (2002). The code of the streets. In S. L. Gabbidon & H. T. Greene (Eds.), *African American classics in criminology and criminal justice* (pp. 293–305). Thousand Oaks, CA: Sage.

Aoun, S. L., & Gregory, R. J. (1998). Mental disorder of Eskimos seen at a community mental health center in western Alaska. *Psychiatric Services, 49*(11), 1485–1487.

Astone, N. M., & McLanahan, S. (1991). Family structure, parental practices, and high school completion. *American Sociological Review, 56,* 309–320.

Baker, A. (1996). *Parents as school partners project: Final report.* New York: National Council of Jewish Women.

Baker, D. P., & Stevenson, D. L. (1987). Mother's strategies for children's school achievement: Managing the transition to high school. *Sociology of Education, 59,* 156–166.

Barbarin, O. (1983). Coping with ecological transitions by Black families: A psycho-model. *Journal of Community Psychology, 11,* 308–322.

Barbarin, O. (1993). Emotional and social development in African American children. *Journal of Black Psychology, 19*(4), 381–390.

Barbarin, O. (2002). Ready or not! African American males in kindergarten. In J. U. Gordon (Ed.), *The African American male in American life and thought.* New York: Nova Science Publishers.

Barbarin, O. (in press). Academic competence of African Americans in kindergarten: Is it just a matter of money. *Education in Urban Society.*

Barbarin, O. A., & Soler, R. E. (1993). Behavioral, emotional, and academic adjustment in a national probability sample of African American children: Effects of age, gender, and family structure. *Journal of Black Psychology, 19*(4), 423–446.

Barona, A., & Garcia, E. E. (1990). *Children at risk.* Washington, DC: National Association of School Psychologists.

Barth, R., Courtney, M., & Berry, M. (1994). Timing is everything: An analysis of the time to adoption and legalization. *Social Work Research, 18,* 139–148.

Baumrind, D. (1972). An exploratory study of socialization effects on Black children: Some Black-White comparisons. *Child Development, 43,* 261–267.

Becker, G., Ainlay, S., & Coleman, L. (1986). *The dilemma of difference: Multi-disciplinary perspectives of stigma.* New York: Plenum.

Best, D., Rawaf, S., Rowley, J., Floyd, K., Manning, V., & Strang, J. (2001). Ethnic and gender differences in drinking and smoking among London adolescents. *Ethnicity and Health, 6*(1), 51–57.

Blaser, M. J. (1983). Epidemiologic characteristics of child homicides in Atlanta, 1970–1980. *Pediatrician, 12,* 63–67.

Bradley, C. B., McMurray, R. G., Harrell, J. S., & Deng, S. (2000). Changes in common activities of 3rd through 10th graders: The CHIC study. *Medicine and Science in Sports and Exercise, 32*(12), 2071–2078.

Brody, G. H., Flor, D. L., & Gibson, N. M. (1999). Linking maternal efficacy beliefs, developmental goals, parenting practices, and child competence in rural single-parent African American families. *Child Development, 70*(5), 1197–1208.

Chavez, E. L., Oetting, E. R., & Swain, R. C. (1994). Dropout and delinquency: Mexican-American and Caucasian non-Hispanic youth. *Journal of Clinical Child Psychology, 23,* 47–55.

Christoffel, K. K. (1990). Violent death and injury in U.S. children and adolescents. *American Journal of Disease and Children, 144,* 697–706.

Clark, R. M. (1983). *Family life and school achievement: Why poor black children succeed or fail.* Chicago: University of Chicago Press.

Coleman, J. S. (1987). The relations between school and social structure. In M. T. Hallinan (Ed.), *The social organization of schools: New conceptualizations of the learning process* (pp. 177–204). New York: Plenum Press.

Comer, J. P. (1988). Educating poor minority children. *Scientific American, 259*(5), 42–48.

Cosden, M., Elliott, K., Noble, S., & Kelemen, E. (1999). Self-understanding and self-esteem in children with learning disabilities. *Learning Disability Quarterly, 22*(4), 279–290.

Cosden, M., Zimmer, J., Reyes, C., & Gutierrez, M. (1995). Kindergarten practices and first grade achievement for Latino Spanish-speaking and Anglo students. *Journal of School Psychology, 33*(2), 123–141.

Cosden, M., Zimmer, J., & Tuss, P. (1993). The impact of age, gender, and ethnicity on kindergarten entry and retention decisions. *Educational Evaluation and Policy Analysis, 15,* 209–222.

Costello, E. J., Angold, A., & Burns, B. J. (1996). The Great Smoky Mountains study of youth: Goals, designs, methods, and the prevalence of DSM-III-R disorders. *Archives of General Psychiatry, 53,* 1129–1136.

Costello, E. J., Costello, A. J., & Edelbrock, C. (1988). Psychiatric disorders in pediatric primary care: Prevalence and risk factors. *Archives of General Psychiatry, 45,* 1107–1116.

Costello, E., Farmer, E., Angold, A., Burns, B., & Erkanli, A. (1997). Psychiatric disorders among American Indian and White youth in Appalachia: The Great Smoky Mountains study. *American Journal of Public Health, 87,* 827–832.

Costello, E. J., Keeler, G. P., & Angold, A. (2001). Poverty, race/ethnicity, and psychiatric disorder: A study of rural children. *American Journal of Public Health, 91,* 1494–1499.

Curry, G. D., Ball, R., & Fox, R. J. (1994). *Gang crime and law enforcement record-keeping (Research in brief).* Washington, DC: National Institute of Justice.

Curry, G. D., & Spergel, I. (1988). Gang homicide, delinquency, and community. *Criminology, 26,* 381–405.

Curry, G. D., & Spergel, I. A. (1992). Gang involvement and delinquency among Hispanic and African American adolescent males. *Journal of Research in Crime and Delinquency, 29,* 273–291.

De La Rosa, M., Vega, R., & Radisch, M. A. (2000). The role of acculturation in the substance abuse behavior of African-American and Latino adolescents: Advances, issues, and recommendations. *Journal of Psychoactive Drugs, 32*(1), 33–42.

DuPaul, G. J., Power, T. J., Anastopoulous, A. D., Reid, R., McGoey, K. E., & Ikeda, M. (1997). Teacher ratings of attention deficit hyperactivity disorder symptoms factor structure and normative data. *Psychological Assessment, 9*(4), 436–444.

Eccles, J. S., & Harold, R. D. (1993). Parent/school involvement during the early adolescent years. *Teacher College Record, 94*(3), 568–587.

Edman, J. L., Andrade, N. N., Glipa, J., Foster, J., Danko, G. P., Yates, A., Johnson, R. C., McDermott, J. F., & Waldron, J. A. (1998). Depressive symptoms among Filipino American adolescents. *Cultural Diversity and Mental Health, 4*(1), 45–54.

Esposito, C. (1999). Learning in urban blight: School climate and its effect on the school performance of urban, minority, low-income children. *School Psychology Review, 28*(3), 365–377.

Federal Bureau of Investigation. (1996). *Uniform crime reports 1995.* Washington, DC: Government Printing Office.

Fernandez, R. M., Paulsen, R., & Hirano-Nakanishi, M. (1989). Dropping out among Hispanic youth. *Social Science Research, 18,* 21–52.

Fisher, C. B., Wallace, S. A., & Fenton, R. E. (2000). Discrimination distress during adolescence. *Journal of Youth and Adolescence, 29,* 679–695.

Fletcher, A. C., Darling, N. E., Steinberg, L., & Dornbusch, S. M. (1995). The company they keep: Relation of adolescents' adjustment and behavior to their friends' perceptions of authoritative parenting in the social network. *Developmental Psychology, 31,* 300–310.

Flores, G., Bauchner, H., Feinstein, A. R., & Nguyen, U. D. T. (1999). The impact of ethnicity, family income, and parental education on children's health and use of health services. *American Journal of Public Health, 89*(7), 1066–1071.

Fritzberg, G. J. (2001). Less than equal: A former urban schoolteacher examines the causes of educational disadvantagement. *The Urban Review, 33*(2), 107–129.

Garcia Coll, C. (1990). Developmental outcome of minority infants: A process-oriented look into our beginnings. *Child Development, 61,* 270–289.

Garcia Coll, C., & Magnuson, K. (2000). Cultural differences as sources of developmental vulnerabilities and resources. In J. P. Shonkoff & S. J. Meisels (Eds.), *Handbook of early childhood intervention* (2nd ed., pp. 94–114). New York: Cambridge University Press.

Glover, S. H., Pumariega, A. J., Holzer, C. E., Wise, B. K., & Rodriguez, M. (1999). Anxiety symptomatology in Mexican-American adolescents. *Journal of Family Studies, 8*(1), 47–57.

Goffman, I. (1986). *Stigma.* New York: Simon & Schuster.

Goffman, L., & Leonard, J. (2000). Growth of language skills in preschool children with specific language impairment: Implications for assessment and intervention. *American Journal of Speech & Language Pathology, 9*(2), 151–161.

Graham, S. (1992). Most of the subjects were white and middle class. *American Psychologist, 47,* 629–639.

Griffith, J. (1996). Relation of parental involvement, empowerment, and school traits to student academic performance. *The Journal of Educational Research, 90,* 33–41.

Grossman, J., & Shigaki, 1. S. (1994). Investigation of familial and school-based risk factors for Hispanic Head Start children. *American Journal of Orthopsychiatry, 64*(3), 456–467.

Guerra, N. G., Huesmann, L. R., Tolan, P. H., Van-Acker, R., & Eron, E. (1995). Stressful events and individual beliefs as correlates of economic disadvantage and aggression among urban children. *Journal of Consulting and Clinical Psychology, 63*(4), 518–528.

Halle, T. G., Kurtz-Costes, B., & Mahoney, J. L. (1997). Family influences on school achievement in low-income African-American children. *Journal of Educational Psychology, 90*(3), 527–537.

Hart, B., & Risley, T. (1995). *Meaningful differences in the everyday experiences of young American children.* Baltimore: Paul H. Brookes.

Henderson, A. T., & Berla, N. (1994). *A new generation of evidence: The family is critical to student achievement.* St. Louis, MO: Danforth Foundation, and Flint, MI: Mott (C. S.) Foundation.

Hill, N. E., & Bush, K. (2001). Relations between parenting environment and children's mental health among African American and European American mothers and children. *Journal of Marriage and Family, 63,* 954–966.

Hogan, P. T., & Siu, S. (1988). Minority children and the child welfare system: An historical perspective. *Social Work, 33*(6), 493–498.

Hughes, D., & Chen, L. (1999). The nature of parents' race-related communications to children: A developmental perspective. In L. Balter & C. S. Tamis-LeMonda (Eds.), *Child psychology: A developmental perspective* (pp. 467–490). Philadelphia: Psychology Press/Taylor & Francis.

Irwin, M. H., & Roll, S. (1995). The psychological impact of sexual abuse of Native American boarding school children. *Journal of the American Academy of Psychoanalysis, 23*(3), 461–473.

Jain, A., Sherman, S. N., Chamberlin, L. A., Carter, Y., Powers, S. W., & Whitaker, R. C. (2001). Why don't low-income mothers worry about their preschoolers being overweight? *Pediatrics, 107*(5), 1138–1146.

Jenkins, L. E. (1989). The Black family and academic achievement. In G. L. Berry & J. K. Asaneb (Eds.), *Black students: Psychosocial issues and academic achievement* (pp. 138–152). Thousand Oaks, CA: Sage.

Jessor, R. (1992). Risk behavior in adolescence: A psychosocial framework for understanding and action. *Developmental Review, 12*(4), 374–390.

Kapp, S. A., McDonald, T. P., & Diamond, K. L. (2001). The path to adoption for children of color. *Child Abuse and Neglect, 25,* 215–229.

Kashani, J. H., & Orvaschel, H. (1988). Anxiety disorders in mid-adolescence: A community sample. *American Journal of Psychiatry, 145,* 960–964.

Kellam, S. G., Branch, J. D., Agrawal, K. C., & Ensminger, M. E. (1975). *Mental health and going to school: The Woodlawn program of assessment, early intervention and evaluation.* Chicago: University of Chicago Press.

Kominski, R., & Adams, A. (1992). Educational attainment in the United States: March 1991 and 1990. *Current Population Reports,* P-20, No. 462.

Kunitz, S. J., Gabriel, K. R., Levy, J. E., Henderson, E., Lampert, K., McCloskey, J., Quintero, G., Russell, S., & Vince, A. (1999). Risk factors for conduct disorder among Navajo Indian men and women. *Social Psychiatry and Psychiatric Epidemiology, 34*(4), 180–189.

Kunitz, S. J., Gabriel, K., Ruben, L., Jerrold, E., Henderson, E., Lampert, K., McCloskey, J., Quintero, G., Russell, S., & Vince, A. (1999). Alcohol dependence and conduct disorder among Navajo Indians. *Journal of Studies of Alcohol, 60*(2), 159–167.

Lambert, M. C., Weisz, J. R., Knight, F., & Desrosiers, M. F. (1992). Jamaican and American adult perspectives on child psychopathology: Further exploration of the threshold model. *Journal of Consulting and Clinical Psychology, 60*(1), 146–149.

Leadbeater, B. J., & Bishop, S. J. (1994). Predictors of behavior problems in preschool children of inner-city Afro-American and Puerto Rican adolescent mothers. *Child Development, 65*(2), 638–648.

Lequerica, M., & Hermosa, B. (1995). Maternal reports of behavior problems in preschool Hispanic children: An exploratory study in preventive pediatrics. *Journal of the National Medical Association, 87*(12), 861–868.

Luster, T., & McAdoo, H. (1996). Family and child influences on educational attainment: A secondary analysis of the High/Scope Perry Preschool data. *Developmental Psychology, 32*(1), 26–39.

McClelland, D. C. (1955). *Studies in motivation.* East Norwalk, CT: Appleton-Century-Crofts.

McLoyd, V. C. (1998). Socioeconomic disadvantage and child development. *American Psychologist, 53*(2), 185–204.

Millstein, R. A. (1993). The national impact of alcohol and drug problems and HIV infection and AIDS among the poor and underserved. *Journal of Health Care for the Poor and Underserved, 3*(1), 21–29.

Montgomery, L. E., Kiely, J. L., & Pappas, G. (1996). The effects of poverty, race, and family structure on US children's health: Data from the NHIS, 1978 through 1980 and 1989 through 1991. *American Journal of Public Health, 86*(10), 1401–1405.

Morton, T. D. (1999). The increasing colorization of America's child welfare system: The overrepresentation of African-American children. *Policy and Practice of Public Human Services, 57*(4), 23–30.

Muller, C., Katz, S. R., & Dance, L. J. (1999). Investing in teaching and learning: Dynamics of the teacher-student relationship from each actor's perspective. *Urban Education, 34*(3), 292–337.

Murray, V. M., & Brody, G. H. (1999). Self-regulation and self-worth of Black children reared in economically stressed, rural, single mother-headed families: The contribution of risk and protective factors. *Journal of Family Issues, 20*(4), 458–484.

Myers, H. F., & Taylor, S. (1998). Family contributions to risk and resilience in African American children. *Journal of Comparative Family Studies, 29*(1), 215–229.

Nahulu, L. B., Andrade, N. N., Makini, G., Yuen-Noelle, Y. C., McDermott, J. F., Danko, G. P., Johnson, R. C., & Waldron, J. A. (1996). Psychosocial risk and protective influences in Hawaiian adolescent psychopathology. *Cultural Diversity and Mental Health, 2*(2), 107–114.

National Youth Gang Center. (1997). *1995 National Youth Gang Survey.* Washington, DC: U.S. Department of Justice, Office of Justice Programs, Office of Juvenile Justice and Delinquency Prevention.

Neal, A. M., Lilly, R. S., & Zakis, S. (1993). What are African American children afraid of? *Journal of Anxiety Disorders, 7,* 129–139.

Neal, A. M., & Turner, S. M. (1991). Anxiety disorders research with African Americans: Current status. *Psychological Bulletin, 109,* 400–410.

O'Brien-Caughy, M., Randolph, S. M., & O'Campo, P. J. (2002). The Afrocentric Home Environment Inventory: An observational measure of the racial socialization features of the home environment for African American preschool children. *Journal of Black Psychology, 28*(1), 37–52.

Ogbu, J. U. (1978). *Minority education and caste: The American system in cross-cultural perspectives.* New York: Academic Press.

Ogbu, J. U. (1981). Origins of human competence: A cultural-ecological perspective. *Child Development, 52*(2), 413–429.

Ogbu, J. U. (1987). Variability in minority school performance: A problem in search of an explanation. *Anthropology and Education Quarterly, 18*(4), 312–334.

Ortega, A. N., Gergen, P. J., Paltiel, A. D., Bauchner, H., Belanger, K. D., & Leaderer, B. P. (2002). Impact of site of care, race, and Latino ethnicity on medication use for childhood asthma. *Pediatrics, 109*(1), 131–136.

Pang, V. O. (1991). The relationship of test anxiety and math achievement to parental values in Asian-American and European-American middle school students. *Journal of Research and Development in Education, 24,* 1–10.

Phinney, J. S. (1996). When we talk about American ethnic group, what do we mean? *American Psychologist, 51,* 918–927.

Randolph, S. M., Koblinsky, S. A., Beemer, M. A., Roberts, D. D., & Letiecq-Bethany, L. (2000). Behavior problems of African American boys and girls attending Head Start programs in violent neighborhoods. *Early Education and Development, 11*(3), 339–356.

Reyna, C. (2000). Lazy, dumb, or industrious: When stereotypes convey attribution information in the classroom. *Educational Psychology Review, 12*(1), 85–110.

Ripple, C., & Luthar, S. S. (1998). *Long-term predictors of academic adjustment and high school dropout among inner-city adolescents.* (Manuscript submitted for publication.)

Roberts, R. E., Chen, Y. W., & Solovitz, B. L. (1995). Symptoms of DSM-III-R major depression among Anglo, African, and Mexican American adolescents. *Journal of Affective Disorders, 36*(1–2), 1–9.

Roberts, R. E., & Sobhan, M. (1992). Symptoms of depression in adolescence: A comparison of Anglo, African, and Hispanic Americans. *Journal of Youth and Adolescence, 216*(6), 639–651.

Safren, S. A., Gonzalez, R. E., Horner, S. A., Gonzalez, R. E., Horner, K. J., Leung, A. W., Heimberg, R. G., & Juster, H. R. (2000). Anxiety in ethnic minority youth: Methodological and conceptual issues and review of the literature. *Behavior Modification, 24*(2), 147–183.

Salisbury, J., Rees, G., & Gorard, S. (1999). Accounting for the differential attainment of boys and girls at school. *School Leadership and Management, 19*(4), 403–426.

Schreiber, G. B., Robins, M., Striegel-Moore, R., Obarzanek, E., Morrison, J. A., & Wright, D. J. (1996). Weight modification efforts reported by Black and Euro-American preadolescent girls: National Heart, Lung, and Blood Institute Growth and Health Study. *Pediatrics, 98*(1), 63–70.

Shonkoff, J., & Phillips, D. (Eds.). (2000). *From neurons to neighborhoods: The science of early childhood development.* Washington, DC: National Academy Press.

Siegl, J. M., Aneshensel, C. S., Taub, B., Cantwell, D. P., & Driscoll, A. K (1998). Adolescent depressed mood in a multiethnic sample. *Journal of Youth and Adolescence, 27*(4), 413–427.

Steele, C. M. (1997). A threat in the air: How stereotypes shape intellectual identity and performance. *American Psychologist, 52,* 613–629.

Steele, C. M. (1999, August). Thin ice: "Stereotype Threat" and Black college students. *Atlantic Monthly,* pp. 44–54.

Stehno, S. M. (1990). The elusive continuum of child welfare services: Implications for minority children and youths. *Child Welfare, 69*(6), 551–562.

Sue, S., & Zane, N. W. (1985). Academic achievement and socioemotional adjustment among Chinese university students. *Journal of Counseling Psychology, 32*(4), 570–579.

Swanson, J. W., Linskey, A. O., Quintero, S-Ruben, & Pumariega-Andres, J. (1992). A binational school survey of depressive symptoms, drug use, and suicidal ideation. *Journal of the American Academy of Child and Adolescent Psychiatry, 31*(4), 669–678.

Thorkildsen, R., & Stein, R. S. (1998). Is parent involvement related to student achievement? Exploring the evidence. *Research Bulletin, 22,* 17–20.

U.S. Department of Education. (1994). *Strong families, strong schools.* Washington, DC: Author.

U.S. Department of Health and Human Services. (2001). *Mental health: Culture, race, and ethnicity—A supplement to mental health: A report of the Surgeon General.* Rockville, MD: U.S. Department of Health and Human Services, Substance Abuse and Mental Health Services Administration, Center for Mental Health Services.

Vazsonyi, A. T., & Flannery, D. J. (1997). Early adolescent delinquent behaviors: Associations with family and school domains. *Journal of Early Adolescence, 17*(3), 271–293.

Vega, W. A., Gil, A. G., & Wagner, E. (1998). Cultural adjustments and Latino adolescent drug use. In W. Vega & A. G. Gil (Eds.), *Drug use and ethnicity in early adolescence* (pp. 125–148). New York: Plenum Press.

Ventura, S. J., Martin, J. A., Curtin, S. C., & Mathews, T. J. (1999). Births: Final data for 1997. *National Vital Statistics Reports, 47*(18). Hyattsville, MD: National Center for Health Statistics.

Wagenaar, T. C., & Coates, R. D. (1999). Race and children: The dynamics of early socialization. *Education, 120*(2), 220–236.

Walker-Barnes, C. J., & Mason, C. A. (2001). Ethnic differences in the effects of parenting on gang involvement and gang delinquency: A longitudinal, hierarchical linear modeling perspective. *Child Development, 72*(6), 1814–1831.

Waller, A. E., Baker, S. P., & Szocka, A. (1989). Childhood injury deaths: National analysis and geographic variations. *American Journal of Public Health, 79,* 310–315.

Weisz, J. R., & Sigman, M. (1993). Parent reports of behavioral and emotional problems among children in Kenya, Thailand, and the United States. *Child Development, 64*(1), 98–109.

Zimmerman, R. S., Khoury, E. L., Vega, W. A., & Gil, A. G. (1995). Teacher and parent perceptions of behavior problems among a sample of African American, Hispanic, and non-Hispanic White students. *American Journal of Community Psychology, 23*(2), 181–197.

CHAPTER 4

GENDER DIFFERENCES IN CHILDHOOD AND ADOLESCENCE

CATHRYN C. POTTER

University of Denver

Are girls and boys different? If so, how do they differ? How should professionals working with children and youth take these differences into account in designing and implementing interventions? These are not questions that are easily answered. The influence of gender is quite complex—especially when viewed in interaction with other individual characteristics and broader societal conditions. In this chapter, the focus is on key gender differences that inform assessment and intervention.

Although girls and boys share many attributes and experiences during their formative years, there are also differential patterns in the risks they face. It is more probable that boys will display externalizing mental health problems, such as conduct disorder (Eisenburg, Martin, & Fabes, 1996). At all ages, boys are more likely to engage in physical aggression and, during the teen years, are more likely to commit violent acts and to be victims of physical violence (Crick, 1996; OJJDP, 2000). Consequently, boys are more liable to be involved with the juvenile justice system (Snyder, 1997). It is also more probable that they will take some kinds of risks. For example, boys are more likely to try to use illegal substances, drive under the influence, and ignore seatbelt and helmet laws (Grossman, 2000; Johnston, O'Malley, & Bachman, 2001; Lightfoot, 1997). Compared to girls, adolescent boys are more likely to die from accidents and from homicide (Grossman, 2000; OJJDP, 2000). Although boys report less suicidal ideation than girls, they are more likely to successfully complete suicide attempts than are girls (Spirito, Bond, Kurkjian, Devost, Bosworth, & Brown, 1993).

Girls have different risk patterns. They are much more liable to be victims of sexual assault by strangers, romantic partners, and family members (OJJDP, 2000). They are more likely to experience internalizing mental health problems, such as depression and anxiety, and to attempt suicide than are boys (Spirito et al., 1993). Girls are more likely to endanger their health by extreme dieting practices and to be diagnosed with eating disorders (Rogers, Resnick, Mitchell, & Blum, 1997). Their links to some risky behaviors come through relationships. For example, although girls drive under the influence less often than boys do, they are quite likely to ride with someone who is driving under the influence (Millstein

& Erwin, 1987). They are also at risk for early sexual activity (Wilcox, 1999). Although girls form a small minority of juvenile delinquents (some 20 percent), they are more likely to be involved for status offenses (such as truancy, running away, being out of control of parent, etc.) and for some crimes such as prostitution (Poe-Yamagato & Butts, 1996).

It is not possible to examine all aspects of gender differences in one chapter. Therefore this chapter focuses on a few areas, at differing system levels, where gender differences are especially important in designing assessment and intervention. These include the following:

- The understanding of the self
- Peer relationships and experiences
- School performance and life aspirations
- Family relationships

As you read, keep a few thoughts in mind. First, the focus is on one part of a lifelong journey from childhood through adulthood. Girls are on their way to womanhood and boys to manhood; concerns of children and adolescents cannot be divorced from the concerns of women and men. Second, much of the gender literature is fragmented along disciplinary lines, although attention to integrating knowledge across research traditions is becoming more common (Eckes & Trautner, 2000; Johnson et al., 1999). You may want to explore new findings and approaches in the coming years. At the end of the chapter, a few sources are recommended to begin that exploration.

Take a few minutes to read the case studies on Angie and Jason. If you were to begin working with Angie and/or Jason, where would you start? What information would you privilege by moving it forward in your thinking? What system levels would you target? What do Angie and Jason need in order to support their development?

CASE STUDY
ANGIE

You meet Angie at a family service clinic. Her mother, Diane, sought an appointment for Angie, saying that she was concerned about Angie's falling grades and generally bad attitude. In your interviews with Angie and with her mother, you learn the following things.

Angie is 14 years old. She is the oldest of three children living with their mother in a single-family home in a lower-middle-class neighborhood. She considers her brothers to be the bane of her existence ("so incredibly dumb"), and is having much conflict with her mother about such things as clothing, curfew, and dating ("My mom is so lame"). Angie is in the eighth grade this year, having made the transition to junior high last year. She had been an A student in elementary school, with interests in science and in history. Now she is floundering in school and says, "I'm not really good at anything anymore. Besides, the teachers don't even know I'm there."

Diane chose Angie's junior high because of its academic reputation ("Angie is really smart") and because "it is in a better part of town." In elementary school, Angie had a large group of friends, many of whom played on the same softball team. Many of these girls went to another school, but Angie still has three best friends from that group. Until recently, the group numbered five girls, but one "turned on us, I mean like a total bitch! She started all kinds of rumors and stuff. I can't believe it happened. We used to tell each other everything. And the other girls at school, I don't have enough money to be *their* friends, and they are really *mean*. Well, a few of them are OK, but you wouldn't believe what kids with money get into." Angie has continued to play softball with her team, but has recently been erratic about attending games and practices "because Jason thinks it takes too much time, and the coach says Jason ought to lighten up."

Angie is in love with 16-year-old Jason. Says Angie: "We are, like, glued together. I think about him all the time! He just got his license, and his uncle gave him a van. Can you believe my mom doesn't like me to ride with him? I mean, if you just got your license then you are probably the best driver you'll ever be since you haven't forgotten anything from the test." Jason is "gorgeous." Angie feels she should certainly lose "at least 10 pounds—maybe 20. You have to look good!" Angie and Jason have not had sexual intercourse, but Angie says, "He *is* 16, so probably I'll have to pretty soon."

Angie's parents divorced when she was 10 years old, following her mother's discovery that her father had begun fondling Angie at age 9. She has not seen her father since then, although she hears about him from her paternal grandparents. According to Angie, "He's really into drugs and really messed up. He used to work construction, but now he's just one of those drugged-out biker guys." Diane is a bank teller and attends college part time, majoring in business administration. Says Diane: "We are headed for the middle class—someday!" Diane sought counseling for Angie when the sexual abuse was discovered. The therapist saw both Angie and her mother, and the two together for almost a year. Both report that counseling was helpful. Says Angie: "Hey, it's the only reason I'm even willing to talk to *you*."

On her thoughts about herself, Angie says, "I don't know, I don't know. Really, I don't know who I am. I look back, and the old me was really strong and stupid, and going to do it all. But the world isn't like that really.... Now, it's all fuzzy and no one hears me, not even Jason. Well, sometimes my friends do, but maybe they are slipping away too. I think about this stuff a lot, then I just get so tired, I can't do anything."

CASE STUDY

JASON

You meet Jason, age 16, and his parents at a family service agency that also provides diversion services to the local juvenile court. Jason was referred for counseling following a car accident in which he lost control of the van and crashed into a tree. Fortunately, none of his six passengers was injured. Although Jason was not driving under the influence, there were open cans of beer in the car. He was referred to the diversion program in lieu of facing a liquor law violation charge.

Jason lives with his parents, both professionals, and an older sister and younger brother in a comfortable, upper-middle-class section of town. He has always been an athletic kid and plays baseball for the high school team. His teammates are his primary peer group. When not practicing or playing baseball, they spend time mountain biking or, recently, tinkering with the engine on Jason's van. Jason's parents feel that these boys are all "good kids." As his father states, "We don't have to pay much attention to what Jason is up to. He pretty much comes and goes as he pleases."

For the most part, Jason is a good student, bringing home primarily Bs. His parents report that during the last few months, he seems to have lost his concentration, and his grades are slipping. In addition, he seems to be angry with everyone. Always a quiet boy, Jason converses even less with his parents and siblings. Says his mother, "I just don't know what he is thinking or feeling." His Dad adds, "He's just a regular kid."

Jason's parents blame some of the recent changes in Jason on his relationship with Angie, age 14. They worry that she is too young for Jason, and see her as too "forward" ("They talk every night on the phone. If he doesn't call her, she calls him"). Jason's mom notices that if Jason calls Angie and she isn't home, he seems distracted and angry until he can reach her. "I just don't know what kind of hold she has on him."

In private conversation with Jason, you find him difficult to talk with. He answers most questions with short sentences. He denies having any problems and has difficulty describing his feelings. He blames the accident on "too much noise in the van," and says, "I'll never take that many guys anywhere again." He denies having any knowledge of the origin of the beer, saying, "I wouldn't rat anyone out even if I did know." He reluctantly acknowledges that "lots of kids have drugs and alcohol at school. It's easy to get. Everyone does it—at least a little bit."

Jason has difficulty articulating the pros and cons of his relationship with Angie. He says simply that he loves her, that they are "alike," and that he doesn't understand why she can't spend most of her free time with him. He doesn't like her softball team because "they practice and play at different times from my team. It cuts into our time together." He also thinks her teammates are loud and boisterous ("You should hear some of the stuff they say to each other"). Jason doesn't quite understand girls in general: "They talk all the time! They always want to talk about how they feel. What is the point?" He is very uncomfortable discussing the sexual aspect of their relationship, but does say he is "prepared" and carries a condom.

Jason wants to know "what I have to do to be finished with this court stuff."

GENDER RESEARCH IN SOCIAL AND DEVELOPMENTAL PSYCHOLOGY

During the last 40 years, gender differences have been largely addressed with a focus on cognition and on social roles, and specifically cognitive schemes that guide perceptions and behavior (Olson, Roese, & Zanna, 1996). Both social and developmental psychology focus on the ways boys and girls differ, and both fields propose competing explanations for those differences. The social psychology perspective generally frames questions about gender differences in the here and now, whereas the developmental approach focuses on patterns of change over time. A social psychology perspective places more emphasis on the role of current environmental influences, whereas the developmental perspective focuses more on internal mechanisms, such as cognitive schema, and on early family influences (Eckes & Troutner, 2000).

If we step beyond the group of researchers devoted specifically to gender research, developmental research often takes a gender-neutral approach in seeking to understand adolescence. Moreover, basic research in developmental and social psychology is not often formulated to guide intervention with youth experiencing difficulties. Attention to crafting an understanding of gender-specific intervention approaches and assessing the effectiveness of those interventions is largely missing in the literature. Still, there are practical implications of the literature on gender differences for those serving children and youth.

VIEWING DEVELOPMENT FROM THE WOMEN'S PSYCHOLOGY PERSPECTIVE

As already noted, many domains of human development have been examined from a gender-neutral point of view. Scholars interested in the psychology of women question this approach, arguing that the prevailing research strategies conceptualized adolescent development from a male-centered perspective. They argue that the development of girls and women is substantially different from that of boys and men, and that a specific focus on the female experience is needed (Brown, 1998; Gilligan, 1990, 1993). Much of the research in this tradition uses samples consisting only of girls, and has been qualitative in nature (e.g., Brown & Gilligan, 1992). This approach is in keeping with a feminist goal of highlighting experiences and voices not commonly examined in the literature; however, the absence of comparison groups leaves open the possibility that observations about girls may apply equally well to boys (Eccles, Barber, Jozefowicz, Malenchuk, & Vida, 1999). Certainly, we know more about the inner lives of girls than we do of boys.

Drawing on a reformulation of psychodynamic theory, some argue that early family experiences lead boys and girls on differing paths, with the paths of girls supporting the development of relational skills rather than an individualistic orientation (Chodorow, 1978). This process involves gender-differentiated individuation such that boys are seen as separating from the mother in early childhood, whereas girls do so in adolescence. For example, in early childhood, boys develop an understanding of themselves as different from their mothers, but girls continue to deepen their identification with the feminine role model. Thus, when boys and girls face the developmental task of separating during adolescence, they approach the task from different places, and for girls the task may be more profound. On the other hand, girls spend their childhood more connected to the caregiver, thus giving them greater opportunity to develop a relational orientation; boys pursue a more individuated path. This theoretical orientation is based on reinterpretation of data used in the formulation of Freudian and Eriksonian theory. It may be used to explain observed gender differences in gender identification, relational orientation, and emotional expressiveness in childhood (Dorney, 1995; Fabes & Martin, 1991; Swann & Wyer, 1997) and in qualitative findings related to adolescent crisis among girls (Gilligan, Lyon, & Kammer, 1990).

In contrast, some argue for a broader socio-historical and cultural view of development (Wersch, del Rio, & Alvarez, 1995) in which individual human development is seen as being driven strongly by social and cultural forces. From this perspective, one cannot understand gender differences without explicit attention to the role of patriarchy in both family and society. Patriarchal systems value attributes seen as "male" over those seen as "female," and grant certain privileges to boys that are not granted to girls. For example, parents and teachers may privilege traditionally male interests (e.g., math, science, and sports), and may actually see girls as unable to excel in these areas. Boys may be expected to be leaders and take charge, whereas girls may be seen as "pushy" if they attempt to do so.

In recent qualitative research with rural girls in Colorado, girls describe being passed over as managers or being denied opportunities to employ their skills using farm machinery in favor of boys with no prior experience. These girls also note that the result is lowered income and influence for girls in the work place (Demmler, Potter, Ramsey, & Jacobson, 2000). Patriarchal systems affect the development of boys as well. Boys must learn to manage privilege and power and must conform to social expectations of masculine behavior.

UNDERSTANDING THE SELF

What does it mean to be a girl? Or to be a boy? What gender differences do we see in child and adolescent understanding and experience?

Gender Identity and Social Development

The ability to identify gender and apply gender stereotypes begins early in life for girls and for boys. Children can accurately distinguish adult gender by 2 years of age and the gender of other children by age 3 (Fagot & Leinbach, 1993). By age 3, children have clear ideas about gender stereotypes (boys hit people and girls cry a lot [Kuhn, Nash, & Brucken, 1978]); these ideas continue to gain complexity through childhood. Children's stereotypes become more flexible with age (Signorella, Bigler, & Liben, 1993) and the concepts of masculinity and femininity become increasingly important. Between ages 8 and 11, girls become more androgynous and less bound by gender stereotypes, and boys and girls behave more similarly. During this time, girls tend to be strong, self-confident, and outspoken—attributes that are generally supported by the social world (Basow & Rubin, 1999; Dorney, 1995.) At around age 11, this flexibility diminishes; both boys and girls become more rigid in their understanding of gender (Hill & Lynch, 1983).

These changes coincide with entry to puberty and with changes in the social world, such as the organization of school, the importance of peers and sexual attractiveness, and increased performance pressures from parents. Adolescent girls use more gender stereotypes than they did in their preteen years (Basow & Rubin, 1999), but they are more flexible than their male peers (Galambos, Almeida, & Peterson, 1990). That is, adolescent girls and boys attribute many individual differences in behavior to gender differences, but girls are more likely than are boys to see a wide range of behaviors and attributes as appropriate for females. For example, girls may see an active interest in sports as gender appropriate, whereas boys may see such interest as lying in the male domain. Many studies have found that girls are more likely to view themselves as expressive (versus instrumental) and interdependence oriented (versus individualistic) (Bem, 1981; Lippa, 1995; McGuire & McGuire, 1987; Swan & Wyer, 1997). Across all age groups, the communications of girls are more "other-directed, warm and mitigated, and less dominant, status asserting, aggressive and task-oriented than males' speech" (Carli & Bukatko, 2000, p. 321). In spite of this, there appear to be few gender differences in the *ability* to decode information about others' emotional states and to take multiple perspectives, although adolescent girls appear to be more likely to *use* perspective-taking and emotional decoding skills than are boys (Davis & Franzoni, 1991; Eisenberg, Martin, & Fabes, 1996). That is, although girls seem to display more advanced social-cognitive skills, this may be a matter of preference and practice rather than ability.

Compared to boys, girls report greater frequency, intensity, and duration of many emotional states, including surprise, shyness, shame, sadness, and guilt. Boys are more likely to deny experiencing these emotions (Perry, Perry, & Weiss, 1989; Zahn-Waxler, Cole, & Barret, 1991). Adolescent girls also report greater intensity of both positive and negative emotions than do boys (Fujita, Diener, & Sandvik, 1991), and girls are often perceived as expressing more emotions—except anger (Fabes & Martin, 1991). These differences may be related to family socialization, given that parents are less accepting of girls' anger, while being more supportive of other emotional expressions (Eisenberg et al., 1996).

Researchers on the psychology of women have described the entry into adolescence as a time of crisis for adolescent girls (Brown & Gilligan, 1992). Girls increasingly realize that their understanding of the world is in conflict with societal expectations, and this provokes the crisis. They become gradually aware of the accommodations that society demands from them, of the importance of appearance and role conformity and of the limits on their aspirations. As a result, they come to discredit their feelings and understandings, experiencing increased self-doubt (Hill & Lynch, 1983). Brown and Gilligan (1992) describe the loss of congruence between the internal and external self among adolescent girls. Indeed, girls seem to lose contact with their inner world, experiencing it as fragmented and hard to access (Gilligan, Lyon, & Kammer, 1990). This loss of "voice" may be characteristic of girls' entry to adolescence, and it is in stark contrast to the vibrant, feisty, confident understanding of self they experienced prior to adolescence.

It is not clearly known if this phenomenon varies for girls from differing ethnic cultures, socioeconomic statuses, or sexual orientations. Certainly variations would be expected because the experiences of girls are so deeply rooted in the culture of everyday life and in the inner struggles they face. Moreover, we do not know if boys experience a similar loss, perhaps manifested in different domains. These gaps in the qualitative literature make it difficult to draw firm conclusions about how boys and girls differ in this regard.

Self-Esteem

Extensive discussions have focused on diminished self-esteem among adolescent girls (AAUW, 1990; Gilligan et al., 1990; Pipher, 1994). These patterns do exist, but the story is a complex one. For example, although adolescent girls report lower self-esteem than do boys, the drop in self-esteem across adolescence is similar for both genders (Eccles, Wigfield, Flanagan, Miller, Reuman, & Yee, 1989). Gender patterns in self-esteem vary by domain and by ethnicity, and they are affected by social structures, such as whether a school transition is to middle school or to junior high (Simmons & Blyth, 1987). Although global self-esteem is lower for girls during adolescence, there is considerable variability by domain, with boys being more confident in their athletic and mathematical abilities and girls more confident in English and social abilities (Winston, Eccles, & Senior, 1997).

Self-esteem among African American girls appears higher than that of both European American girls and African American boys, and it is less likely to drop over time (Rotheram-Borus, Dopkins, Sabate, & Lightfoot, 1996). African American girls are most confident in their social and athletic abilities and less confident about their school-related abilities. Girls of color who rate themselves as having strong ethnic identities have higher self-esteem than do those who self-identify as mainstream or bicultural (Rotheram-Borus et al., 1996). European American girls (and not African American girls) who mature early have lower self-esteem (Eccles et al., 1999).

Some have argued that the risk for lowered self-esteem among European American girls is caused by unrealistic societal expectations of feminine beauty (e.g., Wolfe, 1991). Certainly body image, the relative assessment of one's physical attributes in comparison to an external societal norm, is an important issue for adolescent girls. Striegel-Moore (1997) argues that the tension between ideals for beauty and the experience of puberty is exacerbated by an interpersonal orientation and by the importance of beauty in the conception of femininity. It is normative for adolescent girls to experience intense body image dissatisfaction; however, this seems to apply somewhat more for European American girls (Attie & Brooks-Gunn, 1989). Excessive dieting and eating disorders may stem, in part, from pathological occupation with body image. Although only 1 to 3 percent of adolescent girls meet diagnostic criteria for eating disorders (Hoek, 1991), girls are much more likely than boys to engage in extreme patterns of dieting and to develop serious eating-related problems (Rogers et al., 1997).

Depression

By adulthood, women are twice as likely to report depressive symptoms and 1.5 times more likely than men to be diagnosed with clinical depression (Nolen-Hoeksema, 1990). During childhood, depression appears to manifest differently in girls and boys. For example, boys appear more likely to exhibit some depressive symptoms, such as behavioral disturbance, self-derogation, and physiological complaints, whereas girls are more likely to display other symptoms, such as dysphoria. Differences in the prevalence of depression emerge during early adolescence around the eighth grade (Petersen et al., 1991). By age 15, girls are twice as likely to be depressed as are boys, displaying higher incidence of both depressive disorder and subclinical depressive symptoms (Nolen-Hoeksema & Girgus, 1994).

It appears that girls and boys differ in their styles of coping with negative events and with dysphoria. During adolescence, boys are more likely to externalize and girls are more likely to internalize negative events (Levit, 1991). In several studies, Nolen-Hoeksema has demonstrated that females are more apt to engage in a passive, ruminating coping style that focuses cognition on symptoms, causes, and consequences of depression. In contrast, males are more likely to take an active, behavioral approach to mitigating symptoms (Nolen-Hoeksema, 1987, 1991; Noel-Hoeksema & Girgus, 1994). These differing styles of coping are associated with longer, deeper depressive episodes for girls. Involvement in sports activities appears protective against depressed mood for girls (Gore, Farrell, & Gordon, 2001). Girls also face greater challenges in adolescence, including increased social pressure to be socially compliant (Nolen-Hoeksema, 1991), and greater risk for negative events, including sexual victimization (Peterson et al., 1987). These contribute to risk for depression.

Finally, numerous studies suggest that adolescent girls are at increased risk for suicidal ideation and attempt, although boys are more likely to complete an attempt. Male attempters are also more likely to display serious intentionality prior to the attempt (Spirito et al., 1993). Nevertheless, the typical suicide attempter is a young adolescent female who ingests drugs (Hoberman & Garfinkle, 1988). Data from the 1999 Youth Risk Behavior Survey indicate that 18.3 percent of girls report having made a plan regarding suicide attempt during the past 12 months, as compared to 10.9 percent of boys (Centers for Disease Control, n.d.a). The increased risk for attempt among girls may be driven by depression (Spirito et al., 1993) and by a history of sexual abuse (Lipschitz, Winegar, Nicolaou, Hartnick, Wolfson, & Southwick, 1999), although the exact mechanisms here are not well understood.

THE RELATIONAL WORLD

As noted previously, research from a number of perspectives indicates the experience of self is more relationally oriented for girls than is the experience of self for boys. That is, girls appear to be more interested in and skillful at establishing and maintaining strong patterns of communication. They see themselves as relational beings. We might then expect to see gender differences in the nature of friendship, aggression, and romance.

Friendship

For all children, positive experiences of friendship are related to development and to psychological functioning (Crick, 1996). Friendships increase interpersonal skills, sensitivity, and understanding of others (Laursen, 1993; Schulman, 1993; Youniss, 1980; Youniss & Smollar, 1985). Girls spend more time with their friends, have smaller groups of friends, share more with their friends, and expect and get more from their friends (kindness, loyalty, empathetic understanding) (Belle, 1999; Clark & Bittle, 1992; Parker & Asher, 1987; Savin-Williams & Berndt, 1990; Wong & Csikszentmihalyi, 1991). Boys are more likely to have activity-centered relationships that are organized as a function of participation in sports or other activities, such as serving as a class officer, joining the marching band, or simply playing video games with friends. Boys disagree more often with friends and tend to be more controlling and less cooperative in their play with others (Berndt, Perry, & Miller, 1988; Leaper, 1991).

In early adolescence, girls begin to prefer dyadic relationships and their friendships become more intimate, self-disclosing, and stable over time. In contrast, boys continue to congregate in larger groups, and disclose less information with close friends. Girls are more likely to discuss problems with close friends. Boys are more likely to seek sources they see as having expertise with the issue at hand (Furman & Buhrmester, 1985, 1992). When girls have intimate friendships, they are less likely than boys to seek out new friends (Savin-Williams & Berndt, 1990); however, they are more likely to seek new friends following betrayal or loss of friendship than are boys (Way, 1996).

Most qualitative research on girls' friendships has focused on European American, middle-class girls (Brown, Way, & Duff, 1999); however, the few studies of ethnically and socioeconomically diverse samples have found some different patterns. Qualitative research highlights class-related differences among adolescent girls in friendships. Working-class girls are more likely to solidify relationships with other girls in response to perceived threats, whereas middle-class girls are more likely to struggle to maintain relationships in a structure of hierarchical, popularity-oriented social cliques (Eder, 1985; Evans & Eder, 1993). Maintaining popularity, for white middle-class girls requires a complex negotiation of "meanness" and power (Merten, 1997). Working-class girls often use ritual teasing of each other as a way to distance from dominant culture roles and to respond to environmental pressures. This ritual teasing is not about "meanness," power, and competition but rather it is characterized by group solidarity and social support (Eder, 1991, 1993; Way, 1998; Ward, 1996). For example, Eder (1993) reports an exchange among girls in which one girl, temporarily ousted by the group, begins a ritual teasing about sexual encounters. The activity eventually unites all the girls in laughing and restores group solidarity as they discuss their thoughts about romance and ambivalence about sexual activity.

Girl #1: You are gonna say #*# Oh, Bob it feels so good!
Girl #2: You ain't gonna hear that because I ain't doing nothing!
Girl #1: Oh, little bit higher Bobbie, little bit higher #*#....
Girl #3: If she seems to be crying, it's a moment of joy.

Aggression

Crick and colleagues (Crick, 1995, 1996; Grotpeter & Crick, 1996; Rys & Bear, 1997) have explored the nature of aggression among children and adolescents. In contrast to the common understanding of aggression as being either verbal or physical in nature, Crick has examined another type of aggression—relational aggression. Relational aggression is characterized by behaviors aimed at hurting others through relationships (e.g., gossip and rumor-spreading or threatening to withdraw friendship). Compared to boys, girls of all ages appear more likely to engage in relationally aggressive acts. They are also more likely to be hurt by such acts. In contrast, boys appear more likely to behave in physically aggressive ways. Boys and girls are equally likely to use verbal aggression. Both boys and girls see these forms of aggression as gender linked, and those who behave in nonnormative aggressive ways (girls who are physically aggressive and boys who are relationally aggressive) pay an emotional and social price (Crick, 1996).

Romance

Romantic experiences in adolescence are embedded in the individual cultures of the teens involved, the broader teen culture, and the specific peer culture in which the dyad is embedded (Coates, 1999). Teen culture is rapidly changing, as is the diversity of adult relationships that adolescents see around them (Graber, Britto, & Brooks-Gunn, 1999). Nevertheless, a few observations from research can be made. Sexual activity among adolescents has become normative in American society (Graber, Brooks-Gunn, & Galen, 1998) and is viewed by adolescents as an important part of teen life (Sugland, Wilder, & Chandra, 1996). In 1999, 49.9 percent of high school students (grades 9–12) reported having had sexual intercourse. Youth appear to be engaging in sexual activity at earlier ages. High school freshmen are 2.4 times as likely to report having engaged in sexual intercourse prior to age 13 than are high school seniors (11.7 percent compared to 4.8 percent) (Centers for Disease Control, n.d.b). Adult views have not kept pace; in fact, adults heartily disapprove (Smith, 1994).

In many ways, romantic relationships are a hallmark of adolescence in western societies. Love is the central theme in some 73 percent of popular rock music songs (Christenson & Roberts, 1998), and adolescent-oriented TV serials most commonly focus on romance and sex themes (Ward, 1995). Indeed, by middle adolescence, teens become preoccupied with romantic feelings (Medora, Goldstein, & Von der Hellen, 1994; Savin-Williams & Berndt,

1990). These relationships can positively affect teens' social competence and self-esteem (Neeman, Hubbard, & Masten, 1995; Samet & Kelly, 1987); however, early romantic relationships are associated with psychological, behavioral, and school difficulties for girls (Cauffman & Steinberg, 1996; Grinder, 1996; Neeman et al., 1996).

Adolescents display wider emotional swings than do adults, and many of these emotions focus on romantic relationships (Larson & Richards, 1994). These relationships are sources of both positive emotions, such as love and affection, and negative emotions, such as anxiety, anger, and jealousy. Introduction to this world of emotion is initiated in part by biological changes in puberty (Richards & Larson, 1993). However, romantic feelings are also related to romantic scripts. For example, Simon, Eder, and Evans (1992) in a qualitative study of sixth- to eighth-grade girls found a shared norm that "one should always be in love." These scripts can intensify both positive and negative emotions—emotions over which adolescents may have relatively little control (Larson, Clore, & Wood, 1999). Cognitively, adolescents are just developing some basic elements of emotional cognition, including the ability to differentiate emotions from experiences that create them, to separate one's own emotions from those of others, to consider intentions of others, and to differentiate complex emotional states. For these reasons, the emotions of romance cloud judgment among adolescents even as they contribute to the development of emotional intelligence over time (Larson et al., 1999).

Gender differences abound in the experience of adolescent romance. Adolescent girls emphasize the nature of the relationship, whereas adolescent boys more often focus on the sexual aspects (Cimbalo & Nowell, 1993; Hong & Faedda, 1994). Although the "double standard" regarding the social acceptability of sexual relationships in general and "cheating" in specific is diminishing (Michael, Gagnon, Laumann, & Kolata, 1994; Smith, 1994), it still plays an important part in the ways adolescents view their own sexual relationships, and those of others. Many teens report having had distorted ideas about what to expect from sexual relationships, and girls are especially likely to say they "wished they had waited" (De Gaston, Jensen, & Weed, 1995). The good news: As both girls and boys get older, they use more mature approaches to choosing partners and establishing relationships based on mutual interests (Furman, Brown, & Feiring, 1999).

As boys and girls move through adolescence, they spend more time and derive more support from romantic relationships (Furman & Buhrmester, 1992; Richards, Crowe, Larson, & Swarr, 1998). Girls are more likely to emphasize self-disclosure, support, and jealousy when describing their romantic relationships (Feiring, 1996). Some argue that lower levels of self-disclosure by boys in romantic relationships stem from the norms set with male friends rather than from differential desires for self-disclosure (Aires, 1987). Regardless of its source, this pattern continues into adulthood (Orlofsky, 1993). The pattern also holds in terms of self-disclosure to researchers examining romantic relationships, as the following quote illustrates:

> Well over ten years ago, I set out to interview pubescents about puberty. If there are more reluctant interview subjects then I have never come across them, and I soon started asking for teenagers' recollections instead. Teenage boys didn't have much more to say than pubescents, but when I asked teenage girls about puberty they rushed into four- and five-hour narratives about sexual and romantic life. How I looked when he first saw me; how he stuck

to me like glue; what we did that first night; how when he kissed me I felt like in a Harlequin novel; how he told me he loved me but how could I be sure; how he stayed with me after the baby and that was how I knew he really cared; how I told her off before I hit her; what I said, felt, wanted, what he meant, what she answered, what I felt when she said he felt because she said she felt, because I had…. (Thompson, 1995, p. 1)

Although romance is often a mutual choice, sexual activity need not be. Adolescent girls are at significant risk for coercive sexual relationships. In 1999, 12.5 percent of high school girls reported having experienced coerced sexual intercourse, as compared to 5.2 percent of boys (Centers for Disease Control, n.d.c). Between 60 and 75 percent of girls who have intercourse before age 15 report forced sexual experiences, and 60 percent of girls who become pregnant during adolescence have been sexually abused in some way prior to the pregnancy (AGI, 1994; Moore et al., 1989). Over half of sexual assaults against adolescent girls take place in dating relationships (Ross, 1988). However, girls are not likely to report dating violence. When they do seek help, they seek it from friends (Calhoun & Atkeson, 1991).

Considerable research indicates that social cognition about dating violence and rape is important in affecting behavior for both girls and boys. Social cognition is affected by societal rape myths. Teens of both genders who believe such myths are less likely to identify coercion, even if the victim said "no" (Jenkins & Dambrot, 1987). Up to one-third of girls see dating violence as a sign of love (Roscoe & Kelsey, 1986). Violent boys report motives for dating violence that include anger and jealousy and say they use violence to exert power and to control behavior (Burke, Stets, & Pitog-Good, 1989; Gamache, 1991). Witnessing family violence increases the risk that girls will experience date rape and increases the risk that boys will assault their dates (Jaffe, Sudermann, & Reitzel, 1992).

EDUCATION AND LIFE ASPIRATIONS

Gender differences in educational performance are hotly debated (AAUW, 1990, 1992, 1996). In 1974, Maccoby and Jacklin found patterns of gender difference favoring boys in several domains, including mathematics, verbal abilities, and spatial abilities. Recent research indicates that test-score differences have declined greatly; however, there remain considerable gender differences in the academic areas adolescents choose to pursue, and in the quality of the education they receive.

By high school, boys perform better than girls on standardized math tests (Eccles, 1985; Hyde, Fennema, & Lamon, 1990). However, meta-analyses of many studies of math ability indicate that in the general population, the gender difference may actually favor girls (Hyde et al., 1990). There no longer appear to be any gender differences in general verbal ability, although girls tend to do better on many subscales. Gender differences in spatial ability have been suggested as reasons for differences in interest in math and science. Again, however, differences are declining. Large differences favoring boys exist in only a few areas, and the difference lies in speed rather than in accuracy (Eisenberg et al., 1996).

These small differences in cognitive abilities do not appear to be large enough to explain the variations seen in interest and participation in academic domains. By high school, girls are taking less math and science and more language and literature. These differences are related to career choices, and persist into the college years, where girls are more likely to major in the arts and social sciences and boys are more likely to major in math, science, engineering, and business (AAUW, 1992). Parental beliefs about the abilities of children are related to performance (Eisenberg et al., 1996). Jacobs (1991) found that parental gender stereotypes have both a direct and indirect influence on children's abilities, by influencing children's beliefs about themselves. For example, even though girls have higher grades in math, boys have higher confidence in their math abilities, with these differences largely explained by parental stereotypes. By entry to adolescence, parental confidence is the best predictor of performance, serving as a stronger predictor than previous academic record (Eccles et al., 1982).

Differential educational experiences are well documented, although equality may be improving as schools and teachers explicitly consider gender in designing educational programs (AAUW, 1996; Eisenberg et al., 1996; Sadker & Sadker, 1994). Teachers may treat girls and boys differently, often supporting gender stereotypes. For example, Gold, Crombie, and Noble (1987) found that girls seen by the teacher as compliant were assessed as more capable than girls whose behavior was more active and confrontational, even when actual ability levels were the same. This pattern did not hold for boys. Girls are given less access to instructional time in areas such as math and science, and instructional materials are often gender biased (AAUW, 1991, 1992, 1996; Eisenberg et al., 1996; Purcell & Stewart, 1990). Qualitative work on experiences of adolescent girls reveals the importance of relationships with teachers and of a rigorous, equality-oriented environment (DeZolt & Henning-Stout, 1999).

> The teachers here, they just care about us. Like they don't just tell us what to do in class and forget about us. It's like we're real people with stuff going on in our lives. They make us work, too, real hard. But you want to because they believe we can do it, and we can. Not like in other schools I've been where they think you're just stupid or something and give you worksheets and stuff. (Genella, high school senior, as quoted in DeZolt & Henning-Stout, 1999, p. 258)

Are these qualities of a learning environment equally applicable to boys? Many would argue that they are. Are the qualities more salient for girls? That is, are they more likely to affect girls' level of engagement in learning? Researchers on the psychology of women argue yes, but without better research on boys' educational preferences we cannot be sure.

FAMILY CONNECTIONS

Although adolescence is typically seen as a time of life that emphasizes distance from family, relationships between adolescents and their families remain important influences. For both genders, a positive, mutual relationship with mom and an adaptive family system are predictors of good relationships between older teens and their families (Robinson, 2000). However, boys and girls treat their families differently in some ways, and they are treated differently by their families in some ways. For example, girls tend to disclose more of their affective lives to parents than boys (Papini, Farmer, Clark, Micka, & Barnett, 1990). Boys are given more autonomy during adolescence (Bumpus, Crouter, & McHale, 2001).

Warm, supportive family relationships are protective factors for both boys and girls, whereas family conflict is associated with many psychological and social problems (Fraser, 1998). Similarly, poor parenting practices are risk factors for many antisocial behaviors (Loeber, Farrington, Stouthamer-Loeber, & Van Kammen, 1998; Rodgers, 1999). Lower family cohesion and social support are associated with higher life stress among urban girls, whereas engaging in problem solving strategies is protective (Weist, Freedman, Paskewitz, & Proescher, 1995). With regard to substance abuse in early adolescence, family influences are more important in predicting substance use for girls than for boys. However, by late adolescence, both boys and girls are more influenced by peers and by lowered self-esteem than by family relationships (Green, 1995).

Parental monitoring of adolescent behavior is a protective factor at all ages (Green, 1995). There is an art to parental monitoring, however. Increased parental attempts at psychological control of girls serve to increase the likelihood of risky sexual behavior; on the other hand, consistent, pragmatic parental monitoring of behavior is protective (Santelli & Beilenson, 1992). Balancing supervision and protection with exposure to appropriate developmental challenges may be a theme of effective parenting for adolescents. And it may be particularly challenging for parents of girls, since parents of girls, as compared to parents of boys, often seek greater control (von der Lipp, 1998).

Given the centrality of mothers in many conceptions of family stability and in women's psychology conceptions of adolescent development, examining what is known about mother-daughter relationships has clear practice implications. The relationship between mothers and daughters is not a matter of personality match; mothers and daughters find ways to relate even when their approaches to life are very different (Morrison, 1995). The quality of the relationship, especially with regard to communication, is related to the mother's sense of competence as a parent (Suhrhoff, 1997). Girls without histories of problem behaviors are most likely to remember calm discussions with their mothers (Zweifel, 1995). De Waal (1993) engaged in lengthy interviews with 50 adolescent girls over a period of three years. These girls described a changing power balance between girls and mothers as interactions moved from a command framework to a negotiation framework. Mothers begin to use persuasion rather than force, and daughters use manipulation rather than conflict as both seek to maximize their own positions.

We cannot leave the topic of family relationships without emphasizing that girls are at greater risk for sexual abuse within their family contexts than are boys. Girls make up more than 80 percent of victims of incest (OJJDP, 2000). The onset of sexual abuse begins most often when girls are aged 8 to 12 (Finkelhor & Baron, 1986), but often continues into adolescence. Certainly the effects of sexual abuse are seen in adolescence. A history of sexual abuse is associated with problems for adolescent girls, including depression and suicide, early sexual activity and teen pregnancy, and juvenile delinquency. In addition, many girls experience a "sleeper effect," where the emotional effects of sexual abuse are experienced at later developmental stages (Finkehor & Berliner, 1995). Girls who have experienced child sexual abuse or date rape are more likely to experience fear, anger, loss of trust, flashbacks, sexual dysfunction, and symptoms of post-traumatic stress disorder (Miller, Monson, & Norton, 1995; Roth, Wayland, & Woolsy, 1990; Sorensen & Bowie, 1994). Thomlinson

(1998) notes, "The factors that appear to promote recovery from sexual abuse include support from a non-offending, caring parent; a high level of parental upset; early help seeking responses to the family crisis; a family history of skillful conflict management and high family cohesion" (p. 63).

THEMES IN GENDER DEVELOPMENT: PRACTICE PRINCIPLES

As you read this chapter, you may have been drawing some conclusions about the ways boys and girls differ. Although it is wise to be careful with these broad conclusions, there is also value in naming them and considering their implications. As you examine the following list, consider whether you might argue for adding other conclusions. Why might you draw additional conclusions? What would you like to know to be more certain about your conclusions?

- Girls and boys use gender stereotypes to define self and guide behavior and choices. This use of "role scripts" in early childhood and adolescence shapes identity. It is important to explore the ways gender stereotypes may be contributing to problem behaviors and to risk for problem behaviors. An important first step is simply talking with children and youth about their understanding of gender.

- Societal views of gender influence family, peer, and institutional cultures, such as school climate. These cultures may be more or less supportive of the development of girls and boys. Professionals can support or seek to change these cultural structures. This decision should be based on the degree to which children's social settings are characterized by rigidified and gendered opportunities. Research suggests that both girls and boys benefit when there are many opportunities for involvement and when opportunities are not highly gendered.

- Girls talk a lot more than boys do! They are more relational, and they are more comfortable with emotional disclosure. Boys are more active and task oriented. Assessment and intervention strategies that rely exclusively on "talk" may not be as effective in engaging boys. Conversely, highly structured task approaches may not be as effective in engaging girls.

- On balance, definitions of self among girls are more relational than they are among boys. Congruent with their understanding of self, girls' friendships, romantic relationships, and family relationships tend to be based on greater self-disclosure and display of emotion, higher levels of communication, and greater use of relational aggression. The quality of a relationship is of great importance to girls. For this reason, building trust through talk and commitment to genuine, lasting relationships may be important in interventions for girls. For example, a girl's helping professional might not seek to make, and then break, a strong relationship with the girl in a short-term intervention setting. It would be more appropriate to create a strong, mentoring relationship in the natural social network.

- The understanding of self for boys is more likely to be grounded in an assessment of task competence, individuality, and competition. Congruent with this, boys' social networks are more focused on shared activities, including risk-taking activities. Communication is more task oriented and less emotional, and boys are more likely to choose physical aggression when angry. For this reason, intervention with boys should be perceived by boys as "doing" something important. It might be grounded, for example, in adventurous activities that teach life lessons.

■ Assessment should be based on an understanding of the common and different risks that confront girls and boys. For example, both boys and girls experience declines in self-esteem during adolescence, but these declines manifest in different ways. For girls, assessment of depression, suicidal ideation, and engagement in self-harming behaviors (e.g., excessive dieting) is important. Attention must also be afforded current and historical sexual victimization. For boys, assessment should include focus on engagement in dangerous, risky activities, poor anger management, and propensity for use of violence as a problem-solving strategy. For boys also, assessment should include focus on the cognitions supporting behavior, especially those reasoning patterns linking emotions, desires for power and control, and behavior with others.

■ Adolescence may be a time of particular vulnerability for girls, although there is considerable debate on this point. Most scholars would agree that social structures place more limits on the behaviors and aspirations of girls during adolescence. Exploring the meaning and impact of gender on female experiences is important. Many would argue for explicitly connecting experiences of gender to larger social issues, such as gender discrimination.

■ Peer relationships provide children and youths with opportunities for emotional support, shared work, and adventure. Boys may experience work and adventure as related to task accomplishment. In contrast, girls may experience them as relational. Youth of color and lower SES youth may derive resilience against lowered self-esteem from peer networks that provide a sense of solidarity. In contrast, the peer networks for majority youth may be more competitive and less supportive. To date, these differences are not well incorporated into interventions. We should consider how knowledge of these differences might be advantaged in the design of social and problem-solving skills training for children and youths.

■ Love isn't easy. Gender differences in communication styles, emotionality, self-disclosure, conceptions of love, and readiness for physical intimacy make romance a particularly dangerous and exciting event in adolescent life. Girls may be better prepared for the intense emotions of romantic love, but both girls and boys may have difficulty making sense of the impact of emotions on judgment. Girls who engage in early sexual relationships face risks that may be grounded in the mismatch between cognitive abilities and relational orientations and skills. Intervention should engage youth in discussion about love, sexual activity, and the social cognition that supports healthy, loving relationships.

■ Because parental relationships with children and adolescents are grounded in gendered styles of communication, emotionality, and self-disclosure, intervention with parents may need to address gender preferences in behavior and interests, and the ways parents might wish to expand their children's experiences and thinking. Interventions that strengthen family cohesion and parent-child relationships appear supportive of child development in general.

■ In adolescence, parental monitoring of children's behavior is associated with favorable developmental outcomes. On balance, research suggests that parents may give boys too much room for independent decision making, and girls too little. In any case, intervention often should focus on parental monitoring and supervision. The art of parental supervision lies in implementing clear expectations and pragmatic, monitoring strategies in the context of increasingly negotiated solutions. Decision making involving parents and children shifts from a parental fiat model to a mutual decision-making model during adolescence.

■ The term *Hardiness Zone* is used to describe ecological spaces that support normal development as well as resiliency characteristics (Debold, Wesen, & Brookins, 1999; Oullette, 1993). These ecological spaces take place in dyads, groups, families, school settings, sports organizations, places of religious worship—all the places that young people live their lives. While the principles discussed above are important considerations for the design of interventions with high-risk children and youth, they are equally important for supporting the normal relationships and settings in which young people live.

GENDER-SPECIFIC INTERVENTION

Given developmental differences in girls and boys, to what degree might gender-specific intervention approaches be warranted? A *gender-specific intervention* is one in which the issues related to gender take a primary place in the design and implementation of the intervention and where intervention is likely to take place in gender segregated groups. Although there has been some discussion of gender-specific interventions for specific problem domains, such as juvenile delinquency (e.g., Potter, 1998), there is little, if any, intervention research supporting the efficacy of these approaches. Without clear evidence of the efficacy of gender-specific interventions, we might ask what interventions work well with both genders? Unfortunately, the existing research on adolescent intervention often fails to ask this question. For example, three recent texts examining the evidence for child and adolescent mental health interventions fail to address gender as an issue, even when examining effective interventions with adolescent depression (Carr, 2000; Epstein, Kutash, & Duchnowski, 1998; Hibbs & Jensen, 1996).

One exception to the general lack of attention to gender in evaluating program effectiveness is found in research on Multi-Systemic Therapy (MST), an intensive family-based intervention that has been evaluated with mixed gender groups in several random-assignment studies with delinquent and substance abusing youth. In general, MST families report more cohesion and MST youth demonstrate decreased peer aggression, self-reported delinquency, arrests and substance abuse compared to control group youth. In all studies, the intervention is equally effective for boys and girls (Henggeler, Schoenwald, Borduin, Rowland, & Cunningham, 1998). Multi-Systemic Therapy's emphasis on teaching parents effective communication and monitoring skills and promoting effective collaboration with the systems in which their children live may be one reason for its success with both boys and girls.

Although the MST research sets an example for an approach to examining gender differences in therapeutic outcomes, we are left with other important questions. For what problem areas might gender-specific interventions be designed? What problem areas are best addressed with coeducational and/or gender-neutral intervention approaches? What elements of gender-specific programs are most beneficial to girls? Are these elements also beneficial to boys, or should we choose others? When should a helping professional choose a gender-specific approach over a gender-neutral approach? When should girls and boys be treated together in groups or in couples? The answers to the questions are not known, from an empirical point of view.

What, then, are the pragmatic implications of our growing knowledge of gender differences? Gender-specific interventions may be most appropriate under two circumstances:

1. When the social problem relates primarily to one gender
2. When the intervention seeks to change general gender preferences or behaviors

Gender-specific approaches should be the standard approach for social problems where either boys or girls are the primary population affected. For girls, these areas include sexual abuse and dating violence, eating disorders, and adolescent depression. Similarly, we should consider developing gender-specific interventions for girls experiencing problems in areas where girls are a small minority, such as juvenile delinquency and violence. Girls exhibiting these problems are often seen as gender incongruent, a view that may bring its own risks. In addition, interventions in these areas are most likely to have been designed and tested with largely male populations. The reverse argument holds as well, of course. For example, boys facing recovery from sexual abuse or eating disorders require gender-specific intervention because the problem areas are less common for boys and intervention approaches have been primarily targeted and tested with girls. Similarly, juvenile justice interventions for boys might take a gender-specific approach because boys are greatly overrepresented in this population.

Finally, when a helping professional seeks to affect gender norms, even if those norms are not universally seen as problematic, gender-specific intervention should be considered. For example, intervention in school settings to increase interests in math and science among girls might consider a gender-specific strategy. Similarly, interventions to increase relational abilities among boys might consider a gender-specific approach. School-based bullying prevention programs that seek to intervene in patterns of aggression might choose a gender-specific approach, given the clear evidence regarding gender differences in aggression.

CONCLUDING THOUGHTS

Gender is an important factor in shaping the experiences of children and adolescents. Girls and boys face differing risks and opportunities as they move toward adulthood. Although they share many attributes, boys and girls also employ differing strategies as they negotiate relationships with family, friends, romantic partners, and the major social systems in which they live. To date, most interventions do not explicitly address gender, and the professional literature does not give clear guidelines about when and how we might best take gender into consideration.

All intervention with young people is grounded in developmental context, and gender is an important aspect of developmental context. If we are to intervene effectively with children and adolescents, it is important to actively consider gender as we design, implement, and evaluate interventions. This is significant when we are creating interventions for both girls and boys that support varying styles and approaches. It is also important when we seek to change gender norms or provide gender-specific interventions for gender-specific problems. It is equally important as we create everyday living spaces for children and youth. This is challenging and exciting work—work that has the potential to increase our effectiveness in preparing children and youth for happy and healthy adult lives.

DISCUSSION QUESTIONS: ANGIE AND JASON

Having examined some of the gender issues in child and adolescent development, reread the case studies for Jason and Angie at the beginning of this chapter and answer the following questions:

1. Has your thinking changed about how you might approach intervention with these young people? What changed and why? What information do you now privilege by moving it forward in your thinking?

2. What are the important relationships and settings in which Angie and Jason live? How do these relationships and settings support their development? How might they be strengthened?

3. Are there new relationships or settings that might be accessed or created to support the development of these young people? Explain.

4. How would you choose to intervene with Angie and/or Jason? What kinds of interventions would you want to consider? Why? Would you consider an intervention focusing on Angie and Jason as a couple? Why or why not?

5. If interaction with a professional is an important intervention, what characteristics should this helping relationship have? How might these characteristics be similar or different for Angie and Jason?

SUGGESTED READINGS

Eckes, T., & Trautner, H. M. (Eds.). (2000). *The developmental social psychology of gender.* Mahwah, NJ: Erlbaum.

Eisenberg, N., Martin, C. L., & Fabes, R. A. (1996). Gender development and gender effects. In D. C. Berliner & R. C. Calfee (Eds.), *Handbook of educational psychology* (pp. 358–396). New York: Simon & Schuster Macmillan.

Furman, W., Brown, B. B., & Feiring, C. (Eds.). (1999). *The development of romantic relationships in adolescence.* New York: Cambridge University Press.

Johnson, N. G., Roberts, M. C., & Worell, J. (1999). *Beyond appearance: A new look at adolescent girls.* Washington, DC: American Psychological Association.

Way, N. (1998). *Everyday courage: The lives and stories of urban teenagers.* New York: New York University Press.

REFERENCES

Aires, E. (1987). Gender and communication. In P. Shaver & C. Hendrick (Eds.), *Review of personality and social psychology* (Vol. 7, pp. 149–176). Beverly Hills: Sage.

Alan Guttmacher Institute. (1994). *Sex and America's teenagers.* New York: Author.

American Association of University Women. (1990). *Shortchanging girls, shortchanging America: Full data report.* Washington, DC: Author.

American Association of University Women. (1992). *The AAUW report: How schools shortchange girls.* Washington, DC: Author.

American Association of University Women. (1996). *Girls in middle school: Working to succeed in school.* Washington, DC: Author.

Attie, I., & Brooks-Gunn, J. (1989). Development of eating problems in adolescent girls: A longitudinal study. *Developmental Psychology, 25,* 70–79.

Basow, S. A., & Rubin, L. R. (1999). Gender influences on adolescent development. In N. G. Johnson, M. C. Roberts, & J. Worell (Eds.), *Beyond appearance: A new look at adolescent girls* (pp. 25–52). Washington, DC: American Psychological Association.

Belle, D. (1999). *Children's social networks and social supports.* New York: Wiley.

Bem, S. L. (1981). Gender schema theory: A cognitive account of sex typing. *Psychological Review, 88,* 354–364.

Berndt, T. J., Perry, T. B., & Miller, K. E. (1988). Friends' and classmates' interactions on academic tasks. *Journal of Educational Psychology, 80,* 506–513.

Brody, L. (1991). *Gender emotion and the family.* Cambridge, MA: Harvard University Press.

Brown, L. M. (1998). *Raising their voices: The politics of girls' anger.* Cambridge, MA: Harvard University Press.

Brown, L. M., & Gilligan, C. (1992). *Meeting at the crossroads: Women's psychology and girls' development.* New York: Ballantine Books.

Brown, L. M., Way, N., & Duff, J. L. (1999). The others in my I: Adolescent girls' friendships and peer relations. In N. G. Johnson, M. C. Roberts, & J. Worell (Eds.), *Beyond appearance: A new look at adolescent girls* (pp. 205–226). Washington, DC: American Psychological Association.

Bumpus, M., Crouter, A., & McHale, S. M. (2001). Parental autonomy granting during adolescence: Exploring gender differences in context. *Developmental Psychology, 37,* 163–173.

Burke, P. J., Stets, J. E., & Pitog-Good, M. A. (1989). Gender identity, self-esteem and physical and sexual abuse in dating relationships. In M. A. Pitog-Good & J. E. Stets (Eds.), *Violence in dating relationships: Emerging social issues* (pp. 72–93). New York: Praeger.

Calhoun, K. S., & Atkeson, B. M. (1991). *Treatment of rape victims: Facilitating psychological adjustment.* New York: Pergamon Press.

Carli, L. L., & Bukatko, D. (2000). Gender, communication and social influence: A developmental perspective. In. T. Eckes & H. M. Trautner (Eds.), *The developmental social psychology of gender* (pp. 295–331). Mahwah, NJ: Erlbaum.

Carr, A. (Ed.). (2000). *What works with children and adolescents: A critical review of psychological interventions with children, adolescents and their families.* Philadelphia: Taylor and Francis.

Cauffman, E., & Steinberg, L. (1996). Interactive effects of menarcheal status and dating on diet and disordered eating among adolescent girls, *Developmental Psychology, 32,* 631–635.

Centers for Disease Control. (n.d.a). Youth Risk Behavior surveillance system, Survey Results: Unintentional Injuries/Violence, 1999 National Survey. Retrieved March 20, 2002, from http://apps.nccd.cdc.gov/YRBSS/GraphV.asp?Site=XX&Cat=1&Qnum=Q24&Year=1999&ByVar=Q2.

Centers for Disease Control. (n.d.b). Youth Risk Behavior surveillance system, Survey Results: Sexual Behaviors, 1999 National Survey. Retrieved March 20, 2002, from http://apps.nccd.cdc.gov/YRBSS/GraphV.asp?Site=XX&Cat=4&Qnum=Q58&Year=1999&ByVar=Q2.

Centers for Disease Control. (n.d.c). Youth Risk Behavior surveillance system, Survey Results: Sexual Behaviors, 1999 National Survey. Retrieved March 20, 2002, from http://apps.nccd.cdc.gov/YRBSS/GraphV.asp?Site=XX&Cat=1&Qnum=Q21&Year=1999&ByVar=Q2.

Chodorow, N. (1978). *The reproduction of mothering: Psychoanalysis and the sociology of gender.* Berkeley: University of California Press.

Christenson, F. G., & Roberts, K. F. (1998). *It's not only rock and roll.* Cresskill, NJ: Hampton Press.

Cimbalo, R. S., & Novell, D. O. (1993). Sex differences in romantic love attitudes among college students. *Psychological Reports, 73,* 15–18.

Clark, M. L., & Bittle, M. L. (1992). Friendship expectations and the evaluation of present friendships in middle childhood and early adolescence. *Child Study Journal, 22,* 115–135.

Coates, D. L. (1999). The cultured and culturing aspects of romantic experience in adolescence. In W. Furman, B. B. Brown, & C. Feiring (Eds.), *The development of romantic relationships in adolescence* (pp. 330–363). New York: Cambridge University Press.

Crick, N. R. (1995). Relational aggression: The role of intent attributions, feelings of distress and provocation type. *Development and Psychopathology, 7,* 313–322.

Crick, N. R. (1996). The role of overt aggression, relational aggression, and prosocial behavior in the prediction of children's future social adjustment. *Child Development, 67,* 2317–2327.

Davis, M. H., & Franzoi, S., (1996). Stability and change in adolescent self-consciousness and empathy. *Journal of Research in Personality, 25,* 70–87.

De Gaston, J. F., Jensen, L., & Weed, S. (1995). A closer look at adolescent sexual activity. *Journal of Youth and Adolescence, 24,* 465–479.

de Waal, M. (1993). In J. van Mens-Verhulst & K. Schreurs (Eds.), *Daughtering and mothering: Female subjectivity reanalyzed* (pp. 35–43). Florence, KY: Taylor & Francis/Routledge.

Debold, E., Brown, L. M., Weseen, S., & Brookins, G. K. (1999). Cultivating hardiness zones for adolescent girls: A reconceptualization of resilience in relationships with caring adults. In N. G. Johnson, M. C. Roberts, & J. Worell (Eds.), *Beyond appearance: A new look at adolescent girls* (pp. 181–204). Washington, DC: American Psychological Association.

Demmler, J., Potter, C., Jacobson, C., & Ramsey, M. (2000). *The status of girls in Colorado: Full data report.* Denver: Colorado Women's Foundation.

DeZolt, D. M., & Henning-Stout, M. (1999). Adolescent girls' experiences in school and community settings. In N. G. Johnson, M. C. Roberts, & J. Worell (Eds.), *Beyond appearance: A new look at adolescent girls* (pp. 253–272). Washington, DC: American Psychological Association.

Eccles, J., Barber, B., Jozefowicz, O. M., & Vida, M. (1999). Self-evaluations of competence, task values, and self-esteem. In N. B. Johnson, M. C. Roberts, & J. Worell (Eds.), *Beyond appearance: A new look at adolescent girls* (pp. 53–83). Washington, DC: American Psychological Association.

Eccles, J. S., Frome, P., Yoon, K. S., Freedman-Doan, C., & Jacobs, J. (2000). Gender-role socialization in the family: A longitudinal approach. In T. Eckes & H. M. Trautner (Eds.), *The developmental social psychology of gender* (pp. 295–331). Mahwah, NJ: Erlbaum.

Eccles, J. S., Wigfield, A., Flanagan, C. A., Miller, C., Reuman, D. A., & Yee, D. (1989). Self-concepts, domain values and self-esteem: Relations and changes at early adolescence. *Journal of Personality, 57,* 283–310.

Eckes, T., & Trautner, H. M. (Eds.). (2000). *The developmental social psychology of gender.* Mahwah: Erlbaum.

Eder, D. (1985). The cycle of popularity: Interpersonal relations among female adolescents. *Sociology of Education, 58,* 154–165.

Eder, D. (1991). Serious and playful disputes: Variation in conflict talk among female adolescents. In A. D. Grimshaw (Ed.), *Conflict talk: Sociolinguistic investigations of arguments in conversations* (pp. 67–84). Cambridge: Cambridge University Press.

Eder, D. (1993). "Go get ya a french!" Romantic and sexual teasing among adolescent girls. In D. Tannen (Ed.), *Gender and conversational interaction* (pp. 17–31). Oxford, England: Oxford University Press.

Eisenberg, N., Martin, C. L., & Fabes, R. A. (1996). Gender development and gender effects. In D. C. Berliner & R. C. Calfee (Eds.), *Handbook of educational psychology* (pp. 358–396). New York: Simon & Schuster Macmillan.

Epstein, M. H., Kutash, K., & Duchnowski, A. (1998). *Outcomes for children and youth with emotional and behavioral disorders and their families: Programs and evaluation best practices.* Austin, TX: Pro-Ed.

Evans, C., & Eder, D. (1993). "No exit": Processes of social isolation in the middle school. *Journal of Contemporary Ethnography, 22,* 139–170.

Fabes, R. A., & Martin, C. L. (1991). Gender and age stereotypes of emotionality. *Personality and Social Psychology Bulletin, 17,* 532–540.

Fagot, B. I., & Leinback, M. D. (1985). Gender identity: Some thoughts on an old concept. *Journal of the American Academy of Child Psychiatry, 24,* 684–688.

Feiring, C. (1996). Concepts of romance in 15-year-old adolescents. *Journal of Research on Adolescence, 6*(2), 181–200.

Finkelhor, B., & Baron, L. (1986). High-risk children. In D. Finkelhor (Ed.), *A sourcebook on child sexual abuse.* Beverly Hills: Sage.

Finkelhor, D., & Berliner, L. (1995). Research on the treatment of sexually abused children: A review and recommendations. *Journal of the American Academy of Child and Adolescent Psychiatry, 34,* 1–16.

Finkelhor, D., & Ormord, R. (2000, June). Characteristics of crimes against juveniles. *Juvenile Justice Bulletin,* Office of Juvenile Justice and Delinquency Prevention.

Fraser, M. W. (Ed.). (1997). *Risk and resiliency in childhood: An ecological perspective.* Washington, DC: National Association of Social Workers.

Fujita, F., Diener, E., & Sandvick, E. (1991). Gender differences in negative affect and well-being: The case for emotional intensity. *Journal of Personality and Social Psychology, 61,* 427–434.

Furman, W., & Buhrmester, D. (1985). Age and sex differences in perceptions of networks of personal relationships. *Child Development, 21,* 1016–1024.

Furman, W., & Wehner, E. A. (1997). Adolescent romantic relationships: A developmental perspective. In S. Shulman & W. A. Collins (Eds.), *Romantic relationships in adolescence: Developmental perspectives* (pp. 21–36). San Francisco: Jossey-Bass.

Galambos, H. L., Almeida, D. M., & Petersen, A. C. (1990). Masculinity, femininity, and sex role attitudes in early adolescence: Exploring gender intensification. *Child Development, 61,* 1905–1914.

Gamache, D. (1991). Domination and control: The social context of dating violence. In B. Oevy (Ed.), *Dating violence: Young women in danger* (pp. 69–83), Seattle, WA: Seal Press.

Gilligan, C. (1990). Joining the resistance: Psychology, politics, girls, and women. *Michigan Quarterly Review, 29*(4), 501–536.

Gilligan, C. (1993). *In a different voice: Psychological theory and women's development.* Cambridge, MA: Harvard University Press.

Gilligan, C., Lyons, N. P., & Hammer, T. (Eds.). (1990). *Making connections: The relational world of adolescent girls at the Emma Willard School.* Cambridge, MA: Harvard University Press.

Gold, D., Crombie, G., & Noble, S. (1987). Relations between teachers' judgments of girls' and boys' compliance and intellectual competence. *Sex Roles, 16,* 351–358.

Gore, S., Farrell, F., & Gordon, J. (2001). Sports involvement as protection against depressed mood. *Journal of Research on Adolescence, 11*(1), 119–130.

Graber, J. A., Britto, P. R., & Brooks-Gunn, J. (1999). What's love got to do with it: Adolescents' and young adults' beliefs about sexual and romantic relationships. In W. Furman, B. B. Brown, & C. Feiring (Eds.), *The development of romantic relationships in adolescence* (pp. 364–395). New York: Cambridge University Press.

Graber, J. A., Brooks-Gunn, J., & Galen, B. R. (1988). Betwixt and between: Sexuality in the context of adolescent transitions. In R. Jessor (Ed.), *New perspectives on adolescent risk behavior* (pp. 270–316). New York: Cambridge University Press.

Grassmick, H., Hagan, J., Blackwell, B., & Arnekleve, B. (1996). Risk preferences and patriarchy: Extending power-control theory. *Social Forces, 75*(1), 177–199.

Green, W. (1995). Family, peer and self factors as predictors of male and female adolescent substance use at 9th and 12th grade. *Dissertation Abstracts International: Section B: The Sciences and Engineering, 55*(9), 2771.

Grinder, R. E. (1966). Relations of social dating attractions to academic orientation and peer relations. *Journal of Educational Psychology, 57,* 27–34.

Grossman, E. C. (2000). The history of injury control and the epidemiology of child and adolescent injuries. *The Future of Children, 10*(1), 23–52.

Grotpeter, J., & Crick, N. (1996). Relational aggression, overt aggression, and friendship. *Child Development, 67,* 2328–2338.

Henggeler, S. W., Schoenwald, S. K., Borduin, C. M., Rowland, M. D., & Cunningham, P. B. (1998). *Multisystemic treatment of antisocial behavior in children and adolescents.* New York: Guilford Press.

Hibbs, E. D., & Jensen, P. S. (1996). *Psychosocial treatments for child and adolescent disorders: Empirically based strategies for clinical practice.* Washington, DC: American Psychological Association.

Hill, J. P., & Lynch, M. E. (1983). The intensification of gender-related role expectations during early adolescence. In J. Brooks-Gunn & A. C. Peterson (Eds.), *Girls at puberty: Biological and psychological perspectives* (pp. 201–230). New York: Plenum.

Hoberman, H. M., & Garfinkel, B. D. (1988). Completed suicide in children and adolescents. *Journal of the American Academy of Child and Adolescent Psychiatry, 27,* 689–695.

Hoek, H. W. (1991). The incidence and prevalence of anorexia nervosa and bulimia nervosa in primary care. *Psychological Medicine, 21,* 455–460.

Hong, S. M., & Faedda, S. (1994). Ranking of romantic acts by an Australian sample. *Psychological Reports, 74,* 471–474.

Hyde, J. S., Fennema, E., & Lamon, S. J. (1990). Gender differences in mathematics performance: A meta-analysis. *Psychological Bulletin, 107,* 139–155.

Jacobs, J. E. (1991). Influence of gender stereotypes of parent and child mathematics attitudes. *Journal of Educational Psychology, 83,* 518–527.

Jaffe, P. G., Sudermann, M., & Reitzel, D. (1992). Working with children and adolescents to end the cycle of violence: A social learning approach to intervention and prevention programs. In R. DeV. Petrs, R. J. McMahon, & V. L. Quinsey (Eds.), *Aggression and violence through the life span* (pp. 83–99). Newbury Park, CA: Sage.

Jenkins, M. J., & Dambrot, F. H. (1987). The attribution of date rape: Observers' attitudes and sexual experiences and the dating situation. *Journal of Applied Social Psychology, 17,* 875–895.

Johnson, N. C., Roberts, M. C., & Worell, J. (Eds.). (1999). *Beyond appearance: A new look at adolescent girls.* Washington, DC: American Psychological Association.

Johnston, L. D., O'Malley, P. M., & Bachman, J. G. (2001). *Monitoring the future: National survey results on drug use, 1975–2000, Volume 1.* Washington, DC: National Institute of Drug Abuse.

Kuhn, D., Nash, S. C., & Brucken, L. (1978). Sex role concepts of two and three-year-old children. *Child Development, 49,* 445–451.

Larson, R., & Richards, M. (1994). *Divergent realities: The emotional lives of mothers, fathers and adolescents.* New York: Basic Books.

Larson, R. W., Clore, G. L., & Wood, G. A. (1999). The emotions of romantic relationships: Do they wreak havoc on adolescents? In W. Furman, B. B. Brown, & C. Feiring (Eds.), *The development of romantic relationships in adolescence.* New York: Cambridge University Press.

Laursen, B. (Ed.). (1993). *New directions for child development: Vol. 60, Close friendships in adolescence.* San Francisco: Jossey-Bass.

Leaper, C. (1991). Influence and involvement in children's discourse: Age, gender and partner effects. *Child Development, 62,* 797–811.

Levit, D. B. (1991). Gender differences in ego defenses in adolescents: Sex roles as one way to understand the differences. *Journal of Personality and Social Psychology, 61,* 992–999.

Lightfoot, C. (1997). *The culture of adolescent risk-taking.* New York: Guilford.

Lippa, R. (1995). Gender-related individual differences and psychological adjustment. *Journal of Personality and Social Psychology, 69,* 1184–1202.

Lipschitz, D. S., Winegar, R. K., Nicolaou, A. L., Hartnick, E., Wolfson, M., & Southwick, S. M. (1999). Perceived abuse and neglect as risk factors for suicidal behavior in adolescent inpatients. *The Journal of Nervous and Mental Disease, 187,* 32–39.

Loeber, R., Farrington, D. P., Stouthamer-Loeber, M., & Van Kammen, W. B. (1998). *Antisocial behavior and mental health problems: Explanatory factors in childhood and adolescence.* Mahwah, NJ: Erlbaum.

Macoby, E. E., & Jacklin, C. N. (1974). *The psychology of sex differences.* Stanford, CA: Stanford University Press.

McGuire, W. J., & McGuire, C. V. (1987). Significant others in self-space: Sex differences and developmental trends in the social self. In J. Suls (Ed.), *Psychological perspectives on the self* (Vol. 1, pp. 71–96). Hillsdale, NJ: Erlbaum.

Medora, N. P., Goldstein, A., & Von der Hellen, C. (1994). Variables related to romanticism and self esteem in pregnant teenagers. *Adolescence, 28,* 159–171.

Merton, D. (1997). The meaning of meanness: Popularity, competition, and conflict among junior high school girls. *Sociology of Education, 70,* 175–191.

Michael, R. T., Gagnon, J. H., Laumann, E. O., & Kolata, G. (1994). *Sex in America.* Boston: Little, Brown.

Miller, B. C., Monson, B. H., & Norton, M. C. (1995). The effects of forced sexual intercourse on white adolescent females. *Child Abuse and Neglect, 19,* 1289–1301.

Millstein, J. S., & Irwin, C. (1987). Accident-related behaviors in adolescents: A biopsychosocial view. *Alcohol, Drugs, and Driving, 4,* 21–29.

Moore, K. A., Nord, C. W., & Peterson, J. L. (1989). Nonvoluntary sexual activity among adolescents. *Family Planning Perspectives, 21,* 110–114.

Morisson, S. (1995). Mother-daughter personality match: Its effects on level of adjustment in the adolescent. *Dissertation Abstracts International: Section B: The Sciences and Engineering, 55*(2-A), 0719.

Neeman, H., Hubbard, J., & Masten, A. S. (1995). The changing importance of romantic relationship involvement to competence from late childhood to late adolescence. *Development and Psychopathology, 7,* 727–750.

Nolen-Hoeksema, S. (1987). Sex differences in unipolar depression: Evidence and theory. *Journal of Personality and Social Psychology, 101,* 259–282.

Nolen-Hoeksema, S. (1990). *Sex differences in depression.* Stanford, CA: Stanford University Press.

Nolen-Hoeksema, S., & Girgus, J. S. (1994). The emergence of gender differences in depression during adolescence. *Psychological Bulletin, 115,* 424–443.

Office of Juvenile Justice and Delinquency Prevention. (2000). *Juvenile offenders and victims: 1999 National Report.* Washington, DC: U.S. Department of Justice.

Olsen, J. M., Roese, N. J., & Zanna, M. P. (1996). Expectancies. In E. T. Higgins & A. W. Kruglanski (Eds.), *Social psychology: Handbook of basic principles* (pp. 211–238). New York: Guilford.

Orlofsky, J. L. (1993). Intimacy status: Theory and research. In J. E. Marcia, A. S. Waterman, D. R. Matteson, S. L. Archer, & J. L. Orlofsky (Eds.), *Ego identity: A handbook for psychosocial research* (pp. 111–133). New York: Springer-Verlag.

Ouellette, S. (1993). Inquiries into hardiness. In L. Goldberger & S. Breznitz (Eds.), *Handbook of stress: Theoretical and clinical aspects* (2nd ed., pp. 77–100). New York: Free Press.

Papini, D., Farmer, F., Clark, S., & Snell, W. (1988). An evaluation of adolescent patterns of sexual self-disclosure to parents and friends. *Journal of Adolescent Research, 3,* 387–401.

Parker, J., & Asher, S. R. (1987). Peer acceptance and later personal adjustment: Are low-accepted children "at risk"? *Psychological Bulletin, 102,* 357–369.

Perry, D. G., Perry, L. C., & Weiss, R. J. (1989). Sex differences in the consequences that children anticipate for aggression. *Developmental Psychology, 25,* 312–319.

Peterson, A. C., Sarigiani, P. A., & Kennedy, R. F. (1991). Adolescent depression: Why more girls? *Journal of Youth and Adolescence, 20,* 247–271.

Pipher, M. (1994). *Reviving Ophelia.* New York: Ballantine Books.

Poe-Yamagata, E., & Butts, J. A. (1996). *Female offenders in the juvenile justice system.* Washington, DC: U.S. Department of Justice, Office of Justice Programs, Office of Juvenile Justice and Delinquency Prevention.

Potter, C. (1999). Violence and aggression in girls. In J. Jenson & M. Howard (Eds.), *Prevention and treatment of violence in children and youth: Etiology, assessment, and recent practice innovations.* Washington, DC: NASW Press.

Purcell, P., & Stewart, L. (1990). Dick and Jane in 1989. *Sex Roles, 22,* 177–185.

Resnick, M. D., Bearman, P. E., Blum, R., Bauman, K. S., Harris, K. M., Jones, J., Tabor, J., Beuhring, T., Sieving, R., Shew, M., Ireland, M., Bearinger, L. H., & Udry, J. R. (1997). Protecting adolescents from harm: Findings from the National Longitudinal Study on Adolescent Health. *Journal of the American Medical Association, 278,* 823–831.

Richards, M. H., Crowe, P. A., Larson, R., & Swarr, A. (1998). Developmental patterns and gender differences in the experience of peer companionship during adolescence. *Child Development, 69,* 154–163.

Richards, M. H., & Larson, R. (1993). Pubertal development and the daily subjective states of young adolescents. *Journal Research on Adolescence, 32*(2), 145–169.

Robinson, L. (2000). Interpersonal relationship quality in young adulthood: A gender analysis. *Adolescence, 35*(140), 775–784.

Rodgers, K. (1999). Parental processes related to sexual risk-taking behaviors of adolescent males and females. *Journal of Marriage and the Family, 61*(1), 99–109.

Rodgers, L., Resnick, M. D., Mitchell, J. E., & Blum, R. W. (1997). The relationship between socioeconomic status and eating disorders in a community sample of adolescent girls. *International Journal of Eating Disorders, 22,* 15–23.

Roscoe, B., & Kelsey, T. (1986). Dating violence among high school students. *Psychology, 23,* 53–59.

Ross, M. P. (1988). Hidden rape: Sexual aggression and victimization in a national sample in higher education. In A. W. Burgess (Ed.), *Sexual assault* (Vol. II, pp. 3–25). New York: Garland.

Roth, S., Wayland, K., & Woolsey, M. (1990). Victimization history and victim-assailant relationship as factors in recovery from sexual assault. *Journal of Traumatic Stress, 3,* 169–180.

Rotheram-Borus, M. J., Dopkins, S., Sabate, N., & Lightfoot, M. (1996). Personal and ethnic identity, value and self-esteem among Black and Latino adolescent girls. In B. J. Leadbeater & N. Way (Eds.), *Urban girls: Resisting stereotypes, creating identities* (pp. 35–52). New York: New York University Press.

Rys, G., & Bear, G. (1997). Relational aggression and peer relations: Gender and developmental issues. *Merill-Palmer Quarterly, 43,* 87–106.

Sadker, M., & Sadker, D. (1994). *Failing at fairness: How America's schools cheat girls.* New York: Scribner.

Samet, N., & Kelly, E. W. (1987). The relationship of steady dating to self esteem and sex role identity among adolescents. *Adolescence, 22,* 231–245.

Santelli, J. S., & Beilenson, P. (1992). Risk factors for adolescent sexual behavior, fertility and sexually transmitted diseases. *Journal of School Health, 62,* 271–279.

Savin-Williams, R. C., & Berndt, T. J. (1990). Friendship and peer relations. In S. Feldman & G. R. Elliott (Eds.), *At the threshold: The developing adolescent* (pp. 277–307). Cambridge, MA: Harvard University Press.

Schulman, S. (1993). Close friends in early and middle adolescence: Typology and friendship reasoning. In B. Laursen (Ed.), *New directions for child development: Vol. 60, Close friendships in adolescence* (pp. 55–71). San Francisco: Jossey-Bass.

Signorella, M. L., Bigler, R. S., & Liben, L. S. (1993). Developmental differences in children's gender schemata about others: A meta-analytic review. *Developmental Review, 13,* 147–183.

Simmons, R. B., & Blyth, D. A. (1987). *Moving into adolescence: The impact of pubertal change and school context.* Hawthorn, NY: Aldine de Gruyter.

Simon, R., Eder, D., & Evans, C. (1992). The development of feeling norms underlying romantic love among adolescent females. *Social Psychology Quarterly, 55,* 29–46.

Smith, T. W. (1994). Attitudes towards sexual permissiveness: Trends, correlates, and behavioral connections. In A. S. Rossi (Ed.), *Sexuality across the life course* (pp. 63–97). Chicago: University of Chicago Press.

Sorensen, S. B., & Bowie, P. (1994). Vulnerable populations: Girls and young women. In L. Eron & J. Gentry (Eds.), *Violence and youth: Psychology's response. Vol. II. Papers of the American Psychological Association Commission on Violence and Youth.* Washington, DC: American Psychological Association.

Spirito, A., Bond, A., Kurkjian, J., Devost, L., Bosworth, T., & Brown, L. K. (1993). Gender differences among adolescent suicide attempters. *Crisis, 14,* 178–184.

Streigel-Moore, R. H. (1997). Risk factors for the development of eating disorders. In M. S. Jacobson, N. H. Golden, & C. E. Irwin (Eds.), *Adolescent nutritional disorders: Prevention and treatment* (pp. 98–109). New York: New York Academy of Sciences.

Sugland, B. W., Wilder, K. J., & Chandra, A. (1996). *Sex, pregnancy, and contraception: A report of focus group discussions with adolescents.* Washington, DC: Child Trends.

Suhrhoff, E. T. (1997). Maternal constellations revisited in the wake of parenting. *Dissertation Abstracts International: Section B: The Sciences and Engineering, 59*(5-B), 2702.

Swan, S., & Wyer, R. S. (1997). Gender stereotypes and social identity: How being in the minority affects judgments of self and others. *Personality and Social Psychology Bulletin, 23,* 1265–1276.

Thomlison, B. (1998). Risk and protective factors in child maltreatment. In M. W. Fraser (Ed.), *Risk and resilience in childhood: An ecological perspective.* Washington, DC: NASW Press.

Thompson, S. (1994). What friends are for: On girls' misogyny and romantic fusion. In J. Irvine (Ed.), *Sexual cultures and the construction of adolescent identities* (pp. 228–249). Philadelphia: Temple University Press.

Thompson, S. (1995). *Going all the way: Teenage girls' tales of sex, romance and pregnancy.* New York: Hill and Wang.

von der Lippe, A. (1998). Are conflict and challenge sources of personality development? Ego development and family communication. In E. Skoe & A. von der Lippe (Eds.), *Personality development in adolescence: A cross national and life span perspective* (pp. 38–60). Florence, KY: Taylor and Francis/Routledge.

Ward, J. V. (1996). Raising resisters: The role of truth-telling in the psychological development of African-American girls. In B. J. Leadbeater & N. Way (Eds.), *Urban girls: Resisting stereotypes, creating identities* (pp. 35–52). New York: New York University Press.

Ward, L. M. (1995). Talking about sex: Common themes about sexuality in the primetime television programs children and adolescents view most. *Journal of Youth and Adolescence, 24,* 595–615.

Way, N. (1996). Between experiences of betrayal and desire: Close friendships among urban adolescents. In B. J. Leadbeater & N. Way (Eds.), *Urban girls: Resisting stereotypes, creating identities* (pp. 35–52). New York: New York University Press.

Way, N. (1998). *Everyday courage: The lives and stories of urban teenagers.* New York: New York University Press.

Weist, M., Freedman, A., Paskewitz, D., & Proescher, E. (1995). Urban youth under stress: Empirical identification of protective factors. *Journal of Youth and Adolescence, 24*(6), 705–721.

Wertsch, J. V., del Rio, P., & Alvarez, A. (Eds.). (1995). *Sociocultural studies of mind.* New York: Cambridge University Press.

Wilcox, B. L. (1999). Sexual obsessions: Public policy and adolescent girls. In N. G. Johnson, M. C. Roberts, & J. Worell (Eds.), *Beyond appearance: A new look at adolescent girls* (pp. 333–354). Washington, DC: American Psychological Association.

Winston, C., Eccles, J. S., & Senior, A. M. (1997). The utility of an expectancy/value model of achievement for understanding academic performance and self esteem in African-American and European-American adolescents. *Zeitschrift fur Padagogische Psychologie, 11,* 177–186.

Wolfe, N. (1991). *The beauty myth.* New York: Anchor Books.

Wong, M., & Csikszentmihalyi, M. (1991). Affiliation motivation and daily experience: Some issues on gender differences. *Journal of Personality and Social Psychology, 60,* 154–164.

Youniss, J. (1980). *Parent and peers in social development: A Sullivan-Piaget perspective.* Chicago: University of Chicago Press.

Youniss, J., & Smollar, J. (1985). *Adolescent relations with mothers, fathers and friends.* Chicago: University of Chicago Press.

Zahn-Waxler, C., Cole, P. M., & Barrett, K. C. (1991). Guilt and empathy: Sex differences and the implications for the development of depression. In J. Garber & K. A. Dodge (Eds.), *The development of emotion regulation and disregulation* (pp. 243–272). Cambridge: Cambridge University Press.

Zweifel, L. J. (1995). Effects of adolescent pubertal maturation and parental midlife development in mother-daughter relationships. *Dissertation Abstracts International: Section B: The Sciences & Engineering, 55*(7-B), 3032.

CHAPTER 5

SOCIAL WORK PRACTICE WITH GAY AND LESBIAN CHILDREN AND ADOLESCENTS

JOHN F. LONGRES
University of Washington

WILLIAM S. ETNYRE
University of Washington

Social services directed at supporting children and adolescents who are, or will grow up to be, gay or lesbian are a relatively recent occurrence. Before the rise of the lesbian and gay movement, services for "nontraditional" children took place in mainstream mental health services and were focused largely on preventing or "curing" homosexual conduct (Dunkle, 1994; Silverstein, 1996). After the Stonewall Riots in 1969, gays and lesbians began to develop affirming health and human services aimed at the adults making up the movement. There was a good deal of hesitancy about developing services for children and adolescents, as adult gays and lesbians felt vulnerable to accusations that they would prey on the young or "recruit" them into an "unnatural lifestyle" (Herdt & Boxer, 1988; Berger & Purchin, 1995). The emergence of services for children and adolescents derived as much from the conscious outreach of gay and lesbian adults as from the work of such allied communities as parents and friends of gays and lesbians (PFLAG) and the various safe schools coalitions that began forming in the late 1970s.

Today, most large and many medium-sized cities have services specifically for children and adolescents who identify as gay, lesbian, or bisexual, as well as those who are questioning their sexuality (GLBQ). Services are provided in private practices, free-standing agencies, and larger, more mainstream settings. Adult gays and lesbians who recognize the need to treat youth in multidimensional ways largely provide the services. Services range from drop-in centers to full-scale social service programs. These advocate against discrimination, work to alter hostile family and school environments, socialize GLBQ children into a healthy adulthood, and treat troubled GLBQ children and adolescents.

Many existing services also work with transgender children and adolescents under the rubric of sexual minority. Such children may share many of the same experiences as GLBQ children but should not be clinically confused with them (Klein, 1999). Transgender children differ from gay and lesbian children in that they have a strong identification with their anatomical opposite sex. Transgender children present extreme forms of gender nonconformity: They are likely to strongly avoid clothing and play activities associated with their anatomical sex, depict themselves in drawings as people of the opposite sex, and behave stereotypically "sissy" or hyper-masculine. Such children often feel that they are trapped in the body of a boy or a girl while deeply believing that they are, in fact, not a boy or a girl. More importantly, many transgender individuals do not think of themselves as gay or lesbian. It is common for transgender people, especially female to male—to have a heterosexual orientation—that is, to be attracted to the opposite sex. Although the American Psychiatric Association describes such children as suffering from a gender identity disorder (GID) (Mallon, 1999b), it has put together a committee to restudy this issue before the publication of the *DSM V* (Mallon, 1999a). Although transgender children should not be ignored and although there may in fact be overlap between transgender and gay and lesbian children, we will focus on gay and lesbian children and adolescents.*

In this chapter, we define sexual orientation and estimate the prevalence of gay and lesbian adolescents in the United States. We also discuss the social construction of sexual orientation in contemporary society and give attention to issues of cultural diversity. In addition, we review theories of sexual orientation, especially with regard to the contention that a gay or lesbian orientation represents pathology and comes about as a result of poor parenting. Since adolescence is a time of identity formation, we focus largely on the "coming-out" process, drawing from the literature and from the lives of two teenagers. In the process, however, we call attention to the limitations of a coming-out model when working with youth who have been severely abused or neglected as children. Throughout, we take up issues related to an affirming social work practice with GLBQ children and youth and their families.

SEXUAL ORIENTATION AND ITS PREVALENCE

Sexual orientation refers to the object of a person's predominant sexual, erotic, and affectional desires (Isay, 1996; Bell & Weinberg, 1978; Kinsey, 1948). One may desire a person of the opposite sex, of the same sex, or of both sexes. The idea of sexual orientation—that is, classifying people according to the object of their sexual desire—is a rather new idea. The word *homosexual* was coined in Germany in 1869 and entered English in 1892 (Downing, 1989). Today, *gay, lesbian,* and *bisexual* are replacing the term *homosexual.* These terms continue to classify people according to sexual object choice but add the notion of an identity, including a lifestyle and worldview. Although the gay and lesbian rights movement is having an enormous international impact, different ways of thinking

*For more information on practice with transgender children and youth, see G. P. Mallon Guest, ed., "Social Services with Transgendered Youth," *Journal of Gay and Lesbian Social Services,* 10, 3/4 (1999).

about sexuality prevail outside a western, industrial context. Even within industrial societies, different ideas about sexuality may be evident depending on social class and ethnic status (Valocchl, 1998).

Researchers have only begun to study same-sex behavior, desires, or identity among adolescents. During the past decade, five studies using large representative samples and one study surveying the entire student body of a large school district have asked questions that enable us to estimate the prevalence of same-sex-oriented youth (cited in Safe Schools Coalition of Washington [SSCA], 1999). Four studies oversampled adolescents of color in two states (Vermont and Massachusetts) and in two cities (Seattle and San Francisco). The fifth study focused exclusively on Native American youth from 55 tribes attending reservation schools (SSCA, 1999).

As with adults, the prevalence of same-sex-oriented adolescents varied as a function of the way the questions were asked. Table 5.1 indicates that when asked to declare their sexual orientation (%GLB), between 1.1 and 4.5 percent acknowledged a gay, lesbian, or bisexual identity. When asked to acknowledge same-gender sexual experiences (%SGE), the percent ranges from 0.2 to 4.4. (The low 0.2 percent found in San Francisco is likely to do with the fact that the students were asked if they had ever had "intercourse," a term that is confusing when applied to same-sex experiences.) Same-gender attraction (%SGA) and fantasies (%SGF) were asked in only two studies and produced percents ranging from 2.8 to 5.1. Table 5.1 suggests that Native American adolescents (Minnesota and NAIAHS) were not significantly different from other children in the way they responded to these questions. Although not shown in the table, adolescents from other ethnic groups did not differ significantly from their white, non-Hispanic counterparts in answering the questions.

In interpreting these results, the reader should keep in mind that the studies were not designed specifically to estimate the prevalence of GLB adolescents. Although confidentiality was promised, it may be that many teens did not sufficiently trust the researchers to honestly answer the questions. Moreover, since adolescence is a time when identity may be emerging and confusing, the data probably underestimate the number of children who may eventually come to acknowledge GLB identities, experiences, attractions, and fantasies. Finally, those that do identify as GLB during adolescence probably represent a special kind of child, one who is forced "out" because of a high degree of gender nonconformity and/or

TABLE 5.1   Estimating the Prevalence of Gay and Lesbian Youth: The Results of Studies Inquiring into Sexual Orientation

LOCATION	SAMPLE SIZE	GRADE LEVEL	%GLB	%SGE	%SGA	%SGF
Minnesota	36,254	7–12	1.1	1.0	5.1	2.8
NAIAHS	13,254	7–12	1.6	1.3	4.4	4.4
Massachusetts	3,982	9–12	2.0	3.0	na	na
Vermont	8,636	8–12	na	4.4	na	na
San Francisco	1,914	9–12	na	0.2	na	na
Seattle	8,406	9–12	4.5	na	na	na

Source: Safe Schools Coalition of Washington, March 1999, *Eighty-Three Thousand Youth: Selected Findings of Eight Population Based Studies,* http//:www.safeschools-wa.org/quant-intro.

one who is self-assured enough to withstand peer and family pressure to conform to heterosexual expectations.

CULTURAL ISSUES IN SEXUAL ORIENTATION

As indicated, the concept of sexual orientation categorizes people according to sexual object choice and has come to refer to a set of psychosocial attributes. Many lesbians and gays no longer view themselves in purely sexual terms (i.e., homosexual) but in social and moral terms as well. A gay or lesbian orientation is an identity that encompasses involvement in an emerging community, including recreational, social, and political activities, and, most of all, in gay pride (Herdt & Boxer, 1992; Cass, 1996; Troiden, 1988).

Gays and lesbians have generated a unique culture—that is, a set of norms and values by which they align themselves. This is not to say that there is consensus; as with any community, there are considerable variations and competing opinions. This is also not to say that every gay and lesbian accepts the norms, for as the data already described suggest, many do not accept the idea of a gay or lesbian identity. Nevertheless, among those who do identify, a decidedly white, middle-class set of norms dominates (Valocchl, 1998). There is a growing tendency to emphasize stable and committed unions between same-sex partners of a similar generation. Coupling with partners very different in age, and particularly those under age, is increasingly taboo. Having and raising children of their own is not unusual, especially among lesbian couples. Becoming upstanding pillars of the community is also encouraged, as gay men and lesbians commit themselves to community activities from the development of formal organizations to the development of a myriad of social, recreational, and special-interest clubs and voluntary associations.

A set of moral attitudes serves as the glue of the emerging community. Most lesbians and gays consider themselves to be an oppressed minority struggling for social justice. They reject the idea that they are abnormal or deviant or even that they live at the fringe of society. They often argue that sexual orientation is rooted in genetics and that they have been gay or lesbian all their lives. *Homophobia,* a fear of same-sex relationships, and *heterosexism,* the anti-lesbian and anti-gay norms that pervade mainstream society, are seen as real obstacles to be overcome. "Gay pride" symbolizes the struggle against injustice and the drive to be positively included in America's multicultural mix. Coming out is an open, political statement aimed at challenging heterosexist institutions.

This vision of sexual orientation forms the context of mental health and social service interventions, including those directed at children and adolescents. Gay and lesbian affirming social services for adolescents and young adults help them deal with the trauma of growing up in a heterosexist society, offer them a haven for coming out, and socialize them into the emerging norms and values of the lesbian and gay communities (Herdt & Boxer, 1988; Cassese, 2000).

Issues in Working with Clients of Color

Although the lesbian and gay rights movement is having a strong influence both nationally and internationally, this dominant view of sexual orientation is foreign to recent immigrants and many in the broader African, Asian, Latino, and Native American communities.

When working with adolescents of color, clinicians need to be especially sensitive to three issues: degree of homophobia confronted, understanding of sexual orientation, and racism in the lesbian and gay community.

Level of Homophobia.   A high degree of homophobia is typical in many communities of color. In spite of the universality of homosexual conduct (Greenberg, 1988, pp. 77–79; Murray & Roscoe, 1998; Murray, 2000), it is not unusual to hear claims that homosexuality was unknown prior to the negative influence of western countries (Jones & Hill, 1996; Nakajima, Chan, & Lee, 1996). Although some practitioners in nonwestern societies are progressive (Sik-ying Ho, 1999), it appears that most continue to believe homosexuality is pathological (Nakajima, Chan, & Lee, 1996).

Native American people may not quite fit this generalization. Many American Indian societies believed in a third and fourth gender—neither male nor female (Williams, 1986; Roscoe, 1998).* In some of these, if a boy or girl showed signs of being "two spirit" (the term presently being used among Native people), rituals often celebrated their "coming out." Two-spirit people combined elements of male and female apparel and often served as shamans. Third-sex women often went to battle as warriors while third-sex men served as nurses and concubines. The coming of Christianity severely altered these practices; Jacobs (1977, p. 22) cautions that two-spirit people today are often "beaten, disowned, and disavowed." She also notes that many tribal people publicly deny their existence or claim that such behavior is a western invention. However, relatively benign attitudes toward homosexuality are believed to persist among more traditional American Indians.[†]

Understanding of Sexual Orientation.   For many people of color, the notion of "gay or lesbian" has more to do with physical appearance and demeanor and sexual role taking than with sexual object choice. A feminine-acting woman or a masculine-acting man might not necessarily see themselves, or be treated by others, as lesbian or gay in spite of being involved in a same-sex relationship. Even among Native Americans, two-spirit people did not have sexual relations with each other. They entered into marriages with one-spirit "men" and "women," who, in spite of having sex with someone of the same sex, were never considered two-spirit (Tafoya & Wirth, 1996; Williams, 1986).

Given strong homophobia and different cultural beliefs about same-sex sex, adolescents of color will feel special pressure to conform to traditional expectations. Sik-ying Ho (1999) describes the pressure felt by men in Hong Kong who are trying to assume a gay identity. She provides the example of a young man who is trying to come out while also dealing with his sense of duty toward his mother and respect for Chinese family values. His traditional mother, while slowly adjusting to her son's gayness, can't help but feel

---

*It is unclear just how many of the estimated 400 Indian Nations believed in third-sex people at the time of colonialization. Although anthropologists often did not inquire into it, it is likely that the majority of tribes did believe in it, including Nations from every part of the present-day United States (the Crow, Algonkian, Winnebago, Miami, Navajo, Blackfoot, Zuni, Lakota, Arapaho, Pueblo, Cheyenne, Kansa, Osage, Omaha, Kwakiutl, Ojibway, Piegan, and Mohave). See Roscoe (1998).

[†]This observation was obtained from personal communication with Karina Walters, Associate Professor of Social Work, University of Washington. Tafoya (1996) makes a similar contention.

her son should care for her, marry and provide children, and not dream of sharing a life with a man. Herdt and Boxer (1988) provide another example, that of Hoong, an adolescent who came to the United States from southeast Asia as a young child. After seeing a gay newspaper in his room, Roong's younger brother said, "You must never tell this to mother and father. If you do that, everything will be ruined. If you are gay, you have to go away" (p. 157).

Racism.   In addition to homophobia and different understanding of sexual orientation, adolescents of color must confront racism in the predominantly white lesbian and gay communities. Many struggle with issues of "Where do I belong?" To be gay or lesbian in the African, Asian, and Latino American communities is to feel rejected, especially if the adolescent does not conform to gender-role expectations. The rejection is compounded when they also feel rejected by the white gay and lesbian community. Not surprisingly, people of color often struggle with whether their gayness or their ethnicity comes first (Walters, 1998; Icard, 1996; Nakajima, Chan, & Lee, 1996). Are they a gay black or a black gay? Are they a Native American lesbian or a lesbian Native American? Do they build their lives around their ethnicity, even if it means suppressing sexual desires secondary to respecting traditional norms? Do they build their lives around their gayness, even if it means confronting racism daily and feeling alienated from family?

Many of the services for gay and lesbian adolescents serve culturally diverse youth. Becca Hutcheson, past program coordinator for Seattle's Lambert House, estimates that over 60 percent of the youth using the services are of color (personal communication, 2001). Herdt and Boxer (1988) and Grossman and Kerner (1998) report similar statistics for the youth using Chicago's Horizons and New York's Hetrich-Martin Institute, respectively. These centers offer hope that the next generation will overcome the racial divide that marked previous generations of lesbians and gays.

THEORIES OF SEXUAL ORIENTATION

Gay and lesbian affirming clinical practice gives little attention to understanding the origin of same-sex desire. Following the standard used in practice with heterosexual children and youth, homosexual desire is taken as a given that requires no explanation. Affirming services do not make sexual orientation problematic: It is neither a pathology in need of change nor an underlying cause of a presenting problem. The focus is on alleviating problems in living and improving social functioning (Malyon, 1982).

However, it is not uncommon for youth, especially in periods of depression, to speculate negatively about the origins of their same-sex desires. They may believe that having been a victim of sexual abuse made them lesbian or gay. Others may believe that they have not tried hard enough or that they are being tested or lack faith in God. Similarly, it is not unusual for distressed parents to inquire about the causes of their children's sexual orientation, or, more specifically, to express concern that they may have done something wrong to cause their child to be lesbian or gay (Mallon, 1994).

McDougall (1998) has collected a series of letters written by Australian parents that describe their reactions when learning of their child's gay or lesbian identity. Concern about whether they did something wrong in raising their child is one of the most commonly acknowledged initial reactions. The following excerpts serve as case examples:

EXAMPLE 1

My initial feelings of anger and guilt are still with me, despite it being two years since my daughter told me of her homosexuality....

There's the guilt because my beautiful daughter is flawed. Was it my fault? Did I love her so much that she learned a woman's love is the only worthy thing? Or did I err in teaching her that girls are as good as the boys they're forced to compete with? Should I have let her play the sports she showed talent for, water-polo and cricket? A good mother might have forced her to play with dolls, and sit at home with her knitting and sewing. (pp. 17–18)

EXAMPLE 2

When I was asked if I could write this letter my first reaction was, "What a great idea," then as the days went by and I gave it more thought I would feel the tears come to my eyes as my mind went back to that period about ten years ago when I thought my world had been shattered. My son—gay! Where did I go wrong, how did I make my son like this? My guilt overwhelmed me and I sank into the depths of despair. (p. 45)

As Example 1 suggests, some parents will not easily adjust to their child's sexual orientation. In particular, those with strongly held religious, moral, or culturally based convictions about the necessity for marriage and family are likely to need many years to resolve the internal conflicts arising from their child's homosexuality. In many instances, however, adolescents and their parents will not require lengthy explanations. Parents are often put at ease by reassurances that same-sex desires are not brought about by poor parenting. The real work with parents is likely to focus on fears of stigmatization and grief about dreams for grandchildren. Similarly, parents as well as young lesbians and gays are put at ease by knowing that they are not alone and that their sexual identity need not hinder them from becoming productive and contributing members of society. When basically healthy parents and children worry about possible negative origins of same-sex desire, they often need reassurance that they are good people caught up in an unjust, heterosexist society.

Research on the origins of sexual orientation can nevertheless shed light on some central concerns of adolescents and parents: whether homosexuality is genetic, whether it is brought about by "bad" parenting, and whether lesbians and gays can grow up to be psychologically healthy.

There is a good deal of recent interest in the possible genetic origins of sexual orientation. The best answer to this question is that genetics is undoubtedly important, but so is environment. Studies of identical twins are particularly important in that, having the same genetic makeup, one would expect to find that identical twins would have the same sexual orientation. Genetic studies of identical twins, however, report that about 52 percent of male twins and 48 percent of female twins have the same sexual orientations (Pillard, 1996). Although this suggests that genetics cannot be ruled out, the lack of perfect heritability indicates that environmental influences are also important.

Given the heterosexism that permeates most societies, it should not be surprising that some research, especially that using clinical samples and questionable methodology, supports the notion that same-sex desire is a sign of pathology brought about by poor parenting. Bieber and colleagues (1988), for instance, surveyed the opinions of psychoanalysts who were treating homosexual and heterosexual men during the 1950s. The researchers concluded that homosexuality was caused by the combination of an overly attentive mother and a hostile or detached father. Nicolosi (1991), using a sample of men receiving reparative therapy, believes that homosexuality is brought about by problems between fathers and pre-oedipal sons, which lead to "failure to internalize male gender identity" (p. xvi). Psychoanalytic studies of lesbianism also suggest pathology in the form of penis envy, disordered identification with father, failed identification with mother, disturbances of early mother/child relations, and premature genital awareness (Magee & Miller, 1996)

The bulk of the research done with nonclinical samples, however, indicates that homosexual conduct is neither pathological nor brought about by poor parenting. In a series of well-designed studies, Hooker (1957, 1965, 1967, 1972) demonstrated that homosexual men could not be distinguished from heterosexual men in their psychological functioning. Gonsoriek (1982) reviewed more than 20 psychometric studies—13 of men and 10 of women—and found little evidence to indicate that adult heterosexuals and homosexuals differed significantly in their psychological profiles. He concluded that the "studies overwhelmingly suggest that homosexuality per se is not related to psychopathology or psychological adjustment" (p. 79). Friedman (1988) reviewed the literature on gay men and concluded, "Studies of adult homosexual men indicate that global psychopathology is not more common among them than among heterosexual controls" (p. 213). Furthermore, he found that "most adult homosexual males are not effeminate, and many experience themselves as adequately masculine and are so experienced by others" (p. 212).

There is a paucity of studies on the psychological health of children who grow up to be gay or lesbian. Surveys of adult gay and lesbians indicate that many, although by no means all, report gender nonconformity in childhood (some degree of effeminacy/differentness in boys and some degree of masculinity/differentness in girls) (Bell et al., 1978, 1981). Friedman (1988), however, argues that gender nonconformity is best seen as one element in the origin of homosexuality and not a singular cause of it, since gender nonconformity in childhood is also reported by significant numbers of nonclinical heterosexual adults (Bell et al., 1978, 1981). With respect to other characteristics, Herdt and Boxer (1988, p. 207) report on an unpublished study that found that gay and lesbian adolescents were *no* more likely to feel anxiety, confusion, or insecurity than heterosexual youth. As might be expected, given the stress of coming out in the context of high school, lesbian and gay youth were more likely to feel vulnerable, depressed, and vigilant (suspicious of the behaviors of others).

With regard to parenting, Bell and colleagues (1981) surveyed nearly 1,000 homosexual and 500 heterosexual adult men and women to test Bieber's propositions about family patterns. Using a racially mixed sample, they found little evidence to support a theory of poor parenting. Although the configuration of dominant mother and withdrawn father was readily apparent among homosexuals, it was also apparent among a significant number of heterosexuals. Green (1987) conducted a 15-year prospective study of "sissy" boys in an effort to understand the genesis of sexual orientation in men. He, too, failed to find support for Bieber's propositions on family dynamics.

GAY AND LESBIAN IDENTITY DEVELOPMENT:
COMING OUT

Theories of coming out are a central component of working with gay, lesbian, and bisexual adolescents. These theories describe the process whereby an individual takes on a sexual identity and sensitize social workers to the events and issues with which young clients will deal. These theories also provide a statement of successful outcomes from which to evaluate clinical intervention: Mentally healthy adult lesbians and gays are those who accept their orientation; are proud of their identity; build a network of supportive lesbian and gay friends, including a life partner; and participate openly in the larger society (Coleman, 1982; Troiden, 1979, 1988; Cass, 1979).

As indicated, coming-out theories are rooted in middle-class, western thinking and may not apply as well when working with children of recent immigrants, children of color, or children from working-class backgrounds. Taking on a gay or lesbian identity or living openly within the gay community may not be possible for many youth. Clinicians should demonstrate accurate empathy by sympathizing with the constraints that may be operating and by helping clients to seek the best adaptation within them. As Sik-ying Ho (1999) shows, helping clients and their families make even modest accommodations to traditional expectations around sexual orientation, family obligations, and religious beliefs is a form of social action.

Although coming-out theories describe a set of psychosocial experiences, their cultural and political context cannot be ignored. Herdt and Boxer (1988) describe coming out as "death and rebirth" (p. 166). Growing up in a heterosexist society instills in people the belief that everyone, including oneself, has heterosexual desires and will participate in the cultural rituals of dating, courtship, marriage, children, and grandchildren. Coming out puts an end to this belief and replaces it with an expanded vision of what it means to be human. Coming out is a political act because it requires individuals to reject a stigmatized identity and stand up against discrimination (Isay, 1986; Downey & Friedman, 1996). It is also a moral act because in being reborn, gays and lesbians create a broader sense of right and wrong built around the rightness of their love (Herdt & Boxer, 1988). Children and adolescents who come out should therefore be seen as demonstrating strength and resilience in the face of a hostile environment.

Coming-out theories are in keeping with a person-in-environment perspective. The pace of coming out and the kinds of adjustments made during the coming-out process are seen as a function of interaction between individuals and their social environment. Troiden (1979, 1988) uses symbolic interactionism to describe identity formation in the context of self and other expectations. Cass (1979, 1996) uses a constructionist approach that gives attention to sociocultural as well as psychological determinants of identity development. As a result of changes that have taken place in psychodynamic thinking, gay-affirming social workers may also find useful ideas in ego-psychology, object relations, self-psychology, and intersubjective theories (Drescher, 1996; Magee & Miller, 1996; Cohler & Galatzer-Levy, 1996; Etnyre, 2001).

Coming-out theories are developmental theories and thus usually define a series of stages through which same-sex-oriented people pass. The theories were proposed as a response to the Stonewall riots of 1969 and therefore reflected the experiences of that generation. The majority in that generation came out during early adulthood, after leaving home, going to college, getting a job, or joining the military. For that reason, coming out tended to be seen as a long and slow process of self-discovery. Today, there appears to be a shorter time period between sensing one's desires, acting on them, and being open about them. Thus, the home, the local community, and the high school are now the contexts for coming out for many youth. For instance, Herdt and Boxer (1988, p. 181) found in their sample of 202 youth that boys and girls first experience same-sex attraction around age 10. On average, the boys had their first same-sex sexual experience at age 13, whereas girls had theirs at around age 15. The age at which girls and boys acknowledged or self-disclosed their gay or lesbian orientation was around 16. By the time they turn 20 years old, many young people have told their parents and have become fully active in the lesbian and gay community.

With respect to children and adolescents, coming out logically includes an initial sense of differentness, a time when one becomes aware of sexual yearnings and acts on them, and a time when one enters into friendships, which leads to self- and other-disclosure (Dank, 1971; Coleman, 1982; Ponse, 1980, 1984; Cass, 1979, 1984; Troiden, 1979, 1988). But the particulars—when a youth first realizes, experiences sex, forms friendships with gay and lesbian adolescents, tells parents, or goes public—follow no logical order. As Troiden (1988) noted, coming out is nonlinear and open ended, and this is especially true for younger people today.

Stages of coming out are best understood figuratively—that is, as a set of common experiences whose order may vary depending on gender, race, class, personality and family characteristics, and happenstance. In the next section, we divide coming out heuristically into two basic experiences: a set of initial experiences in which expectations about a heterosexual life die and a second set of experiences around integrating into the lesbian or gay community. We do not demarcate a separate set of experiences for coming out to parents. When working with children and adolescents, parents are likely to be involved throughout the coming-out experience.

A third set of experiences, those related to "going public," can be identified but will not be discussed here. Going public often includes attending proms, marching in gay rights parades, and learning to be utterly open about one's sexual orientation in all aspects of daily life. Although these are important experiences and support personality development, they are best seen as extensions of earlier coming-out experiences. The clinical issues of self-understanding and issues related to family of origin, friendships, sexual functioning, and sexual relationships will be the major foci of intervention, regardless of where a young adult may be in the coming-out process.

Throughout our presentation, we will illustrate a number of early and later coming-out experiences by citing Rita Reed's (1997) informative biographies of an adolescent gay boy and an adolescent lesbian. We do this as a way of helping clinicians hear the voices of fairly typical lesbian and gay adolescents—those that they are likely to see in their practice.

Early Coming-Out Experiences:
The End of Heterosexual Expectations

The first indication of a lesbian or gay orientation is likely to be a sense of "differentness." A girl may see herself as a tomboy and prefer to play with boys, or the boy may not like rough and tumble activities and prefer to play with girls. Of course, differentness may not be reflected in gender nonconformity: Children who will grow up GLB may simply sense an attraction to same-sex peers at the same time that they might prefer hanging out with opposite-sex peers. Rita Reed (1997) relates the differentness felt by 17-year-old James Nabozny, from a working-class family in rural Wisconsin, in the years before he came out:

> I knew from an early age that I was different. In kindergarten we played house and, like, the model was—man marries woman and they have kids. The strange thing was I wanted to marry a man, but I didn't want to be the woman. It was confusing and lots of times I ended up playing the mother, just so I could be married to the man. That seemed ok in kindergarten but as I got older people didn't think it was ok anymore. (p. 80)

Children who find themselves in these circumstances often feel alone, isolated, and somehow in the wrong. In an effort to cope with disapproval, many make an effort to be more like their peers. This may lead to identity foreclosure where, unable to accept their differentness, they strive to suppress it (Cass 1979, 1996). They may take on a "false self" (Winnicott, 1960)—that is, suppressing homo-erotic urges and developing a heterosexual persona (Maylon, 1993). Not unusually, this attempt to fit in leads to making jokes about "queers," belittling or shunning other gender-nonconforming peers, or participating in queer bashing even while continuing to feel homosexual desire (Beard & Glickauf-Hughes, 1994; Stein & Cabaj, 1996). Amy Grahn, the 17-year-old suburban girl described by Rita Reed (1997), attempted to be more like her heterosexual peers but soon gave up in favor of being herself.

> I guess I've always been kind of a tomboy [but] in the seventh grade I changed. I did that junior high thing...tried to be like everybody else. It was that makeup thing, yeah, I tried to conform and fit in.
>   But I didn't like it. I just wanted to be me and wear jeans and feel however I wanted to feel, be comfortable. (p. 20)

The way parents react to gender-nonconforming children is extremely important. Psychodynamic theories that see the origin of homosexuality in the failure of children to identify with the gender roles of their parents may have it wrong. Parents who disapprove of "prehomosexual" children may instill feelings of guilt, self-hate, and low self-esteem (Hanson & Hartman, 1996). For instance, parents may push their children to conform. Girls may be encouraged—indeed, forced—to wear dresses and learn "lady-like" behavior, and boys may be forced into sports or other activities in the hope of "making a man out of him." If the child fails at these endeavors or refuses to conform, parents may begin to reject their child, which in turn creates rejection of parents on the part of the child. Amy Grahn remembered:

> My dad tried to make a rule when I was in grade school that I would wear a dress once a week to school. I said forget that idea. That's not happening here...No way was I going to wear a dress to school. (p. 23)

James Nabozny believed his parents suspected he was gay and sent him to live with his religious aunt and uncle when he was in the seventh grade. He ended up running away from them.

> We'd pray about me being gay every night. It was really getting very difficult to be there and I just felt like I was this big old pervert. I ran away, back to my parents' house, to tell my mom I didn't want to be there anymore.

> My aunt called the police, and that got the juvenile officer involved.... So in front of my parents, social worker, and Al-A-Teen sponsor, the police officer came right out and asked me if I was gay. I said yes. (Reed, 1997, p. 81)

Some parents do react negatively to their gay or lesbian child. Herdt and Boxer (1988) report that 6 of the 202 adolescents they interviewed were thrown out of their homes. In today's more progressive climate, many parents, after an initial negative reaction, eventually come around and become supportive. Some 90 percent of gay and lesbian youth can think of at least one adult who really cared for them. Roughly 53 percent of harassed youth agreed that their family loved them and gave them support when needed (SSCA, 1999). Some parents will be extremely sensitive and supportive and may even help their child come out.

Amy Grahn recounted the proactive and positive way her parents reacted to her differentness:

> I hadn't given my parents much credit. I pushed myself away.... Then...my mom...her exact words were, "Your dad and I are wondering if you're dealing with your sexuality." I said, "No" and went to my room.... I came back out five minutes later and said, "Yes, and so what if I am?"
>
> Their response was positive. It was like we love you, no matter what. From that moment it's been nothing but support from them. (Reed, 1997, p. 29)

Relationships with heterosexual peers are often very bad. Middle and high school youth are uncertain about their sexuality and often defend against anxiety by taunting and abusing others. This may be especially true for boys. Marsiglio (1993) found that 89 percent of male teenagers thought male same-sex acts were disgusting and only 12 percent said they would definitely befriend an openly gay male. D'Augelli (1996) speculates that the stigma associated with same-sex behaviors may be greater now due to the association of AIDS with gay males.

Sexual orientation-based harassment in high schools ranks third after ethnic and gender harassment (SSCW, 1999). Nevertheless, around 34 percent of gay- and lesbian-identified students and 6 percent of heterosexual-identified students were the targets of offensive behavior because of their perceived orientation. Gay and lesbian teens were the victim of offensive sexual comments (82 percent), stolen property (50 percent), threats of physical injury (19 percent), and actual injuries that required medical treatment (15.2 percent). Some 19 percent were in physical fights, 24 percent felt afraid and unsafe at school, and 22 percent missed at least one day of school during the past 30 days because of fear (SSCW, 1999).

Amy Grahn's high school peers, including her basketball teammates, shunned her:

> I thought I had some pretty good friends in the seventh grade, but in eighth grade I realized I didn't.... They just stopped hanging out with me when I was more myself. (Reed, 1997, p. 20)

James Nabozny also had a hard time at school.

> In the seventh grade...people said I walked like a girl. They called me fag, queer, homo. It escalated to pushing me around in the locker room, you know, telling me to quit looking at them when we were changing. (Reed, 1997, p. 80)

As a consequence of harassment, emerging gay and lesbian adolescents experience other problems as they try to make their way through high school. Almost all studies show that a large number of lesbian and gay adolescents contemplate, attempt, and, in some cases, commit suicide (WSSC, 1999). Hartstein (1996) suggests that boys are likely to attempt suicide in the early stages of coming out, whereas girls are likely to attempt suicide after the break-up of an affair. James Nabozny and Amy Grahn attempted suicide, both during their initial coming out. James remembered,

> I just couldn't see going through what I had been going through for four more years [of high school]...I could run away or I could kill myself. I thought about two things when I tried to kill myself: either that somebody would realize that I needed help...or I'd just die and it would be over with. So I took a whole bunch of pills—everything in the medicine cabinet.
>
> I tried to kill myself again early in the ninth grade, so my parents put me with another aunt and uncle so I could go to a different school district. The school was better, but my aunt and uncle weren't. (Reed, 1997, p. 82)

It is not surprising that school can be a bad experience for children who are gender nonconforming. Youth who are harassed because of their perceived sexual orientation are more likely to experience lower grades; to sniff inhalants and use marijuana, cocaine, and LSD; and to take laxatives to lose weight (WSSC, 1999). Neither Amy nor James graduated with their high school class. Harassment, along with general anxieties about their emerging identities, produced lower grades, led to switching schools, and finally to dropping out. Both, however, eventually completed their GED requirements.

On a positive note, gay and lesbian youth are often resilient in the face of peer harassment and can find support among teachers. Many of them do graduate on time with their classmates. Some 74 percent of those who experienced harassment continued to maintain a grade-point average of A or B and 64 percent had at least one adult at school to whom they could go for help or to talk (SSCW, 1999). We need also to recognize the number of students who fight back and challenge the pervasive heterosexual norms found in school systems. The *New York Times* recently reported that gay and lesbian student organizations are to be found throughout urban and suburban school districts (Baker, 2001).

Along the early path to coming out, adolescents often begin to experiment with sex. Some of the experiences may be heterosexual, and this raises the possibility that they might be able to have it both ways, stay within the heterosexual norms of society but also fulfill homosexual desires. Herdt and Boxer (1988) report that some 80 percent of the girls and 60 percent of the boys in their study had a heterosexual experience around age 14 (p. 181). For girls, this was often before their first encounter with another girl; for boys, it generally followed an encounter with another boy.

Although our cultural construction of sexual orientation is bifurcated into gays and lesbians, with bisexuals often treated with mistrust (Fox, 1995), recent studies suggest that sexual orientation is best seen as multidimensional (Klein, Sepekoff, & Wolf, 1985) and continuous (Haslam, 1997). Yet, Herdt and Boxer (1988, p. 132) found that the youth in their study did not think of themselves as bisexual. Although they were capable of sexual experiences with members of the opposite sex, most did not find the experience satisfactory. They also tended to mistrust bisexuals, being especially concerned about the ability to love a person of one gender while having relations with a person of another. Moreover, they also worried about what it meant to be left by a bisexual who would run off with someone of the opposite sex. Herdt and Boxer suggest that those youth who do identify as bisexual are more conflicted about their sexuality or use bisexuality as a transient label that allows them to more easily pass from straight to lesbian or gay. It might also be that bisexuality cannot be understood through the eyes of lesbians and gays. True bisexuality might have its own psychosocial origin and its own coming-out experiences (Fox, 1995).

By way of summary, the early coming-out experiences are marked by developmentally appropriate confusion over sexual identity. Pre-gay and pre-lesbian adolescents are likely to see themselves as different and to feel isolated and lonely. Having been raised in a heterosexist society, they will often believe that they have done something wrong and should be punished. They rightly fear the negative reactions of their family as well as the harassment they suffer at the hands of peers. Adolescents are caught in a developmental crisis, between strong heterosexual expectations and their deep uncertainty about fulfilling those expectations.

Social workers need to be alert for harassed, isolated, and lonely children who appear gender nonconforming. Regardless of setting, social workers should be aware of available resources and ready to make referrals to local services or, in areas where these may not be available, to important resources such as PFLAG. (See Resources section at end of chapter.) In extreme cases, social workers might find themselves advocating on behalf of children with school and community leaders and, in some instances, angry parents.

In working directly with youth, affirming practitioners are nonjudgmental and supportive. Practitioners should not assume a gay or lesbian orientation. They should build a relationship that permits adolescents to verbalize their thinking and to work out their identity, whether it is gay, straight, or bisexual. Social workers must be patient as they help adolescents resolve their anxieties and fears. Assessing for suicidal ideation should be a primary concern. Therapists who rush the process or underestimate the intense crisis provoked by coming out can do considerable harm. The following example suggests that premature labeling can lead to serious consequences.

> Mr. C was admitted to a psychiatric unit after a suicide attempt at age 17. On admission, he revealed…that he had taken an overdose after he had seen a peer counselor at a local gay and lesbian social service agency because he thought he might be gay. When the counselor confirmed his fears by suggesting that he probably was gay, the patient felt confused, hopeless and suicidal. (Hartstein, 1996, p. 830)

Later Coming-Out Experiences: Making Friends

As adolescents confirm their sexual orientation, they also start connecting with similarly oriented friends and searching for dates and partners. Troiden (1988) refers to this period as the *actual coming-out stage* because this is the time when a person goes from self-disclosure to disclosure to the world. Although the literature has focused a lot on early coming-out issues, less attention has been given to making friends and sexual relationships. Given the importance of friends and partners to personality development (Harris, 1998), this is a serious oversight in the literature. Here, we draw from the lives of Amy Grahn and James Nabozny as well as our own reflections to sketch out some issues in meeting friends and finding romance.

Meeting Friends.   For many youth, finding gay friends creates considerable joy. James Nabozny recounted his joy upon making a gay friend:

> I met Jessey, my best friend, when I was twelve and he was eleven. We both were so relieved to finally talk to someone about it. We talked about guys, created a fantasy world for ourselves, and cut out pictures of boys. I felt as if the black-and-white world I had lived in was now alive with color. Someone else finally shared my secret. (Reed, 1997, p. 80)

Yet, adolescents can be quite ambivalent about meeting gay or lesbian persons. They may long for a friend but they may also fear the implications of entering into the lesbian and gay world. Herdt and Boxer (1988) describe the behaviors of adolescents coming to Horizons, a Chicago multicultural youth service, for the first time. Many youth find it very difficult to enter the building even after locating it. They often fret and fear for weeks and months, circling the block or wandering the neighborhood trying to muster up the courage to enter.

Why such fear? The coming-out process involves death and rebirth in the context of a heterosexist world. Two explanations are likely: fear of being found out and fear of becoming the stereotypes they internalized while being raised in a heterosexist society. First, it is one thing for youth to sense their differentness and even act on it furtively; it is quite another thing to be open about their sexuality. They are especially afraid of how their parents might react but they also worry about the reactions of straight friends. Many youth learn about gay- and lesbian-oriented places through their friends, often in negative ways: "That's where fags hang out." Going to one of these places raises the fear of being found out. Second, once their dream of a heterosexual life is over, adolescents must learn how to be gay or lesbian, and this conjures up all the stereotypes they have internalized. They are so used to thinking of lesbians and gays as wildly deviant and sinful people that all sorts of anxiety about being in their company are conjured up. Adolescents can especially fear older lesbians and gays. Boys worry they will be attacked by "chicken hawks" (older men who prey on boys) and girls fear "lesbian witches" who will whisk them away (Herdt & Boxer, 1988). Beyond this, they fret about what will become of them: "Will I 'catch' AIDS?" or "Will I be converted into a 'diesel dyke' man-hater or a 'screaming queen' woman-hater?"

With the growth of social and human services, lesbian and gay adolescents often meet their first friends through the groups they attend. Herdt and Boxer (1988) describe a specially designed rap group for "new people" at Horizons. The group process is used to help adolescents work through their anxieties and prepare them, should they decide they are lesbian or gay, to enter the community. The group leader, who is usually only a few years older than the new people, is trained to make no assumptions about their sexual orientation and to maintain clear friendship and sexual boundaries. Once in the group, the adolescents deal with such issues as "What are gay people like?" and "What do people on the outside think about gays?" They discuss issues related to family, friends, and schools. They talk about suicide and HIV/AIDS. They discuss bisexuality and list the positives and negatives of taking on a gay or lesbian identity. Herdt and Boxer (1988) pay special attention to how the "new people" behave in these groups. Considerable tension and long silences mark many of the sessions. It is not unusual for newcomers to give false names or use nicknames; confidentiality is obviously an important concern. Some adolescents drop out or go in and out of the group as they try to sort out the issues on their own. Talking about sex and suicide are particularly difficult topics. Magical or defensive thinking is readily apparent.

Adolescents wonder if their straight friends are correct in saying that if you hang out around gay people, it will rub off on you, that that is how you become gay. Many also wonder whether their same-sex desires might go away if they worked hard to hide or ignore them.

Most of those teens who go through a group process as described by Herdt and Boxer (1988) eventually get caught up in sorting out their anxieties and begin to make friends in the group and through the group to the larger youth community. This is often a liberating time, as gay and lesbian adolescents often feel, for the first time, that they have friends and have found their niche.

Yet, liberty can extol a price. As adolescents enter the gay and lesbian worlds, new dilemmas arise with family and friends. The difficulties arise as much from tensions in the home as from the influence of peers and the yearnings of teenagers for independence. Joining the lesbian and gay youth culture is a heady experience that often produces conflict with parents or parent substitutes. Locating a niche, becoming independent, and stabilizing one's life takes time. Although her parents were completely supportive, Amy still found them too restrictive, and moved out against their will.

Barely 17 years old, Amy Grahn was having a great time hanging out with the girls she met at her group. Her parents had set up a rule about sleeping over at friends' houses: Her brother could not sleep over at girls' houses, and Amy could not sleep over at boys' houses. After the family acknowledged her lesbianism, the rules had to change. Amy could stay over at girls' houses, if the parents met the girl first, and Amy could invite a girlfriend to her house, but the two had to sleep in separate rooms (Reed, 1997, p. 33). Amy felt constrained living with her suburban family while becoming more and more immersed in the urban lesbian community:

> I felt really stuck, so far away from the city and the people I wanted to hang out with.... There were always restrictions on the car. I could only make it to the [Twin] cities twice a week. It wasn't enough for me. No way! I had to be home by midnight. I hated that. I wanted to stay out and party.... I was skipping school.... I hated it. I was so over school, so done. I didn't have any friends there. All my friends were out of school. Sheila was a rugby buddy. She knew I wanted to move out, so she offered to let me live with her. I moved out when my mom was in Florida...she asked me to wait till she got back. I didn't want to.... My dad didn't agree with what I was doing. (Reed, 1997, p. 51).

James Nabozny, after an assault by heterosexual peers at the start of the eleventh grade, ran away to the city in search of a new life. He ended up on the streets of Minneapolis going from one friend's house to another.

> When I got off the bus, I was very afraid.... My biggest fear was that I'd be hungry—like homeless and hungry. The major thing was that I didn't want [was] to have to be a prostitute to survive. I always said that if I was hungry or if I had to sell myself...I would go home.... I stayed quite a few places. I mean, I'd meet somebody and he'd say, "You want to stay at my house?" I'd say, "Sure." (Reed, 1997, p. 85)

Living on the streets is a fairly common event for many young runaways. Besides prostitution, adolescents can get caught up in panhandling and petty criminal activities.

Involvement in drug use is likely. The Safe School Coalition of Washington (1999) reports that more than 33 percent of gay and lesbian youth said they engaged in high risk or heavy drug use. Around 50 percent or more of those who experienced anti-gay harassment smoked cigarettes and had been in a physical fight in the recent past. Some 33 percent had used marijuana and 38 percent had sniffed inhalants. Over 23 percent had used cocaine and LSD. Becca Hutcheson, of Seattle's Lambert House, suggests that social workers need to be more involved in working with street kids. She said that young, often troubled, teenagers come in to use the range of supportive services she provides. By age 16, many have drifted away into street life, only to return as more stable, though sometimes criminally sophisticated, young adults (personal communication).

After three months on the street, James went back home for a visit but made it clear it was only a visit:

> By Christmas I was really homesick. I called my mom.... I said: "This is the way it is. Either you let me come home for the holidays and let me move back down here afterwards or you won't see me until I turn eighteen." She agreed and they came to get me. (Reed, 1997, p. 85)

Unlike a lot of adolescents in similar circumstances, James did not go back to street life. He returned to the Twin Cities with a clear purpose. He wanted to find a job, finish high school, and become a stable person. This led him to seek a foster family through the Metropolitan Community Church. He moved in with a gay couple who called James's parents and obtained their support. James got a job, went back to school, and learned a lot from his foster parents, but he also learned that gay parents may not be any easier to live with than straight parents.

> The situation with the guys wasn't everything that I wanted it to be.... [One] always criticized me. Nothing I did was good enough.... I paid rent, my own car payment and insurance, worked full-time, went to school, and did most of the housework—at least I thought so. It was never enough.... I know there have to be rules, but I felt like they wanted a twelve-year old so they could raise him, discipline him, and all this stuff. I was already grown up and beyond where I needed all the discipline, rules and structure. (Reed, 1997, p. 97)

Finding Romance. Dating, sex, and love often follow directly from friendships. Gay and lesbian teens share all the same insecurities as heterosexual teens. Finding dates and having sex are important steps in self-acceptance, self-esteem, and the eventual transition into an independent and happy adult life (Coleman, 1982; Troiden, 1979, 1988). Yet, many adolescents fear no one will find them attractive. They spend a lot of time examining their skin and facial features, and worrying about their weight, height, and body image. As an indication of these worries, the Safe Schools Coalition of Washington (1999) reports that some 22 percent of youth who have been harassed because of their sexual orientation have vomited or taken laxatives to lose weight during the previous 30 days. Herdt and Boxer (1988) capture the feelings of a young and insecure boy having sex for the first time:

> It was someone I met [in the group]. It was the end of winter and it was cold. We didn't do too much.... We kissed and felt each other. I was really nervous. I couldn't come. I jerked him off.... It lasted four months. It was okay. I didn't feel bad. I thought things went awfully quick; it was something I wanted. (p. 147)

Many lesbian and gay adolescents are excluded from the "normal" developmental experiences that help heterosexual youth to better understand their desires and develop their capacity for intimate relationships (Isay, 1996). As a consequence, they often lack the normative adolescent experiences of "puppy love," dating in groups, introducing dates to parents, dealing with jealousies, breaking up, and the like. For example, lesbian and gay adolescents feel the same desire as heterosexual youth to introduce parents to their dates. Even when seemingly estranged, adolescents still would like their parents to meet their dates, to feel their approval, and to reformulate their parent-child relationship in more adult ways. Bringing someone home in the hopes of gaining family respect and approval is a big event. James Nabozny had had a series of brief sexual encounters before meeting someone he thought he wanted to bring home to meet his parents. The event proved disastrous, as his working-class family rejected the "effeminate" boy James brought home.

> It was a big event in my life—the first time I took a boyfriend home to meet my parents.... It was not good at all...they didn't like him, he was too effeminate. When I am on Lake Superior ...I get butch, very adventurous. I just knew that this wasn't for my boyfriend. It was the last place in the whole world he wanted to be.... He had to walk barefoot and the rocks were hurting his feet. This was the beginning of the end of our relationship. I mean, I wanted somebody who'd be able to walk through these rocks with me. (Reed, 1997, p. 103–104)

In Amy's case, she was rejected when a girlfriend brought her home. In this case, the girlfriend wasn't "out" with her parents and so bringing Amy home provoked a coming-out experience that ended badly and, as with James, led to the end of the romance.

Although bringing a date home and finding rejection might lead to further depression and alienation, resilient youth can actually learn something about themselves. James learned that he really did not want an "effeminate" partner. Although he had been a "sissy boy," he found a new sense of masculinity once he started dating. The next boyfriend he brought home was more masculine and was from the same socioeconomic background, and the homecoming went very well, indeed.

As this example shows, early dating experiences are important in helping adolescents understand their own social and sexual needs. In James's case, he learned through interaction with his parents. Amy learned it from getting in touch with her own feelings. She dated a lot of girls before she found someone she liked, and in the process, she discovered things about herself she hadn't realized. Although she presented herself as quite masculine and was popular among feminine women, she was in fact not attracted to them:

> I thought it was great that these women just wanted me, but they weren't my type at all. Too femmie! I mean, I kinda like a butch girl. (Reed, 1997, p. 58)

When lesbian and gay adolescents meet someone they really fall for, the intensity of the romance can be strong. James Nabozny summarizes the wonderful effects of his first serious romance:

> He was my first true love. Being close to him felt better than anything I've ever felt. It was the first time in my whole life that I knew somebody was in my life who cared a lot about

me, not because I was their son or I was a relative, but because of who I was. He liked me for who I was, not for any other reason. (Reed, 1997, p. 108)

If the romance goes badly, as it usually does at this age, the experience can be equally devastating. Having separated from the heterosexual world, lesbian and gay adolescents sometimes assume that romance with a same-sex partner will prove magically stable and permanent. When the romance goes wrong, homophobic stereotypes may come back to haunt them and may cause then to rekindle their wish for a heterosexual orientation.

This did not happen to James and Amy in spite of their first loves ending sadly. The young woman Amy fell in love with was a little older, in college, less into drinking and partying than Amy was, somewhat bisexual, and less out to her parents. The relationship proved difficult and ended after the girlfriend moved from her college dorm, their refuge, and went home for the summer. Although they saw each other a couple of times over the summer, by the time September came, the girlfriend had lost interest in Amy. Amy grieved for a long time and for almost a year lost all desire to date. James's romance eroded as he learned the boyfriend used alcohol and pot, and completely came apart when he realized that the boy who "liked me for who I was" was also seeing other guys on the side.

It is the end of my life, that's what it feels like anyway.... I can't quit crying. I'm sick to my stomach. I threw up three times last night. It's to the point where I want to hurt myself physically.... I want to know why, dammit, why is he doing this to me? Why after telling me he loved me...why say one day, "Well I don't love you anymore"? (Reed, 1997, p. 125)

For young gay men and bisexual women, the specter of AIDS hangs heavily over their sexual lives. Although adults (over age 24) are far more likely to be HIV positive, the likelihood of infection among adolescents (ages 13 to 24) has grown consistently. In 1996, adolescents constituted 4 percent of all newly diagnosed cases (Center for Disease Control, 1998). Although many fear AIDS, youth cannot really imagine anything but a long and healthy life. They have a tendency to believe that they are invulnerable because they only have sex after dating someone for a long time, or are attracted only to people who are healthy and monogamous, or are only with other adolescents, who they assume cannot be infected. When a friend or partner does become infected, they can feel extremely vulnerable. Some may begin to question their gayness, others may find the situation too difficult to talk about and go into denial, and still others may relive memories of family death and separation. Herdt and Boxer (1988) describe the effects on an adolescent group when one of their members contracted and died of AIDS. They quote a young African American who had "thought about this a lot...how people said that if you practice homosexuality you would go to hell" (p. 156). They also relate the effects on a southeast Asian youth who had lost many family members in the killing fields: "I thought when I came to America this was all over; I was safe and secure. And here I find that being homosexual, I must deal with the same problem" (p. 158).

By way of summary, as adolescents become more accepting of their sexual orientation, social workers will find themselves working on a range of issues associated with making friends, finding romance, and continuing relationships with parents, including foster parents. At this time, the use of support groups (for adolescents as well as parents) can be very helpful. Although they will often be hesitant in joining, groups offer adolescents the possibility of friends, dates, and romance—the very things they were missing before accepting their orientation. Furthermore, groups are a safe place for adolescents to deal with issues such as self-esteem, body image, appropriate dating behavior, multicultural issues, HIV and safe sex practices, alcohol and drug use, dealing with parents, seeking independence, and educational achievement.

There are insufficient data on whether social workers in mainstream mental health agencies lead support or psychotherapeutic groups for lesbian and gay teens. An attempt to uncover such services among Seattle mainstream agencies found no such groups. In most emerging lesbian and gay adolescent services—such as Horizons in Chicago and Lambert House in Seattle—nonprofessional peers, not much older than the adolescents they serve, facilitate the support groups. (Parent support groups, such as PFLAG, also tend to be run by other parents.) In many of these services, social workers or other trained helping professionals are involved in training facilitators and developing or refining psychoeducational units to be used in the groups. They are also likely to be available for adolescents who need one-on-one counseling and therapy.

Although homophobia and heterosexism provide the context for coming out, not all the difficulties experienced by lesbian and gay adolescents can be attributed to societal oppression. Downey and Friedman (1996) distinguish between primary and secondary forms of internalized homophobia. Coming-out theories highlight primary homophobia, the internalized attitudes and values of a hostile society that make positive adaptation to a gay or lesbian identity difficult. Coming-out theories start with the assumption of a psychologically healthy individual—adolescents like Amy and James—who can take advantage of basic supportive services as they confront the challenges of taking on a gay or lesbian identity.

Secondary internalized homophobia is experienced by gays and lesbians who have suffered early "primary" abuse, including physical and sexual abuse and neglect, or have been exposed to family violence, alcoholism, and mental illness. Said another way, internalized homophobia is secondary in youth whose primary problems result from early life trauma. Such youth are often unable to take advantage of supportive services because of the mental and personality disorders they suffer. Downey and Friedman (1996) observe that these youth often have "negative therapeutic reactions," (p. 47) especially when things seem to be going well for them. Although at times they can be charming, they are riddled with guilt, project hostility on others, and often provoke hostility from others, even therapists. Their coming-out difficulties are therefore much more complicated and require uncovering or insight-oriented therapeutic approaches. Although beyond the scope of this chapter, clinicians working with such adolescents will need to draw from the practice literature on trauma and its sequelae (Herman, 1992; Downey & Friedman, 1996; Rosenberg, 2000; Cassese, 2000; Cassese & Mujica, 2000).

In providing counseling or therapy, clinicians need to be able to distinguish between basically healthy youth who are experiencing the normal vicissitudes of coming out and those youth whose experiences are mediated by personality and mental disorders rooted in dysfunctional family patterns. For basically healthy youth, supportive therapeutic interventions are appropriate, but for those with unresolved childhood and family issues, clinicians will have to be prepared to use other therapeutic models.

SUMMARY AND GUIDELINES FOR PRACTICE

As many as 5 percent of youth either identify themselves as gay, lesbian, or bisexual, or admit to same-sex experiences, attractions, and fantasies. Many of these—and others who will question their sexuality at a later time—will find their way into services. What kinds of guidelines should be available to inform clinical practice? We offer the following:

1. In keeping with social work values, clinicians should support children and adolescents as they struggle to understand their sexual orientation, be it gay, lesbian, bisexual, or heterosexual. An affirming practice is one that does not make sexual orientation problematic. It neither encourages a heterosexual adaptation nor does it assume a homosexual one.

2. When working with children and young teens, social workers must exercise patience and gentleness. Although gays and lesbians have made a positive impact on society, coming out is still a confusing and difficult experience. At all times, social workers need to assess for suicidal feelings and thoughts.

3. Clinicians should also expect to assume the roles of broker and advocate when working with the children and adolescents. Familiarity with resources is essential, as is the ability to work with parents, teachers, school officials, and others to protect youth against harassment or physical harm.

4. The role of the practitioner is to enable those gay or lesbian adolescents who do come out to achieve a healthy sexual identity, including the ability to develop supportive friendships, enter into mature and stable sexual relationships, and be open in community life. Appropriate treatment begins with a thorough assessment of the client's sexual orientation, level of sexual identity formation, stigmatizing experiences, and degree and type of internalized homophobia.

5. Healthy adolescents—such as James and Amy—will benefit from supportive therapy as they deal with various coming-out issues. Much of this can take place in the context of peer support groups. Social workers can train facilitators and influence the topics discussed in support group sessions. They can also work one-to-one with adolescents who are dealing with difficult friendship, dating, and parental relationships.

6. Some adolescents will suffer from a variety of problems because of early life abuse and neglect. These youth will likely not benefit from supportive services but will require uncovering forms of therapy. Practice strategies derived from working with people who have experienced trauma will prove useful.

7. Sexual orientation is a social construction rooted in contemporary western norms. Although many urban services are proudly multicultural, clinicians should not assume that all adolescents are alike. Adolescents of color—as well as those from working-class families and those with fundamentalist religious beliefs—may be engulfed in a different set of parental and community expectations. Furthermore, adolescents of color are likely to experience racial prejudice within the gay and lesbian communities. Social workers will need to be aware of cultural factors that place the client between "a rock and a hard place," negotiating the dilemma of coming out versus maintaining allegiance to family and cultural values.

In coming to an end, we would like to reflect on the issue of self-disclosure. Social workers in lesbian and gay services are generally open about their own sexual orientation.

But what happens in mainstream or traditional services where the workers' sexual orientation may not be public knowledge? Unlike Amy and James, a number of adolescents and their parents may go out of their way to avoid lesbian and gay services. The literature addressing this issue is clear: Gay and lesbian clinicians should self-disclose. Cabaj and Stein (1996) and Cornett (1993, 1995) argue that failure to disclose tacitly reinforces cultural disapproval of homosexuality. Isay (1996) presents case examples showing that clients entered into a better therapeutic relationship after the clinician self-disclosed. We suggest a flexible approach focused on two interrelated issues: the attitudes and beliefs of the worker and the timing of disclosures.

The primary issue is the attitudes and beliefs of the worker; this is both a personal as well as organizational issue. To the extent that a social worker is not gay affirming, this should be made clear to agency staff as well as to children and their families. Given ethical and effectiveness considerations, we believe that agencies ought to establish a policy that encourages pairing gay-affirming practitioners with adolescents who are questioning their orientation. The policy should also incorporate general social work guidelines regarding confidentiality, consent for treatment, and duty to inform when the client is in danger to self and others. Establishing such policies will require deliberating on homophobia, as it has influenced the lives of heterosexual as well as lesbian and gay social workers. Thus, in working with any family, practitioners, backed by agency policy, should be clear that sexual orientation cannot be effectively changed and that their role is to help adolescents understand their sexual inclinations and develop healthy sexual identities. Their role also includes working to help parents better understand their children and continue to provide them with love and support.

Whether a social worker self-discloses will be a function of the circumstances of a particular case. To the extent that a parent or child directly asks about the worker's orientation, the worker should stress the agency's policy on gay affirmation and proceed to self-disclose. If clients do not ask, it is still important to discuss the philosophy behind a gay-affirming practice, but it may not always be necessary to self-disclose. Where a good relationship exists without knowledge of the worker's orientation, workers may not need to self-disclose. Where clients are uneasy and the worker believes that his or her orientation may be an issue, open discussion may ease the discomfort and allow therapeutic work to proceed.

DISCUSSION QUESTIONS

1. Describe what is meant by "a gay-affirming practice with children and adolescents." Do you think you will be able to provide an affirming practice? What kinds of personal and professional obstacles might you have to confront in order to be an affirming practitioner?

2. Lesbians and gays are a diverse group of people. Describe the emerging norms of the gay and lesbian community and how they are reflected in practice. How might these norms influence effective practice with children and adolescents of color, or who are immigrants or the children of immigrants?

3. If a mother asked you why her daughter was a lesbian, how would you respond?

4. What is meant by "coming out"? Do only homosexual adolescents come out or do heterosexual adolescents also come out? How might the coming-out experience be different for heterosexual and homosexual adolescents?

5. Identify and describe some common experiences associated with early coming out. As a social worker, how might you work with adolescents having these experiences?

6. Identify and describe some common experiences associated with later coming out. As a social worker, how might you set up support group services or directly counsel adolescents having these experiences?

7. What is the difference between internalized primary and secondary homophobia? What implications for practice with gay and lesbian adolescents derive from this distinction?

RESOURCES

GLSEN (Gay, Lesbian, Straight Education Network): 121 W. 27th Street, Suite 804, New York, NY 10001. 212-727-0135. http://www.glsen.org/

This is the largest national organization working to end anti-gay bias in America's public, private, and parochial schools. Established nationally in 1994, GLSEN now has over 80 chapters working in communities across the country. The network envisions a future in which every child learns to respect and accept all people, regardless of sexual orientation or gender identity.

OutProud! The National Coalition for Gay, Lesbian, Bisexual and Transgender Youth: 369 Third Street, Suite B-362, San Rafael, CA 94901. http://www.outproud.org/

This organization provides advocacy, information, and resources for teens, including news on current events, coming-out stories, school resources, online brochures, local sources of friendship and support, and coverage of political issues and activities.

PFLAG (Parents and Friends of Lesbians and Gays): 1726 M Street NW, Suite 400, Washington, DC. http://www.pflag.org

This grass-roots organization of parents and friends now has chapters in over 400 cities across the United States. They are an excellent resource for parents, regardless of the age of their gay or lesbian child.

Same Gender Loving Black Youth: http://www.youthresource.com/feat/poc/aaring.htm

This website connects African American same-gender-loving youth and provides information on coming out, relevant awareness events, books about African American youth, and links to other gay and lesbian youth of color.

Utopia: Asian Gay & Lesbian Resources: http://www.utopia-asia.com/

This is the Internet's first Asian gay and lesbian resource website. *Time Magazine* and the BBC World Service have recommended this site.

Youth.Org: http://www.youth.org/

This information service is run by volunteers. It was created to help self-identifying gay, lesbian, bisexual, and questioning youth to have a safe online space where they can be themselves and meet other teens.

REFERENCES

Baker, A. (2001, April 23). Being you. Plus a corsage: Gay proms hit suburbia. *New York Times*, pp. A1, A18.

Beard, J., & Glickauf-Hughes, C. (1994). Gay identity and sense of self: Rethinking male homosexuality. *Journal of Gay and Lesbian Psychotherapy, 2(2),* 21–37.

Bell, A., & Weinberg, M. (1978). *Homosexualities.* New York: Simon and Schuster.

Bell, A., Weinberg, M., & Hammersmith, S. (1981). *Sexual preference: Its development in men and women.* Bloomington: Indiana University Press.

Berger, R., & Purchin, A. (1995). Gay and lesbian youth. *Journal of Gay and Lesbian Social Services, 3(4),* 69–72.

Bieber, I., Bieber, T., Dain, H., Dince, H., Drellich, M., Grand, H., Gundlach, R., Kremer, M., Rifkin, A., & Wilbur, C. (1988). *Homosexuality.* Northvale, NJ: Aronson.

Cabaj, R., & Stein, T. (1996). Foreword. In R. Cabaj & S. Stein (Eds.), *The textbook of homosexuality and mental health* (pp. xxxiii–xliii). Washington, DC: American Psychiatric Press.

Cass, V. (1979). Homosexual identity formation: A theoretical model. *Journal of Homosexuality, 7(2/3),* 219–235.

Cass, V. (1984). Homosexual identity formation: Testing a theoretical model. *The Journal of Sex Research, 20(2),* 143–167.

Cass, V. (1996). Homosexual orientation identity formation: A Western phenomenon. In R. Cabaj & S. Stein (Eds.), *The textbook of homosexuality and mental health* (pp. 227–252). Washington, DC: American Psychiatric Press.

Cassese, J. (2000). Integrating the experience of childhood sexual trauma in gay men. *JGLSS, 12(1/2),* 1–19.

Cassese, J., & Mujica, E. (2000) Cross cultural perspectives in treating the gay male trauma survivor. *Journal of Gay and Lesbian Social Services, 12(1/2),* 153–182.

Center for Disease Control. (1998). *Trends in the HIV-AIDS Epidemic: 1998.* http://www.cdc.gov/hiv/stats/trends98.pdf

Cohler, B., & Galatzer-Levy, R. Sexual orientation and maintenance of personal integrity. In R. Cabaj & S. Stein (Eds.), *The textbook of homosexuality and mental health* (pp. 207–223). Washington, DC: American Psychiatric Press.

Coleman, E. (1982). Developmental stages of the coming-out process. In W. Paul, J. Weinrich, J. Gonsiorek, & M. Hotvedt (Eds.), *Homosexuality: Social, psychological, and biological issues* (pp. 149–158). Beverly Hills: Sage.

Cornett, C. (1993). Dynamic psychotherapy of gay men: A view from self psychology. In C. Cornett (Ed.), *Affirmative dynamic psychotherapy with gay men* (pp. 45–76). Northvale, NJ: Aronson.

Cornett, C. (1995). *Reclaiming the authentic self: Dynamic psychotherapy with gay men.* Northvale, NJ: Aronson.

Dank, B. (1971). Coming out in the gay world. *Psychiatry, 34,* 189–197.

D'Augelli, A. (1996). Lesbian, gay, and bisexual development during adolescence and young adulthood. In R. Cabaj & T. Stein (Eds.), *Textbook of homosexuality and mental health* (pp. 267–288). Washington, DC: American Psychiatric Press.

Downey, J., & Friedman, R. (1996). The negative therapeutic reaction and self-hatred in gay and lesbian patients. In R. Cabaj & T. Stein (Eds.), *The textbook of homosexuality and mental health* (pp. 471–484). Washington, DC: American Psychiatric Press.

Downing, C. (1989). *Myths and mysteries of same sex love.* New York: Continuum.

Drescher, J. (1996). Psychoanalytic subjectivity and male homosexuality. In R. Cabaj & T. Stein (Eds.), *The textbook of homosexuality and mental health* (pp. 173–189). Washington, DC: American Psychiatric Press.

Dunkle, J. (1994). Counseling gay male clients: A review of treatment efficacy research: 1975–present. *Journal of Gay and Lesbian Psychotherapy, 2(2),* 1–19.

Etnyre, W. S. (2001). *Fostering a self-affirming identity in gay men.* Unpublished comprehensive exam, Smith College for Social Work, Northampton, MA.

Fox, R. C. (1995). Bisexual identities. In A. R. D'Augelli & C. J. Patterson (Eds.), *Lesbian, gay, and bisexual identities over the lifespan: Psychological perspectives* (pp. 48–86). New York: Oxford University Press.

Freidman, R. (1988). *Male homosexuality: A contemporary psychoanalytic perspective.* New Haven, CT: Yale University Press.

Freidman, R., & Downey, J. (1998). Psychoanalysis and the model of homosexuality as psychopathology: A historical overview. *The American Journal of Psychoanalysis, 58(3),* 249–270.

Gonsiorek, J. (1982). Introduction. In W. Paul, J. Weinrich, J. Gonsiorek, & M. Hotvedt (Eds.), *Homosexuality: Social, psychological, and biological issues* (pp. 57–70). Beverly Hills: Sage.

Green, R. (1987). *The "sissy boy syndrome" and the development of homosexuality.* New Haven, CT: Yale University Press.

Greenberg, D. F. (1988). *The construction of homosexuality.* Chicago: University of Chicago Press.

Grossman, A., & Kerner, M. (1998). Self-esteem and supportiveness as predictors of emotional distress in gay male and lesbian youth. *The Journal of Homosexuality, 35(2),* 25–39.

Hanson, G., & Hartmann, L. (1996). Latency development in prehomosexual boys. In R. Cabaj & T. Stein (Eds.), *Textbook of homosexuality and mental health* (pp. 253–266). Washington, DC: American Psychiatric Press.

Harris, J. R. (1998) *The nurture assumption: Why children turn out the way they do.* New York: The Free Press.

Hartstein, N. (1996). Suicide risk in lesbian, gay, and bisexual youth. In R. Cabaj & S. Stein (Eds.), *The textbook of homosexuality and mental health* (pp. 819–837). Washington, DC: American Psychiatric Press.

Haslam, N. (1997). Evidence that male sexual orientation is a matter of degree. *Journal of Personality and Social Psychology, 73(4),* 862–870.

Herdt, G. (1992). Coming out as a rite of passage. In G. Herdt (Ed.), *Gay culture in America: Essays from the field* (pp. 29–67). Boston: Beacon.

Herdt, G., & Boxer, A. (1988). *Children of Horizons: How gay and lesbian teens are leading a new way out of the closet.* Boston: Beacon.

Herman, J. L. (1992). *Trauma and recovery.* New York: Basic Books.

Hooker, E. (1957). The adjustment of the male overt homosexual. *Journal of Projective Techniques, 21,* 18–31.

Hooker, E. (1965). Male homosexuals and their worlds. In J. Marmor (Ed.), *Sexual inversion.* New York: Basic Books.

Hooker, E. (1967). The adjustment of the male overt homosexual. *Journal of Psychology, 31,* 18–30.

Hooker, E. (1972). Homosexuality. In Department of Health, Education and Welfare, *NIMH task force on homosexuality: Final report and background papers.* Pub. # (HSM) 72-9116, pp. 11–22. Washington, DC: GPO.

Icard, L. (1996). Assessing the psycho-social well-being of African American gays: A multidimensional perspective. *Journal of Gay and Lesbian Social Services, 5(2/3),* 25–49.

Irvin, F. S. (1988). *Resilience and vulnerability among gay and lesbian youth.* Unpublished paper presented at the Annual Meeting of the American Psychological Association. (Reported in Herdt & Boxer, 1988, p. 207.)

Isay, R. (1986). The development of sexual identity in homosexual men. *Psychoanalytic Study of the Child, 41,* 467–489.

Isay, R. (1996). Psychoanalytic therapy with gay men. In R. Cabaj & T. Stein (Eds.), *The textbook of homosexuality and mental health* (pp. 451–469). Washington, DC: American Psychiatric Press.

Jacobs, S. (1997). Is the "North American Berdache" merely a phantom in the imagination of western social scientists? In S. Jacobs, T. Wesley, & S. Lang (Eds.), *Two-Spirit People* (pp. 21–43). Urbana: University of Illinois Press.

Jones, B., & Hill, M. (1996). In R. Cabaj & S. Stein (Eds.), *The textbook of homosexuality and mental health* (pp. 549–563). Washington, DC: American Psychiatric Press.

Kinsey, A., Pomeroy, W., & Martin, C. (1948). *Sexual behavior in the human male.* Philadelphia: Saunders.

Kinsey, A., Pomeroy, W., Martin, C., & Gebhard, P. (1953). *Sexual behavior in the human female.* Philadelphia: Saunders.

Klein, F., Sepekoff, B., & Wolf, T. (1985). Sexual orientation: A multi-variable dynamic process. *Journal of Homosexuality, 11(1/2),* 35–49.

Klein, R. (1999). Group work practice with transgendered male to female sex workers. *JGLSS, 10(3/4),* 95–109.

Magee, M., & Miller, D. C. (1996). Psychoanalytic views of female homosexuality. In R. Cabaj & S. Stein (Eds.), *The textbook of homosexuality and mental health* (pp. 191–206). Washington, DC: American Psychiatric Press.

Mallon, G. (1994). Counseling gay and lesbian youth. *Journal of Gay and Lesbian Social Services, 3/4(1),* 75–91.

Mallon, G. (1999a). Knowledge for practice with transgendered children. *Journal of Gay and Lesbian Social Services, 10(4),* 1–18.

Mallon, G. (1999b). Practice with transgendered children. *Journal of Gay and Lesbian Social Services, 10(4),* 49–64.

Malyon, A. (1982). Psychotherapeutic implications of internalized homophobia in gay men. *Journal of Homosexuality, 7,* 59–69.

Malyon, A. (1993). Psychotherapeutic implications of internalized homophobia in gay men. In C. Cornett (Ed.), *Affirmative dynamic psychotherapy with gay men* (pp. 77–92). Northvale, NJ: Aronson.

Marsiglio, W. (1993). Attitudes toward homosexual activity and gays as friends: A national survey of heterosexual 15 to 19 year-old males. *Journal of Sex Research, 30,* 12–17.

McDougall, B. (1998). *My child is gay: How parents react when they hear the news.* St. Leonards, NSW, Australia: Allen & Unwin.

Michaels, S. (1996). The prevalence of homosexuality in the United States. In R. Cabaj & S. Stein (Eds.), *The textbook of homosexuality and mental health* (pp. 43–63). Washington, DC: American Psychiatric Press.

Minton, H., & Mattson, S. (1998). Deconstructing heterosexuality: Life stories from gay New York. *Journal of Homosexuality, 36(1),* 43–61.

Murray, S. O., & Roscoe, W. (Eds.). (1998). *Boy-wives and female husbands: Studies in African homosexualities* (pp. xii–xxii). New York: St. Martin's Press.

Nakajima, G., Chan, Y., & Lee, K. (1996). In R. Cabaj & S. Stein (Eds.), *The textbook of homosexuality and mental health* (pp. 563–582). Washington, DC: American Psychiatric Press.

Nicolosi, J. (1991). *Reparative treatment of male homosexuality.* Northvale, NJ: Aronson.

Pillard, R. C. (1996). Homosexuality from a familial and genetic perspective. In R. Cabaj & S. Stein (Eds.), *The textbook of homosexuality and mental health* (pp. 115–128). Washington, DC: American Psychiatric Press.

Ponse, B. (1980). Lesbians and their worlds. In E. Marmor (Ed.), *Homosexual behavior: A modern reappraisal* (pp. 157–175). New York: Basic Books.

Reed, R. (1997). *Growing up gay: The sorrows and joys of gay and lesbian adolescence.* New York: Norton.

Roscoe, W. (1998). *Changing ones: Third and fourth genders in Native North America.* New York: St. Martin's Griffin.

Rosenberg, L. (2000). Phase oriented psychotherapy for gay men recovering from trauma. *Journal of Gay and Lesbian Social Services, 11(1/2),* 37–74.

Safe Schools Coalition of Washington. (March, 1999). *Eighty-three thousand youth: Selected findings from eight population based studies.* http://www.safeschools-wa.org/quant.mh.html.

Sik-ying Ho, P. (1999). Developing a social constructionist therapy approach for gay men and their families in Hong Kong. *Journal of Gay and Lesbian Social Services, 9(4),* 69–97.

Silverstein, C. (1993). The borderline personality disorder and gay people. In C. Cornett (Ed.), *Affirmative dynamic psychotherapy with gay men* (pp. 117–149). Northvale, NJ: Aronson.

Stein, T., & Cabaj, R. (1996). Psychotherapy with gay men. In R. Cabaj & S. Stein (Eds.), *The textbook of homosexuality and mental health* (pp. 413–432). Washington, DC: American Psychiatric Press.

Tafoya, R. (1996). Native two-spirited people. In R. Cabaj & S. Stein (Eds.), *The textbook of homosexuality and mental health* (pp. 603–620). Washington, DC: American Psychiatric Press.

Tafoya, T., & Wirth, D. (1996). Native American two-spirit men. *Journal of Gay and Lesbian Social Services, 5(2/3),* 51–69.

Troiden, R. (1979). Becoming homosexual: A model of gay identity acquisition. *Psychiatry, 42,* 362–373.

Troiden, R. (1988). *Gay and lesbian identity.* Dix Hills, NY: General Hall.

Valocchl, S. (1999). The class-inflected nature of gay identity. *Social Problems, 46(2),* 207–234.

Walters, K. L. (1998). Negotiating conflicts in allegiances among lesbians and gays of color: Reconciling divided selves and communities. In G. Mallon (Ed.), *Foundations of social work practice with gay and lesbian persons* (pp. 47–75). New York: Harrington Park Press.

Williams, W. (1986). *The spirit and the flesh.* Boston: Beacon.

Winnicott, D. (1960). Ego distortions in terms of true and false self. In D. Winnicott (Ed.), *The maturational processes and the facilitating environment* (pp. 140–152). London: Hogarth.

CHAPTER 6

POVERTY AND CHILD DEVELOPMENT

Promising Interventions

MIRIAM R. LINVER
Columbia University

ALLISON SIDLE FULIGNI
UCLA

MAGDALENA HERNANDEZ
Columbia University

JEANNE BROOKS-GUNN
Columbia University

The number of children and adolescents in the United States currently living in poverty is staggering; poverty continues to be a pervasive problem into the twenty-first century. Although children's poverty rates increased steadily throughout the 1980s and the early 1990s, recent statistics suggest poverty in this country may be leveling off (Dalaker, 2001). The poverty rate for children from birth to age 18 years was 18.3 percent in 1980 and 16.2 percent in 2000 (Dalaker, 2001). Even with this downward trend, over 11 million children currently live in poverty. Poverty does not strike children at random; young children,

Note: For an expanded discussion of child and family interventions, see Fuligni and Brooks-Gunn (2000). Funders for this paper include the NICHD Research Network on Child and Family Well-Being; the National Institute on Early Childhood Development and Education, the Office of Educational Research and Improvement, U.S. Department of Education; the Office of the Assistant Secretary of Planning and Evaluation, U.S. Department of Health and Human Services; and the National Institute for Child Health and Human Development. We are grateful to Lori Mielcarek for her assistance in the preparation of this chapter. Address correspondence via e-mail to Miriam Linver, MRL23@columbia.edu, or mail to National Center for Children and Families, Box 39, 525 W. 120th St., Teachers College, Columbia University, New York, NY 10027.

ethnic minority children, and immigrant children are more likely to live in poverty compared to older, nonminority, and nonimmigrant children. In 1995, for example, 21 percent of all children under age 18 lived in poor families, but 24 percent of children age 6 and under lived in poor families (Corcoran & Chaudry, 1997). In 2000, 9.4 percent of white non-Hispanic children lived in poverty, compared to 14.5 percent of Asians, 28.0 percent of Hispanics, and 30.9 percent of black children (Dalaker, 2001). First-generation immigrant children are more likely to live in poverty than children in native-born families.

In this chapter, (1) we consider how poverty matters for children in three main outcome domains: health and physical development; socioemotional and behavioral functioning; and cognitive development and academic achievement; (2) we investigate the pathways through which these domains operate; (3) we examine multiple interventions for children and adolescents that may counteract some of the negative effects of living in poverty, including family-level interventions for families with young children, early childhood education programs, and a variety of interventions for adolescents; and (4) we discuss the implications of family, school, and neighborhood poverty for children and their families. Although evidence is mixed, we conclude that programs that employ multiple approaches (e.g., in-kind transfers, early childhood education, and home visiting) may work best to raise families out of poverty.

DEFINITIONS OF POVERTY

Poverty can be defined in various ways, including timing, depth, and duration of poverty. The measurement of "official" U.S. poverty is based on a set of income thresholds that were developed in the 1960s and are adjusted each year for changes in the cost of living using the Consumer Price Index. In 2000, U.S. *poverty thresholds* for families of three and four persons were $13,470 and $17,761, respectively. A method of comparing poverty across households is to examine the *income-to-needs ratio*; this is calculated by dividing each household's income by its corresponding poverty threshold. In 2000, children (as well as other family members) living in a four-person household whose income was $53,283 would have income-to-needs ratios of 3.0 ($53,283/$17,761); members of four-person households with a total household income of only $8,881 would each have an income-to-needs ratio of 0.5. By definition, an income-to-needs ratio of 1.0 indicates that a family income is equal to the U.S. poverty threshold for any given year (Duncan, Brooks-Gunn, & Klebanov, 1994). Some researchers have argued that the poverty threshold bar is set too low, as families living just above the poverty line still struggle to make ends meet (Hernandez, 1997); although their income may be sufficient for survival, it falls behind that of the surrounding community. These researchers suggest that a more accurate threshold for determining families who have adequate income is 150 percent of the poverty line. There have been some attempts to alter the poverty line, by including benefits such as Temporary Assistance for Needy Families (TANF), Earned Income Tax Credit (EITC), and the like in calculations (Betson & Michael, 1997).

More children than adults in the United States currently live in poverty, for several reasons. First, children of single mothers are more likely to live in poverty than children in two-parent households; household earnings are higher in two-parent families than in single-mother households both because two-parent families may have two wage earners and because, on average, men earn higher salaries than women. Second, the poverty line is defined by the number of people living in a household; if there are more children in a household, more income is needed in the household for all family members to be above the poverty line. Since children do not contribute income to the family, if there are more children in a household, it is more likely that the family will fall below the poverty line than if there are fewer or no children. This problem is compounded in single-mother households. Third, even if transfer income (such as TANF) is included in total income (census data on income do not include transfer income; Dalaker, 2001), income for most families would remain at under 150 percent of the poverty line. Thus, although families with children are more likely to receive benefits, they are still living in economically poor conditions.

THEORETICAL FRAMEWORKS FOR STUDYING THE EFFECTS OF POVERTY ON CHILDREN

Researchers have documented the negative outcomes of living in poverty for children; few have systematically controlled for family characteristics that may be correlated with poverty (e.g., single-parent family, mother's age, mother's schooling), or have measured the effects of timing, depth, and duration of poverty on children (Brooks-Gunn & Duncan, 1997). Children and adolescents who experience poverty are at risk for maladaptive outcomes in several domains, including health, cognitive development, academic achievement, and socioemotional functioning. The association between poverty and negative outcomes persists across varied definitions of poverty (e.g., poverty threshold, income, income-to-needs ratio, persistent poverty, transient poverty) and diverse outcome criteria. In the next section, we review research on the effects of poverty on children and adolescents. Our discussion spans multiple developmental periods (prenatal, infancy, early childhood, middle childhood, and adolescence) and is structured according to outcome areas. We consider three main outcome domains: (1) health and physical development; (2) socioemotional and behavioral functioning; and (3) cognitive development and academic achievement.

Child and adolescent development occurs within several distinct but interrelated ecological systems, including the family, the neighborhood, the school, and the wider network of community and government institutions (Bronfenbrenner & Crouter, 1983). Two main perspectives have emerged in the literature to explain how income matters for children's development, given the influence of these ecological systems on children's developmental outcomes. One focuses on the effect of income through a family's ability to invest resources in children's development (Becker & Thomes, 1986; Haveman & Wolfe, 1994; Mayer, 1997); the other emphasizes the effect of income through parents' emotional well-being and parenting practices (Conger & Elder, 1994; Elder & Caspi, 1988).

We consider poverty's distal and proximal influences on child and adolescent well-being, through family-, school-, and neighborhood-level resources. It is important to note that risk factors within and between ecological levels frequently co-occur, so that children and adolescents who experience poverty are also likely to experience additional risk factors. Cumulative effects of multiple risk factors are greater than the additive combination of the effects of individual risks (Liaw & Brooks-Gunn, 1994; Sameroff, Seifer, Baldwin, & Baldwin, 1993; Sameroff, Seifer, Zax, & Barocas, 1987).

Poverty is a dynamic phenomenon; some researchers emphasize the nonlinear nature of its effects (Bane & Ellwood, 1996; Corcoran & Chaudry, 1997; Duncan & Rodgers, 1988), whereas others claim poverty's effects on children and families follows a linear relation (Mayer, 1997). An example of nonlinear poverty effects was reported by Duncan, Yeung, Brooks-Gunn, and Smith (1998); these researchers found that the association between income and a number of years of completed schooling or high school completion was stronger for children in low-income families (<$20,000) than those in middle- and high-income families. Studies of the effects of the duration of poverty have also highlighted the importance of considering the effects of deep, persistent, and early poverty versus short, intermittent poverty. Smith, Brooks-Gunn, and Klebanov (1997) found that persistent poverty had stronger associations with cognitive test scores than transient poverty in 3- to 8-year-old children. In the following sections, we include more detailed discussions of the effects of poverty on children's and adolescents' outcomes, across multiple domains and contexts. We then discuss how interventions may lessen the effects of living in poverty for particular populations, giving examples of specific interventions that have been implemented.

EFFECTS OF POVERTY ON CHILDREN AND ADOLESCENTS

When controlling for other family demographic characteristics that are associated with poverty (and that could account in part for links between income and children's development), poverty is still a predictor of more negative child outcomes, although the size of the association is reduced (Blau, 1999; Mayer, 1997). Poverty effects are also seen when studies use sibling models (looking at differences in siblings' school completion rates based on income levels during their childhoods; Duncan et al., 1998). Poverty effects seem to be strongest during the preschool and early school years, when low income is persistent and when poverty is deep (i.e., less than one-half the poverty threshold; Brooks-Gunn & Duncan, 1997).

Health and Physical Development

The detrimental effects of poverty emerge as early as the prenatal period. Pregnant women who experience poverty are less likely to receive timely prenatal care, are more likely to smoke, and are at risk for delivering low birth weight (2,500 grams or less) and "small for gestational age" infants than higher-income pregnant women (Kleinman & Kessel, 1987; Klerman, 1991; McGauhey & Starfield, 1993; Starfield, Shapiro, Weiss, et al., 1991). Delayed immunizations, inadequate well-baby care, neonatal mortality, and lead poisoning are more common among low-income than higher-income infants and children (Brody, Pirkle, Kramer, et al., 1994; Corman & Grossman, 1985; National Center for Health Statistics, 2000). The discrepancy in health care use extends through childhood and adolescent years, with poor children and adolescents frequently lacking regular medical care providers and relying on emergency room visits (Federal Interagency Forum on Child and Family Statistics, 1999; National Center for Health Statistics, 2000). Untreated dental problems and inadequate dental care are more common among children and adolescents from low-income families than among those from higher-income families (National Center for Health Statistics, 2000).

Some evidence shows that persistent poverty is more detrimental than transient poverty for children's health outcomes. In several studies, poor nutritional status was found to be associated with concurrent poverty at ages 2 to 17 (Lewit & Kerrebrock, 1997) and, more powerfully, with persistent poverty at ages 5 to 7 (Korenman & Miller, 1997; Miller & Korenman, 1994). Poor nutritional status, in turn, is associated with poorer health, as well as lower cognitive, behavioral, and emotional functioning in childhood and adolescence (Brown, 1987; Physician Task Force on Hunger in America, 1985).

Links between poverty and physical well-being may be associated with medical care and health insurance. However, in studies of adult populations, access to health care does not totally eliminate SES disparities (Adler et al., 1994). Nevertheless, the receipt of adequate health services ensures access to preventive services and medical assistance that aid in the identification and treatment of potentially serious medical conditions (American Academy of Pediatrics, 1995). Health insurance coverage is a particularly powerful determinant of the receipt of adequate health care (Newacheck et al., 1996; Wood et al., 1990). Poor and near-poor (children from families with incomes under 125 percent of the poverty line) children are more likely to lack health insurance coverage than children from higher-income families (Mills, 2000). Adolescents from poor families are three times as likely to be uninsured than adolescents from families with incomes greater that 200 percent of the poverty line (National Center for Health Statistics, 2000). Government-funded health insurance programs (Medicaid, State Children's Health Insurance Program [S-CHIP]) provide a safety net for low-income families, but the enrollment rates, and accompanying service utilization rates, of low-income children and youth still lag behind those of children and adolescents from higher-income families using private health insurance.

Children and adolescents in poor families are clearly at risk across several indicators of health and physical well-being. Although here we discuss three outcome areas separately (health, socioemotional and behavior functioning, and cognitive development), it is important to note that difficulties in one domain can lead to or aggravate difficulties in another area. For example, low birth weight (which is more likely in poor children) is associated with cognitive difficulties, grade failure, and lower school achievement during childhood and adolescence (Klebanov, Brooks-Gunn, & McCormick, 1994; McCarton et al., 1997). Low scores on measures of cognitive and verbal ability are associated with increased risk for delinquency and antisocial behavior, above and beyond the effects of socioeconomic status (Farrington, 1987; Moffitt, 1993). We now turn to associations of poverty with socioemotional and cognitive outcomes.

Socioemotional and Behavioral Functioning

An estimated one in ten children experience potentially impairment-causing mental illnesses (Burns et al., 1995; Shaffer et al., 1996). Comorbity among emotional and behavioral difficulties—including ADHD, depression, conduct disorders, antisocial behavior, and drug use—is not uncommon (Spencer et al., 1999). Early conduct problems and antisocial behavior are the strongest predictors of later delinquency and mental health problems (Ramey & Campbell, 1991; Farrington, 1987; Moffit, 1990; Moffit & Silva, 1988; Pierce, Ewing, & Campbell, 1999; Reid, Patterson, & Snyder, 2002).

Parents of poor children are more likely than parents of nonpoor children to report that their child has ever had an emotional or behavioral problem and been treated for such problems (Korenman, Miller, & Sjaastad, 1995; McLeod & Shanahan, 1993). Family income and poverty status, over and above maternal education and family structure, have small-to-moderate direct effects on young children's externalizing (e.g., aggressive) and internalizing (e.g., anxiety) behaviors (Brooks-Gunn, Duncan, Klebanov, & Sealand, 1993; Duncan, Brooks-Gunn, & Klebanov, 1994; Klebanov, Brooks-Gunn, & McCormick, 1994; Smith et al., 1997). Patterson and colleagues (Patterson & Narrett, 1990) found that family income was a stronger predictor of children's conduct and peer relations than ethnicity and household composition.

Living in poverty is associated with a variety of other socioemotional and behavior problems. Early childhood poverty has been associated with depression that persists until late childhood, as well as antisocial behavior, adolescent anxiety, and adolescent hyperactivity (McLeod & Shanahan, 1996; Pagani et al., 1997). Compared with nonpoor peers, young children living in persistent poverty have higher internalizing problem scores; research is mixed whether current poverty status or persistent poverty is related to children's externalizing behavior problems (Duncan et al., 1994; McLeod & Shanahan, 1993). Analysis of the National Longitudinal Study of Youth (NLSY) indicates that the effects of deep poverty (less than one-half of the poverty threshold) on children's behavior problems persist through age 8 (Smith, Bastiani, & Brooks-Gunn, 1998). Similarly, family poverty is associated with parent reports of emotional and behavior problems among children aged 3 to 17 years in the 1988 National Health Interview Survey Child Health Supplement (Brooks-Gunn & Duncan, 1997).

Cognitive Development and Academic Achievement

Family income is more strongly associated with cognitive outcomes for young children than with socioemotional outcomes. In the National Longitudinal Study of Youth-Child Supplement (NLSY-CS) and the Infant Health and Development Program (IHDP), income associations were found when examining various measures of income, as discussed earlier, and various cognitive indicators, such as verbal, achievement, and intelligence test scores (Smith et al., 1997). Even after controlling for mothers' education, effect sizes for family income on 3- to 8-year-old children's test scores ranged from .20 to .32 (Alexander & Entwisle, 1988; Duncan et al., 1994; Klebanov, Brooks-Gunn, McCarton, & McCormick, 1998; Smith et al., 1997). Children living in persistent poverty had cognitive scores six to nine points lower than those of children who had never lived in poverty (Smith et al., 1997). Children who repeat a grade are at greater risk for several specific behavioral disorders, such as attention deficit hyperactivity disorder, obsessive compulsive disorder, overanxious disorder, and major depressive disorder (Velez, Johnson, & Cohen, 1989). Children who demonstrate low scores on early measures of school achievement, verbal IQ, and verbal ability are at risk for delinquent and antisocial behavior.

Although there is overwhelming evidence that poverty is associated with cognitive and academic disadvantage, the effects of the *timing* of poverty are less clear. Analyses of IHDP and NLSY longitudinal data did not find a significant association between the timing of poverty and early cognitive test scores (Smith et al., 1997). However, using data from the Panel Study of Income Dynamics (PSID), Duncan and colleagues (Duncan et al., 1998) found that early poverty was more strongly associated with years of schooling than later poverty. In particular, persistent poverty has more detrimental effects on IQ, school achievement, and socioemotional functioning than does transient poverty, although children in both groups generally do worse than children who have never been poor (Smith, Brooks-Gunn, & Kohen, 2001).

EFFECTS OF SCHOOL EXPENDITURES

There has been some debate as to the effects of school expenditure on student outcomes. In his widely cited review of the determinants of student achievement, Hanushek (1986) found no systematic relation between expenditures and student achievement. Others, most notably Greenwald and colleagues (Greenwald, Hedges, & Laine, 1996; Hedges, Laine, & Greenwald, 1994), have found that expenditure has a strong positive association with educational outcomes. Although the direct assocation between school expenditures and student achievement requires further examination, more recent studies suggest that students in schools located in high-poverty neighborhoods are at a disadvantage when considering several school characteristics, including class size, teacher experience, teacher qualifications, and classroom technology. Both correlational and experimental research suggest that reduced class sizes lead to higher academic achievement (Finn & Achilles, 1990; Glass et al., 1982; Mosteller, 1995), particularly for primary-grade-age minority and disadvantaged students (Finn, 1998; Robinson & Wittebols, 1986; U.S. Department of Education, 1998). Low-SES schools are more likely to have class sizes that exceed the recommended range.

Teacher qualifications—most markedly teacher education and experience—are positively associated with student achievement (Darling-Hammond, 2000; U.S. Department of Education, 2000a). Inexperienced teachers (under four years of experience) are disproportionately represented in high-poverty schools, as is teacher attrition (Henke et al., 1997; U.S. Department of Education, 2000b). U.S. Department of Education estimates indicate that 64 percent of all unqualified teachers work in high-poverty schools (although high-poverty schools employ 38 percent of all teachers; U.S. Department of Education, 1999).

Classroom technology, including computer and Internet use, has received increasing attention as a vehicle for student learning. The use of computers to teach discrete skills has been associated with greater student learning, especially for children from low-income families (President's Committee of Advisors on Science and Technology, 1997). Poor students, however, have less access to computers and the Internet than children from higher-income families (Anderson & Ronnkvist, 1999; U.S. Department of Education, 2000b). Some estimates indicate that low-SES schools lag three to four years behind high-SES schools in their computer technology (Becker, 2000).

Equal access to high-quality education is considered to be an entitlement for all children regardless of socioeconomic status. Research indicates, however, that children from low-income families are greatly disadvantaged along several indicators of school quality and that this disadvantage can lead to later difficulties in educational achievement and related domains.

EFFECTS OF NEIGHBORHOOD POVERTY

Although researchers have recently turned their attention to neighborhoods as important influences on child outcomes (Brooks-Gunn, Duncan, & Aber, 1997; Leventhal & Brooks-

Gunn, 2000), few studies have been able to disentangle the effects of neighborhood poverty from other neighborhood features, such as distribution of unemployment, family structure, education, and welfare receipt. Poor children are twice as likely to live in unsafe neighborhoods than their peers, for example (Federman, Garner, Short, et al., 1996). This area of inquiry is further complicated by lack of individual-level data; consequently, there is frequent reliance on aggregate neighborhood data. Studies suggest that neighborhood affluence is associated with children's achievement and cognitive outcomes, while neighborhood poverty is associated—although less robustly—with children's behavioral outcomes. Studies of neighborhood-level data suggest that neighborhood poverty is associated with the high occurrence of health problems among low-income children (Starfield, 1992). Lower rates of prenatal health care and higher rates of low birth weight births have been associated with neighborhood poverty in studies using individual-level data (Gould & LeRoy, 1988; Collins & David, 1990; O'Campo et al., 1997). Residing in a high-SES neighborhood has been associated with children's verbal, intelligence, and reading achievement test scores at ages 3 through 6 (Brooks-Gunn et al., 1993; Chase-Lansdale et al., 1997; Chase-Lansdale & Gordon, 1996; Duncan et al., 1994; Klebanov, Brooks-Gunn, McCarton, & McCormick, 1998). The disadvantages of living in a poor neighborhood continue into late childhood and adolescence; living in a low-SES neighborhood was significantly linked to children's affiliation with deviant peers for 10- to 12-year-olds and adolescents (Brody et al., 2001).

INTERACTIONS BETWEEN POVERTY AND CHILD CHARACTERISTICS

Poverty does not affect all children equally, and such differences are magnified as children grow through adolescence and into young adulthood. A child's age, gender, and ethnicity all influence how he or she is affected by living in poverty, however poverty is defined.

Younger children may be more vulnerable to the effects of living in poverty than are older children. Children who live in poverty during the preschool years have lower rates of school completion than children and adolescents who experience poverty only in later years (Duncan et al., 1998; Baydar, Brooks-Gunn, & Furstenberg, 1993). It is possible that other factors correlated with low income, such as poor-quality schooling, may add to children's lowered educational outcomes (Alexander & Entwisle, 1988).

Poverty rates among African American and Latino families living in the United States are two to three times higher than that of European Americans (Dalaker, 2001). As such, it is important to examine the differential effects of poverty on ethnically diverse groups of children. The developmental trajectories of ethnic minority children also may differ from that of majority children's trajectories for health, cognitive, and socioemotional outcomes, due to past and present racial discrimination and oppression (Garcia Coll et al., 1996; McLoyd, 1990; Wilson, 1987).

Boys growing up in poverty may be more vulnerable to family disturbances than are girls. For example, when children are exposed to maternal depression and anxiety during infancy, boys are more likely to demonstrate higher levels of externalizing behavior problems during preschool and childhood (Shaw, Vondra, Hommerding, Keenan, & Dunn, 1994; Wall & Holden, 1994). Boys from poor families are also likely to demonstrate more externalizing behavior problems in elementary school (Bolger, Patterson, Thompson, & Kupersmidt, 1995).

During the teenage years, in contrast, girls and boys are affected differently by poverty (Juarez, Viega, & Richards, 1997). Fathers' rejecting and neglecting behaviors affect the psychosocial functioning of adolescent girls, but not boys (Elder, Nguyen, & Caspi, 1985). Parents' employment loss intensifies parent-child conflicts more for boys than for girls at adolescence (Conger, Conger, & Elder, 1997).

REVIEW OF PROMISING INTERVENTIONS

Interventions aimed at reducing the effects of poverty on children and adolescents have taken a multitude of approaches, based on the wide-reaching domains of influence of poverty on children's and youths' development (the consequences) as well as the various mechanisms by which poverty has been hypothesized to be affecting those outcomes (the pathways). Some intervention programs have focused primarily on treating the consequences of growing up in poverty, by providing remedial services such as physical care (developmental screenings, referrals to medical and mental health service providers, and comprehensive health care coverage) and/or early care and education services designed to support children's social, emotional, and cognitive development.

Prevention strategies often focus on one or more of the pathways by which poverty influences child and adolescent well-being. McLoyd (1989; McLoyd, Jayaratne, Ceballo, & Borquez, 1994) has proposed that family poverty affects children because of parents' psychological experience of financial strain, which reduces parents' likelihood of parenting in a style that is supportive of children's development. Interventions influenced by this theoretical model might seek to provide mental health or social support to the parent, to reduce his or her psychological distress and enhance his or her parenting, and/or might provide alternate caregiving settings for the child, in which caregivers provide nurturance and cognitive stimulation.

Early education intervention programs for children of low-income families have been evolving since their first appearance in the 1960s. Several program models have emerged, including center-based programs that provide early education and other services directly to low-income children at a preschool-like center, home-visiting programs that provide parenting support and other services to families during visits to their own homes, and comprehensive family support programs that serve multiple members of the family by offering parenting support and/or education as well as early childhood education and other social supports. Family support programs may be center-based or home-visiting programs, or may combine both types of service delivery.

The service delivery approach of early intervention programs has been linked to the domains of functioning that they have successfully improved. The strongest effects of intervention programs on young children's cognitive and language development have been documented in programs that provide developmentally appropriate early education services directly to the children, such as the Perry Preschool Program, the Infant Health and Development Program (IHDP), and Head Start (although the smaller programs have shown stronger effects than large-scale programs like Head Start; Barnett, 1995). On the other hand, programs that provide home-based parenting services may have stronger effects on parenting domains compared to child domains.

Family-Level Interventions

The family has been considered as a mechanism by which low income and poverty affect young children in many types of interventions, including home visiting programs and family literacy programs. These programs focus their service delivery on the child, mother, and/or family; effects on child outcomes depend on the focus of the intervention; for example, some programs show weaker effects on children but stronger effects on mothers.

Home Visiting Programs.   Home visiting programs focus on the services of a professional (such as a nurse) or paraprofessional who visits the home on a periodic basis (such as weekly or monthly). Service delivery often begins in the prenatal period and continues through a designated period of the child's life (a few months or years). These programs focus on improving parenting, as well as promoting preventive health care use. A well-known example of a home visiting program is the Nurse Home Visitation Program (NHVP; Olds, Henderson, Kitzman, Eckenrode, Cole, & Tatelbaum, 1999), aimed at promoting children's health and development. Other programs have focused on demonstrating to parents intellectually stimulating ways of interacting with their children. An example of this type is the Parents as Teachers (PAT) program, which served parents of diverse socioeconomic backgrounds with children from birth to age 3; it attempted to instruct parents to be their children's "first teachers" (Wagner & Clayton, 1999). A second example of this type of program is the Home Instruction Program for Preschool Youngsters (HIPPY), designed specifically for low-income parents of preschoolers (Baker, Piotrkowski, & Brooks-Gunn, 1999). The home visit component of the HIPPY program model includes twice-monthly visits by paraprofessionals. During these visits, the home visitor engages the parent in role-playing, child-focused, educational activities (Britto, Fuligni, & Brooks-Gunn, in press).

Home visiting programs can provide direct services for children, their families, or both; when these programs do not provide direct services for children, they tend to report fewer effects on child cognitive outcomes. Comprehensive reviews of home visiting programs have found that only one-third to two-thirds have documented immediate positive gains for children's cognitive scores (Benasich, Brooks-Gunn, & Clewell, 1992; Olds & Kitzman, 1993). For example, the NHVP reported no intervention effects for children at ages 3 and 4 years, except for children of mothers who smoked heavily during pregnancy. These children of heavy-smoking mothers exhibited significant gains in IQ at 3 and 4 years of age (Olds et al., 1999). The HIPPY program was designed specifically to enhance preschool children's cognitive skills and school readiness, but the program provided treatment only to the parents. A recent evaluation of HIPPY has revealed there were some effects on children's cognitive outcomes, although effects were not found consistently (Baker et al., 1999). Similarly, the PAT program, which provided monthly home visits to teach mothers about positive parenting and stimulating their children, found only modest and inconsistent effects on child cognitive outcomes in two recent demonstrations (Wagner & Clayton, 1999).

The IHDP provided medical, developmental, and social assessments for all participants during the three years of the program. The intervention group received (1) home visits weekly for the first year and biweekly for the next two years; (2) a full-day, year-round, center-based, educational day-care program from for the second two years of the program (children were ages 1 to 3 years); and (3) a series of parent group meetings every other month in the second two years. The program demonstrated both short-term and long-term effects on children's cognitive development. Positive effects on cognitive test scores were found for both heavier low birth weight (LBW; 2001–2500 g) and lighter low birth weight (2000 g) groups, although the effect was about twice as large for the heavier than the lighter LBW groups (Brooks-Gunn, Klebanov, Liaw, & Spiker, 1993; Infant Health and Development Program, 1990). The mean effect size for cognitive test scores was 7 points for the lighter LBW group and 13 points for the heavier LBW group. Sustained effects at age 5 years were reported for the heavier, but not the lighter, LBW children; children in the intervention group had higher cognitive scores than the follow-up-only group (the difference was about 4 points on the verbal Wechsler Preschool and Primary Scale of Intelligence [WPPSI] and 6 points on the Peabody Picture Vocabulary Test–Revised [PPVT–R] for the heavier LBW group; Brooks-Gunn et al., 1994a).

In addition to impacts on cognitive outcomes, there are also documented effects of home visiting programs on children's social and emotional development; for example, short-term gains in social skills, reduction of problem behaviors, and improved quality of mother-child interactions have been reported (Olds & Kitzman, 1993). The IHDP reported significant impacts on problem behaviors through the term of the intervention; these effects were sustained at ages 5 and 8 only for heavier low birth weight children (Brooks-Gunn, Klebanov, Liaw, & Spiker, 1993; Hill, Waldfogel, & Brooks-Gunn, 2002; McCarton et al., 1997).

Family Literacy Programs.   Family literacy programs focus on an intergenerational relationship and are designed to enhance the skills of both a young child as well as one or more family members in order to improve overall family well-being, especially for families in poverty (St. Pierre & Swartz, 1995). Improvements are therefore expected to occur for both child and parent. These programs usually offer a combination of early childhood education, adult education, and parenting education, provided either exclusively in center-based settings or via a combination of center- and home-based services. Children are expected to benefit both from the child-focused component as well as indirectly through impacts on parenting and home environment. Improved educational and occupational status of participating adults is expected to influence family resources and well-being; parenting education is expected to improve both the provision of cognitively stimulating parent-child activities and the amount of literacy-related materials available in the home (St. Pierre & Swartz, 1995).

Many evaluations of family literacy programs lack experimentally rigorous designs compared to the home visiting programs previously described; positive program effects have still been documented for preschool cognitive outcomes as well as for school readiness (Philliber, Spillman, & King, 1996; St. Pierre, Ricciuti, & Creps, 1998; St. Pierre, Swartz, Gamse, Murray, Deck, & Nickel, 1995; Tao, Gamse, & Tarr, 1998). No long-term cognitive outcomes have been examined in longitudinal studies, so it is not known whether these benefits persist beyond program completion. Social and emotional outcomes for children in family literacy programs have not been examined either immediately or longitudinally.

Family literacy programs also have documented some effects on parents' own literacy skills and on the number of reading materials they provide for children in the home (Heberle, 1992; Richardson & Brown, 1997; St. Pierre & Swartz, 1995; Tao, Swartz, St. Pierre, & Tarr, 1997). Not all programs have impacts on parents, however; in the Even Start program, there were no treatment-control differences on measures of parent-child reading interactions or parents' educational expectations for their children. As well, there were no pretest/posttest differences on maternal depression or family income and resources (St. Pierre et al., 1995).

Early Childhood Education Interventions

Research on family-focused interventions suggests that providing a service to the child directly may have the strongest impact on children's outcomes. The provision of high-quality, developmentally appropriate, center-based child care has been a central focus of many interventions for low-income families. Examples of such programs include the Perry Preschool Program and Head Start. Many of these programs included an additional component that included services for the family, such as the Perry Preschool Program, the Houston Parent Child Development Center (Houston PCDC), the Chicago Child-Parent Center Program (Chicago CPC), and the IHDP. The Perry Preschool Program intervention consisted of daily 2½-hour center-based classes as well as 1½-hour teacher home visits (both from October through May each year). The Chicago CPC provided comprehensive services, including health and social services as well as parental involvement; eventually, a full-day kindergarten component was added. The Houston PCDC program included, in the first year, home visits by a paraprofessional educator designed to provide the mother with improved skills in teaching her infant, with a focus on language development. In the second year, mothers and children participated in four half-day center settings per week; these sessions emphasized child cognitive and language development, child rearing, health, and safety.

The effectiveness of center-based early childhood interventions has been summarized in several reviews (Barnett, 1995; Brooks-Gunn, Berlin, & Fuligni, 2000; Bryant & Maxwell, 1997; Currie, 2001; Farran, 2000; Karoly et al., 1998; Yoshikawa, 1995). Table 6.1 summarizes short- and long-term consequences for children and adolescents of a variety of interventions. Overall, findings demonstrate positive effects on children's IQ scores, which are strongest when the intervention begins in infancy (Brooks-Gunn, McCarton, Casey, et al., 1994a; Campbell & Ramey, 1994; IHDP, 1990). Significant effects are also found for programs serving preschoolers (Royce, Darlington, & Murray, 1983). Long-term effects on math and reading scores have been reported among young adults who attended model preschool programs (Campbell, Ramey, Pungello, Sparling, & Miller-Johnson, in press). Other long-term effects of high-quality early education interventions include higher rates of education, reduction of delinquent behaviors, and less involvement with the criminal justice system even into adolescence and young adulthood (Reynolds, Temple, Robertson, & Mann, 2001; Schweinhart, Barnes, Weikart, Barnett, & Epstein, 1993). One review noted indirect effects of early childhood education programs on reducing antisocial and delinquent behaviors through program effects on both early childhood cognitive abilities as well as parents' parenting skills (Yoshikawa, 1995).

TABLE 6.1 Impacts on Children of Early Intervention Programs, by Type

PROGRAM TYPE	EFFECTS FOUND	CITATIONS
HOME VISITING PROGRAMS	Short-term boost in IQ & achievement; fewer special education classes	Gray & Klaus, 1970; Gray & Ramsey, 1982
	Fewer ER visits	Olds, Henderson, & Kitzman, 1994; Olds, 1996
PRESCHOOL/CENTER-BASED PROGRAMS	Short-term boost in IQ and achievement; long-term higher achievement levels; better high school graduation rate; less grade repetition	Schweinhart & Weikart, 1980; Schweinhart et al., 1993; Reynolds, 1994; Reynolds, 1997; Reynolds & Temple, 1995; Ramey & Campbell, 1991
	Less crime/delinquency in adolescence and adulthood	Schweinhart et al., 1993; Barnett, 1993
	Higher income; less welfare participation as adults	Schweinhart et al., 1993; Barnett, 1993
FAMILY-FOCUSED HOME VISITING INTERVENTIONS THAT ALSO PROVIDE A CENTER- OR PRESCHOOL-BASED COMPONENT	Fewer behavior problems in childhood	Johnson & Breckenridge, 1982
	Short-term and long-term gains in IQ; positive long-term effects on achievement	Johnson & Walker, 1991; Honig & Lally, 1982; Ramey et al., 1985; Brooks-Gunn et al., 1994a; McCarton et al., 1997
	Less crime/delinquency in adolescence	Lally, Mangione, & Honig, 1988

Source: Adapted from Karoly and colleagues (1998).

Overall, early interventions have been found to make a difference in the lives of children and families living in less optimal environments, such as in poverty. Table 6.2 summarizes some of these effects on parents. Note that six out of seven studies reporting on parenting behaviors found that program participation improved the quality and sensitivity of parent-child interactions, but only two of four studies assessing children's home environment found positive effects of program participation (Brooks-Gunn et al., 2000).

Family-focused intervention programs target child outcomes both directly and indirectly through parents and families. Although Table 6.1 indicates that programs may have a number of impacts on parenting and family functioning, few evaluations include tests of indirect pathways (Brooks-Gunn et al., 2000). A notable exception is an analysis of Abecedarian and the Carolina Approach to Responsive Education (CARE) programs, which tested both the quality of home environment as well as parental authoritarian attitudes as possible mediators of program effects on children (Burchinal et al., 1997). These analyses

TABLE 6.2   Impacts on Parents of Early Intervention Programs, by Type

PROGRAM TYPE	PARENTING EFFECT FOUND	CITATIONS
HOME VISITING PROGRAMS	Greater maternal workforce participation and reduced use of welfare and food stamps	Kitzman et al., 1997; Olds, Henderson, Chamberlin, & Tatelbaum, 1986, 1988; Olds, Henderson, & Kitzman, 1994; Olds, Henderson, Kitzman, & Cole, 1995; Olds, Henderson, Tatelbaum, & Chamberlin, 1986; Olds et al., 1997
	More supportive and less harsh parenting	Barrera, Rosenbaum, & Cunningham, 1986; Field, Widmayer, Stringer, & Ignatoff, 1980; Gray & Ruttle, 1980; Larson, 1980; Lieberman, Weston, & Pawl, 1991; Madden, O'Hara, & Levenstein, 1984; Olds et al., 1988; Olds et al., 1994
	More stimulating home environments in some programs and more developmentally appropriate child-rearing attitudes	Barrera et al., 1986; Erickson, Korfmacher, & Egeland, 1992; Field et al., 1980; Gray & Ruttle, 1980; Larson, 1980; Olds et al., 1994; Osofsky, Culp, & Ware, 1988; Ross, 1984
FAMILY-FOCUSED INTERVENTIONS THAT ALSO PROVIDE A CENTER-BASED COMPONENT	Positive effects on maternal education and employment	Andrews et al., 1982; Brooks-Gunn, McCormick, Shapiro, Benasich, & Black, 1994b; Field, Widmayer, Greenburg, & Stoller, 1982; Seitz & Apfel, 1994
	Positive effects on maternal mental health	Klebanov, Brooks-Gunn, & McCormick, 2001; Schweinhart, Barnes, Weikart, Barnett, & Epstein, 1993

Source: Adapted from Brooks-Gunn, Berlin, and Fuligni (2000).

demonstrated a direct effect of the quality of home environment on children's cognitive test scores, although none of this effect was mediated through the effect of the intervention on the home environment (because no treatment effect on the home environment was found). No direct association of parents' authoritarian attitudes and child outcomes was found, so parenting could not be tested as a mediator. Evaluation research that tests these pathways is essential for assessing the effects of interventions that seek to influence children's outcomes through changes in family and home environment.

Interventions with Adolescents

Recently, growing public support has emerged for programs targeted at adolescents' after-school hours; specifically, these programs can provide adolescents with enriching experiences that can enhance their socialization and other skills (Roth & Brooks-Gunn, 2002).

Several interventions have been evaluated. For example, Big Brother/Big Sister is a mentoring program for youth from single-parent families; a random assignment evaluation found reductions in drug and alcohol use, and improvements in school performance and relationships with peers and family. The effects were stronger for minority youth (Tierney, Groosman, & Resch, 1995). A second model intervention is the Quantum Opportunities Program, a community-based, year-round, four-year multifaceted program (including tutoring, mentoring, direct instruction, community service, and college and job placement) for youth from families receiving public assistance beginning in the ninth grade. By the end of high school, youth who had participated in the program showed increases in academic skills and educational expectations, but no differences in dropout or childbearing rates. One year after the end of the program, however, participants were significantly more likely to have graduated from high school or received their GED, be in postsecondary school, and have fewer children (Hahn, Leavitt, & Aaron, 1994). The Woodrock program uses a human relations curriculum for youth in inner-city Philadelphia schools to promote their antidrug focus. An evaluation found better school attendance, improved race relations, and less drug and alcohol use among participants (LoSciuto, Hilbert, Fox, Porcellini, & Lanphear, 1999).

Overall, programs that incorporate more elements of a youth development framework are associated with more positive outcomes for adolescents. Such programs seek to enhance not only adolescents' skills but also their confidence in themselves and their future, their character, and their connections to other people and institutions by creating environments, both at and away from the program, where youth can feel supported and empowered. Additionally, interventions that promote an adult-adolescent relationship (though not limited to mentoring) and that provide continued support throughout the adolescent years were most effective (Roth & Brooks-Gunn, 2002; Roth, Brooks-Gunn, Murray, & Foster, 1998).

Several interventions have focused on helping teen parents improve their parenting skills, with the broader goal of increasing self-sufficiency in the context of welfare reform. Two such examples are the Teenage Parent Demonstration (TPD; Kisker, Rangarajan, & Boller, 1998) and the New Chance Observational Study (Zaslow & Eldred, 1998). Both programs targeted teen mothers (ages 16 to 22 for New Chance and ages 17 to 19 for TPD). Overall, very few positive effects were found on parenting skills and behaviors of teen mothers; in some cases, parenting was negatively affected (Reichman & McLanahan, 2001). Unlike other parenting interventions, however, TPD and New Chance did not include parent education through frequent home visits, and the intervention did not begin very soon after the birth of the child (children were ages 6 months to 8 years in TPD, and between 30 and 60 months in New Chance). Thus, it is not necessarily surprising that strong effects of these interventions were not found.

CONCLUSIONS

Poverty is a problem for child development across multiple domains— health; socioemotional functioning; and cognitive development, school readiness, and achievement. Although poverty has both deleterious and pervasive effects on child development, it may be difficult to disentangle the effects of poverty from the effects of other risk factors, including, for example, ethnicity, immigrant status, and gender. As detailed in this chapter, poverty is indirectly related to child outcomes, as it limits access to education, health care, and high-quality neighborhoods and schools. In addition, poverty is related to familial factors, such as parenting and parent mental health, which are also related to child and adolescent outcomes. Researchers are cautioned to examine the effects of poverty on child development carefully; advanced statistical and methodological techniques are available to examine complex models that can take into account a variety of contexts and covariates. More importantly, it is essential to design studies and formulate research questions that can address the complex relations and contexts linking poverty to children's developmental outcomes. Practitioners who think about developmental psychopathology must navigate these waters with care; poverty is only one of many factors in children's and adolescents' social and developmental disorders. Those who work with children and adolescents should assess poor children within their broader contexts, considering other related characteristics that make up the environment in which they live.

Research on some of the pathways by which poverty affects children can help inform interventions designed to offset effects of poverty on children and adolescents. These pathways can include parental mental health, parenting, family income, and parents' education. For very young children, evaluations of a variety of programs have demonstrated that high-quality direct child care services can improve developmental outcomes. More sophisticated approaches to improving family functioning and, indirectly, child outcomes, have been designed and implemented. It is more difficult, however, to document the indirect effects of these programs on children's developmental outcomes.

Important questions about the nature of intervention services, and their ultimate goals, are raised. Keeping ultimate goals of improving outcomes for children and families in mind, what types of services will be most beneficial for families? If a single mother is moving from welfare to work, perhaps secure, high-quality child care will improve her emotional well-being more effectively than parenting classes, which can add to logistical family scheduling stresses rather than reducing them. Data from a variety of research studies demonstrate many assistance programs and interventions that might be beneficial for children in poverty. These include nutrition/WIC programs, income supplements, parent job training and placement, parental mental health care resources, parenting education, as well as direct child education.

DISCUSSION QUESTIONS

1. Which interventions are most salient for children and adolescents in poverty, and why?

2. What are the most important short- and long-term effects of early intervention programs? How should these intervention effects be measured and defined?

3. Should intervention programs that are designed to help children and adolescents in poverty focus on child outcomes (consequences), family processes (pathways), or both? Explain.

SUGGESTED READINGS

Brooks-Gunn, J., Fuligni, A. S., & Berlin, L. J. (Eds.). (in press). *Early child development in the 21st century: Profiles of current research initiatives.* New York: Teachers College Press.

Duncan, G., & Brooks-Gunn, J. (Eds.). (1997). *Consequences of growing up poor.* New York: Russell Sage Foundation.

Fuligni, A. S., & Brooks-Gunn, J. (2000). The healthy development of children: SES disparities, prevention strategies, and policy opportunities. In B. D. Smedley & S. L. Syme (Eds.), *Promoting health: Intervention strategies from social and behavioral research* (pp. 170–216). Washington, DC: National Academy Press.

Luthar, S. S. (1999). *Poverty and children's adjustment.* Thousand Oaks, CA: Sage.

REFERENCES

Adler, N. E., Boyce, T., Chesney, M. A., Cohen, S., Folkman, S., Kahn, R. L., & Syme, S. L. (1994). Socioeconomic status and health: The challenge of the gradient. *American Psychologist, 49,* 15–24.

Alexander, K. L., & Entwisle, D. R. (1988). Achievement in the first 2 years of school: Patterns and process. *Monographs of the Society for Research in Child Development, 53*(2).

American Academy of Pediatrics. (1995). Recommendations for preventive pediatric health care. *Pediatrics, 96,* 712.

Anderson, R. E., & Ronnkvist, A. (1999). *The presence of computers in American schools.* Irvine, CA: Center for Research on Information Technology and Organizations.

Andrews, S. R., Bluementhal, J. B., Johnson, D. L., Kahn, A. J., Ferguson, C. J., Lasater, T. M., Malone, P. E., & Wallace, D. B. (1982). The skills of mothering: A study of Parent Child Development Centers (New Orleans, Birmingham, Houston). *Monographs of the Society for Research in Child Development, 6*(198).

Baker, A. J. L., Piotrkowski, C. S., & Brooks-Gunn, J. (1999). The Home Instruction Program for Preschool Youngsters (HIPPY). *Future of Children, 9,* 116–133.

Bane, M. J., & Ellwood, D. T. (1996). *Welfare realities: From rhetoric to reform.* Cambridge, MA: Harvard University Press.

Barnett, W. S. (1993). Benefit-cost analysis of preschool education: Findings from a 25-year follow-up. *American Journal of Orthopsychiatry, 63,* 500–508.

Barnett, W. S. (1995). Long-term effects of early childhood programs on cognitive and school outcomes. *The Future of Children: Long Term Outcomes of Early Childhood Programs, 5,* 25–50.

Barrera, M. E., Rosenbaum, P. L., & Cunningham, C. E. (1986). Early home intervention with low-birth weight infants and their parents. *Child Development, 57,* 20–33.

Baydar, N., Brooks-Gunn, J., & Furstenberg, F. F. (1993). Early warning signs of functional illiteracy: Predictors in childhood and adolescence. *Child Development, 64,* 815–829.

Becker, G. S., & Thomes, N. (1986). Human capital and the rise and fall of families. *Journal of Labor Economics, 4,* S1–S139.

Becker, H. J. (2000). Who's wired and who's not: Children's access to and use of computer technology. *The Future of Children, Children and Computer Technology, 10.* Retrieved July 14, 2002 from http://www.futureofchildren.org.

Benasich, A. A., Brooks-Gunn, J., & Clewell, B. C. (1992). How do mothers benefit from early intervention programs? *Journal of Applied Developmental Psychology, 13,* 311–362.

Betson, D. M., & Michael, R. T. (1997). Why are so many children poor? *The Future of Children, 7,* 25–54.

Blau, D. M. (1999). The effect of income on child development. *The Review of Economics and Statistics, 81,* 261–276.

Bolger, K. E., Patterson, C. J., Thompson, W. W., & Kupersmidt, J. B. (1995). Psychosocial adjustment among children experiencing persistent and intermittent family economic hardship. *Child Development, 66,* 1107–1129.

Britto, P. R., Fuligni, A. S., & Brooks-Gunn, J. (in press). Home words abound: Home environments as a context for promoting literacy and academic achievement in young children. In T. Gullota & M. Bloom (Eds.), *Encyclopedia of primary prevention and health promotion.* New London, CT: Kluwer Academic/Plenum Publishers.

Brody, D. J., Pirkle, L., Kramer, R., Flegal, K. M., Matte, T. D., Gunter, E. W., & Paschal, D. C. (1994). Blood lead levels in the U.S. population. *Journal of the American Medical Association, 272,* 277–281.

Brody, G. H., Ge, X., Conger, R., Gibbons, F. X., Murry, V. M., Gerrard, M., & Simons, R. L. (2001). The influence of neighborhood disadvantage, collective socialization, and parenting on African American children's affiliation with deviant peers. *Child Development, 72,* 1231–1246.

Bronfenbrenner, U., & Crouter, A. C. (1983). The evolution of environmental models in developmental research: Vol. 1. History, theory and methods. In W. Kessen (Ed.), *Handbook of child psychology* (pp. 357–414). New York: Wiley.

Brooks-Gunn, J., Berlin, L. J., & Fuligni, A. S. (2000). Early childhood intervention programs: What about the family? In J. P. Shonkoff & S. J. Meisels (Eds.), *Handbook of early childhood intervention* (2nd ed., pp. 549–588). New York: Cambridge University Press.

Brooks-Gunn, J., & Duncan, G. J. (1997). The effects of poverty on children. *Future of Children, 7,* 55–71.

Brooks-Gunn, J., Duncan, G., & Aber, J. L. (Eds.). (1997). *Neighborhood Poverty: Context and consequences for children (Volume 1). Policy implications in studying neighborhoods (Volume 2).* New York: Russell Sage Foundation.

Brooks-Gunn, J., Duncan, G. J., Klebanov, P. K., & Sealand, N. (1993). Do neighborhoods influence child and adolescent development? *American Journal of Sociology, 99,* 353–395.

Brooks-Gunn, J., Klebanov, P. K., Liaw, F. R., & Spiker, D. (1993). Enhancing the development of low birth weight, premature infants: Changes in cognition and behavior over the first three years. *Child Development, 64,* 736–753.

Brooks-Gunn, J., McCarton, C., Casey, P., McCormick, M., Bauer, C., Berenbaum, J., Tyson, J., Swanson, M., Bennett, F., Scott, D., Tonascia, J., & Meinert, C. (1994a). Early intervention in low birth weight, premature infants: Results through age 5 years from the Infant Health and Development Program. *Journal of the American Medical Association, 272,* 1257–1262.

Brooks-Gunn, J., McCormick, M., Shapiro, S., Benasich, A. A., & Black, G. (1994b). The effects of early education intervention on maternal employment, public assistance, and health insurance: The Infant Health and Development Program. *American Journal of Public Health, 84,* 924–931.

Brown, J. L. (1987). Hunger in the U.S. *Scientific American, 256,* 37–41.

Bryant, D., & Maxwell, K. (1997). The effectiveness of early intervention for disadvantaged children. In M. J. Guralnick (Ed.), *The effectiveness of early intervention* (pp. 23–46). Baltimore: Brookes.

Burchinal, M. R., Campbell, F. A., Bryant, D. M., Wasik, B. H., & Ramey, C. T. (1997). Early intervention and mediating processes in cognitive performance of children of low-income African American families. *Child Development, 68,* 935–954.

Burns, B. J., Costello, E. J., Angold, A., Tweed, D., Stangl, D., Farmer, E. M., & Erkanli, A. (1995). Children's mental health service use across service sectors. *Health Affairs, 14,* 147–159.

Campbell, F., & Ramey, C. (1994). Effects of early intervention on intellectual and academic achievement: A follow-up study from low-income families. *Child Development, 65,* 684–698.

Campbell, F. A., Ramey, C. T., Pungello, E., Sparling, J., & Miller-Johnson, S. (in press). Early childhood education: Young adult outcomes as a function of differing treatment. *Applied Developmental Science.*

Chase-Lansdale, P. L., & Gordon, R. A. (1996). Economic hardship and the development of five- and six-year-olds: Neighborhood and regional perspectives. *Child Development, 67,* 3338–3367.

Chase-Lansdale, P. L., Gordon, R. A., Brooks-Gunn, J., & Klebanov, P. K. (1997). Neighborhood and family influences on the intellectual and behavioral competence of preschool and early school-age children. In J. Brooks-Gunn, G. J. Duncan, & J. L. Aber (Eds.), *Neighborhood poverty: Context and consequences for children* (Vol. 1, pp. 79–118). New York: Russell Sage Foundation.

Collins, J. W., Jr., & David, R. J. (1990). The differential effect of traditional risk factors on infant birthweight among blacks and whites in Chicago. *American Journal of Public Health, 80,* 679–681.

Conger, R. D., Conger, K. J., & Elder, G. H. (1997). Family economic hardship and adolescent adjustment: Mediating and moderating processes. In G. J. Duncan & J. Brooks-Gunn (Eds.), *Consequences of growing up poor* (pp. 288–310). New York: Russell Sage Foundation.

Conger, R. D., & Elder, G. H. (1994). *Families in troubled times: Adapting to change in rural America.* New York: Aldine de Gruyter.

Corcoran, M. E., & Chaudry, A. (1997). The dynamics of children in poverty. *The Future of Children, 7,* 40–54.

Corman, H., & Grossman, M. (1985). Determinants of neonatal mortality rates in the U.S.: A reduced form model. *Journal of Health Economics, 4,* 213–236.

Currie, J. (2001). *A fresh start for Head Start?* Children's Roundtable Report #5. Washington, DC: Brookings Institution.

Dalaker, J. (2001). Poverty in the United States: 2000. *U.S. Census Bureau, Current Population Reports, Series P60–214.* Washington, DC: U.S. Government Printing Office.

Darling-Hammond, L. (2000). Teacher quality and student achievement: A review of state policy evidence. *Education Policy Analysis Archives, 8.* Available: http://olam.ed.asu.edu/epaa/v8n1/.

Duncan, G. J., Brooks-Gunn, J., & Klebanov, P. K. (1994). Economic deprivation and early childhood development. *Child Development, 65,* 296–318.

Duncan, G. J., & Rodgers, W. L. (1998). Longitudinal aspects of childhood poverty. *Journal of Marriage and the Family, 50,* 1007–1021.

Duncan, G. J., Yeung, W. J., Brooks-Gunn, J., & Smith, J. R. (1998). How much does childhood poverty affect the life chances of children? *American Sociological Review, 63,* 406–423.

Elder, G. H., & Caspi, A. (1988). Economic stress in lives: Developmental perspectives. *Journal of Social Issues, 44,* 25–45.

Elder, G., Van Nguyen, T., & Caspi, A. (1985). Linking family hardship to children's lives. *Child Development, 56,* 361–375.

Erickson, M. F., Korfmacher, J., & Egeland, B. (1992). Attachments past and present: Implications for therapeutic intervention with mother-infant dyads. *Development and Psychopathology, 4,* 495–507.

Farran, D. C. (2000). Another decade of intervention for children who are low income or disabled: What do we know now? In J. P. Shonkoff & S. J. Meisels (Eds.), *Handbook of early childhood intervention* (2nd ed.). New York: Cambridge University Press.

Farrington, D. P. (1987). Early precursors of frequent offending. In J. Q. Wilson & G. C. Loury (Eds.), *From children to citizens: Families, schools, and delinquency prevention* (pp. 27–50). New York: Springer-Verlag.

Federal Interagency Forum on Child and Family Statistics. (1999). *America's children: Key national indicators of well-being.* Washington, DC: Author.

Federman, M., Garner, T. I., Short, K., Cutter IV, W. B., Kiley, J., Levine, D., McDough, D., & McMillen, M. (1996). What does it mean to be poor in America? *Monthly Labor Review Online, 119,* 1–15.

Field, T., Widmayer, S., Greenberg, R., & Stoller, S. (1982). Effects of parent training on teenage mothers and their infants. *Pediatrics, 69,* 245–269.

Field, T. M., Widmayer, S. M., Stringer, S., & Ignatoff, E. (1980). Teenage, lower-class, black mothers and their preterm infants: An intervention and developmental follow-up. *Child Development, 51,* 426–436.

Finn, J. (1998). *Class size and students at risk: What is known? What is next?* Washington, DC: US Department of Education, Office of Educational Research and Improvement, National Institute on the Education of At-Risk Students.

Finn, J., & Achilles, C. (1990). Answers and questions about class size: A statewide experiment. *American Educational Research Journal, 27,* 557–577.

Fuligni, A. S., & Brooks-Gunn, J. (2000). The healthy development of young children: SES disparities, prevention strategies, and policy opportunities. In B. D. Smedley & S. L. Syme (Eds.), *Promoting health: Intervention strategies from social and behavioral research* (pp. 170–216). Washington, DC: National Academy of Sciences.

Garcia Coll, C., Surrey, J., & Weingarten, K. (1996). *Mothering against the odds: Diverse voices of contemporary mothers.* Wellesley, MA: Jean Baker Miller Training Institute.

Glass, G., Cahen, L., Smith, M., & Filby, N. (1982). *School class size.* Beverly Hills, CA: Sage.

Gould, J. B., & LeRoy, S. (1988). Socioeconomic status and low birth weight: A racial comparison. *Pediatrics, 82,* 896–904.

Gray, S. W., & Klaus, R. A. (1970). The early training project: A seventh year report. *Child Development, 41,* 909–924.

Gray, S. W., & Ramsey, B. K. (1982). The early training project: A life-span view. *Human Development, 25,* 48–57.

Gray, S. W., & Ruttle, K. (1980). The Family-Oriented Home Visiting Program: A longitudinal study. *Genetic Psychology Monographs, 102,* 299–316.

Greenwald, R., Hedges, L. V., & Laine, R. D. (1996). The effect of school resources on student achievement. *Review of Educational Research, 66,* 361–396.

Hahn, A., Leavitt, T., & Aaron, P. (1994). *Evaluation of the Quantum Opportunities Program (QOP): Did the program work?* Waltham, MA: Center for Human Resources, Brandeis University.

Hanushek, E. A. (1986). The economics of schooling: Production and efficiency in public schools. *Journal of Economic Literature, 24,* 1141–1177.

Haveman, R., & Wolfe, B. (1995). The determinants of children's attainments: A review of methods and findings. *Journal of Economic Literature, 33,* 1829–1878.

Heberle, J. (1992). PACE: Parent and child education in Kentucky. In T. G. Sticht, M. J. Beeler, & B. A. McDonald (Eds.), *The intergenerational transfer of cognitive skills: Vol. I. Programs, policy, and research issues* (pp. 136–148). Norwood, NJ: Ablex.

Hedges, L. V., Laine, R. D., & Greenwald, R. (1994). Does money matter? A meta-analysis of studies of the effects of differential school inputs on student outcomes. *Educational Researcher, 23,* 5–14.

Henke, R. R., Choy, S. P., Chen, X., Geis, S., & Alt, M. N. (1997). *America's teachers: Profile of a profession, 1993–94* (NCES 97–460). Washington, DC: National Center for Education Statistics.

Hernandez, D. J. (1997). Poverty trends. In G. J. Duncan & J. Brooks-Gunn (Eds.), *Consequences of growing up poor* (pp. 18–34). New York: Russell Sage Foundation.

Hill, J. L., Waldfogel, J., & Brooks-Gunn, J. (2002). Assessing differential impacts: The effect of high-quality child care on children's cognitive development. *Journal of Policy Analysis & Management, 21,* 601–627.

Honig, A. S., & Lally, R. (1982). The family development research program: Retrospective review. *Early Childhood Development and Care, 10,* 41–62.

Infant Health and Development Program. (1990). Enhancing the outcomes of low-birth-weight, premature infants: A multisite, randomized trial. *Journal of the American Medical Association, 263,* 3035–3042.

Johnson, D. L., & Breckenridge, J. N. (1982). The Houston parent-child development center and the primary prevention of behavior problems in young children. *American Journal of Community Psychology, 10,* 305–316.

Johnson, D. L., & Walker, T. (1991). A follow-up evaluation of the Houston parent-child development center: School performance. *Journal of Early Intervention, 15,* 226–236.

Juarez, S. C., Viega, B., & Richards, M. H. (1997, April). *The moderating effect of family environment on exposure to violence and PTSD symptoms.* Paper presented at the biennial conference of the Society for Research on Child Development, Washington, DC.

Karoly, L. A., Greenwood, P. W., Everingham, S. S., Hoube, J., Kilburn, M. R., Rydell, C. P., Sanders, M., & Chiesa, J. (1998). *Investing in our children: What we know and don't know about the costs and benefits of early childhood interventions.* Santa Monica, CA: RAND.

Kisker, E., Rangarajan, A., & Boller, K. (1998). *Moving into adulthood: Were the impacts of mandatory programs for welfare-dependent teenage parents sustained after the programs ended?* Princeton, NJ: Mathematica Policy Research.

Kitzman, H., Olds, D. L., Henderson, C. R., Hanks, C., Cole, R., Tatelbaum, R., McConnochie, K. M., Sidora, K., Luckey, D. W., Shaver, D., Engelhardt, K., James, D., & Barnard, K. (1997). Effect of prenatal and infancy home visitation by nurses on pregnancy outcomes, childhood, childhood injuries, and repeated childbearing: A randomized controlled trial. *Journal of the American Medical Association, 278,* 644–652.

Klebanov, P. K., Brooks-Gunn, J., McCarton, C., & McCormick, M. C. (1998). The contribution of neighborhood and family income to developmental test scores over the first three years of life. *Child Development, 69,* 1420–1436.

Klebanov, P. K., Brooks-Gunn, J., & McCormick, M. C. (1994). Classroom behavior of very low birth weight elementary school children. *Pediatrics, 94,* 700–708.

Klebanov, P. K., Brooks-Gunn, J., & McCormick, M. C. (2001). Maternal coping strategies and emotional distress: Results of an early intervention program for low birth weight young children. *Developmental Psychology, 37* (5), 654–667.

Kleinman, J. C., & Kessel, S. S. (1987). Racial differences in low birth weight: Trends and risk factors. *New England Journal of Medicine, 317,* 749–753.

Klerman, L. (1991). *Alive and well?* New York: National Center for Children in Poverty, Columbia University.

Korenman, S., & Miller, J. E. (1997). Long-term poverty and child health in the United States: Analysis of the NLSY. In G. J. Duncan & J. Brooks-Gunn (Eds.), *Consequences of growing up poor* (pp. 70–99). New York: Russell Sage Foundation.

Korenman, S., Miller, J. E., & Sjaastad, J. E. (1995). Long-term poverty and child development in the United States: Results from the NLSY. *Children and Youth Services Review, 17,* 127–155.

Lally, J. R., Mangione, P. L., & Honig, A. S. (1988). The Syracuse University Family Development Research Program: Long-range impact of an early intervention with low-income children and their families. In D. R. Powell (Ed.), *Parent education in early intervention: Emerging directions in theory, research, and practice.* Norwood, NJ: Ablex.

Larson, C. P. (1980). Efficacy of prenatal and postpartum home visits on child health and development. *Pediatrics, 66,* 191–197.

Leventhal, T., & Brooks-Gunn, J. (2000). The neighborhoods they live in: Effects of neighborhood residence upon child and adolescent outcomes. *Psychological Bulletin, 126,* 309–337.

Lewit, E. M., & Kerrebrock, N. (1997). Population based growth stunting. *Future Child, 7,* 149–156.

Liaw, F., & Brooks-Gunn, J. (1994). Cumulative familial risks and low birth weight children's cognitive and behavioral development. *Journal of Clinical Child Psychology, 23,* 360–372.

Lieberman, A. F., Weston, D. R., & Pawl, J. H. (1991). Preventive intervention and outcome with anxiously attached dyads. *Child Development, 62,* 199–209.

LoSciuto, L., Hilbert, S. M., Fox, M. M., Porcellini, L., & Lanphear, A. (1999). A two-year evaluation of the Woodrock Youth Development Project. *Journal of Early Adolescence, 19,* 488–507.

Madden, J., O'Hara, J., & Levenstein, P. (1984). Home again: Effects of the mother-child home program on mother and child. *Child Development, 55,* 636–647.

Mayer, S. E. (1997). *What money can't buy: Family income and children's life chances.* Cambridge, MA: Harvard University Press.

McCarton, C., Brooks-Gunn, J., Wallace, I., Bauer, C., Bennett, F., Bernbaum, J., Broyles, R., Casey, P., McCormick, M., Scott, D., Tyson, J., Tonascia, J., & Meinert, C. (1997). Results at age 8 years of early intervention for low birthweight premature infants: The Infant Health and Development Program. *Journal of the American Medical Association, 277,* 126–132.

McGauhey, P. S., & Starfield, B. (1993). Child health and the social environment of white and black children. *Social Science and Medicine, 36,* 867–874.

McLeod, J. D., & Shanahan, M. J. (1993). Poverty, parenting and children's mental health. *American Sociological Review, 58,* 351–366.

McLeod, J. D., & Shanahan, M. J. (1996). Trajectories of poverty and children's mental health. *Journal of Health and Social Behavior, 37,* 207–220.

McLoyd, V. C. (1989). Socialization and development in a changing economy: The effects of paternal job and income loss on children. *American Psychologist, 44,* 293–302.

McLoyd, V. C. (1990). The impact of economic hardship on black families and children: Psychological distress, parenting, and socioemotional development. *Child Development, 61,* 311–346.

McLoyd, V. C., Jayaratne, T. E., Ceballo, R., & Borquez, J. (1994). Unemployment and work interruption among African American single mothers: Effects on parenting and adolescent socioemotional functioning. *Child Development, 65,* 562–589.

Miller, J. E., & Korenman, S. (1994). Poverty and children's nutritional status in the United States. *American Journal of Epidemiology, 140,* 233–243.

Mills, R. J. (2000). Health insurance coverage: 1999. *Current Population Reports* (P60-211). Washington, DC: U.S. Census Bureau.

Moffitt, T. E. (1990). Juvenile delinquency and attention deficit disorder: Boys' developmental trajectories from age 3 to age 15. *Child Development, 61,* 893–910.

Moffitt, T. E. (1993). The neuropsychology of conduct disorder. *Development and Psychopathology, 5,* 135–152.

Moffitt, T. E., & Silva, P. A. (1988). Self-reported delinquency, neuropsychological deficit, and history of attention deficit disorder. *Journal of Abnormal Psychology, 16,* 553–569.

Mosteller, F. (1995). The Tennessee study of class size in the early grades. *The Future of Children, 5,* 113–127.

National Center for Health Statistics. (2000). *Health, United States.* Hyattsville, MD: Author.

Newacheck, P. W., Hughes, D. C., & Stoddard, J. J. (1996). Children's access to primary care: Differences by race, income, and insurance status. *Pediatrics, 7*, 26–32.

O'Campo, P., Xue, X., Wang, M. C., & Caughy, M. (1997). Neighborhood risk factors for low birthweight in Baltimore City: A multi-level analysis. *American Journal of Public Health, 87*, 1113–1118.

Olds, D. L. (1996, November). *Reducing risks for childhood-onset conduct disorder with prenatal and early childhood home visitation.* Paper presented at the American Public Health Association Pre-Conference Workshop: Prevention Science and Families: Mental Health Research and Public Health Policy Implications, New York.

Olds, D. L., Eckenrode, J., Henderson, C. R., Jr., Kitzman, H., Powers, J., Cole, R., Sidora, K., Morris, P., Pettitt, L., & Luckey, D. (1997). Long-term effects of home visitation on maternal life course and child abuse and neglect: 15-year follow-up of a randomized trial. *Journal of the American Medical Association, 278*, 637–643.

Olds, D. L., Henderson, C. R., Chamberlin, R., & Tatelbaum, R. (1986). Preventing child abuse and neglect: A randomized trial of nurse home visitation. *Pediatrics, 78*, 65–78.

Olds, D. L., Henderson, C. R., Chamberlin, R., & Tatelbaum, R. (1988). Improving the life-course development of socially disadvantaged mothers: A randomized trial of nurse home visitation. *American Journal of Public Health, 78*, 1436–1445.

Olds, D. L., Henderson, C. R., & Kitzman, H. J. (1994). Does prenatal and infancy nurse home visitation have enduring effects on qualities of parental caregiving and child health at 25–50 months of life? *Pediatrics, 93*, 89–98.

Olds, D. L., Henderson, C. R., Kitzman, H. J., & Cole, R. (1995). Effects of prenatal and infancy nurse home visitation on surveillance of child maltreatment. *Pediatrics, 95*, 365–372.

Olds, D. L., Henderson, C. R., Kitzman, H. J., Eckenrode, J. J., Cole, R. E., & Tatelbaum, R. C. (1999). Prenatal and infancy home visitation by nurses: Recent findings. *Future of Children, 9*, 44–65.

Olds, D. L., Henderson, C. R., Tatelbaum, R., & Chamberlin, R. (1986). Improving the delivery of prenatal care and outcomes of pregnancy: A randomized trial of nurse home visitation. *Pediatrics, 77*, 16–28.

Olds, D. L., & Kitzman, H. (1993). Review of research on home visiting for pregnant women and parents of young children. *The Future of Children, 3*, 53–92.

Osofsky, J. D., Culp, A. M., & Ware, L. M. (1988). Intervention challenges with adolescent mothers and their infants. *Psychiatry, 51*, 236–241.

Pagani, L., Boulerice, B., Tremblay, R. E., & Vitaro, F. (1997). Behavioral development in children of divorce and remarriage. *Journal of Child Psychology and Psychiatry, 38*, 769–781.

Patterson, G. R., & Narrett, C. M. (1990). The development of a reliable and valid treatment program for aggressive young children. Special Issue. Unvalidated, fringe, and fraudulent treatment of mental disorders. *International Journal of Mental Health,19*, 19–26.

Philliber, W. W., Spillman, R. E., & King, R. (1996). Consequences of family literacy for adults and children: Some preliminary findings. *Journal of Adolescent and Adult Literacy, 39*, 558–565.

Physician Task Force on Hunger in America. (1985). *Hunger in America: The growing epidemic.* Middletown, CT: Wesleyan University Press.

Pierce, E. W., Ewing, L. J., & Campbell, S. B. (1999). Diagnostic status and symptomatic behavior of hard-to-manage preschool children in middle childhood and early adolescence. *Journal of Clinical Child Psychology, 28*, 44–57.

President's Committee of Advisors on Science and Technology, Panel on Educational Technology. (1997). *Report to the President on the use of technology to strengthen K–12 education in the United States.* Washington, DC: The White House.

Ramey, C. T., Bryant, D. M., Sparling, J. J., & Wasik, B. H. (1985). Educational interventions to enhance intellectual development: Comprehensive day care versus family education. In S. Harel & N. Anastasiow (Eds.), *The "at-risk" infant: Psychological, social, and medical aspects* (pp. 75–85). Baltimore, MD: Paul H. Brookes.

Ramey, C. T., & Campbell, F. A. (1991). Poverty, early childhood education, and academic competence: The Abecedarian experiment. In A. Huston (Ed.), *Children reared in poverty* (pp. 190–221). New York: Cambridge University Press.

Reichman, N. E., & McLanahan, S. S. (2001). *Self-sufficiency programs and parenting interventions: Lessons from New Chance and the Teenage Parent Demonstration.* SRCD Social Policy Report, Vol 15.

Reid, J. B., Patterson, G. P., & Snyder, J. J. (2002). *Antisocial behavior in children and adolescents: A developmental analysis and the Oregon model for intervention.* Washington, DC: APA Books.

Reynolds, A. J. (1994). Effects of a preschool plus follow-up intervention for children at risk. *Developmental Psychology, 30,* 787–804.

Reynolds, A. J. (1997, April). *Long-term effects of the Chicago Child-Parent Center Program through age 15.* Paper presented at the biennial meeting of the Society for Research on Child Development, Washington, DC.

Reynolds, A. J., & Temple, J. A. (1995). Quasi-experimental estimates of the effects of a preschool intervention. *Evaluation Review, 19,* 347–373.

Reynolds, A. J., Temple, J. A., Robertson, D. L., & Mann, E. A. (2001). Long-term effects of an early childhood intervention on educational achievement and juvenile arrest: A 15-year follow-up of low-income children in public schools. *Journal of the American Medical Association, 285,* 2339–2346.

Richardson, D. C., & Brown, M. (1997). *Family Intergenerational Literacy Model. Fact sheet and impact statements.* Oklahoma City, OK: National Diffusion Network.

Robinson, G., & Wittebols, J. H. (1986). *Class size research: A related cluster analysis for decision making.* Arlington, VA: Educational Research Service.

Ross, G. S. (1984). Home intervention for premature infants of low-income families. *American Journal of Orthopsychiatry, 54,* 263–270.

Roth, J. L., & Brooks-Gunn, J. (2002). What is a youth development program? Identifying defining principles. In R. M. Lerner, F. Jacobs, & D. Wertlieb (Eds.), *Promoting positive child, adolescent, and family development: A handbook of program and policy innovations (Vol. 2: Enhancing the life chances of youth and families: Contributions of programs, policies and service systems)* (pp. 197–223). Thousand Oaks, CA: Sage.

Roth, J. L., Brooks-Gunn, J., Murray, L., & Foster, W. (1998). Promoting healthy adolescents: Synthesis of youth development program evaluations. *Journal of Research on Adolescence, 8,* 423–459.

Royce, J. M., Darlington, R. B., & Murray, H. W. (1983). Pooled analyses: Findings across studies. In *As the twig is bent...Lasting effects of preschool programs.* Hillsdale, NJ: Erlbaum.

Sameroff, A. J., Seifer, R., Baldwin, A., & Baldwin, C. (1993). Stability of intelligence from preschool to adolescence: The influence of social and family risk factors. *Child Development, 64,* 80–97.

Sameroff, A. J., Seifer, R., Barocas, R., Zax, M., & Greenspan, S. (1987). Intelligence quotient scores of 4-year old children: Social and environmental risk factors. *Pediatrics, 79,* 343–350.

Sameroff, A. J., Seifer, R., Zax, M., & Barocas, R. (1987). Early indicators of developmental risk: The Rochester Longitudinal Study. *Schizophrenia Bulletin, 13,* 383–393.

Schweinhart, L. J., Barnes, H. V., Weikart, D. P., Barnett, W. S., & Epstein, A. S. (1993). *Significant benefits: The High/Scope Perry Preschool Study through age 27.* Ypsilanti, MI: High/Scope Press.

Schweinhart, L. J., & Weikart, D. P. (1980). Young children grow up: The effects of the Perry Preschool Program on youths through age 15. *Monographs of the High/Scope Educational Research Foundation, No. 7.* Ypsilanti, MI: High/Scope Educational Research Foundation.

Seitz, V., & Apfel, N. H. (1994). Parent-focused intervention: Diffusion effects on siblings. *Child Development, 65,* 677–683.

Shaffer, D., Gould, M. S., Fisher, P., Trautment, P., Moreau, D., Kleinman, M., & Flory, M. (1996). Psychiatric diagnosis in child and adolescent suicide. *Archives of General Psychiatry, 53,* 339–348.

Shaw, D. S., Vondra, J. I., Dowdell-Hommerding, K., Keenan, K., & Dunn, M. (1994). Chronic family adversity and early child behavior problems: A longitudinal study of low-income families. *Journal of Child Psychology and Psychiatry, 35,* 1109–1122.

Smith, J. R., Bastiani, A., & Brooks-Gunn, J. (1998). Poverty and mental health. In H. Friedman (Ed.), *Encyclopedia of mental health, Vol. 3* (pp. 219–228). San Diego, CA: Academic Press.

Smith, J. R., Brooks-Gunn, J., & Klebanov, P. K. (1997). The consequences of living in poverty for young children's cognitive and verbal ability and early school achievement. In G. J. Duncan & J. Brooks-Gunn (Eds.), *Consequences of growing up poor* (pp. 132–189). New York: Russell Sage Foundation.

Smith, J. R., Brooks-Gunn, J., Kohen, D., & McCarton, C. (2001). Transitions on and off AFDC: Implications for parenting and children's cognitive development. *Child Development, 72*(5), 1512–1533.

Spencer, T., Biederman, J., & Wilens, T. (1999). Attention-deficit/hyperactivity disorder and comorbidity. *Pediatric Clinics of North America, 46,* 915–927.

Starfield, B. (1992). Effects of poverty on health status. *Bulletin of the New York Academy of Medicine, 68,* 17–24.

Starfield, B., Shapiro, S., Weiss, J., Liang, K., Ra, K., Paige, D., & Wang, X. (1991). Race, family income, and low birth weight. *American Journal of Epidemiology, 134,* 1167–1174.

St. Pierre, R. G., Ricciuti, A., & Creps, C. (1998). *Synthesis of state and local Even Start evaluations: Draft.* Cambridge, MA: Abt Associates.

St. Pierre, R. G., & Swartz, J. P. (1995). The Even Start Family Literacy Program. In S. Smith (Ed.), *Advances in applied developmental psychology: Vol. 9. Two generation programs for families in poverty: A new intervention strategy* (pp. 37–66). Norwood, NJ: Ablex.

St. Pierre, R. G., Swartz, J. P., Gamse, B., Murray, S., Deck, D., & Nickel, P. (1995). *National evaluation of the Even Start Family Literacy Program: Final report.* Washington, DC: U.S. Department of Education.

Tao, F., Gamse, B., & Tarr, H. (1998). *National evaluation of the Even Start Family Literacy Program: 1994–1997 final report.* Washington, DC: U.S. Department of Education, Planning and Evaluation Service.

Tao, F., Swartz, J., St. Pierre, R., & Tarr, H. (1997). *National evaluations of the Even Start Family Literacy Program.* Washington, DC: U.S. Department of Education.

Tierney, J. P., Grossman, J. B., & Resch, W. N. L. (1995). *Making a difference: An impact study of Big Brothers/Big Sisters.* Philadelphia: Public/Private Ventures.

U.S. Department of Education. (1998). *Reducing class size: What do we know?* Washington, DC: Author.

U.S. Department of Education. (1999). *The initial report of the secretary on the quality of teacher preparation.* Washington, DC: Author.

U.S. Department of Education. (2000a). *Monitoring school quality: An indicators report* (NCES 2001-030). Washington, DC: National Center for Education Statistics.

U.S. Department of Education. (2000b). *Internet access in public schools and classrooms: 1994–99* (NCES 2000-086). Washington, DC: National Center for Education Statistics.

Velez, C. N., Johnson, J., & Cohen, P. (1989). A longitudinal analysis of selected risk factors for childhood psychopathology. *Journal of the American Academy of Child and Adolescent Psychiatry, 28,* 861–864.

Wagner, M. M., & Clayton, S. L. (1999). The parents as teachers: Results from two demonstrations. *Future of Children, 9,* 91–115.

Wall, J. E., & Holden, E. W. (1994). Aggressive, assertive, and submissive behaviors in disadvantaged, inner-city preschool children. *Journal of Clinical and Child Psychology, 23,* 382–390.

Wilson, W. J. (1987). *The truly disadvantaged: The inner city, the underclass, and public policy.* Chicago: University of Chicago Press.

Wood, D. L., Hayward, R. A., Corey, C. R., Freeman, H. E., & Shapiro, M. F. (1990). Access to medical care for children and adolescents in the United States. *Pediatrics, 86,* 666–673.

Yoshikawa, H. (1995). Long-term effects of early childhood programs on social outcomes and delinquency. *The Future of Children, 5,* 51–75.

Zaslow, M., & Eldred, C. (Eds.). (1998). *Parenting behavior in a sample of young mothers in poverty: Results of the New Chance Observational Study.* New York: Manpower Demonstration Research.

CHAPTER 7

PREVENTION AND TREATMENT STRATEGIES TARGETING PHYSICAL CHILD ABUSE AND NEGLECT

NEIL B. GUTERMAN
Columbia University

RICHARD A. EMBRY
Columbia University

An anonymous caller to the child abuse hotline reported that a neighbor, Ms. T., was seen hitting her 11-year-old daughter, Shandra, with "excessive force." A child protective services worker assigned to the case visited the home and reported that there were five adults and three children living in a two-bedroom apartment. Ms. T is the mother of two of the three children, Shandra and 14-month-old Kevin; the other adults and child were described by Ms. T as relatives. During her visit to the home, the worker observed that there was little furniture and there were no beds in the apartment, and speculated that drugs were likely sold in the apartment. One of the adults in the home reported to her that there was occasionally no food in the home for the children, and that sometimes the children spent the night at their maternal aunt's home. The worker also observed that the skin on Kevin's arms, legs, and upper torso was red and peeling, and required immediate medical attention. Kevin was admitted to the local hospital and found to have advanced skin infections. He was kept in the hospital for treatment and observation, although no evidence of bruises or other external signs of injury were observed on Kevin or the other children. Although the protective services worker noted the presence of risk in her report, the report of child abuse was unsubstantiated at the time.

Although some controversy continues to surround our understanding of what precisely constitutes physical child abuse and neglect,* practitioners and scholars most often adopt as a working definition those acts of commission or omission by parents or responsible caregivers that result in or pose substantial risk of injury or harm to a child (c.f. Dubowitz & Guterman, in press; DePanfilis & Salus, 1992). Organized efforts to address the problem of physical child abuse and neglect have been identifiable for more than a century in the United States; however, it was not until the latter half of the twentieth century that professionalized clinical intervention was initiated seeking to address the problem. The "discovery" of the "battered child syndrome" in the 1950s and early 1960s has long been credited with the initiation of a national movement that spurred the development of federal and state policies, programs, and clinical interventions aimed at preventing and treating the problem of child maltreatment in the United States (c.f. Lindsey, 1994). During this time, the nation's child protective services system was established and institutionalized, and several major policy initiatives established a legal and programmatic framework within which the problem of child maltreatment is presently addressed. In the face of these broad developments, the problem of physical child abuse and neglect has remained a remarkably persistent one in the United States. Indeed, from the 1960s onward, reported incidents of child maltreatment continued to climb sharply upward, until just the last several years when reports of child maltreatment have appeared to level off (see Figure 7.1). Although part of this rapid increase is likely due to increased public awareness and motivation to identify the problem to authorities, it is also likely that these numbers reflect an actual increase in the problem of physical child abuse and neglect in America over the last several decades (c.f. Guterman, 2000).

THE INCIDENCE OF PHYSICAL CHILD ABUSE AND NEGLECT

Although a variety of child maltreatment forms are reported to the nation's child protective services system, cases of physical child abuse and neglect constitute approximately 80 percent of all reports made in the United States. Child neglect is the most commonly reported form of child maltreatment, typically representing well over half of the reported cases of child maltreatment annually; physical abuse typically represents approximately one-quarter of all annual reports (e.g., U.S. Department of Health and Human Services, 2001). Of these forms of child maltreatment, most data sources indicate that the younger the child, the higher the risk of victimization, particularly in its most severe forms (see Figure 7.2). For example, data reported to the federal government in 1999 indicate that almost nine out of ten child maltreatment fatalities occurred in children 5 years old or younger, and that 43 percent of all child maltreatment related fatalities occurred during the first year of life (U.S. Department of Health and Human Services, 2001).

---

*This chapter does not attend to the important problems of child sexual abuse or emotional abuse/neglect; rather, it maintains a specific focus on the interrelated problems of physical abuse and neglect, involved in approximately 80 percent of child maltreatment cases reported to child protective services systems in the United States (U.S. Department of Health and Human Services, 2001).

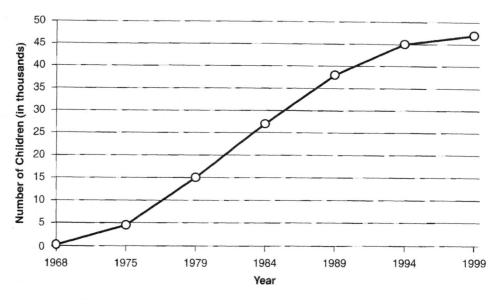

FIGURE 7.1   Estimated Number of Children Reported for Child Maltreatment in the United States from 1968 to 1999

Source: Based on available data in McCurdy and Daro (1993) and Peddle and Wang (2001).

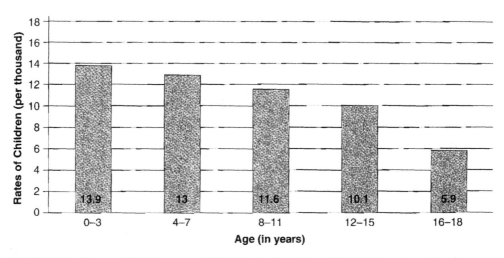

FIGURE 7.2   Rates of Children per 1,000 Substantiated for Child Maltreatment by Age, in the U.S., 1999

Source: Adapted from United States Department of Health and Human Services (2001).

A look at the demographic patterns associated with child maltreatment indicate that impoverished families and families of color are significantly overrepresented in studies of official child maltreatment reports (e.g., Jason et al., 1982; Lauderdale et al., 1980; Spearly & Lauderdale, 1983). However, it must be noted that such findings hold a number of biases related to professional reporting patterns and the increased exposure to public authorities faced particularly by impoverished families. Population-based studies that do not rely on protective services data have been able to overcome many of these biases. Findings from such studies still consistently indicate greater abuse and neglect rates among impoverished families (especially among the "poorest of the poor"), but they also show a conflicting picture with regard to the relationship between ethnicity and maltreatment risk. These studies have persistently struggled to tease apart the complex interplay between socioeconomic pressures, minority group status, and the array of interrelated psychosocial risks that may accompany minority group status and that, themselves, may serve to heighten maltreatment potential (e.g., National Research Council, 1993; Cazenave & Straus, 1979; Connelly & Straus, 1992; Chaffin, Kelleher, & Hollenberg, 1996). Further advances remain to be forged in clarifying the definition, labeling, and incidence of physical child abuse and neglect in order to capture a clearer picture of how maltreatment risk may manifest differentially across groups (c.f. Korbin, 1994).

DEVELOPMENTAL SEQUELAE ASSOCIATED WITH PHYSICAL ABUSE AND NEGLECT

For children surviving physical abuse and neglect, the effects of such experiences vary according to the nature of the maltreatment experiences, the child's age, the available supports and resources, and other ongoing life stressors. Studies have nonetheless discerned an array of medical, cognitive, and psychosocial sequelae associated with experiences of physical child abuse and neglect. These have included both immediate and longer-term outcomes:

- Physical injuries such as subdural hemorrhages, retinal hemorrhages, burns, or bone fractures (Lancon et al., 1998; Bonnier et al., 1995)
- Neurological damage (Perry et al., 1995, 1997; Lewis, 1992; Dykes, 1986; Bonnier et al., 1995)
- Delayed physical growth (Drotar, 1992; Money, 1977)
- Problems with social relationships, developing trust, and forming attachments (Cohn, 1979; Kinard, 1979; Carlson et al., 1989; Egeland & Sroufe, 1981; Dodge et al., 1994; Main & Solomon, 1986; Kaufman & Cicchetti, 1989)
- Problems with self-regulation of emotions (Shields et al., 1994; Cicchetti et al., 1993)
- Heightened aggression, externalizing behavior problems, and later criminal activities (Dykman et al., 1997; Maxfield & Widom, 1996; Polansky et al., 1981; Aber, 1990; Salzinger et al., 1984; Hoffman-Plotkin & Twentyman, 1984; Main & George, 1984; Herrenkohl & Herrenkohl, 1981; Cummings et al., 1994)

- Heightened depression, low self-esteem, and increased risk for suicidal ideation and behavior (Silverman et al., 1996; Gaensbauer & Mrazek, 1981; Allen & Tarnowski, 1989; Oates et al., 1985; Kazdin et al., 1985)
- Symptoms of post-traumatic stress disorder (Dykman et al., 1997)
- Increased risk for substance and/or alcohol abuse in later life (Widom & White, 1997; Malinosky-Rummell & Hansen, 1993)
- Cognitive and language deficits (Hoffman-Plotkin & Twentyman, 1984; Perry et al., 1983; Azar et al., 1988; Fantuzzo, 1990; Kolko, 1992; Allen & Oliver, 1982; Allen & Wasserman, 1985; Cicchetti & Beeghly, 1987)

It is an unfortunate fact that the younger the victim, the more devastating the consequences are likely to be. In addition to facing heightened risk for fatality, very young children are at inordinate risk for such profound problems resulting from maltreatment as nonorganic failure to thrive, shaken baby syndrome, mental retardation, impaired growth and dwarfism, brain injuries, blindness, or injuries to other parts of the body (National Research Council, 1993; Mrazek, 1993; Frank et al., 1985). Recent advances in neurological assessment technology have soberingly documented a variety of neurological sequelae stemming from early childhood maltreatment and holding particularly disturbing implications for later life, including brain contusions, intracranial hemorrhages, brain atrophy, and alterations in the development of the limbic system of the brain linked with memory, emotions, and basic drives (Teicher et al., 1996; Ito et al., 1993; Frank et al., 1985; Cheah et al., 1994). Although evidence is not yet conclusive given the multiple ongoing influences throughout childhood, physical abuse and neglect experienced early in childhood appears to heighten risk later in life for some of the most intractable social and mental health problems facing the American public, including adult crime and juvenile delinquency, depression, school failure, and alcohol and substance abuse (National Research Council, 1993).

ETIOLOGY OF PHYSICAL CHILD ABUSE AND NEGLECT

Evidence from several decades of research has identified a wide array of factors that appear to contribute to the likelihood that a child will be physically abused and/or neglected. These factors have commonly been organized according to a multileveled rubric, often using what has been termed an *ecological* or *ecological developmental* framework (e.g., Garbarino, 1977; Belsky, 1980; Cicchetti & Lynch, 1993). This framework highlights that physically abusive and/or neglectful behavior derives from the complex set of transactions within and between:

- The *micro-system* representing the parent and child and their interactions
- The *meso-* and *exo-systems* in which the parent-child dyad are embedded, including the settings, networks of relationships, and institutions in which the parent and child socialize and are sustained
- The *macro-system* comprised of overarching social structural elements within which the meso- and exo-systems are themselves lodged (Bronfenbrenner, 1977; Garbarino, 1980, 1977; Belsky, 1980)

Although it is beyond the scope of this chapter to comprehensively present the known etiological findings related to physical child abuse and neglect,* we will highlight some of the clearest themes in the existing etiological research. In the parent-child *microsystem,* the primary attachments that parents have formed with their own parent figures during childhood appears as a key etiological factor, particularly in the degree to which parents themselves experienced abuse or neglect (e.g., Egeland et al. 1988; George, 1996; Widom, 1989; Zuravin et al., 1996). Although little evidence supports the popular assumption that the presence of parental mental illness, in a general sense, is associated with maltreatment risk, several specific problematic aspects of socioemotional functioning have been linked with maltreating parenting. Parents at risk of physical abuse and neglect often exhibit depression and low self-esteem (e.g., Ethier et al., 1995; Kotch et al., 1995; Chaffin et al., 1996; Nair et al., 1997; Christensen et al., 1994; Culp et al., 1989). Problems in the abuse of alcohol or other psychoactive substances have also been specifically linked with maltreatment risk (Chaffin et al., 1996; U.S. Department of Health and Human Services, 1999), especially during the early childhood years with approximately half of all substantiated cases of child maltreatment involving substance or alcohol abuse affecting children 4 years of age or younger (National Center on Child Abuse and Neglect, 1993). As well, maltreating parents have often been observed to hold specific deficits in social coping skills, including a hyperresponsivity to child-related stimuli and deficits in reading and responding to social cues (e.g., Pruitt & Erickson, 1985; Milner & Crouch, 1998). Further, maltreating parents often report feeling "out of control" in their lives and frequently hold an external locus of control orientation (Ellis & Milner, 1981; Gynn-Orenstein, 1981; Nurius Lovell & Maggie, 1988; Stringer & LaGreca, 1985; Wiehe, 1986).

Work by Bugental and colleagues (1999) and Patterson and colleagues (Patterson, 1982; Reid & Patterson, 1989) has demonstrated that abusive or neglectful parent-child interactions can, in part, be understood as resulting from a cyclical pattern of parent-child interactions. This cyclical pattern can be seen, for example, when a child's behavior is perceived as difficult or stressful by a parent and responded to in an coercive or insecure fashion, provoking still further difficult or stressful behaviors from the child, promoting a potential downward cyclical spiral toward abusive parental behaviors. Also (and consistent with the "learned helplessness" theory of Seligman, 1975), parents may respond to child behaviors perceived as difficult or stressful by withdrawing, becoming depressed, and showing decreased responsiveness and sensitivity to their children's cues (e.g., Murray et al., 1996; Donovan et al., 1998). It has been shown that children responded to in such ways tend to display "dysregulated" behavioral patterns through excessively demanding behaviors, excessive crying, or exhibiting their own depressive behavior patterns (Cox et al., 1987; Field, 1992, 1998). Such dyadic interaction processes may spiral downward over time into neglectful parenting behaviors. Importantly, findings by Field (1998), indicate that a dyadic depressive, potentially neglectful interaction may have biochemical substrates and may appear at birth or even in *utero.*

Nineteen-year-old Mercedes, a recent immigrant from Mexico, brought her 3-month-old baby boy in for a well-baby visit to the local health clinic. At the

---

*For a more in-depth discussion of the etiology of physical child abuse and neglect, refer to National Research Council (1993), Guterman (2000), and Trickett and Schellenbach (1998).

time, the doctor referred her to the clinic social worker, as she had expressed concerns over the stability of her living situation. Mercedes conveyed to the social worker that she had been living with her husband, but that she recently left him after he stabbed her in the leg with a knife during an argument. She stated that she had entered a domestic violence shelter with her baby and that she had been living there for a week. The social worker noted that Mercedes appeared to have a depressed affect, was in need of emergency cash, and tended to minimize the violence with her husband. Mercedes had not finished high school, spoke little English, and had been unemployed since arriving in the United States two years prior. Mercedes agreed to meet with the social worker during her next scheduled well-baby visit, but did not return to the clinic until eight months later, when her baby contracted an ear infection and bronchitis. The social worker learned at that time that Mercedes had returned to live with her husband, and had reported another incident of domestic violence where she had been hospitalized for contusions and abrasions to the face and upper torso. Although there was no evidence of physical injury to the baby, he appeared to the worker as very fussy and highly reactive to the busy clinic environment. Concerned over the well-being of the child, the clinic social worker decided to contact child protective services for fear that the baby was at risk of child neglect and ongoing exposure to family violence.

Parents at risk of physical abuse or neglect may not only experience interactions with their children as stressful but also often face an array of life stressors both within the family and the broader *meso-system* in which family life is embedded (e.g., Kotch et al., 1999; Browne, 1988; Rodriguez & Gren, 1997; Hilson & Kupier, 1994; Kolko et al., 1993). Studies have documented that stressors such as material deprivation, unemployment, multiple life events, and geographic moves are associated with heightened risk for child maltreatment (e.g., Crittenden, 1999; Chan, 1994; Straus & Kantor, 1987; Justice et al., 1985). As well, family strife, particularly the presence of domestic violence, has often been found to co-occur at high rates in cases of physical child abuse and neglect, especially in its most severe forms. For example, studies of children suspected of being maltreated seen in hospital settings have reported that between 45 percent and 59 percent of mothers showed evidence of being battered by their partners (McKibben, De Vos, & Newberger, 1991; Stark & Flitcraft, 1988), and domestic violence has been shown to be present in over 40 percent of child maltreatment fatalities (Oregon Children's Services Division, 1993; Child Fatality Review Panel, 1993; Felix & McCarthy, 1994). In this regard, it is important to point out that fathers or male partners are highly overrepresented as perpetrators in cases of fatal child abuse (Brewster et al., 1998; Krugman, 1985; Margolin, 1992).

One of the central stressors identified in maltreatment risk is that of family poverty. Studies have found that families reported to child protective services systems are more likely to be single mothers, have unemployed fathers, receive public assistance, and/or live in poor neighborhoods (e.g., Hampton & Newberger, 1985; Coulton et al., 1995; Drake & Pandey, 1996; Lindsey, 1994; Zuravin, 1989; Ards, 1989). As summarized by Pelton (1994), "There is overwhelming and remarkably consistent evidence…that poverty and low income are strongly related to child abuse and neglect and to the severity of child maltreatment" (pp. 166–167). At the same time, it is also important to emphasize that a vast majority of impoverished families are never identified as maltreating their children (e.g., Sedlack & Broadhurst, 1996). What such findings suggest is that although economic impoverishment is one of the most consistently observed predictors of physical child abuse and neglect risk, it must been considered in combination with other risk and protective factors that may modify the risk for future physical child abuse and neglect (c.f. Chapter 2 of this book).

Social networks and the characteristics of the communities in which families live have often been considered as factors that may play a role in protecting from, or, conversely, as contributing to maltreatment risk, particularly in ways they may alter the relationship between parents' perceived stresses (such as those that are socioeconomically derived) and their parenting behaviors. Research spanning four decades has consistently discerned important links between problematic aspects of families' social networks and heightened child maltreatment risk (e.g., Young, 1964; Salzinger et al., 1983; Adamakos et al., 1986; Straus & Smith, 1992; Gaudin et al., 1993; Chan, 1994; Coohey, 1996). Studies have tended to report that, when compared with nonmaltreating families, maltreating families have smaller, less dense social networks with whom they carry out less contact and reciprocal exchanges (e.g., Course et al., 1990; Kotelchuck, 1982; Salzinger et al., 1983; Crittenden, 1985; Elmer, 1967; Lovell & Hawkins, 1988). It has also been reported that maltreatment risk is higher for families living in community settings characterized by a lack of cohesion among neighbors, where community life consists of instability, disorganization, and high degrees of community violence (Coulton et al., 1995; Korbin, 1994; Richters & Martinez, 1993; Osofsky, 1993).

Finally, although a highly complex issue, *macro-systemic* cultural, economic, and historical influences have been considered for some time in the ways they may shape the risk for child maltreatment. The role of culture, for example, has most frequently been considered in the means by which cultural messages convey norms of parenting behavior, along with sanctions and allowances for a variety of parenting practices (Korbin, 1994, 1987; Finkelhor & Korbin, 1988). Wide variation has been noted across cultural contexts regarding culturally accepted and normative supervisory arrangements, the number and nature of caregivers, disciplinary and indigenous medical practices employed with children (e.g., Korbin, 1994; Fischler, 1985; Ritchie & Ritchie, 1981). For example, corporal punishment that may appear to be physical abuse within some cultural contexts may be wholly acceptable and defined as normative within other contexts (Solheim, 1982). Given this, what may be accepted as normative child-rearing patterns within a specific cultural context may be misconstrued across cultural boundaries as child maltreatment, especially in situations where professionals must enact child protection laws and policies derived from a majority cultural value system (e.g., Gray & Cosgrove, 1985). It has been argued that these reasons provide partial explanation for an overrepresentation of nonmajority group families in studies using official child protective services data (e.g., Jason et al., 1982; Lauderdale et al., 1980; Spearly & Lauderdale, 1983). Although a great many questions still remain with regard to the many dynamics that influence and lead to physical child abuse and neglect, we nonetheless have developed a substantial body of knowledge that can be drawn from in considering efforts to prevent and to treat physical child abuse and neglect when it occurs.

UNTANGLING "PREVENTION" VERSUS "TREATMENT" OF PHYSICAL CHILD ABUSE AND NEGLECT

Efforts to "prevent" and to "treat" physical child abuse and neglect have often been confused in practice. The Child Abuse Prevention and Treatment Act (Public Law 93–247 and its amendments), which governs the nation's present institutional response to the problem, although including both the words *prevention* and *treatment* in its title, has primarily promoted intervention after child maltreatment has already taken place. Until very recently, the notion of prevention most commonly connoted prevention of the *recurrence* of physical child abuse and neglect *after* its onset, or prevention of the need for out-of-home placement when maltreatment was found to be present and threaten a child's remaining at home safely (oftentimes termed *family preservation* services). However, in just the last decade, intervention strategies aimed at the prevention of physical child abuse and neglect *before the fact* have rapidly emerged as a clearly identifiable and increasingly adopted strategy in communities across the United States. Although some scholars have attempted to identify and label varying forms of child maltreatment prevention and intervention using terminology drawn from the fields of medicine and public health (such as "primary/secondary/ tertiary" prevention or "universal/selected/indicated" intervention), we find that these categories hold somewhat fuzzy boundaries, and do not well reflect the realities of child maltreatment programs and practices in operation. Given this, we instead adopt the labels of *prevention* and *treatment* here to describe the range of intervention strategies aimed at the problem of physical child abuse and neglect. In this context, *prevention* denotes intervening before maltreatment has been identified by formal authorities, whereas *treatment* denotes intervening to address the problem after it has been identified. As treatment efforts have historically preceded prevention efforts, lodged within the prevailing child protection and child welfare systems, we will examine these first.

TREATMENT OF PHYSICAL CHILD ABUSE AND NEGLECT

Michael, a 7-year-old white boy, was removed from the custody of his parents as a result of child neglect. Upon a visit to the home, the protective services worker observed that there was no heat and little food in the refrigerator and cabinets. It was also reported that Michael had witnessed ongoing partner violence between his parents, including at least one episode in which his mother held a knife to his father's throat while threatening to kill him. Michael's parents had been arrested in the past for growing marijuana in their home and were reported to smoke marijuana regularly in Michael's presence.

Following one episode of domestic violence, Michael's mother was arrested and involuntarily hospitalized for 72 hours at a nearby hospital. Michael's mother also made a death threat toward the protective services worker. The mother was court ordered to attend an anger management course and to receive a psychiatric evaluation, both of which she refused.

Owing to the onset of deafness 10 years prior as well as declining eyesight due to macular degeneration, Michael's father was largely dependent on

Michael's mother for communication outside the home and for transportation. Because of the father's disability, the family received government assistance, was described as poor, and had a history of frequent moves.

Michael was placed into foster care and initially described by his foster mother as verbally and physically aggressive to her and to his peers, and by school staff as developmentally delayed. In addition, Michael's foster mother reported that he wet his bed four nights a week, had frequent nightmares, and feared his biological mother would kill him.

After two foster placements failed as a result of Michael's aggressive behavior, Michael was placed in a therapeutic foster care program that included weekly home visits by a master's-level caseworker providing individual child therapy, child management instruction with the foster parents, and case management services. Services also included family therapy and monitoring of visits with the biological parents to support reunifying Michael with his biological parents. Michael also attended a kindergarten program that included instruction in stress management and cognitive behavioral methods to improve his impulse control and decrease his aggressive behavior with others. The child was also evaluated to rule out neurological factors that might influence his functioning.

Michael's father showed some motivation to meet court-ordered goals. He stated he would seek a parenting class, receive psychotherapy, attend weekly drug testing, and pursue mobility services and independence skill development.

After nine months of therapeutic foster care services, Michael's foster mother reported that Michael's behavior had improved appreciably. His aggression toward her and toward peers had diminished, and his bedwetting had ceased. His nightmares had subsided, and his behavior at kindergarten was reported to have improved. Efforts were initiated to terminate parental rights, and Michael's foster mother expressed interest in adopting him.

After a child protective services investigation to determine the presence of physical abuse or neglect, a child maltreatment victim may remain in the home—with or without ongoing child welfare system oversight—or the child may be removed from the home for safety and placed in an out-of-home setting. Such out-of-home settings may include foster care with relatives or nonrelatives, specialized treatment (or therapeutic) foster care, group home placement, or placement in an intensive residential treatment facility. Decisions regarding out-of-home placement and the provision of specific services are typically determined by a variety of factors, including an assessment of immediate risk for further maltreatment, the clinical need of child victims and adult perpetrators, service availability, local child welfare system policies and practices, and the role of the courts (Rossi, 1992). The services provided may seek to address the effects of maltreatment on the child, and/or seek to prevent the recurrence of child maltreatment by working with the parent(s) or family. Cases of child maltreatment are typically served within a complex service matrix that may include involvement of the child welfare system, law enforcement, and mental health and health care systems. Representatives of these different systems may view child maltreatment from very different perspectives, operate under different policy frameworks, and hold conflicting opinions regarding both child and family service needs and case goals. This complex service environment—when coupled with challenging, crisis-prone child and parent circumstances—can frequently result in case decisions and accompanying service plans that may appear haphazard and urgent.

Interventions targeting children and families affected by physical child abuse and neglect are varied, and a comprehensive review of treatment interventions for child maltreatment is beyond the scope of this chapter.* We highlight here interventions that have received some positive empirical support and that may be offered to children and families being served across the continuum of child welfare system services. The interventions chosen reflect differing theoretical models and intervention targets. We present interventions that primarily target the child as a primary service recipient, interventions that service the family as a primary recipient, and interventions that take an integrated approach.

Child-Focused Treatment Strategies

Children who are abused and neglected often require treatment to address the negative developmental, behavioral, and emotional consequences of their maltreatment. While sometimes involving others, such as foster parents or teachers, the primary aim of such interventions is to ameliorate the effects of physical abuse and/or neglect in children. One such well-developed program is the Early Intervention Foster Care (EIFC) program developed by Fisher, Chamberlain, and colleagues at the Oregon Social Learning Center (Fisher, Ellis, & Chamberlain, 1999; Fisher & Chamberlain, 2000; Fisher, Gunnar, Chamberlain, & Reid, 2000). The EIFC specifically applies principles of social learning theory developed by Patterson, Reid, and Dishion (1992) to the treatment needs of maltreated preschool children residing in specialized therapeutic foster care homes. Social learning theory as applied to this population focuses on the effective use of rewards and punishments to manage child behavior with a particular emphasis on avoiding harsh and ineffective responses to challenging child misbehavior. Specific child service needs that are addressed by the EIFC include behavior and conduct problems, difficulties with emotional regulation, and developmental delays.

Children in the EIFC are served by a multidisciplinary team that includes the foster parents, clinical team supervisor, foster parent consultant, early childhood development interventionist, and a family therapist. Foster parents are given an intensive preservice training that stresses the use of behavioral reinforcement techniques, the need for close supervision and positive engagement of children, the use of contracts and rewards for increasing prosocial behavior, and the use of time-out and other consequences for setting limits on behavior (Fisher, Ellis, & Chamberlain, 1999). Daily telephone contact is made with foster parents to track child functioning, provide support, and modify child management strategies. Weekly home visits are also made by the foster parent consultant, and weekly agency-based foster parent support groups are also provided. Services provided to the children include interventions to remediate developmental delays (Bricker, 1989) and attendance at weekly therapeutic play groups. Additionally, services designed to support

---

*Refer to Cohn and Daro (1987), Wolfe and Wekerle (1993), Kolko (1998), and Oates and Bross (1995) for more in-depth examination of treatment interventions for cases of physical child abuse and neglect.

permanency in the child's placement may be provided to biological, adoptive, or long-term foster parents.

A small pilot study utilizing a quasi-experimental design examined the effectiveness of the EIFC model on child and foster parent adjustment during the initial months of the foster placement (Fisher, Gunnar, Chamberlain, & Reid, 2000). This study, conducted on a sample of 30 children and their foster parents, reported positive changes on child behavior, parenting practices of foster parents, foster parent stress, and a biological indicator linked with emotional regulation in children.

The resilient peer treatment (RPT) model of Fantuzzo and colleagues (Fantuzzo et al., 1996; Fantuzzo et al., 1988) was developed to promote the social development of withdrawn maltreated preschoolers. This treatment, which is influenced by developmental and ecological theories, pairs maltreated preschoolers with highly social resilient peers—called play buddies—in a classroom or preschool play setting. In a study conducted by Fantuzzo and colleagues (1996), peers were involved in 15 play sessions over two months. Before each play session, an adult play supporter oriented the resilient peer to a play area that included typical preschool toys, such as blocks, cars, dolls, and toy telephones. The play supporter also reminded the resilient peer of successful play activities that they had participated in with the withdrawn child during prior sessions. An outcome study utilizing a sample of 46 children and an experimental design examined the effectiveness of RPT and found that those preschoolers who received RPT had significant improvements in positive peer relations and a decrease in social isolation at treatment completion and at two-month follow-up when compared to those in a randomly assigned control group.

Intensive day treatment services are designed to promote strong teacher-child relationships and school learning, while also encouraging children to build positive peer relations, positive self-esteem, and appropriate management of feelings. Culp and colleagues (Culp, Heide, & Richardson, 1987; Culp, Little, Letts, & Lawrence, 1991) have examined the benefits of intensive day treatment services for preschool-aged maltreated children in a study utilizing a quasi-experimental design and a sample of 70 children. Children in the program attended six hours a day, five days a week, across an average of 8 months of service, and were served in group settings that included a 2 to 1 staff to child ratio. The program also included individual child and parent counseling, parent education classes, and crisis intervention services. A quasi-experimental evaluation of the program found that children receiving intensive day treatment services had significantly higher fine motor, gross motor, and language development skills, and especially notably higher scores in the areas of cognitive and social/emotional functioning. Developmental delays evident at pretest were comparatively remediated at discharge. A separate study conducted by Culp, Little, Letts, and Lawrence (1991) also reported improvements in self-concept for those children receiving day treatment services.

Family-Based Treatment Strategies

Given evidence linking a variety of parent, child, and parent-child interactional factors to child maltreatment risk, and the fact that a significant proportion of maltreated children remain with their parents, some researchers have examined the effectiveness of family-based treatment strategies. These interventions attempt both to prevent the recurrence of maltreatment and to address the negative effects of prior maltreatment on child behavior and family relations.

Kolko (1996a) examined the effects of individual cognitive behavioral treatment and family therapy on maltreatment recurrence, risk for future maltreatment, and the negative effects of physical abuse on the child victim. Forty-seven children and parents were randomly assigned to receive individual cognitive behavioral treatment (CBT), family therapy (FT), or regular community service (RCS), and were followed up 12 months later. All service conditions included both office-based and home-based services.

Parents and children receiving individual cognitive behavioral therapy were each provided parallel individual services utilizing social learning theory-based interventions. Child sessions addressed their views of family violence, coping and self-control strategies, utilization of social supports, and personal safety strategies. Parent interventions addressed similar topics and included training in behaviorally oriented child management methods with a focus on contingency training. The cognitive behavioral therapy component was structured to address intrapersonal and interpersonal issues with each child and parent in a manner that was consistent across families. For example, clinic-based interventions for both children and parents typically focus on a key concept (e.g., self-control strategies) including review of written materials, behavioral rehearsal, and discussion of home practice assignments. Subsequent home-based interventions focused on individualized application of the same materials, continued behavioral rehearsal, and supportive counseling (Kolko, 1996b).

Parents receiving family therapy were provided services designed to reflect an interactional or ecological model. Treatment focused on families gaining an understanding of coercive family processes and improving communication and problem-solving abilities. Family therapy services were composed of three phases: engagement, skills building, and application/termination. Families receiving regular community services were provided a more heterogeneous mix of services, including in-home services, parent education, and homemaker skills training.

All three services were linked with significant improvements in parental anger, child management skills, age-appropriate expectations for children, and parental substance abuse. Families receiving cognitive behavioral treatment or family therapy, when compared against families receiving regular community services, showed improvements in parent-to-child violence, child abuse potential, children's externalizing behavior problems, parental stress, and family cohesion. In contrast, families receiving regular community services reported greater improvements in family functioning.

Another promising family-focused strategy is the multifamily group therapy (MFGT) approach. Multifamily group therapy aims to improve family functioning by bringing together two or more families of parents with their children to meet with a professional therapist. The validation and support provided between participants are seen as primary helping agents. Meezan and O'Keefe (1998) report on the evaluation of an MFGT intervention on the risk for child maltreatment and family functioning. This study utilized an experimental design with a sample of 81 families—half of whom were nonwhite and one-third of whom were college graduates. The theoretical focus of the MFGT in this study was diverse and included elements of family systems and structural family therapy, group therapy, behavior modification, cognitive behavioral therapy, reality therapy, parent education, and crisis intervention. Families attending the MFGT service met weekly for an average of 2.5 hours across eight months, accompanied by five to seven other families and a team of four clinicians.

Families receiving MFGT were compared against a randomly assigned group of families receiving family therapy that included elements of structural family therapy, behavior modification, and cognitive behavioral therapy. The study reported that although both groups improved in their utilization of social support as a result of intervention, the MFGT group attended services for a longer period of time, had fewer dropouts, and received more services when compared to the family therapy group. Importantly, on the whole, those families receiving MFGT dropped below a clinical risk level on the Child Abuse Potential Inventory, whereas those receiving family therapy did not.

Integrated Treatment Models

Integrated treatment approaches to child- and family-based problems typically place a heavy emphasis on addressing a wide range of family needs—from concrete necessities required for daily living to the mental health needs of family members. Additionally, both clinical and case management services are typically delivered within a highly coordinated, flexible service model. Services are frequently delivered in the client home, the community, and the office, and staff are frequently available on an as-needed basis. Two well-studied integrated treatment models, both of which incorporate an ecological framework into their interventions, are the ecobehavioral Project 12-Ways model developed by Lutzker and colleagues (Lutzker, 1984; Lutzker, Bigelow, Doctor, Gershater, & Greene, 1998; Watson-Perczel, Lutzker, Greene, & McGimpsey, 1988) and the multisystemic treatment model developed by Henggeler and colleagues (Brunk, Henggeler, & Whelan, 1987; Henggeler, Schoenwald, Borduin, Rowland, & Cunningham, 1998).* These two intervention models hold many similarities: Both attempt to respond to the complex array of factors that can contribute to the risk for child maltreatment. Both incorporate elements of behavioral and cognitive behavioral methods into their intervention models. Both have been applied to maltreatment populations as well as nonmaltreatment populations. And, perhaps most importantly, both can claim some support for their efficacy from fairly rigorous evaluation studies.

The ecobehavioral Project 12-Ways model developed by Lutzker and colleagues is designed to address those child, parent, and family factors that contribute to child physical abuse and neglect. An array of assessment and intervention services are delivered in an individualized fashion within the client's home and other community settings (Lutzker, 1984; Lutzker, Bigelow, Doctor, Gershater, & Greene, 1998; Watson-Perczel, Lutzker, Greene, & McGimpsey, 1988). Service plans may consist of a core of services, including the following: parent training, health and nutrition counseling, problem-solving skills training, stress management training for parents, child behavior management training, activity training, personal hygiene training, home safety improvement, money management, marital counseling, alcohol and other drug treatment referral, and parent support groups.

---

*Perhaps the most well known model of integrated services—the Homebuilder's model—is not included in this chapter because of the limited empirical support for its effectiveness (Schuerman, Rzepnicki, & Littell 1994). Other researchers, however, argue that such findings have limited applicability to the Homebuilder's model (Bath & Haapala, 1994).

For behavioral in-home training, parents are taught the use of clear verbal commands, contingent praise, time out, and the use of token economies to improve their child management skills. Cognitive behavior therapy techniques that are utilized for anger management and stress management may include deep muscle relaxation training. Parents and children may also receive communication and assertiveness training, or training in organizing positive social time with their children (Lutzker, 1984).

Project 12-Ways has been carefully evaluated utilizing several different study designs ranging from single-subject to quasi-experimental group designs (Tertinger, Greene, & Lutzker, 1984; Lutzker & Rice, 1987; Wesch & Lutzker, 1991). The findings from the studies utilizing a quasi-experimental design are based on an analysis of data from 352 families served by the program and 358 comparison families who received regular community services. These findings indicate a modest but statistically significant improvement in subsequent rates of reported abuse, neglect, placement, or adoption when compared against the comparison group. Ongoing follow-ups, however, have reported some "wash out" of program effects after five years.

Multisystemic treatment (MST), developed by Henggeler, Bourdin, and colleagues, adopts the broad general systems theory of von Bertalanffy (1968), the ecological theories of Bronfenbrenner (1979), and the family systems treatment strategies developed by Minuchin, Haley, and others (Brunk, Henggeler, & Whelan, 1987; Henggeler, Schoenwald, Borduin, Rowland, & Cunningham, 1998). Problem behavior is conceptualized as deriving from micro-system, meso-system, and macro-system sources, and family members are viewed as engaging in predictable patterns of interactions that mutually influence one another, as well as the extrafamilial environment. The MST model also draws from the empirical literature to identify what is currently known about the precursors and causes of the problem and designs interventions accordingly (Henggeler, Schoenwald, Borduin, Rowland, & Cunningham, 1998). Assessment and intervention is focused on all three system levels, including a close examination of family behavior patterns, parenting practices, and child behavior.

Current models of MST utilize an in-home time-limited treatment approach. Staff carry small caseloads of three to six families and frequently work in a team format. Staff are available to families around the clock, and make daily contact either by telephone or face to face (Henggeler et al., 1998).

Service plans are individualized and staff do not follow a structured manualized method of intervention like staff in Project 12-Ways. Instead, assessment and treatment follow the nine core principles listed in Figure 7.3. Although MST is delivered according to these principles, a priority is given to interventions that have empirically determined effectiveness. For example, referral to or provision of psychodynamically oriented play therapy for children would be discouraged, whereas cognitive behaviorally based child or family treatment would be encouraged because of the stronger empirical support for these latter approaches.

The effectiveness of MST shows promising results with a variety of clinical populations, including delinquent youth, children with serious emotional disturbances, adolescent sexual offenders, and maltreating families. The effectiveness of an early version of MST on maltreating families was examined by Brunk, Henggeler, and Whelan (1987) in a study utilizing an experimental design with a sample of 43 families—43 percent of whom were African American. Findings in this study indicated that when compared against a randomly

FIGURE 7.3   **MST Treatment Principles**

1. The primary purpose of assessment is to understand the fit between the identified problems and their broader systemic context.
2. Therapeutic contacts emphasize the positive and use systemic strengths as levers for change.
3. Interventions are designed to promote responsible behavior and decrease irresponsible behavior among family members.
4. Interventions are present focused and action oriented, targeting specific and well-defined problems.
5. Interventions target sequences of behavior within and between multiple systems that maintain the identified problems.
6. Interventions are developmentally appropriate and fit the developmental needs of the youth.
7. Interventions are designed to require daily or weekly effort by family members.
8. Intervention effectiveness is evaluated continuously from multiple perspectives with providers assuming accountability for overcoming barriers to successful outcomes.
9. Interventions are designed to promote treatment generalization and long-term maintenance of therapeutic change by empowering caregivers to address family members' needs across multiple systemic contexts.

Source: S. W. Henggeler, S. K. Schoenwald, C. M. Borduin, M. D. Rowland, & P. B. Cunningham. *Multisystemic Treatment of Antisocial Behavior in Children and Adolescents* (New York: Guilford Press, 1998). Reprinted by permission.

assigned group of families receiving parent training, MST families showed greater improvements in parental control of child behavior and child compliance. In addition, neglectful parents became more responsive to their child's behavior after receiving multisystemic treatment. Families receiving parent training showed greater reductions in parent social problems, and both treatment approaches were able to report statistically significant reductions in parent psychiatric symptomatology and parental stress as well as improved family functioning (Brunk, Henggeler, & Whelan, 1987). Larger-scale clinical trials of more recent models of MST are now being conducted with physically abused adolescents and their families.

Summary

Interventions to treat the problem of physical child abuse and neglect after it has occurred have demonstrated their promise in promoting important competencies in children, parents, and families, and in reducing maltreatment recurrences and associated child problems such as withdrawal, aggression, impaired social skills, and noncompliant behavior. Findings from outcome studies suggest that children and families can benefit from interventions that target specific behaviors that are antecedents and consequences of child maltreatment.

Despite these promising evaluation results, it is also clear that the present empirical base holds significant methodological limitations and that existing intervention models may have significant theoretical shortcomings as well. For example, with the exception of the studies conducted by Lutzker and colleagues, all of the studies reviewed were conducted with fairly small sample sizes, which constrains researchers' abilities to evaluate the effectiveness of interventions. Three out of the seven studies reviewed here utilized a quasi-experimental (nonrandom assignment) design, which limits researchers' capacity to demonstrate that positive treatment outcomes occur as a direct result of the intervention. Four of the studies reviewed did no follow-up data collection to assess the stability of gains achieved over time. Finally, half of the interventions that had a family focus failed to collect data on maltreatment recurrence—a principle outcome indicator in child maltreatment intervention research (see Oats & Bross, 1995, for further discussion of methodological limitations of this knowledge base). Such limitations indicate that considerable effort is still necessary to develop and rigorously evaluate treatment models to address physical child abuse and neglect after it has occurred.

From a theoretical standpoint, intervention models have not yet well attended to commonly co-occurring problems in cases of physical child abuse and neglect requiring specialized attention, such as in instances where substance abuse or domestic violence is present. As examples, although models studied by Kolko (1996) and Meezan and O'Keefe (1998) reported that between one-fourth and one-third of the parents served had a history of substance abuse problems, no information is provided on specific program elements targeting substance use as it affects parenting behavior. Further, the majority of other program models overlook reporting on parents' potential substance use concerns. Such oversight is notable, considering the evidence regarding the prevalence of parental substance abuse among children and families under child protective supervision and the increased risk for child maltreatment among families with an alcohol-abusing parent (Murphy, Jellinek, Quinn, & Smith, 1991; U.S. Department of Health and Human Services, 1993; National Committee to Prevent Child Abuse, 1996). Thus, attention to more specialized and tailored models promises to forge still further advances in the treatment of physical child abuse and neglect after they occur.

PREVENTION OF PHYSICAL CHILD ABUSE AND NEGLECT

Whereas treatment interventions aim to alleviate the psychosocial sequelae found in maltreated children and to improve family functioning, preventive interventions aim to address underlying etiological factors that breed later physical child abuse and neglect, and to do so *before* maltreatment has had a chance to erupt. The target population for which treatment interventions are designed is determined by families' entry into the protective services system, where maltreatment has been specifically identified as the problem of concern. In contrast, no single central entry point exists to identify a population of at-risk families who have not yet abused or neglected their children. Instead, at-risk families may access a wide variety of formal helping systems, including health care, schools, child care, mental health, and substance abuse systems. Given this, interventions aimed at preventing physical child abuse and neglect before it occurs are found in many niches, serving a variety of populations within differing institutional contexts. As is evident, an important precursory challenge of any maltreatment preventive approach is to appropriately identify families for preventive intervention, and then to configure the intervention to the needs of families identified as at risk, once targeted. Should *all* families receive some intervention to prevent physical child abuse and neglect or just some? If only some families are to receive intervention, which ones, and how are these to be identified? And based on answers to these questions, then, what specific services should these families receive?

These questions have proven vexing ones for efforts at delivering effective intervention aimed at preventing physical child abuse and neglect before the fact. Very limited efforts in the United States have been expended to attempt to prevent physical child abuse and neglect by targeting all families (often termed *universal* interventions), but a growing national movement has emerged that aims to target and serve families identified as at risk but where no maltreatment has yet been identified. Although families at risk for future physical abuse or neglect may be identified via a range of service systems (e.g., education, Head Start, mental health), the large majority of programs delivering preventive interventions are lodged within health care systems, since these serve as near-universal access points whereby virtually all at-risk families may be located early for preventive services during the perinatal period.

Although some prevention programs have sought to serve all families giving birth to a child within an identified health care system, the majority of programs target services to families believed to be at higher risk for future maltreatment, in an effort to allocate resources most efficiently. Screening and risk assessment of families, although appearing sensible from an economic standpoint, have raised a host of complicated and problematic intervention issues and have important implications for the future of maltreatment prevention. Targeting families through risk screening for maltreatment, for example, raises issues of additional costs, the potential stigma associated with being positively screened, and, most troubling, the many and persistent problems with the accuracy of risk screens to detect future maltreatment (c.f. Caldwell et al., 1988; McDonald & Marks, 1991). Screening processes can also "drive" the nature of services delivered by determining the pool of served families and their attendant service needs (c.f. Guterman, 1999). Although it is beyond the scope of this chapter to examine the difficulties associated with risk screening to appropriately target services to at-risk families, it is important to recognize that without a sound targeting strategy that is closely integrated with services delivered, even the most rigorously designed and tested preventive interventions are likely to be mismatched and therefore ineffective (c.f. Guterman, 2000, for further discussion).

Early Home Visitation Interventions

A variety of models aimed at preventing physical child abuse and neglect have been tested, but perhaps the most visible and most carefully studied are early home visitation service programs. Home visitation services typically engage families deemed to be at risk during prenatal clinic visits or in a hospital at the point of birth. They then assign a home visitor to deliver parenting education and case management assistance in families' homes. Home visitors typically deliver ongoing parenting guidance to at-risk families oftentimes through a child's first several years of life. Home visitors also serve as a referral hub for families who may benefit from being linked up with public assistance, Medicaid, mental health, substance abuse, domestic violence services, or other community supports. Home visiting services have become increasingly available, in part, given an array of largely positive, though some mixed, outcomes attributed to home visitation services linked not only with physical child abuse and neglect risk reduction but also with positive child developmental, parenting, maternal, and child health outcomes (Guterman, 2000; MacLeod & Nelson, 2000).

Among the most notable of early home visitation model programs is the Prenatal/Early Infancy Nurse Home Visitation Program, first developed and studied by David Olds and colleagues in Elmira, New York (e.g., Olds et al., 1999; Kitzman et al., 1997). The program is grounded in human ecology, self-efficacy, and attachment theories, and has been refined over the past 20 years. The program specifically targets low-income primiparous (first-time) mothers and initiates weekly services prenatally, tapering off until the child reaches 2 years of age. Services are delivered by nurse home visitors, addressing such concerns as developmental milestones, maternal sensitivity, and home safety. Primary support persons are encouraged to be involved at specifically designated sessions, and ongoing coordination of services takes place with primary physicians and other appropriate heath and social service agencies in the community (Kitzman et al., 1997; Olds, 1982; Olds et al., 1999).

An initial well-executed evaluation study of 400 families reported a select but broad array of positive outcomes in home-visited families in comparison to randomly assigned control-group families. Intervention services were linked with lower rates of official child maltreatment reports among low-income unmarried teen mothers. As well, home-visited mothers reported fewer subsequent pregnancies and fewer months of public assistance, and infants were seen fewer times in the hospital emergency room. Perhaps most impressively, a recent follow-up study when the children were 15 years old continued to report lower child maltreatment rates in home-visited families, and among the low-income unmarried mothers, fewer subsequent births, shorter time spans on public assistance, fewer problems with substance or alcohol abuse, and less criminal involvement (Olds et al., 1997).

A second notable early home visitation program is the Hawaii Healthy Start program, which has been adopted by Prevent Child Abuse America as a model from which to seek to disseminate home visiting programs throughout communities across the United States. While also providing long-term in-home services to at-risk families like those in the Olds Prenatal/Early Infancy Nurse Home Visitation Program, the Hawaii Healthy Start model differs in several important respects: Hawaii Healthy Start programs utilize individual psychosocial screens to seek to identify the highest-risk families in services, and services are delivered by intensively trained paraprofessionals rather than nurses. In addition, parents need not be primiparous (first-time only), and services are planned to last three or more years, typically until the child enters Head Start or kindergarten. Beyond a very promising preliminary evaluation of the program, more recent carefully controlled studies have reported less positive findings, allowing a reconsideration of program components that may need to be extended or modified (e.g., Duggan et al., 1999; Daro & Harding, 1999). Despite this, however, early home visitation services hold unique strengths in providing in-home hands-on support that can address some of the important parent-child interactional elements linked with maltreatment risk, as well as in assisting families to link up with important formal resources that may assist them in their parenting young children.

Social Support Preventive Interventions

Home visiting interventions, although promising, are also limited by design in their capacity to address some of the more potent etiological influences identified in physical child abuse and neglect, particularly those derived from meso-system–level stresses and pressures found in families' social networks and in their community settings. Several social support intervention models have preliminarily sought to address some of these broader contextual challenges by helping at-risk parents overcome social isolation and more effectively tap informal support networks for material, emotional, and informational support necessary to parent children. Social support programs offer the additional opportunity of providing companionship with other parents who share similar concerns, assisting them to feel more connected to one another and to the broader struggles of parenting.

Schinke, Barth, and colleagues have reported on social support skills training groups for pregnant and parenting teens. In a study of 70 teens, promising improvements were seen in social skills and social supports as a result of participation (Barth & Schinke, 1984; Schinke et al., 1986). Likewise, the Social Network Intervention Project (SNIP) of Gaudin and colleagues engaged parents at risk of child neglect in social skills training and linked them with mutual aid groups and neighborhood helpers. Parents receiving SNIP services reported improvements in their social networks and a broad range of parenting attitudes linked with child neglect (Gaudin, Wodarski, Arkinson, & Avery, 1990–91). Similarly, Guterman (2000, 2001) has reported promising preliminary outcomes linked with parents' involvement in an empowerment support group for high-risk substance abusing parents, including positive changes in parents' social networks, reported stresses, sense of control, and child behavior problems. This model has since been expanded and integrated with early home visitation services, and is under evaluation on a larger scale.

Perhaps the largest-scale social support intervention in practice is one that integrates professional clinical guidance indirectly—namely, Parents Anonymous self-help groups. Such groups, like other self-help groups, are run by parents who have identified themselves as at risk of abusing their children. Initially founded in 1970, Parents Anonymous groups have expanded across the United States, and provide support to an estimated 100,000 parents per year (Rafael & Pion-Berlin, 1999). Participants set their own agendas in Parents Anonymous groups and often address parenting and family communication skills. Participating parents are encouraged to contact one another outside the group meetings for support, and to begin to take leadership and responsibility in the group functioning. Importantly, Parents Anonymous has developed into a national movement and organization that provides technical assistance and that advocates changes in the policies and programming that may aid in addressing the problem of child abuse on a larger scale. As with other self-help movements in the United States, there is a paucity of carefully controlled outcome data on the effectiveness of Parents Anonymous. An initial evaluation found that participating parents self-reported changes in parenting behaviors, more appropriate child developmental expectations, and reduced incidence of child abuse (Rafael & Pion-Berlin, 1999). Recently, the U.S. Office of Juvenile Justice and Delinquency Prevention initiated an effort to study Parents Anonymous under more carefully controlled conditions.

Universal Prevention Strategies

Universal preventive strategies addressing the problem of physical child abuse and neglect are analogous to other universal preventive health strategies such as child immunization or water fluoridation in that they seek to prevent by intervening with an entire population, regardless of identified risk. Given that universal interventions are received by all, such strategies avoid potential stigma that may accompany the targeting and associated labeling of at-risk groups. Although some efforts have been made to engage in broad-based public campaigns—for example, through the distribution of educational parenting magazines for parents of infants (Laurendeau et al., 1991), or by providing all new parents with educational materials about the risks of shaking babies (e.g., Showers, 1992)—precious little empirical evidence is available that sheds light on the efficacy of such universal strategies. Given the expenses associated with such broad strategies, coupled with a high societal value in the United States on protecting individual liberties and privacy, universal prevention strategies have received less attention to date, and efforts to enact broad policies, such as "no spanking zones" in communities, have not fared well (e.g., Wong, 1999). Nonetheless, evidence from a ban on corporal punishment enacted in Sweden in 1979 suggests that such publicly based strategies, if enacted, hold the potential to substantially influence public attitudes and behaviors related to physical abuse or neglect (e.g., Durrant, 1999), although the available evidence is far from conclusive.

CONCLUSIONS

Although we have made important headway in addressing the problem of physical child abuse and neglect in the last half century, the scientific knowledge base from which to guide our prevention and treatment efforts remains in its infancy. Major gaps remain in understanding, for example, how to treat victims of physical abuse in contrast to those of physical neglect, how to prevent physical abuse and neglect in substance abusing or domestically violent families, and, perhaps most troubling, how to prevent maltreatment-related child fatalities. Historically speaking, we presently have highly promising knowledge about intervention models that address the problem of physical child abuse and neglect in a broad way. However, important knowledge gaps still exist that might assist us in tailoring intervention strategies to the specific needs of individual families and risk subgroups, whether these are families with specific mental health issues, families who are impoverished, or families who are socially isolated. We must recognize that ongoing large-scale efforts are required in the practice arena to stem the tide of physical abuse and neglect, and to develop a systematic knowledge base that can guide our practices in sound and reliable ways.

DISCUSSION QUESTIONS

1. Findings suggest that early childhood presents the period of highest risk for physical child abuse and neglect, particularly in its most severe forms. Why might this be the case?

2. What appear as the major causal factors linked with physical child abuse and neglect?

3. Choose one preventive or treatment intervention model reviewed in this chapter. Discuss the reasons for its demonstrated impact in addressing physical abuse and neglect, and consider possible limitations to the model.

4. In light of what is known about the consequences of physical child abuse and neglect, propose new or additional methods of intervention that might address some of the most

common sequelae of maltreatment, and do not presently form a core aspect of current intervention models.

5. Considering some of the primary etiological factors in physical child abuse and neglect, propose new or additional preventive intervention strategies that may effectively interrupt the chain of events leading to later maltreatment.

SUGGESTED READINGS

Guterman, N. B. (2000). *Stopping child maltreatment before it starts: Emerging horizons in early home visitation services.* Thousand Oaks, CA: Sage.

Lutzker, J. (Ed.). (1998). *Handbook of child abuse research and treatment.* New York: Plenum Press.

National Research Council. (1993). *Understanding child abuse and neglect.* Washington, DC: National Academy Press.

Reece, R. (Ed.). (2000). *Treatment of child abuse: Common ground for mental health, medical, and legal practitioners.* Baltimore: Johns Hopkins University Press.

Trickett, P. K., & Schellenbach, C. J. (1998). *Violence against children in the family and the community,* Washington, DC: American Psychological Association.

Wolfe, D. A., McMahon, R. J., & Peters, R. D. (1997). *Child abuse: New directions in prevention and treatment across the lifespan.* Thousand Oaks, CA: Sage.

REFERENCES

Aber, J. L., Allen, J. P., Carlson, V., & Cicchetti, D. (1990). The effects of maltreatment on development during early childhood: Recent studies and their theoretical, clinical and policy implementations. In D. Cicchetti & V. Carlson (Eds.), *Child maltreatment: Theory and research on causes and consequences* (pp. 579–619). New York: Cambridge University Press.

Adamakos, H., Ryan, K., Ullman, D. G., Pascoe, J., Diaz, R., & Chessare, J. (1986). Maternal social support as a predictor of mother-child stress and stimulation. *Child Abuse and Neglect, 10,* 463–470.

Allen, D., & Tarnowski, K. (1989). Depressive characteristics of physically abused children. *Journal of Abnormal Child Psychology, 17,* 1–11.

Allen, R. E., & Oliver, J. M. (1982). The effects of child maltreatment on long term development. *Child Abuse & Neglect, 6,* 299–305.

Allen, R. E., & Wasserman, G. A. (1985). Origins of language delay in abused infants. *Child Abuse & Neglect, 9,* 335–340.

Ards, S. (1989). Estimating local child abuse. *Evaluation Review, 13,* 484–515.

Azar, S. T., Barnes, K. T., & Twentyman, C. T. (1988). Developmental outcomes in abused children: Consequences of parental abuse or a more general breakdown in caregiver behavior? *Behavior Therapist, 11,* 27–32.

Barth, R. P., & Schinke, S. P. (1984, November) Enhancing the social supports of teenage mothers. *Social Casework: The Journal of Contemporary Social Work.*

Belsky, J. (1980). Child maltreatment: An ecological integration. *American Psychologist, 35*(4), 320–335.

Bonnier, C., Nassogne, M. C., & Evrard, P. (1995). Outcome and prognosis of whiplash shaken infant syndrome: Late consequences after a symptom-free interval. *Developmental Medicine & Child Neurology, 37*(11), 943–956.

Brewster, A. L., Nelson J. P., Hymel, K. P., Colby D. R., Lucas, D. R., McCanne T. R., & Milner, J. S. (1998). Victim, perpetrator, family, and incident characteristics of 32 infant maltreatment deaths in the United States Air Force. *Child Abuse and Neglect, 22,* 91–101.

Bricker, J. D. (1989). *Early intervention for at-risk and handicapped infants, toddlers, and preschool children.* Palo Alto, CA: VORT.

Bronfenbrenner, U. (1977). Toward an experimental ecology of human development. *American Psychologist, 32*(7), 513–531.

Browne, D. H. (1988). The role of stress in the commission of subsequent acts of child abuse and neglect. *Early Child Development & Care, 31*(1–4), 27–33.

Brunk, M. A., Henggeler, S. W., & Whelan, J. P. (1987). Comparison of multisystemic therapy and parent training in the brief treatment of child abuse and neglect. *Journal of Consulting & Clinical Psychology, 55*(2), 171–178.

Bugental, D., Blunt, L., Judith E., Lin, E. K., McGrath, E. P., & Bimbela, A. (1999). Children "tune out" in response to the ambiguous communication style of powerless adults. *Child Development, 70*(1), 214–230.

Caldwell, R. A., Bogat, G. A., & Davidson, W. S. (1988). The assessment of child abuse potential and the prevention of child abuse and neglect: A policy analysis. *American Journal of Community Psychology, 16*(5), 609–624.

Carlson, V., Cicchetti, D., Barnett, D., & Braunwald, K. (1989). Disorganized/disoriented attachment relationships in maltreated infants. *Developmental Psychology, 25*(4), 525–531.

Cazenave, N., & Straus, M. (1979). Race, class, network embeddedness and family violence: A search for potent support systems. *Journal of Comparative Family Studies, 10*(3), 282–300.

Chaffin, M., Kelleher, K., & Hollenberg, J. (1996). Onset of physical abuse and neglect: Psychiatric, substance abuse, and social risk factors from prospective community data. *Child Abuse & Neglect, 20*(3), 191–203.

Chan, Y. C. (1994). Parenting stress and social support of mothers who physically abuse their children in Hong Kong. *Child Abuse and Neglect, 18*(3), 261–269.

Cheah, I. G., Kasim, M. S., Shafie, H. M., & Khoo, T. H. (1994). Intracranial haemorrhage and child abuse. *Annals of Tropical Paediatrics, 14*(4): 325–328.

Christensen, M. J., Brayden, R. M., Dietrich, M. S., & McLaughlin, F. (1994). The prospective assessment of self-concept in neglectful and physically abusive low income mothers. *Child Abuse & Neglect, 18*(3), 225–232.

Cicchetti, D., & Beeghly, M. (1987). Symbolic development in maltreated youngsters: An organizational perspective. *New Directions for Child Development, 36.*

Cicchetti, D., & Lynch, M. (1993). Toward an ecological/transactional model of community violence and child maltreatment: Consequences of children's development, *Psychiatry, 56.* 96–118.

Cohn, A. H. (1979). Effective treatment of child abuse and neglect. *Social Work,* 513–519.

Cohn, A. H., & Daro, D. (1987). Is treatment too late? What ten years of evaluative research tell us. *Child Abuse & Neglect, 11*(3), 433–442.

Connelly, C. D., & Straus, M. A. (1992). Mother's age and risk for physical abuse. *Child Abuse and Neglect, 16*(5), 709–718.

Coohey, C. (1996). Child maltreatment: Testing the social isolation hypothesis. *Child Abuse and Neglect, 20*(3), 241–251.

Coulton, C. J., Korbin, J. E., Su, M., & Chow, J. (1995). Community level factors and child maltreatment rates. *Child Development, 66,* 1262–1276.

Course, S. J., Schmid, K., & Trickett, P. K. (1990). Social network characteristics of mothers in abusing and nonabusing families and their relationships to parenting beliefs. *Journal of Community Psychology, 18*(1), 44–59.

Cox, A. D., Puckering, C., Pound, A., & Mills, M. (1987). The impact of maternal depression in young children. *Journal of Child Psychology, Psychiatry and Allied Disciplines, 28*(6), 917–928.

Crittenden, P. M. (1985). Social networks, quality of child rearing, and child development. *Child Development, 56,* 1299–1313.

Crittenden, P. M. (1998). Dangerous behavior and dangerous contexts: A 35-year perspective on research on the developmental effects of child physical abuse. In P. K. Trickett & C. J. Schellenbach (Eds.), *Violence against children in the family and the community* (pp. 11–38). Washington, DC: American Psychological Association Press.

Culp, R. E., Culp, A. M., Soulis, J., & Letts, D. (1989). Self-esteem and depression in abusive, neglecting, and nonmaltreating mothers. *Infant Mental Health Journal, 10*(4), 243–251.

Culp, R. E., Heide, J. S., & Richardson, M. T. (1987). Maltreated children's developmental scores: Treatment versus nontreatment. *Child Abuse and Neglect, 11,* 29–34.

Culp, R. E., Little, V., Letts, D., & Lawrence, H. (1991). Maltreated children's self-concept: Effects of a comprehensive treatment program. *American Journal of Orthopsychiatry, 61*(1), 114–121.

Cummings, E. M., Hennessy, K. D., Rabideau G. J., & Cicchetti, D. (1994). Responses of physically abused boys to interadult anger involving their mother. *Development & Psychopathology, 6,* 31–41.

Daro, D., & Harding, K. (1999). Healthy Families America: Using research to enhance practice. *The Future of Children, 9*(1), 152–176.

DePanfilis, D., & Salus, M. K. (1992). *Child protective services: A guide for caseworkers.* Washington, DC: U.S. Department of Health and Human Services.

Dodge, K. A., Pettit, G. S., & Bates, J. E. (1994). Effects of physical maltreatment on the development of peer relations. *Development and Psychopathology, 6*(10), 43–56.

Drake, B., & Pandey, S. (1996). Understanding the relationship between neighborhood poverty and specific types of child maltreatment. *Child Abuse and Neglect, 20*(11), 1003–1018.

Drotar, D. (1992). Prevention of neglect and nonorganic failure to thrive. In D. J. Willis, E. W. Holden, & M. Rosenberg (Eds.), *Prevention of child maltreatment: Developmental and ecological perspectives* (pp. 115–149). New York: John Wiley.

Dubowitz, H., & Guterman, N. B. (in press). Preventing child neglect and physical abuse. In A. Giardino (Ed.), *Child maltreatment—A clinical guide and reference,* 3rd ed. Maryland Heights, MO: GW Medical Publishing.

Duggan, A. K., McFarlane, E. C., Windham, A. M., Rohde, C. A., Salkever, D. S., Fuddy, L., Rosenberg, L. A., Buchbinder, S. B., & Sia, C. J. (1999). Evaluation of Hawaii's Healthy Start Program. *The Future of Children, 9*(1), 66–91.

Durrant, J. E. (1999). Evaluating the success of Sweden's corporal punishment ban. *Child Abuse and Neglect, 23*(5), 435–448.

Dykes, L. (1986). The whiplash shaken infant syndrome: What has been learned? *Child Abuse & Neglect, 10,* 211–221.

Dykman, R. A., McPherson, B., Ackerman, P. T., Newton, J. E., Mooney, D. M, Wherry, J., & Chaffin, M. (1997). Internalizing and externalizing characteristics of sexually and/or physically abused children. *Integrative Physiological & Behavioral Science, 32*(1), 62–74.

Egeland, B., Jacovitz, D., & Sroufe, L. A. (1988). Breaking the cycle of abuse. *Child Development, 59,* 1080–1088.

Egeland, B., & Sroufe, L. A. (1981). Attachment and early maltreatment. *Child Development, 52,* 44–52.

Ellis, R. H., & Milner, J. S. (1981). Child abuse and locus of control. *Psychological Reports, 48*(2), 507–510.

Elmer, E. (1967). *Children in jeopardy.* Pittsburgh: University of Pittsburgh Press.

Ethier, L. S., Lacharite, C., & Couture, G. (1995). Childhood adversity, parental stress, and depression of negligent mothers. *Child Abuse & Neglect, 19*(5), 619–632.

Fantuzzo, J. W. (1990). Behavioral treatment of the victims of child abuse and neglect. *Behavior Modification, 14,* 316–339.

Fantuzzo, J., Jurecic, L., Stovall, A., Hightower, A. D., Goins, C., & Schachtel, D. (1988). Effects of adult and peer social initiations on the social behavior of withdrawn, maltreated preschool children. *Journal of Consulting and Clinical Psychology, 56*(1), 34–39.

Fantuzzo, J., Sutton-Smith, B., Atkins, M., Meyers, R., Stevenson, H. H., Coolahan, K., Weiss, A., & Manz, P. (1996). Community-based resilient peer treatment of withdrawn maltreated preschool children. *Journal of Consulting and Clinical Psychology, 64*(6), 1377–1386.

Field, T. (1992). Infants of depressed mothers. *Development and Psychopathology, 4*(1), 49–66.

Field, T. (1998). Maternal depression: Effects on infants and early intervention. *Preventive Medicine: An International Devoted to Practice & Theory, 27*(2), 200–203.

Fischler, R. S. (1985). Child abuse and neglect in American Indian communities. *Child Abuse & Neglect, 9,* 95–106.

Fisher, P. A., & Chamberlain, P. (2000). Multidimensional treatment foster care: A program for intensive parenting, family support, and skill building. *Journal of Emotional and Behavioral Disorders, 8*(3), 155–164.

Fisher, P. A., Ellis, B. H., & Chamberlain, P. (1999). Early intervention foster care: A model for preventing risk in young children who have been maltreated. *Children's Services: Social Policy, Research, and Practice, 2*(3), 159–182.

Fisher, P. A., Gunnar, M. R., Chamberlain, P., & Reid, J. B. (2000). Preventive intervention for maltreated preschool children: Impact on children's behavior, neuroendocrine activity, and foster parent functioning. *Journal of the American Academy of Child and Adolescent Psychiatry, 39*(11), 1356–1364.

Frank, Y., Zimmerman, R., & Leeds, N. M. (1985). Neurological manifestations in abused children who have been shaken. *Developmental Medicine & Child Neurology, 27*(3), 312–316.

Gaensbauer, T. J., & Mrazek, D. A. (1981). Differences in the patterning of affective expression in infants. *Journal of the American Academy of Child and Adolescent Psychiatry, 20*, 673–691.

Garbarino, J. (1977, November). The human ecology of child maltreatment: A conceptual model for research. *Journal of Marriage and the Family*, 721–735.

Garbarino, J. (1980). *Protecting children from abuse and neglect: Developing and maintaining effective support systems for families.* San Francisco: Jossey-Bass.

Gaudin, J. M., Wodarski, J. S., Arkinson, M. K., & Avery, L. S. (1990–91). Remedying child neglect: Effectiveness of social network interventions. *Journal of Applied Social Sciences, 15*, 97–123.

George, C. (1996). A representational perspective of child abuse and prevention: Internal working models of attachment and caregiving. *Child Abuse and Neglect, 20*(5), 411–424.

Gray, E., & Cosgrove, J. (1985). Ethnocentric perception of childrearing practices in protective services. *Child Abuse & Neglect, 9*, 389–396.

Guterman, N. B. (1999). Enrollment strategies in early home visitation to prevent physical child abuse and neglect and the "universal versus targeted" debate: A meta-analysis of population-based and screening-based programs, *Child Abuse and Neglect, 23*(9), 863–890.

Guterman, N. B. (2000). *Stopping child maltreatment before it starts: Emerging horizons in early home visitation services,* Thousand Oaks, CA: Sage.

Guterman, N. B. (2001, June). *Strengthening early home visitation through parental empowerment and informal network development.* Presented at the Eighth Annual Colloquium of the American Professional Society on the Abuse of Children, Washington, DC.

Gynn-Orenstein, J. S. (1981). The relationship between moral reasoning, locus of control, emotional empathy, and parenting profile in physically abusing mothers. *Dissertation Abstracts International, 42*(5-B), 2056–2057.

Hampton, R. L., & Newberger, E. H. (1985). Child abuse incidence and reporting by hospitals: Significance of severity, class, and race. *American Journal of Public Health, 75*(1), 56–60.

Henggeler, S. W., Schoenwald, S. K., Borduin, C. M., Rowland, M. D., & Cunningham, P. B. (1998). *Multisystemic treatment of antisocial behavior in children and adolescents.* New York: Guilford Press.

Herrenkohl, R., & Herrenkohl, E. (1981). Some antecedents and developmental consequences of child maltreatment. In R. Rizley & D. Cicchetti (Eds.), *New directions for child development, development perspectives on child maltreatment* (pp. 57–76). San Francisco: Jossey-Bass.

Hillson, J. M. C., & Kupier, N. A. (1994). A stress and coping model of child maltreatment, *Clinical Psychology Review, 14*(4), 261–285.

Hoffman-Plotkin, D., & Twentyman, C. (1984). A multimodal assessment of behavioral cognitive deficits in abused and neglected preschoolers. *Child Development, 55*, 794–802.

Ito, Y., Teicher, M. H., Glod, C. A., Harper, D., Magnus, E., & Gelbard, H. A. (1993). Increased prevalence of electrophysiological abnormalities in children with psychological, physical, and sexual abuse. *Journal of Neuropsychiatry & Clinical Neurosciences, 5*(4), 401–408.

Jason, J., Amereuh, N., Marks, J., & Tyler, C. (1982). Child abuse in Georgia: A method to evaluate risk factors and reporting bias. *American Journal of Public Health, 72*(12), 1353–1358.

Justice, B., Calvert, A., & Justice, R. (1985). Factors mediating child abuse as a response to stress. *Child Abuse and Neglect, 9*(3), 359–363.

Kaufman, J., & Cicchetti, D. (1989). The effects of maltreatment on school-aged children's socioemotional development: Assessments in a day camp setting. *Developmental Psychology, 15*, 516–524.

Kazdin, A., Moser, J., Colbus, D., & Bell, R. (1985). Depressive symptoms among physically abused and psychiatrically disturbed children. *Journal of Abnormal Psychology, 94*, 298–307.

Kinard, E. M. (1979). The psychological consequences of abuse for the child. *Journal of Social Issues*, 82–100.

Kitzman, H., Olds, D. L., Henderson, C. R., Hanks, C., Cole, R., Tatelbaum, R., Mcconnochie, K. M., Sidora, K., Luckey, D. W., Shaver, D., Engelhart, K., James, D., & Barnard, K. (1997). Effect of prenatal and infancy home visitation by nurses on pregnancy outcomes, childhood injuries, and repeated childbearing. *Journal of the American Medical Association, 278*(8), 644–652.

Kolko, D. (1992). Characteristics of child victims of physical violence: Research findings and clinical implications. *Journal of Interpersonal Violence, 7*(2), 244–276.

Kolko, D. (1996a). Individual cognitive behavioral treatment and family therapy for physically abused children and their offending parents: A comparison of clinical outcomes. *Child Maltreatment, 1* (4), 322–342.

Kolko, D. (1996b). Clinical monitoring of treatment course in child physical abuse: Psychometric characteristics and treatment outcomes. *Child Abuse and Neglect, 20*(1), 23–43.

Kolko, D. (1998). Treatment and intervention for child victims of violence. In P. Trickett & C. Schellenbach (Eds.), *Violence against children in the family and the community.* Washington, DC: American Psychological Association.

Kolko, D. J., Kazdin, A. E., Thomas, A. M., & Day, B. (1993). Heightened child physical abuse potential: Child, parent, and family dysfunction. *Journal of Interpersonal Violence, 8*(2), 169–192.

Korbin, J. (1994). Sociocultural factors in child maltreatment. In G. B. Melton & F. D. Barry (Eds.), *Protecting children from abuse and neglect: Foundations for a new national strategy* (pp. 182–223). New York: Guilford.

Kotch, J. B., Browne, D. C., Dufort, V., & Winsor, J. (1999). Predicting child maltreatment in the first 4 years of life from characteristics assessed in the neonatal period. *Child Abuse & Neglect, 23*(4), 305–319.

Kotch, J. B., Browne, D. C., Ringwalt, C. L., & Stewart, P. W. (1995). Risk of child abuse or neglect in a cohort of low-income children. *Child Abuse & Neglect, 19*(9), 1115–1130.

Kotelchuck, M. (1982). Child abuse and neglect: Prediction and misclassification. In R. Starr (Ed.), *Child abuse prediction: Policy implications* (pp. 67–104). Cambridge, MA: Ballinger.

Krugman, R. D. (1985). Fatal child abuse: Analysis of 24 cases. *Pediatrician, 12*, 68–72.

Lancon, J. A., Haines, D. E., & Parent, A. D. (1998). Anatomy of the shaken baby syndrome. *Anatomical Record, 253*(1), 13–18.

Larner, M. B., Stevenson, C. S., & Behrman, R. E. (1998). Protecting children from abuse and neglect: Analysis and recommendations. *The Future of Children, 8*(1), 4–22.

Lauderdale, M., Valiunas, A., & Anderson, R. (1980). Race, ethnicity, and child maltreatment: An empirical analysis. *Child Abuse and Neglect, 4*(3), 163–169.

Laurendeau, M., Gagnon, G., Desjardins, M., Perreault, R., & Kischuk, N. (1991). Evaluation of an early, mass media parental support intervention. *Journal of Primary Prevention, 11*(3), 207–225.

Lewis, D. O. (1992). From abuse to violence: Psychological consequences of maltreatment. *Journal of the American Academy of Child and Adolescent Psychiatry, 31*(3), 383–391.

Lindsey, D. (1994). *The welfare of children.* New York: Oxford University Press.

Lovell, M. L., & Hawkins, J. D. (1988). An evaluation of a group intervention to increase the personal social networks of abusive mothers. *Children and Youth Services Review, 10,* 175–188.

Lutzker, J. (1984). Project Twelve Ways: Treating child abuse and neglect from an ecobehavioral perspective. In R. F. Dangel & R. Polster (Eds.), *Parent training: Foundations of research and practice.* New York: Guilford Press.

Lutzker, J., Bigelow, K. M., Doctor, R. M., & Kessler, M. L. (1998). Safety, health care, and bonding within an ecobehavioral approach to treating and preventing child abuse and neglect. *Journal of Family Violence, 13*(2), 163–185.

MacLeod, J., & Nelson, G. (2000). Programs for the promotion of family wellness and the prevention of child maltreatment: A meta-analytic review. *Child Abuse and Neglect, 24*(9), 1127–1149.

Main, M., & George, C. (1985). Response of abused and disadvantaged toddlers to distress in agitates: A study in the daycare setting. *Developmental Psychology, 21,* 407–412.

Main, M., & Solomon, C. (1986). Discovery of a new insecure-disorganized, disoriented attachment pattern. In T. B. Brazelton & M. Yogman (Eds.), *Affective development in infancy* (pp. 95–12). Norwood, NJ: Ablex.

Malinosky-Rummell, R., & Hansen, D. J. (1993). Long-term consequences of childhood physical abuse. *Psychological Bulletin, 114*(1), 68–79.

Margolin, L. (1992). Child abuse by mothers' boyfriends: Why the overrepresentation? *Child Abuse and Neglect, 16,* 541–551.

Maxfield, M. G., & Widom, C. S. (1996). The cycle of violence. Revisited 6 years later. *Archives of Pediatrics & Adolescent Medicine, 150*(4), 390–395.

McCurdy, K. & Daro, D. (1993). *Current trends in child abuse reporting and fatalities: The results of the 1992 annual fifty state survey.* Chicago: National Committee for the Prevention of Child Abuse.

McDonald, T. P., & Marks, J. (1991). A review of risk factors assessed in child protective services, *Social Services Review, 65,* 112–132.

McKibben, L., De Vos, E., & Newberger, E. H. (1991). Victimization of mothers of abused children: A controlled study. In R. L. Hampton (Ed.), *Black family violence* (pp. 75–83). Lexington, MA: Lexington Books.

Meezan, W., & O'Keefe, M. (1998). Evaluating the effectiveness of multifamily group therapy in child abuse and neglect. *Research on Social Work Practice, 8*(3), 330–353.

Milner, J. S., & Crouch, J. L. (1998). Physical child abuse: Theory and research. In R. Hampton (Ed.), Family violence prevention and treatment (2nd ed.). Newbury Park, CA: Sage.

Money J. (1977). The syndrome of abuse dwarfism (psychosocial dwarfism or reversible hyposomatotropism). *American Journal of Diseases of Children, 131*(5), 508–513.

Mrazek, P. J. (1993). Maltreatment and infant development. In C. H. Zeanah, Jr. (Ed.), *Handbook of infant mental health* (pp.159–170). New York: Guilford Press.

Murphy, J., Jellineck, M., Quinn, D., & Smith, G. (1991). Substance abuse and serious child maltreatment: Prevalence, risk, and outcome in a court sample. *Child Abuse and Neglect, 15,* 197–211.

Murray, L., Fiori-Crowley, A., Hooper, R., & Cooper, P. (1996). The impact of postnatal depression and associated adversity on early mother-infant interations and later infant outcomes. *Child Development, 67*(5), 2512–2526.

Nair, P., Black, M. M., Schuler, M., Keane, V., Snow, L., Rigney, B. A., & Magder, L. (1997). Risk factors for disruption in primary caregiving among infants of substance abusing women. *Child Abuse & Neglect, 21*(11), 1039–1051.

National Committee to Prevent Child Abuse. (1996). The relationship between parental alcohol or other drug problems and child maltreatment. *NCPCA Fact Sheet #14.* Chicago.

National Research Council. (1993). *Understanding child abuse and neglect.* Washington, DC: National Academy Press.

Nurius, P. S., Lovell, M., & Maggie, E. (1988). Self-appraisals of abusive parents: A contextual approach to study and treatment. *Journal of Interpersonal Violence, 3*(4), 458–467.

Oates, K., & Bross, D. (1995). What have we learned about treating child physical abuse? A literature review of the last decade. *Child Abuse and Neglect, 19*(4), 463–473.

Oates, R. K., Forrest, D., & Peacock, A. (1985). Self-esteem of abused children. *Child Abuse and Neglect, 9,* 159–163.

Okun, A., & Parker, J. G. (1994). Distinctive and interactive contributions of physical abuse, socioeconomic disadvantage, and negative life events to children's social, cognitive, and affective adjustment. *Development & Psychopathology, 6,* 77–98.

Olds, D. (1982). The prenatal/early infancy project: An ecological approach to prevention. In J. Belsky (Ed.), *In the beginning: Readings in infancy* (pp. 270–285). New York: Columbia University Press.

Olds, D. L., Eckenrode, J., Henderson, C. R., Kitzman, H., Powers, J., Cole, R., Sidora, K., Morris, P., Pettitt, L. M., & Luckey, D. (1997). Long-term effects of home visitation on maternal life course and child abuse and neglect: Fifteen year follow-up of a randomized trial. *Journal of the American Medical Association, 278*(8), 637–643.

Olds, D., Henderson, C. R., Kitzman, H. J., Eckenrode, J. J., Cole, R. E., & Tatelbaum, R. C. (1999). Prenatal and infancy home visitation by nurses: Recent findings. *The Future of Children, 9*(1), 44–65.

Osofsky, J. D., Wewers, S., Hamn, D. M., & Fick, A. C. (1993). Chronic community violence: What is happening to our children? *Psychiatry, 56,* 36–45.

Patterson, G. (1982). *Coercive family process.* Eugene, OR: Castalia.

Patterson, G., Reid, J. B., & Dishion, T. J. (1992). *A social learning approach 4: Antisocial boys.* Eugene, OR: Castalia.

Peddle, N., & Wang, C. T. (2001). *Current trends in child abuse prevention, reporting, and fatalities: The 1999 fifty state survey*. Chicago: Prevent Child Abuse America.

Pelton, L. (1994). The role of material factors in child abuse and neglect. In G. B. Melton & F. D. Berry (Eds.), *Protecting children from abuse and neglect: Foundations for a new national strategy*, (pp. 131–181). New York: Guilford Press.

Perry, B. D., Pollard, R. A., Blakeley, T. L., Baker, W. L., & Vigilante, D. (1995). Childhood trauma, the neurobiology of adaptation and use-dependent development of the brain: How states become traits. *Infant Mental Health Journal, 16*(4), 271–291.

Perry, M. A., Doran, L. D. & Wells, E. A. (1983). Developmental and behavioral characteristics of the physically abused child. *Journal of Clinical Child Psychology, 12,* 320–324.

Polansky, N. A., Chalmers, M. A., Buttenwieser, E., & Williams, D. P. (1981). *Damaged parents: An anatomy of child neglect*. Chicago: University of Chicago Press.

Pruitt, D. L., & Erickson, M. R. (1985). The child abuse potential inventory: A study of concurrent validity. *Journal of Clinical Psychology, 41,* 104–111.

Rafael, T., & Pion-Berlin, L. (1999, April). Parents Anonymous: Strengthening families. *Juvenile Justice Bulletin*. Washington DC: Office of Juvenile Justice and Delinquency Prevention.

Reid, J. B., & Patterson, G. R. (1989). The development of antisocial behaviour patterns in childhood and adolescence. *European Journal of Personality, 3*(2), 107–119.

Richters, J. E., & Martinez, P. (1993). The NIMH Community Violence Project: I. Children as victims and witnesses to violence. *Psychiatry, 56,* 7–21.

Ritchie, J., & Ritchie, J. (1981). Child rearing and child abuse: The Polynesian context. In J. Korbin (Ed.), *Child abuse and neglect: Cross-cultural perspectives* (pp. 186–294). Berkeley, CA: University of California Press.

Rodriguez, C. M., & Green, A. J. (1997). Parenting stress and anger expression as predictors of child abuse potential. *Child Abuse & Neglect, 21*(4), 367–377.

Rossi, P. (1992). Assessing family preservation programs. *Children and Youth Services Review, 14,* 77–97.

Salzinger, S., Kaplan, S., & Artemyeff, C. (1983). Mothers' personal social networks and child maltreatment. *Journal of Abnormal Psychology, 92*(1), 68–76.

Salzinger, S., Kaplan, S., Pelcovitz, D., Samit, C., & Krieger, R. (1984). Parent and teacher assessment of children's behavior in child maltreating families. *Journal of the American Academy of Child Psychiatry, 23,* 458–464.

Schinke, S. P., Schilling, R. F., Barth, R. P., Gilchrist, L. D., & Maxwell, J. S. (1986). Stress-management intervention to prevent family violence. *Journal of Family Violence, 1*(1), 13–26.

Sedlack, A. J., & Broadhurst, D. D. (1996). *Third national incidence study of child abuse and neglect: Final report*. Washington, DC: U.S. Department of Health and Human Services.

Seligman, M. E. P. (1975). *Helplessness: On Depression, Development, and Death*. San Fransisco: W. H. Freeman.

Showers, J. (1992). "Don't shake the baby": The effectiveness of a prevention program. *Child Abuse and Neglect, 16*(1), 11–18.

Silverman, A. B., Reinherz, H. Z., & Giaconia, R. M. (1996). The long-term sequelae of child and adolescent abuse: A longitudinal community study. *Child Abuse & Neglect, 20*(8), 709–723.

Solheim, J. S. (1982). A cross-cultural examination of use of corporal punishment on children: A focus on Sweden and the United States. *Child Abuse & Neglect, 6*(2), 147–154.

Spearly J., & Lauderdale, M. (1983). Community characteristics and ethnicity in the prediction of child maltreatment rates. *Child Abuse and Neglect, 7,* 91–105.

Stark, E., & Flitcraft, A. H. (1988). Women and children at risk: A feminist perspective on child abuse. *International Journal of Health Services, 18,* 97–118.

Straus, M., & Kantor, G. (1986). Stress and child abuse. In R. Helfer & R. S. Kempe (Eds.), *The battered child* (4th ed., pp. 42–59). Chicago: University of Chicago Press.

Straus, M. A., & Smith, C. (1992). Family patterns and child abuse. In M. A. Straus & R. J. Gelles (Eds.), *Physical violence in American families* (pp. 245–262). New Brunswick, NJ: Transaction Publishers.

Stringer, S. A., & LaGreca, A. M. (1985). Correlates of child abuse potential, *Journal of Abnormal Child Psychology, 13*(2), 217–226.

Teicher, M. H., Ito, Y., Glod, C. A., Schiffer, F., & Gelbard, H. A. (1996). Neurophysiological mechanisms of stress response in children. In C. R. Pfeffer (Ed.), *Severe stress and mental disturbance in children* (pp.59–84). Washington, DC: American Psychiatric Press.

Trickett, P. K., & Schellenbach, C. J. (Eds.). (1998). *Violence against children in the family and the community*. Washington, DC: American Psychological Association.

U.S. Department of Health and Human Services. (1993). *A report to Congress 1993: Study of child maltreatment in alcohol abusing families*. Washington, DC: Administration for Children and Families, National Center on Child Abuse and Neglect.

U.S. Department of Health and Human Services, (1999). *Blending perspectives and building common ground: A report to Congress on substance abuse and child protection*. Washington, DC: U.S. Government Printing Office.

U.S. Department of Health and Human Services, Administration on Children, Youth and Families. (2001). *Child maltreatment, 1999: Reports from the states to the National Child Abuse and Neglect Data System*. Washington, DC: Government Printing Office.

Watson-Perczel, M., Lutzker, J., Greene, B. F., & McGimpsey, B. J. (1988). Assessment and modification of home cleanliness among families adjudicated for child neglect. *Behavior Modification, 12*(1), 57–81.

Widom, C. S. (1989). The cycle of violence. *Science, 244*(4901), 160–166.

Widom, C. S., & White, H. R. (1997). Problem behaviours in abused and neglected children grown up: Prevalence and co-occurrence of substance abuse, crime and violence. *Criminal Behaviour & Mental Health, 7*(4), 287–310.

Wiehe, V. (1986). Empathy and locus of control in child abusers. *Journal of Social Service Research, 9*, 2–3, 17–30.

Wolfe, D.A., & Wekerle, C. (1993). Treatment strategies for child physical abuse and neglect: A critical progress report. *Clinical Psychology Review, 13*(6), 473–500.

Wong, E. (1999, January 27). Oakland panel rejects no-spanking proposal. *Los Angeles Times*, p. A3.

Young, L. (1964). *Wednesday's children: A study of child neglect and abuse*. New York: McGraw-Hill.

Zuravin, S. J. (1989). The ecology of child abuse and neglect: Review of the literature and presentation of data. *Violence and Victims, 4*(2), 101–120.

Zuravin, S., McMillen, C., DePanfilis, D., & Risley-Curtiss, C. (1996). The intergenerational cycle of child maltreatment: Continuity versus discontinuity. *Journal of Interpersonal Violence, 11*(3), 315–334.

CHAPTER 8

SEXUAL ABUSE OF CHILDREN AND ADOLESCENTS

SANDRA J. KAPLAN

*North Shore University Hospital
and New York University School of Medicine*

The sexual abuse of children and adolescents is a major public health problem. In 1998, 1.6 per 1,000 U.S. children and adolescents (a total of 103,845) were sexually abused (United States Department of Health and Human Services [USDHHS], 2000). During the past two decades, research has clarified correlates of sexual abuse and studied the efficacy of assessment and treatment approaches. Organizations of mental health professionals have developed guidelines for the care of sexually abused children, and these advances have informed clinical practice.

DEFINITION AND INCIDENCE

There are three major sources of national epidemiological data on child maltreatment: the Third National Incidence Study (NIS-3; U.S. Department of Health and Human Services, 1996), the Reports from the States to the National Child Abuse and Neglect Data System (NCANDS; USDHHS, 2000), and population surveys (Finkelhor, Moore, Hamby, & Strauss, 1997). The NIS-3 provides the definition of sexual abuse used throughout this chapter:

> Child and adolescent sexual abuse involves a child under 18 years of age having experienced one of the following types of sexual acts: intrusion defined as evidence of oral, anal, or genital penile penetration or anal or genital digital or other penetration; molestation with genital contact, but without evidence of intrusion; or other acts which were not known to have involved genital contact with areas of a child's body (e.g., fondling of breasts or buttocks, exposure) or inadequate or inappropriate supervision of sexual activities when the perpetrator was a parent, parent substitute, or other.

The NIS-3 sampled child protective services, law enforcement, juvenile probation, public health, hospital, school, day-care, mental health, and social service agencies in counties throughout the United States for three months in 1993. It reported increased incidence of sexual abuse compared to the two previous incidence studies of 1980 and 1986. It estimated the rate to be 217,700 (3.2 per 1,000), compared to 119,200 (1.9 per 1,000) in 1986, and 42,900 (0.7 per 1,000) in 1980. In 1993, girls were estimated to have been targets of sexual abuse more often than boys (4.9 per 1,000, compared to 1.6 per 1,000) (USDHHS, 1996).

The more recent Reports from the States to the National Child Abuse and Neglect Data System (USCHHS, 2000) presents data collected for 1998 by state child protective service agencies, but not from multiple agencies, as did the NIS-3. The NCANDS report estimates that 1.6 per 1,000 children and adolescents in the United States (a total of 103,845) were documented by child protective services as having been sexually abused, representing 11.5 percent of the total 903,000 documented children and adolescent maltreatment cases. Again, girls were more often the target than boys, 2.3 versus 0.6 per 1,000, respectively. Male parents, male relatives, or other males acting alone were perpetrators in more than half (55.9 percent) the cases documented that year, and 29 percent involved females as perpetrators. Approximately 4 percent of children were sexually abused by female parents acting alone, and in 12 percent of cases, both parents were perpetrators. The average ages of sexual abuse victims were 10.4 years for girls and 8.6 years for boys.

Population surveys represent the third major source of national epidemiological child abuse data. During a national survey of the child disciplinary practices of 1,000 parents (Finkelhor et al., 1997), 5.7 percent reported that their children had been sexually abused at any time prior to the survey, and 1.9 percent reported that their children had been sexually abused in the year prior to the survey. Sexual abuse was reported as equal in frequency for boys and girls. Sexual abuse cases included in this survey were more likely to have been disclosed if parents had been sexually abused themselves, were from lower socioeconomic groups, or were from single-parent families.

RISK FACTORS FOR CHILD SEXUAL ABUSE

Risk factors for child sexual abuse found during a survey of women age 21 and older include maternal and paternal alcohol abuse, perceptions of mothers and fathers as rejecting and not nurturing, and not having lived with both biological parents prior to age 16 (Vogeltanz et al., 1999). The cases of sexual abuse documented in the 1998 Survey of Child Protective Services revealed that risk factors for child sex abuse included female gender, and being approximately age 10 years if a female target and approximately age 9 years if a male target (USDHHS, 2000). As mentioned, in their survey of disciplinary practices, Finkelhor and colleagues (1997) found lower socioeconomic status, single parenthood, and parental history of childhood sexual abuse to be risk factors for the sexual abuse of children.

The phenomenon of recantation of child sexual abuse allegations made by the child or adolescent tempers how we view the epidemiological studies, as well as possible opportunities for protective and therapeutic interventions for children and adolescents. Bradley and Wood (1996) found that of 249 state-validated child sexual abuse cases, 4 percent were recanted following disclosure of abuse. Pressure from a caregiver was found to have occurred in half of these cases. Gonzalez and colleagues (1993) reported that 27 percent of children who disclosed sexual abuse in therapy later recanted.

CLINICAL ASPECTS

All children and adolescents suspected of being sexually abused require assessments, which include physical examinations by clinicians with training in forensic data collection and interviews by persons with special training in methods of interviewing that do not predispose the child to confirm abuse when it has not taken place. After confirmation of sexual abuse, children and adolescents and their caregivers should have comprehensive mental health evaluations to define problems and obtain any needed interventions.

Findings on Physical Examination, Biochemical and Physiological Test Results

At the physical examination, children who have been sexually abused may have some or all of the following signs: abrasions or bruises of the external genitalia, distortion or attenuation of the hymen, alterations in anorectal tone, sexually transmissible diseases, and pregnancy (American Medical Association, 1994). However, it is important to understand that because fondling is the most prevalent form of child sexual abuse, most often there are no physical findings.

There have been few studies of the biological correlates of abuse that have included children or adolescents as subjects. Herman-Giddens, Sandler, and Friedman (1988) have reported earlier onset of menarche among girls who have been sexually abused than among those who have not, and Kendall-Tackett and Simon (1988) found that adult women who reported childhood sexual abuse also reported earlier onset of menarche. Sexual abuse has been associated with changed hormone levels and fluctuations of both the hypothalamic-pituitary-adrenal axis (HPA) and the hypothalamic-pituitary-gonadal axis (HPG). Putnam and colleagues (1991) reported higher morning cortisol levels in girls who had been sexually abused than in those who had not, and De Bellis and colleagues (1994) found increased urinary secretion of the catecholamine homovanillic acid.

Adults with post-traumatic stress disorder (PTSD), the most common psychiatric diagnosis among victims of abuse, have been found to respond to chronic trauma with a state of hyperarousal, including increased heart rate (Pitman, Van Der Kolk, Orr, & Greenber, 1990). Ito and associates (1993) found more frontotemporal and anterior region brain electrophysiological abnormalities on electroencephalograph (EEG) among physically or sexually abused children admitted to child and adolescent psychiatric in-patient services than among those who had not suffered abuse.

Psychiatric, Scholastic, and Social Findings

Child sexual abuse increases risk for several childhood and adolescent psychiatric diagnoses: Major Depressive Disorders (Flisher et al., 1997), Conduct Disorder (Livingston et al., 1993), and Somatization Disorder (Pribor, Yutzy, Dean, & Wetzel, 1993). It has also been linked to disordered eating behavior, particularly bulimia (Douzinas, Fornari, Goodman, Sitnick, & Packman, 1994). Kendall-Tackett and colleagues (1993) reviewed the literature on the effects of child sexual abuse and found that between 21 and 36 percent of victims showed no short-term symptoms, but the remaining children showed varied patterns of symptoms. These included (in descending order of frequency) sexualized behaviors, PTSD, poor self-esteem, anxiety, fear, depression, suicidal ideation, somatic complaints, aggressive behavior, running away, and substance abuse. Additionally, some authors have reported on the relationship between child sexual abuse and Dissociative Identity Disorder (DID)(Ross, 1994; Putnam, 1991; Miller, 1989; Putnam, Zahn, & Post, 1990).

Sexualized Behaviors.   Problems with the modulation of sexual impulses have been reported frequently in victims of sexual abuse. Sexually abused children (Friedrich, 1993) and adolescents (Trickett & Putnam, 1993) have been found to differ significantly in their displays of sexual behaviors and attitudes from peers who have not been abused. The severity of sexualized behavioral problems associated with sexual abuse is increased if physical as well as sexual abuse occurred (Friedrich, 1997).

PTSD.   Wolfe, Sas, and Wekerle (1994) found Post-Traumatic Stress Disorder to be the most consistently reported diagnosis associated with childhood sexual abuse victimization, as did Avery, Massat, and Lundy (2000). Herman (1992) noted that the constellations of symptoms and severity of impairment are frequently not sufficient to warrant a *DSM-IV-TR* (APA, 2000) diagnosis of PTSD, but that victims of sexual abuse often present with a constellation of symptoms similar to those of victims of other types of interpersonal trauma. Herman and Van Der Kolk (1994) have described this constellation as Complex PTSD, which may include difficulties with affect regulation, self-concept, dissociative symptoms, relations with others, and somatization.

Livingston, Lawson, and Jones (1993) found that the likelihood of an abused child developing PTSD is predicted by the total number of family-related stressors to which he or she was exposed. Mannarino and Cohen (1996) identified family adaptability and the intensity of parental response to the disclosure of sexual abuse as predictors of the intensity of the child's symptoms. Fering, Taska, and Lewis (1999) noted that increased severity of emotional and behavioral symptoms is associated with adolescent age at the time of sexual abuse.

Poor Self-Esteem, Anxiety, Fear, and Somatic Complaints.   Sexually abused children appear to have "impaired" self-concepts, and this is more evident in older children than younger children (Barnett, Vondra, & Shonk, 1995; Cole & Putnam, 1992). Spacarelli (1994) reported self-blame for abuse. Friedrich (1994) has hypothesized that the increased somatic symptomatology of survivors of both childhood physical and sexual abuse (e.g., Leserman et al., 1996) is related to the heightened and distorted focus on the physical self that follows sexually abusive experiences.

Depression and Suicidal Ideation.   Koverola, Pound, Hagger, and Lytle (1993) identified a relationship between childhood depression and sexual abuse, and Zuravin and Fontanella (1999) noted that for girls it is a risk factor for depression in adulthood. Several researchers have reported increased suicidal behavior among survivors of intrafamilial sexual abuse (Dinwiddie et al., 2000; Wozencraft, Wagner, & Pellegrin, 1991).

Aggressive and Risk-Taking Behavior.   Sexual abuse is linked to increased aggressive behaviors among adolescent victims (Fergusson & Horwood, 1999) and among adults who were sexually abused as children (Widom & Ames, 1994). Lewis (1992) hypothesized that child physical or sexual abuse exacerbates preexisting psychobiological vulnerabilities. Cicchetti (1991) has hypothesized that increased risk taking by abused children is related to the difficulties they have modulating their arousal levels. Riggs and McHorney (1990) documented that sexually abused (and physically abused) children and adolescents are more likely to take part in high-risk behaviors, such as cigarette smoking and alcohol and drug abuse than peers who have not suffered abuse. Johnson (1996) found that people who had been abused as children had greater numbers of sexual partners, earlier onset of sexual activity, and more frequent unprotected sex.

Dissociative Identity Disorder.   Over 90 percent of adults who carried a diagnosis of Dissociative Identity Disorder (formerly Multiple Personality Disorder, MPD) are reported to have had histories of physical or sexual abuse (Ross 1994), and Putnam and colleagues have found that traumatic amnesia and dissociation are responses associated with sexual abuse. The most common symptoms of dissociation in childhood are trance-like states, in which a child stares and is inattentive and unresponsive. Putnam (1991) has suggested that dissociation enables the child to avoid the frightening and overwhelming feelings that accompany abuse. Initially, such dissociation may be helpful to the traumatized child, but it may impede recovery by interfering with processing of the strong emotions and cognitions associated with abuse, and it also interferes with cognitive performance and can impair functioning in school.

Dissociative Identity Disorder presents with some persistent physiological responses. It has been found to be associated with changes in optical functioning (Miller, 1989), as well as varying skin conductance, respiration, skin temperature, and heart rate that coincide with changes in *personality alters* (Putnam, Zahn, & Post, 1990). Putnam (1991) also has reported different evoked potentials for visual images and electroencephelographic patterns according to *alter.*

Social Functioning.   Not surprisingly, Johnson also found that sexual abuse correlates with social problems, including fewer close friends and more conflict with parents. Hazzard and colleagues (1995) found that the relationship between mother and daughter significantly predicts internalizing and externalizing behavioral problems, and Paradise, Rose, Sleeper, and Nathanson (1994) found that the psychiatric status of the mother predicts outcomes of sexually abused children generally.

School Performance.   Children's success in school also is reduced by sexual abuse. Eckenrode, Laird, and Dorris (1993) identified impaired cognitive and language abilities and school functioning: specifically delays in verbal development, impaired academic achievement, higher rates of absenteeism, retention, and placement in special classes.

ASSESSMENT AND TREATMENT

Most mental health practitioners agree that when sexual abuse is confirmed, children and adolescents should be assessed to determine appropriate referrals for mental health treatments.

However, social service agencies and juvenile courts refer only a minority of victims for treatment (Chapman & Smith, 1987). The gap in mental health needs assessments and treatment referrals for these children may be accounted for in several ways, including a lack of available personnel in child protective services for tasks other than those that focus on assessing the needs of children for protection as well as a lack of available and affordable child mental health services dedicated to serving maltreated children and their families.

Special Issues in Interviewing Children and Adolescents When Abuse Is Suspected

Because there has been increasing recognition that, under certain circumstances, children may develop false memories of abuse (Ceci & Bruck, 1993), practitioners must be sensitive to the role that interviewing plays in work with children who may have been abused. In particular, Ceci and Bruck found that preschool children are vulnerable to confusion and false memories because of faulty interview techniques. Several studies have found that children are most likely to be misled during interviews if (1) they feel it is preferable to "guess" or "pretend" rather than to acknowledge "not knowing" (Saywitz & Moan-Hardie, 1994); (2) their memories are "weak" (Saywitz, Goodman, Nicholas, & Moan, 1991); (3) they are confused about "adult" language that does not take the child's developmental level into account (Saywitz et al., 1991); (4) the interviewer is seen as unfriendly, intimidating, or authoritarian (Goodman, Batterman-Faunce, & Kenney, 1992); or (5) the interviewer has preconceived bias about the event (Ceci & Bruck, 1993).

A general consensus exists that while using open-ended questions during interviews carries lowest risk for confusion, such questions generate the least information. Leading questions that pressure a child to agree with the interviewer, however, can lead to a permanent distortion of memory of what happened. Saywitz and Goodman (1996) reported that clinicians may profitably use questions that are more focused but that avoid leading a child reluctant to discuss abuse. For example, the question, "Tell me about your dad. What do you like about him?" may generate information that the child would otherwise not volunteer. In order to minimize suggestibility in forensic interviews, Reed (1996) has recommended that interviewers systematically clarify to children what is expected of them by teaching them to say specifically when they are confused or do not know answers to questions.

Boat and Everson (1988) and White (1991) have developed interview guidelines for use with anatomically detailed dolls that have been used to facilitate children's identification of body parts. However, no assessment techniques with anatomically correct dolls have been found to provide definitive evidence that a child has been abused. Consensus has emerged that these dolls should not be used in isolation as a diagnostic test for child sexual abuse, although some clinicians have reported that they may help children who are better able to show than to tell what happened (APSAC, 1995). Based on their research, Bruck and colleagues (1995) have recommended that these dolls be used with caution, because they have been associated with false reports of the sexual abuse of preschoolers. In addition, there is no evidence that anatomically correct dolls are superior as interview aides to anatomical drawings or regular dolls.

Psychosocial Interventions

Systematic evaluations of the effectiveness of a variety of treatments (Becker, Alpert, Big-Foot, & Bonner, 1995; Finkelhor & Berliner, 1995) have taken place during the past decade. Most of these use either cognitive-behavioral (Cohen & Mannarino, 1993, 1998; Deblinger & Heflin, 1996; Deblinger, McLeer, & Henry, 1990) or structured group psychotherapy approaches (Deluca, Hazen, & Cutler, 1993; Larzelere, Collins, & Collins, 1993). Studies report that sexually abused children show improvement in some symptoms after even a relatively brief course of treatment. After an extensive review of the empirical literature on treatment of sexually abused children, Finkelhor and Berliner (1995) conclude that, although there remains a need for large-scale randomized trials, research lends support for the effectiveness of abuse-focused directive therapies compared to less trauma-focused treatments.

Because sexually abused children may present with a wide variety of symptom patterns, further research is needed to determine the most effective treatment approaches for particular constellations of symptoms. For example, there is evidence that aggressive and sexualized behaviors may be more resistant to change than such "internalized" symptoms as depression or anxiety (Larzelere et al., 1993). Therefore, specialized treatment strategies for sexualized behaviors may be indicated (Gil & Johnson, 1993; Ryan, 1991). The optimum therapeutic intervention strategies for the approximately 40 percent of sexually abused children without demonstrable associated symptomatology (Kendall-Tackett et al., 1993) remain to be determined.

In recent years, there has been a growing consensus that the most effective therapeutic approaches in dealing with children who have been abused are those that use structured and direct approaches focused on integrating feelings related to the abuse (Finkelhor & Berliner, 1995; Friedrich, 1994; James, 1994). These trauma-focused therapies emphasize helping children to organize and express their memories, feelings, and attributions regarding the trauma in a manner that facilitates their viewing abuse as something bad that happened to them, rather than as indicating stigma or destiny.

One recent area of research offers opportunities to design effective cognitive-based therapies that focus on correcting victims' negative attributions associated with self-blame, depression, and anger regarding their traumatic experiences. Kolko and Feiring (2002) have reported that dimensions of attributions that need to be considered include locus of control (internal-external), stability, and controllability (one's ability to control the onset and offset of a particular event).

James (1994) has recommended an approach to treatment that includes having the child return at later developmental stages, as needed, for subsequent therapy. This allows the child to "work through" the meaning of trauma in light of new stages of development. Often during adolescence or adulthood, victims of childhood incest begin to understand and recognize their experience as traumatic. Consideration of the need for "booster treatments" at different developmental stages, however, needs to be balanced with the danger that long-term therapy may induce children to have permanent views of themselves as "victims."

Most therapies include parallel treatment of the parents to educate them about the effects of abuse and methods of helping their children deal with its aftermath. Abusive parents are at high risk for depression, antisocial personality disorder, and substance abuse

(Kaplan, Pelcovitz, Ganeles, & Salinger, 1990). Diagnosis and treatment of the psychiatric disorders of parents of abused children is an important component of the child's treatment. As mentioned earlier, the mother's psychiatric status has an important effect on behaviors and outcomes, particularly for girls.

Medications

Few of the studies of the efficacy of psychopharmacologic treatments of PTSD (or of other mental disorders associated with abuse) have had abused children as subjects. Studies of adults have most often relied on clinical reports or on open trials and have suggested that psychopharmacologic interventions may be helpful adjuncts to psychotherapy, but will generally not suffice as isolated treatment. Carbamazepines and benzodiazepines have been found to be helpful in lessening affective instability (Friedman, 1988). There is little evidence, however, that either of these medications improve the full spectrum of PTSD symptoms. Two double-blind studies of tricyclic antidepressants (Davidson et al., 1990; Frank, Kosten, Giller, & Dan, 1988) and one study of monoamine oxidase inhibitors (Frank et al.) have found these medications to be moderately helpful in treating PTSD. Van Der Kolk and colleagues (1994) reported that Fluoxetine diminished the sense of numbing, affect dysregulations, impaired relationships with others, and loss of sustaining beliefs reported by persons with PTSD. Brady, Sonne, and Roberts (1995) reported that Sertraline decreased symptoms of PTSD, depression, and alcohol cravings among substance abuse treatment patients with PTSD. Several double-blind studies did not find antidepressants to be helpful in treating adults with PTSD, but they have been criticized for measuring the effectiveness of the medication for only four-week periods (Reist et al., 1989). Famularo, Kinscherff, and Fenton (1988) found that Propranolol (given at a dose of 2.5 mg per kilogram) was effective in lessening hyperarousal and hypervigilance in child victims of physical or sexual abuse diagnosed with PTSD. Terr (1989) also has recommended the use of Propanolol or other beta-blockers for traumatized children as an adjunct to behaviorally based treatments (Terr, 1989, 1991). Fluoxetine-induced responses of depressive symptoms were greater in bulimic patients with histories of physical or sexual abuse than in those with no abuse histories (McCarthy, Goff, Baer, Cioffi, & Herzog, 1994). Reduced symptoms of aggression, hyperarousal, and sleep problems in preschool children with severe PTSD have been reported with use of Clonidine (Harmon & Riggs, 1996).

PREVENTING SEXUAL ABUSE OF CHILDREN AND ADOLESCENTS

The focus in preventing sexual abuse has been on educating children, though the results on the efficacy of education-oriented prevention trials have been mixed. Programs tend to be based in schools and typically aim to teach children to differentiate "good" from "bad" touch, to deal with abusers' efforts to keep the abuse a secret, and what children should do if sexual abuse is attempted. Children are usually told that the abuser may be someone they know and that if abuse occurs, they are never at fault (Wolfe, Repucci, & Hart, 1995).

Although Berrick and Gilbert (1991) found that children's knowledge about sexual abuse increases after these programs, they did not find evidence that such knowledge translates into children's ability to take appropriate action. For example, Pelcovitz and colleagues (1992) described 22 young school-aged children in Long Island, New York, who had been sexually abused by a school employee but did not disclose the abuse, despite having received prevention training before and during the abuse. Some of the reasons the children gave for not reporting it were that they were confused about what the prevention program had told them to do in the case of abuse, they feared retaliation by the abuser, and they were concerned that they would be blamed by their parents for the sexual activities associated with the abuse.

Several researchers (Berrick & Gilbert, 1991; Wolfe et al., 1995) have questioned the adequacy of most prevention programs to teach preschoolers even basic concepts of abuse prevention. In particular, Berrick and Gilbert reported that preschoolers who were exposed to sexual abuse prevention curricula often found the material in these programs to be confusing, suggesting their inappropriateness for children at that developmental stage. Kraizer, Witte, and Fryer (1989), however, found that when the curriculum is sensitive to children's developmental level, is of sufficient length, and includes the active involvement through role-play and other participatory techniques, prevention can be taught adequately, even to preschoolers.

Whether or not these programs are effective at preventing sexual abuse, Finkelhor and Strapko (1992) have suggested that they can be effective in prompting sexually abused children to disclose the abuse. A strategy for the future, perhaps, might be to develop programs that include parents more actively, because the focus of prevention efforts addressed in current programs rests primarily on the children.

Ethical and Legal Issues

Work with children who have been sexually abused raises complex ethical and legal issues for the practitioner. To begin with, clinicians may seek guidance from their professional organizations, most of which have issued guidelines for evaluating children and adolescents when physical and sexual abuse is suspected. (See in particular Bernet [1997] on the Guidelines of the American Academy of Child and Adolescent Psychiatry; the American Professional Society on the Abuse of Children [1990, 1995]; the American Psychological Association [1994]; the American Academy of Pediatrics [1999]; and the American Medical Association [1994].)

Additionally, throughout the United States, states have statutes mandating that professionals in physical and mental health care, social services, law enforcement, and education report suspected cases of child sexual abuse. It is essential for clinicians to understand their local statutes and to be aware of laws and investigatory and prosecutorial procedures that may be used by agencies responsible for investigating allegations as they gather information. This knowledge may help the clinician collaborate more effectively with social services, legal, and law enforcement professionals charged with protecting children—at the very least, this knowledge will help practitioners protect the children in their care. To learn more, clinicians may consult with supervisors of local child protective service field offices (usually in County Departments of Social Services [DSSs]) about general procedures or specific cases. In addition, hospitals with pediatric services often have multidisciplinary child protection committees that can provide consultation.

Clinicians who are subpoenaed to testify in cases where they have clinical knowledge related to a specific case or who serve as expert witnesses on abused children in general may consult with any of a number of legal advisors: from the state district attorney's office, as a witness in a prosecution; with attorneys who advise DSS child protective services workers; or with legal counsel available through their workplaces or whom they have retained themselves.

CONCLUSION

Up to 5.7 percent of children in the United States have been sexually abused (Finkelhor et al., 1997). Sexual abuse is correlated with emotional and behavioral problems—including the traumatic sexualization of victims. Children who have been abused also show higher rates of suicidal behavior, substance abuse, and psychiatric disorders, including PTSD.

Despite the high prevalence and mental health consequences of childhood sexual abuse, there are insufficient efforts being made either to prevent abuse or to provide mental health services for its victims. Part of the problem is the failure to perform routine mental health assessments either during the investigatory or case planning periods by state child protective services or to make referrals after the legal process that follows such a report. Because successful treatment for the child requires treatment for the family as a whole, we need more specialized treatment programs for both children and their families.

There have, however, been exciting advances regarding care of victims of sexual abuse. Both psychotherapies and medications can be used to ameliorate the behavioral and emotional consequences of abuse. Specific interviewing strategies have been developed to help the clinician avoid altering the child's memory of the event, and thereby interfering with either prosecution of the offense or with the child's later treatment. Interdisciplinary mental health practice has much to contribute in terms of increased understanding of the etiology of sexual abuse and advocacy for more effective preventive and rehabilitative intervention programs.

■ ■ ■ ■ ■

CASE STUDY
JANET

Janet, a 10-year-old fifth-grade student, began crying during a school-based sex abuse prevention educational presentation. When approached by her teacher after class, Janet told her that her father often "touched my private parts." The teacher then made a child abuse report to the state department of social services. Janet stayed after school in the principal's office with her teacher. A representative from the county child protective service office arrived at school and interviewed Janet.

Janet told the protective service worker that her mother worked as a nurse from 6:00 P.M. to 6:00 A.M. and that her father cared for her and her 5-year-old brother while her mother worked. Her father worked from 8:00 A.M. to 4:00 P.M. as a computer programmer. Janet said that most nights after he tucked her brother into his bed in his own room, her father came into her bed. She stated that he then took off his underpants, cuddled up to her, touched her private parts and had her touch his. She stated that her father rubbed up against her and that yellow "toothpaste like stuff came out his private." The child protective service worker took Janet to the nearby emergency room, where she was examined by a pediatrician and interviewed by a team that included a pediatric social worker and a resident in child and adolescent psychiatry.

A pediatric culposcope was used in the examination of Janet. She was found to have a dilated and scarred hymen and vaginal discharge, which was cultured to test for possible venereal disease. With the aid of male and female anatomically detailed dolls used during her interview for possible sexual abuse, she was able to identify body parts correctly. Nonleading questions were used during this interview. She again disclosed that her father had touched her genitals and that "yellow toothpaste" came out of his penis while he was in bed with her when her mother was at work. She also disclosed that her father had told her not to tell her mother, because her mother would become upset and might divorce him and call the police. She said that her father told her that he would go to jail if the police came and that they would be poor if he couldn't work, because he would go to jail. Janet was rewarded with a secret present only to be known to the two of them each month. Janet said that the abuse began with her father touching her when she was 8 years old and in the third grade. She also said that when she began fifth grade, he began putting his private part inside her.

A psychiatric evaluation was done at the time of the physical examination. It revealed that Janet was an anxious child who feared retribution by her mother and father because of having disclosed sexual abuse. She was fearful that her mother would be angry with her and that her father would go to jail. She said that it would be her fault if he went to jail and if her parents got divorced. Janet said that she was "a bad girl." She spoke of attempts to avoid her father and of being afraid of him. She reported that she had thoughts all day of him touching her private parts and of feeling numb and like someone other than herself was being touched by her father. She spoke of not wanting to sleep in her bed and of recurrent nightmares of being chased by her father, and of her mother not wanting to help her escape from him. She reported that she had been having trouble concentrating in school, and that she was only getting "satisfactories" in reading and mathematics on her report card, even though since first grade, she had gotten "excellents" in reading and in mathematics.

The child presented no evidence of sustained depressive symptoms or of suicidal plan, attempt, or ideation. There was no evidence of thought disorders or a history of cigarette or other substance use.

Janet was diagnosed as having PTSD and she, her mother, and her brother were referred to the child abuse mental health treatment program located in the nearby teaching hospital. Her father was arrested. Subsequently, he was released on bail and told not to return home. Janet's child mental health program referred him to a treatment program for sexual offenders.

Janet was treated with cognitive behavioral therapy in a group with other girls who had been sexually abused. Her mother was evaluated and diagnosed as having Major Depressive Disorder. She was treated with individual psychotherapy and antidepressant medication. Janet's mother also attended supportive group therapy with the mothers of the girls in Janet's psychotherapy group. Her father was prosecuted, convicted, and imprisoned for one year. During that time and after his release, he received cognitive behavioral and group therapy and was allowed supervised visits with his children. After two years in an out-patient treatment program for sex offenders and after marital therapy with his wife, he was permitted to join in psychotherapy sessions with his children. He was permitted to return to his home three years after his arrest. His wife then only worked day shifts, and he continued to be on parole.

DISCUSSION QUESTIONS

1. How is Janet's case typical of child sexual abuse cases? In what ways are Janet's reactions typical or atypical?

2. Do you believe that the use of anatomically correct dolls was necessary and appropriate in assessing whether sexual abuse had taken place? Why or why not?

3. If you had had to interview Janet, what questions would you have asked to elicit the information she provided?

4. Which of the therapeutic strategies mentioned in this case would be available in your community? What others not mentioned here would be available?

SUGGESTED READINGS

Friedrich, W. N. (1990). *Psychotherapy of sexually abused children and their families.* New York: W. W. Norton.
Jones, D. P. H. (1992). *Interviewing the sexually abused child.* London: Gaskell.

REFERENCES

American Academy of Pediatrics. (1999). Guidelines for the evaluation of sexual abuse of children: Subject review. (RE9819). *Pediatrics, 103*(1), 186–191. Available online at http://www.aap.org/policy/re9819.html.
American Medical Association. (1994). *Diagnostic and treatment guidelines on child sexual abuse.* Chicago: Author.
American Professional Society on the Abuse of Children (APSAC). (1990). *Guidelines for psychological evaluation of suspected sexual abuse in young children.* Chicago: Author.
———. (1995). *Practice guidelines: Use of anatomical dolls in child sexual abuse assessment.* Chicago: Author.
American Psychiatric Association. (APA). (2000). *Diagnostic and statistical manual of mental disorders (4th ed.) (DSM-IV-TR).* Washington, DC: Author.
American Psychological Association. (1994). *Guidelines for child custody evaluations in divorce proceedings.* Washington, DC: Author.
Avery, L., Massat, C. R., & Lundy, M. (2000). Posttraumatic stress and mental health functioning of sexually abused children. *Child and Adolescent Social Work Journal, 17(1),* 19–34.
Barnett, D., Vondra, J. I., & Shonk, S. M. (1996). Self-perceptions, motivation, and school functioning of low-income maltreated and comparison children. *Child Abuse and Neglect, 20(5),* 397–410.
Becker, J. V., Alpert, J. L., BigFoot, D. S., & Bonner, B. (1995). Empirical research on child abuse treatment: Report by the child abuse and neglect treatment working group. *Journal of Clinical Child Psychology, 24,* 23–46.
Bernet, W. (1997). Practice parameters for the forensic evaluation of children and adolescents who may have been physically or sexually abused. *Journal of the American Academy of Child Adolescent Psychiatry, 36,* 423–442.
Berrick, J. D., & Gilbert, N. (1991). *With the best of intentions: The child sexual abuse prevention movement.* New York: Guilford.
Boat, B. W., & Everson, M. D. (1988). Use of anatomical dolls among professionals in sexual abuse evaluations. *Child Abuse & Neglect, 12,* 171–179.

Bradley, A. R., & Wood, J. M. (1996). How do children tell? The disclosure process in child sexual abuse. *Child Abuse & Neglect, 20,* 881–889.

Brady, K. T., Sonne, S. C., & Roberts, J. M. (1995). Sertraline treatment of comorbid posttraumatic stress disorder and alcohol dependence. *Journal of Clinical Psychiatry, 56,* 502–505.

Ceci, S., & Bruck, M. (1993). Suggestibility of the child witness: A historical review and synthesis. *Psychological Bulletin, 113,* 403–439.

Chapman, J. R., & Smith, B. (1987). Response of social service and criminal justice agencies to child sexual abuse complaints. *Response to the Victimization of Women and Children, 10,* 7–13.

Cicchetti, D. (1991). Toward the development of a transactional model of risk taking and self regulation. In L. P. Lipsitt & L. L. Mitnick (Eds.), *Self-regulatory behavior and risk taking: Causes and consequences* (pp. 165–198). Norwood, NJ: Ablex.

Cohen, J. A., & Mannarino, A. P. (1993). A treatment model for sexually abused preschool children. *Journal of Interpersonal Violence, 8(1),* 115–131.

———. (1998). Interventions for sexually abused children: Initial treatment findings. *Child Maltreatment, 3(1),* 17–26.

Cole, P., & Putnam, F. W. (1992). Effect of incest on self and social functioning: A developmental psychopathology perspective. *Journal of Consulting and Clinical Psychology, 60,* 174–184.

Davidson, J., Kudler, H. S., Smith, R., Mahorney, S. L., Lipper, S., Hammett, E., Saunders, W. B., & Cavenar, J. O., Jr. (1990). Treatment of PTSD with amitriptyline and placebo. *Archives of General Psychiatry, 48,* 259–269.

De Bellis, M. D., Lefter, L., Trickett, P. K., & Putnam, F. W. (1994). Urinary catecholamine excretion in sexually abused children. *American Academy of Child and Adolescent Psychiatry, 33,* 320–327.

Deblinger, E., & Heflin, A. H. (1996). *Treating sexually abused children and their nonoffending parents: A cognitive behavioral approach.* Thousand Oaks, CA: Sage.

Deblinger, E., McLeer, S. V., & Henry, D. (1990). Cognitive behavioral treatment for sexually abused children suffering post-traumatic stress. *Journal of the American Academy of Child & Adolescent Psychiatry, 29,* 747–752.

De Luca, R., Hazen, A., & Cutler, J. (1993). Evaluation of a group counseling program for preadolescent female victims of incest. *Elementary School Guidance and Counseling, 28,* 104–114.

Dinwiddie, S., Heath, A. C., Dunne, M. P., Bucholz, K. K., Madden, P. A. F., Slutske, W. S., Bierut, L. J., Statham, D. B., & Martin, N. G. (2000). Early sexual abuse and lifetime psychopathology: A co-twin control study. *Psychological Medicine, 30,* 41–52.

Douzinas, N., Fornari, V., Goodman, B., Sitnick, T., & Packman, L. (1994). Eating disorders and abuse. *Child Psychiatric Clinics of North America, 3,* 777–796.

Eckenrode, J., Laird, M., & Doris J. (1993). School performance and disciplinary problems among abused and neglected children. *Developmental Psychology, 29,* 53–62.

Famularo, R., Kinscherrf, R., & Fenton, T. (1988). Propranolol treatment for childhood PTSD, acute type. *American Journal of Disorders of Children, 142,* 1244–1247.

Feiring, C., Taska, L., & Lewis, M. (1999). Age and gender differences in children's and adolescents' adaptation to sexual abuse. *Child Abuse and Neglect, 23,* 115–128.

Fergusson, D. M., & Horwood, L. J. (1999). Prospective childhood predictors of deviant peer affiliations in adolescence. *Journal of Child Psychology & Psychiatry & Allied Disciplines, 40(4),* 581–592.

Finkelhor, D., & Berliner, L. (1995). Research on the treatment of sexually abused children: A review and recommendations. *Journal of the American Academy of Child and Adolescent Psychiatry, 34,* 1408–1423.

Finkelhor, D., Moore, D., Hamby, S. L., & Straus, M. A. (1997). Sexually abused children in a national survey of parents: Methodological issues. *Child Abuse and Neglect, 21(1),* 1–9.

Finkelhor, D., & Strapko, N. (1992). Sexual abuse prevention education: A review of evaluation studies. In D. Willis, E. W. Holden, & M. S. Rosenberg (Eds.), *The prevention of child maltreatment: Developmental and ecological perspectives* (pp. 150–167). New York: Wiley.

Flisher, A. J., Kramer, R. A., Hoven, C. W., Greenwald, S., Alegria, M., Bird, H. R., Canino, G., Connell, R., & Moore, R. E. (1997). Psychosocial characteristics of physically abused children and adolescents. *Journal of the American Academy of Child and Adolescent Psychiatry, 36,* 123–131.

Frank, J., Kosten, T., Giller, E. L. Jr., & Dan, E. (1988). A randomized clinical trial of phenelezine andimipramine for PTSD. *American Journal of Psychiatry, 145,* 1289–1291.

Friedman, M. (1988). PTSD and carbamazepine. *American Journal of Psychiatry, 145,* 281–285.

Friedrich, W. N. (1993). Sexual victimization and sexual behavior in children: A review of recent literature. *Child Abuse and Neglect, 17,* 59–66.

———. (1994). Individual psychotherapy for child abuse victims. *Child Psychiatric Clinics of North America, 3,* 797–812.

———. (1997). *Manual for the child sexual behavior inventory.* Available from Psychological Assessment Resources, Inc., 16204 N. Florida Avenue, Lutz, FL 33549.

Gil, E., & Johnson, T. C. (1993). *Sexualized children: Assessment and treatment of sexualized children who molest.* Rockville, MD: Launch Press.

Gonzalez, L. S., Waterman, J., Kelly, R. J., McCord, J., & Oliveri, M. K. (1993). Children's patterns of disclosures and recantations of sexual and ritualistic abuse allegations in psychotherapy. *Child Abuse and Neglect, 17,* 281–289.

Goodman, G. S., Batterman-Faunce, J. M., & Kenney, R. (1992). Optimizing children's testimony: Research and social policy issues concerning allegations of child sexual abuse. In D. Cichetti & S. Toth (Eds.), *Child abuse, child development and social policy.* Norwood, NJ: Ablex.

Harmon, R. J., & Riggs, P. D. (1996). Clinidine for posttraumatic stress disorder in preschool children. *Journal of the American Academy of Child and Adolescent Psychiatry, 35,* 1247–1249.

Hazzard, A., Celano, M., Gould, J., Lawry, S., & Webb, C. (1995). Predicting symptomatology and self-blame among child sex abuse victims. *Child Abuse & Neglect, 19,* 707–714.

Herman, J. L. (1992). Complex PTSD: A syndrome in survivors of prolonged and repeated trauma. *Journal of Traumatic Stress, 5,* 377–392.

Herman-Giddens, M. E., Sandler, A. D., & Friedman, N. E. (1988). Sexual precocity in girls: An association with sexual abuse? *American Journal of Diseases of Children, 142,* 431–433.

Ito, Y., Teicher, M. H., Glod, C. A., Harper, D., Magnus, E., & Gelbard, H. A. (1993). Increased prevalence of electrophysiological abnormalities in children with psychological physical and sexual abuse. *Journal of Neuropsychiatry and Clinical Neurosciences, 5,* 401–408.

James, B. (1994). *Handbook for treatment of attachment-trauma problems in children.* New York: Free Press.

Johnson, P. G. (1996). *A study of the sexual abuse of adolescents and their subsequent behavior.* Unpublished thesis, Wurzweiler School of Social Work, Yeshiva University, New York.

Kaplan, S. J., Pelcovitz, D., Ganeles, D., & Salzinger, S. (1990). Psychopathology of parents of abused and neglected children and adolescents. In M. Lenherr & P. Welch (Eds.), *Selected readings in child abuse and neglect* (pp. 162–168). Denver: University of Colorado Health Sciences Center.

Kendall-Tackett, K. A., & Simon, A. F. (1988). Molestation and the onset of puberty: Data from 365 adults molested as children. *Child Abuse and Neglect, 12,* 73–81.

Kendall-Tackett, K. A., Williams, L. M., & Finkelhor, D. (1993). Impact of sexual abuse on children: A review and synthesis of recent empirical studies. *Psychological Bulletin, 113,* 164–180.

Kolko, D. J., & Feiring, C. (2002). "Explaining why": A closer look at attributions in child abuse victims. *Child Maltreatment, 7(1),* 5–8.

Koverola, C., Pound, J., Hagger, A., & Lytle, C. (1993). Relationship of child sexual abuse to depression. *Child Abuse and Neglect, 17,* 393–400.

Kraizer, S., Witte, S. S., & Fryer, G. E. (1989, September/October). Child sexual abuse prevention programs: What makes them effective in protecting children? *Children Today,* 23–27.

Larzelere, R. E., Collins, L., & Collins, R. A. (1993). *During and post-treatment effects of group therapy for sexual victimization.* Proceedings of the conference on responding to child maltreatment. San Diego: San Diego Children's Hospital.

Leserman, J., Drossman, D. A., Li, Z., Toomey, T. C., Nachman, G., & Glogau, L. (1996). Sexual and physical abuse history in gastroenterology practice: How types of abuse impact health status. *Psychosomatic Medicine, 58,* 4–15.

Lewis, D. O. (1992). From abuse to violence: Psychophysiological consequences of maltreatment. *Journal of the American Academy of Child and Adolescent Psychiatry, 31,* 383–391.

Livingston, R., Lawson, L., & Jones, J. G. (1993). Predictors of self-reported psychopathology in children abused repeatedly by a parent. *Journal of the American Academy of Child and Adolescent Psychiatry, 32,* 948–953.

Mannarino, A., & Cohen, J. (1996). Family related variables and psychological symptom formation in sexually abused girls. *Journal of Child Sexual Abuse, 5,* 105–120.

McCarthy, M. K., Goff, D. C., Baer, L., Cioffi, J., & Herzog, D. B. (1994). Dissociation, childhood trauma and the response to fluoxetine in bulimic parents. *International Journal of Eating Disorders, 15,* 219–226.

Miller, S. D. (1989). Optical differences in cases of multiple personality disorder. *Journal of Nervous & Mental Disease, 177(8),* 480–486.

Paradise, J., Rose, L., Sleeper, L., & Nathanson, M. (1994). Behavior, family function, school performance, and predictors of persistent disturbance in sexually abused children. *Pediatrics, 93,* 452–459.

Pelcovitz, D., Adler, N., Kaplan, S., Packman, L., & Krieger, R. (1992). The failure of a school-based child sexual abuse prevention program. *Journal of the American Academy of Child and Adolescent Psychiatry, 33,* 305–312.

Pitman, R. K., Van der Kolk, B. A., Orr, S. P., & Greenber, M. S. (1990). Nalaxone—Reversible analgesic response to combat-related stimuli in posttraumatic stress disorder. *Archives of General Psychiatry, 47,* 541–544.

Pribor, E. F., Yutzy, S. H., Dean, J. T., & Wetzel, R. D. (1993). Briquet's syndrome, dissociation, and abuse. *American Journal of Psychiatry, 50,* 1507–1511.

Putnam F. W. (1991). Dissociative disorders in children and adolescents. A developmental perspective. *Psychiatric Clinics of North America, 14(3),* 519–531.

Putnam, F., Zahn, T., & Post, R. M. (1990). Differential autonomic nervous system activity in multiple personality disorder. *Psychiatry Research, 31,* 251–260.

Reed, L. D. (1996). Findings from research on children's suggestibility and implications for conducting child interviews. *Child Maltreatment, 1,* 105–120.

Reist, C., Dauffmann, C., Haier, R., Sangdahl, C., DeMet, E. M., Chica-DeMet, A., & Nelson, J. N. (1989). A controlled trial of desipramine in 18 men with PTSD. *American Journal of Psychiatry, 146,* 513–516.

Riggs, S., Alario, A. J., & McHorney, C. (1990). Health risk behaviors and attempted suicide in adolescents who report prior maltreatment. *Journal of Pediatrics, 116,* 815–821.

Ross, C. A. (1994). *The Osiris Complex: Case studies in multiple personality disorder.* Toronto: University of Toronto Press.

Ryan, G. (1991). Perpetration prevention: Primary and secondary. In G. Ryan & S. Lane (Eds.), *Juvenile sexual offending: Causes, consequences and correction.* Lexington, MA: D. C. Heath.

Saywitz, K. J., & Goodman, G. S. (1996). Interviewing children in and out of court: Current research and practical implications. In J. Briere, L. Berliner, J. Bulkley, et al. (Eds.), *The APSAC handbook on child maltreatment* (pp. 297–318). Thousand Oaks, CA: Sage.

Saywitz, K. J., Goodman, G. S., Nicholas, E., & Moan, S. (1991). Children's memories of physical examinations involving genital touch: Implications for reports of child sexual abuse. *Journal of Consulting and Clinical Psychology, 59,* 682–691.

Saywitz, K., & Moan-Hardie, S. (1994). Reducing the potential for distortion of childhood memories. *Consciousness and Cognition, 3,* 408–425.

Spaccarelli, S. (1994). Stress, appraisal, and coping in child sexual abuse: A theoretical and empirical review. *Psychological Bulletin, 116(2),* 340–362.

Terr, L. C. (1989). Family anxiety after traumatic events. *Journal of Clinical Psychiatry, 50,* 15–19.

———. (1991). Childhood traumas: An outline and overview. *American Journal of Psychiatry, 148,* 10–20.

Trickett, P. K., & Putnam, F. W. (1993). Impact of child sexual abuse on females: Toward a developmental, psychobiological integration. *Psychological Science, 4,* 81–87.

U.S. Department of Health and Human Services, Administration for Children and Families, Administration on Children, Youth and Families. (1996). *The third National Incidence Study of child abuse and neglect (NIS-3).* Washington, DC: U.S. Government Printing Office.

U.S. Department of Health and Human Services, Administration on Children, Youth and Families. (2000). *Child maltreatment 1998: Reports from the states to the National Child Abuse and Neglect Data System.* Washington, DC: U.S. Government Printing Office.

Van Der Kolk, B. A., Dreyfuss, D., Michaels, M., Shera, D., Berkowitz, R., Fisler, R., & Saxe, G. (1994). Fluoxetine in posttraumatic stress disorder. *Journal of Clinical Psychiatry, 55,* 517–522.

Vogeltanz, N. D., Wilsnack, S. C., Harris, T. R., Wilsnack, R. W., Wonderlich, S. A., & Kristjanson, A. F. (1999). Prevalence and risk factors for childhood sexual abuse in women: National survey findings. *Child Abuse & Neglect, 23(6),* 579–592.

White, S. (1991). Using anatomically detailed dolls in interviewing preschoolers. In C. Schaefer, K. Gitlund, & D. Sandgrund (Eds.), *Play, diagnosis and assessment.* New York: Wiley.

Widom, C. S., & Ames, M. A. (1994). Criminal consequence of childhood sexual victimization. *Child Abuse and Neglect, 18,* 303–318.

Wolfe, D. A., Sas, L., & Wekerle, C. (1994). Factors associated with the development of posttraumatic stress disorder among child victims of sexual abuse. *Child Abuse and Neglect, 18,* 37–50.

Wolfe, D., Reppucci, N. D., & Hart, S. (1995). Child abuse prevention: Knowledge and priorities. *Journal of Clinical Child Psychology, 24* (supplement).

Wozencraft, T., Wagner, W., & Pellegrin, A. (1991). Depression and suicidal ideation in sexually abused children. *Child Abuse and Neglect, 15,* 505–511.

Zuravin, S. J., & Fontenella, C. (1999). The relationship between child sexual abuse and major depression among low income women: A function of growing up experiences? *Child Maltreatment, 4(1),* 3–12.

CHAPTER 9

SCHOOL-BASED INTERVENTIONS FOR STUDENTS WITH EMOTIONAL AND BEHAVIORAL DISORDERS

K. RICHARD YOUNG
Brigham Young University

MICHELLE MARCHANT
Brigham Young University

LYNN K. WILDER
Brigham Young University

Societal changes over the last two decades have resulted in an increasing number of children being identified as at risk. Many of these children will develop serious patterns of antisocial behavior and/or emotional disturbances (Walker, Colvin, & Ramsey, 1995). Increasing numbers of students in our nation's schools are exhibiting aggressive and disruptive behavior beyond minor incidents that may typically occur during the course of normal classroom activities (Nelson & Carr, 1999). Such behavior has become one of the most pressing issues in schools today (Algozzine & Kay, 2002). Despite many years of research and attention toward emotional and behavioral problems in schools, such problems have increased in frequency and intensity.

Trends in society seem to promote aggressive behavior as a solution to interpersonal conflict (Walker et al., 1995). Students frequently bring their antisocial behavior, which has been learned and reinforced in their out-of-school environments, to school. This interferes with the development and maintenance of an environment that is safe, secure, and conducive to learning. Teachers and school administrators face continuous behavioral challenges on a daily basis as they attempt to maintain safe and orderly classroom environments, where teachers are permitted to teach and where all students can learn (Algozzine & Kay, 2002; Nelson, Crabtree, Marchand-Martella, & Martella, 1998; Sugai, Sprague, Horner, & Walker, 2000).

During the past decade, the role of schools in respect to problem behavior has drastically changed. Traditionally, the primary role of schools was academic instruction. Today, schools are expected to assume a major role in changing students' problem behaviors. Filling this role requires administrators, general education teachers, special education teachers, school psychologists, social workers, counselors, and other related services personnel to bring together programs and services to help students and teachers deal with a wide variety of both internalizing and externalizing behavior disorders.

Educators across the country must address problem behavior as part of their daily assignment, in addition to teaching academic content (Nelson & Carr, 1999). Addressing antisocial behavior is critical because there is a direct relationship between academic failure, underachievement, and poor social adjustment (Algozzine & Kay, 2002; Kazdin, 1987; Patterson, 1982). If schools do not attend to the emotional and behavioral needs of students on a broad scale, it is unlikely that they will create the conditions necessary for academic success for many of the students.

The purpose of this chapter is to provide practical guidelines for school personnel as a foundation for the development of schoolwide programs for (1) the social, emotional, and behavioral development of all students within a school; (2) the prevention of emotional and behavioral disorders in students at risk; and (3) the treatment of students already struggling with serious emotional and behavioral difficulties. Five major areas of consideration are discussed within the chapter:

1. Understanding risk and protective factors that provide the foundation for the content, assessments, and interventions at all levels of the school program
2. Establishing a comprehensive assessment system, including a screening process for at-risk students, that provides for a functional analysis of problem behavior, examines the environment for factors that add to the problem (e.g., coercive behavior management practice, family difficulties), and searches for protective factors that could be used as resources to alleviate risk (e.g., faculty that are sensitive to multicultural issues, strong interpersonal relationships with significant adults or mentors)
3. Implementing multiple levels of intervention within the school (i.e., primary, secondary, and tertiary)
4. Designing interventions for high-risk youth that are comprehensive in nature (i.e., addresses multiple risk and protective factors) and intensive in scope (e.g., includes a variety of settings and school personnel, families, mentors)
5. Involving parents and family members in the intervention process

Meeting behavioral and emotional needs of students is a challenge for schools for several reasons. First, the Individuals with Disabilities Education Act (IDEA, 1997) includes a definition for "seriously emotionally disturbed" that is considered restrictive by professional groups that have challenged the definition. Another problem has been the avoidance of using labels such as *seriously emotionally disturbed* or *emotional/behavioral disorders*. This, in turn, has often resulted in a failure (1) to adequately screen for such problems, (2) to identify and intervene early, (3) to intervene in a comprehensive manner, and/or (4) to develop and implement prevention programs.

The problem of improper and/or inadequate treatment is further complicated because school personnel typically do not use a precise classification system such as *DSM-IV-TR* (American Psychiatric Association, 2000) but include a wide range of disorders (e.g., anxiety disorders, depression, schizophrenia, conduct disorders) under a single label such as *seriously emotionally disturbed* or *emotional/behavioral disorders*. This broad use of a label often results in an insufficient intervention plan. However, to provide services using special education funds, such a definition must be used.

DEFINITION OF EMOTIONAL AND BEHAVIORAL DISORDERS

In order to provide special education services to a student, a school team must decide whether the student qualifies as emotionally/behaviorally disordered using the comprehensive assessment information. From a school perspective, this may not be as easy to determine as it may first appear, because professionals (e.g., psychologists, school workers, counselors, teachers, special educators, state and local school administrators) and federal and state educational agencies have, for many years, disagreed on a definition of emotional and behavioral disorders (Kauffman, 2000). One definition (Bower, 1981) was adopted by the U.S. Office of Education and thus became, with modifications, the federal definition governing the classification and special education placement of students thought to have emotional and/or behavioral disorders. Based on Bower's article (1981) the Individuals with Disabilities Education Act (IDEA, 1997) defined *emotionally disturbed* as follows:

   (i) The term means a condition exhibiting one or more of the following characteristics over a long period of time and to a marked degree, *which adversely affects educational performance:*
       (A) An inability to learn which cannot be explained by intellectual, sensory, or health factors;
       (B) An inability to build or maintain satisfactory interpersonal relationships with peers and teachers;
       (C) Inappropriate types of behavior or feelings under normal circumstances;
       (D) A general, pervasive mood of unhappiness or depression; or
       (E) A tendency to develop physical symptoms or fears associated with personal or school problems.
   (ii) *The term includes children who are schizophrenic* [or autistic]. *The term does not include children who are socially maladjusted, unless it is determined that they are seriously emotionally disturbed.* (45 C.F.R. 121a.5[b][8][1978])

Although this basic definition has been in place for over two decades (since P.L. 94-142, 1975) with only minor changes, it has been criticized as illogical, subjective, and even inappropriate by professionals and organizations (Council for Children with Behavioral Disorders Executive committee, 1987; Forness & Knitzer, 1992; Kauffman, 1986).

The National Mental Health and Special Education Coalition, a group of professionals representing more than a dozen professional associations and advocacy groups, collaborated on the following definition:

   I. The term *emotional or behavioral disorder* means a disability characterized by behavioral or emotional responses in school programs so different from appropriate age, cultural, or ethnic norms that they adversely affect educational performance, including academic, social, vocational or personal skills, and which:

(a) is more than a temporary, expected response to stressful events in the environment;

(b) is consistently exhibited in two different settings, at least one of which is school-related; and

(c) persists despite individualized interventions within the education program, unless, in the judgment of the team, the child or youth's history indicates that such interventions would not be effective.

Emotional or behavioral disorders can co-exist with other disabilities.

II. This category may include children or youth with schizophrenia disorders, affective disorders, anxiety disorders, or other sustained disturbances of conduct or adjustment when they adversely affect educational performance in accordance with Section I. (Forness & Knitzer, 1992, p. 13)

Kauffman (2000) reported that the coalition-proposed definition has been endorsed by more than 30 professional and advocacy groups that are "working toward incorporation into federal laws and regulations" (p. 32). Although many professionals advocate for this definition, school personnel recognize that schools typically are required to use the IDEA definition. When the IDEA definition is used, students are typically labeled as "Seriously Emotionally Disturbed" (SED). When the coalition definition is used, students are more likely to be referred to as "Emotionally/Behaviorally Disordered" (EBD).

PREVALENCE

An important issue, related to which definition to accept, is *prevalence*, the number of school-age children and youth with emotional and behavioral disorders. Prevalence estimates are the basis for allocating funds, establishing budgets, hiring staff, and developing and implementing treatment programs; and these estimates vary widely. Factors influencing this variation include a methodology of estimating prevalence that is not well developed, differences in definitions of SED and EBD accepted by different researchers, influences of social policy and economic factors, and other sources of bias. In addition, government estimates tend to be very conservative. Recent surveys suggest a range of 3 to 6 percent to be a reasonable estimate (Anderson & Werry, 1994; Brandenburg, Friedman, & Silver, 1990; Costello, Messer, Bird, Cohen, & Reinherz, 1998); however, the percent of students that are actually classified and served as having emotional and behavioral disorders varies across states from .05 to 2 percent (Kauffman, 2000). The use of the IDEA definition somewhat deflates the prevalence.

GENDER, ETHNIC, AND SOCIOECONOMIC PREVALENCE INFORMATION

The percent of students classified as having emotional/behavioral disorders varies significantly according to student gender and ethnicity. Overrepresentation of certain groups in the broad umbrella category of emotional disturbance used in schools is problematic. For instance, Coutinho, Oswald, and Forness (2002), using data that the Office of Civil Rights collected in 1998 to report on the status of civil rights in the nation's schools, indicated that (1) white males were 3.8 times as likely as white females to be identified as EBD, (2) African American females were 1.4 times more likely than white females to be identified as EBD, (3) African American males were 5.5 times more likely to be identified as white females, and (4) Native American males were identified more than would be expected given their percentage in the normal population.

Coutinho and colleagues (2002) also reported that EBD classification was related to student socioeconomic status. Identification increases with poverty for African American males (markedly) and females and for Hispanic males. It decreases slightly for white males and females in poverty, hence the disproportionality. African Americans living in communities with high poverty rates are at greatest risk of any of the ethnic groups of EBD identification. Native Americans are at greatest risk of EBD identification when they live in nonwhite communities. Both student characteristics and community socioeconomic levels influence identification rates.

REVIEW OF RESEARCH

Risk Factors

Better understanding of the factors that put children at risk for emotional and behavioral disorders, along with protective factors, is likely to lead to better school prevention and early intervention programs. Children with consistent and/or challenging behavior problems are commonly labeled as *being at risk,* particularly for emotional and behavioral disorders, antisocial behavior, school failure, and dropping out. The at-risk label is based on numerous risk factors that disrupt the typical social/behavioral development that occurs from childhood into adulthood. *Risk factors* are defined as conditions or influences that increase the likelihood that a child's behavior will deviate from the norm or that a problem condition will persevere into the child's teen and adult years.

As we examine how schools may be part of an effort to prevent the development of emotional and behavioral disorders, it is natural to want to examine factors that can cause the development of emotional and behavioral disorders. Researchers indicate that identifying the factors that lead to emotional/behavioral disorders (EBD) can enable us to intervene and possibly reverse the process (Walker & Sprague, 1999). In studying the contributing causes of emotional/behavioral disorders, educators should examine both risk and protective factors. Kauffman (2000) and Walker and colleagues (1995) are two excellent resources for an in-depth study of such factors, particularly as related to school settings.

Determining specific causal factors for any type of emotional/behavioral disorder is difficult. The focus on risk factors is one of probability: anticipation that the presence or absence of particular events and conditions will increase or decrease the likelihood of a particular outcome for a child (Garmezy, 1987; Quinn & McDougal, 1998). Kauffman (2001) explains:

> When several risk factors come together—for example, poverty, parental antisocial behavior, community violence, and difficult temperament—their effects are not merely additive but multiplicative. That is, two such factors occurring together more than double the probability

that a child will develop a disorder. If a third factor is added the chance of disorder is several times higher yet. (p. 226)

The concept that the more risk factors that are present, the greater the risk for the child to develop a disorder is very important; remember, risk factors are only probabilities. Every individual child is unique; some succumb to the effects of these events and conditions that increase risk, while others are amazingly resilient (Hetherington & Martin, 1986).

Although the concept of risk factors is helpful, note that social scientists have not identified all the potential risk factors that reliably lead to pathology in children, nor have they found all the protective factors that will always produce a resilient child (Kauffman, 2000; Reitman & Gross, 1995). Emotional and behavioral disorders rarely have just one or even two causal factors; the disorder typically is interrelated to multiple factors (Kauffman, 2000). For the purposes of this chapter, we have identified four areas of risk, with specific factors within each area: (1) individual, (2) family, (3) school, and (4) cultural conditions. These risk factors are outlined in Table 9.1, along with references for documentation.

In examining these categories of risk characteristics and their respective risk factors, it is important to understand that they typically have a cumulative effect. A child can start on a path of risk by exposure to one or more factors, which accumulate and then lead to other problem behaviors. The path may continue until the outcomes include serious consequences.

Walker and Sprague (1999) identified the path from risk factor exposure to long-term negative outcomes. The first stage along this path is the exposure of a child to family, neighborhood, and societal risk factors. Factors such as poverty, abuse and neglect, incompetent parenting, or drug and alcohol use by caregivers may increase the probability of a child developing maladaptive behavioral manifestations. These behavioral manifestations might include defiance of adults' instructions, coercive interactive styles, aggression toward peers, inadequate problem-solving skills, and inadequate preparation for school. If a child brings these behavior patterns to school, risks are compounded. Negative short-term outcomes may begin to develop at school. The child may experience peer and/or teacher rejection, academic failure or low achievement, discipline referrals, and truancy. These experiences often culminate in a child being shifted to different school environments and, in fact, the child may even end up attending a number of different schools.

As this path of exposure to risk factors continues, the seriousness of these behaviors accelerates, and ultimately the child experiences "negative, destructive long-term outcomes" (Walker & Sprague, 1999). Long-term outcomes—such as school failure and dropout, delinquency, drug and alcohol use, gang membership, and violent or criminal acts—can eventually lead to serious adult deviant behaviors. Commonly, youth who walk this unfortunate path find themselves being chronically dependent on the welfare system and/or incarceration in correctional facilities. Therefore, prevention, early identification, and intervention are important because the frequency and intensity of problem behaviors exhibited by students in the elementary school years often increase over time, progressing from the risk level to the more serious level of clinical significance (Kamps, 2002).

When specific and comprehensive services are delayed, the prognosis for successful intervention significantly declines. There is a practice in many of our schools of either ignoring or mislabeling students who exhibit early signs of emotional and behavior disorders as *learning disabled*, rather than directly dealing with these problems with intensive inter-

TABLE 9.1 Risk Factors for Emotional/Behavioral Disorders

CATEGORY AND RISK FACTORS	DOCUMENTATION
I. INDIVIDUAL CHARACTERISTICS	
A. Noncompliant to adults; teases, annoys, or interferes with others; disruptive	Forehand & McMahan, 1981; Morgan & Jenson, 1988; Patterson, 1982, 1983; Walker et al., 1995
B. Nervous and anxious; impulsive; becomes upset under pressure; distractible; has difficulty in attending and concentrating; overly dependent on teachers (adults); lack of social readiness.	Kauffman, 2000; McKinney, Mason, Peterson, & Glifford, 1975; Shinn, Ramsey, Walker, Stieber, & O'Neill, 1987; Shores, Jack, Gunter, Ellis, Debriere, & Behby, 1993; Walker et al., 1995
C. Socially incompetent; lacks essential social skills; has difficulty in building friendships and social supports; is verbally and/or physically aggressive toward peers; bullies; has difficulty adapting to environmental changes	Farmer, Farmer, & Gut, 1999; Farmer & Hollowell, 1994; Shores, 1987; Young et al., 1997
D. Lack of communication skills; language disorders; deficient in social language	Giddan, Bade, Rickenberg, & Ryley, 1995; Rogers-Adkinson & Griffith, 1999
II. FAMILY CHARACTERISTICS	
A. *Family stressors:* poverty, alcohol and drug abuse, parent criminality, single caregivers, and violence in the home	Kupersmidt, Griesler, DeRosier, Patterson, & Davis, 1995; Walker et al., 1995
B. *Child abuse:* physical, psychological, and sexual	Cicchetti & Toth, 1995; Kauffman, 2000; Levendosky, Okum, & Parker, 1995; Widom, 1997
C. *Family dysfunction:* frequent quarrels, lack of rules, interactions that are negative-aggressive escalations	Kauffman, 2000; Patterson et al., 1992
D. *Inconsistent and coercive parenting:* anger, meanness, failure to enforce rules, hostility, shouting, threats, physical discipline (e.g., spanking)	Kauffman, 2000; O'Leary, 1995; Patterson, 1986; Patterson et al., 1992; Reid & Eddy, 1997
III. SCHOOL CHARACTERISTICS (E.G., CLASSROOM CONDITION, TEACHER BEHAVIOR, ADMINISTRATION)	
A. Failure to clarify expectations for standards of achievement and civility	Kauffman, 2000; Walker, 1995; Walker et al., 1995
B. Inappropriate expectations for students (e.g., teacher bias because of diagnostic label, low expectations of potential performance)	Henderson & Fox, 1998; Kauffman, 2000; Mayer, Nafpaktitis, Butterworth, & Hollingsworth, 1987
C. Failure to accommodate individual differences; rigid and inflexible treatment of students	Coleman & Gilliam, 1983; Foster, Ysseldyke, & Reese, 1975; Hallahan & Kauffman, 2000; Kauffman, 2000; Lewin, Nelson, & Tollefson, 1983

(continued)

TABLE 9.1   CONTINUED

CATEGORY AND RISK FACTORS	DOCUMENTATION
D. Inconsistent management of behavior (e.g., lack of structure, inconsistent use of punishment and/ or praise and reinforcement, unpredictable consequences)	Hetherington & Martin, 1986; Kauffman, 2000; Reid & Eddy, 1997; Walker et al., 1995
E. Failure to provide appropriate academic instruction (e.g., students not properly placed in curriculum, academic activities become aversive, using ineffective instructional strategies, not teaching critical skills)	Coleman & Vaughn, 2000; Dawson et al., 2000; Gunter & Denny, 1998; Gunter, Denny, Jack, Shores, & Nelson, 1993; Gunter, Hummel, & Conroy, 1998; Gunter & Reed, 1997; Kauffman, 2000; Shores & Wehby, 1999
F. Undesirable models of school conduct (e.g., inappropriate teacher examples of conduct, undue attention to misconduct of other students, failure to attend to and reward appropriate behavior)	Bandura, 1986; Hallenbeck & Kauffman, 1995; Kauffman, 2000; Rutter et al., 1979; Walker et al., 1995
IV. CULTURAL CONDITIONS	
A. Poverty, ethnicity, economic status	Achenbach & Edelbrock, 1981; Banks & Banks, 1997; Bolger, Patterson, Thompson, & Kupersmidt, 1995; Delpit, 1995; Dinges, Atlis, & Vincent, 1997; Felner, Brand, DuBois, Adan, Mulhall, & Evans, 1995; Guerra, Huesmann, Tolan, VanAcker, & Eron, 1995; Hart & Risley, 1995; Hodgkinson, 1995; Kauffman, 2001; Short, 1997; Walker & Sprague, 1999; Yung & Hammond, 1997
B. Peer group influence (e.g., peer pressure, deviant peer group, peer rejection, gang affiliation, absence of a positive peer group)	Farmer et al., 1999; Farmer & Hollowell, 1994; Kauffman, 1999; Kauffman, 2000; Long & Brendtro, 1992; Patterson et al., 1992; Walker, Stieber, & O'Neill, 1990; Walker, Shinn, O'Neill, & Ramsey, 1987, Walker et al., 1995; Walker & Sprague, 1999
C. Media (e.g., violence, pornographic, and electronic games material)	American Psychological Association, 1993; Huesmann, Moise, & Podalski, 1997; Kauffman 2000; Walker et al., 1995; Walker & Sprague, 1999

ventions when signs first appear. Students with serious behavior problems are often mis-classified in primary grades (e.g., considered to have a learning disability instead of emotional/behavioral disorders), but the behavior patterns of these students continue to accelerate until during the middle school years it finally becomes obvious that they have serious emotional/behavioral disorders. To avoid misclassifying students with problem behavior, schools should implement systematic screening programs for early identification of students who have risk factors for emotional/behavioral disorders.

The long-term social and financial implications of children and youth who are on the path to or already have emotional/behavioral disorders are enormous. Clearly, preventing the development of emotional/behavioral disturbances in children at risk will save valuable personal and economic resources and increase the productivity of a segment of our society that currently contributes little and consumes much. It will also provide immediate benefit to our public schools in that learning environments will become secure, safe and conducive to learning for all.

The most critical issue for school systems to recognize and understand is that students who are on the destructive path of developing emotional/behavioral disorders can be identified and receive services. In fact, Walker and colleagues (1995) and Kamp (2002) indicated that antisocial children (including those who develop severe emotional/behavior disorders) can be identified in preschool and the early elementary years. Procedures and instruments for the early identification of children exhibiting these risk behaviors are available (Drummond, 1993; Walker, Severson, & Feil, 1994). One such instrument is the Systematic Screening for Behavior Disorders.

The Systematic Screening for Behavior Disorders (SSBD) (Walker & Severson, 1992) is a multiple-gating screening instrument designed to identify at-risk elementary-age students; it is typically administered schoolwide. In Stage 1, the classroom teachers rank 10 students who display externalizing behavior problems and 10 who display internalizing behavior problems. Stage 2 consists of the teacher identifying the three highest-ranked students from each category and completing the teacher rating scales that indicate patterns in the students' behavior, both adaptive and maladaptive. These students advance to Stage 3 if they meet the normative criteria and cutoff points. During Stage 3, two structured observations are conducted. One observation is done in the classroom to assess academic engaged time and the second observation is done on the playground to evaluate social behavior. Students who meet or exceed the criteria of Stage 3 are referred to child study teams for additional evaluations and assessments to determine whether they qualify as emotionally/behaviorally disordered. (See Walker & Severson, 1992, for further details about this instrument.)

Protective Factors

The impact of risk factors on an individual child may be tempered or counteracted by certain protective factors. *Protective factors* are characteristics that shield one from negative influences and help to establish a more stable environment. They are events and conditions that increase the probability that the child will be resilient and they include factors such as flexible temperament, supportive family, positive social skills, successful involvement in school activities, and attachment to community activities. Just as heightened risk is a function of the number of risk factors, resiliency can be a function of the number of protective factors.

Building protective factors is a promising strategy that contributes to the reduction of risk factors while concurrently teaching resilience. Protective factors—such as child's temperament; a significant adult to nurture and guide the child; accomplishments in the areas of sports, music, or drama—can help to strengthen a child to a point that the risk factors are minimized, resulting in a child who is successful at school, in the home, and/or in the community.

In addition to early identification of at-risk students, schools can develop and implement prevention programs that help promote protective factors with all students. Table 9.2 identifies key behaviors that need to be taught and strengthened in youth in order to help

TABLE 9.2   Characteristics of Successful Students and Supporting Documentation

Researchers have identified the following categories of behaviors that characterize students who are successful and have noted that these behaviors are not typical of at-risk students.

CHARACTERISTICS OF SUCCESSFUL STUDENTS	DOCUMENTATION

A. Teacher-preferred behavior
  1. Follows instructions
  2. Follows class rules
  3. Accepts correction
  4. Works cooperatively with peers
  5. Does not argue and whine
  6. Behaves appropriately in nonclassroom settings
	Algozzine & Kay, 2001; Garmezy, 1987; Rutter, 1990; Walker & Epstein, 2001; Walker, Horner, Sugai, Bullis, Sprague, Bricker, & Kauffman, 2000; Kauffman, 1992; Kerr & Zigmond, 1986; Patterson et al., 1992; Reid, 1993; Walker & McConnell, 1988; Young, West, Marchant, Morgan, & Mitchem, 1997

B. Peer-preferred behavior
  1. Interacts positively with others
  2. Is not verbally and physically aggressive with others
  3. Praises and encourages others
  4. Respects the rights of others
	Dodge, 1985; Dodge, Coie, & Brakke, 1982; Kamps & Kay, 2002

C. Academic-related behavior
  1. Stays on task
  2. Gains attention appropriately
  3. Asks for help or clarification when needed
  4. Completes and turns in assignments
  5. Has good work habits
	DeBaryshe, Patterson, & Capaldi, 1993; Epstein, Kinder, & Bursuck, 1989; Kauffman, 1993; Kupersmid & Patterson, 1987; Lloyd, Hallahan, Kauffman, & Keller, 1991

protect them against risk factors. Table 9.3 outlines the characteristics of the school programs that have been highly successful in developing these protective factors.

The following case study illustrates how a school student support team, using the information in Tables 9.1 through 9.3, can identify, assess, and develop an intervention plan for an at-risk student in the context of a schoolwide prevention program.

CASE STUDY
RODRIGUEZ

Rodriguez, a 10-year-old Hispanic American male, lived in a two-parent home in a low-socioeconomic neighborhood. Rodriguez's family consisted of three children, Rodriguez being the oldest. His parents were of Hispanic descent and had lived in the United States for 15 years. They were bilingual, and although they spoke Spanish in the home, both parents had good conversational English and Rodriguez's English skills were assessed to be more than adequate for academic instruction.

TABLE 9.3   Characteristics of Effective Prevention Programs and Supporting Research

CHARACTERISTICS OF EFFECTIVE PREVENTION PROGRAMS	SIGNIFICANT RESEARCH STUDIES AND REPORTS

I. Focus on building new behaviors and skills by
   A. Teaching adaptive and responsible patterns of social behavior to students
   B. Providing many response opportunities
   C. Providing feedback and reinforcement
   D. Providing school wide social skills instruction
   E. Extending social skills instruction and behavior management to the home
	Alberg, Petry, & Eller, 1994; Algozzine & Kay, 2002; Algozzine & White, 2002; Biglan, 1995; Kamps, 2002; Kamps & Kay, 2002; Maheady & Sainato, 1985; Marchant & Young, 2001; Mayer, 1995; Rutter, 1990; Walker, 1995; Young et al., 1997

II. Providing multiple levels of service, including primary, secondary, and tertiary	Algozzine & Kay, 2001; Kamps & Tankersley, 1996

III. Including research-based strategies that promote
   A. Many opportunities to teach, practice, and reinforce new alternative behavior
   B. Maintenance of behaviors across time via
      1. Frequent reviews of material
      2. Planned booster sessions if behavior drops below a predetermined criterion
	Botvin et al., 1995; Kazdin, 1987; Marchant & Young, 2001

C. Mentoring (for students of diverse cultures) and multicultural teacher competencies	Campbell-Whatley, Algozzine & Obiakor, 1997; Guetzloe, 1997; Obiakor, 1999; Wilder, Jackson, & Smith, 2001

D. Generalization of behaviors across social contexts by
      1. Teaching students to correctly use new skills in multiple social settings
      2. Providing opportunities to practice in those settings
	Drabman, Spitalnik, & O'Leary, 1973; Nelson & Carr, 1999; Peterson, Young, West, & Peterson, 1999; Rhode, Morgan, & Young, 1983; Smith, Young, West, Morgan, & Rhode, 1988; Young et al., 1997

IV. Identifying skill deficits early and providing skill building and multilevel interventions immediately	Kamps & Tankersley, 1996; Algozzine & Kay, 2001; Loeber, 1982; Reid & Patterson, 1989; Tremblay, Paganikurtz, Vitaro, Massie, & Pihl, 1995; Walker et al., 1995; Walker, Kavanagh, Golly, Stiller, Severson, & Feil, 1995

V. Establishing high expectations for success and emphasizing noncoercive behavioral support by
   A. Establishing and teaching clear rules
   B. Using praise consistently to recognize appropriate behavior
   C. Minimizing use of punishment
	Gottfredson, Gottfredson, & Hybl, 1993; Mayer & Butterworth, 1979; Sulzer-Azaroff & Mayer, 1991; Young, Black, Marchant, Mitchem, & West, 2000

VI. Teaching self-management skills and monitoring progress frequently and consistently	Kazdin, 1987; Mitchem & Young, 2001; Mitchem, Young, West, & Benyo, 2001; Tolan & Guerra, 1994; Young, West, Smith, & Morgan, 1991; Young et al., 1997
VII. Developing a curriculum that is practical, feasible, and acceptable to regular education teachers and students	Gall, Borg, & Gall, 1986; Mitchem & Young, 2001; Tolan, Guerra, & Kendall, 1995

Teachers and administrators at Rodriguez's school reported that communicating with his parents was challenging, not because of language, but because the parents had had negative experiences with teachers and school systems in the past. Although they displayed anger toward school personnel (e.g., yelling at teachers during conferences, making accusations toward the school), they did show concern for their son's welfare. In the past, Rodriguez was temporarily placed in foster care due to parental neglect and abuse; however, the family was reunited. While their son was in foster care, the parents attended parenting classes. At the time of the referral, both parents worked; therefore, after-school supervision of the children was left to babysitters or to Rodriguez.

Rodriguez had many characteristics typical of children in a fifth-grade class, but often his behavior was not typical. His teacher referred him to the school at-risk youth prevention and early intervention team (referred to hereafter as the "student support team") because he exhibited the following: physical aggression, property damage, swearing, and obscene gestures. He also displayed a depressed affect. According to his teacher, Rodriguez ignored directions, created disturbances during class, interacted inappropriately with peers, and rarely completed academic work accurately. The teacher was particularly concerned about his violent reactions to adult feedback regarding his behavior. She provided these data via the Systematic Screening for Behavior Disorders (SSBD) assessment instrument (Walker & Severson, 1992), which all teachers in the school were asked to complete on high-risk students (described earlier).

After screening, a comprehensive assessment was necessary for possible special education classification and the development of appropriate interventions. In the case of Rodriguez, the school student support team (consisting of the principal, assistant principal, school psychologist, and a behavioral specialist) decided that a comprehensive assessment was needed, as Rodriguez was ranked as the top student with externalizing behavior problems in his fifth-grade class, as indicated on the SSBD. His assessment battery consisted of the School Archival Records Search (SARS) (Walker, Block-Pedego, Todisi, & Severson, 1991), a Functional Behavioral Assessment (Gresham, Watson, & Skinner, 2001), the Wechsler Intelligence Scale for Children–Revised (WISC–III) (Wechsler, 1991), the Woodcock-Johnson III Achievement Battery (Woodcock, McGrew, & Mather, 2001), the Behavioral Objective Sequence (BOS) (Braaten, 1998), and the Social Skills Rating Scale (SSRS—Teacher, Student, and Parent Form) (Gresham & Elliot, 1990). The student support team was careful to consider cultural bias in the use of these instruments, observations, and rating scales. The WISC–III and Woodcock-Johnson III, like most tests, have culturally loaded items, and teacher bias might be a factor in the observations and in the scoring of the rating scales (Winzer & Mazurek, 1998).

The School Archival Records Search (SARS) (Walker et al., 1991) revealed that Rodriguez had attended four schools in the past two years and was never considered for retention or special education services. However, he had received Title I Services for mathematics. The search of records indicated that Rodriguez had an average of six office referrals for behavioral incidents per month during both fourth and fifth grades. He had worked with the school counselor once a week in an effort to strengthen his social behavior.

A functional behavioral assessment was conducted to determine both the function and contexts of Rodriguez's problem behavior. A structured interview was completed with his teacher as part of this assessment. This interview revealed that Rodriguez enjoyed interacting with his peers, especially in a group context, as well as having one-on-one time with adults. Unfortunately, he also exhibited behaviors that were disturbing to classmates and teachers, such as destroying school materials, teasing students, stealing, sleeping in class, bullying other students, and disrupting the class. Medication once taken for behavior control had been discontinued. The results of the interview indicated that one or more of these identified problem behaviors occurred daily. Problem behaviors occurred in multiple settings (e.g., on the playground, on the school bus, in the cafeteria, and in the classroom). The teacher stated that Rodriguez exhibited these behaviors in the presence of a variety of adults (i.e., teachers, playground supervisors, paraeducators). Further, the teacher believed that Rodriguez did not have a positive relationship of trust and respect with any significant adult at school or at home, nor did he have close friendships with other students.

After the structured interview was completed, a direct observation of Rodriguez in his class was conducted using an ABC (Antecedent, Behavior, Consequence) analysis form (Cooper, Heron, & Heward, 1987; Witt, Daly, & Noell, 2000). The observation suggested that much of Rodriguez's behavior was designed primarily to get attention from adults and other students. He did not appear to use negative behavior to avoid or escape academic work or other activities, and his behavior did not appear to express cultural conflict.

In addition to collecting information about Rodriguez's problem behaviors, the team members asked the teacher to complete a strength-based behavioral rating scale, the *Behavioral Objective Sequence* or BOS (Braaten, 1998), to determine his developmental level of prosocial skills, so that a positive, individualized behavioral support program (BSP) could be designed. Although the BOS currently is not normed for specific ethnic/racial groups, Wilder, Murray, and Shepherd (2000) conducted a study that compared teacher ratings of students with learning and behavior problems from four different ethnic/racial groups on the BOS: Hispanic Americans, African Americans, European Americans, and Native Americans. The researchers found that a few items functioned differently for these groups; however, the items on the BOS are largely a reflection of the traditional school prosocial culture and not biased toward any group in particular. Teachers should be aware of ways that behaviors of cultural groups typically differ from the school culture. (See subsequent sections in this chapter on multicultural and socioeconomic factors).

Strength-based or skills-based assessment instruments (e.g., the BOS [Braaten, 1998] or Epstein's *Behavior and Emotional Rating Scale* [Epstein & Sharma, 1998]) are valuable tools for busy professionals since rating scale items, positively stated, translate directly into objectives for a student's individualized education plan (IEP) or any behavioral support plan. A strength-based approach allows parents, professionals, and the student to recognize what is going right as well as what deficits a student may have. This approach establishes positive expectations for the student and sets the context for good relations between the professionals, the parents, and the student (Epstein, 1999). The results from the BOS rating scale indicated that Rodriguez's strengths were consistent school attendance, good personal hygiene, appropriate conversation skills, accepting help from adults on routine nonacademic and academic tasks, participating (at least minimally) in group-focused class activities, responding well to praise, and verbalizing that he has friends (interestingly, this is a contradiction from the observation).

Results from the Social Skills Rating Scale—Parent Form (SSRS) (Gresham & Elliot, 1990) indicated that at home and in the neighborhood, Rodriguez appeared to make friends easily; however, he bullied younger siblings and alternated between appropriate social behavior with family members and displaying depressed affect. The results from the Teacher Form (Gresham & Elliot, 1990) suggested that he used free time in an acceptable way and volunteered to help peers with classroom tasks; however, he did not initiate conversation or interactions with peers, make friends easily, or follow directions from adults. The data also indicate that he is excessively impulsive and fidgety. Rodriguez's data from the Student Form (Gresham & Elliot, 1990) indicated that he believed that he made friends, followed teacher directions, and controlled his temper. However, Rodriguez did recognize that he does not know how to join in games and activities.

In addition to the behavioral information already noted, the teacher reported that Rodriguez was on grade level in his academic work, despite his disruptive and off-task behavior.

The WISC-R IQ test revealed a full-scale score of 112. His academic achievement as tested with the Woodcock-Johnson III Achievement Test was within the normal range for all subscales except Math Calculation, Math Fluency, Passage Comprehension, and Reading Vocabulary. The scores on these four subscales may be early indicators of future academic difficulties.

Using the current federal definition (described earlier), school teams in some states might not qualify Rodriguez for special education services since his academic performance was on grade level. As the team at Rodriguez's school reviewed his assessment and needs, they determined he met their criteria to be classified as having an emotional/behavioral disorder. The team's decision was supported by the assessment results that indicated that Rodriguez's behavioral and emotional responses (1) were so different from his peers that they adversely affected his social and personal skills, (2) consistently occur in the classroom and on the playground, and (3) persisted despite attempted prereferral interventions. These results aligned directly with the coalition's definition (described earlier, Forness & Knitzer, 1992). The team anticipated that without intense services from various sources, Rodriguez's behavior would continue to deteriorate; thus, Rodriguez was identified as emotionally/behaviorally disordered. The school team also discussed multicultural and socioeconomic considerations relevant to Rodriguez.

Peers sometimes referred to Rodriguez, who is dark skinned, by using racial epithets. He teased his peers in retaliation, and his talking out and other negative adult attention-seeking behavior increased after teasing incidents. Belittling, degrading, and drawing undue attention to a person's skin color or ethnic origin commonly result in behaviors similar to those displayed by Rodriguez. Teachers sometimes ignore these behaviors among their students; some even participate in blatant or couched racism themselves.

Multicultural Factors

Professionals who work with students from diverse cultures who have emotional/behavioral disorders must never ignore bullying directed toward these students (Guetzloe, 1997; Wilder, 2002); they should "take a stand with the student and not against him or her" (Long, 1997, p. 245), offering responsive, caring, and kind adult help. Rodriguez should receive such support when others bully him, and his teacher should never allow him to bully others. Prejudicial beliefs (e.g., considering a certain group of students as lazy or less intelligent, less athletic, less friendly, or even *deserving of bullying*) decry the principle of individualization, a hallmark of special education (Hardman, Drew, & Egan, 1999), and counteract the constitutional principles of liberty and human rights in a democracy.

Although avoiding stereotypes and viewing students as individuals is of paramount importance for professionals working with students from diverse cultures, Hispanic American students—like other ethnic, cultural, or socioeconomic groups—usually have some social behaviors in common (Delgado Rivera & Rogers-Adkinson, 1997). Professionals should be aware of student social behaviors that may be related to culture in order to better address their students' educational needs, teaching them more efficiently and effectively.

For example, in cases like that of Rodriguez, it might be useful to know that some Hispanic students tend to be more comfortable with a cooperative interaction style than with the more prevalent competitive style of classroom interactions (Carraquillo, 1991). In addition, Hispanic students may feel more comfortable than others with close physical contact and frequent emotional expressions (except anger), and some may interpret a lack of such contact from the teacher as rejection (Lynch & Hanson, 1992). Hispanic students are often taught by their parents to avoid eye contact with adults as a sign of respect (Harry, 1994). This is sometimes problematic for teachers. Such students also have a relaxed concept of time. This puts them at a disadvantage in classrooms where on-time behavior is greatly valued and thus reinforced, and a relaxed concept of time is punished. This variable may also affect Hispanic students' performance on assessments, since many standardized tests have time limits (Hamayan & Domico, 1991). School personnel must be aware of cultural factors and be educated as to how they should interact with students from diverse backgrounds.

Socioeconomic Factors

In reference to the case study, both of Rodriguez's parents worked, and the family income was marginally adequate. Low SES is not uncommon among students with emotional/behavioral difficulties. In addition to multicultural factors, school professionals should consider socioeconomic factors as they work with students with emotional/behavioral challenges. Poverty negatively impacts the life of any child, regardless of race or ethnicity (Hodgkinson, 1995). Achenbach and Edelbrook (1981) found teachers' behavioral ratings of students varied more according to student SES than they did across races; professionals rated students with low SES as exhibiting the most problematic behavior of any group. Wilder (1999) found that for students with EBD, students' self-assessment of behavior was most unlike the teachers' assessment of that same behavior when students had low socioeconomic status.

Socioeconomic status is a powerful predictor of school failure, antisocial behavior, and mental illness (Coutinho et al., 2002). Werner and Smith (1992) found that low SES was the single-greatest predictor of mental illness in children and youth before age 18. In addition, students with low SES consistently perform lower than other students at all grade levels in academic achievement. They are also more likely to be identified with behavior problems, to be suspended from school, and to be referred for special education services than students with middle socioeconomic status (Grossman, 1991).

Students with low socioeconomic status "are more likely to require warmth and support in addition to good instruction and to need more encouragement for their efforts and praise for their successes" (Brophy, 1986, p. 1073). Peers may tease students with low SES for wearing unfashionable secondhand clothing, for smelling like they haven't bathed or brushed their teeth, for their lack of trendy toys, or for their lack of school supplies. Students with low SES frequently have less than sufficient health and dental care, which often results in poor school attendance. They are additionally at risk of school failure for their lack of access to current technology and library facilities after school hours and for their lack of access to productive after-school activities such as clubs, sports teams, community centers, religious organizations, and service-learning opportunities—all forms of participation that can serve as protective factors to curb inappropriate social behavior. Of course, teachers have an obligation to do what they can to alleviate these problems for students (see Wilder, 2002). As with multicultural factors, low SES factors affect every child differently.

As school personnel offer their best efforts in attempting to solve the problems of students with emotional problems and behavioral difficulties in schools, they cannot design truly effective interventions without considering multicultural and socioeconomic factors that impact children and youth in schools. They must also consider prevention and intervention strategies at multiple levels.

Multilevel Interventions

All students are at risk to some degree; risk is a continuum from a few minor factors to multiple serious factors. Educators have learned that prevention and intervention must occur at multiple levels. Researchers have identified three levels of intervention: primary, secondary, and tertiary (Algozzine & Kay, 2002; Sprague & Walker, 2000; Walker et al., 1995). All students need some level of positive behavior support. *Primary or universal interventions* are schoolwide systems, such as teaching social skills, establishing and delivering effective instruction, and implementing a schoolwide discipline plan (such a plan typically serves the needs of 90 percent or more of students). The main purpose of primary interventions is to promote positive social development, as well as prevent the onset of emotional/behavioral disorders and antisocial behavior by improving the environment for all students.

Secondary interventions provide services to approximately 7 percent of students who do not respond positively to the primary interventions and who are at risk for serious behavior problems. Typically, secondary interventions target classrooms and small groups. *Tertiary interventions,* which are intensive and individualized, are applicable to 3 percent of the students. The purpose of tertiary interventions is to prevent additional decline of a student's behavior and ameliorate current problems by designing a plan that is specifically tailored for the student with severe and chronic problem behaviors (Algozzine & Kay, 2002; Sprague & Walker, 2000; Walker et al., 1995).

In the case study, the faculty at Rodriguez's elementary school had previously selected and implemented a schoolwide discipline plan and social skills training as primary interventions for their student body. However, neither of these strategies prevented Rodriguez from continuing to develop ongoing problem behaviors. Eventually, his behavior became problematic for other students, faculty, and staff, as well as for Rodriguez himself; therefore, a team of educators determined that it was necessary to design a behavioral support plan to meet Rodriguez's individual needs and to help him build protective factors.

Behavioral Support Plan

The purpose of a behavioral support plan is to translate the data from the comprehensive assessment conducted by the team of professionals into strategies that meet the individual needs of students (Gresham, Watson, & Skinner, 2001). How does one design and implement a behavioral support plan from the results of a functional behavior assessment (FBA) and other behavioral assessments such as the BOS and SSRS? First, the team of educators (e.g., teachers, school psychologists, and administrators) determine the function of the child's problem behavior(s) from the results of the FBA. For example, a student's behavior might occur primarily for the function of getting attention, or the purpose might be avoiding difficult academic assignments. The team then explores possible interventions and procedures for decreasing inappropriate behavior while increasing alternative prosocial behavior.

A critical component of the behavioral support plan is to identify the student's strengths and to further develop his or her prosocial behavior that may be overshadowed by the problem behavior(s).

A behavioral support plan can consist of one or a combination of the following procedures: (1) preliminary strategies, (2) instructional strategies, (3) reinforcement procedures, and (4) correction procedures. The purpose of the preliminary strategies is to use preventative measures in an effort to reduce the occurrence of the problem behavior, such as making changes in the people who are present when the problem behavior is likely to occur or modifying expectations/routines. Instructional strategies are implemented to teach the child a replacement behavior, often referred to as a *target behavior.* For example, the student may require instruction in the area of social, communication, or self-management skills. As was mentioned previously, the BOS (Braaten, 1998) is a valuable tool because its rating scale items translate directly into developmentally appropriate objectives that can be used to design an instructional program to directly teach a child the skills he or she needs to be successful.

Another possible intervention is to implement reinforcement procedures—specifically, identifying potential reinforcers, establishing specific behavior criteria, determining a schedule of reinforcement, and identifying a delivery system. This procedure may be in the form of a self-monitoring strategy, behavioral contracts, group contingencies, home note system, token economy, and so forth (Rhode, Jenson, & Reavis, 1992). Often, sincere, specific praise is powerful enough to improve behavior (Latham, 1998). Brief praise notes commending specific behavior are also very effective. Sometimes it is necessary to couple reinforcement procedures with correction procedures, such as using precision commands, corrective teaching, or response costs (Rhode et al., 1992; Young et al., 1997). An educator can select from these procedures when designing a behavioral intervention plan customized for individual students' needs.

The following is a discussion of how Rodriguez's comprehensive behavior assessment in the case study was interpreted and what behavioral interventions ensued. The common problem behavior (discovered by way of the various assessment instruments, i.e., the functional behavioral assessment, BOS, and SSRS) was seeking attention from adults and other students, in the form of yelling, teasing, destroying school materials, and bullying. This attention-seeking behavior was found to be a problem primarily in the classroom and on the playground. The behaviors identified by the team as replacement behaviors for Rodriguez's inappropriate attention-seeking behaviors included (1) the use of appropriate language and raising his hand to get the teacher to respond to his personal needs and wishes, (2) appropriate participation in group social activities, (3) following teacher instructions, and (4) staying on task during independent work time (Braaten, 1998). The team chose to begin working on these behaviors in an effort to help Rodriguez feel success both in the classroom and on the playground.

Researchers have found that a combination of classroom and playground interventions decrease problem behaviors while increasing appropriate behaviors (Eddy, Reid, & Fetrow, 2000; Walker et al., 1995). Eddy and associates (2000) implemented social skills instruction in elementary classrooms and unstructured free play on the playground in an effort to reduce students' physical aggression and inattentive behavior. They reported that the interventions produced statistically significant results on reducing these problem behaviors.

Furthermore, the researchers indicated significant improvement in the students' positive behavior. Based on this research and Rodriguez's needs, two interventions were designed to help Rodriguez acquire the two identified behaviors—one for the classroom and the other for the playground.

One component of the classroom intervention consisted of social skills instruction in How to Get the Teacher's Attention, How to Follow Instructions, and How to Ask to Participate (Young, West, Marchant, Morgan, & Mitchem, 1997). The special education teacher and Rodriguez's general education teacher accepted the responsibility to team teach social skills to the entire class in an effort to build Rodriguez's social behavior in a general education context. The Direct Teaching Sequence, a preteaching strategy that requires both verbal repetition and behavioral rehearsal of the social skill, was used to teach these skills (Marchant & Young, 2001). Using this didactic, interactive method to practice social skills has been documented to produce prosocial behavior that is significantly better than that generated through the use of therapeutic and or problem-solving skills (Walker et al., 1995; Kazdin, 1997).

In the case study, the purpose for providing social skills training in Rodriguez's general education classroom versus providing the training exclusively in a pullout setting was threefold. First, the team believed that all students in the classroom could benefit from the instruction. Second, researchers reported that in order for children and youth with antisocial behavior to alter their behavior, their peers should also be involved in the social skills training (Walker et al., 1995). When peers are included in the training sessions, they are more likely to accept, rather than reject, the child into settings (e.g., playground) that are apart from the training setting because the peers have witnessed the student's ability to use prosocial behavior. This was an important element for Rodriguez's behavioral support plan because he needed to learn how to cooperate with his classmates.

Generalization of the social skills from one context to another is the third reason for teaching the skills in a large-group setting (Walker et al., 1995). After Rodriguez acquired the social skill in a small-group or one-on-one context, he needed to transfer the skills to other settings, such as the classroom and lunchroom, as well as with other adults and children. Rodriguez also needed to learn appropriate classroom survival skills, such as how to get the teacher's attention appropriately; the team felt that this skill was best learned within the context of the classroom.

In a prevention program conducted for students at risk for emotional disturbance, the researchers investigated the impact of classwide social skills instruction, peer tutoring, and positive behavior management on inappropriate behaviors (Kamps, Kravits, Rauch, Kamps, & Chung, 2000). They reported that the inappropriate behaviors—specifically, aggression, out-of-seat, and negative verbalizations—were significantly reduced and that an increase in academic engagement and behavior compliance transpired concurrently.

In the case of Rodriguez, verbal teacher praise, a reinforcement procedure, was identified as a second component for the classroom intervention, due to the findings from the results of the Behavioral Objective Sequence that indicated that Rodriguez responded well to praise. Kauffman, Mostert, Trent, and Hallahan (1998, p. 51) stated that "positive reinforcement is the staple of good behavior management." Praise is one of the most natural, positive reinforcers for teachers to use in their daily routine. Considering this information, the team recommended that the general education teacher wear a MotivAider® (Behavioral

Dynamics, 2000), a device that vibrates at the end of a preprogrammed interval that serves as a prompt for the teacher to deliver a praise statement. Rodriguez's teacher agreed to wear this device in order to increase her praise rate. In addition, each staff member who worked with Rodriguez made an effort to write at least one praise note per day that specifically described the appropriate behavior that they observed him using in class or in other areas of the school.

The playground intervention consisted of structured practice of the social skill referred to as How to Ask to Participate, with a self-monitoring strategy. It was determined that the school counselor would invite Rodriguez and two or three other fifth-graders to his office two times per week. First, the counselor reviewed the social skill (e.g., How to Ask to Participate) with the group. Then the group played a game or participated in an activity. This provided structured practice for rehearsing and using the skill.

In addition, Rodriguez was given a self-monitoring card that he took with him during his recesses. This card had a place for him to write what activity he participated in and with whom he participated; there were also boxes for the playground supervisor's initials and his own initials. The playground supervisor wrote her initials in the box if Rodriguez had participated appropriately—no bullying, teasing, or other inappropriate behavior. Similarly, Rodriguez wrote his initials in an adjacent box if he felt that he had used appropriate social skills on the playground. If the playground supervisor and Rodriguez agreed that appropriate behavior had been used, he received 5 points, which were later exchanged for tangible reinforcers. If the supervisor recorded that Rodriguez's behavior was appropriate, but Rodriguez disagreed, he received 3 points. The inverse results of this scenario resulted in zero points.

Self-management is a set of strategies that a person uses to alter his or her own behavior, frequently to make a behavior less aversive to others and to replace a problem behavior with a behavior that is likely to be more productive (Young et al., 1991). Two potential benefits of teaching students to manage their own behavior are (1) the teacher's (or staff's) responsibility for primarily managing the student's problem behavior is decreased and (2) the student learns to take responsibility for his or her own behavior (Cole & Bambara, 1992; Young et al., 1991). In a study conducted by Rhode, Morgan, and Young (1983), six students with emotional and behavior disorders used a self-management treatment procedure to maintain appropriate behavior in both special and general education classroom settings via self-recording combined with teacher's matching of their behavior on a fixed-interval schedule. Analysis of the results of the study indicated that students acquired and maintained high levels of appropriate classroom behavior.

Research by Rhode and colleagues (1983) indicated that self-management can be a successful procedure for children and youth who have behavior problems. Additional research suggested that the use of self-management is a procedure that teachers find acceptable and feasible (Mitchem & Young, 2001). In Rodriguez's case, the teacher and playground supervisor determined the self-monitoring intervention was feasible and acceptable because their responsibility was minimal. Furthermore, as of Rodriguez's developed cooperative social skills, he became personally aware of and more responsible for his daily behavior on the playground with the use of the self-monitoring strategy.

The points Rodriguez earned for self-monitoring his playground activities were exchanged for both social and tangible reinforcers. The special education teacher talked with

Rodriguez to determine his preference of reinforcers, a strategy recommended by Kauff-man and associates (1998) to assess reinforcers that are appealing and potentially effective for students. The survey and teacher interview indicated that he preferred interacting with his peers in a group or spending time on the computer playing games. Thus, Rodriguez exchanged the points he earned for time with peers, structured activities, and playing computer games by himself or with a selected friend approved by the general education teacher.

In an effort to provide Rodriguez with mentors (i.e., older students, big brothers, adults) who could help him to build more protective factors in his life, the counselor and special education teacher chose to alternate days where they would spend one-on-one time with Rodriguez in both leisure and educational activities. Both Rodriguez and these faculty members shared in selecting the activities, which included eating lunch together, reading, playing a board game, working on homework, and so forth. To make mentoring an even more salient intervention, they located a mentor from the Hispanic American community who could consistently spend time with Rodriguez.

Considering that the origins of behavior problems are associated with conditions in the home and community, it seemed logical that the parents become involved in altering their children's behavior (Marchant & Young, 2001). As the team evaluated the needs of Rodriguez and his parents, they recognized that the parents' willingness to enhance their relationship with their son was a strength that should be built on to assist Rodriguez as an individual and his family at large. A united effort between parents and schools provides consistency needed to develop appropriate behavior (Kauffman et al., 1998). When parents are involved in the teaching of social skills, the overall effectiveness of a program is enhanced because of the increased number of settings and change agents involved in strengthening the child's behavior; as a result, the overall impact on the child's prosocial behavior is likely to be heightened (Marchant & Young, 2001, Walker et al., 1995).

Thus, another intervention that the school chose to offer the parents was a parent coach to teach and support them in the use of positive parenting skills in their home on a weekly basis. The parent coach provided them with a skills-based approach designed to teach Rodriguez appropriate behavior, such as compliance, coupled with positive reinforcement strategies. Rodriguez and his parents participated in role-plays in order to practice the positive behavior and parenting skills. During these role-plays, the parent coach provided positive and corrective feedback. She also visited the home at times that were identified by the parents as challenging for positive parent-child interactions and offered suggestions to the parents as to how to specifically change their behavior in an effort to improve their interaction with Rodriguez.

Marchant and Young (2001) conducted a study in which a parent coach assisted parents in acquiring and implementing positive parenting skills, including preteaching and corrective teaching strategies of a social skill, giving positive reinforcement, and delivering appropriate instructions. The parents successfully learned and used the skills-based teaching techniques and the positive reinforcement strategies to improve their children's compliance. The analysis of the data suggests that these techniques were successful in altering the children's behavior. In addition, the parents and children's opinion were evaluated and the results indicated that the procedures and strategies were effective, feasible, and acceptable by both parents and children.

CASE STUDY OUTCOMES
RODRIGUEZ

Toward the conclusion of Rodriguez's fifth-grade school year, the team reconvened to assess his progress. As they evaluated the data from the behavioral support plan, they discovered a variety of outcomes. One positive outcome, as indicated by both informal observation and the self-monitoring data, was that Rodriguez's peer-to-peer social skills had significantly improved. Specifically, his ability to ask to participate in activities was much more appropriate than before the social skills and self-monitoring interventions. Rodriguez's classmates reported that they now enjoyed Rodriguez joining in classroom and playground games. Due to this finding, the team recommended that social skills instruction and the self-monitoring procedures continue into the sixth grade.

Unfortunately, the same level of improvement was not seen in Rodriguez's academic and school behavior. However, the team noted glimpses of progress as they reviewed samples of his daily classroom assignments and test scores. The teacher reported that Rodriguez more frequently got her attention appropriately, but he still required substantial practice and support in this area. Therefore, the team suggested that the plan that was established for classroom behavior during Rodriguez's fifth-grade year also be resumed during the sixth-grade year.

Another profitable outcome of the behavioral support plan was that the mentor, Juan, from the Hispanic American community decided to enroll Rodriguez in an after-school community program where Juan volunteered. The results from this were many. First, it offered Rodriguez a replacement for the unstructured time that he had previously experienced during his after-school hours. Second, the social interaction was yet another venue in which Rodriguez could practice appropriate peer-to-peer skills. And finally, it provided an opportunity for Juan to spend time with Rodriguez in both group and one-on-one contexts. Rodriguez's behavior at the community center, where the after-school program was conducted, indicated that he enjoyed the environment and people with whom he interacted. He also reported to his parents and the school counselor that he wanted to continue to spend time with Juan because he was "cool and nice." Thus, the team decided that a mentor was a valuable part of the behavioral support plan and that the relationship should be maintained throughout the summer and into the next year.

As viable members of the behavioral support team, the parents committed to continue to collaborate closely with Rodriguez's teacher and those invested in Rodriguez's academic and social development during the upcoming year. They expressed a desire to continue to receive assistance from the parent coach.

Overall, Rodriguez's progress in his social development proved satisfactory to the behavioral support team. The most rewarding outcome from the behavioral support plan was Rodriguez's comment to his mother that he liked school now because he had friends and felt better about doing his schoolwork. By the end of the year, the team noticed his depressed affect had changed into one of happiness, as indicated by his contagious smile and energy to participate in home, school, and after-school activities.

The success with Rodriguez was due, to a large degree, to personnel focusing on four key components of a systematic school plan discussed in this chapter. First, school personnel were aware of the concept of risk and protective factors and the need for systematic screening for at-risk students. Second, they used a comprehensive approach to assessment, including a functional behavioral assessment to identify the functions of target behaviors. Third, the school had in place a multiple-levels approach to services, including a primary level of prevention and early intervention (e.g., schoolwide social skills instruction and praise notes). Finally, they had a functioning student support team to plan and implement secondary and tertiary interventions. This team developed a comprehensive "positive behavior support plan (PBSP)" that had impact on Rodriguez's life. The PBSP was both comprehensive (i.e., addressed Rodriguez's multiple needs) and intensive in nature (i.e., was implemented in multiple settings and with multiple persons).

CONCLUSION

Lane, Gresham, and O'Shaughnessy (2002) examined the EBD literature and concluded the following:

> Many schools do not take advantage of current knowledge about early identification and prevention/intervention strategies for children with learning difficulties and/or emotional or behavioral problems. Too many schools have a policy of waiting for teachers to refer children who are having academic and/or behavioral difficulties *after* problems appear rather than identifying children who are at risk *before* problems occur (also see Forness, Kavale, MacMillan, Asarnow, & Duncan, 1996; Lane, 1999; Torgesen & Wagner, 1998). Because of the progressive nature of many learning and social/emotional difficulties, it is essential that more schools adopt proactive practices. (p. 5)

A compelling body of research demonstrates that most children at risk for emotional and behavioral disorders are responsive to systematically planned and implemented prevention and early intervention programs (Lane et al., 2002).

DISCUSSION QUESTIONS

1. How can protective factors (flexible temperament, supportive family, positive social skills, successful involvement in school activities, and attachment to community activities) be facilitated for or taught to students with EBD and their families?

2. How should school personnel use deficit-based and strength-based assessment information to develop a combination of strategies that provide positive supports for the student at risk?

3. How does culture affect behavior for students with emotional/behavioral disorders?

4. How do professionals minimize or avoid cultural bias in assessing, placing, and instructing students with EBD?

These examples of research-validated practice are frequently used in school programs for students with emotional/behavioral disorders. Additional readings for intervention strategies are listed below.

SUGGESTED READINGS

Beck, R. (1997–2000). *RIDE: Responding to Individual Differences in Education: Elementary school level*. Longmont, CO: Sopris West.

Breen, M. J., & Fiedler, C. R. (1996). *Behavioral approach to assessment of youth with emotional/behavioral disorders*. Austin, TX: ProEd.

Epstein, M. H., & Sharma, J. M. (1998). *Behavioral and Emotional Rating Scale.* Austin, TX: Pro-Ed.

Goldstein, A. (1999). *The Prepare Curriculum: Teaching prosocial competencies.* Champaign, IL: Research Press.

Goldstein, A. P., & McGinnis, E. (1997). *Skillstreaming series.* Champaign, IL: Research Press.

Greenwood, C. (1997). *Together we can: Classwide peer tutoring to improve basic academic skills.* Longmont, CO: Sopris West.

Latham, G. (1998). *Keys to classroom management.* North Logan, UT: P & T ink.

Obiakor, F. (1994). *The eight step multicultural approach: Learning and teaching with a smile.* Dubuque, IA: Kendall/Hunt.

Reid, J., & Patterson, G. R. (1991). Early prevention and intervention with conduct problems: A social interactional model for the integration of research and practice. In G. Stoner, M. Shinn, & H. M. Walker (Eds.), *Interventions for achievement and behavior problems* (pp. 715–740). Silver Spring, MD: National Association of School Psychologists.

Rhode, G., Jenson, W., & Reavis, H. K. (1992). *The tough kid book: Practical classroom management strategies.* Longmont, CO: Sopris West.

Sheridan, S. M., (1995–2000). *The tough kid social skills book.* Longmont, CO: Sopris West.

Sitlington, P. L., Clark, G. M., & Kolstoe, O. P. (2000). *Transition education & services for adolescents with disabilities.* Boston: Allyn and Bacon.

Sprick, R., & Howard, L. (1995). *Teacher's encyclopedia of behavior management.* Longmont, CO: Sopris West.

Walker, H. (1995). *The acting out child: Coping with classroom disruption.* Longmont, CO: Sopris West.

Walker, H. (1999). *First step to success.* Longmont, CO: Sopris West.

Walker, H. M., Block-Pedego, A., Todis, B., & Severson, H. (1991). *School archival records search (SARS): User's guide and technical manual.* Longmont, CO: Sopris West.

Wechsler, D. (1991). *Wechsler Intelligence Scale for Children* (3rd ed.). San Antonio, TX: The Psychological Corporation.

Young, K. R., West, R. P., Smith, D. J., & Morgan, D. P. (1991–2000). *Teaching self-management strategies to adolescents.* Longmont, CO: Sopris West.

REFERENCES

Achenbach, T. M., & Edelbrock, C. S. (1981). Behavior problems and competencies reported by parents of normal and disturbed children aged four through sixteen. *Monographs for the Society of Research in Child Development, 46* (1, Serial No. 188).

Alberg, J., Petry, C., & Eller, A. (1994). *A resource guide for social skills instruction.* Longmont, CO: Sopris West.

Algozzine, B., & Kay, P. (Eds.). (2002). *Preventing problem behaviors: A handbook of successful prevention strategies.* Thousand Oaks, CA: Corwin Press.

Algozzine, B., & Kay, P. (2002). Promising practices for preventing problem behaviors. In B. Algozzine & P. Kay (Eds.), *Preventing problem behaviors: A handbook of successful prevention strategies.* Thousand Oaks, CA: Corwin Press.

Algozzine, B., & White, R. (2002). *Preventing behaviors using schoolwide discipline.* Thousand Oaks, CA: Corwin Press.

American Psychiatric Association. (2000). *Diagnostic and statistical manual of mental disorders* (4th ed.) (Text rev.) Washington, DC: Author.

American Psychological Association. (1993). *Violence and youth: Psychology's response.* Washington, DC: Author.

Anderson, J., & Werry, J. S. (1994). Emotional and behavioral problems. In I. B. Pless (Ed.), *The epidemiology of childhood disorders* (pp. 304–338). New York: Oxford University Press.

Baca, L. M., & Cervantes, H. T. (1998). *The bilingual special education interface* (3rd ed.). Upper Saddle River, NJ: Prentice-Hall.

Bakken, J. P., & Aloia, G. F. (1999). Transitioning multicultural learners with exceptionalities. In F. E. Obiakor, J. O. Schwenn, & A. F. Rotatori (Eds.), *Advances in special education: Multicultural education for learners with exceptionalities* (Vol. 12, pp. 217–232). Stamford, CT: JAI Press.

Bandura, A. (1986). *Social foundations of thought and action: A social cognitive theory.* Upper Saddle River, NJ: Prentice-Hall.

Banks, J. A., & Banks, C. A. (Eds.). (1997). *Multicultural education: Issues and perspectives* (3rd ed.). Boston: Allyn and Bacon.

Biglan, A. (1995). Translating what we know about the context of antisocial behavior into lower prevalence of such behavior. *Journal of Applied Behavior Analysis, 28,* 479–492.

Bolger, K. E., Patterson, C. J., Thompson, W. W., & Kupersmidt, J. B. (1995). Psychosocial adjustment among children experiencing persistent and intermittent family economic hardship. *Child Development, 66,* 1107–1129.

Bos, C. S., Coleman, M., & Vaughn, S. (2002). Reading and students with E/BD: What do we know and recommend? In K. L. Lane, F. M. Gresham, & T. E. O'Shaughnessy (Eds.), *Interventions for children with or at risk for emotional and behavioral disorders* (pp. 87–103). Boston: Allyn and Bacon.

Botvin, G. J., Schinke, S., & Orlandi, M. A. (1995). School-based health promotion: Substance abuse and sexual behavior. *Applied and Preventive Psychology, 4,* 167–184.

Bower, E. M. (1981). *Early identification of emotionally handicapped children in school* (3rd ed.). Springfield, IL: Thomas.

Braaten, S. (1998). *Behavioral Objective Sequence.* Champaign, IL: Research Press.

Brandenburg, N. A., Friedman, R. M., & Silver, S. E. (1990). The epidemiology of childhood psychiatric disorder: Prevalence findings from recent studies. *Journal of the American Academy of Child and Adolescent Psychiatry, 29,* 76–83.

Brophy J. (1986). Teacher influences on student achievement. *American Psychologist, 41,* 1069–1077.

Campbell-Whatley, G. D., Algozzine, B., & Obiakor, F. (1997). Using mentoring to improve academic programming for African American male youths with mild disabilities. *The School Counselor, 44,* 362–366.

Carraquillo, A. L. (1991). *Hispanic children and youth in the United States: A resource guide.* New York: Garland Publishing.

Cicchetti, D., & Toth, S. L. (1995). A developmental psychopathology perspective on child abuse and neglect. *Journal of the American Academy of Child and Adolescent Psychiatry, 34,* 541–565.

Cole, C. L., & Bambara, L. M. (1992). Issues surrounding the use of self-management intervention in the school. *School Psychology Review, 21*(2), 193–201.

Coleman, M. C., & Gilliam, J. E. (1983). Disturbing behaviors in the classroom: A survey of teacher attitudes. *Journal of Special Education, 17,* 121–129.

Coleman, M., & Vaughn, S. (2000). Reading interventions for students with emotional/behavioral disorders. *Behavioral Disorders, 25,* 93–104.

Cooper, J. O., Heron, T. E., & Heward, W. L. (1987). *Applied behavior analysis.* Upper Saddle River, NJ: Merrill/Prentice-Hall.

Costello, E. J., Messer, S. C., Bird, H. R., Cohen, P., & Reinherz, H. Z. (1998). The prevalence of serious emotional disturbance: A re-analysis of community studies. *Journal of Child and Family Studies, 7,* 411–432.

Council for Children with Behavioral Disorders Executive Committee. (1987). Position paper on definition and identification of students with behavioral disorders. *Behavioral Disorders, 13,* 9–19.

Coutinho, M. J., Oswald, D. P., & Forness, S. R. (2002). Gender and sociodemographic factors and the disproportionate identification of culturally and linguistically diverse students with emotional disturbance. *Behavioral Disorders, 27*(2), 109–125.

Dawson, L., Venn, M. L., & Gunter, P. L. (2000). The effects of teacher versus computer reading models. *Behavioral Disorders, 25,* 105–113.

DeBaryshe, B. D., Patterson, G. R., & Capaldi, D. M. (1993). A performance model for academic achievement in early adolescent boys. *Development Psychology, 29,* 795–804.

Delgado, B. M., & Rogers-Adkinson, D. (1999). Educating the Hispanic-American exceptional learner. In F. E. Obiakor, J. O. Schwenn, & A. F. Rotatori (Eds.), *Advances in special education: Multicultural education for learners with exceptionalities* (Vol. 12, pp. 53–71). Stamford, CT: JAI Press.

Delgado Rivera, B., & Rogers-Adkinson, D. (1997). Culturally sensitive interventions: Social skills training with children and parents from culturally and linguistically diverse backgrounds. *Intervention in School and Clinic, 33,* 75–80.

Delpit, L. (1995). *Other people's children: Cultural conflict in the classroom.* New York: New Press.

Dinges, N. G., Atlis, M. M., & Vincent, G. M. (1997). Cross-cultural perspectives on antisocial behavior. In D. M. Stoff, J. Breiling, & J. D. Maser (Eds.), *Handbook of anti-social behavior* (pp. 463–473). New York: Wiley.

Dodge, K. (1985). A social information processing model of social competence in children. In M. Perlmutter (Ed.), *Minnesota symposium in child psychology* (Vol. 18, pp. 107–135). New York: Academic Press.

Dodge, K., Coie, J., & Brakke, N. (1982). Behavior patterns of socially rejected and neglected adolescents: The roles of social approach and aggression. *Journal of Abnormal Child Psychology, 10,* 389–410.

Dooley, E. A., & Voltz, D. L. (1999), Educating the African-American exceptional learner. In F. E. Obiakor, J. O. Schwenn, & A. F. Rotatori (Eds.), *Advances in special education: Multicultural education for learners with exceptionalities* (Vol. 12, pp. 15–32). Stamford, CT: JAI Press.

Drummond, T. (1993). *The Student Risk Screening Scale (SRSS).* Grants Pass, OR: Josephine County Mental Health Program.

Eddy, J. M., Reid, J. B., & Fetrow, R. A. (2000). An elementary school-based prevention program targeting modifiable antecedents of youth delinquency and violence: Linking the interests of families and teachers (LIFT). *Journal of Emotional and Behavioral Disorders, 8*(3), 165–175.

Epstein, M. (1999). Using strength-based assessment in programs for children with emotional and behavioral disorders. *Beyond Behavior, 9*(2), 25–27.

Epstein, M. H., Kinder, D., & Bursuck, B. (1989). The academic status of adolescents with behavioral disorders. *Behavioral Disorders, 14,* 157–165.

Epstein, M. H., & Sharma, J. M. (1998). *Behavioral and Emotional Rating Scale.* Austin, TX: Pro-Ed.

Farmer, T. W., Farmer, E. M. Z., & Gut, D. (1999). Implications of social development research for school based interventions for aggressive youth with emotional and behavioral disorders. *Journal of Emotional and Behavioral Disorder, 7,* 130–136.

Farmer, T. W., & Hollowell, J. H. (1994). Social networks in mainstream classrooms: Social affiliations and behavioral characteristics of students with EBD. *Journal of Emotional and Behavioral Disorders, 2,* 143–155.

Felner, R. D., Brand, S., DuBois, D., Adan, A. M., Mulhall, P. F., & Evans, E. G. (1995). Socioeconomic disadvantage, proximal environmental experiences, and socioemotional and academic adjustment in early adolescence: Investigation of a mediated effects model. *Child Development, 66,* 774–792.

Forehand, R., & McMahon, R. (1981). *Helping the noncompliant child.* New York: Guilford Press.

Forness, S. R., Kavale, K. A., MacMillan, D. L., Asarnow, J. R., & Duncan, B. B. (1996). Early detection and prevention of emotional or behavioral disorders: Developmental aspects of systems of care. *Behavioral Disorders, 21,* 226–240.

Forness, S. R., & Knitzer, J. (1992). A new proposed definition and terminology to replace "serious emotional disturbance" in Individuals with Disabilities Education Act. *School Psychology Review, 21,* 12–20.

Foster, G. G., Ysseldyke, J. E., & Reese, J. H. (1975). "I wouldn't have seen it if I hadn't believed it." *Exceptional Children, 41,* 469–473.

Franklin, M. E. (1992). Culturally sensitive instructional practices for African-American learners with disabilities. *Exceptional Children, 59,* 115–122.

Gall, M. D., Borg, W. R., & Gall, J. P. (1996). *Educational research* (6th ed.). White Plains, NY: Longman.

Garmezy, N. (1987). Stress, competence, and development. Continuities in the study of schizophrenic adults, children vulnerable to psychopathology, and the search for stress-resistant children. *American Journal of Orthopsychiatry, 57,* 159–174.

Giddan, J. J., Bade, K. M., Rickenberg, D., & Ryley, A. T. (1995). Teaching the language of feelings to students with severe emotional and behavioral handicaps. *Language, Speech, and Hearing Services in the Schools, 26,* 3–13.

Gottfredson, D. C., Gottfredson, G. D., & Hyble, L. G. (1993). Managing adolescent behavior: A multiyear, multischool study. *American Educational Research Journal, 30,* 179–215.

Gresham, F. M., & Elliot, S. N. (1990). *Social skills rating system.* Circle Pines, MN: American Guidance Service.

Gresham, F. M., MacMillan, D. L., & Bocain, K. M. (1996). Behavioral earthquakes: Low frequency, salient behavioral events that differentiate students at-risk for behavioral disorders. *Behavioral Disorders, 21,* 277–292.

Gresham, F. M., Watson, T. S., & Skinner, C. H. (2001). Functional behavioral assessment: Principles, procedures, and future directions. *School Psychology Review, 30*(2), 156–172.

Grossman, H. (1991). Special education in a diverse society: Improving services for minority and working class students. *Preventing School Failure, 36*(1), 19–27.

Guerra, N. G., Huesmann, L. R., Tolan, P. H., Van Acker, R., & Eron, L. D. (1995). Stressful events and individual beliefs as correlates of economic disadvantage and aggression among urban children. *Journal of Consulting and Clinical Psychology, 63,* 518–528.

Guetzloe, E. (1997). The power of positive relationships: Mentoring programs in the school and community. *Preventing School Failure, 41*(3), 100–105.

Gunter, P. L., & Denny, R. K. (1998). Trends and issues in research regarding academic instruction of students with emotional and behavioral disorders. *Behavioral Disorders, 24,* 44–50.

Gunter, P. L., Denny, R. K., Jack, S. L., Shores, R. E., & Nelson, C. M. (1993). Aversive stimuli in academic interactions between students with serious emotional disturbance and their teachers. *Behavioral Disorders, 18,* 265–274.

Gunter, P. L., Hummel, J. H., & Conroy, M. A. (1998). Increasing correct academic responding: An effective intervention strategy to decrease behavior problems. *Effective School Practices, 17*(2), 36–54.

Gunter, P. L., & Reed, T. M. (1997). Academic instruction of children with emotional and behavior disorders using scripted lessons. *Preventing School Failure, 42,* 33–37.

Hallenbeck, B. A., & Kauffman, J. M. (1995). How does observational learning affect the behavior of students with emotional or behavioral disorders? A review of research. *Journal of Special Education, 29,* 45–71.

Hamayan, E. V., & Domico, J. S. (1991). Developing and using a second language. In E. V. Hamayan and J. S. Domico (Eds.), *Limiting bias in the assessment of bilingual students* (pp. 40–75). Austin, TX: Pro-Ed.

Hardman, M. L., Egan, M. W., & Drew, C. J. (1999). *Human exceptionality: Society, school, and family* (6th ed.). Boston: Allyn and Bacon.

Harris & Associates. (1994). *Pilot survey of young African American males in four cities.* New York: Commonwealth Fund.

Harry, B. (1994). Behavioral disorders in the context of families. In R. L. Peterson & Ishii-Jordan (Eds.), *Multicultural issues in the education of students with behavioral disorders* (pp. 149–161). Cambridge, MA: Brookline Books.

Hart, B., & Risley, T. R. (1995). *Meaningful differences in the everyday experience of young American children.* Baltimore: Brookes.

Henderson, H. A., & Fox, N. A. (1998). Inhibited and uninhibited children: Challenges in school settings. *School Psychology Review, 27,* 492–505.

Hetherington, E. M., & Martin, B. (1986). Family factors and psychopathology in children. In H. C. Quay & J. S. Werry (Eds.), *Psychopathological disorders of childhood* (3rd ed., pp. 332–390). New York: Wiley.

Hodgkinson, H. L. (1995). What should we call people? Race, class, and the census for 2000. *Phi Delta Kappan, 77,* 173–179.

Huesmann, L. R., Moise, J. F., & Podolski, C. (1997). The effects of media violence on the development of antisocial behavior. In D. M. Stoff, J. Breiling, & J. D. Maser (Eds.), *Handbook of antisocial behavior* (pp. 181–193). New York: Wiley.

Kamps, D. M. (2002). Preventing problems by improving behavior. In B. Algozzine & P. Kay (Eds.), *Preventing problem behaviors: A handbook of successful prevention strategies.* Thousand Oaks, CA: Corwin Press.

Kamps, D. M., & Kay, P. (2002). Preventing problems through social skills instruction. In B. Algozzine & P. Kay (Eds.), *Preventing problem behaviors: A handbook of successful prevention strategies.* Thousand Oaks, CA: Corwin Press.

Kamps, D. M., Kravits, T., Rauch, J., Kamps, J. L., & Chung, N. (2000). A prevention program for students with or at risk for ED: Moderating effects of variation in treatment and classroom structure. *Journal of Emotional and Behavioral Disorders, 8*(3), 141–154.

Kamps, D. M., & Tankersley, M. (1996). Prevention of behavioral and conduct disorders: Trends and research issues. *Behavioral Disorders, 22,* 41–48.

Kauffman, J. M. (1986). Educating children with behavior disorders. In R. J. Morris & B. Blatt (Eds.), *Special education: Research and trends* (pp. 249–271). New York: Pergamon.

Kauffman, J. M. (1992). Foreword. In K. R. Howe & O. B. Miramontes (Eds.), *The ethics of special education* (pp. xi–xvii). New York: Teachers College Press.

Kauffman, J. M. (1993). How we might achieve the radical reform of special education. *Exceptional Children, 60,* 6–16.

Kauffman, J. M. (2000). *Characteristics of emotional and behavioral disorders of children and youth* (7th ed.). Upper Saddle River, NJ: Merrill.

Kauffman, J. M., Mostert, M. P., Trent, S. C., & Hallahan, D. P. (1998). *Managing classroom behavior* (2nd ed.). Boston: Allyn and Bacon.

Kazdin, A. (1987). *Conduct disorders in childhood and adolescence.* London: Sage.

Kazdin, A. E. (1997). Acceptability of child treatment techniques: The influence of treatment, efficacy, and side effects. *Behavior Therapy, 12,* 493–506.

Kerr, M. M., & Zigmond, N. (1986). What do high school teachers want? A study of expectations and standards. *Education and Treatment of Children, 9,* 239–249.

Kupersmidt, J. B., Griesler, P. C., DeRosier, M. E., Patterson, C. J., & Davis, P. W. (1995). Childhood aggression and peer relations in the context of family and neighborhood factors. *Child Development, 66,* 360–375.

Kupersmidt, J. B., & Patterson, C. J. (1987). *Interim report to the Charlottesville Public Schools on children at risk.* Unpublished manuscript, University of Virginia, Charlottesville.

Lane, K. L. (1999). Young students at risk for antisocial behavior: The utility of academic and social skills interventions. *Journal of Emotional and Behavioral Disorders, 7*(4), 211–223.

Lane, K. L., Gresham, F. M., & O'Shaughnessy, T. E. (2002). *Interventions for children with or at risk for emotional and behavioral disorders.* Boston: Allyn and Bacon.

Lane, K. L., Gresham, F. M., & O'Shaughnessy, T. E. (2002). Identifying, assessing, and intervening with children with or at risk for behavior disorders: A look to the future. In K. L. Lane, F. M. Gresham, & T. E. O'Shaughnessy (Eds.), *Interventions for children with or at risk for emotional and behavioral disorders* (pp. 319–326). Boston: Allyn and Bacon.

Latham, G. I. (1998). *Keys to classroom management.* North Logan, UT: P&T ink.

Levendosky, A. A., Okun, A., & Parker, J. G. (1995). Depression and maltreatment as predictors of social competence and social problem-solving skills in school-aged children. *Child Abuse and Neglect, 19,* 1183–1195.

Lewin, P., Nelson, R. E., & Tollefson, N. (1983). Teacher attitudes toward disruptive children. *Elementary School Guidance and Counseling, 17,* 188–193.

Lindberg, J., & Marchant, M. (under review). The motivaider: A useful device for applied behavior analysts. *Journal of Applied Behavior Analysis.*

Lloyd, J. W., Hallahan, D. P., Kauffman, J. M., & Keller, C. E. (1991). Academic problems. In T. R. Kratochwill & R. J. Morris (Eds.). *The practices of child therapy* (2nd ed., pp. 145–173). New York: Pergamon.

Lochman, J. E. (1992). Cognitive-behavioral intervention with aggressive boys: Three year follow-up and preventative effects. *Journal of Consulting and Clinical Psychology, 60,* 426–432.

Loeber, R. (1982). The stability of antisocial and delinquent child behavior: A review. *Child Development, 53,* 1431–1446.

Long, N. J. (1974). In J. M. Kauffman & C. D. Lewis (Eds.), *Teaching children with behavior disorders: Personal perspectives* (pp. 168–195). Upper Saddle River, NJ: Merrill/Prentice-Hall.

Long, N. J. (1997). The therapeutic power of kindness. *Reclaiming Children and Youth, 5*(4), 242–246.

Long, N., & Brendtro, L. (1992). Gangs, guns and kids [Special Issue]. *Journal of Emotional and Behavioral Problems, 1*(1).

Lynch, M. J., & Hanson, E. W. (1992). *Developing cross cultural competence: A guide for working with young children and their families.* Baltimore: Brooks.

Maheady, L., Harper, G. F., & Mallette, B. (1991). Training and implementation requirements associated with the use of a classwide peer tutoring system. *Education and Treatment of Children, 14*(3), 177–198.

Maheady, L., & Sainato, D. (1985). The effects of peer tutoring upon the social status and social interaction patterns of high and low status elementary students. *Education and Treatment of Children, 8*(1), 51–65.

Marchant, M., & Young, K. R. (2001). The effects of a parent coach on parents' acquisition and implementation of parenting skills. *Education and Treatment of Children, 24*(3), 351–373.

Mayer, G. R. (1995). Preventing antisocial behavior in the schools. *Journal of Applied Behavior Analysis, 28,* 467–478.

Mayer, G. R., & Butterworth, T. (1979, May). A preventative approach to school violence and vandalism: An experimental study. *Personnel and Guidance Journal,* 436–441.

Mayer, G. R., Nafpaktitis, M., Butterworth, T., & Hollingsworth, P. (1987). A search for the elusive setting events of school vandalism: A correlation study. *Education and Treatment of Children, 10,* 259–270.

McKinney, J. D., Mason, J., Perkerson, K., & Clifford, M. (1975). Relationship between classroom behavior and academic achievement. *Journal of Educational Psychology, 67,* 198–203.

Mitchem, K. J., & Young, K. R. (2001). Adapting self-management procedures for classwide use: Acceptability, feasibility, and effectiveness. *Remedial and Special Education, 22*(2), 75–88.

Mitchem, K. J., Young, K. R., West, R. P., & Benyo, J. (2001). CWPASM: A classwide peer-assisted self-management program for general education classrooms. *Education and Treatment of Children, 24*(2), 111–140.

Morgan, D. P., & Jenson, W. R. (1988). *Teaching behaviorally disordered students: Preferred practices.* Columbus, OH: Charles E. Merrill.

Morningstar, M. E., Turnbull, A. P., & Turnbull, M. R. (1996). What do students with disabilities tell us about the importance of family involvement in the transition from school to adult life? *Exceptional Children, 62*(3), 249–260.

MotivAider. (2000). Thief River Falls, MA: Behavioral Dynamics.

Mulvey, E. P., Arthur, M. W., & Reppucci, N. D. (1993). Prevention and treatment of juvenile delinquency: A review of the research. *Clinical Psychology Review, 13,* 133–167.

Nelson, R., & Carr, B. A. (1999). *Think Time Strategy for schools: Bringing order to the classroom.* Longmont, CO: Sopris West.

Obiakor, F. E. (1999). Multicultural education: Powerful tool for educating learners with exceptionalities. In F. E. Obiakor, J. O. Schwenn, & A. F. Rotatori (Eds.), *Advances in special education: Multicultural education for learners with exceptionalities* (pp. 1–14). Stamford, CT: JAI Press.

O'Leary, S. G. (1995). Parental discipline mistakes. *Current Directions in Psychological Science, 4,* 11–13.

Patterson, G. R. (1982). *Coercive family process: Vol. 3. A social learning approach.* Eugene, OR: Castalia Press.

Patterson, G. R. (1983). *Longitudinal investigation of antisocial boys and their families* [Research grant from the National Institute of Mental Health]. Eugene: Oregon Social Learning Center.

Patterson, G. R. (1986). Performance models for antisocial boys. *American Psychologist, 41,* 432–444.

Patterson, G. R., Reid, J. B., & Dishion, T. J. (1992). *Antisocial boys.* Eugene, OR: Castalia.

Peterson, L. D., Young, K. R., West, R. P., & Peterson, M. H. (1999). Effects of student self-management on generalization of student performance to regular classrooms." *Education and Treatment of Children, 22*(3), 357–372.

Quinn, K. P., & McDougal, J. L. (1998). A mile wide and a mile deep: Comprehensive interventions for children and youth with emotional and behavioral disorders and their families. *School Psychology Review, 27,* 191–203.

Reid, J. (1993). Prevention of conduct disorder before and after school entry: Relating intervention to developmental findings. *Development and Psychopathology, 5,* 243–262.

Reid, J. B., & Eddy, J. M. (1997). The prevention of antisocial behavior: Some considerations in the search for effective interventions. In D. M. Stoff, J. Breling, & J. D. Maser (Eds.), *Handbook of antisocial behavior* (pp. 343–356). New York: Wiley.

Reid, J. B., & Patterson, G. R. (1989). The development of antisocial behavior patterns in childhood and adolescence. *European Journal of Personality, 3,* 107–119.

Reitman, D., & Gross, A. M. (1995). Familial determinants. In M. Hersen & R. T. Ammerman (Eds.), *Advanced abnormal child psychology* (pp. 87–104). Hillsdale, NJ: Erlbaum.

Rhode, G., Morgan, D. P., & Young, K. R. (1983). Generalization and maintenance of treatment gains of behaviorally handicapped students from resource rooms to regular classrooms using self evaluation procedures. *Journal of Applied Behavior Analysis, 16(2),* 171–188.

Rogers-Adkinson, D., & Griffith, P. (Eds.). (1999). *Communication disorders and children with psychiatric and behavioral disorders.* San Diego: Singular.

Rutter, M. (1990). Psychosocial resilience and protective mechanisms. In J. Rolf, A. S. Masten, D. Cicchetti, K. H. Nuechterlein, & S. Weintraub (Eds.), *Risk and protective factors in the development of psychopathology* (pp. 181–214). Cambridge: Cambridge University Press.

Rutter, M., Maughan, B., Mortimer, P., Ouston, J., & Smith, A. (1979). *Fifteen thousand hours: Secondary schools and their effects on children.* Cambridge, MA: Harvard University Press.

Shinn, M. R., Ramsey, E., Walker, H. M., Stieber, S., & O'Neill, R. E. (1987). Antisocial behavior in school settings: Initial differences in an at risk and normal population. *The Journal of Special Education, 21*(2), 69–84.

Shores, D., & Wehby, J. H. (1999). Analyzing the social behavior of students with emotional and behavioral disorders in classrooms. *Journal of Emotional and Behavioral Disorders, 7,* 194–199.

Shores, R. E. (1987). Overview of research on social interaction: A historical and personal perspective. *Behavioral Disorders, 12,* 233–241.

Shores, R. E., Jack, S. L., Gunter, P. L., Ellis, D. N., DeBriere, T. J., & Wehby, J. H. (1993). Classroom interactions of children with behavior disorders. *Journal of Emotional and Behavioral Disorders, 1,* 27–39.

Short, J. F. (1997). *Poverty, ethnicity, and violent crime.* New York: Westview.

Smith, D. J., Young, K. R., West, R. P., Morgan, D., & Rhode, G. (1988). Reducing the disruptive behavior of junior high school students: A classroom self-management procedure. *Behavioral Disorders, 13*(4), 231–239.

Sprague, J., & Walker, H. (2000). Early identification and intervention for youth with antisocial and violent behavior. *Exceptional Children, 66*(3), 367–379.

Sugai, G., Sprague, J. A., Horner, R. H., & Walker, H. M. (2000). Preventing school violence: The use of office discipline referrals to assess and monitor schoolwide discipline interventions. *Journal of Emotional and Behavioral Disorders, 8,* 94–101.

Sulzer-Azaroff, B., & Mayer, G. R. (1991). *Behavior analysis for lasting change.* Fort Worth, TX: Holt, Rinehart and Winston.

Tindal, G., & Crawford, L. (2002). Teaching writing to students with behavior disorders: Metaphor and medium. In K. L. Lane, F. M. Gresham, & T. E. O'Shaughnessy (Eds.), *Interventions for children with or at risk for emotional and behavioral disorders* (pp. 104–124). Boston: Allyn and Bacon.

Tolan, P. H., Guerra, N. G., & Kendall, P. C. (1995). A developmental-ecological perspective on antisocial behavior in children and adolescents: Toward a unified risk and intervention framework. *Journal of Consulting and Clinical Psychology, 63,* 579–584.

Torgesen, J. K., & Wagner, R. K. (1998). Alternative diagnostic approaches for specific developmental reading disabilities. *Learning Disabilities Research & Practice, 13,* 220–232.

Tremblay, R. E., Paganikurtz, L., Vitaro, F., Massie, L. C., & Pihl, R. O. (1995). A bimodal preventive intervention for disruptive kindergarten boys: Its impact through mid-adolescence. *Journal of Consulting and Clinical Psychology, 63,* 560–568.

Walker, H. M. (1995). *The acting-out child: Coping with classroom disruption* (2nd ed.). Longmont, CO: Sopris West.

Walker, H. M., Block-Pedego, A., Todis, B., & Severson, H. (1991). *School archival records search (SARS): User's guide and technical manual.* Longmont, CO: Sopris West.

Walker, H. M., Colvin, G., & Ramsey, E. (1995). *Antisocial behavior in school: Strategies and best practices.* Pacific Grove, CA: Brooks/Cole.

Walker, H. M., Kavanaugh, K., Golly, A., Stiller, B., Severson, H. H., & Feil, E. G. (1995). *First steps: Intervention strategies for the early remediation of kindergarten behavior problems.* (Available from the Institute on Violence and Destructive Behavior, College of Education, University of Oregon).

Walker, H. M., & McConnell, S. (1988). *The Walker-McConnell Scale of Social Competence and School Adjustment: A social skills rating scale for teachers.* Austin, TX: Pro-Ed.

Walker, H. M., & Severson, H. H. (1990). *Systematic Screening for Behavior Disorders (SSBD): A multiple gating procedure.* Longmont, CO: Sopris West.

Walker, H. M., & Severson, H. H. (1992). *Systematic screening for behavior disorders.* Longmont, CO: Sopris West.

Walker, H. M., Severson, H. H., & Feil, E. G. (1994). *The Early Screening Project: A proven child-find process.* Longmont, CO: Sopris West.

Walker, H. M., Shinn, M. R., O'Neill, R. E., & Ramsey, E. (1987). A longitudinal assessment of the development of antisocial behavior in boys: Rationale, methodology and first year results. *Remedial and Special Education, 8*(4), 7–16, 27.

Walker, H. M., & Sprague, J. R. (1999). The path to school failure, delinquency and violence: Causal factors and some potential solutions. *Intervention in School and Clinic, 35*(2), 67–73.

Walker, H. M., Stieber, S., & O'Neill, R. E. (1990). Middle school behavioral profiles of antisocial and at-risk control boys: Descriptive and predictive outcomes. *Exceptionality, 1,* 61–77.

Wechsler, D. (1991). *Wechsler Intelligence Scale for Children-Revised* (WISC-III). New York: Harcourt Brace Jovanovich.

Werner, E. E., & Smith, R. S. (1992). *Overcoming the odds: High risk children from birth to adulthood.* Ithaca, NY: Cornell University Press.

West, R. P., & Sloane, H. N. (1986). The effects of teacher presentation rate and point delivery rate on classroom disruption, performance accuracy, and response rate. *Behavior Modification, 10,* 167–186.

Widom, C. S. (1997). Child abuse, neglect, and witnessing violence. In D. M. Stoff, J. Breling, & J. D. Maser (Eds.), *Handbook of antisocial behavior* (pp. 159–170). New York: Wiley.

Wilder, L. K. (1999). *Student versus teacher perception of student behavior for youth with emotional/behavioral disorders: Accurate assessment.* Doctoral Dissertation, Lansing, MI: UMI.

Wilder, L. K. (2002). The homeless are people too: Including homeless students in educational programming. In P. Grant, F. E. Obiakor, & E. Dooley (Eds.), *Educating all learners.* Springfield, IL: Charles C. Thomas.

Wilder, L. K., Jackson, A. P., & Smith, T. B. (2001). Secondary transition of multicultural learners: Lessons from the Navajo Native American experience. *Preventing School Failure, 45*(3), 119–124.

Wilder, L. K., Murray, F., & Shepherd, T. (2000). *Strength-based assessment of behavior across cultures.* Unpublished raw data.

Winzer, M. A., & Mazurek, K. (1998). *Special education in multicultural contexts.* Upper Saddle River, NJ: Prentice-Hall.

Witt, J. C., Daly, E. M., & Noell, G. (2000). *Functional assessments.* Longmont, CO: Sopris West.

Young, K. R., Black, S., Marchant, M., Mitchem, K. J., & West, R. P. (2000, August). A teaching approach to discipline: An alternative to punishment. *Marriage and Families,* 9–15.

Young, B. R., & Hammond, W. R. (1997). Antisocial behavior in minority groups: Epidemiological and cultural perspectives. In D. M. Stoff, J. Breiling, & J. D. Maser (Eds.), *Handbook of antisocial behavior* (pp. 474–495). New York: Wiley.

Young, K. R., West, R. P., Marchant, M., Morgan, J. C., & Mitchem, K. J. (1997). *Prevention Plus: A comprehensive program for the prevention of antisocial behavior.* Logan: Utah State University, Institute for the Study of Children, Youth, and Families at Risk.

Young, K. R., West, R. P., Smith, D. J., & Morgan, D. P. (1991). *Teaching self-management strategies to adolescents.* Longmont, CO: Sopris West.

CHAPTER 10

AUTISTIC SPECTRUM DISORDERS
Assessment and Intervention

MARK C. HOLTER
University of Michigan

Autism is a neurological disorder identified in early childhood. It afflicts the core of socialization with a profound impact on communicative, cognitive, and emotional development. While autism cannot currently be "cured," recent evidence has demonstrated that early intervention can significantly improve the outcome in a wide range of areas. This chapter reviews recent work in diagnosis and assessment, as well as the common elements of effective programming for children with autism. Two case studies are provided to illustrate the information.

Autism is a severe and lifelong developmental disorder. People with autism have profound difficulties relating socially and communicating with others. It is part of a larger group of disorders referred to as the *autistic spectrum disorders (ASD)* or the *pervasive developmental disorders (PDD)*. Once thought to be rare, recent research reveals that autism affects approximately one in 1,000 persons, and the broader category of ASD affects about one in 500, affecting three times as many boys as girls (Fombonne, 1998; Bryson & Smith, 1998; Burd & Kerbeshian, 1988; Cialdella & Mameile, 1989; Bryson, 1996). Thus, autism is more prevalent than muscular dystrophy, Down syndrome, deafness, or childhood cancer (Dawson, 1999). Autism usually manifests itself within the first two years of life and can cause severe impairment in language, cognition, and communication. Though many children with autism make great strides through early intervention, most people with autism will never marry, have a job, or live independently (Goode, Rutter, & Howlin, 1994). Half of all autistic children will not develop functional vocal speech (Prizant, 1983; Lord & Rutter, 1994; Paul, 1987). Adults with autism whose level of cognitive and communication skills allow for independent living and sustained employment have persistent problems in social interaction (Goode et al., 1994). Until the late 1980s, conventional wisdom was that little could be done for children with autism. Recent success with intensive intervention has led to a newfound, if cautious, sense of optimism within the field.

DIAGNOSIS AND CLASSIFICATION

Diagnosis

Autism as a diagnostic concept was first used in 1943 by Leo Kanner in his clinical description of a group of 11 children with marked deficits in social relatedness, including delayed or lack of language ability, and an inordinate need for routine. By the late 1970s, the diagnosis was made based on three major domains of dysfunction, with specific criteria for each domain: (1) qualitative impairment in reciprocal social interaction, (2) qualitative impairment in verbal and nonverbal communication and in imagination, and (3) restricted repertoire of activities and interests. In 1980, the term *Pervasive Developmental Disorder (PDD)* was introduced and included in the American Psychiatric Association's Manual (*DSM-III*). Although no specific criteria were provided for PDD, a child is diagnosed if exhibiting, from the first several years of life, difficulties in social, language, emotional, and/or cognitive domains combined with significant impairment of functioning. Autism is the most specifically defined example of PDD in the *DSM-IV* (see Figure 10.1).

Assessment

The symptoms of autism are present and measurable by 18 months of age (NRC, 2001), a point by which many parents have begun to suspect problems in their child's development (Filipek et al., 2000). The main characteristics differentiating autism from other developmental disorders before 3 years old involve behavioral deficits in eye contact, orienting to one's name, joint attention behaviors, pretend play, imitation, nonverbal communication, and language development (NRC, 2001).

Children with autistic spectrum disorders (ASDs) vary across numerous dimensions such as intellectual capacity, communicative ability, and degree of behavioral deviance. Consequently, assessments involve direct observation as well as interviews of parents and other service providers such as social workers and teachers. An important goal of assessment is to describe an individual's functioning across the domains of verbal ability, social competence, receptive and expressive language skills, abilities of daily living, and so on. Assessments that provide detailed descriptions of functioning abilities provide the basis for intervention programs (Volkmar, Klin, Marans, & Cohen, 1996). Assessments should identify strengths to be enhanced rather than only skills deficits, so that programs can be designed to help individuals reach their maximum potential. A comprehensive developmental approach to the assessment of a young child with autistic spectrum disorder is guided by the following principles (Klin, Carter, Volkmar, Cohen, Marans, & Sparrow, 1997):

1. Assessment of multiple areas of functioning, including current abilities, behavioral presentation, and functional adjustment.
2. Adoption of a developmental perspective. In light of the presence of mental retardation in the majority of individuals with autism, it is important to interpret their functioning within the context of overall developmental level.
3. Variability of skills is typical. It is important to delineate a profile of strengths and weaknesses rather than an overall summary or global score. Similarly, it is equally important not to generalize from an isolated or "splinter" skill to an overall impres-

FIGURE 10.1   Diagnostic Criteria for Autistic Disorder

A. A total of at least six items from (1), (2), and (3), with at least two from (1), and one each from (2) and (3):

1. Qualitative impairment in social interaction, as manifested by at least two of the following:
   (a) marked impairment in the use of multiple nonverbal behaviors such as eye-to-eye gaze, facial expression, body postures, and gestures to regulate social interaction.
   (b) failure to develop peer relationships appropriate to developmental level
   (c) lack of spontaneous seeking to share enjoyment, interests, or achievements with other people (e.g., by a lack of showing, bringing, or pointing out objects of interest)
   (c) lack of social or emotional reciprocity

2. Qualitative impairments in communication as manifested by at least one of the following:
   (a) delay in, or total lack of, the development of spoken language (not accompanied by an attempt to compensate through alternative modes of communication such as gesture or mime)
   (b) in individuals with adequate speech, marked impairment in the ability to initiate or sustain a conversation with others
   (c) stereotyped and repetitive use of language or idiosyncratic language
   (d) lack of varied, spontaneous make-believe play or social imitative play appropriate to developmental level

3. Restricted repetitive and stereotyped patterns of behavior, interests, and activities, as manifested by at least one of the following:
   (a) encompassing preoccupation with one or more stereotyped and restricted patterns of interest that is abnormal either in intensity or focus
   (b) apparently inflexible adherence to specific, nonfunctional routines or rituals— stereotyped and repetitive motor mannerisms (e.g., hand or finger flapping or twisting, or complex whole body movements)
   (c) persistent preoccupation with parts of objects

B. Delays or abnormal functioning in at least one of the following areas, with onset prior to age 3 years: (1) social interaction, (2) language as used in social communication, or (3) symbolic or imaginative play.

C. The disturbance is not better accounted for by Rett's Disorder or Childhood Disintegrative Disorder.

Source: Reprinted with permission from the *Diagnostic and Statistical Manual of Mental Disorders, Fourth Edition, Text Revision.* Copyright 2000 American Psychiatric Association.

sion of the level of functioning, thereby misrepresenting the child's capacities for learning and adaptation.

4. Variability of behavior across settings is typical. A child's behavior will vary according to the nature of the environment in terms of familiarity, degree of structure provided, and complexity of the environment. Consequently, the assessment should address issues of facilitating and detrimental environments.

5. Assessment of functional adjustment. Results of assessments obtained in highly structured situations must be interpreted in the broader context of a child's daily levels of functioning and response to real-life demands.

6. Assessment of the impact of social disability on behavior and performance.
7. Assessment of behavioral difficulties impact on functioning and intervention plans.

The assessment process should be structured with the use of various diagnostic instruments and behavioral rating checklists. These include the Autism Diagnostic Interview–Revised (ADI–R; Lord, Rutter, & Le Couteur, 1994), the Autism Diagnostic Observation Schedule–Generic (ADOS–G; Lord, Risi, Lambrecht, Cook, Leventhal, DiLavore, et al., 2000), the Childhood Autism Rating Scale (CARS; Schopler, Reichler, & Renner, 1988), and the Autism Behavior Checklist (ABC; Krug, Arick, & Almond, 1980). Table 10.1 provides psychometric properties and general information for these instruments. The case study of Jane (presented later in this chapter) illustrates one family's realization of their daughter's developmental delays, and provides a detailed account of the assessment and diagnostic process.

Autism has been reported to co-occur with a number of other developmental, psychiatric, and medical conditions. Mental retardation is present in about 75 percent of persons

TABLE 10.1   Assessment Instruments in Autism

INSTRUMENT	RELIABILITY AND VALIDITY	INFORMATION
ABC Autism Behavior Checklist (Krug et al., 1980)	The instrument is sensitive in identifying autism but tends to overdiagnose autism in individuals without the disorder (Volkmar et al., 1987). It is not as reliable as the CARS or ADI-R.	Designed to be completed by teachers. It is comprised of a series of dichotomous items weighted relative to how strongly they predict a diagnosis of autism.
ADI-R Autism Diagnostic Interview-Revised (Lord et al., 1993)	Good to excellent reliability and validity in diagnosing autism in preschool children (Lord et al., 1994). It is specifically linked to *DSM-IV* diagnostic criteria.	A semi-structured, investigator-based interview for caregivers of children and adults for whom autism or pervasive developmental disorders is a possible diagnosis.
ADOS-G Autism Diagnostic Observation Schedule-Generic (Lord et al., 2000)	ADOS scores have demonstrated good levels of reliability and validity in discriminating between children with autism and children with nonautistic developmental disabilities (Lord et al., 2000).	A semi-structured, standardized assessment of social interaction, communication, play, and imaginative use of materials for individuals suspected of having autism spectrum disorders.
CARS Childhood Autism Rating Scale (Schopler et al., 1988)	High interrater reliability and internal consistency (Schopler et al, 1988). Demonstrated high convergent validity (with ABC and ADI).	Based on trained rater's observation of behavior during a structured situation. This behavior-rating scale helps to identify children with autism and to distinguish them from developmentally disabled children who are not autistic. Scores falling within the autistic range can be divided into two categories: mild-to-moderate and severe.

with autism, although a substantial minority of individuals have cognitive abilities in the average or above-average range. Individuals with autism are also vulnerable to a range of behavioral difficulties such as hyperactivity, obsessive-compulsive disorders, self-injury, stereotypy, and affective symptoms (Volkmar, Klin, & Cohen, 1997). Seizure disorders of various types are the most common co-occurring medical condition, developing in about 25 percent of persons with autism by early adulthood (Minshew, Sweeney, & Bauman, 1997). A multiaxial approach to differential diagnosis is necessary and provides the contextual basis for classifying intellectual, communicative and other abilities.

Epidemiology

Prevalence and Incidence. The increased demands for autism-related services has focused attention on the apparent rise in prevalence rates. A synthesis of more than 20 studies conducted in 10 countries, with a population base of 4 million or more children, found a rate of 7.5 per 10,000 to reflect the results of studies conducted since 1987 (Fombonne, 1998). The same studies report a rate of 12.5 per 10,000 for atypical autism/PDD, producing an overall rate of 20 cases per 10,000, or 1 in 500 children. The rise in incidence from previous estimates can be explained by more complete diagnoses and increased awareness of the expression of autism in individuals at either end of the spectrum (severely cognitively impaired or more cognitively capable) (Fombonne, 1998). However, there is currently a lack of reliable epidemiological data on borderline autistic conditions such as PDD and Asperger's Syndrome.

The ratio of males to females is 3:1, or 4:1 for more classic autism, while it approaches 2:1 in studies using broader definitions (Bryson, 1997). Girls with the disorder tend to have more severe symptoms and greater cognitive impairment (Fombonne, 1998). To date, research has not revealed differing prevalence on the basis of race or ethnicity.

Etiology. Early causal theories of autism were completely behavioral and faulted deficits in parenting during infancy or early childhood (Bettelheim, 1967). Today, there is broad consensus among clinicians and researchers that ASDs are the behavioral manifestations of underlying neurobiological pathology. Recent research attempts to integrate genetic, neurochemical, and developmental approaches (e.g., Minshew, Sweeney, & Bauman, 1997). Studies have not so far been able to uncover a single overarching neural etiology.

The evidence for a genetic component to autism is fairly clear. The fact that boys are predominantly affected remains unexplained but would seem to have a genetic rather than environmental basis. Parents of an autistic child are five to seven times more likely to have a second autistic child than are parents with unaffected children. In identical twins, the odds of concurrent autism are 90 percent, compared to 2 to 3 percent for fraternal twins (Szatmari & Jones, 1998). The fact that there is not complete concordance between identical twins suggests other factors must modify the genetic predisposition to the disorder.

Some environmental risk factors are known. In utero exposure to rubella or to birth-defect-causing substances such as ethanol and valproic acid increase the chances of the development of autism. Children born to mothers who had taken thalidomide during pregnancy in the late 1950s and early 1960s had an incidence of autism that was 30 times higher than the general population (Stromland, Nordin, Miller, Akerstrom, & Gillberg, 1994). Environmental triggers do appear to account for at least some cases of autistic regression, suggesting the plausibility of genetically vulnerable children affected by environmental stressors. Research has not yet reached the point where it can determine how the multiple genetic and environmental factors combine to make some but not all persons display symptoms.

Efforts are currently underway to determine, at the behavioral level, which symptoms of autism are consequences of underlying neuropsychological deficit, and which symptoms result from abnormal development stemming from these deficits. For instance, impaired ability to interpret facial expressions is an important deficit of autism. Although the deficit may be neurological in origin, its presence continually hampers autistic children's language acquisition to the extent that learning depends on the pleasure of mastery as well as a sense of tangible social rewards (see Rapin & Dunn, 1997, for a full discussion). Advances in the field of neuroscience are providing a deeper understanding of neurodevelopment, but there is still very little known about the functioning of the brain during the early years of life and during the course of early development. Future studies will help clarify the causal pathways that lead to the clinical expression of ASDs. Until more conclusive research leads to the identification of specific genetic and neurological pathologies in the etiology of autism, a model based on the interplay between genetic, neurology, and environment best explains the etiology of autism.

REVIEW OF RESEARCH

Autism is a developmental disorder affecting a wide range of developmental domains, hence the term *pervasive developmental disorder*. The extent of impairment differs greatly among individuals, and the areas of functioning for each individual will vary over the course of his or her life. The diverse developmental research on ASDs includes inquiry into the domains of socialization, communication, as well as cognition and emotion.

Social Dysfunction

Unlike neurotypical infants and toddlers who are motivated to spend a good deal of energy on establishing social relationships with caregivers, autistic infants are less likely to seek comfort from their parents or to take pleasure in interaction with their parents (DeMyer, 1979). For instance, in each case study in this chapter, Jane and Temple were resistant to physical touch and did not allow their parents to provide comfort (see case studies later in this chapter). Specific areas of social deficit include:

- Avoiding eye contact (Volkmar, Cohen, & Paul, 1986)
- Absence of joint attention (i.e., the ability to share with another person the experience of a third object or event) (Lewy & Dawson, 1992)
- Lack of interest in imitation (Smith & Bryson, 1994)
- Lack of symbolic play skills (where children play with toys such as dolls or cars in the way intended) and reciprocal play skills (where there is a back-and-forth between two people, such as when rolling a ball) (Stone & Caro-Martinez, 1990)
- Deficits in engaging in social behaviors or recognizing emotions in others (Klin & Volkmar, 1993)

Language and Communicative Development

Most children with autism begin to speak late and develop speech at significantly slower rates than normally developing children (Le Couteur, Rutter, Lord, Rios, Robertson, Holdgrafter, et al., 1989). In descriptions by their parents, about one-quarter of children with autism acquired some words by 18 months of age but then lost them (Kurita, 1985). For individuals who do develop functional speech, areas of language deficit include articulation abnormalities (Rutter, Mawhood, & Howlin, 1992), abnormal use of words and phrases (Rutter, 1970), and echolalia (i.e., repeating of words and phrases spoken by someone else) (Prizant, 1983). For children showing limited progress with vocal language programs, alternative communication methods, such as sign language (Kiernan, 1983) or Picture Exchange Communication System (PECS), have proven effective in increasing the rate of interaction between children and their listeners (Bondy & Frost, 1998). Consistent with the research cited, the case studies illustrate that neither Jane nor Temple had any expressive language at 2 years of age.

Cognition and Emotional Development

Normally developing infants have the innate capacity to respond to the emotional states of other human beings—for instance, by using their mother's emotional state to guide their behavior (Sigman, Dissanayake, Arbelle, & Ruskin, 1997). Although young children with autism are able to understand other people as agents of action (e.g., someone to feed me), they are often unable to understand other persons as having a unique perspective that can be shared. It is unclear the extent to which children with autism can distinguish among manifestations of emotion as demonstrated through facial expressions and gestures. The ability of children with autism to appreciate their own and other people's mental states (e.g., beliefs, desires, intentions, perceptions) and to understand the links between mental states and action is referred to as *theory of mind*. Because persons with autism are impaired in social interactions that require knowledge of other people's mental states, it is posited that they lack a theory of mind. For instance, children were presented with a hypothetical scenario in which a character is shown the location of an object and is then absent when an object is moved and therefore does not know that the object is in a new location. The child is asked where the character thinks the object is. Normal 4-year-olds, as well as children with Down syndrome with moderate degrees of mental disability, were both able to pass the test easily. In contrast, the majority of children with autism "failed" the test by indicating that the character would think the object was in its new location rather than the previous placement (Baron-Cohen, Leslie, & Frith, 1985). In other words, children with autism fail to attend to the important information because the character was absent while the object was moved, the character's mental state would differ from the child's own state. Fifteen years of subsequent study by various researchers has provided strong evidence for the existence of a theory of mind (Baron-Cohen & Swettenham, 1997).

Course and Outcome

Recent follow-up studies of adults with autism suggest that a number of factors related to early development are associated with outcomes later in life. The most important prognostic indicator is the acquisition of at least simple communicative language by the age of 6 years (Howlin & Goode, 1998). Intellectual capacity, particularly verbal IQ scores, have been the most consistent predictor of adult independence and functioning (Howlin, 1997). About 70 to 80 percent of children with autism achieve IQ scores in the mentally retarded range, and of these, most score in the moderate to severe range of mental retardation (Sigman, Dissanayake, Arbelle, & Ruskin, 1997; Wing & Gould, 1979). Children who were not testable or with nonverbal IQ scores below the range of 55 to 60 remained highly dependent as adults (Howlin & Goode, 1998). Recent studies have highlighted the importance of early intensive intervention in altering the course of autism by improving functioning (Dawson & Osterling, 1997; NRC, 2001). Early intensive interventions are comprehensive programs that address the multiple problems displayed by preschool-aged children with autism in areas of language, cognition, socialization, self-help, motor skills, and so on, and are intensive in that these services are offered with a low staff-to-child ratio (1:1 to 1:3) for about 27 hours per week.

Older studies found little evidence that socioeconomic factors or ratings of family adequacy were correlated with later outcomes (DeMyer, Barton, DeMyer, Norton, Allan, & Steele, 1973). It is important to note that these studies took place before the advent of early intensive intervention for children with autism. Early intensive intervention is now recognized as a best practice (NRC, 2001), but because it is more costly than the services presently offered, school systems vary greatly in their willingness or ability to implement these programs. In the absence of publicly funded interventions that meet current definitions of best practices, parents with the resources to do so implement home-based programs at a cost of up to $60,000 annually (Jacobson & Mulick, 2000), while other parents make do with the resources offered through existing systems of care. The case study of Jane demonstrates that she was able to continue to receive services after her move to a new location because her family had the resources to hire legal representation to advocate for services as well as to fund an interim home-based program. Services are most likely not provided equitably across socioeconomic groups. Since access to services is related to socioeconomic status, there is reason to believe that access to interventions, and hence improved outcomes, are correlated with income levels.

REVIEW OF PROMISING INTERVENTIONS

Systems of Care Issues

Autism is associated with a wide range of symptom expression. Each child requires a unique comprehensive program of services provided by professionals across a range of disciplines. The constellation of needed services will change over time, congruent with the individual's developmental change over the life course. The passage of Public Law 94-142 guarantees the right of children with disabilities to a free and appropriate education. Schools are the mandated providers of these services between the ages of 3 and 21. Consequently, services delivered through the education system (including special education, some form of behavior modification, and other services) are the integral aspect of the treatment of autism in children and adolescents (Volkmar, Cook, & Pomeroy, 1999). Educational programs often include ancillary services such as speech/language therapy, occupational therapy, and physical therapy. Many parents seek additional services outside of the school system, such as behavior modification, pharmacological interventions or other health-related services. The case study of Jane illustrates the wide variety of ancillary services accessed by young children with autism. Coordination of services from various providers is important, and social workers trained to provide case management and advocacy can play a crucial role in the intervention process of individuals with autism.

Promising Interventions

Recent research on interventions for children with autism has highlighted the importance of early intervention in favorably affecting outcomes. Indeed, research on effectiveness has generated much attention and provided a sense of hope in helping individuals with autism attain their maximum potential. This section reviews interventions throughout childhood and adolescence, beginning with those offered to preschool-aged children.

Early Intervention. Unlike most preschool-aged children with disabilities who participate in programs with other children of mixed disabilities, children with autism more likely participate in programs specially designed to address their particular needs. The differences in theoretical orientation of the various intervention approaches have been strongly debated. The most fundamental disagreements over early intervention approaches is between an Applied Behavior Analysis (ABA) approach, as defined by Ivar Lovaas and his colleagues, and a developmental framework represented by a range of professionals including Rogers and Pennington (1991) and Greenspan and Weider (1998). Although a detailed account of the differences in approaches is beyond the scope of this chapter, the following discussion summarizes and contrasts the viewpoints.

Behavioral Approach. A basic assumption underlying the behavioral approach developed by Ivar Lovaas is that because autistic children do not learn from their everyday environments, a comprehensive and intense training environment must be created (i.e., at least 40 hours a week for two or more years). In addition, parent training is crucial so that the child is subjected to the system throughout the entire waking day. In general, the first year focuses on reducing self-stimulatory and aggressive behaviors. The second year focuses on teaching language and play with peers, and the third year focuses on pre-academic tasks and expression of emotions (Lovaas, 1987). However, the actual intervention is individualized based on careful behavioral assessment of the child and conditions in the environment that can be used to help the child acquire skills through behavioral procedures. At age 3, Jane (case study) began this model of one-on-one intervention for 30 hours a week, following the curricular focus outlined earlier.

Research spanning three decades demonstrates the efficacy of applied behavioral methods in reducing inappropriate behavior and in increasing communication, learning, and appropriate social behavior. The first attempt to use group comparison to study outcomes of a behavioral intervention was carried out by Lovaas and colleagues (Lovaas, 1987; McEachin, Smith, & Lovaas, 1993). Nineteen children with autism were treated intensively with behavior therapy for two years and compared with two control groups. Follow-up of the experimental group in first grade, in late childhood, and in adolescence found that nearly half the experimental group but almost none of the children in the matched control group were able to participate in regular schooling. A number of other research groups have provided at least a partial replication of the Lovaas model (see Rogers, 1998).

Developmental Approach.   There is a wide variety of developmental programs, but their common characteristic is that they are child directed. The developmental or play-based approach posits that developing skills in autistic children should be modeled on naturally occurring patterns in typical social situations and not explicitly taught. As opposed to a didactic behavioral approach, the developmental intervention follows the lead of the child, making the child in control of the stimulation rather than a passive recipient (Rogers & Lewis, 1989; Greenspan & Weider, 1998). The environment in which the intervention takes place is structured to provide opportunities for communication, with the child initiating interactions while the communication partner follows the lead (NRC, 2001).

Only three developmentally based models have published outcome data, and only one of these is a controlled study. The Treatment and Education of Autistic and Related Communication Handicapped Children (TEACCH) model was shown to be effective in improving behavior and learning of children with autism (Schopler, Reichler, & Renner, 1971). A more recent controlled study examined the effects of adding TEACCH interventions for a half-hour per day in the homes of 11 preschoolers who were also enrolled in other intervention programs. The children demonstrated significant gains across domains, including imitation, fine and gross motor development, and cognitive skills (Ozonoff & Cathcart, 1998). The LEAP Program (Learning Experiences...An Alternative Program for Preschoolers and Parents) is a combined developmental/behavioral curriculum implemented in an integrated setting. Children participating in the program made significant gains in language, behavior, intellectual level, and developmental rates (Hoyson, Jamieson, & Strain, 1984). Follow-up at 24 months reported significant reduction of symptoms and placement of about half the children in regular classrooms (though the use of classroom support is not described) (Strain, Kohler, & Goldstein, 1996). Rogers and colleagues (1986, 1989) have described the effects of a developmentally oriented, 22-hour per week, center-based treatment model (the "Denver model") that emphasizes play, language, cognition, and social relations. Two studies thus far have established that children receiving the intervention demonstrated significant gains in developmental rates, symbolic play skills, and positive social interactions with parents (Rogers, Herbison, Lewis, et al., 1986; Rogers & Lewis, 1989). The Denver model was replicated in four Colorado preschool sites, with children receiving the program demonstrating accelerated developmental progress (Rogers, Lewis, & Reis, 1987).

Characteristics of Effective Early Interventions.   In spite of conceptual and theoretical differences between the various approaches to intervention, they share a number of common elements. A recent review of interventions for children with autism (Dawson & Osterling, 1997) and a report by the National Research Council (NRC, 2001) have suggested that the source of positive outcomes across these different models may be due to common elements involved rather than to program philosophy. The following summarizes several common elements of effective early intervention programs for young children with autism:

■ *Curriculum content.* The curricula of the programs emphasize five basic skill domains, including the following abilities: (1) to attend to elements of the environment that are essential for learning, especially to social stimuli; (2) to imitate others; (3) to comprehend and use language; (4) to play appropriately with toys; and (5) to interact socially with others.

■ *Highly supportive teaching environments and generalization strategies.* Structured classroom settings are balanced with the use of naturalized teaching settings to improve generalization skills in real-world settings. The programs first try to establish core skills in highly structured environments and then work to generalize these skills to more complex, natural environments.

■ *Predictability and routine.* The programs are highly structured and organized according to written schedules of activities. Since the behavior of children with autism is easily disrupted by changes in environment and routine, the programs adopt strategies to assist the child with transitions from one activity to another.

■ *A functional approach to problem behaviors.* Since young children with autism often show problem behaviors, the programs first try to prevent the development of these behaviors by structuring the environment. If problem behaviors persist, the programs use a functional approach that involves the following steps: (1) recording the behavior, (2) developing a hypothesis about the function that behavior serves for the child, (3) changing the environment to support appropriate behavior that allows the child to cope effectively with the situation, and (4) teaching appropriate behaviors to replace problem behaviors.

■ *Plans for transition from the preschool classroom.* Most programs have specific plans of preparing for a child's transition from the intensive setting into mainstream school settings. The programs teach "survival" skills that children will need later on in order to function independently in preschool or school classrooms. In some models, program staff visit the school to understand expectations, as well as the facilitate visits by school staff to the program to understand the unique functioning and needs of the individual child. In the case illustrations, Jane and Temple were both able to transition to a normal classroom setting that included extra support.

■ *Family involvement.* The programs include parents as a critical component in the intervention for young children with autism. Family involvement is an important factor for success of a program because parents can provide unique insight into creating an intervention plan and can provide additional hours of intervention. Including parents in the intervention can also help children achieve greater maintenance and generalization of skills and can help reduce parents' stress levels. Both case studies illustrate the critical importance of the family to the overall success of an intervention.

In addition to the identified core elements, the programs share a number of other common attributes. All the programs emphasize the importance of starting the intervention as soon as a child is suspected of having an autistic spectrum disorder, since less restrictive placement outcomes in later age have been demonstrated for children who began intervention early (NRC, 2001). Program intensity results from a high number of hours (an average of 27 hours per week) and a staff to student ratio of 1:1 for the younger children and up to 1:3 for developmentally more advanced preschoolers. Further, the programs are directed and implemented by teams with extensive training and experience within the field of autistic spectrum disorders. The programs have developed standardized training protocols so that they can be implemented in other locations. Finally, each model has mechanism for the ongoing tracking of the progress of individual children, allowing for adjustments in the child's intervention plan.

The emerging research provides support for the premise that interventions incorporating the preceding program characteristics result in developmental acceleration for the children, as well as reduction in autistic symptomatology (Rogers, 1998; Dawson & Osterling, 1997). However, early detection and behavioral intervention are not enough for many children. Approximately 50 percent of children with autism have poor outcomes despite intensive early intervention, and even those who do respond well often continue to have significant behavioral disturbances that affect their ability to form relationships, work, and live independently (Dawson & Osterling, 1997). The fact that not all the children benefit to the same extent demonstrates that child characteristics (e.g., level of cognitive functioning), as well as variability in families (e.g., ethnicity, level of education, socioeconomic status), interact with treatment effectiveness. The individualization of treatment is made increasingly possible with the broadening of intervention programs and the ability to specify important child characteristics through assessment tools and procedures. The pathways connecting child and environmental variables to treatment processes and outcomes will be clarified with further research. The goal is to be able to determine the most effective choice of intervention processes based on the characteristics of the individual child, the family, and the environment.

Pharmacological Treatment.   Medication does not provide a cure for autism but, in the context of an individualized treatment plan, can enhance the person's ability to benefit from educational and behavioral modification interventions (McDougle, 1997). Pediatricians may not have the necessary expertise to monitor medication trials appropriately. In such cases, the consultation of a psychiatrist with experience in treating children with autism with the particular medication should be sought. The use of medication to reduce behaviors should always include a plan for teaching the desired replacement behaviors. Siegal (1996) believes that a medication trial may be necessary if one or more of the following criteria are met:

1. There is behavior that is such a problem that the child is frequently injuring himself or others.
2. Behavioral approaches have been tried with little or no success.
3. Problem behaviors are present in more than one setting.
4. Problem behaviors interfere with the child's ability to learn.
5. The potential benefits of the drug will likely outweigh possible short- or long-term side effects.

Pharmacological interventions with infants and young children are generally best avoided. The antipsychotic drug haloperidol has been shown to be effective in the treatment of behavioral disturbances associated with autism, although a significant number of children develop dyskinesias as a side effect (Campbell et al., 1997). Two of the selective serotonin reuptake inhibitors (SSRIs), clomipramine (Gordon, State, Nelson, Hamburger, & Rapoport, 1993) and fluoxetine (McDougle et al., 1996), have shown positive results, although in young children clomipramine was not found to be therapeutic and caused negative side effects (Sanchez et al., 1996). Preliminary studies of some of the newer atypical neuroleptic medications suggest that they may have fewer side effects than conventional antipsychotics such as haloperidol, but controlled studies are needed before firm conclusions can be drawn about any possible advantages in safety and efficacy over traditional agents (Scahill & Koenig, 1999).

Mainstreaming School-Aged Children with Autism.   As a child ages out of preschool programs that are often designed specifically for the developmental and behavioral challenges posed by autism, the issue arises of whether to retain the child in a specialized classroom or to transition the child to a regular classroom. The present educational policy favors the inclusion of children with special needs in regular classroom settings. Unfortunately, in many school systems, the necessary supports are not available to successfully implement integration. Given the nature of social deficits in autism, there is reason to believe that children with autism may not be as able as mentally retarded, nonautistic children to benefit from such an approach. As such, the individual needs of the child should be key in considering alternative educational arrangements. The level of competence in social skills should be considered as important as cognitive functioning in choosing an appropriate setting.

A number of programs have focused on social skills training. For instance, the LEAP Program, described earlier, emphasizes social skills training (Hoyson, Jamieson, & Strain, 1984). The Early Childhood Social Skills Program contains curricular elements taught using a prescribed sequence. The specific social skills include (1) making offers and requests to share, (2) offering play suggestions, (3) making offers and requests to give assistance, (4) showing affection, and (5) giving compliments (Kohler, et al., 1995). Some children with autism have difficulty sustaining attention in regular classroom settings and do better in smaller, structured classrooms, whereas others do well in traditional settings as long as supports, such an aide, are in place. Attempts have been made to develop integrated models. For example, Quill (1990) described an integrated model implemented in a Massachusetts school district that included active parent involvement, the availability of consultative services and technical support to faculty and family members, individually designed integration plan, a peer buddy program to improve social acceptance among peers, an ecological approach to curriculum development, and behavior management techniques. The program's comprehensiveness could allow for successful inclusion of students with autism but demands extensive resources that many school districts would be currently unwilling or unable to meet.

Residential Placement.   Although the majority of children with autism now live with their families rather than in institutional or group home settings, out-of-home care may be necessary if the child is a danger to self or others. If serious attempts to control injurious behavior through intensive behavioral and medication therapies have failed, residential placement should be seriously considered (Siegal, 1996). In a study of families who had placed their developmentally disabled adult children out of home with those who had not, Sherman (1988) found that, relative to other developmental disorders, adults with autism are three times more likely to be placed outside of the home than to remain with their families. The reasons included severity of disability, behavioral disruptions, as well as availability of formal and informal sources of assistance (Sherman, 1988). Residential programs that are designed for persons with autism are preferable to other group settings because the staff are trained in the use of behavior management approaches unique to helping persons with autism avoid problem behaviors (Van Bourgondien & Schopler, 1990).

Adolescent Children with Autism.   As children with autism move into early adolescence, their cognitive functioning remains relatively stable and is fairly consistent with middle childhood performance. Difficult behaviors that were tolerated in childhood become more problematic, as the child's size can be perceived as threatening to others in the community. It was in adolescence that Temple Grandin (see case study) experienced increased anxiety and behavioral problems, leading to her expulsion from school. Programs for adolescents need to actively work on behavioral management techniques for aggressive and self-injurious behaviors. Sexual maturation creates behavioral problems owing to the lack of appropriate social skills and understanding. These issues can usually be resolved with a combination of sexual education (Randall & Parker, 1999) and consistent behavioral teaching techniques (Mesibov & Handlan, 1997).

Some communities have specialized community-based programs for adolescents and adults with autism. Programs such as Division TEACCH in North Carolina offers a full continuum of educational programs as well as an array of residential and vocational programs specifically for people with autism across the lifespan. This program is based on a structured teaching approach in which environments are organized with concrete visual information. Parents are included as co-therapists and taught strategies for working with their children. Programming is based on individualized assessments of a child's strengths and learning style, interests, and needs. Some programs offer similar educational and vocational programs in conjunction with a community-based residential setting. Programming for adolescents with autism is currently expanding, and their ability to benefit from services is increasing due to the recent advent of early intervention (Mesibov & Handlan, 1997).

As children with autism approach adulthood, decisions around living arrangements need to be addressed. Some families feel that care for their adult children is best provided at home, others see supporting the child to leave the home as part of the normal developmental process of aging into adulthood. For those individuals needing supported living arrangements, planning for out-of-home placement should begin as high school graduation approaches or when school district funding is coming to an end (age 22). The type of living arrangement should be adjusted to the developmental level of independence that can be achieved. Options range from a group home and day treatment program for individuals with severe to moderate retardation, to a group home with a sheltered work program for those with less severe retardation. For higher-functioning persons, a group home or supported housing option combined with job coaching at an appropriate employment setting may be ideal.

Social skills training as individuals prepare for adulthood emphasizes (1) life skills for integrated community living, (2) vocational preparation, (3) functional academics, and (4) community-based instruction to aid generalization (Berkell, 1992). An example is the READDY curriculum, which contains job skills, interpersonal social skills, and job-related activities of daily living (Berkell, 1992). The literature on programs for adolescents and adults remains descriptive and could benefit from well-controlled studies.

Working with Families.   Working with individuals with autism often means a high level of involvement with the person's family. Attention must be given to helping families cope with issues that arise in the care of their child. Providing such support benefits the entire family and hence the treatment process itself. Parents of children with autism are vulnerable to the effects of long-term stress brought on by having to care for a child with a chronic disability. The case study of Jane provides a detailed account of the stress experienced by parents of children with autism. Parents, especially mothers, tend to report feelings of guilt, inadequacy about parenting ability, tension, and physical symptoms (DeMeyer, 1979). It is quite common for one parent, usually the mother, to give up outside employment or career (with subsequent loss of income) because of the time commitments of caring for a disabled child and the general lack of appropriate child care. Participation in "normal" social activities (play dates, birthday and holiday parties, family get-togethers) becomes harder as the child with autism ages and the developmental gap between the child and peers becomes increasingly pronounced. Some parents feel that their social group changes, as some friends offer greater support and others become more distanced (Intagliata & Doyle, 1984).

Respite care is a support service that families have identified as particularly beneficial to them in their struggle to cope (Salisbury & Intagliata, 1986), and in improving the quality of life of the parents as well as the child's siblings (Wigham & Tovcy, 1994). The users of respite care tend to be those families with limited support networks (Cohen, 1982).

Autism is a lifelong disorder, and social workers involved with individuals with autism provide services over the life course. The need for services changes over time with the needs of the individual. Professionals should be knowledgeable about local services (e.g., support groups, respite care, summer camps, etc.) as well as the efforts of and contact information for local, state, and national advocacy groups (e.g., Autism Society of America). Parent groups provide emotional support as well as instrumental support in the sharing of information and resources (e.g., intervention techniques, therapist references, baby-sitting exchanges, strategies for successful IEPs, reviews of restaurants and other public places that are "autism-friendly"). The Internet has become an important resource in obtaining information and resources on autism, as well as connecting and sharing information with others. Internet chatrooms and listservs can be especially important for parents who are geographically isolated.

Since there is no known cure for autism, it is understandable that a range of treatments have been touted as quite effective despite the lack of evidence. The social worker can play a valuable role in helping families explore the theoretical basis of a proposed treatment, the evidence of effectiveness (or lack thereof), as well as the costs involved. Many untested treatments pose little risk to the child and only a small cost to the family (e.g., auditory therapy), but others pose a potential risk to the child (e.g., toxic doses of megavitamins or injection of sheep brain extract) or disrupt the present educational program. Families should be actively discouraged from pursuing treatments that represent a risk to the child or involve substantial disruption of the child's educational program or the family's life.

The professional needs to have working knowledge of state and federal laws related to special education and related services to school-aged children with autism. The school system bears responsibility for the treatment and costs as mandated by the Individuals with Disabilities Education Act (IDEA) (Public Law 105-17). At the end of 1999, almost 150 court cases were seeking more appropriate educational programs for children with autistic spectrum disorders (Mandlawitz, 1999, as reported in NRC, 2001). Although a number of states have tried to pool funding streams like Medicaid, private insurance, and Federal special education funds to deal with the problem presented by high costs of programming, there remains no systematic strategy or pattern of funding. Since each person's individual education plan (IEP) is ironed out through a series of meetings attended by a range of stakeholders, the professional must be prepared to advocate for the treatment needs of the child rather than abdicate judgment to arbitrary system rules or fiscal considerations (NRC, 2001).

Future Directions for Interventions and Outcomes Research. The number of children being identified as needing special interventions for autistic spectrum disorders has increased in the last 10 years. This makes the development and provision of services to treat the unique needs of this population all the more urgent. The most important considerations in programming have to do with the strengths and weaknesses of the individual child, the age at diagnosis, and early intervention (NRC, 2001). Recent outcome research has demonstrated the effectiveness of interventions for persons with autism. Given the differential outcomes among children with autism, there is a need for research specifying which intervention processes, under which circumstances, are most effective with which subpopulations of these children. Current systems of service provision for children with autism are inadequately responding to their treatment needs. Presently, many people with autism do not reach their potential simply because those serving them are unaware of the best ways to treat autism or lack the skills to carry out these interventions. It is essential that professionals serving persons with autism act as advocates within current systems of care, as well as communicate knowledge of best practices to the broader community.

CASE STUDY
JANE

Jane was the second of three children born to an intact family. Jane's parents, Tom and Mary, had been married for four years at the time of Jane's birth. The pregnancy, labor, and delivery were unremarkable. Mary has a doctorate in biostatistics and was working in an academic position at a northeastern university. Tom had two years of technical training in electronics and had worked in the electronics department of a company, producing electronic components until being laid off when Jane was nine months old. Since that time, Tom has been the children's primary caregiver.

By her 18-month well-visit, Jane had not acquired any words. In consultation with the pediatrician, it was decided to wait and see if language developed by the 2-year check-up. Instead, Mary enrolled Jane in an early intervention program shortly before her second birthday. At 24 months, Jane was assessed by the early intervention program's multidisciplinary team that included a nurse, a speech pathologist, a social worker, and an educator. Using the Michigan Early Intervention Developmental Profile, Jane's cognitive skills were placed at the 10-month level, with repetitive and expressive language at the 8-month level, gross motor skills at the 23-month level, and fine motor skills at the 11-month level. Jane was then referred to the Division of Developmental and Behavioral Pediatrics at the University of Massachusetts Department of Pediatrics, where she was diagnosed with autism by a team made up of a pediatrician, a developmental pediatrician, and a master's-level psychologist. Medical investigations ruled out hearing loss and neurological causes of decreased receptive and expressive language performance.

Jane remained nonverbal at age 2. She developed stereotypies—for example, tapping little figurines against a bookcase for hours. She had frequent daily tantrums caused by barely perceptible changes in family routine or in response to demands such as "It's time for your bath." For the parents, the most distressing behavior was the lack of social connectedness. Jane seemed to look right through her parents or anyone else in her environment. She would not allow her parents to comfort her, actively resisting physical touch.

In her early intervention program, Jane took part in two center-based visits a week in a group setting, as well as a weekly one-hour home visit by a speech pathologist. In addition, Jane received about two hours a week from an occupational therapist and a weekly home visit from a social worker who played with Jane and suggested strategies for involving her in play-based activities. Jane aged out of the early intervention program at age 3 and transitioned into an intensive Applied Behavior Analysis (ABA) program run by the New England Center for Children (NECC). The 30-hour weekly program was delivered by NECC and funded by the public school system. Jane began to make encouraging progress—she began to speak, had reduced stereotypies and fewer aberrant behaviors, and interacted more with her siblings. Jane then began attending an integrated preschool part time, with one-on-one support from her main therapist, with the remainder of her time spent in one-on-one ABA.

When Jane was 4½ years old, the family moved to a small midwestern city. Prior to the move, the family sent her individualized education plan (IEP) to the special education director and asked for a replication. Despite three months of meetings, telephone calls, and emails, there was no plan in place when the school year began. Unwilling to risk losing the progress Jane had made, the family bore the cost of a part-time private preschool and a home-based one-on-one ABA program. The family retained legal counsel to represent them in negotiations with the school district. After mediation, the school system funded both the preschool and the one-on-one ABA programs. Jane was the only child in the district receiving such intensive services. This model of one-on-one ABA coupled with inclusion experiences with typical peers and supported by a one-on-one aide has continued.

Jane, now 7 years old, continues to make progress. She has a sense of humor, is very verbal, enjoys playing with her friends, and is learning in the first-grade environment. Her older brother has subsequently been diagnosed with Asperger's Syndrome and ADHD. Her 4-year-old sister is typically developing.

Mary and Tom report feeling quite supported by their immediate family before and after the disorder manifested itself. Although they were given the name of a local support group at the time of diagnosis, Mary and Tom never joined, feeling they had no energy or time to deal with their personal issues in response to the diagnosis. Mary states, "We were so focused on Jane's issues, between work and researching interventions and negotiating with the schools, etc., taking time to help *us* adjust seemed to be just adding another burden. Good God, getting a babysitter for a child with autism becomes a major endeavor!" Mary has become involved in a local advocacy group comprised of parents of children with autism, representing that group on a task force convened by the school system to implement evidenced-based interventions for children with autism.

Mary and Tom respond differently to the stress related to parenting special needs children. Mary reports that Tom and his family have the mindset that "everything will be OK," whereas she actively seeks out information through reading and talking to people. Mary is a long-range planner on issues such as wills and estate planning. Tom is better than Mary at maintaining consistency in family routines. These differences have caused difficulties for Mary and Tom and, at times, for the kids. Mary and Tom have worked with family counselors to help them "provide a more united front for the kids."

CASE STUDY

DR. TEMPLE GRANDIN

Temple Grandin was diagnosed with autism in 1949 at the age of 2. As a baby, she avoided physical contact with her mother or other caregivers. She displayed perserverative behaviors. Prior to the advent of specialized intervention for children with autism, the treatment of choice was institutionalization. Instead, Temple remained at home and was referred to a speech therapist who ran a special nursery school in her home. Temple describes speech therapy as quite helpful in her acquisition of expressive language. She was able to attend a regular elementary school classroom through the constant effort of her mother, who acted as an advocate by actively negotiating classroom issues. For example, before Temple's first day of attendance, her mother visited the classroom and, together with the teacher, enlisted the help of the other children in facilitating Temple's success. In adolescence, Temple experienced an increase in anxiety symptoms as well as behavioral problems, including constant fighting. Behavioral problems led to her expulsion from high school. She then attended a boarding school for gifted children with emotional problems.

While visiting her aunt's ranch during this period, Temple observed that cattle being handled in a squeeze chute sometimes relaxed after the pressure was applied. With her aunt's help, Temple was herself enclosed in the cattle squeeze chute and found that it provided relief from feelings of anxiety for several hours. Against the wishes of the school psychologist, but with the encouragement of a high school teacher, Temple built her own squeeze machine, modeled after the cattle squeeze chute. Temple describes its two functions: (1) to help relax "nerves" and (2) to provide the comforting feeling of being held. Squeeze machines are manufactured for use by other adults with autism. Temple gives much credit for her subsequent successful career in designing livestock equipment to her high school science teacher, who used her "fixation" on cattle chutes to motivate her to study psychology and science.

Consistent with autistic disorder, Temple experiences problems in functioning in a range of areas including:

- *Speech.* As a young child, Temple had normal receptive language but great difficulties with expressive language.
- *Auditory.* Temple describes her auditory processing as like having a hearing aid with the volume control stuck on "super loud—an open microphone that picks up everything."
- *Tactile/sensory issues.* Temple had extreme tactile sensitivity, such as the aversion to the touch of certain clothing fabrics.
- *Anxiety.* Temple has experienced extreme anxiety, including anxiety attacks, since shortly after her first menstrual period. She began taking antidepressant medication in her mid-thirties, which led to immediate relief of her anxiety symptoms. In addition, the medication has led to a steady improvement in speech, sociability, and posture.

Temple was recently asked if she was missing something in life because of her autism. Her answer illustrates in a very personal way how autism manifests itself in differing perceptions, cognition, and social relations:

> Just in the last couple of years, when I was working on my book, *Thinking in Pictures,* I realized that I am missing something that everybody else has—emotional complexity—and I have replaced it with intellectual complexity. I obtain great satisfaction out of using my intellect. I like to figure things out and solve problems. This really turns me on. When I observe emotional complexity in others, it is sort of a rhythm that goes on between a boyfriend and a girlfriend. I often observe this on airplanes. Sometimes I get to sit next to them. It is similar to observing beings from another planet. The relationship is what motivates them; but for me, it is figuring out how to design something, such as figuring out better ways to treat autism. I use my mind to solve problems and invent things. I get a tremendous satisfaction from inventing things and doing innovative research. We have just finished up several good experiments at the university. We came out with really good results, and it turns me on. My life is basically my work. If I did not have my work, I would not have any life. This brings up the importance of getting autistic people in high school and junior high school interested in something they can turn into a career. They need to build on their talents, such as art work and computer programming. (Edelson, 1996)

Dr. Grandin went on to become a gifted animal scientist, receiving a Ph.D. from the University of Illinois. She is credited with designing one-third of all the livestock-handling facilities in the United States. She teaches courses on livestock handling and facility design at Colorado State University. In addition to her professional career, Dr. Grandin writes and lectures widely on issues related to autism. Dustin Hoffman consulted her as he prepared for his role as an adult with autism in the 1988 film *Rain Man.* In 1998, she was the subject of an award-winning documentary, *Stairway to Heaven,* by renowned filmmaker Errol Morris.

DISCUSSION QUESTIONS

1. What are some ways in which young children could be screened earlier for autistic spectrum disorders?

2. How is a program's theory tied to specific intervention techniques?

3. In advocating for the treatment needs of children with autism, what are the range of systems that need to be addressed?

4. Why is family involvement so important for children with autism?

5. What are some special considerations in working with families of children with autism?

SUGGESTED READINGS

Committee on Educational Interventions for Children with Autism, Division of Behavioral and Social Sciences and Education, National Research Council. (2001). *Educating children with autism.* Washington, DC: National Academy Press.

Grandin, T. (1995). *Thinking in pictures: And other reports from my life with autism.* New York: Doubleday.

Randall, P., & Parker, J. (1999). *Supporting the families of children with autism.* New York: Wiley.

Volkmar, F. R. (Ed.). (1998). *Autism and pervasive developmental disorders* (2nd ed.). New York: Cambridge University Press.

Williams, D. (1994) *Somebody somewhere.* New York: Times Books.

RESOURCES

The Autism Society of America (ASA): http://www.autism-society.org. ASA provides a wide range of services and information to families and educators, organizes a national conference, and publishes *The Advocate,* with articles by parents and autism experts. Local chapters make referrals to regional programs and services as well as sponsor parent support groups. This site offers information on educating children with autism, including a bibliography of instructional materials for and about children with special needs.

Center for the Study of Autism (CSA): http://www.autism.org. The center provides information about autism to parents and professionals, and conducts research on the efficacy of various therapeutic interventions.

REFERENCES

Aman, M. G., & Singh, N. N. (1986). *Manual for the Aberrant Behavior Checklist.* East Aurora, NY: Slosson Educational Publications.

Baron-Cohen, S., Cox, A., Baird, G., Swettenham, J., Nightingale, N., Morgan, K., Drew, A., & Charman, T. (1996). Psychological markers in the detection of autism in infancy in a large population. *British Journal of Psychiatry,* 168, 1–6.

Baron-Cohen, S., Leslie, A. M., & Frith, U. (1985). Does the autistic child have a "theory of mind"? *Cognition,* 21, 37–46.

Baron-Cohen, S., & Swettenham, J. (1997). Theory of mind in autism: Its relationship to executive function and central coherence. In D. J. Cohen & F. R. Volkmar (Eds.), *Handbook of autism and pervasive developmental disorders* (2nd ed., pp. 880–893). New York: Wiley.

Berkell, D. E. (1992). Instructional planning: Goals and practice. In D. E. Berkell (Ed.), *Autism: Identification, education and treatment* (pp. 89–105). Hillsdale, NJ: Erlbaum.

Bettelheim, B. (1967). *The empty fortress: Infantile autism and the birth of the self.* New York: Free Press.

Bondy, A. S., & Frost, L. A. (1998). The picture exchange communication system. *Seminars in Speech and Language,* 19, 373–388.

Bryson, S. (1997). Epidemiology of autism: Overview and issues outstanding. In D. J. Cohen & F. R. Volkmar (Eds.), *Handbook of autism and pervasive developmental disorders* (2nd ed., pp. 41–46). New York: Wiley.

Bryson, S. E. (1996). Brief report: Epidemiology of autism. *Journal of Autism and Development Disorders,* 26, 165–166.

Bryson, S. E., & Smith, I. M. (1998). Epidemiology of autism: Prevalence, associated characteristics, and implications for research and service delivery. *Mental Retardation and Developmental Disabilities Research Reviews,* 4, 97–103.

Burd, L., & Kerbeshian, J. (1988). A North Dakota prevalence study of schizophrenia presenting in childhood. *Journal of the American Academy of Child and Adolescent Psychiatry,* 26, 347–350.

Campbell, M., Armenteros, J. L., Malone, R. P., Adams, P. B., Eisenberg, Z. W., & Overall, J. E. (1997). Neuroleptic-related dyskinesias in autistic children: A prospective, longitudinal study. *Journal of the American Academy of Child and Adolescent Psychiatry,* 36, 835–843.

Cialdella, P., & Mamelle, N. (1989). An epidemiological study of autism in a French department (hone): A research note. *Journal of Child Psychology and Psychiatry and Allied Disciplines,* 30, 165–175.

Cohen, S. (1982). Supporting families through respite care. *Rehabilitation Literature,* 43, 7–11.

Dawson, G. (1999). *The phenotypes of Autism*. Presented at the 1999 meeting of the Sackler-McDonnell Foundation Conference on Genetics, Irvine, CA.

Dawson, G., & Osterling, J. (1997). Early intervention in autism: Effectiveness and common elements of current approaches. In Guralnick M. J., (Ed.), *The effectiveness of early intervention* (2nd ed.). Baltimore: Brookes.

DeMyer, M. K. (1979). *Parents and children in autism*. Washington, DC: Victor H. Winston.

DeMyer, M. K., Barton, S., DeMyer, W. E., Norton, J. A., Allen, J., & Steele, R. (1973). Prognosis in autism: A follow-up study. *Journal of Autism & Childhood Schizophrenia*, 3(3), 199–246.

Dunlap, G., Koegel, R. L., & Egel, A. L. (1979). Autistic children in school. *Exceptional Children*, 45, 552–558.

Edelson, S. (1996). *Interview with Dr. Temple Grandin*. Retrieved January 09, 2002, from http://www.autism.org/interview/temp_int.html

Filipek P. A., Accardo P. J., Ashwal S., Baranek G. T., Cook, E. H. Jr., Dawson, G., et al. (2000). Practice parameter: Screening and diagnosis of autism: Report of the Quality Standards Subcommittee of the American Academy of Neurology and the Child Neurology Society. *Neurology* 55(4), 468–479.

Fombonne, E. (1998). Epidemiology of autism and related conditions. In F. R. Volkmar (Ed.), *Autism and pervasive mental disorders* (pp. 32–63). Cambridge: Cambridge University Press.

Goode, S., Rutter M., & Howlin, P. (1994). *A twenty-year follow-up of children with autism*. Paper presented at the 13th Biennial Meeting of the International Society for the Study of Behavioural Development, Amsterdam, the Netherlands.

Gordon, C. T., State, R. C., Nelson, J. E., et al. (1993). A double-blind comparison of clomipramine, desipramine, and placebo in the treatment of autistic disorder. *Archives of General Psychiatry*, 50, 441–447.

Greenspan, S. I., & Weider, S. (1998). *The child with special needs: Encouraging intellectual and emotional growth*. New York; Perseus.

Howlin, P. (1997). *Autism: Preparing for adulthood*. London: Routledge.

Howlin, P., & Goode, S. (1998). Outcome in adult life for people with autism and Asperger's syndrome. In F. R. Volkmar (Ed), *Autism and pervasive mental disorders* (pp. 209–241). Cambridge: Cambridge University Press.

Hoyson, M., Jamieson, B., & Strain, P. S. (1984). Individualized group instruction of normally developing and autistic-like children. *Journal of Early Child Development*, 8, 152–172.

Intagliata, J., & Doyle, N. (1984). Enhancing social support for parents of developmentally disabled children: training in interpersonal problem solving skills. *Mental Retardation*, 22(1), 4–11.

Jacobson, J. W., & Mulick, J. A. (2000). System and cost research issues in treatments for people with autistic disorders. *Journal of Autism & Developmental Disorders*, 30(6), 585–593.

Kiernan, C. (1983). The use of nonvocal communication techniques with autistic individuals. *Journal of Child Psychology and Psychiatry*, 24, 339–375.

Klin, A., Carter, A., Volkmar, F. R., Cohen, D. J., Marans, W. D., & Sparrow, S. S. (1997). Assessment issues in children with autism. In D. J. Cohen & F. R. Volkmar (Eds.), *Handbook of autism and pervasive developmental disorders* (2nd ed., pp. 411–447). New York: Wiley.

Klin, A., & Volkmar, F. R. (1993). The development of individuals with autism: Implications for the theory of mind hypothesis. In S. Baron-Cohen, H. Tager-Flusberg, & D. Cohen (Eds.), *Understanding other minds: Perspectives from autism* (pp. 317–331). Oxford: Oxford University Press.

Koenig, K., Rubin, E., Klin, A., & Volkmar, F. R. (2000). Autism and the pervasive developmental disorders. In C. H. Zeanah (Ed.), *Handbook of infant mental health* (pp. 298–310). New York: Guilford.

Kohler, F. W., Strain, P. S., Hoyson, M., Davis, L., Donina, W. M., & Rapp, N. (1995). Using a group-oriented contingency to increase social interactions between children with autism and their peers: A preliminary analysis of corollary supportive behaviors. *Behavior Modification*, 19(1), 10–32.

Krug, D. A., Arick, J., & Almond P. (1980). Behavior checklist for identifying severely handicapped individuals with high levels of autistic behavior. *Journal of Child Psychology and Psychiatry*, 21, 221–229.

Kurita, H. (1985). Infantile autism with speech loss before the age of 30 months. *Journal of the American Academy of Child Psychiatry*, 24, 191–196.

Le Couteur, A., Rutter, M., Lord, C., Rios, P., Robertson, S., Holdgrafter, M., & McLennan, J. D. (1989). Autism Diagnostic Interview: A semi-structured interview for parents and care-givers of autistic persons. *Journal of Autism and Developmental Disorders*, 19, 363–387.

Lewy, A. L., & Dawson, G. (1992). Social stimulation and joint attention in autistic young children. *Journal of Abnormal Psychology*, 20(6), 555–566.

Lord, C. (1993). The complexity of social behavior in autism. In S. Baron-Cohen, H. Tager-Flusberg, & D. Cohen (Eds.), *Understanding other minds: Perspectives from autism* (pp. 292–316). Oxford: Oxford University Press.

Lord, C., Risi, S., Lambrecht, L., Cook, E. H. Jr., Leventhal, B. L., DiLavore, P. C., Pickles, A., & Rutter, M. (2000). The autism diagnostic observation schedule-generic: A standard measure of social and communication deficits associated with the spectrum of autism. *Journal of Autism & Developmental Disorders*, 30(3), 205–223.

Lord, C., & Rutter, M. (1994). Autism and pervasive developmental disorders. In M. M. Rutter, L. Hersov, & E. Taylor (Eds.), *Child and adolescent psychiatry: Modern approaches* (3rd ed., pp. 569–593). Oxford: Blackwell.

Lord, C., Rutter, M., & Le Couteur, A. (1994). Autism Diagnostic Interview-Revised: A revised version of a diagnostic interview for caregivers of individuals with possible pervasive developmental disorders. *Journal of Autism and Developmental Disorders*, 24, 659–685.

Lord, C., Storoschuk, S., Rutter, M., & Pickles, A. (1993). Using the ADI-R to diagnose autism in preschool children. *Infant Mental Health Journal*, 14, 234–252.

Lovaas, O. I. (1987). Behavioral treatment and normal educational and intellectual functioning in young autistic children. *Journal of Consulting and Clinical Psychology*, 55, 3–9.

Mandlawitz, M.(1999). *The impact of the legal system on educational programming for young children with autism spectrum disorder.* Paper presented at the First Workshop of the Committee on Educational Interventions for Children with Autism, National Research Council, December 13–14, 1999.

McDougle, C. J. (1997). Psychopharmacology. In D. J. Cohen & F. R. Volkmar (Eds.), *Handbook of autism and pervasive developmental disorders* (2nd ed., pp. 707–729). New York: Wiley.

McDougle, C. J., Naylor, S. T., Cohen, D. J., Volkmar, F. R., Heninger, G. R., & Price, L. H. (1996). A double-blind placebo-controlled study of fluvoxamine in adults with autistic disorder. *Archives of General Psychiatry*, 53, 1001–1008.

McEachin, J. J., Smith, T., & Lovaas, O. I. (1993). Long-term outcome for children with autism who received early intensive behavioral treatment. *American Journal of Mental Retardation*, 97(4), 359–372.

Mesibov, G., & Handlan, S. (1997). Adolescents and adults with autism. In D. J. Cohen & F. R. Volkmar (Eds.), *Handbook of autism and pervasive developmental disorders* (2nd ed., pp. 309–324). New York: Wiley.

Minshew, N. J., Sweeney, J. A., & Bauman, M. L. (1997). Neurological aspects of autism. In D. J. Cohen & F. R. Volkmar (Eds.), *Handbook of autism and pervasive developmental disorders* (2nd ed., (pp. 344–369). New York: Wiley.

National Research Council. (2001). *Educating children with autism.* Committee on Educational Interventions for Children with Autism. In C. Lord & J. P. McGee (Eds.), Division of Behavioral and Social Sciences and Education. Washington, DC: National Academy Press.

Ozonoff, S., & Cathcart, K. (1998). Effectiveness of a home program intervention for young children with autism. *Journal of Autism and Developmental Disorders*, 28, 25–32.

Paul, R. (1987). Natural history. In D. J. Cohen & A. Donnellan (Eds.), *Handbook of autism and pervasive developmental disorders* (pp. 121–132). New York: Wiley.

Prizant, B. M. (1983). Echolalia in autism: Assessment and intervention. *Seminars in Speech and Language*, 4, 63–77.

Quill, K. A. (1990). A model for integrating children with autism. *Focus on Autistic Behavior*, 5, 1–19.

Randall, P., & Parker, J. (1999). *Supporting the families of children with autism.* New York: Wiley.

Rapin, I., & Dunn, M. (1997). Language disorders in children with autism. *Seminars in Pediatric Neurology*, 4(2), 86–92.

Rogers, S. J. (1998). Empirically supported comprehensive treatments for young children with autism. *Journal of Clinical Child Psychology*, 27(2), 168–179.

Rogers, S. J., Herbison, J., Lewis, H., Pantone, J., & Reis, K. (1986). An approach for enhancing the symbolic, communicative, and interpersonal functioning of young children with autism and severe emotional handicaps. *Journal of the Division of Early Childhood,* 10, 135–148.

Rogers, S. J., & Lewis, H. (1989). An effective day treatment model for young children with pervasive developmental disorders. *Journal of the American Academy of Child and Adolescent Psychiatry,* 28, 207–214.

Rogers, S. J., Lewis, H., & Reis, K. (1987). An effective procedure for training early special education teams to implement a model program. *Journal of the Division of Early Childhood,* 11, 180–188.

Rogers, S. J., & Pennington, B. F. (1991). A theoretical approach to the deficits in infantile autism. *Development and Psychopathology,* 3, 137–162.

Rutter, M. (1970). Autistic children: Infancy to adulthood. *Seminars in Psychiatry,* 2, 435–450.

Rutter, M., Mawhood, L., & Howlin, P. (1992). Language delay and social development. In P. Fletcher & D. Hall (Eds.), *Specific speech and language disorders in children: Correlates, characteristics, and outcomes* (pp. 63–78). London: Plenum.

Salisbury, C. L., & Intagliata, J. (Eds.). (1986). *Respite care: Support for persons with developmental disabilities and their families.* Baltimore, MD: Paul H. Brookes.

Sanchez, L. E., Campbell, M., Small, A. M., Cueva, J. E., Armenteros, J. L., & Adams, P. B. (1996). A pilot study of clomipramine in young autistic children. *Journal of the American Academy of Child and Adolescent Psychiatry,* 35, 537–544.

Scahill, L., & Koenig, K. (1999). Pharmacotherapy in children and adolescents with pervasive developmental disorders. *Journal of Child & Adolescent Psychiatric Nursing,* 12(1), 41–43.

Schopler, E., Reichler, R. J., & Renner, B. R. (1988). *The Childhood Autism Rating Scale (CARS).* Los Angeles: Western Psychological Services.

Sherman, B. R. (1988). Predictors of the decision to place developmentally disabled family members in residential care. *American Journal of Mental Retardation,* 92(4), 344–351.

Siegel, B. (1996). *The world of the autistic child: Understanding and treating autistic spectrum disorders.* New York: Oxford University Press.

Siegel, B. (1997). Coping with the diagnosis of autism. In D. J. Cohen & F. R. Volkmar (Eds.), *Handbook of autism and pervasive developmental disorders* (2nd ed., pp. 745–766). New York: Wiley.

Sigman, M., Dissanayake, C., Arbelle, S., & Ruskin, E. (1997). Cognition and emotion in children and adolescents with autism. In D. J. Cohen & F. R. Volkmar (Eds.), *Handbook of autism and pervasive developmental disorders* (2nd ed., pp. 248–265). New York: Wiley.

Smith, I. M., & Bryson, S. E. (1994). Imitation and action in autism: A critical review. *Psychological Bulletin,* 116(2), 259–273.

Stone, W. L. (1997). Autism in infancy and early childhood. In D. J. Cohen & F. R. Volkmar (Eds.), *Handbook of autism and pervasive developmental disorders* (2nd ed., pp. 266–282). New York: Wiley.

Stone, W. L., & Caro-Martinez, L. M. (1990). Naturalistic observations of spontaneous communication in autistic children. *Journal of Autism and Developmental Disorders,* 20, 437–453.

Strain, P. S., Kohler, F. W., & Goldstein, H. (1996). Learning experiences…an alternative program: Peer-meditated interventions for young children with autism. In E. Hibbs & P. Jensen (Eds.), *Psychosocial treatments for child and adolescent disorder* (pp. 573–586). Washington, DC: APA.

Stromland, K., Nordin, V., Miller, M., Akerstrom, B., & Gillberg, C. (1994). Autism in thalidomide embryopathy: A population study. *Developmental Medicine and Child Neurology,* 36(4), 351–356.

Szatmari, P., & Jones, M. B. (1998). Genetic epidemiology of autism and other pervasive developmental disorders. In F. R. Volkmar (Ed.), *Autism and pervasive mental disorders* (pp. 109–129). Cambridge: Cambridge University Press.

Tanoue, O., & Asano, K. (1988). Epidemiology of infantile autism in southern Ibarki, Japan: Difference in prevalence in birth cohorts. *Journal of Autism and Developmental Disorders,* 18, 155–156.

Van Bourgondien, M. E., & Mesibov, G. B. (1989). Diagnosis and treatment of adolescents and adults with autism. In G. Dawson (Ed.), *Autism: New perspectives on diagnosis, nature, and treatment* (pp. 367–385). New York: Guilford.

Van Bourgondien, M. E., & Schopler, E. (1990). Critical issues in the residential care of people with autism. *Journal of Autism and Developmental Disorders,* 20, 391–400.

Volkmar, F. R., Cohen, D. J., & Paul, R. (1986). An evaluation of DSM-III criteria for infantile autism. *Journal of the American Academy of Child Psychiatry,* 25, 190–197.

Volkmar, F. R., Cook, E. H., & Pomeroy, J. (1999). Practice parameters for the assessment and treatment of children, adolescents, and adults with autism and other pervasive developmental disorders. *Journal of the American Academy of Child and Adolescent Psychiatry*, 38, 32–54.

Volkmar, F. R., Klin, A., & Cohen, D. J. (1997). Diagnosis and classification of autism and related conditions: consensus and issues. In D. J. Cohen & F. R. Volkmar (Eds.), *Handbook of autism and pervasive developmental disorders* (2nd ed., pp. 5–40). New York: Wiley.

Volkmar, F. R., Klin, A., Marans, W., & Cohen, D. J. (1996). The pervasive developmental disorders: Diagnosis and assessment. *Child and Adolescent Psychiatry Clinicians of North America*, 5, 967–978.

Volkmar, F. R., Klin, A., Marans, W., & Cohen, D. J. (1997). Childhood disintegrative disorder. In D. J. Cohen & F. R. Volkmar (Eds.), *Handbook of autism and pervasive developmental disorders* (2nd ed., pp. 47–59). New York: Wiley.

Wigham, S., & Tovey, C. (1994, March 3). Sweet success. *Care Weekly*, 12.

Wing, L., & Gould, J. (1979). Severe impairments of social interaction and associated abnormalities. *Journal of Autism and Developmental Disorders*, 9, 11–29.

CHAPTER 11

TREATMENT AND EARLY INTERVENTION FOR SCHIZOPHRENIA

CAROL T. MOWBRAY
University of Michigan

DEBBIE GIOIA-HASICK
University of Michigan

According to the most recent edition of the *Diagnostic and Statistical Manual of the American Psychiatric Association* (*DSM-IV,* APA, 1994), schizophrenia is characterized by delusions, hallucinations, disorganized speech, grossly disorganized or catatonic behavior, and negative symptoms, such as affective flattening and avolition. The disturbance must persist continuously for six months or more and constitute dysfunction in one or more major social/occupational life areas (see Figure 11.1). Despite the apparent parsimony of these criteria, the actual disorder of schizophrenia is extremely heterogeneous over individuals, time, place, culture, age groups, race/ethnicity, and gender. As this variability might imply, our understanding of this disorder is incomplete (Flaum, 1995). Research-based knowledge of early onset schizophrenia is even more limited than for adult schizophrenia. Onset in childhood or early adolescence is thought to have somewhat different etiology and consequences than adult onset; however, some experts regard the former as a totally different disorder (US DHHS, 1999). In this chapter, we include coverage of what is known about schizophrenia in children as well as in adults, discussing extensions of the latter to children and adolescents at risk or with early signs and symptoms, in order to fill knowledge gaps.

EPIDEMIOLOGY

The one-year prevalence of schizophrenia in this country has been reported as 1.3 percent for adults aged 18 to 54 years (US DHHS, 1999) and estimated to be 24 million worldwide

FIGURE 11.1 *DSM-IV* **Diagnostic Criteria for Schizophrenia**

A. *Characteristic symptoms:* Two (or more) of the following must be present for a significant portion of time during a 1-month period (or less if treated successfully):
   (1) delusions
   (2) hallucinations
   (3) disorganized speech (e.g., frequent derailment or incoherence)
   (4) grossly disorganized or catatonic behavior
   (5) negative symptoms (i.e., affective flattening, alogia or avolition)

B. *Social or occupational dysfunction:* Since the onset of the disturbance, one or more major areas of functioning such as work, interpersonal relations, or self-care are markedly below the level achieved prior to onset.

C. *Duration:* Continuous signs of the disturbance for at least 6 months. The 6 month period must include at least 1 month of symptoms that meet Criterion A.

D. *Disorder not attributable to mood or schizoaffective disorder*

E. *Disorder not due to substance abuse or other general medical condition*

F. *Relationship to a Pervasive Development Disorder (PDD):* If there is a prior history of Autistic disorder or PDD, the schizophrenia diagnosis is only given if prominent hallucinations or delusions are present for at least a month

Source: Reprinted with permission from the *Diagnostic and Statistical Manual of Mental Disorders, Fourth Edition, Text Revision.* Copyright 2000 American Psychiatric Association.

for the year 2000 (Desjarlais, Eisenberg, Good, & Kleiman, 1995). Worldwide studies of schizophrenia have been conducted since the 1920s. Until recently, prevalence has varied dramatically across countries (50-fold according to Torrey [1987], from 0.3 to 17 per 1,000). However, the World Health Organization (WHO) studies of schizophrenia, from 1969 to 1986, reported only slight variation in *incidence rates* across countries with culturally and socioeconomically diverse populations (Beiser & Iacono, 1990).

The most interesting aspect of the WHO findings may be the extreme heterogeneity in the *prevalence* of schizophrenia across cultures. The typical outcome and course of schizophrenia varied from a single psychotic episode followed by complete remission without continuing disability (low prevalence) to a chronic unremitting psychotic illness, marked by continuing disability, producing high prevalence rates. Further, according to the WHO studies, outcomes from initial schizophrenia episodes were significantly more favorable in developing countries (Jablensky & Sartorius, 1988); for example, 50 percent of patients in the United States vs. 7 percent in Nigeria had a chronic unremitting course. These findings have been remarkably robust, not explained by sampling bias, diagnostic variation, acute versus insidious onset, selective outcome measures, and so on (Hopper & Wanderling, 2000).

In the United States and worldwide, although there are no established overall gender differences in prevalence of schizophrenia (Hambrecht, Maurer, & Haefner, 1992), consistent gender differences in age of onset have been reported, producing differential rates for males and females in different age groups (Nicole & Shriqui, 1995). Peak incidence in males is between ages 15 and 25; in females, incidence peaks between ages 25 and 35

(Werry & Taylor, 1994). Race/ethnicity differences in the prevalence of schizophrenia have also been reported—most notably that African Americans are diagnosed with schizophrenia at higher rates than Caucasians (US DHHS, 1999), even controlling for symptom presentation (Pavkov, Lewis & Lyons, 1989). This appears, at least in part, to represent a diagnostic bias, because when more structured assessments are used, the racial differences decrease; African Americans formerly diagnosed with schizophrenia receive an affective disorder diagnosis (Neighbors, 1997). Epidemiology studies also consistently find disproportionately higher rates of schizophrenia among inner-city populations, suggesting social drift of these individuals into lower status circumstances (Werry & Taylor, 1994).

However, comparisons of the prevalence of schizophrenia between subgroups (e.g., men vs. women, or among racial/ethnic minorities) or over time are suspect. There are acknowledged validity differences across diagnostic methods and across clinicians, as well as differences in the diagnostic criteria over time and between classification systems. *DSM* criteria have gradually been operationalized, become more narrow and specific, differentiated more subtypes, and required longer duration of active symptom manifestation (Flaum, 1995; Tsuang, Stone, & Faraone, 2000). International Classification of Diseases (ICD-10) differs from *DSM-IV* criteria in accepting a shorter duration and not requiring dysfunction. Some reports comparing national trends over time suggest marked decreases in schizophrenia prevalence for the 1970s–1980s. However, because these changes correspond to the shift in *DSM* from one of the loosest to one of the narrowest diagnostic classification systems, their real meaning is unclear (Werry & Taylor, 1994).

Childhood Schizophrenia

In contrast to the adult population, there have been no national or international epidemiological studies of serious emotional disorders or mental illnesses in children (Asarnow & Asarnow, 1996). This lack of data represents a striking omission for national planning of child and adolescent mental health treatment. Although classification and diagnosis of adults with schizophrenia for research purposes are beset with methodological problems (Coffey, 1998), these problems pale in comparison to the difficulties in performing reliable assessments on children. Few well-tested diagnostic tools are available to accurately assess childhood onset schizophrenia (Caplan, 1989); most assessment measures are adapted versions of those standardized on adults.

Multiple additional explanations exist for the lack of empirical data on childhood schizophrenia. First, researchers often disagree about diagnostic criteria and err on the side of caution and protection of children from the stigma of a difficult psychiatric label. Professionals have been reluctant to create distinctions between transient childhood difficulties and more fixed childhood problems that may later become psychotic disturbance (Mash & Dozois, 1996). Further, a reasonable hesitancy by family and professionals in embracing a diagnostic decision may be prudent, because it is possible that the difficulties may be transient and resolve without treatment. Delaying diagnosis may be a partial explanation for lower rates of child versus adult schizophrenia. However, in itself, this is problematic, because studies suggest that early intervention may reduce subsequent disability in the disorder (McGorry, 1992; Lincoln & McGorry, 1999).

Consensus about core symptoms of childhood schizophrenia is also more difficult due to the rapid change, growth, and development seen in childhood. Developmental peculiarities and poor social functioning are identifiable for childhood onset, prior to formal diagnosis (Eggers & Bunk, 1997; Eggers, Bunk & Krause, 2000). Yet, such behavioral difficulties can also be features of other disorders (Russell, 1989). The low prevalence of childhood schizophrenia might also be attributable to neurocognitive heterogeneity at the onset of the disorder, which is not fully understood. Finally, children sometimes do not reveal their symptoms to significant adults because hallucinations and delusions seem relatively ego-syntonic and therefore not frightening (Russell, 1994). Because the current consensus in the field is to view and treat many childhood psychotic illnesses as continuous with adult-onset forms, we need to understand the developmental life course of illnesses such as schizophrenia, especially in its very early phases (McClellan, 1999; McGorry & Jackson, 1999; Walker, 1991).

Prevalence by Age.   Onset for schizophrenia in childhood is conceptualized in terms of two age-related groupings: (1) very early onset schizophrenia (VEOS; 2–12 years) and (2) early onset schizophrenia (EOS; 13–18 years). In VEOS, the onset of psychotic symptoms occurs before age 12. This disorder is rare, but unfortunately it also carries the worst prognosis (Eggers & Bunk, 1997). Those with a chronic onset pattern before age 12 never seem to fully remit in long-term follow-up. The earliest report of a full diagnosis of schizophrenia occurred in a child of 4.9 years (Russell et al., 1989). The prevalence rate of VEOS is estimated to be one-sixtieth that of adult-onset schizophrenia, affecting approximately 1 in 10,000 children aged 2 to 12 years—clearly an atypical pattern (Asarnow & Asarnow, 1996; Remschmidt et al., 1994).

Early onset schizophrenia (EOS) is diagnosed when a first episode occurs between ages 12 and 18. There is some potential for diagnostic blurring during these years because they may also mark the beginning of prodromal symptoms for adult onset schizophrenia. The onset of active "positive" symptoms typically lasts from 1 to 6 months in EOS, with an acute onset more frequent after age 12 (Eggers & Bunk, 1997; Werry & Taylor, 1994). *Positive symptoms* of schizophrenia (i.e., delusions, hallucinations, and disorganized thoughts and speech) are defined as false perceptions and beliefs not shared by those without the disorder. *Negative symptoms* (i.e., alogia, avolition, and blunted affect) reflect an absence of thoughts and feelings that are normally present in a healthy person but are conspicuously absent in a person with schizophrenia (Mueser & Gingerich, 1994). Early onset schizophrenia may be associated with a worse prognosis than adult-onset schizophrenia, including intellectual decline, because the positive and negative symptoms develop during a critical phase of adolescent development (Jacobsen & Rapoport, 1998). Some illness onsets seem to be linked to pubertal changes, although a clear relationship has not yet been established (Frazier et al., 1997).

Prevalence by Gender.   Higher ratios of males to females (e.g., greater than 3:1) have been reported for early onset cases in some studies (Eggers & Bunk, 1997). Gender differences seem to level out by adolescence. Early vulnerability to the disorder in males may represent gender differences in neurocognitive functioning that are similarly represented in other neurological disorders (Lewine, 1998; Done et al., 1994).

Prevalence by Ethnicity and Culture.   Current research has just begun to explore cultural and ethnic differences in childhood forms of mental disorders. Some studies suggest that earlier onset of schizophrenia in "developing" countries predicts better clinical and social outcomes (Sartorius et al., 1986). Lopez (2000) has recently produced an international review of the social world of childhood mental illness, touching on the important ways that culture defines childhood problem behaviors that may be precursors of severe mental disorders. However, there are no hard data on worldwide childhood schizophrenia rates or their relationship to culture/ethnicity, and researchers caution against prematurely establishing these linkages (Jablensky, 1997).

RESEARCH ON SCHIZOPHRENIA
IN ADULTS AND CHILDREN

Before presenting research describing symptoms and functioning problems associated with schizophrenia, some caveats are necessary. First, schizophrenia is one of the most variable of psychiatric disorders (Tandon, Jibson, Taylor, & DeQuardo, 1995). Debates persist as to whether schizophrenia can be reliably classified into discrete syndromes or whether dimensional or symptom-specific research approaches are more appropriate (Penn, Corrigan, Bentall, Racenstein, & Newman, 1997). The *DSM-IV* includes schizophreniform, schizoaffective, and schizophrenia diagnoses. The result of these considerations is that some research studies may include or exclude particular subtypes; thus, readers need to be aware that conclusions presented in review articles, such as this chapter, are broad-stroke generalizations and that there are many qualifications to their application. Readers should also be aware of the proliferation of recent research on schizophrenia, which is likely to continue into the future. In part, this increase reflects the availability of newer technologies to study brain structures and operations (such as functional MRI) and the desirability of measuring outcomes associated with newer antipsychotic medications and psychiatric rehabilitation methods. This expanded research focus also appears to reflect influences of cognitive psychology in examining the phenomenology of schizophrenia, patients' views of the self (e.g., Davidson, 1994), and the meaning of delusions and hallucinations (Garety & Freeman, 1999).

Significance of the Schizophrenia
Diagnosis for Adults

Schizophrenia is regarded as a bio-psychosocial disorder, and research confirms biological and psychosocial origins and manifestations. The biological basis has been established through comparisons of individuals with schizophrenia diagnoses versus normal controls. The most consistent biological marker is abnormalities in smooth-pursuit eye tracking (Buckley, Buchanan, Schulz, & Tamminga, 1996). Precise characterization of eye-tracking dysfunction in schizophrenia is important. Researchers use a computerized electrooculographic testing and analyzing instrument, which moves a signal slowly across a screen, while keeping the eye steady, and produces multiple measures (Campana, Duci, Gambini, & Scarone, 1999). Eye-tracking dysfunction is also found in relatives of schizophrenic patients (Green, 1998).

Numerous research studies have also identified excessive activity of dopamine (a neurotransmitter) being linked to schizophrenia (Deniker, 1970; Wyatt, 1986; Davis et al., 1991). Some research has found structural deviations in the brain, occurring very early in life: ventricular enlargements (Bogerts & Falkai, 1995; Tsuang & Faraone, 1999; Werry & Taylor, 1994) and abnormalities of limbic and nonlimbic system structures (Bogerts & Falkai, 1995; Buckley, Buchanan, Tamminga, & Schulz, 2000). Positron emission tomography (PET) scans have identified common regions of the brain showing high rates of activity in hallucinating schizophrenia patients (Andreasen, 1997).

Neurological studies have demonstrated consistent cognitive deficits in schizophrenia: "a disruption in fundamental circuitry in the brain, resulting in a generalized deficit in a basic cognitive process" (Mohammed, Paulsen, O'Leary, Arndt, & Andreasen, 1999, p. 754). Based on a review of all published studies of neuropsychological functioning in schizophrenia since 1980, the deficits most consistently reported are (in decreasing order of magnitude) delayed recall, manual dexterity, performance skill, cognitive flexibility and abstraction, attention/concentration, memory acquisition, and verbal skill (Zakzanis, Leach, & Kaplan, 1998). Even in a sample of first-episode, neuroleptic-naive patients compared to controls, Hawkins and colleagues (1999) found significant deficits in many of these cognitive-performance areas. Adults with schizophrenia, overall, have significantly lower IQs than the general population; however, this difference is stable from childhood through adulthood, and predates the onset of schizophrenia (Russell et al., 1997).

CASE STUDY
HETEROGENEITY ILLUSTRATION

Steve is a 35-year-old, single, Jewish male with an illness pattern that has defied most notions of what had previously been understood to be the classic "positive" symptoms of schizophrenia (i.e., auditory hallucinations, delusions). Steve did well in high school and went on to earn a degree in political science at a four-year university. He began to experience neurocognitive decline when he started his postcollege career doing research for political candidates. He persisted in his job for about a year but he could no longer retain and process information like he did in college. This was very frustrating and he became more reclusive, eventually moving out of his apartment, sleeping in his car, and losing the job he loved. His social relationships had always been poor but now they deteriorated to the point where his parents became concerned with his isolation and odd behavior, and brought Steve to a psychiatrist to be evaluated.

It was determined that Steve had a form of schizophrenia characterized by profound cognitive deficits. Steve has a paternal uncle with schizophrenia who has done well on Clozaril, but has a different presentation. Steve was never hospitalized but was prescribed antipsychotic medications as an outpatient for his disorganized and paranoid thinking, but it has helped very little. Testing had shown that Steve had lost IQ points (rare in most forms of schizophrenia) and had profound deficits in neurocognitive task ability (i.e., verbal learning and memory). His deficits require Steve to reside in a structured living program and utilize supported employment services to maintain a service industry job. He is stable but not at his pre-illness level and has never experienced the leaps in recovery attained by others with positive symptom patterns.

In terms of psychiatric symptoms, schizophrenia has often been primarily described in terms of *positive* (first rank) symptoms, such as delusions and hallucinations. The term *first rank* is attributed to Kurt Schneider (1959) and refers to specific delusions and hallucinations deemed to be important for exact diagnosis of schizophrenia. Previously ignored, but now identified as more chronic and persistent, are *negative* symptoms, such as apathy, anhedonia, blunted affect, and social/emotional withdrawal. *Negative* does not refer to a person's attitude, but to a lack of certain characteristics that should be present (NAMI, 2001). Researchers have attempted to classify patients into distinct subtypes of positive and negative symptoms, but the subtypes are not longitudinally stable. Other research has identified secondary negative symptoms, caused by primary symptoms and/or treatment (e.g., medication side effects) (Tandon et al., 1995). Negative symptoms seem to be more common in men with schizophrenia and affective symptoms more so in women (Nicole & Shriqui, 1995).

As summarized by Werry and Taylor (1994), the risk of suicide for people with schizophrenia is similar to that for affective disorders—about 15 percent of those diagnosed, from 20 to 50 times higher than in the general population (MediView, 2001). Most suicides occur within 10 years of diagnosis, and the greatest risks occur following discharge. Of particular concern is an elevated risk of suicide for young men with higher premorbid functioning and expectations for future success.

Some research has investigated which types of symptoms are more significant to long-term outcomes in schizophrenia. Negative symptoms are most consistently related to low functioning and lack of community integration (Gold et al., 1999; US DHHS, 1999). However, other reports identify disorganization (Werry & Taylor, 1994) or cognitive impairments as most influential to functional outcomes, with medium to large effect sizes (Green, Kern, Braff, & Mintz, 2000). This research suggests that learning potential is the mediator between cognitive deficits and functioning outcomes. Thus, cognitive deficits may be particularly significant for explaining the major functional effects of early onset schizophrenia on development. Cognitive deficits diminish skill capacities necessary for community functioning, independent living, and activities of daily living (Green et al., 2000).

Quality of life differences (Katschnig, 1997) and parenting adequacy in schizophrenia have also been researched, although, for the latter, associated deficits are less clearly established (Oyserman, Mowbray, Allen-Meares, & Firminger, 2000; Mowbray, Oyserman, Bybee, & MacFarlane, 2003). A recent and expanding area of research involves social functioning. Individuals diagnosed with schizophrenia display poorer social competence, social cognition, social skills and social problem solving, as well as social insensitivity and indifference. However, it is not yet clear to what extent these deficits represent consumers' reactions to their experiences (institutionalization, stigma), reflect overall deficiencies in information processing, or are specifically connected to the schizophrenia diagnosis (Penn et al., 1997; Silverstein, 1997). Green (1998) has speculated that the major impairment in schizophrenia is an inability to process information from the environment; and, because interpersonal data are complicated and subtle, it is thus not surprising that those with schizophrenia have major deficits in the social area.

Individuals with schizophrenia diagnoses have significantly more health problems: greater prevalence of vision and dental problems, high blood pressure, diabetes, and sexually transmitted diseases, even when controlling for age, race, and gender (US DHHS, 1999). Mortality rates are significantly elevated in comparison to the general population.

At present, it is unclear to what extent these health problems may be side effects of medications, correlates of poverty and unhealthy lifestyles (e.g., overweight), or aspects of the schizophrenia illness.

Finally, of perhaps greatest controversy and consequence for the treatment of adults diagnosed with schizophrenia, are findings related to violence and criminality. Studies of jail and prison populations find higher rates of mental illness, and research on outpatient clients shows more criminality and violence than for the general population (Monahan, 1992; Mulvey, 1994; Torrey, 1994). The clinical variables most predictive of dangerousness are substance abuse, schizophrenia and schizoaffective diagnoses, and psychotic symptoms, especially paranoid delusions and command hallucinations (Link, Andrews, & Cullen, 1992; Steadman, Silver, Monahan, Appelbaum, Robbins, Mulvey, Grisso, Roth, & Banks, 2000). Command hallucinations are voices that tell the person to act or behave in a certain way. The common public perception is that deinstitutionalization resulted in more offending among individuals with serious mental illness. However, population-level studies have failed to confirm this association (Banks, Stone, Pandiani, Cox, & Morschauseret, 2000; Mullen, Burgess, Wallace, Palmer, & Ruschena, 2000; Severson, 2000). Despite this overall deficit picture, many adults with schizophrenia are able to manage this chronic illness and lead fulfilling lives, such as Nobel Prize Laureate John Nash (Nasar, 1998).

Symptoms and Effects of Childhood Schizophrenia

In early onset schizophrenia, the child will typically have delusions or complicated hallucinations. In very early onset schizophrenia, children usually experience simple hallucinations and confused thinking (McClellan, 2000). For example, young children may believe that they are on a TV show; teens may feel that they are being controlled by a TV character, part of a network of others who receive command messages to leave their homes and board a spaceship for their "true" home. Although many children have rich fantasy lives, children with schizophrenia are more distressed by their "fantasies," are unable to separate themselves easily from them, and may hide these thoughts for many years so as to fit in with their peers. They usually have more difficulty with social relationships than children who are just very imaginative. A longitudinal study, comparing data at 11 and 26 years, found that those children with strong psychotic symptoms early in life were twice as likely to have a schizophreniform diagnosis by age 26 (Poulton et al., 2000).

In general, early onset appears to have the following features: (1) a more gradual development of symptoms, (2) more negative symptoms over the illness course, (3) more neuropsychological problems, and (4) more disruption of adult milestones (US DHHS, 1999). A 10-year follow-up of adolescents treated for schizophrenia found poor social adjustment and functional impairments for the majority, suggesting consequences more severe than with adult onset (Lay, Blanz, Hartmann, & Schmidt, 2000).

The risk for substance abuse is particularly high among adolescent males with recent schizophrenia onset as they attempt to self-medicate psychotic and depressive symptoms (Linszen & Lenior, 1999). Depending on the extent of the abuse, this co-occurring disorder can have many repercussions in the lives of those with schizophrenia, including a higher risk of suicide (Mueser et al., 2001). Because addiction also appears to have a strong biological and neurodevelopmental etiology, understanding its relationship with schizophrenia could increase accuracy in targeting onset. The worst-case scenario is one in which the onset of schizophrenia is masked by substance use and therefore remains untreated for long periods of time, almost assuring the probability of a poor outcome.

Economic Burden of Schizophrenia

The cost of schizophrenia cannot be fully measured; however, the following estimates suggest the enormous burden of schizophrenia illness worldwide: In 1990, the total economic burden of schizophrenia was estimated at $32.5 billion. Of this, $17 to $19 billion is attributable to direct medical costs (Rice, 1999; Weiden & Olfson, 1995; Williams & Dickson, 1995), and the remainder to indirect costs such as lost business productivity (Silverstein, 2000).

Families suffer a disproportionate share of economic burden in schizophrenic illness, with cost estimates for families in the United States ranging from $2.5 to $8.6 billion in 1992 (Terkelsen & Grosser, 1990).

ETIOLOGY

Theories of Etiology

Fifty years ago, theory and practice clearly located the cause of schizophrenia within the family—ascribed to the "schizophrenogenic mother" and/or to double-bind family relationships. These concepts are hardly referenced today (Lukens & Thorning, 1998); however, in actual practice, "parent blaming" still exists. A survey of MSW licensed practitioners found that the majority of respondents attributed serious mental illness in children (including schizophrenia and psychosis) to unhealthy parenting, parental dysfunction, and/or deficits (Rubin et al., 1998). Furthermore, professionals sometimes see parents' grief responses over the onset of a child's major mental illness as pathological, and their search for information about the illness as signs of enmeshment and overinvolvement (MacGregor, 1994).

For the past 30 years, the most accepted theories of schizophrenia assume bio-psycho-social etiology, congruent with the manifestations of the illness. "Stress-diathesis" models posit that schizophrenia arises from the impact of the environment on individuals who have a genetic predisposition (Tsuang & Faraone, 1999). These individuals are more vulnerable to stress and therefore less able to respond appropriately to stressors (Walker & Diforio, 1997). A neurodevelopmental model hypothesizes that (1) nongenetic stressors interact with a genetic predisposition to produce an early (pre- or postnatal) abnormality in neural development; (2) the consequent neural disruption is (a) silent until the affected region of the brain is called on-line, later in development, or (b) becomes manifest due to an interaction between affected neurotransmitters and neurohormonal mechanisms of stress responsivity (in adolescence or adulthood); and (3) there is an inverse relationship between the extent of genetic predisposition and the amount of stress necessary to push the individual across a threshold into the schizophrenia spectrum (Green, 1998). Models for the specific neural mechanisms involved in schizophrenia symptom onset have been proposed (Rosso, Cannon, Huttunen, Huttunen, et al., 2000; Walker & Diforio, 1997), suggesting maldevelopment of the brain as early as the second trimester of life (Tsuang et al., 2000).

Some researchers hypothesize a cumulative vulnerability—when an individual's pool of genetic and environmental variables exceeds a certain threshold, he or she will manifest signs of schizophrenia (Tsuang & Faraone, 1999). Other researchers have suggested two types of schizophrenia—one caused primarily by genetic inheritance and responsible for the majority of cases; the other by neurodevelopmental deviance, perhaps 10 to 20 percent of cases (Buckley, 1998; Kendler & Diehl, 1993; Werry & Taylor, 1994). Cannon (1998) summarizes recent research that strongly supports the theory of a genetic-early environment interaction (e.g., labor and delivery complications); that is, birth complications are independent of genetics (not occurring more frequently in unaffected siblings or offspring of adults with schizophrenia) and relate to later schizophrenia diagnosis only in high risk samples (with schizophrenia family histories).

CASE STUDY

ILLUSTRATION OF A LENGTHY PRODROME AND FAMILIAL GENETIC LOADING

Michele has strong family genetics for this disorder. She is a second-generation Japanese American woman whose mother, with a probable diagnosis of schizophrenia, committed suicide when Michele was in high school, and whose older brother, definitely diagnosed with schizophrenia, died from heart and obesity problems that were secondary to his disorder. Michele now feels that her illness began in junior high school. She heard voices at that time but was unable to ask for help since her mother was so preoccupied with her own internal demons. Thus, Michele coped alone for years with all the torment in her brain and with multiple life stressors until she took a knife to her stomach in an attempt to find some final relief. She survived the suicide attempt, was hospitalized, and finally discovered that schizophrenia was the cause of her thought disturbances.

Possibly due to Michele's lengthy prodrome period, medications seemed to have little effect on her symptoms. She suffered tremendously in her 20s with multiple hospitalizations each year. She often became depressed, wondering aloud to her treatment team that "if only" she had received medication earlier in her life, her outcome would have shown improvement in adulthood. Michele vividly remembers the pain of school, social, and family difficulties in high school. She remembers that withdrawal to the safety of her room was both a blessing and a curse.

Now in her early 40s, Michele has halted the pattern of recurrent hospitalizations through medication, education about her disorder, consistent use of cognitive-behavioral strategies, and a strong social network. She has worked as a peer counselor for others in the early phases of schizophrenia and has benefited from courses at the local junior college. Michele has been active in a clubhouse model of community support, has been involved in local theater productions, and has lived independently for years without any of the desperation she experienced initially in her disorder.

Genetic Factors

A genetic basis for schizophrenia has been well established over the last 20 years, utilizing rigorous methodologies (control groups, structured psychiatric assessments, and blind diagnosis). Studies assessing relatives of individuals diagnosed with schizophrenia substantiate that schizophrenia aggregates in families. In those families with schizophrenia present, the risk for a first-degree relative also being diagnosed is 5 to 15 times higher than in relatives of matched controls (Maziade & Raymond, 1995; Kendler & Diehl, 1993). The mean concordance rate for schizophrenia in monozygotic twins is about 46 percent, compared to 14 percent in dizygotic pairs (Rutter, Silberg, O'Connor, & Simonoff, 1999). Studies of children adopted away from mothers with schizophrenia versus controls show highly significant increased prevalence in diagnoses of psychotic disorders in the latter group. Family members of individuals diagnosed with schizophrenia have increased prevalence of schizophrenia-like personality traits (schizotypal and paranoid personality disorders; Rutter et al., 1999) and communication disturbances (Docherty, Gordinier, Hall, & Cutting, 1999), suggesting psychiatric liability. These results have been consistent across studies from Greece (Frangos et al., 1985), Ireland (Kendler et al., 1993), Denmark (Kety et al., 1994), Germany, Norway, and the United States (Kendler & Diehl, 1993). Statistical analyses suggest that the mode of transmission is probably not due to a single gene (Rutter et al., 1999; Tsuang et al., 2000). Accumulating evidence also suggests that neurological factors play a greater role in the development of schizophrenia in males (Nicole & Shriqui, 1995).

Environmental Factors

Biologically based, environmental stressors studied as etiological factors are quite extensive and have included maternal body mass index pre-pregnancy (Schaefer et al., 2000), second trimester exposure to respiratory infections (Brown et al., 2000), fetal hypoxia associated with obstetrical complications (Cannon et al., 2000), perinatal brain damage (Jones et al., 1998), low birth weight (Hultman et al., 1999), fetal malnutrition (Dalman et al., 1999), Rh-factor incompatibility, prenatal exposure to viral infection (Green, 1998), and birth dates during influenza epidemics (Walker & Diforio, 1997; Werry & Taylor, 1994). However, while all these circumstances are significantly associated with schizophrenia-spectrum diagnoses in adulthood, they are also found for other developmental impairments. The vast majority of infants exposed to these complications do *not* develop schizophrenia (Cannon, 1998). Furthermore, most of these factors are also markers for poverty and low social class (Werry & Taylor, 1994).

Psychosocial stressors have been less extensively and/or systematically studied, particularly concerning events in the pre- and postnatal periods. Animal studies suggest that maternal stress during pregnancy increases the likelihood of offspring demonstrating abnormalities in brain structures and behaviors. Human studies have linked maternal prenatal poverty, depression, and exposure to a significant stressor during pregnancy with greater likelihood of bearing children later diagnosed with schizophrenia. A number of unrelated studies also indicate that children at high risk for schizophrenia are more likely to manifest problems or to develop symptoms when themselves exposed to early environmental stressors, such as parental mistreatment, high levels of critical attitudes, dysfunctional adoptive families (US DHHS, 1999; Walker & Diforio, 1997), care in institutional settings (Parnas, Teasdale, & Schulsinger, 1985), and below-average mothering at preschool ages (Jones, Rodgers, Murray, & Marmot, 1994). Thus, although quite incomplete at present, the evidence suggests that genetic risk for schizophrenia combined with environmental neuropsychological and/or early social stressors increase a child's likelihood of schizophrenia in childhood or adulthood, although none of these factors is singularly a definitive predictor.

Special Issues in Childhood Schizophrenia

As in adult schizophrenia, there appear to be many etiological pathways in the complex and often misunderstood disorder of childhood schizophrenia. Two issues have particular relevance: a connection between autism and childhood schizophrenia and the high preponderance of psychiatric disorders in these children's close relatives.

Overall, childhood onset individuals are clearly atypical even among the larger population of persons with schizophrenia. Childhood schizophrenia has core deficits (i.e., neuromotor, expressive, interpersonal) that are congruent with adult forms of the disorder, but that stand out during the early developmental years. These deficits may accurately identify children who are at risk for schizophrenia or they may be indicative of a different disorder. Childhood schizophrenia and autism initially shared a common diagnostic base because both disorders are characterized by abnormal social interactions (Asarnow & Asarnow, 1994). Although they have overlapping features, schizophrenia is typically differentiated by a later age of onset, less impaired intellectual abilities, the presence of hallucinations and delusions, and the tendency to experience relapse and remission (Klinger & Dawson, 1996; Rutter, 1972). Autistic children are characterized by their inability to form human relationships, their use of unusual speech, and their very limited range of activities and interests (Harvard MH Letter, 2001). They may have a tendency toward repetitive actions and extreme responses to objects, either through avoidance or total preoccupation, as well as an inability to respond to social cues (Facts for Families, 2000; Klinger & Dawson, 1996; Gillberg, 2000). These symptom profiles clearly point to two different disorders and distinct etiologies.

Concerning family preponderance, some research suggests that the genetic contribution is greater for child-onset versus adult-onset schizophrenia (Buckley et al., 1996). Why this is the case is not entirely clear, although it does strengthen genetic transmission theories. According to the neurodevelopmental hypothesis, specific neural pathology in schizophrenia may at first be "clinically silent" and then become triggered by internal and external factors to create the onset of the disorder (Weinberger, Berman, & Zec, 1986). Neurodevelopmental damage appears greater in childhood-onset schizophrenia (Rapoport, 1997), particularly in circuits relevant for language (Nicholson, Lenane, Singaracharlu, Malaspina, et al., 2000), although the origin of the damage has not yet been determined.

LIFE COURSE OF SCHIZOPHRENIA

Criteria for schizophrenia specify that symptoms must have been present for six months or more, differentiating it from schizophreniform disorder. However, the prodromal period (from first noticeable symptoms to first prominent symptoms) for schizophrenia is highly variable. A comprehensive Vancouver study of all residents experiencing a first episode of functional psychosis found prodromes up to 20 years long, with a median length of 37.9 weeks, a mean 115.2 weeks, and a SD = 168 (Beiser et al., 1994). The length of the pretreatment period is reportedly a significant predictor of the course of the first psychotic episode (Haefner & Maurer, 1995). The significant variations in symptom onset and course of schizophrenia are illustrated in both case studies in this chapter.

Early Indicators

Recent research has retrospectively collected or accessed information on the childhood and adolescent functioning of adults diagnosed with schizophrenia. The methodologies vary from blind ratings of old home videos of these adults during childhood, to large-scale, population-based, follow-back research (e.g., using perinatal databases). Most studies contrast pre-schizophrenic adults with normal peers. Differentiating characteristics pre-onset include motor coordination (Cannon et al., 1999); social maladjustment at school age (Done, Crow, Johnstone, & Sacker, 1994); late milestones of motor development, speech problems, solitary play preferences, less social confidence, and social anxiety in teenage years (Jones et al., 1994); personality disorders (Lewis, David, Malmberg, & Allebeck, 2000); verbal IQ and mechanical knowledge tests (David et al., 1997); and social functioning, organizational ability, and intellectual functioning (Davidson et al., 1999).

Some studies have contrasted pre-schizophrenic adults with their unaffected siblings, and thus allow possible differentiation of traits with a genetic basis versus traits that are early indicators or prodromal signs of schizophrenia. The characteristics that seem to reflect early indicators (more common in diagnosed individuals than their relatives) include minor physical anomalies (i.e., craniofacial features, finger and palm prints); unusual movements (Rosso et al., 2000); and poor childhood motor coordination, social interaction deficits, and speech problems (Buckley, 1998; Bearden et al., 2000). These indicators are obviously not specific to schizophrenia, but prominent in many developmental disorders, and so may reflect underlying brain damage of children who go on to develop adult schizophrenia (Buckley, 1998).

In contrast, still other research has identified markers common to patients with schizophrenia *and* their adult relatives (vs. relatives of controls or other diagnostic groups): executive functioning, memory (Faraone et al., 1999); attentional deficits (Cornblatt & Keilp, 1994; Kremen et al., 1994); communication disturbances (Docherty, Gordinier, Hall, & Cutting, 1999); perceptual-motor speed, concept formation, and abstraction (Kremen et al., 1994); cognitive tests (Cannon et al., 2000); externalizing behaviors (Amminger et al., 1999); subclinical thought disorder (Dworkin et al., 1991; Maier, Hoechst-Janneck, & Franke, 1995); poor rapport, odd behaviors, social isolation/avoidance or maladjustment (Bearden et al., 2000; Kendler, McGuire, Gruenberg, & Walsh, 1995); and anhedonia/asociality and poor social competence in adolescence (Dworkin et al., 1991). Thus, these factors may be indicators of vulnerability to schizophrenia (components of a clinical syndrome, schizotaxia, that may or may not progress to psychosis; Tsuang et al., 2000). In a unique qualitative study, first-episode patients with schizophrenia described their initial subjective prodromal experiences: a distorted perception of the self, extreme preoccupation and withdrawal into ideas, neurotic features, disturbed thought, and attenuated delusions or perceptions (less than psychotic) (Moller & Husby, 2000).

Long-Term Prospects and Recovery

Beyond the prodrome, the literature has identified subsequent phases of the schizophrenic disorder: (1) an active phase, lasting typically 1 to 6 months, characterized mainly by positive symptoms (Haefner & Maurer, 1995); (2) the recuperative/recovery phase of several months, in which signs of active psychosis disappear or diminish, but functional deficits may remain; and (3) the residual phase, noticeable in about 80 percent of cases where recovery is incomplete and impairments and symptoms continue (Werry & Taylor, 1994). This phasic description, however, rarely applies to individual patients, nor do researchers agree on the percentage of cases which enter the residual phase versus those which evidence remission. One recent study of first-episode schizophrenia reported that out of 50 individuals (with significantly smaller ventricles and with an acute onset), there were 15 different life-course patterns of illness at the 5-year follow-up (DeLisi et al., 1998). Overall, the course of schizophrenia is highly variable. Most individuals experience at least one relapse after the first psychotic episode, usually of positive symptoms and when noncompliant with medications (Robinson et al., 1999). Some individuals experience an erratic pattern of symptoms over their lifetimes, whereas others experience a steady level, ranging from moderate to severe. The first 5 to 10 years are most problematic, either due to the illness itself or to individuals developing better personal treatment and management strategies over time (US DHHS, 1999).

Until the last 20 years, schizophrenia was characterized as a disorder in which recovery never occurred, and progressive deterioration could be expected (Hulbert, Jackson, & McGorry, 1996; Tsuang et al., 2000). A number of longitudinal research studies now disprove this assumption. Gold and colleagues (1999) studied cognitive function in young adults who received treatment early in their illness. Intellectual abilities did not deteriorate; IQs for some patients even improved. The Vermont Longitudinal Study presented landmark research findings following up patients discharged from a state hospital to an innovative community treatment program in the 1950s (Harding et al., 1987). The patients all had confirmed *DSM-III* schizophrenia diagnoses and were among those in the hospital with the poorest prognosis. Yet, at follow-up, two-thirds of this group had restored social functioning and evidenced recovery in terms of work and community integration, and exhibited no current signs of mental illness nor use of psychiatric medications. Ten other recent worldwide studies of patients with schizophrenia, followed for two to four decades, also find wide heterogeneity in outcomes and significant improvements for 33 to 60 percent of the individuals studied (Harding, 1995). These findings imply that the course of the schizophrenia illness may be long and difficult, but that a large percentage of patients do significantly improve, and even recover. Other data suggest that the earlier the intervention, the shorter the time frame for recovery and the better the overall prognosis (discussed later).

RISK AND PROTECTIVE FACTORS

From genetic studies, obviously a major risk factor for developing schizophrenia and related disorders is family history—first-degree relationships and a greater number of relatives with schizophrenia diagnoses pose a greater risk. Risk for experiencing schizophrenia seems to be exacerbated by biological factors (apoxia during birth, infections prenatally) by stress-related experiences of mothers during pregnancy, and of at-risk children during early developmental periods. Thus, good medical and psychosocial care of mothers during pregnancy and the birth process may be a protective factor, as well as minimal stress in childhood environments.

The WHO studies suggest that supportive relationships from the family or the community may minimize the long-term disability associated with schizophrenia. On an individual basis, those with schizophrenia predispositions can perhaps avoid stressful situations by being in positive support relationships with others; stress can also be avoided by a certain degree of social isolation, known as *positive withdrawal* (Green, 1998). The WHO studies further suggest that useful employment (less affected by lingering disability in developing countries) may also slow down or arrest the long-term effects of schizophrenia (Hopper & Wanderling, 2000). Gender can be a protective factor, too, at least in young adulthood. The mechanism involved has not been determined; however, the presence of estrogen is suspected (Harding, 1998). Finally, there is some suggestion that certain personality types may place vulnerable individuals at higher risk for schizophrenia—for example, explosive, paranoid, and schizoid (i.e., magical thinking) personality diagnoses (Hulbert, Jackson, & McGorry, 1996).

REVIEW OF PROMISING INTERVENTIONS

Young adults with a schizophrenic disorder are rarely willing to embrace their diagnosis or the treatment recommended for an illness that is overwhelming, basically frightening, and about which they and their families have little experience or information. They often resist being labeled mentally ill, see themselves as social failures rather than psychiatric patients, and avoid mental health services (Hoffman & Mastrianni, 1992). Despite this opposition, it is incumbent on professionals and advocates to be knowledgeable about and to offer education on the best treatment options available, regardless of whether consumers are ready to partake of services. The following approaches have been identified as efficacious for intervention, relapse prevention, and recovery in adult schizophrenia: (1) pharmacotherapy, (2) psychosocial rehabilitation, (3) assertive community treatment, and (4) family psychoeducation (see Bustillo, Lauriello, Horan, & Keith, 2001; Huxley, Rendall & Sederer, 2000; Mueser, Bond, & Drake, 2001; Silverstein, 2000, for reviews). In describing each approach, we also discuss its relevance for children and adolescents. Next, we summarize treatment guidelines from the Schizophrenia Patient Outcome Research Team (PORT, 1998).

Pharmacotherapy

A major component of psychiatric recovery for most adults is typically some form of antipsychotic medication, even if only for the acute episode. The widespread use of a new class of atypical antipsychotics (i.e., Risperidone, Olanzapine), following a first episode, has led to a quicker return to baseline functioning for many individuals with schizophrenia (Marder & Meibach, 1994). These medications seem to be appreciably better than previously used neuroleptics in reducing positive, negative, and disorganized symptoms of schizophrenia (Ho, 1999); less distressing side-effects are evident and rehospitalization rates are markedly reduced (Conley et al., 1999). There are promising indications that better work recovery may also be associated with the newer medications, but replication studies are needed (Bond & Meyer, 1999; Nuechterlein et al., 2000; Rollins, 2000). However, medication alone is not a panacea—it must be combined with education and rehabilitative treatments (Huxley et al., 2000).

The introduction of many new psychopharmaceutical agents makes medication decisions for schizophrenia much more complex than in past decades (Mellman et al., 2001). Medications are now more likely to be used in combination (polypharmacotherapy) or introduced at various illness stages (Canales et al., 1999). However, some medication-compliant individuals still have symptoms that are nonresponsive to traditional drug therapies (5 to 25 percent, according to Brenner et al., 1990). Psychiatrists are individualizing treatment according to the patient's symptom presentation, based on guidelines for patient care. The step-by-step staging of clinical decision making for medication use is known as *medical algorithms*—a set of rules for addressing treatment issues (Mellman et al., 2001).

The Texas Medication Algorithm Project (TMAP) and the associated Children's Medication Algorithm Project (CMAP) represent major initiatives for clinical understanding and medication direction to optimize treatment response (Miller et al., 1999; Hughes et al., 1999). The former (TMAP) provides basic tools to arrive at consensus for a "best" treatment response when persons have similar psychiatric illnesses. It is important that mental health treatments find effective medications for patients diagnosed with schizophrenia, as poor response to medications may result in substantial recuperative delays that induce some persons to surrender to the patient role prematurely and perhaps limit their opportunities for rehabilitation (Chandler et al., 1999). Unfortunately, the availability of the newer atypical antipsychotics relates to class and race: In a recent study, about one-half of prescriptions for antipsychotics were for the newer medications; however, factors associated with receiving new antipsychotics included race (being white) and having more education (Wang, West, Tanielian, & Pincus, 2000). The newer antipsychotics are substantially more costly than traditional neuroleptics. For example, Risperidone lists at $79/month, and Zyprexa at $177–$451/month (depending on dosage), whereas Haldol is approximately $30/month (VA Cost of Medication, 1999). Some pharmaceutical companies offer a compassionate care program for those who cannot afford medication costs and will authorize inclusion of the medication to the pharmaceutical formulary list for coverage by Medicare/Medicaid when requested.

Table 11.1 displays both novel and traditional neuroleptics currently being prescribed for the treatment of schizophrenia. Advantages and disadvantages of these medications are also presented. For the most part, newer medications are usually recommended for first-episode patients, especially as part of ongoing outpatient treatment. Persons with schizophrenia may need a range of medication options over their life cycle to accommodate personal preferences, changes in effectiveness, and diverse side effects.

A few studies are beginning to tackle the issue of psychotropic medication in children with psychotic symptoms, achieving favorable results (Spencer & Campbell, 1994). Due to the fact that full safety and efficacy of these medications have not been established in young children, their use in childhood schizophrenia is allowed but considered "off-label." Both the National Institute of Mental Health (NIMH) and the FDA are offering incentives to drug companies to conduct studies on children and young adolescents to increase understanding of the usefulness of these pharmaceutical agents. This will require implementing new approaches to clinical trials.

Psychosocial Rehabilitation

Psychosocial rehabilitation (PSR) focuses on the reduction of disability, the promotion of more effective adaptation, and support in attaining success in the individual's roles of choice (Silverstein, 2000). There are numerous important components of PSR.

TABLE 11.1   Novel and Traditional Neuroleptic Medications for Schizophrenia

MEDICATION	YEAR APPROVED	ADVANTAGES	DISADVANTAGES
NOVEL NEUROLEPTICS			
Clozapine (Clozaril)	1988	Use in treatment-resistant patients Rare tardive dyskinesia*	Agranulocytosis***; blood monitoring
Risperidone (Risperdal)	1994	Less EPS**; can be given orally	Weight gain
Olanzapine (Zyprexa)	1996	Improved positive and negative symptoms	Weight gain
Quetiapine (Seroquel)	1997	Improved positive and negative symptoms; less EPS Rare tardive dyskinesia	Weight gain
Ziprasidone (Geodon)	2001	Improved positive and negative symptoms; less EPS	Lengthening QT interval of heartbeat****
Aripiprazole	Phase III trials	Improved positive and negative symptoms	Unknown
TRADITIONAL NEUROLEPTICS			
Chlorpromazine (Thorazine)	1952	Effective with positive symptoms High potency	Severe EPS; tardive dyskinesia
Halperidol (Haldol)	1967	Oral and injectable forms; use in Tourette's disorder	EPS; blurry vision; tardive dyskinesia
Fluphenazine (Prolixin)		Oral and injectable forms; use in bipolar disorder	EPS; blurry vision; tardive dyskinesia
Thioridazine (Mellaril)		Low potency; use in PTSD, infantile autism; antiemetic	EPS; blurry vision; contraindications with other medication; tardive dyskinesia
Trifluoperazine (Stelazine)		Effective with positive symptoms; high potency; antiemetic	EPS; tardive dyskinesia

*Tardive Dyskinesia (TD): involuntary movements of the tongue, face, mouth, jaw, and hands
**Extrapyramidal Side-Effects (EPS): akathesia (restlessness) or akinesia (stiffness)
***Agranulocytosis: a serious condition in which the bone marrow stops producing white blood cells
****Lengthening QT interval of heartbeat shows up as an irregular pattern on EKGs

Social Rehabilitation.   Skills training methods in PSR have repeatedly been found to be effective in the overall treatment of schizophrenia and are recommended as a best clinical practice in some treatment guidelines (Lehman et al., 1998; Dilk & Bond, 1996; Heinssen et al., 2000). Social skills can be effectively taught in individual, family, or group format but effect sizes in the alleviation of symptoms and improved community functioning have not been robust across investigations (DeRubeis & Crits-Christoph, 1998; Huxley et al., 2000).

Vocational Rehabilitation (Education and Employment). These two areas are extremely important to the developmental lives of young adults. Work restoration is an expanding issue in schizophrenia recovery and rehabilitation due to supported employment models and use of atypical neuroleptics. As documented over multiple studies, only one person in five with schizophrenia is able to work in full-time competitive employment (Drake, 1999; Lehman, 1995; Lehman & Steinwachs, 1998). Encouraging young adults with schizophrenia to seek out employment settings they prefer versus utilizing sheltered workshops or other prevocational training had not been the prior norm of vocational rehabilitation (Becker et al., 1996; Danley et al., 1987, 1996). Mueser and colleagues (1997) found that obtaining competitive employment was associated with improved functioning in a range of nonvocational domains, including self-esteem, satisfaction with life, and symptomatology. Functional outcomes (work, school, social) plus intensity of community rehabilitation services seem to be associated with improvement in humanitarian gains such as self-esteem (Brekke & Long, 2000).

Addressing the population's need for postsecondary education is a rapidly growing area. Supported education is a PSR intervention with goals similar to those in the vocational domain: (1) provision of ongoing support, (2) establishing educational competencies, (3) mastering basic foundational skills (i.e., reading, math), (4) normal integration into campus activities and the campus environment, (5) troubleshooting and problem solving with an educational support person or team, (6) encouraging peer support and building interpersonal skills, and (7) a learn-by-doing approach (Mowbray, Collins, & Bybee, 1999). Educational attainments, with supports, have pushed the achievement bar up for most young adults, enhanced a variety of psychosocial domains, and provided possible models for work reentry (Hoffman & Mastrianni, 1993; Mowbray et al., 1999).

Assertive Community Treatment

The Program of Assertive Community Treatment (PACT) is a service-delivery model, providing comprehensive community-based treatment to persons with severe and persisting mental illnesses (Allness & Knoedler, 1998). The PACT program grew out of frustrations that traditional inpatient treatment was not facilitating an adequate transition for individuals into the community. The development of PACT, by Stein and Test (1980), in the early 1970s borrowed features of hospital inpatient care but went beyond the confines of the hospital to create a comprehensive community-based program. The program evolved into an enduring, well-replicated model of continuous community care (Stein & Test, 1980; Bond & Boyer, 1988). The Program of Assertive Community Treatment traditionally has served those who have been the highest utilizers of mental health services, and therefore has had the enormous challenge of demonstrating good outcomes in treatment-resistant individuals with chronic psychiatric disorders. Assertive community treatment models have consistently reduced the rate of rehospitalization and demonstrated a trend toward improved vocational outcomes (Olfson, 1990; Test, 1992; Scott & Dixon, 1995; Chandler et al., 1996).

The National Alliance for the Mentally Ill (NAMI)—an allied group of family members, consumers, mental health professionals, and concerned community members—recognized the benefit of the PACT model in the reduction of stigma. Because of problems in lack of access to and dissemination of sound, evidence-based models, NAMI collaborated on a start-up PACT manual (Allness & Knoedler, 1998) to encourage replication of and adherence to the model's core features. Program goals, philosophies, and descriptions of the responsibilities of each team member are addressed in the manual. The features listed in Figure 11.2 should be incorporated in PACT replications.

Family Psychoeducation

Most young adults with schizophrenia generally live with or near their families after they receive their initial diagnosis. Family social support can be a protective factor in relapse prevention. When symptoms flare, it is vital for consumers to have someone who can negotiate on their behalf for treatment and other essential services. However, some family members experience increased burden as a result of assuming this caregiver role and may develop physical and mental health problems of their own due to the unexpected role change (Spaniol, 1987; Lefley, 1996). It is a commonly held assumption that intervention with education and support can mediate some of the family burden and distress of relatives (Mueser & Glynn, 1999). Local NAMI chapters conduct educational support and advocacy groups. *Journey of Hope* is a multifamily informational group run by a trained family member to provide basic disorder-related information.

In clinical settings, families may receive specific behavioral and supportive interventions to assist them with the management of the illness at home. Behavioral Family Therapy (BFT) is a structured approach to working with families who have a member with a severe and persisting psychiatric disorder. This model emphasizes improved communication and coping skills, provides education, and avoids blaming family members or pathologizing their coping efforts (Mueser & Glynn, 1999). Behavioral Family Therapy and its modifications have been shown to be effective in lowering relapse and rehospitalization rates when compared to standard care (McFarlane, 1990; McFarlane et al., 1995; Tarrier et al., 1989). Findings from cross-cultural studies also support the effectiveness of BFT (Telles et al., 1995; Xiong et al., 1994). A recent review (Huxley et al., 2000) identified family intervention as demonstrating the most promising findings in psychosocial treatment studies. Some concern has been expressed that BFT is less proficient in terms of cost

FIGURE 11.2 Core Features of the PACT Model

1. The PACT multidisciplinary team is the primary provider of services.
2. Services are provided mainly in the community (75 percent or more).
3. The services are highly individualized and are continuous.
4. Optimal treatment consists of antipsychotic medication, individual supportive therapy, crisis intervention, and hospitalization, when necessary.
5. Substance abuse is not an exclusionary criterion.
6. Rehabilitation consists of training in social and daily living skills and work and school support.
7. Families are working members of the PACT team, and regular communication and education about the disorder are emphasized.
8. Support services such as help with housing, legal concerns, medical needs, and transportation are also provided to each individual, as required.

efficiency and long-term impact on family communication patterns (Bellack et al., 2000). Although family interventions are highly effective in preventing relapse, additional research is needed to increase understanding of the treatment model and to apply it in culturally and economically diverse populations. Families can also receive support through a variety of informative websites and state and national conferences. Information is provided at the end of this chapter.

Summary of Usual Care Recommendations in Schizophrenia

In a landmark study, data from client surveys ($n = 719$) in two states' inpatient and outpatient facilities were translated into 12 core treatment recommendations for persons with schizophrenia (Lehman & Steinwachs, 1998). Many disparities exist between what is considered efficacious treatment and what people actually receive in the community. In a concerted effort to examine and translate research in schizophrenia into practical applications based on empirical evidence, the Schizophrenia Patient Outcomes Research Team (PORT; Lehman et al., 1998) made the following recommendations concerning medication, psychological, and family treatments as well as vocational rehabilitation and mental health services:

1. Medication should be used at proper dosage for at least a year following an acute episode, with maintenance treatment at low effective dosages and monitoring for medication side-effects where indicated. For individuals with treatment adherence difficulty, depot medication therapy should be considered.
2. Psychological treatments should be included, at individual and group levels, incorporating support, illness education, and skills training.
3. Family treatments should be offered and should include education about the illness, support, crisis intervention, and problem-solving skills training.
4. Persons with schizophrenia should be offered vocational services as part of their treatment, toward a goal of competitive employment.
5. As mentioned earlier, services for persons with schizophrenia should include ACT with case management as the model for service delivery in the community.

The intent of these guidelines is to move the field forward in a way that will benefit individuals, families, and mental health systems, by establishing some standardization of care for persons with schizophrenia based on empirical research findings. Besides being comprehensive, the multiple treatments targeted at the biopsychosocial difficulties of schizophrenia should be integrated—offered by the same service provider, for ease of access and use by consumers and for coordination among providers.

For childhood schizophrenia, a workgroup of members of the American Academy of Child and Adolescent Psychiatry (AACAP) developed and disseminated practice parameters for treatment based on what is known about the clinical features of this disorder (Practice Parameters, 1997). The guidelines state that treatment should include appropriate doses of antipsychotic medications in conjunction with psychoeducational, psychotherapeutic, and social support programs. Typically, children with schizophrenia receive comprehensive services during an inpatient hospitalization only to have difficulties getting these services in the community and achieving good continuity of care (US DHHS, 2001). Inpatient social workers on child and adolescent units express concern over inadequate educational and social supports for families after hospital discharge. Social workers also may hesitate to give standard referrals because issues related to illness chronicity are often frightening to first-episode families. NAMI publishes a newsletter "for families touched by childhood-onset brain disorders" in response to the need to connect families with more appropriate resources (National Alliance for the Mentally Ill Publication, 2001).

PREVENTION, EARLY INTERVENTION, AND RECOVERY

Psychosocial treatment approaches in childhood schizophrenia have shown significant benefits for children and families in strengthening coping resources and social support systems (Huxley et al., 2000). These interventions are evolving in three important directions: (1) prevention and education, (2) early intervention at the first episode, and (3) maintenance and recovery therapies.

Prevention

Although our knowledge base is currently insufficient to totally prevent schizophrenia, we do have enough information to decrease risk, at least in some subgroups. That is, adults with schizophrenia themselves or having first-degree relatives with this diagnosis are at higher risk of bearing children with schizophrenia-spectrum illnesses. Pregnancy and birth experiences could be monitored and preparations made to avoid or minimize obstetrical complications, maternal stress, exposure to infections, and the other known conditions associated with higher incidence of schizophrenia. Cannon (1998) remarks that in the future, it may be possible to prevent schizophrenia in some at-risk individuals with careful pre- and perinatal monitoring and intervention, to minimize the risk and/or consequences of oxygen deprivation on the fetal brain.

Barankin and Greenberg (1996) recommend that all children of parents with serious mental illnesses be given annual check-ups, much as is the case when parents have other chronic disorders with a genetic basis (e.g., diabetes). The risk of mental illnesses in children of parents with schizophrenia could also be minimized with greater attention from mental health professionals to parenting issues for these mothers and fathers. Although mental health providers rarely pay attention to the parenting needs of clients with diagnosed mental illnesses, or even to the extent to which they are parents (Oyserman, Mowbray, & Zemencuk, 1994), parents have indicated interest in obtaining support when offered (Wang & Goldschmidt, 1996).

An accumulating body of research suggests that more accurate detection and earlier intervention with children and adolescents at risk for schizophrenia can do much to minimize the extent of disability and the long-term duration of the disorder. We have a considerable knowledge base to identify early warning signs for detection of schizophrenia-vulnerability in childhood. Selecting characteristics generally seen in both affected and nonaffected relatives, and extrapolating from the research results reported previously on early indicators (prodromal signs) for children who later develop schizophrenia, suggests that among those genetically at risk, the following five areas may be meaningful risk indicators during childhood: (1) minor physical anomalies (MPAs); (2) finger and palm prints; (3) speech problems; (4) poorer motor coordination in relationship to siblings; and (5) greater social interaction deficits.

CASE STUDY

DIAGNOSTIC UNCERTAINTY IN CHILDHOOD-ONSET SCHIZOPHRENIA

Sean is a handsome African American 8-year-old with beautiful brown eyes. His mother, Janie, has been diagnosed with schizophrenia since she was 19 years old, and now in her 40s, she is stable on low doses of medication. Sean's father does not have the disorder. Having met with a genetic researcher, Janie and her husband felt that they would take the risk of having children because the odds were only 10 percent of passing on the disorder when one parent has been diagnosed. Sean's older sister, Hilary, now age 13, has not exhibited any trace of the illness. Sean, on the other hand, has had school difficulties, particularly in concentrating, that have fueled his frustration and irritability in the classroom and often get him into trouble. His speech has never been very good and he appears to be preoccupied and in his own world much of the time. He does well enough in school to pass, but there have been profound concerns by the school psychologist.

Because childhood-onset schizophrenia is rare, Sean has been treated for a variety of diagnoses ranging from Asperger's syndrome, ADHD, and antisocial personality traits. Sean's understanding of what he is going through has been limited even with social skills training provided in the hospital setting. Occasionally, his judgment has been very poor. He is now in the Neuropsychiatric Hospital to be fully evaluated due to a teacher observation that he was repeatedly mumbling in an audible voice to someone called King.

Sean's parents are seeking some support for the difficult position in which they find themselves. Janie tried a parent's group in the community only to feel like she couldn't begin to relate to the struggles described by parents of 33-year-olds with chronic schizophrenia. The couple felt that they had limited options for continuity of care other than the hospital itself. They also felt guilty that diagnostically they had treated Sean for other conditions and thereby delayed his ability to get efficacious treatment. They are also worried about the long-term effects of starting a child on medication, but no one seems to be able to give them a definitive answer because newer medications have not been used on children for very long and the data are limited.

Early Intervention at Time of First Episode

Three novel treatment interventions have been proposed in the childhood schizophrenia literature: providing schizophrenia education to the family physician, interventions at school sites, and comprehensive programs based on the Early Psychosis Prevention and Intervention Centre (EPPIC) in Australia.

Haefner and Maurer (2000) noted that depression, negative symptoms, and social disability appear to be the main indicators of risk for schizophrenia during the illness prodrome.

Adolescents and children have been at an increasingly greater risk for depression in the past decade. However, a study examining patterns of mental health service use among depressed children and adolescents ($n = 209$, ages 9 to 17) found that 36 percent never received any professional help or prescribed medication (Wu et al., 2001). Because children and adolescents are most likely to see family physicians when difficulties arise, it is important that general practitioners update their screening knowledge for schizophrenia and depression and begin treatment rather than delaying due to referral time-lags or waiting for the full diagnostic picture to unfold (Schulz et al., 2000). Remission can be achieved in a majority of first-episode patients if consistent treatment is maintained over the first year (Lieberman et al., 1993).

In addition to the family physician, school site screening and interventions could address early manifestations of the disorder. At the present time, there are only 1,000 school-based health centers out of approximately 80,000 primary and secondary schools in the United States and only half of those have a mental health component (Kestenbaum, 2000). A multidisciplinary approach has been implemented in some model school-based mental health programs; early studies suggest that the programs are associated with reductions of the disturbing emotional problems that can affect learning and social relationships ("Studies Show Effectiveness of School-Based Mental Health Programs," 2001).

Last, McGorry and colleagues (1999) have focused on treatment lag as a domain of concern, defining a "critical period" for intervention. Birchwood (1999) proposed that intervention in the first three years, before an illness plateau has been reached, yields the greatest opportunity to prevent or limit potential declines due to schizophrenia. By reducing treatment delay, better social recovery, better medication compliance, and relapse prevention are all possible outcomes. The EPPIC model, developed in 1992, has the following objectives:

- Early identification and treatment of primary symptoms of psychotic illness with correspondingly improved access and reduced delays in initial treatment
- Reduction of frequency and severity of relapse
- Reduction of burden for carers and promotion of well-being among family members
- Reduction of secondary morbidity in the postpsychotic phase of illness
- Reduced disruption in social and vocational functioning, and in psychosocial development in the critical period of the early years following onset of illness when most disability tends to accrue

The core services of EPPIC are offered in the community and consist of low-dose neuroleptics, case management, group and family therapies, and a cognitive behavioral model, as detailed in the next section on maintenance therapies. Other research, however, has failed to confirm duration of untreated initial psychosis as predictive of poor long-term outcomes (Ho, Andreasen, Flaum, Nopoulos, & Miller, 2000), suggesting that hypothesized toxic effects of psychosis are complex.

Maintenance and Recovery Therapies in Childhood Episodes

Cognitive Behavioral Therapy (CBT) can be utilized with individuals, parents, children, and the entire family unit. It is most helpful in handling current life situations rather than past history, and with daily functioning rather than personality concerns. It enables persons in therapy to focus on achieving short- and long-term goals and it rewards individuals for achieving success along a continuum. Children resonate to CBT because sessions may remind them of the school environment in that "homework" is given as part of the treatment. Persons with schizophrenia and/or depression respond well to the here-and-now focus of CBT. Lewinsohn and Clarke (1999) concluded that CBT was an effective intervention for adolescent depression.

Jackson and colleagues (1998) developed a variant of CBT called Cognitively Oriented Psychotherapy for Early Psychosis (COPE), which is a growth model of therapy and recovery based on the belief that the person with the disorder can act to shape his or her own outcome after an initial episode. The development of COPE was informed by researchers who do not accord the sole explanation of psychotic disorders to genetics and biochemistry, but honor the point of view of the individual with the disorder and his or her personal stake in recovery (Davidson & Strauss, 1995). It may be entirely possible that developing a mental illness is not always a negative outcome, but it does undoubtedly shape the way a person responds to the world (Jackson et al., 1998). There are four therapeutic phases to this approach: (1) assessment, (2) developing a therapeutic alliance, (3) adaptation of self to the initial illness, and (4) alleviation or prevention of additional disorders (i.e., depression). For more discussion of this model, visit the EPPIC website: www.eppic.org.au.

Conclusions

The future of treatment for childhood-onset schizophrenia involves further exploration and study of all the approaches mentioned. Program evaluations need to focus on long-term functional outcomes for these children. The guidelines proposed by the Surgeon General need implementation and support in community settings. If we can provide access to efficacious treatment, low-cost mental health screening, and treatment for all of our nation's at-risk children and young adults in a variety of service settings, we will be making extraordinary strides in achieving long-lasting societal benefits.

SUMMARY: WHAT IS NEEDED

To improve treatment and interventions for schizophrenic disorders in childhood and adolescence, mental health professionals need to advocate strongly for social action and social change:

■ Biological *and* psychosocial factors are significant in the etiology of schizophrenia, as well as in rehabilitation and recovery. Both areas *must be researched* with methods especially targeted to the developmental needs of children and adolescents. Improved assessment and identification should be paramount as we seek to intervene earlier in a child's life and perhaps short-circuit a more debilitating course. Research dollars are also needed to develop new atypical medications, to test their efficacy with children, to bring down prescription costs, and to increase individual choice, especially when available medications are not effective or have unacceptable side effects.

■ A greater abundance of *humane, respectful, and client-centered services* is needed in all geographic areas. This should include availability of rehabilitation technologies that positively impact the course of schizophrenic disorders, and methods to monitor the quality of treatment that will ensure equitable care, irrespective of disadvantaging factors (Young, Sullivan, Burnam, & Brook, 1998).

■ Increasing *mental health services that attend to family issues* of clients with schizophrenia is an important goal of the Surgeon General's Conference on Children (2001). Services should emphasize family psychoeducation about schizophrenia utilizing materials based on the most current research.

■ The linkage between *schizophrenia and social justice* must be recognized for equitable resource distribution. That is, women versus men with schizophrenia are significantly less likely to have vocational interventions in their treatment plans (Lehman et al., 1998); and many of the purported causes of schizophrenia are related to poverty and social class, as is the paucity of quality services in a given area.

■ Preservice and inservice *training* for mental health professionals regarding etiology, treatment, rehabilitation, and the life course of schizophrenia will sensitize new workers to the salient issues of the disorder and assist experienced clinicians to better target their interventions.

■ All mental health professionals have a responsibility to educate the public so as to *decrease stigma* associated with mental illness and promote access to mental health treatments for all age groups.

■ *Culture* is inextricably linked to schizophrenia. Culture affects the subjective experience of the "identified patient" and how the illness is expressed, including help-seeking, how indigenous clinicians diagnose and treat, and the outcome of a mental illness episode (Castillo, 1997). Few descriptive or treatment studies take culture into account (Johnson-Selfridge & Zalewski, 2001). This needs to change so that the important effects of culture on schizophrenia can be more systematically studied and interventions that are culturally appropriate can be developed and evaluated.

■ For improvements in the outcomes of children and adolescents with schizophrenia to occur, changes in *national policies* are needed. An incredible 70 percent of children and adolescents in need of mental health services do not receive treatment and over 19 million children and adolescents are uninsured (Kestenbaum, 2000).

As a population, we are more aware than ever that there is a crisis of youth violence, depression, and suicide, in part attributable to untreated childhood psychiatric disorders. Because children and adolescents don't vote, we need *a strong national agenda and leadership* for more effective school- and community-based services for youth.

DISCUSSION QUESTIONS

1. What factors seem to account for schizophrenia having a lower prevalence rate in childhood and adolescence?

2. How would you feel about the off-label use of neuroleptic medication for a 9 year old with mild to moderate symptoms of schizophrenia if you were the parent or caretaker of the child? What are the issues for the family? Describe.

3. What community resources and services would you create to assist families in navigating the social and emotional burden of caring for a mentally ill child?

4. Do you feel that juvenile crime and school violence would be lessened if schools were equipped to assess and provide early intervention to children who are troubled? What are the pro's and con's of associating antisocial behavior in children with mental illness? Explain your point of view.

5. What was the attitude towards mental illness in your high school? Can you conceive of any recommendations or policies that would lessen the stigma around mental illness and encourage teens and/or families to come forward for help?

SUGGESTED READING

Shiller, L., & Bennett, A. (1994). *The quiet room: A journey out of the torment of madness.* New York: Warner Books.

RESOURCES

www.aacap.org   The American Academy of Child & Adolescent Psychiatry is a reliable site for medication concerns, research, and answers to questions.

www.nami.org   The National Alliance for the Mentally Ill has a child and adolescent section with a very informative newsletter for parents. It also presents ways to advocate and get involved in local and national chapter activities.

www.eppic.org.au   The Early Psychosis Prevention & Intervention Centre in Melbourne, Australia, details the core features and efficacy of their program.

http://www.medscape.com/mp/rc/schizophrenia   Medscape presents the Schizophrenia Wellness Center, a collection of the latest medical news and information on schizophrenia. The seriousness of schizophrenia presents a significant challenge, and Medscape is helping to meet this challenge by offering a one-stop resource for the latest news, journal articles, summaries from major medical conferences, programs for CME credit, links to valuable patient resources and much more.

REFERENCES

Allness, D. J., & Knoedler, W. H. (1998). *The PACT model of community-based treatment for persons with severe and persistent mental illnesses: A manual for PACT start-up.* Arlington, VA: NAMI.

American Psychiatric Association. (1994). *Diagnostic and statistical manual of mental disorders,* 4th edition. Washington, DC: American Psychiatric Association.

Amminger, G. P., Pape, S., Rock, D., Roberts, S. A., Looser, S., Squires-Wheeler, E., Kestenbaum, C., & Erlenmeyer-Kimling, L. (1999). Relationship between childhood behavioral disturbance and later schizophrenia in the New York High-Risk Project. *American Journal of Psychiatry, 156*(4), 525–530.

Andreasen, N. C. (1997). Neuroimaging techniques in the investigation of schizophrenia. *Journal of Clinical Psychiatry Monograph Series, 15*(3), 16–19.

Asarnow, R. F., & Asarnow, J. R. (1994). Childhood-onset schizophrenia: Editor's introduction. *Schizophrenia Bulletin 20*(4), 591–597.

Asarnow, R. F., & Asarnow, J. R. (1996). Childhood-onset schizophrenia. In E. J. Mash & R. A. Barkley (Eds.), *Child psychopathology*. New York: Guilford Press.

Banks, S. M., Stone, J. L., Pandiana, J. A., Cox, J. F., & Morschauser, P. C. (2000). Utilization of local jails and general hospitals by state psychiatric center patients. *Journal of Behavioral Health Services & Research, 27*(4), 454–459.

Barankin, T., & Greenberg, M. (1996). The impact of parental affective disorders on families. In B. Abosh & A. Collins (Eds.), *Mental illness in the family* (pp. 105–119). Toronto: University of Toronto Press.

Bearden, C. E., Rosso, I. M., Hollister, J. M., Sanchez, L. E., Hadley, T., & Cannon, T. D. (2000). A prospective cohort study of childhood behavioral deviance and language abnormalities as predictors of adult schizophrenia. *Schizophrenia Bulletin, 26*(2), 395–410.

Becker, D. R., Drake, R. E., Farabaugh, A., & Bond, G. R. (1996). Job preferences of clients with severe psychiatric disorders participating in supported employment programs. *Psychiatric Services, 47*(11), 1223–1226.

Beiser, M., Bean, G., Erickson, D., Zhang, J., Iacono, W. G., & Rector, N. A. (1994). Biological and psychosocial predictors of job performance following a first episode of psychosis. *American Journal of Psychiatry, 151*(6), 857–863.

Beiser, M., & Iacono, W. G. (1990). An update on the epidemiology of schizophrenia. *Canadian Journal of Psychiatry, 35*(8), 657–668.

Bellack, A. S., Haas, G. L., Schooler, N. R., & Flory, J. D. (2000). Effects of behavioural family management on family communication and patient outcomes in schizophrenia. *British Journal of Psychiatry, 177*, 434–439.

Bogerts, B., & Falkai, P. (1995). Postmortem brain abnormalities in schizophrenia. In C. L. Shriqui & H. A. Nasrallah (Eds.), *Contemporary issues in the treatment of schizophrenia* (pp. 43–59). Washington, DC: American Psychiatric Press.

Bond, G. R., & Boyer, S. L. (1988). Rehabilitation programs and outcomes. In J. A. Ciardello & M. D. Bell (Eds.), *Vocational rehabilitation of persons with prolonged psychiatric disorders*. Baltimore: Johns Hopkins Press.

Bond, G. R., & Meyer, P. S. (1999). The role of medication in the employment of people with schizophrenia. *Journal of Rehabilitation, 65*(4), 9–16.

Brekke, J. S., & Long, J. D. (2000). Community-based psychosocial rehabilitation and prospective change in functional, clinical, and subjective experience variables in schizophrenia. *Schizophrenia Bulletin, 26*(3), 667–680.

Brenner, H. D., Dencker, S. J., Goldstein, M. J., & Hubbard, J. W. (1990). Defining treatment refractoriness in schizophrenia. *Schizophrenia Bulletin, 16*(4), 551–561.

Brown, A. S., Schaefer, C. A., Wyatt, R. J., et al. (2000). Maternal exposure to infections and adult Schizophrenia spectrum disorders: A prospective birth cohort. *Schizophrenia Bulletin, 26*(2), 287–295.

Buckley, P. F. (1998). The clinical stigmata of aberrant neurodevelopment in schizophrenia. *Journal of Nervous and Mental Disease, 186*(2), 79–86.

Buckley, P. F., Buchanan, R. W., Schulz, S. C., & Tamminga, C. A. (1996). Catching up on schizophrenia. The Fifth International Congress on Schizophrenia Research, Warm Springs, VA, April 8–12, 1995. *Archives of General Psychiatry, 53*, 456–462.

Buckley, P. F., Buchanan, R. W., Tamminga, C. A., & Schulz, S. C. (2000). Schizophrenia research: A progress report, summarizing proceedings of the 1999 International Congress on Schizophrenia Research. *Schizophrenia Bulletin, 26*(2), 411–419.

Bustillo, J. R., Lauriello, J., Horan, W. P., & Keith, S. J. (2001). The psychosocial treatment of schizophrenia: An update. *American Journal of Psychiatry, 158*(2), 163–175.

Cadoret, R. J., Yates, W. R., Troughton, E., Woodworth, G., & Stewart, M. A. (1995). Adoption study demonstrating two genetic pathways to drug abuse. *Archives of General Psychiatry, 52*(1), 42–52.

Campana, A., Duci, A., Gambini, O., & Scarone, S. (1999). An articial neural network that uses eye-tracking performance to identify patients with schizophrenia. *Schizophrenia Bulletin, 24*(4), 789–799.

Canales, P. L., Olsen, J., Miller, A. L., & Crismon, M. L. (1999). Role of antipsychotic polypharmacotherapy in the treatment of schizophrenia. *CNS Drugs, 12*(3), 179–188.

Cannon, M., Jones, P., Huttunen, M. O., Tanskanen, A., Huttunen, T., Rabe-Hesketh, S., & Murray, R. M. (1999). School performance in Finnish children and later development of schizophrenia. *Archives of General Psychiatry, 56,* 457–463.

Cannon, T. D. (1998). Neurodevelopmental influences in the genesis and epigenesis of schizophrenia: An overview. *Applied and Preventive Psychology, 7,* 47–62.

Cannon, T. D., Bearden, C. E., Hollister, J. M., Rosso, I. M., Sanchez, L. E., & Hadley, T. (2000). Childhood cognitive functioning in schizophrenia patients and their unaffected siblings: A prospective cohort study. *Schizophrenia Bulletin, 26*(2), 379–393.

Caplan, R., Guthrie, D., Fish, B., & Tanguay, P. (1989). The Kiddie Formal Thought Disorder Rating Scale: Clinical assessment, reliability, and validity. *Journal of the American Academy of Child and Adolescent Psychiatry, 28*(3), 408–416.

Castillo, R. J. (1997). *Culture & mental illness: A client-centered approach.* Pacific Grove, CA: Brooks/Cole.

Chandler, D., Levin, S., & Barry, P. (1999). The menu approach to employment services: Philosophy and five-year outcomes. *Psychiatric Rehabilitation Journal, 23*(1), 24–33.

Chandler, D., Meisel, J., McGowen, M., Mintz, J., & Madison, K. (1996). Client outcomes in two model capitated integrated service agencies. *Psychiatric Services, 47,* 175–180.

Coffey, M. (1998). Schizophrenia: A review of current research. *Journal of Clinical Nursing, 7*(6), 489–498.

Conley, R. R., Tamminga, C. A., Kelly, D. L., & Richardson, C. M. (1999). Treatment-resistant schizophrenic patients respond to clozapine after olanzapine non-response. *Biological Psychiatry, 46*(1), 73–77.

Cornblatt, B., & Keilp, J. G. (1994). Impaired attention, geneticsm and the pathophysiology of schizophrenia. *Schizophrenia Bulletin, 20*(1), 31–46.

Dalman, C., Allebeck, P., Cullberg, J., Grunewald, C., & Köster, M. (1999). Obstetric complications and the risk of schizophrenia: A longitudinal study of a National Birth Cohort. *Archives of General Psychiatry 56,* 234–240.

Danley, K. S., & Anthony, W. A. (1987). The choose-get-keep model: Serving severely disabled psychiatrically disabled individuals. *American Rehabilitation, 13*(4), 27–29.

Danley, K. S., Rogers, E. S., & MacDonald-Wilson, K. (1996). Supported employment for adults with psychiatric disability: Results of an innovative demonstration project. *Rehabilitation Psychology, 39,* 269–276.

David, A. S., Malmberg, A., Brandt, L., Allebeck, P., & Lewis, G. (1997). IQ and risk for schizophrenia: A population-based cohort study. *Psychological Medicine, 27,* 1311–1323.

Davidson, L. (1994). Phenomenological research in schizophrenia: From philosophical anthropology to empirical science. *Journal of Phenomenological Psychology, 25*(1), 104–130.

Davidson, L., & Strauss, J. S. (1995). Beyond the biopsychosocial model: Integrating disorder, health, and recovery. *Psychiatry, 58,* 44–55.

Davidson, M., Reichenberg, A., Rabinowitz, J., Weiser, M., Kaplan, Z., & Mark, M. (1999). Behavioral and intellectual markers for schizophrenia in apparently healthy male adolescents. *American Journal of Psychiatry, 156*(9), 1328–1335.

Davis, K. L., Kahn, R. S., & Ko, G. (1991). Dopamine in schizophrenia: A review and reconceptualization. *American Journal of Psychiatry, 148*(11), 1474–1486.

DeLisi, L. E., Sakuma, M., Ge, S., & Kushner, M. (1998). Association of brain structural change with the heterogeneous course of schizophrenia from early childhood through five years subsequent to a first hospitalization. *Psychiatry Research: Neuroimaging, 84,* 75–88.

Deniker, P. (1970). Introduction of neuroleptic chemotherapy into psychiatry. In F. Ayd & B. Blackwell (Eds.), *Discoveries in biological psychiatry* (pp. 34–42). Philadelphia: Lippmeyer.

DeRubeis, R. J., & Crits-Cristoph, P. (1998). Empirically supported individual and group psychological treatments for adult mental disorders. *Journal of Consulting & Clinical Psychology, 66*(1), 37–52.

Desjarlais, R., Eisenberg, L., Good, B., & Kleinman, A. (1995). *World mental health: Problems and priorities in low-income countries.* New York: Oxford University Press.

Dilk, M. N., & Bond, G. R. (1996). Meta-analytic evaluation of skills training research for individuals with severe mental illness. *Journal of Consulting and Clinical Psychology, 6,* 1337–1346.

Docherty, N. M., Gordinier, S. W., Hall, M. J., & Cutting, L. P. (1999). Communication disturbances in relatives beyond the age of risk for schizophrenia and their associations with symptoms in patients. *Schizophrenia Bulletin, 25*(4), 851–862.

Done, D. J., Crow, T. J., Johnstone, E. C., & Sacker, A. (1994). Childhood antecedents of schizophrenia and affective illness: Social adjustment at ages 7 and 11. *British Medical Journal, 309,* 699–703.

Drake, R. E., Becker, D. R., Clark, R. E., & Mueser, K. T. (1999). Research on the Individual Placement and Support model of supported employment. *Psychiatric Quarterly, 70*(4), 289–301.

Dworkin, R. H., Bernstein, G., Kaplansky, L. M., & Lipsitz et al. (1991). Social competence and positive and negative symptoms: A longitudinal study of children and adolescents at risk for schizophrenia and affective disorders. *American Journal of Psychiatry, 148*(9), 1182–1188.

Dworkin, R. H., & Lenzenweger, M. F. (1984). Symptoms and the genetics of schizophrenia: Implications for diagnosis. *American Journal of Psychiatry, 141*(12), 1541–1546.

Eggers, C., & Bunk, D. (1997). The long-term course of childhood-onset schizophrenia: A 42 year followup. *Schizophrenia Bulletin, 23*(1), 105–117.

Eggers, C., Bunk, D., & Krause, D. (2000). Schizophrenia with onset before the age of eleven: Clinical characteristics of onset and course. *Journal of Autism and Developmental Disorders, 30*(1), 29–38.

Facts for Families #49: Schizophrenia in children (2000). American Academy of Child and Adolescent Psychiatry, Public Information, Washington DC. Retrieved from http://www.aacp.org/publications/factfam/schizo.htm.

Faraone, S. V., Seidman, L. J., Kremen, W. S., Toomey, R., Pepple, J. R., & Tsuang, M. T. (1999). Neuropsychological functioning among the nonpsychotic relatives of schizophrenic patients: A 4-year follow-up study. *Journal of Abnormal Psychology, 108*(1), 176–181.

Flaum, M. (1995). The diagnosis of schizophrenia. In C. L. Shriqui & H. A. Nasrallah (Eds.), *Contemporary issues in the treatment of schizophrenia* (pp. 83–108). Washington, DC: American Psychiatric Press.

Frangos, E., Athanassenas, S., Tsitourides, S., Katsanou, N., & Alexandrakou, P. (1985). Prevalence of DSM III schizophrenia among the first-degree relatives of schizophrenic probands. *Acta Psychiatrica Scandinavica, 72,* 382–386.

Frazier, J. A., Alaghband-Rad, J., Jacobsen, L., et al. (1997). Pubertal development and the onset of psychosis in childhood onset schizophrenia. *Psychiatry Resource, 70,* 1–7.

Garety, P. A., & Freeman, D. (1999). Cognitive approaches to delusions: A critical review of theories and evidence. *British Journal of Clinical Psychology, 38*(2), 113–154.

Gillberg, C. (2000). Epidemiology of early onset schizophrenia. In H. Remschmidt (Ed.), *Schizophrenia in children and adolescents* (pp. 43–59). New York: Cambridge University Press.

Gold, S., Arndt, S., Nopoulos, P., O'Leary, D. S., & Andreasen, N. C. (1999). Longitudinal study of cognitive function in first-episode and recent-onset schizophrenia. *American Journal of Psychiatry, 156*(9), 1342–1348.

Green, M. F. (1998). *Schizophrenia from a neurocognitive perspective: Probing the impenetrable darkness.* Boston: Allyn and Bacon.

Green, M. F., Kern, R. S., Braff, D. L., & Mintz, J. (2000). Neurocognitive deficits and functional outcome in schizophrenia: Are we measuring the "right stuff"? *Schizophrenia Bulletin, 26*(1), 119–136.

Haefner, H., & Maurer, K. (1995). Epidemiology of positive and negative symptoms in schizophrenia. In C. L. Shriqui & H. A. Nasrallah (Eds.), *Contemporary issues in the treatment of schizophrenia* (pp. 125–154). Washington, DC: American Psychiatric Press.

Haefner, H., & Maurer, K. (2000). The early course of schizophrenia: New concepts for early intervention. In A. Gavin & S. Henderson (Eds.), *Unmet need in psychiatry: Problems, resources, responses* (pp. 218–232). New York: Cambridge University Press.

Hambrecht, M., Maurer, K., & Hafner, H. (1992). Evidence for a gender bias in epidemiological studies of schizophrenia. *Schizophrenia Research, 8,* 223–231.

Harding, C., Brooks, G., Ashikaga, R., Strauss, J., & Breier, A. (1987). The Vermont longitudinal study: II. Long term outcomes of subjects who retrospectively met DSM III criteria for schizophrenia. *American Journal of Psychiatry, 144*(6), 727–825.

Harding, C. M. (1995). The interaction of biopsychosocial factors, time, and course of schizophrenia. In C. L. Shriqui & H. A. Nasrallah (Eds.), *Contemporary issues in the treatment of schizophrenia* (pp. 653–682). Washington, DC: American Psychiatric Press.

Harding, C. M. (1998). Reassessing a person with schizophrenia and developing a new treatment plan. In J. W. Barron (Ed.), *Making diagnosis meaningful: Enhancing evaluation and treatment of psychological disorders* (pp. 319–338). Washington, DC: American Psychological Association.

Harvard Mental Health Letter (2001, June). Autism—Part 1. Vol 17(12), 1–4.

Hawkins, K. A., Mohamed, S., & Woods, S. W. (1999). Will the novel antipsychotics significantly ameliorate neuropsychological deficits and improve adaptive functioning in schizophrenia? *Psychological Medicine, 29*(1), 1–8.

Heinssen, R. K., Liberman, R. P., & Kopelowicz, A. (2000). Psychosocial skills training for schizophrenia: Lessons from the laboratory. *Schizophrenia Bulletin, 26*(1), 21–46.

Ho, B., Andreasen, N. C., Flaum, M., Nopoulos, P., & Miller, D. (2000). Untreated initial psychosis: Its relation to quality of life and symptom remission in first-episode schizophrenia. *American Journal of Psychiatry, 157*(5), 808–815.

Ho, B., Miller, D., Nopoulos, P., & Andreasen, N. C. (1999). A comparative effectiveness study of risperidone and olanzapine in the treatment of schizophrenia. *The Journal of Clinical Psychiatry, 60*(10), 658–663.

Hoffman, F. L., & Mastrianni, X. (1992). The hospitalized young adult: New directions for psychiatric treatment. *American Journal of Orthopsychiatry, 62*(2), 297–302.

Hoffman, F. L., & Mastrianni, X. (1993). The role of supported education in the inpatient treatment of young adults: A two-site comparison. *Psychosocial Rehabilitation Journal, 17*(1), 109–119.

Hopper, K., & Wanderling, J. (2000). Revisiting the developed versus developing country distinction in course and outcome in schizophrenia: Results from IsoS, the WHO Collaborative Followup Project. *Schizophrenia Bulletin, 26*(4), 835–846.

Hughes, C., Emslie, G. J., & Crismon, M. L. (1999). The Texas Children's Medication Algorithm Project: Report of the Texas Consensus Conference panel on medication treatment of childhood major depressive disorder. *Journal of the American Academy of Child & Adolescent Psychiatry, 38*, 1442–1454.

Hulbert, C. A., Jackson, H. J., & McGorry, P. D. (1996). Relationship between personality and course and outcome in early psychosis: A review of the literature. *Clinical Psychology Review, 16*(8), 707–727.

Hultman, C. M., Sparén, P., Takei, N., Murray, R. M., & Cnattingius, S. (1999). Prenatal and perinatal risk factors for schizophrenia, affective psychosis, and reactive psychosis of early onset: Case-control study. *BMJ, 318*, 421–426.

Huxley, N. A., Rendell, M., & Sederer, L. (2000). Psychosocial treatments in schizophrenia: A review of the past 20 years. *Journal of Nervous and Mental Disease, 188*(4), 187–201.

Jablensky, A. (1997). The 100-year epidemiology of schizophrenia. *Schizophrenia Research, 28*(2), 111–125.

Jablensky, A., & Sartorius, N. (1988). Is schizophrenia universal? *Acta Psychiatrica Scandinavica—Supplementum, 344*, 65–70.

Jackson, H., McGorry, P., Edwards, J., et al. (1998). Cognitively-oriented psychotherapy for early psychosis (COPE): Preliminary results. *British Journal of Psychiatry, 172*(33), 93–100.

Jacobsen, L. K., & Rapoport, J. L. (1998). Research update: Childhood-onset schizophrenia: Implications of clinical and neurobiological research. *Journal of Child Psychology & Psychiatry, 39*, 101–113.

Johnson-Selfridge, M., & Zalewski, C. (2001). Moderator variables of executive functioning in schizophrenia: Meta-analytic findings. *Schizophrenia Bulletin, 27*(2), 305–316.

Jones, P., Rodgers, B., Murray, R., & Marmot, M. (1994). Child developmental risk factors for adult schizophrenia in the British 1946 birth cohort. *The Lancet, 344*, 1398–1402.

Jones, P. B., Rantakallio, P., Hartikainen, A., Isohanni, M., & Sipila, P. (1998). Schizophrenia as a long-term outcome of pregnancy, delivery, and perinatal complications: A 28-year follow-up of the 1966 North Finland General Population Birth Cohort. *American Journal of Psychiatry, 155*(3), 355–364.

Katschnig, H. (1997). How useful is the concept quality of life in psychiatry? *Current Opinion in Psychiatry, 10*(2), 337–345.

Kendler, K. S., & Diehl, S. R. (1993). The genetics of schizophrenia: A current genetic-epidemiologic perspective. *Schizophrenia Bulletin, 19*(2), 261–285.

Kendler, K. S., McGuire, M., Gruenberg, A. M., O'Hare, A., Spellman, M., & Walsh, D. (1993). The Roscommon Family Study: I. Methods, diagnosis of probands, and risk of schizophrenia in relatives. *Archives of General Psychiatry 50*, 527–540.

Kendler, K. S., McGuire, M., Gruenberg, A. M., & Walsh, D. (1995). Schizotypal symptoms and signs in the Roscommon Family Study: Their factor structure and familial relationship with psychotic and affective disorders. *Archives of General Psychiatry, 52*, 296–303.

Kestenbaumn, C. J. (2000). How shall we treat the children in the 21st century? *Journal of the American Academy of Child & Adolescent Psychiatry, 39*(1), 1–10.

Kety, S. S. (1994). Genetic and etiologic factors in the etiology of schizophrenia. In S. Matthysse & D. L. Levy (Eds.), *Psychopathology: The evolving science of mental disorder* (pp. 477–487). New York: Cambridge University Press.

Kety, S. S., Wender, P. H., Jacobsen, B., Ingraham, L. J., Jansson, L., Faber, B., & Kinney, D. K. (1994). Mental illness in the biological and adoptive relatives of schizophrenic adoptees: Replication of the Copenhagen Study in the rest of Denmark. *Archives of General Psychiatry, 51,* 442–455.

Klinger, L. G., & Dawson, G. (1996). Autistic disorder. In E. J. Mash & R. A. Barkley (Eds.), *Child psychopathology* (pp. 311–339). New York: Guilford.

Kremen, W. S., Seidman, L. S., Pepple, J. R., & Lyons, M. (1994). Neuropsychological risk indicators for schizophrenia: A review of family studies. *Schizophrenia Bulletin, 20*(1), 103–119.

Lay, B., Blanz, B., Hartmann, M., & Schmidt, M. H. (2000). The psychosocial outcome of adolescent-onset schizophrenia: A 12-year follow-up. *Schizophrenia Bulletin, 26*(4), 801–816.

Lefley, H. P. (1996). *Family caregiving in mental illness.* Thousand Oaks, CA: Sage.

Lehman, A. F. (1995). Vocational rehabilitation in schizophrenia. *Schizophrenia Bulletin, 21*(4), 645–656.

Lehman, A. F., Steinwachs, D. M., Dixon, L. B., Goldman, H. H., Osher, F., Postrado, L., Scott, J. E., Thompson, J. W., Fahey, M., Fischer, P., Kasper, J. A., Lyles, A., Skinner, E. A., Buchanon, R., Carpenter, W. T., Jr., Levine, J., McGlynn, E. A., Rosencheck, R., & Zito, J. (1998). At issue: Translating research into practice: The Schizophrenia Patient Outcomes Research Team (PORT) treatment recommendations. *Schizophrenia Bulletin, 24*(1), 1–10.

Lewine, R. J. (1998) Epilogue: Comments on the origins and development of schizophrenia. In M. F. Lenzenweger & R. H. Dworkin (Eds.), *Origins and development of schizophrenia: Advances in experimental psychopathology.* Washington, DC: American Psychological Association.

Lewinsohn, P. M., & Clarke, G. N. (1999). Psychosocial treatments for depression. *Clinical Psychology Review, 19*(3), 329–342.

Lewis, G., David, A. S., Malmberg, A., & Allebeck, P. (2000). Non-psychotic psychiatric disorder and subsequent risk of schizophrenia: Cohort study. *British Journal of Psychiatry, 177,* 416–420.

Lieberman, J., Jody, D., Geisler, S., Alvir, J., Loebel, A., Szymanski, S., Woerner, M., & Borenstein., M. (1993). Time course and biologic correlates of treatment response in first-episode schizophrenia. *Archives of General Psychiatry, 50,* 369–376.

Lincoln, C., & McGorry, P. D. (1999). Pathways to care in early psychosis: Clinical and consumer perspectives. In P. D. McGorry & H. J. Jackson (Eds.), *The recognition and management of early psychosis: A preventive approach* (pp. 51–79). New York: Cambridge University Press.

Link, B. G., Andrews, H., & Cullen, F. T. (1992). The violent and illegal behavior of mental patients reconsidered. *American Sociological Review, 57,* 275–292.

Linszen, D. H., & Lenior, M. E. (1999). *The recognition and management of early psychosis: A preventive approach.* New York: Cambridge University Press.

Lopez, S. (2000). Cultural psychopathology: Uncovering the social world of mental illness. *Annual Review of Psychology, 51,* 571–598.

Lukens, E. P., & Thorning, H. (1998). Psychoeducation and severe mental illness: Implications for social work and research. In J. B. W. Williams & K. Ell (Eds.), *Advances in mental health research: Implications for practice* (pp. 256–286). Washington, DC: NASW Press.

MacGregor, P. (1994). Grief: The unrecognized parental response to mental illness in a child. *Social Work, 39*(2), 160–166.

Maier, H. C., Hoechst-Janneck, S., & Franke, P. (1995). Subclinical thought disorder in first degree relatives of schizophrenic patients. *Acta Psychiatrica Scandinavica, 92*(4), 305–309.

Malaspina, D., Harlap, S., Fennig, S., Heiman, D., Nahon, D., Feldman, D., & Susser, E. S. (2001). Advancing paternal age and the risk of schizophrenia. *Archives of General Psychiatry 58,* 361–367.

Marder, S. R., & Meibach, R. C. (1994). Risperidone in the treatment of schizophrenia. *American Journal of Psychiatry, 151*(6), 825–835.

Mash, E. J., & Dozois, D. J. (1996). Child psychopathology: A developmental-systems perspective. In E. J. Mash & R. A. Barkley (Eds), *Child psychopathology* (pp. 3–60). New York: Guilford.

Maziade, M., & Raymond, V. (1995). The new genetics of schizophrenia. In C. L. Shriqui & H. A. Nasrallah (Eds.), *Contemporary issues in the treatment of schizophrenia* (pp. 61–79). Washington, DC: American Psychiatric Press.

McClellan, J. (1999). Early-onset psychotic disorders: Course and outcome over a 2-year period. *Journal of the American Academy of Child and Adolescent Psychiatry, 38*(11), 1380–1388.

McClellan, J. (2000). Schizophrenia in children and adolescents. *The Journal of NAMI California, 11*(1), 51–53.

McFarlane, W. R., Link, B., Dushay, R., et al. (1990). Psychoeducation multiple family groups: Four year relapse outcome in schizophrenia. *Family Process, 34,* 127–144.

McFarlane, W. R., Lukens, E., Link, B., Dushay, R., Deakins, S. A., Newmark, M., Dunne, E. J., Horen, B., & Toran, J. (1995). Multiple-family groups and psychoeducation in the treatment of schizophrenia. *Archives of General Psychiatry, 52,* 679–687.

McGorry, P. D. (1992). The concept of recovery and secondary prevention in psychotic disorders. *Australian and New Zealand Journal of Psychiatry, 26,* 3–17.

McGorry, P. D., Edwards, J., Mihalopoulos, C., Harrigan, S. M., & Jackson, H. J. (1996) The Early Prevention and Intervention Centre (EPPIC): An evolving system of early detection and optional management. *Schizophrenia Bulletin, 22,* 305–326.

McGorry, P. D., & Jackson, H. J. (Eds.), (1999). *The recognition and management of early psychosis: A preventive approach.* New York: Cambridge University Press.

Mediview. (2001). New clinical insights for the treatment of schizophrenia and bipolar disorder. *MediView Express Report,* April 25.

Mellman, T. A., Miller, A. L., Weissman, E. M., et al. (2001). Evidence-based pharmacologic treatment for people with severe mental illness: A focus on guidelines and algorithms. *Psychiatric Services, 52*(5), 619–625.

Miller, A. L., Chiles, J. A., Chiles, J. K., et al. (1999). The Texas Medication Algorithm Project (TMAP) schizophrenia algorithms. *Journal of Clinical Psychiatry, 60*(10), 649–657.

Møller, P., & Husby, R. (2000). The initial prodrome in schizophrenia: Searching for naturalistic core dimensions of experience and behavior. *Schizophrenia Bulletin, 26*(1), 217–232.

Monahan, J. (1992). Mental disorder and violent behavior: Perceptions and evidence. *American Psychologist, 47*(4), 11–21.

Mowbray, C. T., Collins, M. E., & Bybee, D. (1999). Supported education for individuals with psychiatric disabilities: Long-term outcomes from an experimental study. *Social Work Research, 23*(2), 89–100.

Mowbray, C. T., Oyserman, D., Bybee, D., & MacFarlane, P. (2003). Parenting of mothers with a serious mental illness: Differential effects of diagnosis, clinical history and other mental health variables. *Social Work Research, 26*(4), 225–240.

Mueser, K. T., Becker, D. R., Torrey, W. C., Xie, H., Bond, G. R., Drake, R. E., & Dain, B. J. (1997). Work and nonvocational domains of functioning in persons with severe mental illness: A longitudinal analysis. *Journal of Nervous and Mental Disease, 185*(7), 419–426.

Mueser, K. T., Bond, G. R., & Drake, R. E. (2001). Community-based treatment of schizophrenia and other severe mental disorders: Treatment outcomes? *Medscape Mental Health, 6*(1), www.medscape.com/medscape/psychiatry/journal/2001/v06.n01/mh3418.mues/mh3418.mues-1.html.

Mueser, K. T., & Gingerich, S. (1994). *Coping with schizophrenia.* Oakland, CA: New Harbinger.

Mueser, K. T., & Glynn, S. M. (1999). *Behavioral family therapy for psychiatric disorders* (2nd ed.). Oakland, CA: New Harbinger.

Mullen, P. E., Burgess, P., Wallace, C., Palmer, S., & Ruschena, D. (2000). Community care and criminal offending in schizophrenia. *Lancet, 355,* 614–617.

Mulvey, E. P. (1994). Assessing the evidence of a link between mental illness and violence. *Hospital and Community Psychiatry, 45*(7), 663–668.

NAMI. (2001). Schizophrenia Fact Sheet. http://www.nami.org/helpline/schizo.htm.

NAMI News. (2001, Winter). Because kids grow up. For families touched by childhood-onset brain disorders. http://www.nami.org/youth/naminews.html.

Nasar, S. (1998). *A beautiful mind.* New York: Simon & Schuster.

Neighbors, H. W. (1997). The (mis)diagnosis of mental disorder in African Americans. *African American Research Perspectives, 3*(1), 1–11.

Nicole, L., & Shriqui, C. L. (1995). Gender differences in schizophrenia. In C. L. Shriqui & H. A. Nasrallah (Eds.), *Contemporary issues in the treatment of schizophrenia* (pp. 225–243). Washington, DC: American Psychiatric Press.

Nicolson, R., Lenane, M., Singaracharlu, S., Malaspina, D., et al. (2000). Premorbid speech and language impairments in childhood-onset schizophrenia: Association with risk factors. *American Journal of Psychiatry, 157*(5), 794–800.

Nuechterlein, K. H. (1986). Childhood precursors of adult schizophrenia. *Journal of Child Psychology and Psychiatry and Allied Disciplines, 27*(2), 133–144.

Nuechterlein, K. H., Gitlin, M. J., Subotnik, K. L., Bartzokis, G., Fogelson, D. L., Siegel, B. V., & Ventura, J. (2000, May). Risperidone is associated with better work recovery after onset of schizophrenia. Presented at the 55th Annual Scientific Convention and program of the Society for Biological Psychiatry, Chicago.

Olfson, M. (1990). Assertive community treatment: An evaluation of the experimental evidence. *Hospital & Community Psychiatry, 41*(6), 634–641.

Oyserman, D., Mowbray, C. T., Allen-Meares, P., & Firminger, K. (2000). Parenting among mothers with a mental illness. *American Journal of Orthopsychiatry, 70*(3), 296–315.

Oyserman, D., Mowbray, C. T., & Zemencuk, J. K. (1994). Resources and supports for mothers with severe mental illness. *Health & Social Work, 19*(2), 132–142.

Parnas, J., Teasdale, T. W., & Schulsinger, H. (1985). Institutional rearing and diagnostic outcome in children of schizophrenic mothers. *Archives of General Psychiatry, 42,* 762–769.

Pavkov, T. W., Lewis, D. A., & Lyons, J. S. (1989). Psychiatric diagnoses and racial bias: An empirical investigation. *Professional Psychology: Research and Practice, 20*(6), 364–368.

Penn, D. L., Corrigan, P. W., Bentall, R. P., Racenstein, J. M., & Newman, L. (1997). Social cognition in schizophrenia. *Psychological Bulletin, 121*(1), 114–132.

Poulton, R., Caspi, A., Moffitt, T. E., et al. (2000). Children's self-reported psychotic symptoms and adult schizophreniform disorder: A 15-year longitudinal study. *Archives of General Psychiatry, 57*(11), 1053–1058.

Practice parameters for the assessment and treatment of children and adolescents with schizophrenia. (1997). *Journal of the Academy of Child & Adolescent Psychiatry, 36*(10S) Supplement, 177S–193S.

Rapoport, J. L. (1997). What is known about childhood schizophrenia. *Harvard Mental Health Letter* excerpt. NAMI website: www.nami.org.

Remschmidt, H. E., Schulz, E., Martin, M., Warnke, A., & Trott, G. (1994). Childhood-onset schizophrenia: History of the concept and recent studies. *Schizophrenia Bulletin, 20,* 631–646.

Rice, D. P. (1999). The economic impact of schizophrenia. *Journal of Clinical Psychiatry, 60*(Suppl 1), 4–6.

Robinson, D., Woerner, M. G., Alvir, J., et al. (1999). Predictors of relapse following response from a first episode of schizophrenia or schizoaffective disorder. *Archives of General Psychiatry, 56*(3), 241–247.

Rollins, A. (2000, October). Presentation at 4th Biennial Research Conference on Work: Informing and enhancing employment practices for persons with serious psychiatric disability through research, Philadelphia.

Rosso, I. M., Bearden, C. E., Hollister, J. M., Gasperoni, T. L., Sanchez, L. E., Hadley, T., & Cannon, T. D. (2000). Childhood neuromotor dysfunction in schizophrenia patients and their unaffected siblings: A prospective cohort study. *Schizophrenia Bulletin, 26*(2), 367–378.

Rosso, I. M., Cannon, T. D., Huttunen, T., Huttunen, M. O., et al. (2000). Obstetric risk factors for early-onset schizophrenia in a Finnish birth cohort. *American Journal of Psychiatry, 157*(5), 801–807.

Rubin, A., Cardenas, J., Warren, K., & King Pike, C. (1998). Outdated practitioner views about family culpability and severe mental disorders. *Social Work, 43*(5), 412–422.

Russell, A. T. (1994). The clinical presentation of childhood-onset schizophrenia. *Schizophrenia Bulletin, 20*(4), 631–646.

Russell, A. T., Bott, L., & Sammons, C. (1989). Phenomenology of schizophrenia occurring in childhood. *Journal of the Academy of Child & Adolescent Psychiatry, 23*(31), 399–407.

Russell, A. J., Munro, J. C., Jones, P. B., Hemsley, D. R., & Murray, R. M. (1997). Schizophrenia and the myth of intellectual decline. *American Journal of Psychiatry, 154*(5), 635–639.

Rutter, M. (1972). Childhood schizophrenia reconsidered. *Journal of Autism and Childhood Schizophrenia, 2,* 315–337.

Rutter, M., Silberg, J., O'Connor, T., & Simonoff, E. (1999). Genetics and child psychiatry: II. Empirical research findings. *Journal of Child Psychology & Psychiatry, 40*(1), 19–55.

Sartorius, N., Jablensky, A., Korten, A., Ernberg, G., et al. (1986). Early manifestations and first-contact incidence of schizophrenia in different cultures: A preliminary report on the initial evaluation phase of the WHO Collaborative Study on Determinants of Outcome of Severe Mental Disorders. *Psychological Medicine, 16*(4), 909–928.

Schaefer, C. A., Brown, A. S., Wyatt, R. J., et al. (2000). Maternal prepregnant body mass and risk of schizophrenia in adult offspring. *Schizophrenia Bulletin, 26*(2), 75–286.

Schneider, K. (1959). *Clinical psychopathology* (5th ed.). New York: Grune & Stratton.

Schulz, S. C., Bass, D., & Vrabel, C. S. (2000). First-episode psychosis: A clinical approach. *Journal of the American Board of Family Practice, 13*(6), 430–439.

Scott, J. E., & Dixon, L. B. (1995). Assertive community treatment and case management for schizophrenia. *Schizophrenia Bulletin, 21*(4), 657–668.

Severson, M. E. (2000). The impact of a state hospital closure on local jails: The Kansas experience. *Community Mental Health Journal, 36*(6), 571–587.

Shenton, M. E., Solovay, M. R., Holzman, P. S., Coleman, M., & Gale, H. J. (1989). Thought disorder in the relatives of psychotic patients. *Archives of General Psychiatry 46,* 897–901.

Silverstein, S. M. (1997). Information processing, social cognition, and psychiatric rehabilitation in schizophrenia. *Psychiatry, 60,* 327–339.

Silverstein, S. M. (2000). Psychiatric rehabilitation of schizophrenia: Unresolved issues, current trends, and future directions. *Applied & Preventive Psychology 9,* 227–248.

Spaniol, L. (1987). *Families of the mentally ill: Coping and adaptation.* New York: Guilford.

Spencer, E. K., & Campbel, M. (1994). Children with schizophrenia: Diagnosis, phenomenology, and pharmacotherapy. *Schizophrenia Bulletin, 20*(4), 713–725.

Steadman, H. J., Mulvey, E. P., Monahan, J., Robbins, P. C., Appelbaum, P. S., Grisso, T., Roth, L. H., & Silverk, E. (1998). Violence by people discharged from acute psychiatric inpatient facilities and by others in the same neighborhoods. *Archives of General Psychiatry, 55,* 393–401.

Stein, L. I., & Test, M. A. (1980). Alternative to mental hospital treatment, I: Conceptual model, treatment program and clinical evaluation. *Archives of General Psychiatry, 37,* 392–397.

Studies show effectiveness of school-based mental health programs. University of Maryland, School of Medicine. Retrieved on 9/15/01 from http://www.umm.edu/news/releases/mental_health.htm.

Tandon, R., Jibson, M. D., Taylor, S. F., & DeQuardo, J. R. (1995). Conceptual models of the relationship between positive and negative symptoms. In C. L. Shriqui & H. A. Nasrallah (Eds.), *Contemporary issues in the treatment of schizophrenia* (pp. 109–124). Washington, DC: American Psychiatric Press.

Tarrier, N., Barrowclough, C., Vaughn, C., & Bamrah, J. S. (1989). Community management of schizophrenia: A two-year follow-up of a behavioral intervention with families. *British Journal of Psychiatry, 154,* 625–628.

Telles, C., Karno, M., Mintz, J., Paz, G., Arias, M., Tucker, D., & Lopez, S. (1995). Immigrant families coping with schizophrenia: Behavioral family intervention v case management with a low-income Spanish-speaking population. *British Journal of Psychiatry, 167,* 473–479.

Terkelsen, K. G., & Grosser, R. C. (1990). Estimating clozapine's cost to the nation. *Hospital and Community Psychiatry: Special Issue: Clozapine, 41*(8), 863–869.

Test, M. A. (1992). The training in community living model. In R. P. Liberman (Ed.), *Handbook of psychiatric rehabilitation* (pp. 153–170). New York: Macmillan.

Thomas, C. R., & Holzer, C. E. (1999). National distribution of child and adolescent psychiatrists. *Journal of the American Academy of Child & Adolescent Psychiatry, 38*(1), 9–16.

Torrey, E. F. (1987). Prevalence studies in schizophrenia. *British Journal of Psychiatry, 150,* 598–608.

Torrey, E. F. (1994). Violent behavior by individuals with serious mental illness. *Hospital and Community Psychiatry, 45*(7), 653–662.

Tsuang, M. T., & Faraone, S. V. (1999). The concept of target features in schizophrenia research. *Acta Psychiatrica Scandinavica, 99* (Suppl. 395), 2–11.

Tsuang, M. T., Stone, W. S., & Faraone, S. V. (1999). Schizophrenia: A review of genetic studies. *Harvard Review of Psychiatry, 7*(4), 189–207.

Tsuang, M. T., Stone, W. S., & Faraone, S. V. (2000). Toward reformulating the diagnosis of schizophrenia. *American Journal of Psychiatry, 157*(7), 1041–1050.

U.S. Department of Health and Human Services (US DHHS). (1999). *Mental health: A report of the Surgeon General.* Rockville, MD: U.S. DHHS, Substance Abuse and Mental Health Services Administration, Center for Mental Health Services, National Institutes of Health, National Institute of Mental Health.

U.S. Department of Health and Human Services (US DHHS). (2001). Surgeon General Conference on Children's Mental Health. http://www.surgeongeneral.gov/cmh/childreport.htm.

VA Cost of Medication. (1999). Retrieved September 15, 2001, from www.stanford.edu/~johnbrks/theCafe/va/medcost.html.

Walker, E. F. (1991). Research on life-span development in schizophrenia. In E. F. Walker (Ed.), *Schizophrenia: A life-course developmental perspective.* San Diego: Academic Press.

Walker, E. F., & Diforio, D. (1997). Schizophrenia: A neural diathesis-stress model. *Psychological Review, 104*(4), 1–19.

Wang, A., & Goldschmidt, V. (1994). Interviews of psychiatric patients about their family situation and young children. *Acta Psychiatrica Scandinavia, 90,* 459–465.

Wang, P. S., West, J. C., Tanielian, T., & Pincus, H. A. (2000). Recent patterns and predictors of antipsychotic medication regimens used to treat schizophrenia and other psychotic disorders. *Schizophrenia Bulletin, 26*(2), 451–457.

Weiden, P. J., & Olfson, M. (1995). Cost of relapse in schizophrenia. *Schizophrenia Bulletin, 21*(3), 419–429.

Weinberger, D. R., Berman, K. F., & Zec, R. F. (1986). Physiologic dysfunction of dorsolateral prefrontal cortex in schizophrenia. *Archives of General Psychiatry, 43,* 114–124.

Werry, J. S., & Taylor, E. (1994). Schizophrenia and allied disorders. In M. Rutter, E. Taylor, & L. Hersov (Eds.), *Child and adolescent psychiatry: Modern approaches* (pp. 594–615). Boston: Blackwell Scientific Publications.

Williams, R., & Dickson, R. A. (1995). Economics of schizophrenia. *Canadian Journal of Psychiatry, 40*(7), Supplement 2, S60–S67.

Wu, P., Hoven, C. W., Cohen, P., et al. (2001). Factors associated with use of mental health services for depression by children and adolescents. *Psychiatric Services, 52*(2), 189–195.

Wyatt, R. J. (1986). The dopamine hypothesis: Variations on a theme. II. *Psychopharmacology Bulletin, 22,* 923–937.

Xiong, W., Phillips, M. R., Xiong, H., Wang, R., Dai, Q., Kleinman, J., & Kleinman, A. (1994). Family-based intervention for schizophrenic patients in China: A randomised controlled trial. *British Journal of Psychiatry Supplement, 165,* 96–102.

Young, A. S., Sullivan, G., Burnam, M. A., & Brook, R. H. (1998). Measuring the quality of outpatient treatment for schizophrenia. *Archives of General Psychiatry, 55*(7), 611–617.

Zakzanis, K. K., Leach, L., & Kaplan, E. (1998). On the nature and pattern of neurocognitive function in major depressive disorder. *Neuropsychiatry, Neuropsychology, & Behavioral Neurology, 11*(3), 111–119.

CHAPTER 12

DEPRESSION DURING THE SCHOOL-AGED YEARS

DAPHNA OYSERMAN

University of Michigan

Depression is a psychobiological reaction that can be provoked in anyone, though much more easily in those with predisposing vulnerabilities (Brockless, 1997). Depression in childhood and adolescence is a common disorder (Lewinson et al., 1993), serious in its consequences when it disrupts normal functioning or attainment of developmental goals (Brent et al., 1997; Kovacs & Bastiaens, 1995; Remschmidt & Schulz, 1995). Research from the past two decades has shown that even very young children get clinically depressed and that the rate of diagnosable depression increases in the early adolescent years (Cantwell & Baker, 1991; Kazdin, 1988). Episodes of depression in childhood and adolescence increase the risk of other negative mental health outcomes (Fleming & Offord, 1990; Peterson et al., 1993) and reduce the likelihood of attaining age-appropriate cognitive, social, and emotional developmental milestones (for a review, see Angold, Costello, & Worthman, 1998). In her review of the literature, Brockless (1997) found *depressed mood* reported by between 14 and 20 percent of child and adolescent respondents in large-scale studies. The percent reporting symptoms meeting criteria for *serious depressive disorder* was lower; 1 to 3 percent of child and 2 to 8 percent of adolescent respondents met criteria for serious depressive disorder.

Social contextual forces such as poverty and family stress increase risk of depression, as does family history of the disorder; however, these stresses are importantly mediated by parenting quality and other buffering factors. Factors that increase risk of depression may also increase risk of other problematic outcomes (Resnick & Burt, 1996). Antecedents of depression such as poverty, problematic neighborhood, family dysfunction, and behavioral markers such as poor school performance and nonconforming/deviant behavior (e.g., early sexual behavior, substance use, truancy-run away)—may or may not present in a particular situation (Resnick & Burt, 1996).

Note: Support while writing this chapter came from NIMH grant numbers R01 MH54321 and R01 MH57495. Support of the Center for Advanced Studies in the Behavioral Sciences, Stanford, is gratefully acknowledged, as is Kirsten Firminger and Carol Carlin's assistance with the reference list.

Depression is part of the everyday discourse of middle-class Americans, but it can mean a variety of different things, from dampened mood within the bounds of normal experience or in response to an adverse event, to a personality trait in which mood is dampened in response to adverse events that would cause little upset in others, to abnormally dampened mood or mood that is dampened for an abnormally long period of time. Thus, *depression* sometimes refers to symptoms of depression and other times refers to meeting specific criteria for a depressive disorder.

This chapter will outline current *definitions* of depression, *methods* of assessing depression, recent evidence about the *prevalence* of depression, *antecedents and consequences* of depression, and information about universal selected and targeted preventive *interventions* relevant to promoting healthy development and reducing the risk of depression in school-aged children and adolescents. Readers of this chapter will learn to identify depression and depressive symptoms and gain an understanding of the antecedents and consequences of depression as well as a sense of applicable intervention approaches.

DEFINITION

Similar to depression in adults, *depression in childhood and adolescence* is a mood state, typically characterized by dysphoric affect (i.e., feeling low, blue, sad, lacking energy; feelings of uselessness and low self-worth; lack of motivation; and inability to concentrate or to feel pleasure in everyday activities) (American Psychiatric Association, 1994; Cicchetti & Toth, 1998). The most widespread criteria to formally assess depression are those of the *Diagnostic and Statistical Manual of Mental Disorders (DSM-IV)* (American Psychiatric Association, 1994). According to these criteria, depression includes mood and physical symptoms and can be either a low mood disorder (unipolar affective disorder) or, less commonly, involve alternating periods of low and high mood (bipolar affective disorder).

Physical symptoms or vegetative signs of depression include weight gain or loss, sleep disorder (insomnia or hypersomnia), psychomotor agitation or retardation, fatigue, other somatic complaints, and suicidal ideation/attempts (American Psychiatric Association, 1994). For children, symptoms of irritability, somatic complaints, and social withdrawal are more salient than low mood; for adolescents, symptoms of motor retardation, hypersomnia, and delusions are more common for than for children (American Psychiatric Association, 1994). Because weight gain is normative in adolescence, this symptom alone may be less relevant in adolescence than adulthood.

A depression diagnosis, according to *DSM-IV* criteria, is appropriate if for *at least two weeks,* a youth experiences core symptoms of dysphoric mood or loss of interest/pleasure in nearly all activities, and at least four of the following "noncore" symptoms: change in sleep, appetite, or weight; decrease in energy; change in psychomotor activity; feelings of worthlessness or guilt; difficulty concentrating or making decisions; recurrent thoughts of death or suicide; or suicide plans/attempts. Perhaps because diagnosis in childhood and adolescence is relatively new, some clinicians adopt a more descriptive approach to diagnosis. That is, they may substitute "depressive equivalents" such as aggressive behavior, refusing to go to school, and other phobic responses for the noncore symptoms, or they may be flexible in the number of noncore symptoms needed to make a preliminary diagnosis, or they may be flexible about the needed duration of symptoms. Substitutions such as these are problematic because depression frequently co-occurs with other disorders, particularly anxiety and avoidant/phobic disorders, and especially for boys, oppositional and conduct disorders, so that these substitutions may blind a clinician to seeing a co-occurring disorder (for reviews, see Allen-Meares et al., in press; Brockless, 1997). Moreover, this flexibility may paradoxically lead to a simpler view or diagnosis than is appropriate in a given circumstance.

Although there is general agreement on the broad definition of depression, clinicians differ in their description of subtypes of depression, depending on its severity, other concomitant symptoms, the existence of precipitating events, and differences in the expression of depression during different developmental phases of childhood. Generally, depression is expressed (can be observed) through inhibition of normal activities, with the importance of overtly dysphoric mood increasing with age. However, it is important to note that when reading literature on depression, readers must ascertain whether the author means (1) dysphoric mood is present; (2) various symptoms are present but not necessarily enough to define as a disorder; (3) a specific cluster of symptoms are present that together define a depressive disorder, but that may be secondary to some other condition; or (4) a specific cluster of symptoms are present with duration and impact on functioning that warrant definition as psychiatric disorder (Cantwell & Baker, 1991). Further, a depressive response may be an adaptive response to stressful life events if it allows children to reassess or pull back from problematic situations. Thus, although depression is not necessarily maladaptive, its symptoms—low energy, low mood, feelings of worthlessness—can interfere with getting help or changing the situation.

METHODS OF ASSESSING DEPRESSION

Although it is possible to assess depression based solely on self-report, input from another source, particularly a parent, is typically considered helpful because use of multiple informants increases reliability and validity of psychiatric diagnosis in children and adolescents (Bird, Gould, & Staghezza, 1992; Piancentini, Cohen, & Cohen, 1992). However, self-report and parent report of depression (low mood; feelings of hopelessness, helplessness, and worthlessness) are likely to vary because parents have less access to the internal states of the child than the child does (Brockless, 1997). Indeed, numerous studies have shown that parents and youth differ significantly in their reports of youth problems, including internalizing (depression and anxiety) and externalizing (aggression, delinquency) (Achenbach et al., 1987; Edelbrock et al., 1985; see Hartos and Power, 2000, for a review). Generally, mothers report more symptoms than do youth (Hartos & Powers, 2000) and the correlation between youth and parent report declines as children enter adolescence (Achenbach et al., 1987).

Depression can be assessed with standardized scales, less structured interviews, observational procedures, and interpretive tools. Standardization is helpful because it allows comparability. However, less structured approaches such as direct observation can be critical in suggesting that a problem may exist. Standardized scales typically ask the youth or another informant (e.g., a parent, teacher, or primary caregiver) to report on the youth's behavior and affect over a period of two weeks prior to the assessment. Behavioral recall is subject to error (for a discussion of problems with recall as related to program evaluation, see Schwarz & Oyserman, 2001). Clinicians should attempt to structure the recall process to help respondents focus on the events of the past weeks that can serve as memory cues. Typically, the assessment goal is twofold: to assess if the youth is currently depressed and to assess symptoms of depression as a baseline against which to gauge success of intervention efforts. Summaries of instruments for measuring depression in childhood and adolescence may be found in Maddox (1997), Murphy, Conoley, and Impara (1994), and Strober and Werry (1986); these sources also provide reliability and validity information. It is important to examine the questions asked in each inventory and decide which scales focus on issues likely to be relevant to the risk of depression in the particular youth or group of youth that are the target of a preventive intervention. Some scales focus more on the mood-relevant symptoms, others more on somatic symptoms. A more comprehensive assessment tool, such as the Child and Adolescent Psychiatric Assessment (CAPA), takes about an hour to administer (Angold et al., 2000).

CONSEQUENCES OF DEPRESSION

Because behavioral "acting out" can mask depression, depression may not necessarily be assessed or treated. Depression may be masked by sexual, aggressive, or other problem behaviors and the type of masking activity may be gendered. Brockless (1997) suggests that in teenage girls, depression can sometimes be masked as an avid pursuit of sexual gratification. Brooks-Gunn and Petersen (1991) conclude that co-occurrence of depression with aggression is more common with boys.

Episodes of depression in childhood and adolescence increase the risk of other negative mental health outcomes (Fleming & Offord, 1990; Peterson et al., 1993) and reduce the likelihood of attaining age-appropriate cognitive, social, and emotional developmental milestones (for a review, see Angold, Costello, & Worthman, 1998). It is particularly critical that depression be prevented where possible; previous episodes of depression are the single-most significant predictor of future episodes of depression (Hammen, 1992). One reason for future risk is that depression may shift cognitive processing style. Depression carries with it a negative cognitive style—depressed individuals see themselves and the world more negatively than nondepressed individuals do. This negative style is sometimes referred to as *depressive realism* and often remains after the episode has remitted. More prosaically, the incapacitation and lack of energy that accompanies depression results in youth falling behind academically, withdrawing from activities that can provide positive reinforcement such as sport and social interchange, leaving youth with less positive reinforcement, a less dense social network, and fewer accomplishments to provide a positive sense of self.

INCIDENCE AND PREVALENCE OF DEPRESSION

Depression is one of the most commonly occurring disorders in childhood and adolescence (Lewinson et al., 1993). Over the past two decades, researchers have documented depression even in very young children, although rates of diagnosable depression increase markedly in the early adolescent years (Cantwell & Baker, 1991; Kazdin, 1988). Using self-report measures, rates as high as 35 percent have been found, but rates are much lower, somewhere between 7.4 percent (for a review, see Jellinek & Synder, 1998) and 5 percent (Brooks-Gunn & Petersen, 1991) for severe depression when stricter *DSM* criteria are used. Before puberty, rates of depression do not differ for boys and girls, but after puberty, girls are twice as likely to have a depressive episode (Jellinek & Synder, 1998). This evidence comes from the United States of America and has either focused on white samples or not analyzed differential rates by racial/ethnic groups. The interplay between gender and racial/ethnic status is just beginning to be studied. African American and white youth do not appear to differ in prevalence of depression, but Latino youth, especially Mexican migrants, appear to be at lower risk, even though they are more likely to come from poor families (a risk increaser) (Hough, 2001). In adolescence, episodes of depression last an average of 5.4 months (Jellinek & Synder, 1998).

REVIEW OF RESEARCH

Psychosocial Risk Factors Related to Increased Risk of Depression

Poverty has a negative effect on the psychological well-being of children (for a review, see Samaan, 1998). Researchers have documented this effect for white children and adolescents (Conger et al., 1999; Elder, Nguyen, & Caspi, 1985), African American children and adolescents (McLeod & Shanahan, 1993), and American Indian children and adolescents (Costello, Farmer, Angold, Burns, & Erkanli, 1997). However, the effects of poverty seem to be buffered somewhat by cultural factors such as spirituality and communal belonging (Samaan, 1998).

Genetic Risk Factors Related to Increased Risk of Depression

Adoption studies document up to an eightfold increase in depression and a fifteenfold increase in suicide among adopted individuals whose biological parents have an affective disorder (Jellinek & Synder, 1998). Children growing up in families with parents with depressive disorder are more likely to develop depression earlier and have a longer duration of episodes of illness (Jellinek & Synder, 1998). Clearly, biology is not destiny; nevertheless, decades of research clearly show that depression runs in families (Hammon, 1997). Intrafamilial transmission of psychopathology is an important factor in the etiology of psychiatric disorder (Kendler, Davis, & Kessler, 1997). That is, risk of depression increases if parents have a depressive disorder. According to Downey and Coyne's (1990) review of the literature, children of parents referred for treatment of depression are six times more likely to receive a diagnosis of major affective disorder than are children without an affectively ill parent.

For these and other mental illness diagnoses, the likelihood of the identified patient's first-degree relatives also having a diagnosis reflects genetic contributions, but environmental circumstances are necessary to trigger genetic vulnerabilities. A number of epidemiological studies have found high rates of diagnosis in children of mentally ill parents, but the diagnoses are not necessarily the same as those of their parents, which may reflect either a more general risk or problems with our current system of diagnosis (US DHHS, 1999).

Heritability indices vary from estimates of 80 percent for bipolar disorder, 75 percent for schizophrenia, to 34 to 48 percent for depression (Rutter, Silberg, O'Connor, & Siminoff, 1999). Thus, the process by which biological risk is transferred is not yet clear. It is possible that the low heritability indices for depression are due to the difficulty in disentangling depression from other diagnosis (error) or the importance of environmental factors in turning on genetic vulnerabilities.

Life Event Factors and Risk of Depression

First, it is unmistakable that undesirable life events increase risk of depression (Kessler, 1997); according to some estimates, half of depressive episodes in young people are preceded by an undesirable event (Goodyer, 2001). Goodyer notes, however, that children do not necessarily perceive events or interpret them the way adults do, so that it is important to understand the child's perspective of the desirability of an event. Second, although generally only events felt to be moderately or severely undesirable increase risk of depressive disorder in school-aged children, children who experience multiple losses are more at risk of depression, even in the face of modestly undesirable events. Third, bereavement seems to increase risk only if it occurs during the school-aged years, not before. Brief separations from parents or other caregivers do not carry a risk for depression, but permanent separations—due to death or removal from the home—can increase risk, depending on the quality of the parent-child bond prior to its disruption and the nature of the caregiving that replaces it (Rutter, 1990). Fourth, in some research, both negative life events and lack of social support have independent negative effects on risk of depression. In other research, negative life events increase the risk of depression only when accompanied by lack of social support (Goodyer, 2001). Finally, though little research on this issue exists, it appears that depression increases subsequent risk of negative life events, particularly lack of continuity (break-ups) in friendships and peer networks (Goodyer, 2001). It appears that early negative events, especially permanent separations, influence children by fostering creation of negative mental images or representations of social relationships. Also, multiple negative events set up conditions for chronic impairment in important relationships that could foster positive mental images or representations of both the self and others in social relationships.

INTERFACE BETWEEN RISK AND PROTECTIVE FACTORS

One useful framework for thinking about depression in childhood and adolescence is Bronfenbrenner's developmental-ecological perspective (1989). Within this framework, individuals develop within a set of embedded contexts. From smallest to largest, these are (1) microsystems (people with whom the individual is in direct contact), (2) meso-systems (systems that indirectly influence individuals by influencing microsystems), and (3) exo-systems (those institutional or sociocultural normative contexts in which micro- and meso-systems are embedded). Each of these factors is part of the constellation of factors influencing risk of depression and individual protective factors such as feelings of competence, optimism about the future, and sense of well-being that can reduce risk of depression. Therefore, interventions can take place at any of these levels. For example, a school-based program can directly influence individual competencies, promote positive peer interactions, or reduce stress, all of which can reduce risk of depressive symptoms.

Individual Competence

Multiple dimensions of competence—including cognitive, social, and emotional competence—can promote positive outcomes and directly or indirectly reduce the risk of depressive symptoms. Social competence can include peer-based competence, competence in romantic relationships, HIV risk reduction behaviors, social skills, and the ability to appropriately engage others in one's school, neighborhood, church, or larger community (Yoshikawa & Seidman, 2000). Some forms of competence among youth represent their response to marginalization due to gender, social class, sexual orientation, race/ethnicity, or religion. In this sense, *competence* means developing a positive sense of identity, including that aspect of identity stigmatized by larger society (Yoshikawa & Seidman, 2000). Because children's self-image is based in part on a growing sense of competence in the domains of childhood—academic, athletic, social, and artistic—success in these areas can be promotive of well-being, but only if successes are seen as markers of current and potential competence, and failures are seen not as permanent setbacks but rather as bumps in the road (Jellinek & Synder, 1998). Interventions targeting competence are typically assumed to reduce risk of depressive symptoms, though this link is not necessarily empirically assessed.

As children become adolescents and begin to imagine their futures, risk of depression may increase in part because adolescents must choose between alternatives that have desirable and undesirable consequences melded together. In particular, adolescents must weigh their life chances if they leave home versus if they stay in the community—especially for youth in rural communities (Crockett et al., 2000), those living in remote areas (Wilson & Peterson, 2000), and those living on reservations (Beauvais, 2000), for whom life chances are more limited if they stay home (in their community) but family bonds will be cut if they don't. Researchers are just being to explore how clusters of competences can promote well-being (and simultaneously reduce risk of negative outcomes such as depression). Preventive interventions that help youth to conceptualize and think through alternatives and to develop strategies for working toward positive and avoiding negative or undesirable consequences are likely to reduce the risk of depression.

Family and Peer Relationships and Supports

Competent parenting—providing warmth, appropriate supervision, structure, and demands—promotes well-being in children. On the other hand, dysfunctional parenting—exhibiting rejection, neglect, maltreatment, and inability to provide appropriate structure—increases the risk of negative mental health outcomes (Resnick & Burt, 1996). Teens and children experiencing repeated out-of-home placements, or living in shelters or on the streets without parental caregiving, are likely to be at greater risk (Resnick & Burt, 1996). Thus, permanency planning (plans to stabilize youths' lives so that they do not experience repeated moves) is likely to reduce risk of depressive symptoms.

As parenting stress increases, parenting is less likely to be competent and therefore less likely to promote well-being of children (Mcloyd, 1990). Parenting is a distinctly stressing role. All parents experience parenting stress to some degree, but parents differ in their stress load and in the domains of parenting in which they feel stressed. Moreover, parenting stress is likely to be child specific because parent and child temperament, needs, and styles interact in the production of stress (Deater-Deckard, 1998). Individual differences in stress load are important because when stress is higher than parents can handle, outcomes for children are likely to be impaired (Deater-Deckard, 1998). Negative outcomes for children include development of a negative sense of self as incompetent and worthless as well as difficulties in development of social skills—due to lack of secure attachment to parents or to problems in the development of parent-child interactions (Hammen, 1992). Children exposed to more stress, including parenting stress, are at risk of depression (Hammen, 1992). Therefore, interventions targeting parental well-being and parenting competency can reduce the risk of child depression.

Parenting quality, style, and strategies are likely to be key elements of how psychopathology is passed to children (Kendler, 1996). Two lines of evidence support this conclusion. First, parental psychopathology is associated with problematic parenting (for a review, see Oyserman, Mowbray, Allen-Meares, & Firminger, 2000). Second, problems in parenting are associated with increased risk of psychopathology in children (for a review, see Beardslee, Versage, & Gladstone, 1998). For example, Johnson, Cohen, Kasen, Smailes, and Brook (2001) followed a representative sample of biological parents and their children from two counties in New York state. They found that although children of parents with psychiatric disorder were at risk of mental disorder, this relationship was significant only in families using maladaptive parenting strategies. Even when parents did not have a psychiatric disorder, these maladaptive parenting strategies increased the risk of psychiatric disorder in children. Thus, parenting quality, style, and strategies are likely influenced by both social contextual factors (e.g., stress) and genetic factors—parents may respond to their child's temperament and their parenting may be shaped by their own psychopathologies (Kendler, 1996).

An emerging literature highlights the influence of family context on depression (Beardslee et al., 1998; Conger et al., 1999). For example, Baldwin, Baldwin and Cole (1993) found that parenting style needs to fit social context. Thus, when families live in neighborhoods with high crime rates, and are stressed due to father absence, maternal low education, lack of employment, or low occupational status, then high parental restrictiveness, high parental demand for teen self-control, and low parental justification or explanation for parenting policies together were correlated with better mental health of teens. In other words, no single parenting pattern is always adaptive or best suited to promoting children's emotional well-being.

Unsurprisingly, given the complexity of the topic, emerging research results both highlight the importance of contextual factors and the difficulty of studying them well. For example, a number of studies have found a correlation between positive relationship with parents, including good communication, and reduced risk of depressive symptoms in adolescence (e.g., Brage & Meredith, 1994). However, this connection between positive parent relationship and adolescent well-being is found only when information on the quality of the relationship and teen well-being are both provided by the same source (either the parent or the youth). Youth and parent reports of the quality of the parent-youth relationship and of youth well-being are not well correlated (for a review, see Hartos & Power,

2000). In an effort to understand why that is so, Hartos and Power (2000) analyzed data from a large racial/ethnically diverse sample of ninth-grade youth and their mothers in Florida. They found subgroups with some youth-mother dyads agreeing (positive correlation between reports) and others systematically disagreeing (negative correlation between reports). What this means for clinicians' attempts to understand teen well-being and the nature of the parent-child relationship is that obtaining data from both sources is needed, and if the sources disagree, then part of the intervention should deal with helping the mother and the youth understand each other's perspective.

School and Neighborhood Context

Social workers have always recognized that neighborhoods and communities are contexts for development. Current research shows that over the past decades, poverty in the United States has become more urban, more spatially concentrated, and more likely to cluster with other indicators of disadvantage, including minority status. That is, residents of neighborhoods of concentrated poverty are more likely to experience other forms of social and economic disadvantage and are disproportionately members of minority groups (Gephart, 2000). However, this does not mean that rural youth are not at risk. Rural areas have suffered decreased population, loss of income, rising rates of youth substance use, and higher levels of high school noncompletion, such that rates of many of the social ills affecting youth depression are midway between levels for inner-city and for suburban youth (Crockett, Shanahan, & Jackson-Newsom, 2000).

Violence and the effects on children and youth of exposure to violence both at home and in the community is an emerging area of research (Margolin & Gordis, 2000). Margolin and Gordis reviewed the literature on the effects of exposure to violence on risk of depression in children and drew several conclusions: Harsh and uncontrollable parenting and parental rejection (as found in abusive home environments) may cause learned helplessness, anxiety, and depression in children because children may interpret the violence they are exposed to as meaning both that they are unsafe and that they are unworthy of being safe—a negative cognition that is carried out of the home and into the world with the child. These reviewers noted that elevated depression risk continues, with evidence for elevated risk two years after abuse has been reported. These effects are particularly pronounced for sexual abuse and among girls. Effects have also been found for children who observed one parent abusing another, or who witnessed violence or were victimized in the community or school, especially if they knew the victimizer.

IMPLICATIONS OF AGE GENDER, RACE/ETHNICITY, SEXUAL ORIENTATION, POVERTY, AND MIGRATION STATUS

Age

Depression that begins in childhood or adolescence is more likely to be associated with later, recurring depressive episodes than depression beginning in adulthood (Kovacs, 1996). The best predictor of future episodes of depression is previous episodes (Hammen, 1992).

Gender

Recent reviews highlight gender differences in the risk of depression. First, from early puberty onward, girls are at greater risk of depression than are boys (Hayward, 1999; Parry, 1989). Second, girls appear more vulnerable to depression when their mothers are depressed (Beardslee et al., 1998). Gender differences in depression change with age and by gender, with girls increasing dramatically in their reports of depression as they attain puberty, such that twice as many postpubertal girls as boys report depression (see Brockless, 1997, for a review). Some suggestions are made that reproductive hormones influence this risk because, for example, women are at more risk from puberty on of "cycling" affective disorders such as mania or bipolar disorder (Parry, 1989). However, this gender difference may not be universal; one study with French teens did not find this gender difference (Bailly et al., 1992).

Race/Ethnicity, Sexual Orientation, Poverty and Migration Status

New studies have begun to explore the ways that race/ethnicity, sexual orientation, poverty, and migration status may influence depression and its consequences (for a review, see Samaan, 1998). Overall, poverty and economic hardship are associated with psychological disorders in children and adolescents (Samaan, 1998), and minority youth, particularly African American youth, are at increased risk of growing up in conditions of poverty (Taylor, Jacobson, & Roberts, 2000). A substantial proportion of school-aged children are resilient in the face of multiple adversities and we are just beginning to understand what may promote well-being and reduce the risk of mental health problems. However, it is clear that independent accumulation of risk factors and the multiplicative effect of one risk factor on the occurrence of another do increase vulnerability to depression (Goodyer, 2001).

Some emerging research shows contextual factors—especially parental poverty, life stress, and social isolation—increase child and adolescent depression by disrupting parenting (Stern, Smith, & Jang, 1999). Using data from the Rochester Youth Development Study, which includes a random stratified sample of Rochester (New York) public school seventh- and eighth-graders, 68 percent African American and 73 percent male, Stern, Smith, and Jang (1999) show that the effects of poverty, life stress, and social isolation on youth depression were all due to the negative effect these factors had on parent distress, appropriate discipline, and supportive parenting. Thus, poverty and other stressors influence children by influencing the quality of the home environment. McLoyd (1990) makes the same point in her study of African American families. Specifically, she argues that poverty and economic loss diminish parents' capacity to provide involved and supportive parenting and that this is an important conduit of the negative effect of poverty on children.

However, some of the results from the research literature on resilience are surprising. For example, an emerging body of research (reviewed in Escobar, Nervi, & Gara, 2000) shows that Mexican-born migrants have better mental health profiles than U.S.-born Mexican Americans (who themselves are indistinguishable from non-Hispanic whites in the United States). This research is important because Mexicans are the largest Hispanic group in the United States, and their size in the general population is increasing. Although no conclusive evidence as to causality exists, Escobar and colleagues (1998, 2000) propose that well-being may be promoted by stronger family ties (termed *familialism* or *familism*) that provide support to family members, a reason for optimism for the future, disengagement from stressful external conditions, and valuation of motherhood, which supports positive neonatal outcomes, and thus the well-being of children.

Resilience does not seem to be common across all minority groups that place a high value on family orientation. For example, there is some evidence that depression and anxiety among American Indian youth is quite high and a cause for concern (for a review, see Beauvais, 2000), and that suicide rates are very high among American Indian youth, particularly boys (Beauvais, 2000). Similarly, although little is known about the mental health within subgroups of Asian American youth, what evidence there is suggests that rates of depression among girls are comparable to those for whites (Leong, Chao, & Hardin, 2000). Asian Americans are, on average, academically competent, but these authors remind readers first that migrant Asian groups are more at risk of school failure, and second that academic competence does not necessarily translate into resilience in the domain of mental health.

PROMISING INTERVENTIONS

A recent review of primary prevention mental health programs for children and adolescents (Durlak, 1998; Durlak & Wells, 1997) highlights that, overall, these programs do show positive effects. Specifically, school-based prevention programs (though not parent-focused interventions) have been found effective, with average participants in programs surpassing performance of control group individuals by 59 to 82 percent. An earlier review of meta-analyses came to similar conclusions, with the addition that behavioral or cognitive behavioral approaches produced better effects than nonbehavioral approaches (LeCroy & Ashford, 1992). That said, as in many other areas of clinical research, not enough is known to state definitively which programs or interventions "work" in which contexts and for whom. Ideally, emerging models of service would have several key characteristics:

1. Children would be viewed as individuals who are simultaneously members of families, peer groups, schools and neighborhoods.
2. Assessment would take into account the child's needs as well as the family's needs.
3. Service would be coordinated so that assessed needs could be met.
4. Interagency linkages would be fostered so that school-based interventions could be coordinated with family-based service provision.
5. Follow-up would take place to be sure that referrals occurred, that services were provided, and that improvements were made.

Prevention Strategies

Two very clear antecedents of depression in children appear to be previous episodes of depression and loss of normal activities (due to long-term illness, loss of social relations due to peer group rejection, death of a close other, etc.) (Brockless, 1997). Loss of normal social relations is likely to reduce chances for positive feedback for social-emotional support, and for other more concrete kinds of support. Depression may leave behind a residue of negative cognitive patterns. Accordingly, a developmental psychopathology model of depression suggests that depression in children results from the complex interplay between interpersonal, cognitive, and stress factors (Hammen, 1992). Cognitive vulnerability includes focus on personal incompetence and unworthiness in appraisals of events and circumstances, and negative "working models" or schemas about oneself and others. Stressful conditions in early and later childhood undermine or erode the development of effective coping and the attainment of developmental milestones. Over time, lack of effective coping and negative working models may produce self-fulfilling prophecies in which youth who fear being rejected end up increasing their chances of being rejected by others in their social context (Hammen, 1992). Cognitions play an important role in depression. First, the child's interpretation of events and circumstances leads him or her to conclude that negative outcomes have occurred and are irredeemable (i.e., they cannot be fixed). Second, these dysfunctionally negative cognitions are also likely to be part of the child's representations of others—his or her social or relational schemas. These negative expectations are likely to lead to maladaptive interpersonal behaviors that contribute to depression.

Therefore, effective primary prevention strategies need to target promotion of effective parenting and other socialization contexts for young children to provide them chances to attain developmental milestones and develop effective coping strategies. Secondary prevention strategies—those for children who lack competencies in the domains of childhood, including social and academic or cognitive domains—need to target these skills to reduce subsequent risk of depression. For children who have previously experienced depression or are currently experiencing depression, additional intervention foci must be on the child's cognitive model or way of making sense of the world and himself or herself.

Four distinct strategies for fostering and bolstering positive, adaptive outcomes are represented in the literature (see Smokowski, 1998, for a review). The first strategy involves *reducing vulnerability* and stress. An example would be teaching youth social skills and safe-sex skills so that they can avoid stressors such as teenaged pregnancy and sexually transmitted diseases, which increase the risk of depression. The second strategy involves *reducing pile-up* of stressors or "risk chains" in which one stressor, such as family poverty, carries with it multiple other stressors, such as inadequate access to health care, parenting stress, and lapses in parental supervision, which increase the risk of child maltreatment and victimization, and later problems with drug and alcohol use, all of which are linked to child and adolescent depression. Interventions focused on this strategy would attempt to break chains and reduce pile-up. An example would be family-based interventions focused on promoting high-quality parenting, including appropriate supervision, warmth, and parental demandingness (that is, pushing children to achieve age-appropriate goals, including those focused on responsibility, initiative, and social obligation). The third strategy involves *increasing resources* to promote positive outcomes. Interventions focused on this strategy would put in place universal or targeted services to promote success; these could be education, health, employment, or recreational services. An example would be providing preschool and after-school programs that support children and youth in attaining social, cognitive and emotional developmental milestones and that provide a safe context for children. The fourth strategy involves *mobilizing protective resources*. Protective resources are factors that buffer risk factors—for example, although maternal mental illness is a risk factor for child depression, presence of a father or other consistently available adult with whom the child has a positive and supporting relationship buffers this risk. An example intervention would be use of a mentoring program for youth who have insufficient adult support or involvement of youth in programs that promote their sense of competence. Instead of breaking risk chains, these interventions focus on building "resilience strings"—a cascade of processes by which youth come to have more resources.

Treatment Strategies

Depression affects children's lives in the sense that it disrupts normal processes of development and contributes to chronic stress. Depression is best considered a disorder in interacting with one's context that results in both further negative consequences and increased risk of future depressive episodes (Hammen, 1992). Clinical depression is a recurrent and sometimes chronic disorder. Negative coping in the form of dysfunctional cognitions (low sense of worth, negative views of one's ability to become competent) and impairment in everyday functioning are simultaneously symptoms of depression, likely antecedents of depression, and likely risk factors for future depression. That is why improving coping is important to treatment of depression.

A recently treated 10-year-old (as cited in Jellinek & Synder, 1998, p. 15) gave the following summary of ways to handle depression: "Talk; be yourself; don't beat yourself up; don't store up your feelings, share them; don't get anxious over every little thing; be kind to yourself." As can be seen, this child balanced admonitions for action ("talk") and for suppression of action ("don't beat yourself up"). Together, these form the interlocking components of depression treatment.

Treatment strategies should take into account both factors generally increasing risk for depression and subgroup specific issues. For example, Wisdom (2001) developed a gender-specific intervention, focused on the needs of adolescent girls. She studied communication patterns of girls who exhibited high versus low depressive symptoms and found that teenaged girls with higher depressive symptoms were less clear and direct in their communications. Direct communicators made clear what they wanted and what their feelings and preferences were, as opposed to indirect communicators, who were vague, expressed little preference, or waited rather than taking a turn at communicating. Because an indirect style is not valued within European American culture (for a review of American culture, see Oyserman, Coon, & Kemmelmeier, 2002), teens with this style are less likely to have rewarding social interchanges. Current tertiary prevention programs for depressed adolescents focus on cognitive-behavioral methods. These programs include increasing participants' involvement in pleasant activities, improving their social skills, and changing negative thoughts to more positive ones.

Because teens who are low income, minority, female, gay-lesbian, or bisexual or transgendered are more at risk of facing negative or stigmatized images about their group and, in some cases, more at risk of abuse and harassment, programs should be tailored to fit their unique needs. Tailoring programs to fit the needs of minority youth, gay-lesbian, bisexual or transgendered youth can include (1) helping youth notice and analyze media messages that negatively stereotype or objectify their group or present it as weak and incompetent in important life domains; (2) defining abuse/harassment (including sexual) and presenting strategies to help avoid/report/deal with ramifications of this; (3) helping youth develop direct communication styles in dealing with outgroups while being culturally sensitive to the communication styles of cultures other than middle-class heterosexual European American ones; (4) discussing ways to preserve a sense of one's own identity while navigating competing demands from family, peer group, school, and romantic partners during adolescence; and (5) discussing self-care techniques to promote positive mental and physical health.

Although service providers are pressed to provide brief interventions by the demands of managed care and other time and cost limitations, it is unlikely that extremely brief intervention (less than eight sessions) will be helpful in alleviating depression (Angold, Costello, Burns, & Erkanli, 2000).

FINAL COMMENTS

Depression in childhood and adolescence is common enough that reducing risk of depression and promoting well-being are often elements of universal preventive interventions in the school-aged years. Since family processes can increase risk, particularly when linked with negative life events and lack of social support, there are a number of plausible targets for intervention. Targeted intervention programs could select high-risk children—that is, children from families where serious mental illness has already been identified, or children whose general circumstance might increase risk (e.g., children with academic or social deficits who might be more at risk of experiencing failures in central domains of childhood). More universal, school-based programs could focus on promoting positive, nonhumiliating student-student and student-teacher interaction. Such intervention might reduce vulnerability to feelings of social neglect or social rejection in all children. Similarly, programs focused on promoting young children's ability to empathize with others and appropriately read and respond to emotion cues could set up a promoting and nonstressing universal context.

DISCUSSION QUESTIONS

1. There is some evidence that the rate of depression among adolescents is increasing. Why might that be?

2. Depression and school failure are associated. What would be the consequences of providing better basic education for children?

3. Migrant children are less at risk of depression than are their American-born counterparts. How could we use this information to develop better preventive interventions?

4. Economic hardship seems to increase the risk of depression via its negative impact on the parent-child relationship. What preventive interventions are viable to target this risk?

5. Depression carries with it a cognitive style that increases risk of subsequent depression. What kinds of interventions are appropriate to reduce the negative consequences of "depressive thinking"?

SUGGESTED READINGS

Durlak, J. (1995) *School-based prevention programs for children and adolescents.* Thousand Oaks, CA: Sage.

Matson, J. L. (1989). *Treating depression in children and adolescents.* New York: Pergamon.

REFERENCES

Achenbach, T., McConaughy, S., & Howell, C. (1987). Child/adolescent behavioral and emotional problems: Implications of cross-informant correlations for situational specificity. *Psychological Bulletin, 101,* 213–232.

Allen-Meares, P., Colarossi, L., Oyserman, D., & DeRoos, Y. (in press). Assessing depression in childhood and adolescence: A guide for social work practice. *Child and Adolescent Social Work Journal.*

American Psychiatric Association. (1994). *Diagnostic and statistic manual of mental disorders* (4th ed.). Washington, DC: Author.

Angold, A., & Costello, J. (2000). The child and adolescent psychiatric assessment (CAPA). *Journal of the American Academy of Child and Adolescent Psychiatry, 39,* 39–48.

Angold, A., Costello, J., Burns, B., Erkanli, Farmer, A. (2000). Effective of nonresidential specialty mental health services for children and adolescents in the "real world." *Journal of the American Academy of Child and Adolescent Psychiatry, 39,* 154–160.

Angold, A., Costello, J., & Worthman, C. (1998). Puberty and depression: The role of age, pubertal status and pubertal timing. *Psychological Medicine, 28,* 51–61.

Bailly, D., Beuscart, R., Collinet, C., Alexandre, J., & Parquet, P. (1992). Sex differences in the manifestations of depression in youth people: A study of French high school students. Part I: Prevalence and clinical data. *European Child and Adolescent Psychiatry, 1,* 135–145.

Baldwin, A., Baldwin, C., & Cole, R. (1993). Stress-resistant families and stress-resistant children. In J. Rolf, A. Masten, D. Cicchetti, K. Nuechterlein, & S. Weintraub (Eds.), *Risk and protective factors in the development of psychopathology* (pp. 257–280). New York: Cambridge University Press.

Beardslee, W. R., Versage, E. M., & Gladstone, T. R. G. (1998). Children of affectively ill parents: A review of the past 10 years. *Journal of the American Academy of Child and Adolescent Psychiatry, 37,* 1134–1141.

Beauvais, F. (2000). Indian adolescence: Opportunities and challenge. In R. Montemayor, G. Adams, & T. Gullotta (Eds.), *Adolescent diversity in ethnic, economic and cultural contexts: Advances in adolescent development, annual book series Vol. 10* (pp. 110–140). Thousand Oaks, CA: Sage.

Bird, H., Gould, M., & Staghezza, B. (1992). Aggregating data from multiple informants in child psychiatry epidemiological research. *Journal of the American Academy of Child and Adolescent Psychiatry, 31,* 78–85.

Brage, D., & Meredith, W. (1994). A causal model of adolescent depression. *Journal of Psychology, 128,* 455–468.

Brent, D. A., Holder, D., Kolko, D., Birmaher, B., Baugher, M., Roth, C., Iyengar, S., & Johnson, B. A. (1997). A clinical psychotherapy trial for adolescent depression comparing cognitive, family, and supportive therapy. *Archives of General Psychiatry, 54,* 877–885.

Brockless, J. (1997). The nature of depression in childhood: Its causes and presentation. In K. N. Dwivedi & V. P. Varma (Eds.), *Depression in children and adolescents* (pp. 9–36). London: Whurr Publishers.

Bronfenbrenner, U. (1989). Ecological systems theory. In R. Vasta (Ed.), *Annals of child development—Six theories of child development: Revised formulations and current issues* (pp. 187–249). Greenwich, CT: JAI Press.

Brooks-Gunn, J., & Petersen, A. (1991). Studying the emergence of depression and depressive symptoms during adolescence. *Journal of Youth & Adolescence: Special Issue: The emergence of depressive symptoms during adolescence, 20,* 115–119.

Cantwell, D. P., & Baker, L. (1991). Manifestations of depressive affect in adolescence. *Journal of Youth and Adolescence, 20,* 121–133.

Cicchetti, D., & Toth, S. L. (1998). The development of depression in children and adolescents. *American Psychologist, 53*, 221–241.

Conger, R., Jewsbury Conger, K., Matthews, L. & Elder, G. Jr. (1999). Pathways of economic influence on adolescent adjustment. *American Journal of Community Psychology: Special Issue: Prevention science, part 1, 27*, 519–541.

Costello, E. J., Farmer, E., Angold, A., Burns, B., & Erkanli, A. (1997). Psychiatric disorders among American Indian and White youth in Appalachia: The Great Smoky Mountains study. *American Journal of Public Health, 87*, 827–832.

Crockett, L., Shanahan, M., & Jackson-Newsom, J. (2000). Rural youth: Ecological and life course perspectives. In R. Montemayor, G. Adams, & T. Gullotta (Eds.), *Adolescent diversity in ethnic, economic and cultural contexts. Advances in adolescent development, annual book series Vol. 10* (pp. 43–74). Thousand Oaks, CA: Sage.

Deater-Deckard, K. (1998). Parenting stress and child adjustment: Some old hypotheses and new questions. *Clinical Psychology: Science and Practice, 5*, 314–332.

Downey, G., & Coyne, J. C. (1990). Children of depressed parents—An integrative review. *Psychological Bulletin, 108*, 50–76.

Durlak, J. (1998). Primary prevention mental health programs for children and adolescents are effective. *Journal of Mental Health, 7*, 463–469.

Durlak, J., & Wells, A. (1997). Primary prevention mental health programs for children and adolescents: A meta-analytic review. *American Journal of Community Psychology, 25*, 115–152.

Edelbrock, C., Costello, A. J., & Dulcan, M. K. (1985). Age differences in the reliability of the psychiatric interview of the child. *Child Development, 56*, 265–275.

Elder, G., Nguyen, T., & Caspi, A. (1985). Linking family hardship to children's lives. *Child Development: Special Issue: Family Development, 56*, 361–375.

Escobar, J. (1998). Immigration and mental health: Why are immigrants better off? *Archives of General Psychiatry, 55*, 781–782.

Escobar, J. I., Nervi, C. H., & Gara, M. A. (2000). Immigration and mental health: Mexican Americans in the United States. *Harvard Review of Psychiatry, 8*, 64–72.

Fleming, J. E., & Offord, D. R. (1990). Epidemiology of childhood depressive disorders: A critical review. *Journal of the American Academy of Child and Adolescent Psychiatry, 29*, 571–580.

Gephart, M. (2000). Neighborhoods and communities as contexts for development. In J. Brooks-Gunn, G. Duncan, & J. Aber (Eds.), *Neighborhood poverty: Context and consequences for children.* (Vol. 1, pp. 1–43). New York: Russell Sage Foundation.

Goodyer, I. (2001). Life events: Their nature and effects. In I. M. Goodyer (Ed.), *The depressed child and adolescent* (2nd ed., pp. 204–232). New York: Cambridge University Press.

Hammen, C. (1992). Cognitive, life stress, and interpersonal approaches to a developmental psychopathology model of depression. *Development and Psychopathology, 4*, 189–206.

Hammen, C. (1997). Children of depressed parents: The stress context. In S. Wolchik & I. Sandler (Eds.), *Handbook of children's coping: Linking theory and intervention* (pp. 131–157). New York: Plenum Press.

Hartos, J. L., & Power, T. G. (2000). Association between mother and adolescent reports for assessing relations between parent-adolescent communication and adolescent adjustment. *Journal of Youth and Adolescence, 29*, 441–450.

Hayward, C. (1999). The emergence of gender differences in psychopathology during adolescence [Abstract]. Presentation at William T. Grant Faculty Scholars Meeting.

Hough, R. (2001). *Health disparities among minority children and adolescents.* Invited address at Research Approaches to Early Treatment and Prevention of Mental Disorders for Minority Children and Adolescents, NIMH Workshop, Division of Services and Intervention Research, Office for Special Populations, and the Division of Mental Disorders, Behavioral Research, and AIDS, Bethesda, MD.

Jellinek, M., & Synder, J. (1998). Depression and suicide in children and adolescents. *Pediatrics in Review, 19*, 255–265.

Johnson, J. G., Cohen, P., Kasen, S., Smailes, E., & Brook, J. S. (2001). Association of maladaptive parental behavior with psychiatric disorder among parents and their offspring. *Archives of General Psychiatry, 58*, 453–460.

Kazdin, A. E. (1988). Childhood depression. In E. J. Mash & L. G. Terdal (Eds.), *Behavioral assessment of childhood disorders* (2nd ed.). New York: Guilford Press.

Kendler, K. (1996). Parenting: A genetic-epidemiologic perspective. *American Journal of Psychiatry, 153,* 11–20.

Kendler, K., Davis, C., & Kessler, R. (1997). The familial aggregation of common psychiatric and substance abuse disorders in the National Comorbidity Survey: A family history study. *British Journal of Psychiatry, 178,* 841–848.

Kessler, R. C. (1997). The effects of stressful life events on depression. *Annual Review of Psychology, 48,* 191–214.

Kovacs, M. (1985). The Children's Depression Inventory (CDI). *Psychopharmacology Bulletin, 21,* 995–998.

Kovacs, M. (1996). Presentation and course of major depressive disorder during childhood and later years of the life span. *Journal of the American Academy of Child and Adolescent Psychiatry, 35,* 705–715.

Kovacs, M., & Bastiaens, L. J. (1995). The psychotherapeutic management of major depressive and dystymic disorders in childhood and adolescence: Issues and prospects. In I. M. Goodyer (Ed.), *The depressed child and adolescent: Developmental and clinical perspectives.* Cambridge, MA: Cambridge University Press.

LeCroy, C., & Ashford, J. (1992). Children's mental health: Current findings and research directions. *Social Work Research & Abstracts, 28,* 13–20.

Leong, F., Chao, R., & Hardin, E. (2000). Asian American adolescents: A research review to dispel the model minority myth. In R. Montemayor, G. Adams, & T. Gullotta (Eds.), *Adolescent diversity in ethnic, economic and cultural contexts. Advances in adolescent development, annual book series* (Vol. 10, pp. 9–42). Thousand Oaks, CA: Sage.

Lewinsohn, R. M., Hops, H., Roberts, R. E., Seeley, J. R., & Andrews, J. A. (1993). Adolescent psychopathology: I. Prevalence and incidence of depression and other DSM-III-R disorders in high school students. *Journal of Abnormal Psychology, 102,* 133–144.

Maddox, T. (Ed.). (1997). *Tests: A comprehensive reference for assessments in psychology, education, and business* (4th ed.). Austin, TX: Pro-Ed.

Margolin, G., & Gordis, E. B. (2000). The effects of family and community violence on children. *Annual Review of Psychology, 51,* 445–479.

McLeod, J. D., & Shanahan, M. J. (1993). Poverty, parenting, and children's mental-health. *American Sociological Review, 58,* 351–366.

McLoyd, V. C. (1990). The impact of economic hardship on Black families and children—Psychological distress, parenting, and socioemotional development. *Child Development, 61,* 311–346.

Murphy, L. L., Conoley, J. C., & Impara, J. C. (Eds.). (1994). *Tests in print IV: An index to tests, test reviews, and the literature on specific tests* (Vols. 1–2). Lincoln: University of Nebraska Press.

Oyserman, D., Coon, H., & Kemmelmeier, M. (2002). Re-examining individualism and collectivism. *Psychological Bulletin, 128,* 3–73.

Oyserman, D., Mowbray, C. T., Meares, P. A., & Firminger, K. B. (2000). Parenting among mothers with a serious mental illness. *American Journal of Orthopsychiatry, 70,* 296–315.

Parry, B. (1989). Reproductive factors affecting the course of affective illness in women. *Psychiatric Clinics of North America, 12,* 207–220.

Petersen, A. C., Compas, B. E., Brooks-Gunn, J., Stemmler, M., Ey, S., & Grant, K. E. (1993). Depression in adolescence. *American Psychologist, 48,* 155–168.

Piancentini, J., Cohen, P., & Cohen, J. (1992). Combining discrepant diagnostic information from multiple sources: Are complex algorithms better than simple ones? *Journal of Abnormal Psychology, 20,* 51–63.

Remschmidt, H., & Schulz, E. (1995). Psychopharmacology of depressive states in childhood and adolescence. In I. M. Goodyer (Ed.), *The depressed child and adolescent: Developmental and clinical perspectives* (pp. 292–324). Cambridge, MA: Cambridge University Press.

Resnick, G., & Burt, M. (1996). Youth at risk: Definitions and implications for service delivery. *American Journal of Orthopsychiatry, 66,* 172–187.

Rutter, M. (1990). Psychosocial resilience and protective mechanisms. In J. Rolf, A. Masten, D. Cicchetti, K. Nuechterlein, & S. Weintraub (Eds.), *Risk and protective factors in the development of psychopathology* (pp. 181–214). New York: Cambridge University Press.

Rutter, M., Silberg, J., O'Connor, T., & Simonoff, E. (1999). Genetics and child psychiatry: I. Advances in quantitative and molecular genetics. *Journal of Child Psychology and Psychiatry and Allied Disciplines, 40,* 3–18.

Samaan, R. (1998). The influences of race, ethnicity and poverty on the mental health of children. *Journal of Health Care for the Poor and Underserved, 11,* 100–110.

Schwarz, N., & Oyserman, D. (2001) Asking questions about behavior: Cognition, communication, and questionnaire construction. *American Journal of Evaluation, 22,* 127–160.

Smokowski, P. (1998). Prevention and intervention strategies for promoting resilience in disadvantaged children. *Social Service Review, 72,* 337–364.

Stern, S. B., Smith, C. A., & Jang, S. J. (1999). Urban families and adolescent mental health. *Social Work Research, 23,* 15–27.

Strober, M., & Werry, J. S. (1986). The assessment of depression in children and adolescents. In N. Sartorius & T. A. Ban (Eds.), *Assessment of depression* (pp. 324–342). Berlin: Springer-Verlag.

Taylor, R., Jacobson, L., & Roberts, D. (2000). Ecological correlates of the social and emotional adjustment of African American adolescents. In R. Montemayor, G. Adams, & T. Gullotta (Eds.), *Adolescent diversity in ethnic, economic and cultural contexts. Advances in adolescent development, annual book series* (Vol. 10, pp. 208–234). Thousand Oaks, CA: Sage.

U.S. Department of Health and Human Services (US DHHS). (1999). *Mental health: A report of the Surgeon General.* Rockville, MD: US DHHS, Substance Abuse and Mental Health Services Administration, Center for Mental Health Services, National Institutes of Health, National Institute of Mental Health.

Wilson, S., & Peterson, G. (2000). Growing up in Appalachia: Ecological influences on adolescent development. In R. Montemayor, G. Adams, & T. Gullotta (Eds.), *Adolescent diversity in ethnic, economic and cultural contexts. Advances in adolescent development, annual book series* (Vol. 10, pp. 75–109). Thousand Oaks, CA: Sage.

Wisdom, J. (2001). *Gender-specific depression prevention for adolescent girls.* Presentation to the Society for Prevention Research.

Yoshikawa, H., & Seidman, E. (2000). Competence among urban adolescents in poverty: Multiple forms, contexts and developmental phases. In R. Montemayor, G. Adams, & T. Gullotta (Eds.), *Adolescent diversity in ethnic, economic and cultural contexts. Advances in adolescent development, annual book series* (Vol. 10, pp. 9–42). Thousand Oaks, CA: Sage.

CHAPTER 13

PREVENTION AND INTERVENTION IN YOUTH SUICIDE

MARK J. MACGOWAN

Florida International University

Suicide is the third leading cause of death among 10 to 19-year-olds (National Center for Injury Prevention and Control, 2002). This chapter describes youth suicide from a public health perspective involving a four-stage problem-response continuum: defining the problem, risk and protective factor identification, intervention evaluation, and implementation (Potter, Rosenberg, & Hammond, 1998). The chapter will emphasize the latter areas, providing a review of prevention, intervention, and postvention related to youth suicide. Here, the terms *suicidality* and *suicidal* refer to both suicidal behaviors (attempts and completions) and suicidal ideation (thoughts and plans of suicide). Case examples will illustrate the efforts to prevent and intervene in youth suicide.

DESCRIPTION OF THE PROBLEM

Suicide rates are highest among older adolescents (see Figure 13.1). The rates have steadily declined since 1994, but remain high. Researchers attribute the decline to a reduction in rates of alcohol and other drug abuse and to an increase in the use of prescribed antidepressants (American Academy of Child and Adolescent Psychiatry, 2001). Fewer young adolescents die by suicide. Among this group, the suicide rates have generally increased since 1981, but the rate dropped in 1999, as can be seen in Figure 13.1.

Suicide rates are much higher for boys than girls. One researcher noted, "Holding all other factors constant, young males are 2.5 times more likely than young females to commit suicide" (Hussey, 1997, p. 223). Researchers attribute the differences in suicide rates to the use of lethal methods among boys, higher rates of depression among girls, and "socialization regarding culturally acceptable forms of self-destructive behaviors" (Lewinsohn, Rohde, Seeley, & Baldwin, 2001, p. 428).

Among racial groups, American Indian/Alaskan Native youth have the highest rates of suicide (see Figure 13.2). White youth have the next highest mortality rate, which has de-

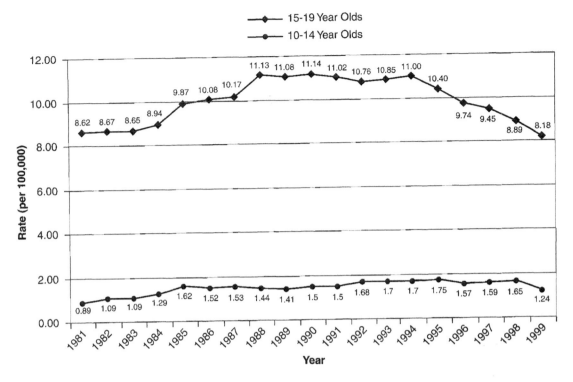

FIGURE 13.1   Youth Suicide Rates by Age Group, 1981–1999

Note: Age-adjusted rates. Standard population is 1940, all races, both sexes.

Source: National Center for Injury Prevention and Control, Center for Disease Control (Customized injury mortality report, accessed March 2, 2002, from the World Wide Web, http://webapp.cdc.gov/sasweb/ncipc/mortrate.html).

creased since 1993. The suicide rates among African American and Asian/Pacific Islander youth appear to follow similar courses, narrowing the gap between the rates for these groups and those of whites. The rates among African American youth increased 105 percent from 1980 until the mid-nineties (U.S. Public Health Service, 1999), resulting in a larger net increase in suicides among African Americans than whites (Centers for Disease Control and Prevention, 1998). The rate has since declined, but remains substantially higher than that of 1981 (possible reasons for the increase are discussed in the next section). The rates among Asian/Pacific Islanders have declined since peaking in 1992, and the rate is now lower than in 1981.

Mortality data on Hispanic/Latinos have been available only since 1990 for most states, and 1997 for all states. The problems with forced-choice ethnic/racial categories and that persons of Hispanic origin may be of any race make comparisons with other groups problematic. Because there were too few youths identified as nonwhite Hispanics, Figure 13.3 includes data concerning white Hispanics. The rates peaked in 1995 and have since declined.

Official data do not exist on suicide among gay, lesbian, and bisexual (GLB) adolescents. These youth are at considerable risk for suicide (Garofalo, Wolf, Kessel, Palfrey, &

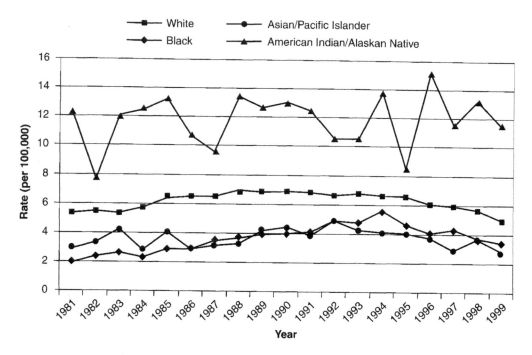

FIGURE 13.2   Suicide Rates per 100,000, Ages 10–19, by Race, 1981–1999

Note: Age-adjusted rates. Standard population is 1940, all races, both sexes.

Source: National Center for Injury Prevention and Control (Center for Disease Control, Customized injury mortality report, accessed from the World Wide Web on March 2, 2002, http://webapp.cdc.gov/sasweb/ncipc/mortrate.html).

DuRant, 1998; Proctor & Groze, 1994; Remafedi, 1999; Russell & Joyner, 2001; Safren & Heimberg, 1999), particularly males (McDaniel, Purcell, & D'Augelli, 2001). Estimates suggest that the suicide rates for GLB youth may be as much as two to three times higher than the rates among non-GLB youth (U.S. Public Health Service, 1999).

RISK AND PROTECTIVE FACTORS

This section describes some of the risk and protective factors related to suicidality (for an expanded discussion, see Macgowan, in press). A *risk factor* is "a measurable characteristic, variable, or hazard that increases the likelihood of development of an adverse outcome" (Móscicki, 1999, p. 44). Risk factors may be distal and proximal (Móscicki, 1999). *Proximal risk factors* are triggers or precipitants to suicide but are neither necessary nor sufficient. *Distal risk factors* are potentiating influences and are a necessary condition for suicide. One or two risk factors alone do not elevate risk, but the co-occurrence and interaction provide sufficient and necessary conditions for attempted or completed suicide (Móscicki, 1999).

Table 13.1 outlines the risk factors from individual, interpersonal, and environmental perspectives. The most commonly examined risk factors have been individual, followed by

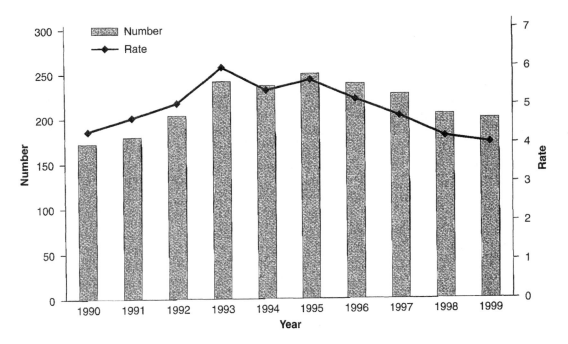

FIGURE 13.3   Suicides and Suicide Rates per 100,000, Ages 10–19, by Whites of Hispanic Origin, 1990–1999

Note: Age-adjusted rates. Standard population is 1940. Reports on Hispanic Origin exclude data from the following states: Oklahoma 1990–96; New Hampshire 1990–92; Louisiana, 1990–91. The figure excludes nonwhite Hispanics as there were 10 or fewer deaths reported every year (rates based on 20 or less are considered unstable).

Source: National Center for Injury Prevention and Control, Center for Disease Control (Customized injury mortality report, accessed from the World Wide Web on March 4, 2002, http://webapp.cdc.gov/sasweb/ncipc/mortrate.html).

family, school, and neighborhood conditions. Little research has focused on broad environmental conditions. The presence of any one of the risk factors in Table 13.1 is generally insufficient for suicide among youth with normal functioning. However, risk heightens when factors accumulate. In addition, certain factors may combine creating risk clusters. One cluster that appears to substantially heighten risk for suicidal behaviors is a combination of mood disorders, alcohol and other drug use, and conduct problems (Andrews & Lewinsohn, 1992; Brent, Baugher, Bridge, Chen, & Chiappetta, 1999; Brent et al., 1988; Brent, Perper, Moritz, Allman, et al., 1993; Brent, Perper, Moritz, Baugher, Roth, et al., 1993; Garrison, McKeown, Valois, & Vincent, 1993; Kovacs, Goldston, & Gatsonis, 1993; Renaud, Brent, Birmaher, Chiappetta, & Bridge, 1999; Shaffer et al., 1996; Young et al., 1995).

A second cluster is the presence of some of the preceding mental health problems and having access to lethal means of suicide. Having a firearm in the home is a significant risk factor for suicide (Brent et al., 1991; Brent, Perper, Moritz, Baugher, & Allman, 1993; Brent, Perper, Moritz, Baugher, Schweers, et al., 1993; Shah, Hoffman, Wake, & Marine, 2000). The presence of a firearm in the home of a youth with one or more comorbid problems adds substantial risk. Youth with psychiatric illness (Brent et al., 1991), conduct

TABLE 13.1   Risk and Protective Factors for Youth Suicide

SYSTEM LEVEL	RISK FACTORS[1]	PROTECTIVE FACTORS[1]

INDIVIDUAL CHARACTERISTICS

	<ul><li>Older (suicide)</li><li>Male (suicide), female (attempts)</li><li>Genetics (suicide, attempts)</li><li>Possible reduced neurobiological functioning (suicide, attempts)</li><li>Epilepsy (suicide)</li><li>Mood disorder, particularly depression (suicide)</li><li>Hopelessness (suicide)</li><li>Cognitive deficits (poor problem-solving, negative attribution, self-criticism)</li><li>AOD use (suicide)</li><li>Violence, impulsive aggression (attempts, ideation)</li><li>Conduct disorder (suicide)</li><li>Legal/disciplinary problems (suicide)</li><li>Previous suicide attempt and suicide ideation (suicide)</li><li>Suicidal communication (suicide)</li><li>Reluctance to seek help</li></ul>	<ul><li>Younger (suicide)</li><li>Reason for living, survival and coping beliefs (among attempters)</li><li>Separation anxiety disorder, among younger youth (attempts)</li></ul>

FAMILY, SCHOOL, & NEIGHBORHOOD CONDITIONS

Family	<ul><li>Family psychopathology (distal) (attempts): Depressed parents (ideation, behaviors); Suicide in family; Suicide attempt by mother and parental substance abuse</li><li>Physical/sexual abuse (attempts)</li><li>Family conflict (proximal)(suicide, attempts, ideation)</li><li>Low parental monitoring (attempts, ideation)</li><li>Poor parental-child communication and divorce (risk of suicide)</li></ul>	<ul><li>Harmonious and supportive family relationships (attempts, ideation)</li><li>Connection with responsible adults</li></ul>
Peer	<ul><li>Loss/disruption of a romantic relationship (suicidal behaviors)</li></ul>	
School	<ul><li>Poor school performance (suicide, attempts)</li></ul>	
Neighborhood/ Community	<ul><li>Suicide imitation/contagion (proximal) (suicide)</li><li>Access to lethal means (proximal) (suicide)</li></ul>	<ul><li>Restriction to lethal means (suicide)</li></ul>

TABLE 13.1   CONTINUED

SYSTEM LEVEL	RISK FACTORS[1]	PROTECTIVE FACTORS[1]
BROAD ENVIRONMENTAL CONDITIONS	<ul><li>Increase in proportion of adolescents in U.S., competition for services among psychologically vulnerable children</li><li>Highly goal-directed and competitive countries such as the United States</li><li>Major changes in family and social norms</li><li>Lowering the legal drinking age (for ages affected; that is, the 18- to 20-year-olds)</li></ul>	<ul><li>Opportunities for services</li><li>Availability and quality of mental health services, retention in services (ideation)</li></ul>

Note: Consult Macgowan (in press) for a detailed discussion of these risk factors.

[1]Notes in parentheses indicate whether the risk is associated with suicide, attempted suicide, or suicidal ideation, if known.

disorder and previous mental health treatment (Shah et al., 2000), or depression and substance abuse (Brent et al., 1988) are at higher risk for suicide when a firearm is in the home.

A third cluster is the co-occurrence of interpersonal conflict (with family and/or girlfriend/boyfriend) and conduct problems (Wagner, 1995). Conflict with parents and with boy/girlfriends, disruption of a romantic attachment, and legal or disciplinary problems were more likely to be associated with youth who had died by suicide than controls (Brent, Perper, Moritz, Baugher, Roth et al., 1993; King, Schwab-Stone, et al., 2001; Marttunen, Aro, & Lonnqvist, 1993).

Protective factors are "internal and external forces that help children resist or ameliorate risk. Like risk factors, protective factors include dispositional, familial, and extrafamilial characteristics. In aggregate, they are the positive forces that contribute to adaptive outcomes in the presence of risk" (Fraser, 1997, pp. 3–4). In contrast with the risk factors, little research has identified factors that protect youth from suicide. Table 13.1 summarizes some of the common protective factors.

Across diverse groups, there are variations in risk and protective factors. Table 13.2 includes risk and protective factors related to gender, race/ethnicity, and sexual orientation. A common protective factor across racial and ethnic groups appears to be attachment to family and traditional culture. For example, familism among Hispanics/Latinos seems protective: "One behavioral referent to familism is family members' obligation to help one another. Working together, family honor and the strength of family cohesion may act as disincentives for suicides or suicide attempts" (Zayas, 1987, p. 9). To explain the dramatic rise in suicide rates among young African Americans, researchers have pointed to an assimilation process in which protective elements associated with cultural distinctiveness have given way to factors of the dominant society that heighten risk for suicide. For example, strong support systems and religious beliefs and devotion, characteristic of traditional, insular African American communities (Gibbs, 1997; Neeleman, Wessely, & Lewis, 1998), have helped keep suicide rates relatively low (Shaffer, Gould, & Hicks, 1994).

TABLE 13.2 Risk and Protective Factors by Diverse Groups

GROUP	RISK FACTORS[1]	PROTECTIVE FACTORS[1]
GENDER		
Females	■ Mood disorder (suicide)[2] ■ Previous suicide attempt (suicide)[2] ■ Social phobia with comorbid depression (ideation, attempts) ■ Alcohol use and conduct disorder (attempt) ■ Tobacco and over-the-counter-drug use (girls) (ideation, attempts) ■ Learning disability (attempts) ■ Chronic illness (ideation) ■ Low self-esteem and substantial family dysfunction (ideation) ■ Dangerous violence (ideation)	■ Emotional well-being (attempts)
Males	■ Previous suicide attempt (suicide)[2] ■ Mood disorder (suicide)[2] ■ AOD abuse (suicide)[2] ■ Aggressive behavior and violence (suicidal behavior) ■ Disruptive behavior (attempt) ■ Chronic stress (ideation)	■ High grade point average (attempts)
RACE/ETHNICITY		
African American	■ Erosion of cultural distinctiveness; increase in SES; rise in secularism ■ Increased availability of firearms; separation from a parental figure; insomnia; neglect; AOD abuse; suicidal ideation; failing grades (attempts)	■ Strong social support system; multigenerational support; strong religious beliefs and devotion (suicidal behaviors)
Hispanic/Latinos	■ Acculturation stress (e.g., perceived discrimination, language conflicts, perceived poor life chances); family; school; psychiatric problems (suicides, attempts) ■ Latinas: sociocultural; family variables; mother-daughter factors; psychological variables (depression, low self-concept)(attempts)	■ Family honor, familism
American Indian/Alaska Native	■ Friends/family members with suicidal behaviors; somatic symptoms; physical/sexual abuse; health problems; AOD use; special education classes; treatment for emotional problems; gang involvement; access to a firearm (attempts)	■ Discussing problems with family or friends; emotional health; attachment to family (attempts)

TABLE 13.2 Risk and Protective Factors by Diverse Groups

GROUP	RISK FACTORS[1]	PROTECTIVE FACTORS[1]
Gay, Lesbian and Bisexual Youth	■ Psychiatric disorders (suicide) ■ Parent relations, school environment, and negative self-perception; depression; gender nonconformity; early awareness and disclosure of homosexuality; stress; violence; lack of support; school drop-out; family problems; acquaintances' suicide attempts; homelessness; substance abuse; loss of friends due to the youth's sexual orientation; loneliness; current suicidal ideation (attempts)	■ Strong parent relations, favorable school environment, positive self-perception (attempts)

Note: Consult Macgowan (in press) for a detailed discussion of these risk factors.

[1]Notes in parentheses indicate whether the risk is associated with suicide, attempted suicide, or suicidal ideation, if known.

[2]The American Academy of Child and Adolescent Psychiatry (2001) considers these factors high risk for suicide.

However, through assimilation, youth become exposed to risk factors, including the erosion of cultural distinctiveness (through accelerating pace of occupational, residential, political, and educational integration) (Shaffer et al., 1994), an increase in SES status (introducing stress associated with the new social environment with its more acceptable method of coping with depression and hopelessness) (Feldman & Wilson, 1997; Gould, Fisher, Parides, Flory, & Shaffer, 1996), a rise in secularism (Neeleman et al., 1998), and an increased availability and use of firearms (Centers for Disease Control and Prevention, 1998; O'Donnell, 1995).

Risk and protective factors form the basis of assessment and prevention efforts in reducing suicide. The next section reviews some promising assessment instruments, followed by a review of promising prevention and intervention strategies.

ASSESSMENT

Assessment is an important component of suicide prevention and intervention and should be based on the best risk and protection evidence. Further, social workers should strive to select measures with acceptable psychometric properties that are culturally relevant. Measures with limited psychometric evidence should be used cautiously. An extensive critical review of measures related to youth suicide is available (Goldston, 2000). This section highlights a selection of broad-based diagnostic interviews and specific instruments that measure suicidality, and instruments designed for specific racial/cultural groups.

Four semistructured or structured diagnostic instruments with good psychometrics (Goldston, 2000) are the Diagnostic Interview Schedule for Children and Adolescents (DICA; Reich, 2000), the Diagnostic Interview Schedule for Children (DISC; Shaffer,

Fisher, Lucas, Dulcan, & Schwab-Stone, 2000), the Interview Schedule for Children and Adolescents (ISCA; Kovacs, 1997; Sherrill & Kovacs, 2000), and the Child Suicide Potential Scales (CSPS; which include the Spectrum of Suicidal Behavior Scale and the Concepts of Death Scale, Pfeffer, Conte, Plutchik, & Jerrett, 1979).

To measure suicide ideation, two instruments with favorable psychometric properties (Goldston, 2000; Range & Knott, 1997) are the Beck Scale for Suicide Ideation (BSI; Beck & Steer, 1991) and the Suicide Ideation Questionnaire (SIQ; Reynolds, 1988). To assess suicide attempts, one instrument with promising psychometric properties (Goldston, 2000) is the Lethality of Suicide Attempt Rating Scale (Smith, Conroy, & Ehler, 1984).

Researchers have developed a few measures specifically for particular population groups. The Indian Health Service Adolescent Health Survey (Pharris, Resnick, & Blum, 1997) has been widely used to assess suicidality among American Indian and Alaskan Native youth (Goldston, 2000) and includes a number of protective factors. A screening tool for GLB youth is the Challenges and Coping Survey for Lesbian, Gay and Bisexual Youth (D'Augelli & Hershberger, 1993; Hershberger & D'Augelli, 1995; Hershberger, Pilkington, & D'Augelli, 1997), the only measure developed specifically for this population (Goldston, 2000). These measures have relatively unknown psychometric properties (Goldston, 2000) and should be used cautiously.

One strategy to prevent suicide is a multistage assessment screening protocol. Researchers have developed multistage instruments that progress from a brief initial screening instrument to one or two additional assessments using progressively more in-depth instruments to assess suicidality. The next section includes a description of this direct screening strategy in more detail.

PREVENTION, INTERVENTION, AND POSTVENTION

This section describes a selection of outcome studies in prevention, intervention, and postvention (i.e., intervention after a traumatic event), illustrated with case examples.

Prevention Strategies

Prevention may be defined as a "strategy or approach that reduces the likelihood of risk of onset, or delays the onset of adverse health problems or reduces the harm resulting from conditions or behaviors" (U.S. Department of Health and Human Services, 2001, p. 201). Prevention strategies include universal programs focusing on entire populations, selective measures that involve a subgroup of a population whose risk is above average, and indicated approaches involving those who, on examination, manifest a risk factor (Institute of Medicine, 1994).

Universal Prevention.   Universal prevention focuses on a defined population, regardless of risk. Few interventions target risk factors at the broader community level. One widely used approach to reduce the potential for suicide is the crisis hotline. However, studies show that suicide hotlines have little or no impact on the incidence of suicide (American Academy of Child and Adolescent Psychiatry, 2001; Burns & Patton, 2000; Lester, 1997). Other universal prevention strategies focus on smaller populations, such as schools. School-based universal prevention programs include student education, gatekeeper training, and direct screening. Student education programs are primarily intended for youth. In contrast, gatekeeper training programs are for peers and adults in contact with potentially suicidal youth.

Student Education.   Findings from studies of the effectiveness of student education programs are inconclusive. On the one hand, the evidence suggests that knowledge increases after exposure to programs (Abbey, Madsen, & Polland, 1989; Ashworth, Spirito, Colella, & Drew, 1986; Klingman & Hochdorf, 1993; Orbach & Bar-Joseph, 1993; Overholser, Hemstreet, Spirito, & Vyse, 1989). For example, one program (Ashworth et al., 1986) consisted of a six-session structured curriculum that included building knowledge, awareness, and attitudes about suicide, and imparting helping behaviors. The authors reported substantial gains in knowledge and decreases in hopelessness. Subjective reports from the teachers and students indicated that there was an increase in helping behavior.

Another program (Orbach & Bar-Joseph, 1993) involved seven, two-hour sessions that included suicide prevention with other life challenges, such as coping with failure, family issues, stress, and problem solving. As described by the authors, "The program was based on the notion that a gradual, controlled confrontation and exploration of inner experiences and life difficulties related to suicidal behavior accompanied by an emphasis on coping strategies can immunize against self-destructive feelings" (p. 120). At posttest, students in the treatment group had positive gains, including significant reductions in suicidal feelings and ability to cope with problems.

In the face of these gains, there are negative findings (Overholser et al., 1989; Shaffer, Garland, Vieland, Underwood, & Busner, 1991; Shaffer et al., 1990; Spirito, Overholser, Ashworth, Morgan, & Benedict-Drew, 1988; Vieland, Whittle, Garland, Hicks, & Shaffer, 1991). For example, Shaffer and colleagues tested the effects of three interventions intended to raise awareness about suicide, increase knowledge of risk factors and referral strategies, and encourage suicidal youth to disclose their preoccupations. The approaches varied in length of time (1.5 hours, 3 hours, 4 hours) and in who led the curriculum (professionals and educators with experience versus regular teachers with limited training).

In the initial study (Shaffer et al., 1991), most students found the program helpful and knowledge about where to get help increased. However, a small number of students reported that the program made their problems worse or caused distress. An 18-month follow-up of one of the programs (1.5-hour presentation) indicated that students in the program were significantly less likely than controls to seek help for a serious problem and significantly less likely to encourage a depressed friend to seek help (Vieland et al., 1991). Further, "students who entered the program believing that suicide was not a reasonable response to stress were more likely to change their minds after program delivery and consider suicide an understandable, possibly reasonable response to stress" (Shaffer & Craft, 1999, p. 72).

Shaffer and colleagues compared the effects of two of the programs cited above (1.5-hour versus 3-hour presentation) in another study (Shaffer et al., 1990). The researchers found that youth who had attempted suicide had more negative reactions to the programs than nonattempters and there was little evidence that the programs changed their attitudes.

In sum, the research is mixed about the efficacy of universal education efforts focusing on youth. Some evidence suggests that students in these programs gain knowledge related to suicide. However, it is not clear that knowledge gains alone are sufficient to influence behavior. Alarmingly, the findings from a few studies suggest that some youths have increased risk following exposure to student education programs.

Gatekeeper Training.   Gatekeeper training involves instructing youth and adults about how to identify suicidal youth and how to get help. A number of studies have examined the effectiveness of this approach (Davidson & Range, 1999; Fendrich, Mackesy-Amiti, & Kruesi, 2000; Grossman & Kruesi, 2000, p. 185; Kalafat & Elias, 1994; Kalafat & Gagliano, 1996; King & Smith, 2000; Nelson, 1987). For example, in one study (Kalafat & Elias, 1994), the program consisted of a three-session curriculum that emphasized knowledge, attitudes, warning signs, and getting help. After the classes, students had significant gains in knowledge about suicide and significantly more positive attitudes toward getting help and helping potentially suicidal peers than controls. Most students reported that the program helped them, but a small percentage said the opposite. Another small percentage found the classes distressing.

In a second study, Kalafat and colleagues (Kalafat & Gagliano, 1996) tested the effects of small-group discussion over five regular class periods of health class. The classes covered coping skills, explained what mental health counseling was in order to reduce stigma, identified helpful adults in the school, addressed suicide myths and facts, described the role of peers in helping troubled youth, and provided wallet cards and emergency information. Students who received the intervention demonstrated significantly more appropriate responses to vignettes about troubled peers than the control group.

Several programs have involved adult gatekeepers exclusively. In Suicide, Options, Awareness, and Relief (SOAR; King & Smith, 2000), school counselors received eight hours of training on how to conduct student interviews to assess risk for suicide after a suicide threat. After the training, most counselors strongly agreed that they could recognize suicidal warning signs, assess a student's risk for suicide, and offer support to a suicidal student. In addition, most knew the intervention steps to take when a student was at high suicidal risk.

Another program that involved teacher interns included a one-hour suicide prevention module (Davidson & Range, 1999). The training provided information about suicide warning signs and risk factors, offered suggestions for teachers confronted with a suicidal student, and imparted specific community mental health resources. Interns read a vignette about a suicidal student and completed questions about their responses. Compared with pretraining, at posttraining the interns were more likely to report that they would take appropriate action.

Integrating several suicide prevention strategies, the Community Action for Youth Survival (CAYS; Grossman & Kruesi, 2000) included caregiver training (recognizing the danger), means restriction (reducing the risk), and postvention (responding to loss). The authors reported that the CAYS program increased school-based caregivers' knowledge, sense of preparedness, and suicide prevention practice. At four to five months after exposure to the program, gatekeepers were "significantly more likely to make follow-up plans for at-risk youth, educate parents about restricting access to means of suicide, and internally disseminate youth suicide training" (Grossman & Kruesi, 2000, p. 185).

In sum, gatekeeper programs appear to increase knowledge and attitudes toward helping youth, but are limited in scope and methods. For example, many efforts cannot reach students disconnected from school and who are at high risk for suicide (Eggert, Thompson, Herting, & Nicholas, 1994). In addition, few studies measure the effect of these efforts on reducing actual suicidal behavior.

Direct Screening. Whereas student and gatekeeper approaches emphasize breaking the taboo of suicide by openly talking about it and educating general populations about risk factors, direct screening methods focus on finding youth at risk for suicide. One example of a direct screening method involves a three-stage approach (Shaffer & Craft, 1999). At the first stage, all students in a health-related class complete a brief self-administered questionnaire called the Columbia Teen Screen (CTS). The risk-based CTS asks students about current suicidal ideation, lifetime suicide attempts, current symptoms of depression, and problems with alcohol and other drugs. Students with at least one of these risk factors are further assessed using the DISC, described earlier. A computer generates a diagnostic report for a clinician who interviews the student in the third stage. At this stage, the clinician determines whether the student needs a referral for treatment or further evaluation. A case manager contacts the family to ensure follow-through.

In a report on the efficacy of this method involving 2,004 high school students in New York City, Shaffer and Craft (1999) noted that 546 met at least one of the risk factors in the first stage of screening. Only 3 were screen-negative; that is, were at risk, but not detected by the CTS. On the other hand, there were 257 false-positives. This finding strongly indicates the need for the timely administration of the second and third phases to screen out students not actually at risk for suicide. In addition, the researchers need to decrease the number of high false-positives, without increasing the number of false negatives, to reduce potentially negative labeling effects.

The direct screening approach in universal suicide prevention is promising. The American Academy of Child and Adolescent Psychiatry favorably reviewed this approach, with the provisos that identified youth be assured treatment and that contingency arrangements be provided for the uninsured (American Academy of Child and Adolescent Psychiatry, 2001).

Selective Prevention. Given the alarming rates of suicide within American Indian and Alaskan Native (AI/AN) communities, surprisingly little work has gone into preventing suicide among this group. In a recent review of prevention strategies (Middlebrook, LeMaster, Beals, Novins, & Manson, 2001), only one study (LaFromboise & Howard-Pitney, 1994, 1995) involved a sample of adolescents that used an acceptable experimental design (quasi-experiment). The school-based Life-Skills Development Curriculum used a social cognitive development perspective intended "to remediate the behavioral and cognitive correlates of suicide" (LaFromboise & Howard-Pitney, 1995, p. 479) among the Arizona Zuni Pueblo. The researchers found that youth in the intervention group ($n = 69$) scored better at posttest (8 months after pretest) on suicide probability and hopelessness than the comparison group ($n = 59$). Students who received the curriculum also had better problem-solving and suicide intervention skills than the comparison group. The prevention model is notable in that researchers, practitioners, and community members worked together to shape the curriculum to Zuni culture. For example, the curriculum was "tailored to be compatible with Zuni norms, values, beliefs and attitudes; sense of self, space, and time; communication styles; and rewards and forms of recognition" (LaFromboise & Howard-Pitney, 1995, p. 481). In addition, the curriculum included a statement from Zuni leaders about the value of life, a historical review of the ways American Indians have coped with stress, a discussion of culturally specific psychological manifestations of suicide risk, and a presentation of how self-destructive behavior affects community well-being (LaFromboise & Howard-Pitney, 1995).

Indicated Prevention. Prevention programs have been developed and tested specifically for high-risk youth. One example is the multifaceted Reconnecting Youth Prevention Research Program (RY; Eggert et al., 1994; University of Washington School of Nursing, 2002). The program consists of providing social network support and skills training for students at risk of school drop out. It incorporates both risk reduction (e.g., suicide risk behaviors) and protection-enhancement (e.g., enhanced self-esteem, family goals met). The first study (Eggert, Thompson, Herting, & Nicholas, 1995) tested three conditions: (1) an assessment plus a one-semester Personal Growth Class (PGC; $n = 36$); (2) an assessment plus a two-semester PGC ($n = 34$); and (3) an assessment-only condition ($n = 35$). Used in all conditions, the assessment consisted of a comprehensive two-hour interview. The PGC consisted of small groups of 12 students meeting daily during regular class time. Social support occurred within the groups in leader-to-student and peer-to-peer relationships. Skills training consisted of self-esteem enhancement, decision making and personal control (of anger, depression, and stress management), and interpersonal communication. All three conditions included a case manager for support and to keep in touch with families. At posttest at 5 and 10 months, the researchers found that all groups showed decreased suicidality (i.e., frequency of suicide thoughts, suicide threats, and suicide attempts), depression, hopelessness, stress, and anger. All groups also reported increased self-esteem and network social support. However, increased personal control occurred only in the PGC groups. Thus, although participants in the PGC classes improved in all areas, the single-session comprehensive assessment interview was as effective in reducing suicidality.

Subsequent research demonstrated the promise of the RY program and the effectiveness of brief screening and modest social support in reducing suicidal behavior. In one study (Randell, Eggert, & Pike, 2001; Thompson, Eggert, Randell, & Pike, 2001), two brief treatment protocols were tested. The first condition was called Counselors Care (C-CARE), consisting of a single-session comprehensive assessment interview (1.5 to 2 hours) and a brief intervention (1.5 to 2 hours) to enhance personal resources and social support. The second condition included C-CARE plus a 12-session, small-group skills training intervention called Coping and Support Training (CAST). The control condition consisted of a 15- to 30-minute assessment interview followed by a facilitation of social support from parents and school personnel, called "usual services." Students at risk of dropping out and suicidality were randomly assigned to C-CARE, CAST, or to usual services.

In a study ($n = 341$) of the immediate effects of the interventions, the researchers (Randell et al., 2001) found that CAST led to increased personal control, problem-solving coping, and perceived family support. Both CAST and C-CARE led to decreases in depression, enhanced self-esteem, and ability to meet family goals. However, all three conditions showed the same significant decreases in suicide risk behaviors, anger control problems, and family distress.

In a study ($n = 460$) of the immediate and extended (i.e., 9-month) efficacy of the interventions, Thompson and colleagues (Thompson et al., 2001) reported that attitudes toward suicidal behaviors (which included thoughts, threats, attempts) significantly declined in the experimental groups. CAST and C-CARE were more effective than usual services in reducing suicidal ideation, depression, and hopelessness across time. CAST was most effective in building personal control and problem-solving coping. Further, the study found that even brief risk assessment and crisis interventions are effective. These findings are encouraging, as the two interventions reduced not only attitudes toward suicide and suicidal ideation but also associated risk factors.

In sum, the findings from these series of studies involving youth at high risk for suicide suggest that brief, school-based preventive interventions are promising. The work of that group shows that social network support and skills training are efficacious in reducing suicide risk behaviors.

CASE STUDY
JESSE

Jesse is a popular 16-year-old on the school football team. An excellent student, he hoped to get into a good college on a scholarship. Jesse liked to attend parties and drank considerably. Most weekends he would get drunk. At one loud neighborhood party, police arrested him for fighting and intoxication. His parents had been married for 17 years but had been fighting for most of the past two years and talked about separation. Jesse's father, Greg, held a steady job but got drunk every day after work. Greg made demands on his son to achieve both in academics and in sports. Over the last six months, Jesse had hostile feelings toward his parents and feelings of depression. To preserve his image as a strong, self-reliant athlete, Jesse never shared his feelings with others.

The school Jesse attended recently implemented a screening program to identify students at risk for suicide (e.g., Shaffer & Craft, 1999). Jesse completed the screening and felt comfortable indicating his thoughts and feelings on a confidential questionnaire. The screening process identified areas of concern, such as his drinking and feelings of depression. A clinician subsequently interviewed Jesse, who shared that he had had recent thoughts of suicide and had readily available means at his disposal—his father's gun collection. In view of the situation, the clinician referred Jesse for further counseling and assigned a case manager to contact his parents, who reported they were "dismayed" that their son had thoughts of suicide. Jesse shared that he was relieved to share his true feelings and grateful that his father seemed supportive.

Intervention Strategies

Intervention strategies are "intended to prevent an outcome or to alter the course of an existing condition" (U.S. Department of Health and Human Services, 2001, p. 201) and to treat known suicidality and prevent it from recurring. There are few experimental studies of psychosocial treatments involving suicidal youth. In one study (Cotgrove, Zirinsky, Black, & Weston, 1995), youth discharged from a hospital were randomly assigned either to a treatment group consisting of standard treatment and a token ("green card") allowing readmission to the hospital upon demand, or to a control group with standard treatment only. The results showed that the treatment group had a lower suicide attempt rate, but the rate was not statistically different from that of the control group.

Brent and colleagues (Brent et al., 1997) examined the effects of three treatments in reducing depression and suicidality (ideation and attempts) among 107 clinically referred, depressed adolescents. The first condition ($n = 37$) consisted of individual cognitive behavior therapy adapted from Beck's Cognitive Behavioral Therapy (Beck, 1979). The treatment was adapted for adolescents by socializing youth to the treatment model, using concrete examples, exploring autonomy and trust, highlighting cognitive distortions and affective shifts that occur during sessions, and developing problem solving, affect regulation, and social skills. The second condition ($n = 35$) consisted of systemic behavior family therapy that combined functional family therapy (Alexander & Parsons, 1982) and problem solving (Robin & Foster, 1989). The third condition ($n = 35$) was nondirective supportive therapy consisting of the provision of support, affect clarification, and active listening. All conditions also received family psychoeducation about affective illness and its treatment. Over three to four months of treatment, all three conditions reduced suicidal ideation, but cognitive therapy was more effective at reducing major depression than the other treatments.

Other studies have also examined the effects of family interventions. One intervention included problem solving and communication in the context of family work (Harrington et al., 1998). The treatment group offered routine care plus the intervention ($n = 85$), which was compared to routine individual services ($n = 77$) at two- and six-month posttests. The manualized intervention consisted of an assessment session and four home visits by master's-level social workers who directed family communication and problem-solving sessions. At posttests, there were no significant differences in suicidal ideation and hopelessness between the intervention and control groups. However, the intervention reduced suicidal ideation among youth without major depression. Harrington and colleagues noted that the clinical significance of this finding is limited; the ideation scores of nondepressed youth were lower than those of the depressed youth, and nondepressed youth are at relatively low risk for subsequent problems (Pfeffer et al., 1993).

Rotheram-Borus and colleagues completed two studies of a family intervention delivered in an emergency room (ER) after a suicide attempt. The studies intended to determine the effects of the intervention on suicidality and on treatment adherence, a common problem in working with suicidal adolescents (Piacentini et al., 1995; Spirito, Plummer, Gispert, & Levy, 1992; Trautman, Stewart, & Morishima, 1993). The specialized ER care included a videotaped presentation about the dangers of ignoring suicide attempts and the potential benefits of treatment, and delivery of a structured family therapy session while in the ER ($n = 65$). The comparison groups received standard ER care ($n = 75$). Both groups also received a six-session manualized cognitive-behavioral aftercare treatment called Successful Negotiation Acting Positively (SNAP).

In the first study, Rotheram-Borus and colleagues (Rotheram-Borus et al., 1996) examined the immediate effects of the intervention on suicidal ideation and other variables, and on treatment adherence. The results indicated that participants receiving the specialized program were significantly less depressed and had less suicidal ideation than those receiving standard ER care. In addition, those in the specialized program were significantly more likely to attend the SNAP program than those receiving standard ER care.

In the second study (Rotheram-Borus, Piacentini, Cantwell, Belin, & Song, 2000), the long-term (18 months) effects of the family intervention were examined, along with an evaluation of suicide re-attempts. At posttest, rates of suicide re-attempts and suicidal re-ideation were lower than expected and similar across conditions. There were fewer suicide re-attempts in the treatment group (6 in specialized care versus 11 in standard care), but the base rates were too low and samples sizes too small to permit meaningful comparisons. The authors did not expect ideation to improve as "feeling suicidal was normative and a signal for taking behavioral actions to stop progression to suicidal acts" (Rotheram-Borus et al., 2000, p. 1091). The program also resulted in significant improvements in maternal emotional distress and family cohesion among families with children who were symptomatic.

Another approach involving parents of youth after release from the ER utilized means restriction education. Access to lethal means of suicide is a risk factor among vulnerable youth (see Table 13.1). The evidence suggests that restricting access to lethal means in the home may reduce impulsive suicides (Centers for Disease Control and Prevention, 1992; Grossman & Kruesi, 2000; Shaffer, Garland, Gould, Fisher, & Trautman, 1988). The approach provided caregivers with injury prevention education. In one study (Kruesi et al., 1999), most adults in households containing firearms took new action to limit access after the education. In another study (McManus et al., 1997), injury prevention education delivered in the ER was significantly associated with adults restricting access to suicidal means, even when controlling for medical outcome from the attempt.

Group methods have also been used in suicide intervention. In a clinical trial involving youth who had deliberately harmed themselves within the past year, group therapy and routine care ($n = 32$) was compared with routine care alone ($n = 31$) (Wood, Trainor, Rothwell, Moore, & Harrington, 2001). The group approach was "developmental group psychotherapy" and included elements of problem solving, cognitive-behavioral therapy, dialectical behavioral therapy, and psychodynamic group psychotherapy. The stages of treatment included an initial assessment phase, followed by six "acute" group sessions covering the following risk-based topics: relationships, school problems, family problems, anger management, depression and self-harm, and hopelessness. Following the acute phase, youth attended "long-term" weekly group sessions emphasizing group process until they felt ready to leave, a median of eight group sessions over six months of the trial. The results at the seven-month interview were that youth who participated in group therapy were less likely to have repeated deliberate self-harm on two or more occasions than those in routine care. They were also less likely to need routine care, had better school attendance, and had a lower rate of behavioral problems than youth who had received routine care. However, the group treatment did not reduce depression or suicidal thinking, a finding consistent with other research involving adults (Linehan, Armstrong, Suarez, Allmon, & Heard, 1991). This study shows the value of group work in reducing acts of deliberate self-harm.

Social network interventions have also been used to reduce suicidality and increase treatment adherence. Originally called Connect Five, King and colleagues (King, 1999; Vallianatos, 2001) developed an intervention renamed the Youth Nominated Support Team (YNST) that brings together health professionals, other trusted adults, and friends to create a supportive network. The program includes psychoeducation and weekly supportive telephone contacts to the youth's support persons. Preliminary findings revealed that YNST has helped to increase retention and decrease suicidal ideation and depression, particularly among girls (King, Preuss, & Kramer, 2001).

In sum, most of the research reviewed suggests that interventions significantly reduce suicidality. Specifically, individual, group, and social network strategies appear to be effective, but family-based interventions have mixed findings about reducing suicidality.

CASE STUDY
MARIA

Maria is 16 years old with parents who came from Cuba when Maria was age 4. Her parents divorced when she was 9 years old and she now lives with her mother, Rose, in a small apartment in a large southeast city. Maria remained close to her father until he died a few years ago. Over the past months, she has had bitter arguments with her mother about Maria's friends and her boyfriend, Ernesto, with whom Maria has been spending much time. Recently, Maria and her mother got into a big argument that resulted in Maria leaving the house and spending the night with Ernesto. The next morning, Maria and Ernesto had a loud argument that ended with Ernesto leaving for work. Maria went home later that day and ingested some of her mother's medication.

When Maria's mother came home from work, she found her daughter and promptly called for an ambulance that took Maria to the hospital emergency room. The next day, the nurse informed Rose and Maria about a program at the hospital intended to help youth and parents deal with such crises (e.g., Rotheram-Borus et al., 2000; Rotheram-Borus, Piacentini, Miller, Graae, & Castro-Blanco, 1994). Both agreed to participate. While in the program, Rose found out about the importance of not ignoring suicide warning signs, such as statements Maria had made over the past weeks about wanting to "end it all" and visit her "papi." She also learned to secure potentially lethal substances. While in the structured outpatient aftercare program, Rose and Maria learned communication and problem-solving skills they would use during conflict. As follow-up, Maria attended individual counseling to discuss her feelings related to her father. Over the next several months, Maria and Rose related more effectively and Maria's grades began to improve.

Postvention

Postvention is a "strategy or approach that is implemented after a crisis or traumatic event has occurred" (U.S. Department of Health and Human Services, 2001, p. 201). One purpose of the approach is to reduce the likelihood of further suicides through imitation. *Suicide imitation,* or *contagion,* is "a phenomenon whereby susceptible persons are influenced towards suicidal behavior through knowledge of another person's suicidal acts" (U.S. Department of Health and Human Services, 2001, p. 197). Exposure to real or fictional accounts of suicide appears to increase risk for suicide among vulnerable youth (see

Table 13.1). A second purpose of postvention is to help families, friends, and acquaintances cope after a death by suicide. Researchers note that parents of suicide victims experience a qualitatively different bereavement process than parents who lose a child through other causes (Holinger, 1994). Parents of victims often feel guilt, shame, stigmatization, and a sense of failure in parenting (Holinger, 1994).

The literature suggests a range of approaches to help reduce the negative impact of suicide (e.g., Grossman et al., 1995; Mauk, 1996; Morrison, 1987; Newman, 2000), but these studies lack empirical testing. For example, researchers and practitioners have developed media guidelines to prevent the effects of contagion (see Figure 13.4), but there is currently no evidence for their effectiveness. Families and peers of suicide victims are frequently involved in support groups (e.g., Moore & Freeman, 1995) but despite their wide appeal, there is little research on the effectiveness of these groups. Similarly, postvention programs are sometimes offered in schools yet are rarely examined for efficacy. A few studies of these programs have been published, with mixed results.

One study (Hazell & Lewin, 1993) examined postvention in two schools that each experienced a death by suicide. Students were selected to participate if they were close friends of the deceased student. The intervention consisted of a large group counseling session delivered within a week of the suicides. The session focused on the students' understanding of the events that led to the suicides, rumor control, their personal reactions following the suicides, and acknowledgment that students in the group could feel suicidal. The leaders provided resources on getting help for those troubled by the suicides. At an eight-month follow-up, students who attended the counseling sessions ($n = 63$) did not differ from matched controls on a number of outcome variables, including depression, suicidality, or whether they would recommend professional counseling to a suicidal friend.

A second study (Poijula, Dyregrov, Wahlberg, & Jokelainen, 2001) examined the effects of a range of approaches to crisis intervention after six suicides at three schools in Finland. Drawn from the three schools, the sample consisted of 89 homeroom classmates of the victims. The approaches included "adequate" and "inadequate" crisis intervention strategies. Adequate strategies consisted of first talk-throughs (FTT) the day after the suicide and psychological debriefings (PD) conducted by clinical psychologists shortly after the FTT. Inadequate strategies consisted of no contingency plan and an adapted form of PD done by a teacher instead of a psychologist, a week after the suicide. At posttest, there were significant differences in the grief intensity scores between schools. In general, adequate crisis intervention reduced the risk of PTSD and high-intensity grief. The researchers concluded that although youth exposed to a classmate's suicide need adequate crisis intervention, strategies should also include careful screening, referral mechanisms, and follow-up.

The comprehensive CAYS prevention program, reviewed earlier, included a postvention component called "responding to loss" (RTL; Grossman et al., 1995). The CAYS program appeared to increase preparation for suicide, but the effects of RTL after an actual suicide are unknown.

Despite the equivocal research findings, a few practice strategies may be offered. As the contagion effect has been documented in a number of studies, the media guidelines should be followed. In addition, schools should at least adopt "adequate" crisis intervention strategies, as described earlier. Further, the presence in schools of ongoing universal preventive measures, described earlier, may mitigate the effects of suicide contagion. As

FIGURE 13.4   Media Guidelines for Clinicians and Reporters

GENERAL CONCERNS AND RECOMMENDATIONS[1]

- Suicide is often newsworthy, and it will probably be reported. Health-care providers should realize that efforts to prevent news coverage may not be effective, and their goal should be to assist news professionals in their efforts toward responsible and accurate reporting.
- "No comment" is not a productive response to media representatives who are covering a suicide story. Refusing to speak with the media does not prevent coverage of a suicide; rather, it precludes an opportunity to influence what will be contained in the report. Public officials should be prepared to provide a reasonable timetable for giving such answers or be able to direct the media to someone who can provide the answers.
- All parties should understand that a scientific basis exists for concern that news coverage of suicide may contribute to the causation of suicide.
- Some characteristics of news coverage of suicide may contribute to contagion, and other characteristics may help prevent suicide.
- Health professionals or other public officials should not try to tell reporters what to report or how to write the news regarding suicide. If the nature and apparent mechanisms of suicide contagion are understood, the news media are more likely to present the news in a manner that minimizes the likelihood of such contagion.
- Public officials and the news media should carefully consider what is to be said and reported regarding suicide. Reporters generally present the information that they are given. Impromptu comments about a suicide by a public official can result in harmful news coverage.

ASPECTS OF NEWS COVERAGE THAT CAN PROMOTE SUICIDE CONTAGION[2]

- It is misleading to present suicide as the inexplicable act of an otherwise "healthy" person. Acknowledge the multidetermined nature of suicide, particularly the underlying psychiatric problems that may not be immediately apparent to an outside observer.
- Communicate that suicide is preventable by providing models of effective treatment. Provide resources for further information and help.
- Question whether the suicide is unusual or newsworthy. People may not need to be informed about all suicides.
- Be mindful that pictures of the victim and/or grieving relatives and friends may foster a pathological identification with the victim and inadvertently glorify the death.
- Try to oversee headlines. Inappropriate headlines can detract from an otherwise helpful story.
- Limit detailed description of method, to avoid modeling behavior.

[1]Abbreviated from "Suicide Contagion and the Reporting of Suicide: Recommendations from a National Workshop." by Centers for Disease Control and Prevention, 1994, *Morbidity and Mortality Weekly Report, 43*(RR-6), 9–18.

[2]From "Practice Parameter for the Assessment and Treatment of Children and Adolescents with Suicidal Behavior," by the American Academy of Child and Adolescent Psychiatry, 2001, *Journal of the American Academy of Child and Adolescent Psychiatry, 40*(7 Supplement), p. 47S.

an example, the Centers for Disease Control recommends anticipatory planning, including establishing a committee to coordinate responses should suicide occur in a school (Centers for Disease Control and Prevention, 1992). Practitioners should continue to offer direct services, such as supportive group work (Moore & Freeman, 1995), for those close to victims of suicide. However, in view of the limited evidence for effectiveness, practitioners should evaluate outcomes as part of an evidence-based approach (Gibbs & Gambrill, 1999, pp. 235–252).

CASE STUDY
CHANTAL

Chantal, a tenth-grade student, learned that one of her friends had killed himself with his father's hunting rifle. The next day, a second student, a friend of the first victim, killed himself using a handgun. At the news of the first suicide, school administrators implemented their crisis response plan. When contacted by the media, administrators followed guidelines for the reporting of suicides and instructed the media to do the same (Figure 13.4). Administrators brought in school social workers and counselors to provide crisis counseling (e.g., Hazell & Lewin, 1993; Poijula, Wahlberg, & Dyregrov, 2001). Chantal received the news hard. She had gotten into an argument with the first victim the day before and felt enormous guilt. Then the news of the second suicide hit her. She began to withdraw herself from school. Her grades slipped. An astute teacher, who had received the school's crisis response training, reached out to her. The teacher referred Chantal to the school social worker, who contacted and involved her parents. The social worker met with Chantal, who felt relieved that she could talk with someone about her feelings. She shared that at times since the suicides she had thought about suicide. The social worker met with Chantal's parents to help them understand Chantal's feelings and behaviors. The social worker provided the parents with information about suicide warning signs and advised them to remove potentially lethal materials. She continued to meet with Chantal over the next month, observing an improvement in Chantal's feelings, attendance, and grades.

SUMMARY AND CONCLUSIONS

There is growing evidence about what places youth at risk of suicide and, conversely, what protects them. Practitioners need to be aware of the risk factors in meeting with each client (Table 13.1). In addition, social workers should learn to recognize the high-risk factors (Table 13.2, note 2) and cluster risk factors. Depressed youth should be asked whether and how often they think about suicide and whether they have ever attempted suicide (American Academy of Child and Adolescent Psychiatry, 2001). A young person who expresses thoughts or plans of suicide should be closely monitored. In particular, workers should act quickly following an initial suicide communication. In one study of youth in residential treatment, "attempts following an initial suicidal communication were likely to use more lethal methods than were attempts following multiple suicidal communications" (Handwerk,

Larzelere, Friman, & Mitchell, 1998, p. 412). Young persons with a persistent wish to die, or a clearly abnormal mental state, should be admitted for inpatient treatment (American Academy of Child and Adolescent Psychiatry, 2001).

Because not all risk factors are evident, social workers should routinely ask one question related to suicide when meeting with a client. An example might be, "Have you had thoughts about harming yourself?" (Jacobs, Brewer, & Klein-Benheim, 1999, p. 21). If answered in the affirmative, practitioners should undertake (or refer the client for) a specific suicide assessment. Although clinical judgment is often used to determine suicide risk (Jobes, Eyman, & Yufit, 1995), research has shown that it is a poor predictor of suicide potential (Furst & Huffine, 1991). Specific measures of suicidality based on risk and protective factors are available and should be utilized.

Many of the prevention and intervention studies reviewed utilized psychometrically rigorous instruments, although some used home-grown measures that make outcomes across studies difficult to compare. Direct screening programs utilize measures based on the best risk factor evidence. However, researchers need to improve the ability of those measures to reduce the high false-positive rates without compromising accuracy in detecting students at risk of suicide.

In terms of suicide prevention, universal programs emphasizing only student education have mixed results, and in some cases, negative results. A limitation of the programs is that they do not measure actual suicidal behaviors, so the relationship between knowledge and attitude gains and prevention of suicidal behaviors is unknown. The programs do not seem suitable for high-risk students, given the evidence that high-risk groups, such as previous attempters, got worse. The findings would at least suggest that indiscriminate implementation of suicide curricula in the schools is unwise. Indeed, the American Academy of Child and Adolescent Psychiatry does not recommend the approach (American Academy of Child and Adolescent Psychiatry, 2001). The most promising universal approach appears to be direct screening (Shaffer & Craft, 1999), as long as youth identified at risk of suicide receive treatment and that arrangements are made for the uninsured. Selective prevention approaches designed for high-risk subgroups (such as the Zuni Pueblo) are promising. Indicated prevention involving high-risk students suggests that brief, school-based preventive interventions can reduce suicidality.

The intervention research suggests that most of the approaches involving suicide attempters significantly reduce suicidality. Individual, group-based, and social network interventions are promising and family-based interventions have mixed findings about reducing suicidality. However, family-based interventions appear to be efficacious in reducing associated problems. At the case level, parents of children visiting health or mental health settings should be routinely offered suicide and self-injury prevention education (Kruesi et al., 1999; McManus et al., 1997). In addition, youth in treatment for attempted suicide should be continually monitored for suicide risk. In one study (Pfeffer, Peskin, & Siefker, 1992), more than half (55 percent) of the youth who attempted suicide were in treatment at the time.

Two theoretical orientations seem promising across prevention and intervention studies. Social network methods appeared to reduce suicidality among high-risk youth in the RY program (Eggert et al., 1994) and in the YNST intervention (King, 1999; King, Preuss et al., 2001). Cognitive-behavioral theory (CBT) is a frequent part of the strategies reviewed (Brent et al., 1997; Eggert et al., 1994; Harrington et al., 1998; Wood et al.,

2001), helping to contribute to successful outcomes. In addition, the component was included in interventions used across racial/ethnic groups (e.g., AI/AN: LaFromboise & Howard-Pitney, 1994, 1995; Latino: Rotheram-Borus et al., 1996, Rotheram-Borus et al., 2000). Some of the common components of CBT in these studies include monitoring and modification of automatic thoughts, assumptions, and beliefs, and acquisition of problem solving, communication, affect regulation, and social skills.

The evidence of efficacy for postvention is equivocal. Adequate crisis intervention strategies consisting of rapid response counseling by qualified mental health professionals hold promise. Media guidelines, as outlined in Figure 13.4, should be followed. Supportive individual and group services may be offered to relatives, friends, and acquaintances of the young person. However, in cases where the evidence is mixed, social workers should evaluate the outcomes against performance criteria as part of evidence-based practice (Gibbs & Gambrill, 1999, pp. 235–252). For example, a social worker could structure a single-case design (Bloom, Fischer, & Orme, 1999) to assess how an individual or group service reduces guilt or depression as measured by an appropriate clinical instrument (Corcoran & Fischer, 2000).

Methodological limitations affect many of the studies reviewed, and particularly the research on prevention and postvention. In general, the research is affected by small sample sizes resulting in too little power to detect differences between groups, weak research designs, lack of suicidality as an outcome variable, and inadequately tested measures of suicidality. In addition, researchers have undertaken disproportionately little outcome research involving diverse groups, despite high or growing rates of suicide.

In conclusion, except for a few universal prevention programs that reported ill effects, and certain postvention strategies with mixed results, most of the strategies reviewed are either promising or efficacious. In view of the negative findings, practitioners should not apply suicide prevention and postvention strategies with the notion that anything is helpful. Rather, programs should be thoughtfully implemented and monitored for effectiveness. In addition, social workers should utilize programs that are promising or efficacious. Universal direct screening, selective preventions directed at high-risk groups, and brief, school-based preventive interventions are promising. Most of the intervention strategies that involve suicide attempters significantly reduce suicidality. Adequate postvention strategies that include quick response counseling and supportive individual and group work using an evidence-based approach hold promise. The number of tested programs remains small, especially related to diverse groups, but it is growing, and offers good potential for preventing youth suicide.

DISCUSSION QUESTIONS

1. What kind of preventive education about suicide did you have in middle or high school? What were the features of the training? How would you rate it in view of the evidence about its effectiveness?

2. What elements should go into forming a suicide response team in schools? Keep in mind the following areas: coordination, security, media response, and mental health.

3. A common problem in treating suicidal youth is treatment adherence. What are ways to help retain youth in treatment?

4. Using the risk and protection evidence cited in this chapter, what elements should form a part of suicide prevention among Latinos/Hispanics? African Americans? Gay, lesbian and bisexual youth?

5. What would be a potentially effective approach to preventing suicide among youth in runaway shelters?

SUGGESTED READINGS

American Academy of Child and Adolescent Psychiatry. (2001). Summary of the practice parameters for the assessment and treatment of children and adolescents with suicidal behavior. *Journal of the American Academy of Child and Adolescent Psychiatry, 40*(4), 495–499.

Hawton, K., & Heeringen, K. V. (2000). *The international handbook of suicide and attempted suicide.* Chichester, NY: Wiley.

Ivanoff, A., & Fisher, P. (2000). Suicide and suicidal behavior. In A. Gitterman (Ed.), *Handbook of social work practice with vulnerable populations* (2nd ed., pp. 788–819). New York: Columbia University Press.

Jacobs, D. (1999). *The Harvard Medical School guide to suicide assessment and intervention.* San Francisco: Jossey-Bass.

Maris, R. W., Berman, A. L., Silverman, M. M., & Bongar, B. M. (2000). *Comprehensive textbook of suicidology.* New York: Guilford Press.

RESOURCES

American Association of Suicidology: http://www.suicidology.org/
American Foundation of Suicide Prevention: http://www.afsp.org/
Canadian Association for Suicide Prevention: http://www.suicideprevention.ca/CASP/index.html
National Organization for People of Color against Suicide: http://www.nopcas.com/
University of Oxford, Centre for Suicide Research: http://cebmh.warne.ox.ac.uk/csr/

REFERENCES

Abbey, K. J., Madsen, C. H., & Polland, R. (1989). Short-term suicide awareness curriculum. *Suicide & Life-Threatening Behavior, 19*(2), 216–227.

Alexander, J., & Parsons, B. V. (1982). *Functional family therapy.* Monterey, CA: Brooks/Cole.

American Academy of Child and Adolescent Psychiatry. (2001). Practice parameter for the assessment and treatment of children and adolescents with suicidal behavior. *Journal of the American Academy of Child and Adolescent Psychiatry, 40*(7 Supplement), 24S–51S.

Andrews, J. A., & Lewinsohn, P. M. (1992). Suicidal attempts among older adolescents: Prevalence and co-occurrence with psychiatric disorders. *Journal of the American Academy of Child and Adolescent Psychiatry, 31*(4), 655–662.

Ashworth, S., Spirito, A., Colella, A., & Drew, C. B. (1986). A pilot suicidal awareness, identification, and prevention program. *Rhode Island Medical Journal, 69*(10), 457–461.

Beck, A., & Steer, R. (1991). *Manual for the Beck Scale for Suicidal Ideation.* San Antonio, TX: Psychological Corporation.

Beck, A. T. (1979). *Cognitive therapy of depression.* New York: Guilford Press.

Bloom, M., Fischer, J., & Orme, J. G. (1999). *Evaluating practice: Guidelines for the accountable professional* (3rd ed.). Boston: Allyn and Bacon.

Brent, D. A., Baugher, M., Bridge, J., Chen, T., & Chiappetta, L. (1999). Age- and sex-related risk factors for adolescent suicide. *Journal of the American Academy of Child and Adolescent Psychiatry, 38*(12), 1497–1505.

Brent, D. A., Holder, D., Kolko, D., Birmaher, B., Baugher, M., Roth, C., et al. (1997). A clinical psychotherapy trial for adolescent depression comparing cognitive, family, and supportive therapy. *Archives of General Psychiatry, 54*(9), 877–885.

Brent, D. A., Perper, J. A., Allman, C. J., Moritz, G. M., Wartella, M. E., & Zelenak, J. P. (1991). The presence and accessibility of firearms in the homes of adolescent suicides. A case-control study. *Journal of the American Medical Association, 266*(21), 2989–2995.

Brent, D. A., Perper, J. A., Goldstein, C. E., Kolko, D. J., Allan, M. J., Allman, C. J., et al. (1988). Risk factors for adolescent suicide. A comparison of adolescent suicide victims with suicidal inpatients. *Archives of General Psychiatry, 45*(6), 581–588.

Brent, D. A., Perper, J. A., Moritz, G., Allman, C., Friend, A., Roth, C., et al. (1993). Psychiatric risk factors for adolescent suicide: A case-control study. *Journal of the American Academy of Child and Adolescent Psychiatry, 32*(3), 521–529.

Brent, D. A., Perper, J. A., Moritz, G., Baugher, M., & Allman, C. (1993). Suicide in adolescents with no apparent psychopathology. *Journal of the American Academy of Child and Adolescent Psychiatry, 32*(3), 494–500.

Brent, D. A., Perper, J. A., Moritz, G., Baugher, M., Roth, C., Balach, L., et al. (1993). Stressful life events, psychopathology, and adolescent suicide: A case control study. *Suicide & Life Threatening Behavior, 23*(3), 179–187.

Brent, D. A., Perper, J. A., Moritz, G., Baugher, M., Schweers, J., & Roth, C. (1993). Firearms and adolescent suicide. A community case-control study. *American Journal of Diseases of Children, 147*(10), 1066–1071.

Burns, J., & Patton, G. (2000). Preventive interventions for youth suicide: A risk factor based approach. *Australian and New Zealand Journal of Psychiatry, 34*(3), 388–407.

Centers for Disease Control and Prevention. (1992). *Youth suicide prevention programs: A resource guide.* Atlanta, GA: Centers for Disease Control and Prevention.

Centers for Disease Control and Prevention. (1998). Suicide among Black Youths—United States, 1980–1995. *Morbidity and Mortality Weekly Report, 47*(10), 193–196.

Corcoran, K., & Fischer, J. (2000). *Measures for clinical practice: A sourcebook* (3rd ed.). New York: Free Press.

Cotgrove, A. J., Zirinsky, L., Black, D., & Weston, D. (1995). Secondary prevention of attempted suicide in adolescence. *Journal of Adolescence, 18*(5), 569–577.

D'Augelli, A. R., & Hershberger, S. L. (1993). Lesbian, gay, and bisexual youth in community settings: Personal challenges and mental health problems. *American Journal of Community Psychology, 21*(4), 421–448.

Davidson, M. W., & Range, L. M. (1999). Are teachers of children and young adolescents responsive to suicide prevention training modules? Yes. *Death Studies, 23*(1), 61–71.

Eggert, L. L., Thompson, E. A., Herting, J. R., & Nicholas, L. J. (1994). Prevention research program: Reconnecting at-risk youth. *Issues in Mental Health Nursing, 15*(2), 107–135.

Eggert, L. L., Thompson, E. A., Herting, J. R., & Nicholas, L. J. (1995). Reducing suicide potential among high-risk youth: Tests of a school-based prevention program. *Suicide & Life-Threatening Behavior, 25*(2), 276–296.

Feldman, M., & Wilson, A. (1997). Adolescent suicidality in urban minorities and its relationship to conduct disorders, depression, and separation anxiety. *Journal of the American Academy of Child and Adolescent Psychiatry, 36*(1), 75–84.

Fendrich, M., Mackesy-Amiti, M. E., & Kruesi, M. (2000). A mass-distributed CD-ROM for school-based suicide prevention. *Crisis, 21*(3), 135–140.

Fraser, M. W. (Ed.). (1997). *Risk and resilience in childhood: An ecological perspective.* Washington, DC: NASW Press.

Furst, J., & Huffine, C. L. (1991). Assessing vulnerability to suicide. *Suicide & Life-Threatening Behavior, 21*(4), 329–344.

Garofalo, R., Wolf, R., Kessel, S., Palfrey, J., & DuRant, R. (1998). The association between health risk behaviors and sexual orientation among a school-based sample of adolescents. *Pediatrics, 101*(5), 895–902.

Garrison, C. Z., McKeown, R. E., Valois, R. F., & Vincent, M. L. (1993). Aggression, substance use, and suicidal behaviors in high school students. *American Journal of Public Health, 83*(2), 179–184.

Gibbs, J. T. (1997). African-American suicide: A cultural paradox. *Suicide & Life-Threatening Behavior, 27*(1), 68–79.

Gibbs, L. E., & Gambrill, E. D. (1999). *Critical thinking for social workers: Exercises for the helping professions.* Thousand Oaks, CA.: Pine Forge Press.

Goldston, D. B. (2000). *Assessment of suicidal behaviors and risk among children and adolescents.* Bethesda, MD: National Institute of Mental Health.

Gould, M. S., Fisher, P., Parides, M., Flory, M., & Shaffer, D. (1996). Psychosocial risk factors of child and adolescent completed suicide. *Archives of General Psychiatry, 53*(12), 1155–1162.

Grossman, J. A., Hirsch, J., Goldenberg, D., Libby, S., Fendrich, M., Mackesy-Amiti, M. E., et al. (1995). Strategies for school-based response to loss: Proactive training and postvention consultation. *Crisis, 16*(1), 18–26.

Grossman, J. A., & Kruesi, M. J. (2000). Innovative approaches to youth suicide prevention: An update of issues and research findings. In R. Maris, S. Cannetto, J. Macintosh, & M. Silverman (Eds.), *Review of Suicidology* (pp. 170–201). New York: Guilford Press.

Handwerk, M. L., Larzelere, R. E., Friman, P. C., & Mitchell, A. M. (1998). The relationship between lethality of attempted suicide and prior suicidal communications in a sample of residential youth. *Journal of Adolescence, 21*(4), 407–414.

Harrington, R., Kerfoot, M., Dyer, E., McNiven, F., Gill, J., Harrington, V., et al. (1998). Randomized trial of a home-based family intervention for children who have deliberately poisoned themselves. *Journal of the American Academy of Child and Adolescent Psychiatry, 37*(5), 512–518.

Hazell, P., & Lewin, T. (1993). An evaluation of postvention following adolescent suicide. *Suicide & Life-Threatening Behavior, 23*(2), 101–109.

Hershberger, S., & D'Augelli, A. (1995). The impact of victimization on the mental health and suicidality of lesbian, gay, and bisexual youths. *Developmental Psychology, 31*, 65–74.

Hershberger, S., Pilkington, N., & D'Augelli, A. (1997). Predictors of suicide attempts among gay, lesbian, and bisexual youth. *Journal of Adolescent Research, 12*(40), 477–497.

Holinger, P. (1994). Suicide: Intervention and prevention. In P. Holinger, D. Offer, J. Barter, & C. Bell (Eds.), *Suicide and homicide among adolescents* (pp. 103–149). New York: Guilford Press.

Hussey, J. M. (1997). The effects of race, socioeconomic status, and household structure on injury mortality in children and young adults. *Maternal and Child Health Journal, 1*(4), 217–227.

Institute of Medicine. (1994). *Reducing risks for mental disorders: Frontiers for preventive intervention research.* Washington, DC: National Academy Press.

Jacobs, D., Brewer, M., & Klein-Benheim, M. (1999). Suicide assessment: An overview and recommended protocol. In D. G. Jacobs (Ed.), *The Harvard Medical School guide to suicide assessment and prevention* (pp. 3–39). San Francisco: Jossey-Bass.

Jobes, D. A., Eyman, J. R., & Yufit, R. I. (1995). How clinicians assess suicide risk in adolescents and adults. *Crisis Intervention and Time-Limited Treatment, 2*(1), 1–12.

Kalafat, J., & Elias, M. (1994). An evaluation of a school-based suicide awareness intervention. *Suicide & Life-Threatening Behavior, 24*(3), 224–233.

Kalafat, J., & Gagliano, C. (1996). The use of simulations to assess the impact of an adolescent suicide response curriculum. *Suicide & Life-Threatening Behavior, 26*(4), 359–364.

King, C. A. (1999). Connect Five: An innovative youth suicide prevention strategy. *News Link, American Association of Suicidology, 25*(1), 11–12.

King, C. A., Preuss, L., & Kramer, A. (2001). *Efficacy of Youth-Nominated Support Team (YST) for suicidal adolescents: Impacts on adherence to psychopharmacology treatment and psychiatric outcome.* Retrieved February 25, 2002, from http://www.nimh.nih.gov/ncdeu/abstracts2001/ncdeu2059.cfm.

King, K. A., & Smith, J. (2000). Project SOAR: A training program to increase school counselors' knowledge and confidence regarding suicide prevention and intervention. *The Journal of School Health, 70*(10), 402–407.

King, R. A., Schwab-Stone, M., Flisher, A. J., Greenwald, S., Kramer, R. A., Goodman, S. H., et al. (2001). Psychosocial and risk behavior correlates of youth suicide attempts and suicidal ideation. *Journal of the American Academy of Child and Adolescent Psychiatry, 40*(7), 837–846.

Klingman, A., & Hochdorf, Z. (1993). Coping with distress and self harm: The impact of a primary prevention program among adolescents. *Journal of Adolescence, 16*(2), 121–140.

Kovacs, M. (1997). *The Interview Schedule for Children and Adolescents (ISCA): Current and Lifetime (ISCA—C & L) and Current and Interim (ISCA—C & I) versions.* Unpublished instruments, University of Pittsburgh School of Medicine, Western Psychiatric Institute and Clinics, Pittsburgh, PA.

Kovacs, M., Goldston, D., & Gatsonis, C. (1993). Suicidal behaviors and childhood-onset depressive disorders: A longitudinal investigation. *Journal of the American Academy of Child and Adolescent Psychiatry, 32*(1), 8–20.

Kruesi, M. J., Grossman, J., Pennington, J. M., Woodward, P. J., Duda, D., & Hirsch, J. G. (1999). Suicide and violence prevention: Parent education in the emergency department. *Journal of the American Academy of Child and Adolescent Psychiatry, 38*(3), 250–255.

LaFromboise, T. D., & Howard-Pitney, B. (1994). The Zuni Life Skills Development curriculum: A collaborative approach to curriculum development. *American Indian & Alaska Native Mental Health Research, 4*(Mono), 98–121.

LaFromboise, T. D., & Howard-Pitney, B. (1995). The Zuni life skills development curriculum: Description and evaluation of a suicide prevention program. *Journal of Counseling Psychology, 42*(4), 479–486.

Lester, D. (1997). The effectiveness of suicide prevention centers: a review. *Suicide & Life-Threatening Behavior, 27*(3), 304–310.

Lewinsohn, P. M., Rohde, P., Seeley, J. R., & Baldwin, C. L. (2001). Gender differences in suicide attempts from adolescence to young adulthood. *Journal of the American Academy of Child and Adolescent Psychiatry, 40*(4), 427–434.

Linehan, M. M., Armstrong, H. E., Suarez, A., Allmon, D., & Heard, H. L. (1991). Cognitive-behavioral treatment of chronically parasuicidal borderline patients. *Archives of General Psychiatry, 48*(12), 1060–1064.

Macgowan, M. J. (in press). Suicidal behaviors among youth. In M. Fraser (Ed.), *Risk and resilience in childhood* (2nd ed.). Washington, DC: NASW Press.

Marttunen, M. J., Aro, H. M., & Lonnqvist, J. K. (1993). Precipitant stressors in adolescent suicide. *Journal of the American Academy of Child and Adolescent Psychiatry, 32*(6), 1178–1183.

Mauk, G., & Rogers, P. (1996). Building bridges over troubled waters: School-based postvention with adolescent survivors of peer suicide. *Crisis Intervention, 1*(2), 103–123.

McDaniel, J. S., Purcell, D. W., & D'Augelli, A. R. (2001). The relationship between sexual orientation and risk for suicide: Research findings and future directions for research and prevention. *Suicide & Life-Threatening Behavior, 31*(1), 84–105.

McManus, B. L., Kruesi, M. J., Dontes, A. E., Defazio, C. R., Piotrowski, J. T., & Woodward, P. J. (1997). Child and adolescent suicide attempts: An opportunity for emergency departments to provide injury prevention education. *American Journal of Emergency Medicine, 15*(4), 357–360.

Middlebrook, D. L., LeMaster, P. L., Beals, J., Novins, D. K., & Manson, S. M. (2001). Suicide prevention in American Indian and Alaska Native communities: A critical review of programs. *Suicide & Life-Threatening Behavior, 31* (Supplement), 132–149.

Moore, M. M., & Freeman, S. J. (1995). Counseling survivors of suicide: Implications for group postvention. *Journal for Specialists in Group Work, 20*(1), 40–47.

Morrison, J. (1987). Youth suicide: An intervention strategy. *Social Work, 32*(6), 536–537.

Móscicki, E. K. (1999). Epidemiology of suicide. In D. G. Jacobs (Ed.), *The Harvard Medical School guide to suicide assessment and prevention* (pp. 40–51). San Francisco: Jossey-Bass.

National Center for Injury Prevention and Control. (2002). *Customized leading cause of death report, 1999, all races, both sexes.* Retrieved March 2, 2002, from http://webapp.cdc.gov/sasweb/ncipc/leadcaus.html.

Neeleman, J., Wessely, S., & Lewis, G. (1998). Suicide acceptability in African- and white Americans: The role of religion. *Journal of Nervous and Mental Diseases, 186*(1), 12–16.

Nelson, F. L. (1987). Evaluation of a youth suicide prevention school program. *Adolescence, 22*(88), 813–825.

Newman, E. C. (2000). Group crisis intervention in a school setting following an attempted suicide. *International Journal of Emergency Mental Health, 2*(2), 97–100.

O'Donnell, C. R. (1995). Firearm deaths among children and youth. *The American Psychologist, 50*(9), 771–776.

Orbach, I., & Bar-Joseph, H. (1993). The impact of a suicide prevention program for adolescents on suicidal tendencies, hopelessness, ego identity, and coping. *Suicide & Life-Threatening Behavior, 23*(2), 120–129.

Overholser, J. C., Hemstreet, A. H., Spirito, A., & Vyse, S. (1989). Suicide awareness programs in the schools: Effects of gender and personal experience. *Journal of the American Academy of Child and Adolescent Psychiatry, 28*(6), 925–930.

Pfeffer, C. R., Conte, H., Plutchik, R., & Jerrett, I. (1979). Suicidal behavior in latency age children: An empirical study. *Journal of the American Academy of Child Psychiatry, 18,* 679–692.

Pfeffer, C. R., Klerman, G. L., Hurt, S. W., Kakuma, T., Peskin, J. R., & Siefker, C. A. (1993). Suicidal children grow up: Rates and psychosocial risk factors for suicide attempts during follow-up. *Journal of the American Academy of Child and Adolescent Psychiatry, 32*(1), 106–113.

Pfeffer, C. R., Peskin, J. R., & Siefker, C. A. (1992). Suicidal children grow up: Psychiatric treatment during follow-up period. *Journal of the American Academy of Child and Adolescent Psychiatry, 31*(4), 679–685.

Pharris, M. D., Resnick, M. D., & Blum, R. W. (1997). Protecting against hopelessness and suicidality in sexually abused American Indian adolescents. *The Journal of Adolescent Health, 21*(6), 400–406.

Piacentini, J., Rotheram-Borus, M. J., Gillis, J. R., Graae, F., Trautman, P., Cantwell, C., et al. (1995). Demographic predictors of treatment attendance among adolescent suicide attempters. *Journal of Consulting and Clinical Psychology, 63*(3), 469–473.

Poijula, S., Dyregrov, A., Wahlberg, K. E., & Jokelainen, J. (2001). Reactions to adolescent suicide and crisis intervention in three secondary schools. *International Journal of Emergency Mental Health, 3*(2), 97–106.

Poijula, S., Wahlberg, K. E., & Dyregrov, A. (2001). Adolescent suicide and suicide contagion in three secondary schools. *International Journal of Emergency Mental Health, 3*(3), 163–168.

Potter, L., Rosenberg, M., & Hammond, W. (1998). Suicide in youth: A public health framework. *Journal of the American Academy of Child and Adolescent Psychiatry, 37*(5), 484–487.

Proctor, C. D., & Groze, V. K. (1994). Risk factors for suicide among gay, lesbian, and bisexual youths. *Social Work, 39*(5), 504–513.

Randell, B. P., Eggert, L. L., & Pike, K. C. (2001). Immediate post intervention effects of two brief youth suicide prevention interventions. *Suicide & Life-Threatening Behavior, 31*(1), 41–61.

Range, L. M., & Knott, E. C. (1997). Twenty suicide assessment instruments: Evaluation and recommendations. *Death Studies, 21,* 25–58.

Reich, W. (2000). Diagnostic Interview for Children and Adolescents (DICA). *Journal of the American Academy of Child and Adolescent Psychiatry, 39,* 59–66.

Remafedi, G. (1999). Suicide and sexual orientation: Nearing the end of controversy? *Archives of General Psychiatry, 56*(10), 885–886.

Renaud, J., Brent, D. A., Birmaher, B., Chiappetta, L., & Bridge, J. (1999). Suicide in adolescents with disruptive disorders. *Journal of the American Academy of Child and Adolescent Psychiatry, 38*(7), 846–851.

Reynolds, W. M. (1988). *Suicidal Ideation Questionnaire, professional manual.* Odessa, FL: Psychological Assessment Resources.

Robin, A. L., & Foster, S. L. (1989). *Negotiating parent-adolescent conflict: A behavioral-family systems approach.* New York: Guilford Press.

Rotheram-Borus, M. J., Piacentini, J., Cantwell, C., Belin, T. R., & Song, J. (2000). The 18-month impact of an emergency room intervention for adolescent female suicide attempters. *Journal of Consulting and Clinical Psychology, 68*(6), 1081–1093.

Rotheram-Borus, M. J., Piacentini, J., Miller, S., Graae, F., & Castro-Blanco, D. (1994). Brief cognitive-behavioral treatment for adolescent suicide attempters and their families. *Journal of the American Academy of Child and Adolescent Psychiatry, 33*(4), 508–517.

Rotheram-Borus, M. J., Piacentini, J., Van Rossem, R., Graae, F., Cantwell, C., Castro-Blanco, D., et al. (1996). Enhancing treatment adherence with a specialized emergency room program for adolescent suicide attempters. *Journal of the American Academy of Child and Adolescent Psychiatry, 35*(5), 654–663.

Russell, S. T., & Joyner, K. (2001). Adolescent sexual orientation and suicide risk: Evidence from a national study. *American Journal of Public Health, 91*(8), 1276–1281.

Safren, S. A., & Heimberg, R. G. (1999). Depression, hopelessness, suicidality, and related factors in sexual minority and heterosexual adolescents. *Journal of Consulting and Clinical Psychology, 67*(6), 859–866.

Shaffer, D., & Craft, L. (1999). Methods of adolescent suicide prevention. *The Journal of Clinical Psychiatry, 60* (2 Supplement), 70–74.

Shaffer, D., Fisher, P., Lucas, C., Dulcan, M., & Schwab-Stone, M. (2000). NIMH Diagnostic Interview Schedule for Children, Version IV (NIMH DISC-IV): Description, differences from previous versions, and reliability of some common diagnoses. *Journal of the American Academy of Child and Adolescent Psychiatry, 39*, 28–38.

Shaffer, D., Garland, A., Gould, M., Fisher, P., & Trautman, P. (1988). Preventing teenage suicide: A critical review. *Journal of the American Academy of Child and Adolescent Psychiatry, 27*(6), 675–687.

Shaffer, D., Garland, A., Vieland, V., Underwood, M., & Busner, C. (1991). The impact of curriculum-based suicide prevention programs for teenagers. *Journal of the American Academy of Child and Adolescent Psychiatry, 30*(4), 588–596.

Shaffer, D., Gould, M., Fisher, P., Trautman, P., Moreau, D., Kleinman, M., et al. (1996). Psychiatric diagnosis in child and adolescent suicide. *Archives of General Psychiatry, 53*(4), 339–348.

Shaffer, D., Gould, M., & Hicks, R. (1994). Worsening suicide rate in black teenagers. *American Journal of Psychiatry, 151*(12), 1810–1812.

Shaffer, D., Vieland, V., Garland, A., Rojas, M., Underwood, M., & Busner, C. (1990). Adolescent suicide attempters. Response to suicide-prevention programs. *Journal of the American Medical Association, 264*(24), 3151–3155.

Shah, S., Hoffman, R., Wake, L., & Marine, W. (2000). Adolescent suicide and household access to firearms in Colorado: Results of a case-control study. *The Journal of Adolescent Health, 26*(3), 157–163.

Sherrill, J., & Kovacs, M. (2000). The Interview Schedule for Children and Adolescents (ISCA). *Journal of the American Academy of Child and Adolescent Psychiatry, 39*, 67–75.

Smith, K., Conroy, R., & Ehler, B. (1984). Lethality of Suicide Attempt Rating Scale. *Suicide & Life Threatening Behavior, 14*, 214–242.

Spirito, A., Overholser, J., Ashworth, S., Morgan, J., & Benedict-Drew, C. (1988). Evaluation of a suicide awareness curriculum for high school students. *Journal of the American Academy of Child and Adolescent Psychiatry, 27*(6), 705–711.

Spirito, A., Plummer, B., Gispert, M., & Levy, S. (1992). Adolescent suicide attempts: Outcomes at follow-up. *American Journal of Orthopsychiatry, 62*(3), 464–468.

Thompson, E. A., Eggert, L. L., Randell, B. P., & Pike, K. C. (2001). Evaluation of indicated suicide risk prevention approaches for potential high school dropouts. *American Journal of Public Health, 91*(5), 742–752.

Trautman, P. D., Stewart, N., & Morishima, A. (1993). Are adolescent suicide attempters noncompliant with outpatient care? *Journal of the American Academy of Child and Adolescent Psychiatry, 32*(1), 89–94.

U.S. Department of Health and Human Services. (2001). *National strategy for suicide prevention: Goals and objectives for action.* Rockville, MD: U.S. Department of Health and Human Services.

U.S. Public Health Service. (1999). *The Surgeon General's call to action to prevent suicide: At a glance: Suicide among the young.* Retrieved February 25, 2002, from http://www.surgeongeneral.gov/library/calltoaction/fact3.htm.

University of Washington School of Nursing. (2002). *Reconnecting Youth Prevention Research Program.* Retrieved January 3, 2002, from http://www.son.washington.edu/departments/pch/ry/about.asp.

Vallianatos, V. (2001, January). Support plan links suicidal youth to help. *NASW News.*

Vieland, V., Whittle, B., Garland, A., Hicks, R., & Shaffer, D. (1991). The impact of curriculum-based suicide prevention programs for teenagers: An 18-month follow-up. *Journal of the American Academy of Child and Adolescent Psychiatry. 30*(5), 811–815.

Wagner, B., Cole, R., & Schwartzman, P. (1995). Psychosocial correlates of suicide attempts among junior and senior high school youth. *Suicide & Life Threatening Behavior, 25*(3), 358–372.

Wood, A., Trainor, G., Rothwell, J., Moore, A., & Harrington, R. (2001). Randomized trial of group therapy for repeated deliberate self-harm in adolescents. *Journal of the American Academy of Child and Adolescent Psychiatry. 40*(11), 1246–1253.

Young, S. E., Mikulich, S. K., Goodwin, M. B., Hardy, J., Martin, C. L., Zoccolillo, M. S., et al. (1995). Treated delinquent boys' substance use: Onset, pattern, relationship to conduct and mood disorders. *Drug and Alcohol Dependence, 37*(2), 149–162.

Zayas, L. H. (1987). Toward an understanding of suicide risks in young Hispanic females. *Journal of Adolescent Research, 2*(1), 1–11.

CHAPTER 14

WHAT CAN BE DONE TO PREVENT AND ASSIST SCHOOL DROPOUTS?

RUSSELL W. RUMBERGER

University of California, Santa Barbara

Despite the national commitment to reducing high school dropout rates, the high school graduation rate has failed to improve over the last decade. This chapter examines why students drop out of school and what can be done about it. It examines why students drop out, focusing on both individual and institutional factors, and how these factors can or cannot explain differences in dropout rates among social groups. It then examines promising interventions that can address the problem, providing examples of both programmatic and systemic solutions, and discusses the extent to which policy can promote them. Finally, it provides a list of questions for further discussion and some additional readings.

Reducing the number of dropouts has been a national policy concern in the United States for over a decade. In 1990, the nation's governors and the president adopted six national education goals for the year 2000 (U.S. Department of Education, 1990). Goal 2 was to increase the high school graduation rate to 90 percent, with a related objective to eliminate the existing gap in high school graduation rates between minority and nonminority students. To help achieve these goals, in 1994, Congress enacted the Goals 2000: Educate America Act, which has awarded over $1.5 billion to participating states and districts to support communities in the development and implementation of education reforms (U.S. Department of Education, 1998, Appendix A). In addition, numerous programs at the national, state, and local levels have been established to help reduce the number of students who drop out of school.

Despite this increased attention and additional resources, the high school graduation rate has not only failed to improve but it has actually become worse. Between 1988, the year before the education goals were established, and 1999, the high school graduation rate among 18- to 24-year-olds declined from 80 percent to 77 percent (U.S. Department of Education, 2000a, Table 6). Yet, during this period, the proportion of youth completing high school actually remained steady because an increasing number of students completed high school by getting a GED or through other alternative means rather than earning a traditional high school diploma. In 1988, 4 percent of 18- to 24-year-olds completed high school by earning a GED, whereas in 1999, 9 percent did so. The reason the method of high school completion may be important is because some recent studies have questioned whether the economic payoff to a high school equivalency is comparable to a traditional high school diploma (Cameron & Heckman, 1993; Murnane, Willet, & Boudett, 1995, 1997; Murnane, Willet, & Tyler, 2000; Rumberger & Lamb, in press; Tyler, Murnane, & Willet, 2000). This trend may accelerate due to recent policies to increase high school exit requirements.

Each year, about 500,000 youths, or about 5 percent of all high school students, drop out of school (U.S. Department of Education, 2000a, Table 1). But over their entire educational careers, a substantially higher proportion of students quit school sometime over their educational careers. One longitudinal study of young men who were 14 to 21 years of age in 1979 estimated that 37 percent had quit high school for at least a three-month period, even though in 1990, when the young men were 25 to 32 years old, only 14 percent were classified as high school dropouts (Klerman & Karoly, 1994). Another longitudinal study of students who were eighth-graders in 1988 found that 21 percent had dropped out school at some point since eighth grade, even though only 12 percent—roughly half of that number—had not completed high school by 1994 (Rumberger & Lamb, in press).

Dropout rates are particularly high for some racial and ethnic minorities. In 1999, the dropout rates among persons 16 to 24 years old were 7.3 percent for white non-Hispanics, 12.6 for black non-Hispanics, and 28.6 for Hispanics (U.S. Department of Education, 2000a, Table 3). The high dropout rate among Hispanics has been a particular concern for the federal government, which recently issued a report on this problem (Secada et al., 1998).[1]

The next section of this chapter examines why students drop out, focusing on both individual and institutional factors, and how these factors can or cannot explain differences in dropout rates among social groups. Next, the chapter first examines promising interventions that can address the problem, providing examples of both programmatic and systemic solutions, and then discusses the extent to which policy can promote them. The final section of the chapter provides a list of questions for further discussion and some additional readings.

WHY STUDENTS DROP OUT OF SCHOOL

Understanding why students drop out of school is the key to addressing this major educational problem. However, identifying the causes of dropping out is extremely difficult to do because, like other forms of educational achievement (e.g., test scores), it is influenced by an array of proximal and distal factors related to both the individual student and to the family, school, and community settings in which the student lives.

The complexity of this phenomenon is illustrated by the variety of reasons that dropouts report for leaving school. Dropouts from the National Education Longitudinal Study of 1988, which tracked more than 16,000 eighth-graders through high school, reported a wide variety of reasons for leaving school: school-related reasons were mentioned by 77 percent,

---

1. Although dropout rates for Hispanics are indeed high, more than 40 percent of all young Hispanics are foreign-born and more than 40 percent of foreign-born Hispanics never attended school in the United States (McMillen et al., 1997, Table 16). In 1995, the last time these figures were computed, dropout rates among U.S.-born Hispanics was 18 percent, compared to 12 percent for U.S.-born black non-Hispanics, and 9 percent for white non-Hispanics.

family-related reasons were mentioned by 34 percent, and work-related reasons were mentioned by 32 percent (Berktold et al., 1998, Table 6). The most specific reasons were "did not like school" (46 percent), "failing school" (39 percent), "could not get along with teachers" (29 percent), and "got a job" (27 percent). But these reasons do not reveal the underlying causes of why students quit school, particularly those causes or factors that long ago may have contributed to students' attitudes, behaviors, and school performance immediately preceding their decision to leave school. Moreover, if many factors contribute to this phenomenon over a long period of time, it is virtually impossible to demonstrate a causal connection between any single factor and the decision to quit school. Instead, scholars are limited to developing theories and testing conceptual models based on a variety of social science disciplines and using a variety of qualitative and quantitative research methods.

A number of theories have been advanced to understand the specific phenomenon of dropping out (e.g., Finn, 1989; Wehlage et al., 1989). Other theories have been used to explain dropping out as part of larger phenomenon of student achievement (e.g., Coleman, 1988; Newmann et al., 1992; Ogbu, 1992).[2] These theories come from a number of social science disciplines—including psychology, sociology, anthropology, and economics—and identify a range of specific factors related to dropping out. Drawing on these theories, I present two conceptual frameworks that focus on two different perspectives for understanding this phenomenon. One framework is based on an individual perspective that focuses on individual factors associated with dropping out; the other is based on an institutional perspective that focuses on the contextual factors found in students' families, schools, communities, and peers. Both frameworks are useful and, indeed, necessary to understand this complex phenomenon. After presenting each framework and reviewing briefly some empirical evidence that highlights some of the most important factors within each framework, I discuss the extent to which these frameworks can be used to explain differences in dropout rates among social groups, particularly racial and ethnic minorities. In most cases, the factors identified in this review are derived from multivariate statistical models that control for a number of other predictive factors, which suggests that the identified factor has a direct, causal connection with dropping out independent of other causal factors. Yet, statistical models can only suggest but not prove causal connections, so it is better to think of these factors as predictive of dropping out or increasing the risk of dropping out.

Individual Perspective

The first framework is based on an individual perspective that focuses on the attributes of students—such as their values, attitudes, and behaviors—and how these attributes contribute to their decisions to quit school. The conceptual framework views the attitudes and behaviors of students through a particular concept—*student engagement*. Several theories have been developed in recent years that all suggest dropping out of school is but the final

---

2. The extent to which general theories of student achievement can be used to explain the specific phenomenon of school dropout is rarely questioned. Yet theories that may be useful in explaining differences in achievement outcomes, such as test scores or grades, may not necessarily be useful in explaining why some students drop out of school, especially to the extent that dropping out is unrelated to academic achievement as dropout theories suggest.

stage in a dynamic and cumulative process of disengagement (Newmann et al., 1992; Wehlage et al., 1989) or withdrawal (Finn, 1989) from school. Although there are some differences among these theories, they all suggest that there are two dimensions to engagement: *academic engagement,* or engagement in learning, and *social engagement,* or engagement in social dimensions of schooling (Wehlage refers to this as "school membership"). Engagement is reflected in students' attitudes and behaviors with respect to both the formal aspects of school (e.g., classrooms and school activities) and the informal ones (e.g., peer and adult relationships). Both dimensions of engagement can influence the decision to withdraw from school. For example, students may withdraw from school because they quit doing their schoolwork (academic engagement) or because they do not get along with their peers (social engagement).[3]

The framework further posits that engagement and educational achievement are influenced by students' background prior to entering school, including their educational aspirations and past achievement. Finally, the framework suggests reciprocal relationships among these factors that change over time: changes in engagement, stability (dropout and school mobility), and achievement, as students' progress through school affect later attitudes, social relationships, and school experiences. Thus, within this framework, student stability is viewed as both a cause and a consequence of engagement in school.

A large body of empirical research has identified many individual predictors of dropping out that are consistent with this framework. Only some of the most important ones will be reviewed here.[4]

The first group of factors has to do with the relationship between dropping out and other dimensions of educational achievement. One of those dimensions is student mobility. A growing body of research suggests that both residential mobility (changing residences) and school mobility (changing schools) increases the risk of dropping out of high school (Astone & McLanahan, 1994; Haveman et al., 1991; Rumberger, 1995; Rumberger & Larson, 1998; Swanson & Schneider, 1999; Teachman et al., 1996). Some scholars have argued that student mobility represents a less severe form of student disengagement or withdrawal from school (Lee & Burkam, 1992; Rumberger & Larson, 1998). In fact, one study found that the majority of high school dropouts changed high schools at least once before withdrawing, whereas the majority of high school graduates did not (Rumberger et al., 1998). Another factor is academic achievement. Numerous studies have found that poor academic achievement is a strong predictor of dropping out (Ekstrom et al., 1986; Goldschmidt & Wang, 1999; Rumberger, 1995; Rumberger & Larson, 1998; Swanson & Schneider, 1999; Wehlage & Rutter, 1986).

Student engagement has also been shown to predict dropping out even after controlling for the effects of academic achievement and student background. Absenteeism, the most common indicator of overall student engagement, and student discipline problems

---

3. Because engagement concerns both the academic and social aspects of schooling, it provides a more comprehensive concept than some others, such as motivation or effort, that focus on only the academic aspect of schooling.

4. As with all social science research, demonstrating a statistically significant relationship between a predictor variable and dropping out does not establish a causal relationship. Nor does it mean that all students with that risk factor drop out, or that students who don't have the risk factor don't drop out. For example, not all students from low socioeconomic backgrounds drop out, whereas some students from high socioeconomic backgrounds do drop out.

are both associated with dropping out (Bachman et al., 1971; Carbonaro, 1998; Ekstrom et al., 1986; Goldschmidt & Wang, 1999; Rumberger, 1995; Rumberger & Larson, 1998; Swanson & Schneider, 1999; Wehlage & Rutter, 1986). These studies support the idea that dropping out is influenced by both the social and academic experiences of students. In other words, dropping out is not simply a result of academic failure.

Finally, a number of student background characteristics have been shown to predict withdrawal from school. Several demographic variables have been examined in the literature: gender, race and ethnicity, immigration status, and language background (Fernandez, Paulsen, & Hirano-Nakanishi, 1989; Goldschmidt & Wang, 1999; Rumberger, 1983, 1995; Steinberg, Blinde, & Chan, 1984; Velez, 1989). These factors are discussed in more detail later. Other individual attributes have also been shown to predict school dropout, including low educational and occupational aspirations and teenage parenthood (Ekstrom et al., 1986; Rumberger, 1995; Rumberger & Larson, 1998; Newmann et al., 1992; Pirog & Magee, 1997; Swanson & Schneider, 1999; Wehlage & Rutter, 1986).

As mentioned earlier, the framework is based on the idea that student disengagement and withdrawal from school is a long-term process that can be influenced by students' early school experiences. Several studies, based on long-term studies of cohorts of students, have examined the predictors of dropping out from as early as first grade (Alexander et al., 1997; Barrington & Hendricks, 1989; Cairns et al., 1989; Ensminger & Slusacick, 1992; Garnier, Stein, & Jacobs, 1997; Morris, Ehren, & Lenz, 1991; Roderick, 1993). These studies found that early academic achievement and engagement (e.g., attendance, misbehavior) in elementary and middle school predicted eventual withdrawal from high school.

One additional indicator of prior school performance has received considerable attention of late—retention. Historically, a large number of students are retained in school each year. Data from National Education Longitudinal Study suggest that about one in five eighth-graders in 1988 had been retained at least once since first grade (Rumberger, 1995, Table 1). As more states end social promotion and institute high school exit examination, this number will no doubt rise. Already in Texas, which has instituted both policies, one out of every six ninth-grade students in 1996–97 was retained (Texas Education Agency, 1998, Appendix A). Although some recent studies have suggested that retention may have some positive effects on academic achievement (Alexander et al., 1994; Roderick et al., 1999), virtually all the empirical studies to date suggest that retention, even in lower elementary grades, significantly increases the likelihood of dropping out (Goldschmidt & Wang, 1999; Grisson & Shepard, 1989; Jimerson, 1999; Kaufman & Bradby, 1992; Roderick, 1994; Roderick, Nagaoka, Bacon, & Easton, 2000; Rumberger, 1995; Rumberger & Larson, 1998). For example, Rumberger (1995) found that students who were retained in grades 1 to 8 were four times more likely to drop out between grades 8 and 10 than students who were not retained, even after controlling for socioeconomic status, eighth-grade school performance, and a host of background and school factors.

Institutional Perspective

Whereas first framework can provide a way to understand dropping out from an individual perspective, individual attitudes and behaviors are shaped by the institutional settings where people live. This latter perspective is common in such social science disciplines as economics, sociology, and anthropology. Historically, it has been less common in psychology, which has focused more on human behavior itself and less on the social environment in which behavior takes place. But over the last decade, a new paradigm has emerged in the field of developmental psychology called *developmental behavioral science* (Jessor, 1993). This paradigm recognizes that the various settings or contexts in which students live—families, schools, and communities—all shape their behavior. This framework was used by a recent National Research Council Panel on High-Risk Youth, which argued that too much emphasis has been placed on "high-risk" youth and their families, and not enough on the high-risk settings in which they live and go to school (National Research Council, Panel on High-Risk Youth, 1993). This view reflects the new emphasis on contexts and not simply individuals.

Empirical research on dropouts has identified a number of factors within students' families, schools, and communities (and peers) that predict dropping out. Again for brevity, only some of the most important ones are reviewed here.

Family Factors.   Family background is widely recognized as the single-most important contributor to success in school. Although early work by Coleman, Jencks, and others suggested that family background alone could explain most of the variation in educational outcomes (Coleman et al., 1966; Jencks et al., 1972), subsequent research found that much of the influence of family background was mediated through schools. Yet, in virtually all research on school achievement, family background still exerts a powerful, independent influence. But what aspects of family background matter and how do they influence school achievement?

Much of the empirical research has focused on the *structural* characteristics of families, such as socioeconomic status and family structure. Research has consistently found that socioeconomic status, most commonly measured by parental education and income, is a powerful predictor of school achievement and dropout behavior (Bryk & Thum, 1989; Ekstrom et al., 1986; McNeal, 1999; Rumberger, 1983; Rumberger, 1995; Rumberger & Larson, 1998; Pong & Ju, 2000). Research has also demonstrated that students from single-parent and step-families are more likely to drop out of school than students from two-parent families (Astone & McLanahan, 1991; Ekstrom et al., 1986; Goldschmidt & Wang, 1999; McNeal, 1999; Rumberger, 1983; Rumberger, 1995; Rumberger & Larson, 1998; Teachman et al., 1996). However, one recent study found that a change in dissolution of two-parent families did not increase the likelihood of dropping out apart from its effects on income loss (Pong & Ju, 2000).

Until recently, there has been relatively little research that has attempted to identify the underlying *processes* through which family structure influences dropping out. The powerful effects of parental education and income are generally thought to support human capital theory. According to human capital theory, parents make choices about how much time and other resources to invest in their children based on their objectives, resources, and constraints which, in turn, affects their children's tastes for education (preferences) and cognitive skills (Haveman & Wolfe, 1994). Parental income, for example, allows parents to provide more resources to support their children's education, including access to better-quality schools, as well as after-school and summer school programs, and more support for learning within the home.

Sociologist James Coleman argued that human capital (parental education) and financial capital (parental income) were insufficient to explain the connection between family background and school success. He argued that social capital—which is manifested in the relationships parents have with their children, other families, and the schools—also influences school achievement independent of the effects of human and financial capital (Coleman, 1988). Although Coleman relied on indirect measures (e.g., family structure) of social capital in his research, some recent studies with more direct measures of family relationships have confirmed that strong relationships between students and parents reduce the odds of dropping out of school (McNeal, 1999; Teachman et al., 1996).[5] Social capital actually represents part of a larger research literature on the role of families in promoting student achievement, including parental involvement (Epstein, 1990; Suichu & Willms, 1996) and types of parental practices known as "parenting style" (Baumrind, 1991; Dornbusch, Ritter, Leiderman, Roberts, & Fraleigh, 1987; Steinberg, Lamborn, Dornbusch, & Darling, 1992). Empirical studies have found that students whose parents monitor and regulate their activities, provide emotional support, encourage independent decision-making (known as authoritative parenting style), and are generally more involved in their schooling are less likely to drop out of school (Astone & McLanahan, 1991; Rumberger et al., 1990; Rumberger, 1995).

School Factors. It is widely acknowledged that schools exert powerful influences on student achievement, including dropout rates. But demonstrating the influence of schools and identifying the specific school factors that affect student achievement presents some methodological challenges. The biggest challenge is disentangling the effects of student and family background from the effects of school factors. Recent developments in statistical modeling have allowed researchers to more accurately estimate school effects after controlling for the individual background characteristics of students (Lee, 2000; Raudenbush & Willms, 1995).

Four types of school characteristics have been shown to influence student performance: (1) student composition, (2) resources, (3) structural characteristics, and (4) processes and practices. The first three factors are sometimes considered as school inputs by economists and others who study schools because they refer to the "inputs" into the schooling process that are largely "given" to a school and therefore not alterable by the school itself (Hanushek, 1989). The last factor refers to practices and policies that the school does have control over and thus can be used to judge a school's effectiveness (Shavelson et al., 1987). Yet all the characteristics of schools could be altered through policy, as suggested in the next section of this chapter.

Student Composition. Student characteristics not only influence student achievement at an individual level but also at an aggregate or social level. That is, the social composition of students in a school can influence student achievement apart from the effects of student characteristics at an individual level (Gamoran, 1992). Several studies have found that the social composition of schools predicts school dropout rates even after controlling for the

---

5. As Portes (1998) points out, in using the concept of social capital, it is important to distinguish between the relationships themselves and the access to resources that such relationships provide.

individual effects of student background characteristics (Bryk & Thum, 1989; McNeal, 1997b; Rumberger, 1995; Rumberger & Thomas, 2000). Several aspects of student composition have been identified in these studies: the average socioeconomic status of students (Rumberger, 1995; Rumberger & Thomas, 2000); minority composition (McNeal, 1997b; Rumberger, 1995); and the concentration of at-risk students (Byrk & Thum, 1989). The impact of social composition can be quite substantial. For example, Rumberger and Thomas (2000) found that the risk of dropping out of school was 38 percent lower if students attended high versus average SES schools (that is, schools with a one standard deviation higher SES).

School Resources.   Currently, there is considerable debate in the research community about the extent to which school resources contribute to school effectiveness (Hanushek, 1997; Hedges et al., 1994). Several studies suggest that resources influence school dropout rates. Two studies found that the pupil/teacher ratio had a positive and significant effect on high school and middle school dropout rates, even after controlling for a host of individual and contextual factors that might also influence dropout rates (McNeal, 1997b; Rumberger, 1995; Rumberger & Thomas, 2000). One of those studies found that the higher the quality of the teachers as perceived by students, the lower the dropout rate, whereas the higher the quality of teachers as perceived by the principal, the higher the dropout rate (Rumberger & Thomas, 2000).

School Structure.   There is also considerable debate in the research community on the extent to which structural characteristics (e.g., size, location), particularly type of control (public, private), contribute to school performance. This issue has been most widely debated with respect to one structural feature—public and private schools (Bryk et al., 1993; Chubb & Moe, 1990; Coleman & Hoffer, 1987). Although widespread achievement differences have been observed among schools based on structural characteristics, what remains unclear is whether structural characteristics themselves account for these differences or whether they are related to differences in student characteristics and school resources often associated with the structural features of schools. Most empirical studies have found that dropout rates from Catholic and other private schools are lower than dropout rates from public schools, even after controlling for differences in the background characteristics of students (Bryk & Thum, 1989; Coleman & Hoffer, 1987; Evans & Schwab, 1995; Neal, 1997; Rumberger & Thomas, 2000; Sander & Krautman, 1995). Yet, empirical studies have also found that students from private schools typically transfer to public schools instead of or before dropping out, meaning that student turnover rates in private schools are not statistically different than turnover rates in public schools (Lee & Burkam, 1992; Rumberger & Thomas, 2000). School size also appears to influence dropout rates both directly (Rumberger & Thomas, 2000) and indirectly (Bryk & Thum, 1989), although the largest direct effect appears to be in low SES schools (Rumberger, 1995). This latter finding is consistent with case studies of effective dropout prevention schools that suggest small schools are more likely to promote the engagement of both students and staff (Wehlage, Rutter, Smith, Lesko, & Fernandez, 1989).

School Policies and Practices.   Despite all the attention and controversy surrounding the previous factors associated with school effectiveness, it is the area of school processes that many people believe holds the most promise for understanding and improving school performance. Several studies found academic and social climate—as measured by school attendance rates, students taking advanced courses, and student perceptions of a fair discipline policy—predict school dropout rates, even after controlling for the background characteristics of students as well as the resource and structural characteristics of schools (Bryk & Thum, 1989; Rumberger, 1995; Rumberger & Thomas, 2000). Another study using one of the same data sets, but using different sets of variables and statistical techniques, found no effect of academic or social climate on high school dropout rates after controlling for the background characteristics of students, social composition, school resources, and school structure (McNeal, 1997b).

Current research literature on school dropouts suggests two ways that schools affect student withdrawal. One way is indirectly, through general policies and practices that are designed to promote the overall effectiveness of the school. These policies and practices, along with other characteristics of the school (student composition, size, etc.), may contribute to *voluntary* withdrawal by affecting conditions that keep students engaged in school. This perspective is consistent with several existing theories of school dropout and departure that view student engagement as the precursor to withdrawal (Finn, 1989; Wehlage, Rutter, Smith, Lesko, & Fernandez, 1989).

Another way that schools affect turnover is directly, through explicit policies and conscious decisions that cause students to *involuntarily* withdraw from school. These rules may concern low grades, poor attendance, misbehavior, or being over age that can lead to suspensions, expulsions, or forced transfers.[6] This form of withdrawal is school-initiated and contrasts with the student-initiated form mentioned earlier. This perspective considers a school's own agency, rather than just that of the student, in producing dropouts and transfers. One metaphor that has been used to characterize this process is discharge: "Students *drop out* of school, schools *discharge* students" (Riehl, 1999, p. 231). Several studies, mostly based on case studies, have demonstrated how schools contribute to students' involuntary departure from school by systematically excluding and discharging "troublemakers" and other problematic students (Bowditch, 1993; Fine, 1991; Riehl, 1999).

Community and Peers. In addition to families and schools, communities and peer groups can influence students' withdrawal from school. There is at least some empirical evidence that differences in neighborhood characteristics can help explain differences in dropout rates among communities apart from the influence of families (Brooks-Gunn et al., 1993; Clark, 1992; Crane, 1991). Crane (1991) further argues that there is a threshold or tipping point on the quality of neighborhoods that results in particularly high dropout rates in the lowest-quality neighborhoods. Clark (1992), using more recent data, found no evidence of a tipping, but did find that the odds of a boy dropping out of school increased substantially as the neighborhood poverty rate increased from 0 to 5 percent.

Although these studies find that communities do influence dropout rates, they are unable to explain how they do so. Poor communities may influence child and adolescent

---

6. One specific example is the growth of "zero tolerance" (automatic discharge) for violations of school safety rules (Skiba & Peterson, 1999).

development through the lack of resources (playgrounds and parks, after-school programs) or negative peer influences (Brooks-Gunn et al., 1997; Hallinan & Williams, 1990; Wilson, 1987). Community residence may also influence parenting practices over and above parental education and income (Klebanov et al., 1994). Finally, students living in poor communities may also be more likely to have friends as dropouts, which increases the likelihood of dropping out of school (Carbonaro, 1998).

Another way that communities can influence dropout rates is by providing employment opportunities both during and after school. Relatively favorable employment opportunities for high school dropouts, as evidenced by low neighborhood unemployment rates, appears to increase the likelihood that students will drop out, whereas more favorable economic returns to graduating, as evidenced by higher salaries of high school graduates to dropouts, tend to lower dropout rates (Bickel & Papagiannis, 1988; Clark, 1992; Rumberger, 1983). Research has also demonstrated that working long hours in high school can increase the likelihood of dropping out (Goldschmidt & Wang, 1999; Seltzer, 1994), although the impact of working in high school depends on the type of job held and, in some jobs, is more detrimental for females than males (McNeal, 1997a).

Explaining Racial and Ethnic Differences in Dropout Rates

One of the most challenging educational issues facing the United States is understanding and solving the persistent disparities in achievement among racial and ethnic groups. Although much of the focus on this issue has centered on student achievement as measured by grades and test scores (e.g., Jencks & Phillips, 1998; Steinberg et al., 1992), there has been considerable attention to understanding and explaining differences in dropout rates (Fernandez et al., 1989; Ogbu, 1989).

Two general approaches have been used to explain differences in dropout rates among racial and ethnic groups. The first approach is based on the idea that differences in dropout rates and other measures of educational achievement can be explained largely by differences in resources and by human and social capital frameworks that suggest these factors affect achievement similarly for all groups. This approach was used by the National Research Council Panel on High-Risk Youth, which focused its study on the high-risk settings of family, school, and community to explain the poor outcomes of high-risk and minority students (National Research Council, Panel on High-Risk Youth, 1993). Indeed, the family, school, and community conditions for racial and ethnic minorities in the United States are generally much worse than for the white majority. For example, child poverty rates for blacks and Hispanics are more than twice as high as child poverty rates for whites (U.S. Department of Education, 2000b, Table 21). Several empirical studies of dropouts have found that at least half of the observed differences in dropout rates between racial groups can be attributed to differences in family and community characteristics (Fernandez et al., 1989; Rumberger, 1983; Velez, 1989). Some more recent studies have found that black and Hispanic dropout rates are not significantly different from white dropout rates after controlling for differences in family (e.g., SES, family structure) and academic (e.g., prior grades, retention, behavior) background (Bryk & Thum, 1989; McNeal, 1997b; Rumberger 1995; Rumbeger & Thomas, 2000).

The second approach is based on the idea that differences in resources and conventional theories are insufficient to explain differences in achievement among racial and ethnic groups. In particular, critics of the first approach argue that it fails to explain why some minority groups with similar levels of "socioeconomic" background succeed, while other groups do not. Instead, they argue that sociocultural factors—particularly cultural differences in values, attitudes, and behaviors—help explain why some racial and ethnic minorities are successful in U.S. schools and others are not.

Several different sociocultural perspectives have been offered to explain differences in the educational performance of ethnic and racial minorities in the United States. Obgu (1989, 1992) distinguishes between voluntary minorities who came to the United States by their own choosing (e.g., European and Asian Americans) and involuntary minorities who were brought into the United States against their will, either through immigration or domination (e.g., African Americans and early Mexican Americans), and argues that voluntary and involuntary minorities adopt very different attitudes and behaviors toward school.[7] Steinberg, Dornbusch, and Brown (1992) demonstrate that Asians are more successful in school than other ethnic groups because of two cultural beliefs: (1) a belief that not getting a good education will hurt their chances for future success (rather than a belief that a good education will help their chances) and (2) a belief that academic success comes from effort rather than ability or the difficulty of the material.[8] They also find that the contexts of families, schools, and peers influence the achievement of racial and ethnic groups differently. Steele (1997) demonstrates that the social stigma of intellectual inferiority among certain cultural minorities—referred to as *stereotype threat*—contributes to their lower academic achievement. What has yet to be demonstrated empirically is whether these more recent sociocultural perspectives can help explain racial and ethnic differences in dropout rates.

Despite limited empirical evidence, both socioeconomic and sociocultural perspectives may help explain racial and ethnic differences in dropout rates by emphasizing different causal mechanisms. Socioeconomic perspectives focus on the fiscal, human, and social resources of families, schools, and communities and their similar influence on the development of students' values and cognitive abilities across all racial and ethnic groups. Sociocultural perspectives focus on cultural differences in the attitudes and behaviors among racial and ethnic groups that influence school success in both the social and academic arenas.

PROMISING INTERVENTIONS

The preceding analysis of why students drop out suggests several things about what can be done to design effective dropout intervention strategies. First, because dropping out is influenced by both individual and institutional factors, intervention strategies can focus on either

7. Although Obgu's perspective is probably the best known, it also has been subject to considerable debate and criticism (see Ainsworth-Darnell, 1998; Cook & Ludwig, 1997; Matute-Bianchi, 1986; Farkas et al., 1990; Gibson, 1997).

8. Other scholars have also found cultural differences in achievement motivation (Kao and Tienda, 1995; Suarez-Orozco and Suarez-Orozco, 1995).

or both sets of factors. That is, intervention strategies can focus on addressing the individual values, attitudes, and behaviors that are associated with dropping out without attempting to alter the characteristics of families, schools, and communities that may contribute to those individual factors. Many dropout prevention programs pursue such *programmatic strategies* by providing would-be dropouts with additional resources and supports to help them stay in school. Alternatively, intervention strategies can focus on attempting to improve the environmental contexts of potential dropouts by providing resources and supports to strengthen or restructure their families, schools, and communities. Such *systemic strategies* are often part of larger efforts to improve the educational and social outcomes of at-risk students more generally. Both strategies are discussed in more detail later.

Second, because dropping out is associated with both academic and social problems, effective prevention strategies must focus on both arenas. That is, if dropout prevention strategies are going to be effective, they must be *comprehensive* by providing resources and supports in all areas of students' lives.[9] And because dropouts leave school for a variety of reasons, services provided them must be flexible and tailored to their individual needs.

Third, because the problematic attitudes and behaviors of students at risk of dropping out appear as early as elementary school, dropout prevention strategies can and should begin early in a child's educational career. Dropout prevention programs often target high school or middle school students who may have already experienced years of educational failure or unsolved problems. Similarly, dropout recovery programs must attempt to overcome long-standing problems in order to get dropouts to complete school. Consequently, such programs may be costly and ineffective. Conversely, early intervention may be the most powerful and cost-effective approach to dropout prevention.

The overall conclusion is that there are a variety of potentially effective approaches to designing dropout interventions. Given that conclusion, what evidence do we have of the effectiveness of alternative approaches?

Unfortunately, the evidence on the effectiveness of dropout interventions is generally weak for two fundamental reasons. First, there have been relatively few rigorous evaluations of dropout intervention programs. For example, the General Accounting Office surveyed more than 1,000 dropout programs in the fall of 1986, yet it found only 20 rigorous evaluations of the 479 programs that responded to the survey (U.S. GAO, 1987). Second, the evaluations that do exist often fail to demonstrate program effectiveness. For example, Dynarski and Gleason (1998) reviewed the evaluations of 21 dropout prevention programs funded under the federal School Dropout Demonstration Assistance Program (SDDAP) and found that only 3 programs improved dropout or completion rates. Similarly, Slavin and Fashola (1998) conducted a literature search of dropout prevention programs with rigorous, experimental evaluations and found only 2 that were effective.

Despite the dearth of research evidence, case studies of proven or at least promising approaches do exist. They also have identified some of the features that have contributed to their effectiveness.

---

9. Some intervention efforts focus on specific risk-factors related to dropout, such as truancy (see, for example, Baker, Sigmon, & Nugent, 2001). To the extent such interventions help reduce the incidence of that risk factor, they would likely to help reduce dropout rates. But, as the discussion below points out, the most effective dropout prevention strategies address a wide range of factors associated with dropping out.

Programmatic Approaches

There are two programmatic approaches to dropout prevention. One approach is to provide supplemental services to students within an existing school program. The second approach is to provide an alternative school program either within an existing school (school within a school) or in a separate facility (alternative school). Both approaches do not attempt to change existing institutions serving most students, but rather create alternative programs or institutions to target students who are somehow identified as at-risk of dropping out.

Supplemental Programs.   One example of a supplemental yet comprehensive programmatic approach to dropout prevention is the Achievement for Latinos through Academic Success, or ALAS program (Gándara, Larson, Mehan, & Rumberger, 1998). This program was developed, implemented, and evaluated as a pilot intervention program to serve the most at-risk students in a poor, predominantly Latino middle school in the Los Angeles area from 1990 to 1995. The ALAS program specifically targeted two groups of high-risk students: special education students and other students who—because of poor academic performance, misbehavior, and low income—were at greatest risk of school failure. The pilot program served two cohorts of special education students (77 total) and one cohort of 46 high-risk students. Participating students received the intervention program in conjunction with the regular school program for all three years they remained in the target school.

The ALAS program was founded on the premise that the youth and school as well as the family and community contexts must be addressed simultaneously for dropout prevention efforts to succeed. Thus, ALAS consists of a series of specific intervention strategies focused on individual adolescents as well as on three contexts of influence on achievement: the family, the school, and the community. The intervention strategies are designed to increase the effectiveness of actors in each context as well as increase collaboration between them. The following specific interventions are provided by ALAS:

1. *Remediation of the student's ineffective problem-solving skills regarding social interactions and task performance* through 10 weeks of problem-solving instruction and two years of follow-up problem-solving training and counseling[10]
2. *Personal recognition and bonding activities,* such as praise, outings, recognition ceremonies, certificates, and positive home calls to parents for meeting goals or improving behavior to increase self-esteem, affiliation, and a sense of belonging with the school organization[11]

---

10. The 10-week curriculum was taught during a regular one-hour class period for high-risk students and during the resource period for the special education students; the follow-up sessions took place during a one-hour period that all participating students took as an elective, where they received counseling, as needed, along with tutoring and other forms of assistance. For more information on the nature of the problem-solving curriculum, see Larson (1989).

11. Bonding activities were continual and included an open office for ALAS students and their friends to hang out before and after school and during lunch; after-school and in-school tutoring; and holiday school parties. Recognition activities, which occurred frequently, included certificates and small rewards for improving grades or attendance as well as occasional public ceremonies for family and friends. For more details on the nature of the intervention, see Larson and Rumberger (1995).

3. *Intensive attendance monitoring,* including period-by-period attendance monitoring and daily follow-ups with parents, to communicate a personal interest in their attendance
4. *Frequent teacher feedback to parents and students* regarding classroom comportment, missed assignments, and missing homework
5. *Direct instruction and modeling for parents* on how to reduce their child's inappropriate or undesirable behavior and how to increase desirable behavior
6. *Integration of school and home needs with community services*[12]

The program was evaluated using an experimental design where high-risk students were randomly assigned to the treatment or a control group, and where participating special education students were compared to a previous year's cohort of special education students. The evaluation examined enrollment status and credits earned in the final year of the program in ninth grade and in the remaining years of high school after the program ended. Evaluation data on mobility, attendance, failed classes, and graduation credits indicate that the ALAS program had a substantial and practical impact on students who received the intervention (Gándara, Larson, Mehan, & Rumberger, 1998). By the end of ninth grade, students in the comparison group had twice the number of failed classes, were four times more likely to have excessive absences, and were twice as likely to be seriously behind in high school graduation credits. These results appear even more remarkable when considering that the participants in this study represent the most difficult to teach students within a pool of students generally viewed as high risk. Nonetheless, these dramatic effects were not sustained. By the end of twelfth grade, only 32 percent of the ALAS participants and 27 percent of the comparison students had completed high school. This clearly suggests that in order to increase graduation rates, it is necessary to provide an ALAS-type intervention throughout the high school years.

The ALAS dropout prevention program targeted students in middle school who were at risk of dropping out of school. Although the program was successful while the students were receiving the intervention, the effects were not sustained for long after the program ended. This suggests that, at the secondary level, dropout prevention efforts need to be ongoing.

Alternative Programs.   The other programmatic approach to dropout prevention is to create alternative school programs that target only students at risk of dropping out. These programs can either operate within regular schools or as separate, alternative schools. They generally provide a complete but alternative educational program than the one found in regular, comprehensive schools. In addition, they typically provide many of the other support services that are found in supplemental programs.

---

12. This included working with parents and the California work-welfare program to get family food stamps or social security benefits; working with the county mental health department and the school district to get the child into nonpublic school or extra tutoring; and working with public defenders and investigating probation officers to determine the most effective disposition or placement. Most of the services of ALAS were provided by counselor-advocates who managed a caseload of about 25 to 35 students and families, although counselor-advocates consulted regularly. See Larson and Rumberger (1995) for more information.

One well-known example is Central Park East Secondary School (CPESS) in New York City (van Heusden Hale, 2000). The school enrolls 450 public school students in grades 7 through 12, most of whom are from low-income families and many of whom have a history of average or below-average academic achievement. No selection criteria, tests, or interviews are required to attend the school, which is supported by public education funds. Costs per student are the same as other public high schools.

The school offers an intellectually rigorous and creative education normally associated with elite private schools. Classes are small, averaging 20 students, and the day is organized into two-hour periods, allowing teachers and students enough time to engage in concentrated work in specific areas. Students take two main subject groups—mathematics and science, and social studies and the humanities. Besides interdisciplinary college-preparatory courses, the school offers career-oriented apprenticeships. It has established high standards and clear expectations for its students. Student performance is regularly assessed through a process in which students explain their work and hear it criticized. To graduate, they must present seven academic projects in specified subjects over two years and defend them before committees of students, teachers, and other adults, much as a Ph.D. candidate defends a thesis.

Central Park East has developed beneficial relationships with parents and the community. The school has worked over time to connect and involve parents in the school overall and in their own child's schooling. It has also formed a number of partnerships with community agencies. In addition, the school has a community service requirement where students spent one morning a week working in community service jobs.

According to CPESS co-director Brigette Belletiere, four specific practices support the school's success:

- Articulation and maintenance of a clear vision and mission that staff carries out
- Goal-setting in line with the vision
- Allocation of instructional resources to keep class size small
- Providing time for ongoing, job-embedded professional development

The school maintains its progress and continually improves itself through an internal democratic process. The staff develops curricula, assessments, and the criteria for earning a CPESS diploma. They are also held accountable for maintaining the school standards.

Student achievement data documents the school's success. Only 5 percent of the students drop out during their high school years, and more than 90 percent of Central Park East's graduates go on to college. Students have high attendance rates and low incidence of violence.

There have been several evaluations of effective alternative programs: Stern and colleagues (1989) evaluated 11 within-school academy programs in California high schools; Wehlage and colleagues (1989) evaluated 12 alternative and 2 comprehensive schools; and Dynarski and Gleason (1998) evaluated 3 within-school and 6 alternative schools in their study. Although the programs differed in the types of students they enrolled, the curricula and services they provided, and the way they were structured, there appear to be several common features among effective programs:

- A nonthreatening environment for learning
- A caring and committed staff who accepted a personal reasonability for student success

- A school culture that encouraged staff risk taking, self-governance, and professional collegiality
- A school structure that provided for a low student-teacher ratio and a small size to promote student engagement.

Case studies have been able to identify schools and describe the salient features that enable them to keep students enrolled and to eventually graduate. These features are similar to those that have been identified for "effective" schools more generally (e.g., Purkey & Smith, 1985; Newman, 1993). Although the list of specific features varies from one author to another (e.g., Newman, 1993; Purkey & Smith, 1985; Wehlage et al., 1989),[13] they essentially address two basic features of schools: the commitments and competencies of the people (teachers, administrators, and staff) and the organizational structure (size, staffing ratio, curriculum design, services, etc.). It remains unclear whether one feature must change before the other, but both appear to be necessary. For example, simply adopting "progressive" structural changes, such as site-based management or team teaching, may do little if teachers do not have the requisite commitments and competencies (Newman, 1993). At the same time, certain organizational features, such as small size and shared decision making, may be necessary to develop and support teachers' commitment to the institution and to the students it serves (Wehlage et al., 1989). What also remains unclear is the extent to which it may be necessary to recruit teachers and staff with the necessary commitment and competencies before creating a supportive structure.[14]

These reviews clearly illustrate that it is possible to create effective alternative programs to address the needs and promote the learning of students at risk of dropping out. Yet, creating successful alternative programs presents a number of challenges. First, programs can have difficulty in attracting students because of negative perceptions by students, parents, and educators that such schools are a dumping group for "bad" students and that they symbolize the failure of the regular system (Dynarski & Gleason, 1998). Some programs have responded to this problem by restricting entry to more motivated at-risk students, which raises questions about the purpose of such schools. Second, because of their low regard, such programs often have a hard time competing for resources with regular school programs.

Systemic Solutions

Systemic solutions have the potential to reduce dropping out in a much larger number of students by improving some of the environmental factors in families, schools, and commu-

13. Purkey and Smith (1985) generated a list of 13 features of effective schools that are necessary to change the culture of the school. Newman (1993) identified a list of four commitments and competencies required of teachers along with a list of four ideas that he describes as a "loose theory about what is needed to make substantial changes in the current educational system" (p. 9). Wehlage and colleagues (1989) describe a series of qualities in the school staff, the culture, and the structure of successful dropout prevention schools.

14. One issue that is rarely discussed in the literature on effective schools is the extent to which teachers are recruited and selected into effective schools. A private conversation with the principal of Central Park East revealed that teachers in that school are interviewed and selected based on a desired set of commitments and competencies, even through the school provides ongoing professional development for its teachers. Based on their belief that all students can and should succeed in school, the selection of teachers may be especially important.

nities that contribute to dropout behavior. That was the position taken by the National Research Council Panel on High-Risk Youth (1993), which argued:

> The primary institutions that serve youth—health, schools, employment, training—are crucial and we must begin with helping them respond more effectively to contemporary adolescent needs. Effective responses will involve pushing the boundaries of these systems, encouraging collaborations between them and reducing the number of adolescents whose specialized problems cannot be met through primary institutions. (p. 193)

Whereas the promise of systemic solutions to the dropout problem is great, the reality is not. The reason is simply that systemic changes are extremely difficult to achieve because they involve making fundamental changes in the way institutions work individually and within the system in which they are apart. As discussed earlier, research has been able to identify the features of effective secondary schools, which is the first step in the school reform process. But the next step is much harder and thus far has eluded school reformers: *Identifying the resources, technical support, and incentives to transform or restructure existing schools in order to create those features* (Purkey & Smith, 1985).

Although local districts and state and federal governments have instituted a number of programs and policies to support school restructuring at the secondary level, these efforts have not had much success, especially in reducing dropout rates. For example, Dynarski and Gleason (1998) reviewed five school restructuring efforts that were part of the second phase of the federal SDDAP dropout prevention program. These initiatives involved large, multimillion-dollar grants for individual schools to restructure so that more students would stay in school in the first place and hence reduce the need for alternative schools or programs. Yet none of these restructured schools significantly reduced dropout rates in relation to comparable schools. As Dynarski and Gleason pointed out:

> The evaluation did not observe much change, however, or even signs of it beginning. Restructuring schools found it easier to add dropout-prevention services than to change teaching and learning. Some initiatives managed to change teaching and learning to a degree, but the changes were fragile and easily undone if district leadership changed or local political contexts shifted. (p. 14)

They went on to find that there was little consensus about the source of the dropout problem and, in particular, how faculty and staff may have contributed to it. Consequently, few faculty and staff were eager or willing to change what they were doing. Finally, turnover of district administrators undermined support for change. These findings contrast markedly with the characteristics of effective alternative programs presented earlier where teachers felt accountable for students' success and their programs encouraged risk taking.

This study suggests that it may be more difficult to transform existing institutions than to create new ones. This may especially be true when it comes to reducing dropout rates in urban high schools. In their study of 207 urban high schools that were attempting major school reform programs based on the effective schools literature, Louis and Miles (1990) found widespread improvement in a number of areas, such as student behavior, student morale, and staff morale. But even among programs that had implemented their programs for several years and enjoyed improvements in student achievement, improvement in dropout rates were "rarely achieved no matter how long a program had been in operation" (Louis & Miles, 1990, p. 49).

Efforts to restructure secondary schools to reduce dropout rates have proved elusive, and so too have efforts to reform other institutions that serve at-risk youth. One ambitious systemic reform effort was the New Futures Initiative promoted and funded by the Annie E. Casey foundation beginning in 1988. New Futures was an attempt to build new collaborative structures among existing public and private institutions in five cities (Dayton, Ohio; Lawrence, Massachusetts; Little Rock, Arkansas; Pittsburgh, Pennsylvania; Savannah, Georgia) to address the problems of at-risk youth, including school dropout. The key strategy was to establish an oversight collaborative in each city with representation from public- and private-sector agencies to "identify youth problems, develop strategies, and set timelines for addressing these problems, coordinate joint agency activities, and restructure educational and social services" (White & Wehlage, 1995, p. 24). The collaboratives also included case managers who (1) brokered services among the disparate agencies serving at-risk youth and their families, (2) served as advocates for at-risk youth, and (3) served as the "eyes and ears" of the collaboratives by providing information and feedback to the group about what reforms were needed.

Evaluations of this ambitious, systemic reform effort found that it did little to reduce dropout rates and other problems of at-risk youth (Wehlage, Smith, & Lipman, 1992; White & Wehlage, 1995). White and Wehlage (1995) found several generic problems in trying to establish community collaboration:

1. *Slippage between policy and action* because case managers were generally unsuccessful in overcoming the "turf battles" among existing agencies and in getting collaboratives to address them
2. *Discord over reform policies* because of fundamental disagreements over the definitions, causes, and remedies to problems
3. *Disjuncture between policy and community conditions* because of the top-down organization of the collaboratives that resulted in an incomplete understanding of the problems and hence ineffective policies

These problems were clearly evident in New Futures school reforms and paralleled those found in the earlier evaluation of restructured schools. In particular, "most educators in New Futures schools believed that the problems that created at-risk students were problems inside the students, not inside the school and its curriculum" (Wehlage, Smith, & Lipman, 1992, p. 73). Hence, as found in the other systemic reform effort, there was little incentive or support for changing the fundamental functioning of schools.

SUMMARY

Although understanding why students drop out of school is difficult because it is influenced by an array of individual and institutional factors, a review of the theoretical and empirical literature does yield some useful insights into the nature of this problem and what can be done about it. First, dropping out is not simply a result of academic failure, but rather often results from both social and academic problems in school. Second, these problems often appear early in students' school careers, suggesting the need for early intervention. Third, these problems are influenced by a lack of support and resources in families, schools, and communities. These findings suggest that reducing dropout rates will require comprehensive approaches both to help at-risk students address the social and academic problems that they face in their lives and to improve the at-risk settings that contribute to these problems. The challenge is to find the capacity and political will to address this important social problem.

DISCUSSION QUESTIONS

1. What is the value of using two perspectives—an individual and an institutional—in understanding and addressing the problem of school dropouts?

2. What factors that influence school dropout are most amenable to change?

3. Given the existing research knowledge, how would you design a dropout prevention program?

4. What policies should the federal government initiate to help solve the dropout problem?

5. What additional research should be undertaken to better understand this problem?

REFERENCES

Ainsworth-Darnell, J. W., & Downey, D. B. (1998). Assessing the oppositional culture explanation for racial/ethnic differences in school performance. *American Sociological Review, 63,* 536–553.

Alexander, K. K., Entwisle, D. R., & Horsey, C. (1997). From first grade forward: Early foundations of high school dropout. *Sociology of Education, 70,* 87–107.

Alexander, K. L., Entwisle, D. R., & Dauber, S. L. (1994). *On the success of failure: A reassessment of the effects of retention in early grades.* New York: Cambridge University Press.

Astone, N. M., & McLanahan, S. S. (1991). Family structure, parental practices and high school completion. *American Sociological Review, 56,* 309–320.

Astone, N. M., & McLanahan, S. S. (1994). Family structure, residential mobility, and school dropout: A research note. *Demography, 31,* 575–584.

Bachman, J. G., Green, S., & Wirtanen, I. D. (1971). *Youth in transition, Vol. III: Dropping out: Problem or symptom?* Ann Arbor: Institute for Social Research, University of Michigan.

Baker, M. L., Sigmon, J. N., & Nugent, M. E. (2001). *Truancy reduction: Keeping students in school.* Washington, DC: U.S. Department of Justice, Office of Juvenile Justice and Delinquency Prevention.

Barnett, W. S. (1995). Long-term effects of early childhood programs on cognitive and school outcomes. *The Future of Children, 5,* 25–50.

Barrington, B. L., & Hendricks, B. (1989). Differentiating characteristics of high school graduates, dropouts, and nongraduates. *Journal of Educational Research, 82,* 309–319.

Baumrind, D. (1991). Parenting styles and adolescent development. In R. Lerner, A. C. Petersen, & J. Brooks-Gunn (Eds.), *The encyclopedia of adolescence* (pp. 758–772). New York: Garland.

Berktold, J., Geis, S., & Kaufman, P. (1998). *Subsequent educational attainment of high school dropouts.* Washington, DC: U.S. Department of Education.

Betts, J. R., Rueben, K. S., & Danenberg, A. (2000). *Equal resources, equal outcomes? The distribution of school resources and student achievement in California.* San Francisco: Public Policy Institute of California.

Bickel, R., & Papagiannis, G. (1988). Post-high school prospects and district-level dropout rates. *Youth & Society, 20,* 123–147.

Bowditch, C. (1993). Getting rid of troublemakers: High school disciplinary procedures and the production of dropouts. *Social Problems, 40,* 493–509.

Brooks-Gunn, J., Duncan, G. J., & Aber, J. L. (1997). *Neighborhood poverty.* New York: Russell Sage Foundation.

Brooks-Gunn, J., Duncan, G. J., Klebanov, P. K., & Sealand, N. (1993). Do neighborhoods influence child and adolescent development? *American Journal of Sociology, 99,* 353–395.

Bryk, A. S., Lee, V. E., & Holland, P. B. (1993). *Catholic schools and the common good.* Cambridge, MA: Harvard University Press.

Bryk, A. S., & Thum, Y. M. (1989). The effects of high school organization on dropping out: An exploratory investigation. *American Educational Research Journal, 26,* 353–383.

Cairns, R. B., Cairns, B. D., & Necherman, H. J. (1989). Early school dropout: Configurations and determinants. *Child Development, 60,* 1437–1452.

Cameron, S. V., & Heckman, J. J. (1993). The nonequivalence of high school equivalents. *Journal of Labor Economics, 11,* 1–47.

Carbonaro, W. J. (1998). A little help from my friend's parents: Intergenerational closure and educational outcomes. *Sociology of Education, 71,* 295–313.

Catterall, J. S. (November 1987). On the social costs of dropping out of school. *The High School Journal, 71,* 19–30.

Chubb, J. E., & Moe, T. M. (1990). *Politics, markets, and America's schools.* Washington, DC: Brookings Institution.

Clark, R. L. (December 1992). *Neighborhood effects on dropping out of school among teenage boys.* Discussion paper. Washington, DC: The Urban Institute.

Coleman, J. S. (1987). Families and schools. *Educational Researcher, 16,* 32–38.

Coleman, J. S. (1988). Social capital in the creation of human capital. *American Journal of Sociology, 94,* S95–S120.

Coleman, J. S., Campbell, E., Hobson, C., McPartland, J., Mood, F., Weinfeld, F., & York, R. (1966). *Equality of educational opportunity.* Washington, DC: U.S. Government Printing Office.

Coleman, J. S., & Hoffer, T. (1987). *Public and private high schools: The impact of communities.* New York: Basic Books.

Cook, P. J., & Ludwig, J. (1997). Weighing the "burden of 'acting white'": Are there race differences in attitudes toward school. *Journal of Policy Analysis and Management, 16,* 256–278.

Crane, J. (1991). The epidemic theory of ghettos and neighborhood effects on dropping out and teenage childbearing. *American Journal of Sociology, 96,* 1226–1259.

Dornbusch, S. M., Ritter, P. L., Leiderman, P. H., Roberts, D. F., & Fraleigh, M. J. (1987). The relation of parenting style to adolescent school performance. *Child Development, 58,* 1244–1257.

Dynarski, M., & Gleason, P. (1998). *How can we help? What we have learned from federal dropout-prevention programs.* Princeton, NJ: Mathematica Policy Research.

Ekstrom, R. B., Goertz, M. E., Pollack, J. M., & Rock, D. A. (1986). Who drops out of high school and why? Findings from a national study. *Teachers College Record, 87,* 356–373.

Ensminger, M. E., & Slusacick, A. L. (1992). Paths to high school graduation or dropout: A longitudinal study of a first-grade cohort. *Sociology of Education, 65,* 95–113.

Epstein, J. L. (1990). School and family connections: Theory, research, and implications for integrating sociologies of education and family. *Marriage and Family Review, 15,* 99–126.

Evans, W. N., & Schwab, R. M. (1995). Finishing high school and starting college: Do Catholic schools make a difference? *The Quarterly Journal of Economics, 110,* 941–974.

Farkas, G., Grobe, R. P., Sheehan, D., & Shuan, Y. (1990). Cultural resources and school success: Gender, ethnicity, and poverty groups within an urban district. *American Sociological Review, 55,* 127–142.

Fernandez, R. M., Paulsen, R., & Hirano-Nakanishi, M. (1989). Dropping out among Hispanic youth. *Social Science Research, 18,* 21–52.

Fine, M. (1991). *Framing dropouts: Notes on the politics of an urban public high school.* Albany: State University of New York Press.

Finn, J. D. (1989). Withdrawing from school. *Review of Educational Research, 59,* 117–142.

Garnier, H. E., Stein, J. A., & Jacobs, J. K. (1997). The process of dropping out of high school: A 19-year perspective. *American Educational Research Journal, 34,* 395–419.

Gamoran, A. (1992). Social factors in education. In M. C. Alkin (Ed.), *Encyclopedia of educational research* (pp. 1222–1229). New York: Macmillan.

Gándara, P., Larson, K., Mehan, H., & Rumberger, R. (1998). *Capturing Latino students in the academic pipeline.* Berkeley, CA: Chicano/Latino Policy Project.

Gibson, M. A. (1997). Complicating the immigrant/involuntary minority typology. *Anthropology & Education Quarterly, 28,* 431–454.

Goldschmidt, P., & Wang, J. (1999). When can schools affect dropout behavior? A longitudinal multilevel analysis. *American Educational Research Journal, 36,* 715–738.

Grisson, J. B., & Shepard, L. A. (1989). Repeating and dropping out of school. In L. A. Sheppard & M. L. Smith (Eds.), *Flunking grades: Research and policies on retention* (pp. 34–63). New York: Falmer Press.

Hallinan, M. T., & Williams, R. A. (1990). Students' characteristics and the peer-influence process. *Sociology of Education, 63,* 122–132.

Hanushek, E. A. (1989). The impact of differential expenditures on school performance. *Educational Researcher, 18,* 45–51, 62.

Hanushek, E. A. (1997). Assessing the effects of school resources on student performance: An update. *Educational Evaluation and Policy Analysis, 19,* 141–164.

Hanushek, E. A., & Jorgenson, D. W. (Eds.). (1996). *Improving America's schools: The role of incentives.* Washington, DC: National Academy Press.

Haveman, R., & Wolfe, B. (1994). *Succeeding generations: On the effects of investments in children.* New York: Russell Sage Foundation.

Haveman, R., Wolfe, B., & Spaulding, J. (1991). Childhood events and circumstances influencing high school completion. *Demography, 28,* 133–157.

Hedges, L. V., Laine, R. D., & Greenwald, R. (1994). Does money matter? A meta-analysis of studies of the effects of differential school inputs on student outcomes. *Educational Researcher, 23,* 5–14.

Hess, Jr., G. A. (1995). *Restructuring urban schools: A Chicago perspective.* New York: Teachers College Press.

Heubert, J. P., & Hauser, R. M. (Eds.). (1999). *High stakes: Testing for tracking, promotion, and graduation.* Washington, DC: National Academy Press.

Jencks, C., & Phillips, M. (1998). *The black-white test score gap.* Washington, DC: Brookings Institution.

Jencks, C., Smith, M., Bane, M. J., Cohen, D., Gintis, H., Heyns, B., & Michelson, S. (1972). *Inequality: A reassessment of the effects of family and schooling in America.* New York: Basic Books.

Jessor, R. (1993). Successful adolescent development among youth in high-risk settings. *American Psychologist, 48,* 117–126.

Jimerson, S. R. (1999). On the failure of failure: Examining the association between early grade retention and education and employment outcomes during late adolescence. *Journal of School Psychology, 37,* 243–272.

Kao, G., & Tienda, M. (1995). Optimism and achievement: The educational performance of immigrant youth. *Social Science Quarterly, 76,* 1–19.

Kaufman, P., & Bradby, D. (1992). *Characteristics of at-risk students in the NELS:88.* Washington, DC: U.S. Government Printing Office.

Klebanov, P. K., Brooks-Gunn, J., & Duncan, G. J. (1994). Does neighborhood and family poverty affects mother's parenting, mental health and social support. *Journal of Marriage and Family, 56,* 441–455.

Klerman, J. A., & Karoly, L. A. (1994). Young men and the transition to stable employment. *Monthly Labor Review, 117,* 31–48.

Kozol, J. (1991). *Savage inequalities: Children in American schools.* New York: Crown.

Larson, K. A. (1989). Problem solving training for enhancing school achievement in high-risk young adolescents. *Remedial and Special Education, 10*(5), 32–43.

Larson, K. A., & Rumberger, R. W. (1995.). ALAS: Achievement for Latinos through academic success. In *Staying in school: A technical report of three dropout prevention projects for middle school students with learning and emotional disabilities.* Minneapolis: Institute on Community Integration, University of Minnesota.

Lee, V. E. (2000). Using hierarchical linear modeling to study social contexts: The case of school effects. *Educational Psychologist, 35,* 125–141.

Lee, V. E., & Burkam, D. T. (1992). Transferring high schools: An alternative to dropping out? *American Journal of Education, 100,* 420–453.

Levin, H. M. (1986). *Educational reform for disadvantaged students: An emerging crisis.* West Haven, CT: National Educational Association.

Louis, K. S., & Miles, M. B. (1990). *Improving the urban high school: What works and why.* New York: Teachers College Press.

Matute-Bianchi, M. E. (1986). Ethnic identities and patterns of school success and failure among Mexican-descent and Japanese-American students in a California high school: An ethnographic analysis. *American Journal of Education, 95,* 233–255.

McMillen, M. M., Kaufman, P., & Klein, S. (1997). *Dropout rates in the United States: 1995.* Washington, DC: U.S. Government Printing Office.

McNeal, R. B. (1997a). Are students being pulled out of high school? The effect of adolescent employment on dropping out. *Sociology of Education, 70,* 206–220.

McNeal, R. B. (1997b). High school dropouts: A closer examination of school effects. *Social Science Quarterly, 78,* 209–222.

McNeal, R. B. (1999). Parental involvement as social capital: Differential effectiveness on science achievement, truancy, and dropping out. *Social Forces, 78,* 117–144.

Morris, J. D., Ehren, B. J., & Lenz, B. K. (1991). Building a model to predict which fourth through eighth graders will drop out of high school. *Journal of Experimental Education, 59,* 286–293.

Murnane, R. J., & Levy, F. (1996). *Teaching the new basic skills: Principles for educating children to thrive in a changing economy.* New York: Free Press.

Murnane, R. J., Willett, J. B., & Boudett, K. P. (1995). Do high school dropouts benefit from obtaining a GED? *Educational Evaluation and Policy Analysis, 17,* 133–147.

Murnane, R. J., Willett, J. B., & Boudett, K. P. (1997). Does acquisition of a GED lead to more training, post-secondary education, and military service for school dropouts? *Industrial and Labor Relations Review, 51,* 100–116.

Murnane, R. J., Willett, J. B., & Tyler, J. H. (2000). Who benefits from obtaining a GED? Evidence from high school and beyond. *The Review of Economics and Statistics, 82,* 23–37.

National Education Goals Panel. (1999). *National Education Goals report: Building a nation of learners, 1999.* Washington, DC: U.S. Government Printing Office.

National Research Council, Panel on High-Risk Youth. (1993). *Losing generations: Adolescents in high-risk settings.* Washington, DC: National Academy Press.

Natriello, G., McDill, E. L., & Pallas, A. M. (1990). *Schooling disadvantaged children: Racing against catastrophe.* New York: Teachers College Press.

Newmann, F. M. (1993). Beyond common sense in educational restructuring. *Educational Researcher, 22,* 4–13, 22.

Newmann, F. M., Wehlage, G. G., & Lamborn, S. D. (1992). The significance and sources of student engagement. In F. M. Newmann (Ed.), *Student engagement and achievement in American secondary schools* (pp. 11–39). New York: Teachers College Press.

Ogbu, J. U. (1989). The individual in collective adaptation: A framework for focusing on academic underperformance and dropping out among involuntary minorities. In L. Weis, E. Farrar, & H. G. Petrie (Eds.), *Dropouts from school: Issues, dilemmas, and solutions* (pp. 181–204). Albany: State University of New York Press.

Ogbu, J. U. (1992). Understanding cultural diversity and learning. *Educational Researcher, 21,* 5–14.

Orfield, G., Bachmeier, M., James, D. R., & Eitle, T. (1997). Deepening segregation in American public schools: A special report from the Harvard Project on School Desegregation. *Equity and Excellence in Education, 30,* 5–24.

Pirog, M. A., & Magee, C. (1997). High school completion: The influence of schools, families, and adolescent parenting. *Social Science Quarterly, 78,* 710–724.

Pong, S.-L., & Ju, D.-B. (2000). The effects of change in family structure and income on dropping out of middle and high school. *Journal of Family Issues, 21,* 147–169.

Portes, A. (1998). Social capital: Its origins and applications in modern sociology. *Annual Review of Sociology, 24,* 1–24.

Purkey, S. C., & Smith, M. S. (1985). School reform: The district policy implications of the effective schools literature. *The Elementary School Journal, 85,* 354–389.

Raudenbush, S. W., & Willms, J. D. (1995). The estimation of school effects. *Journal of Educational and Behavioral Statistics, 20,* 307–335.

Riehl, C. (1999). Labeling and letting go: An organizational analysis of how high school students are discharged as dropouts. In A. M. Pallas (Ed.), *Research in sociology of education and socialization* (pp. 231–268). New York: JAI Press.

Roderick, M. (1993). *The path to dropping out.* Westport, CT: Auburn House.

Roderick, M. (1994). Grade retention and school dropout: Investigating the association. *American Educational Research Journal, 31,* 729–759.

Roderick, M., Bryk, A. S., Jacob, B. A., Easton, J. Q., & Allensworth, E. (1999). *Ending social promotion: Results from the first two years.* Chicago: Consortium on Chicago School Research.

Roderick, M., Nagaoka, J., Bacon, J., & Easton, J. Q. (2000). *Update: Ending social promotion.* Chicago: Consortium on Chicago School Research.

Rumberger, R. W. (1983). Dropping out of high school: The influence of race, sex, and family background. *American Educational Research Journal, 20,* 199–220.

Rumberger, R. W. (1987). High school dropouts: A review of issues and evidence. *Review of Educational Research, 57,* 101–121.

Rumberger, R. W. (1995). Dropping out of middle school: A multilevel analysis of students and schools. *American Educational Research Journal, 32,* 583–625.

Rumberger, R. W., Ghatak, R., Poulos, G., Ritter, P. L., & Dornbusch, S. M. (1990). Family influences on dropout behavior in one California high school. *Sociology of Education, 63,* 283–299.

Rumberger, R. W., & Lamb, S. P. (in press). The early employment and further education experiences of high school dropouts: A comparative study of the United States and Australia. *Economics of Education Review.*

Rumberger, R. W., & Larson, K. A. (1998). Student mobility and the increased risk of high school drop out. *American Journal of Education, 107,* 1–35.

Rumberger, R. W., Larson, K. A., Palardy, G. A., Ream, R. K., & Schleicher, N. A. (1998). *The hazards of changing schools for California Latino adolescents.* Berkeley, CA: Chicano/Latino Policy Project.

Rumberger, R. W., & Thomas, S. L. (2000). The distribution of dropout and turnover rates among urban and suburban high schools. *Sociology of Education, 73,* 39–67.

Sander, W., & Krautmann, A. C. (1995). Catholic schools, dropout rates and educational attainment. *Economic Inquiry, 33,* 217–233.

Secada, W., Chavez-Chavez, R., Garcia, E., Muñoz, C., Oakes, J., Santiago-Santiago, I., & Slavin, R. (1998). *No more excuses: The final report of the Hispanic dropout project.* Washington, DC: U.S. Department of Education.

Seltzer, M. H. (1994). Studying variation in program success: A multilevel modeling approach. *Evaluation Review, 18,* 342–361.

Shavelson, R., McDonnell, L., Oakes, J., & Carey, N. (1987). *Indicator systems for monitoring mathematics and science education.* Santa Monica, CA: RAND.

Skiba, R., & Peterson, R. (1999). The dark side of zero tolerance: Can punishment lead to safe schools? *Phi Delta Kappan, 80,* 372–376, 381–382.

Slavin, R. E., & Fashola, O. S. (1998). *Show me the evidence! Proven and promising programs for America's schools.* New York: Corwin.

Stanton-Salazar, R. D. (1997). A social capital framework for understanding the socialization of racial minority children and youths. *Harvard Educational Review, 67,* 1–40.

Stecher, B. M., & Bohrnstedt, G. W. (Eds.). (2000). *Class size reduction in California: The 1998–99 evaluation findings.* Sacramento: California Department of Education.

Steele, C. (1997). The threat in the air: How stereotypes shape intellectual identity and performance. *American Psychologist, 52,* 613–629.

Steinberg, L., Blinde, P. L., & Chan, K. S. (1984). Dropping out among language minority youth. *Review of Educational Research, 54,* 113–132.

Steinberg, L., Dornbusch, S. M., & Brown, B. B. (1992). Ethnic differences in adolescent achievement. *American Psychologist, 47,* 723–729.

Steinberg, L., Lamborn, S. D., Dornbusch, S. M., & Darling, N. (1992). Impact of parenting practices on adolescent achievement: Authoritative parenting, school involvement, and encouragement to succeed. *Child Development, 63,* 1266–1281.

Suarez-Orozco, M. M., & Suarez-Orozco, C. E. (1995). The cultural patterning of achievement motivation: A comparison of Mexican, Mexican immigrant, Mexican American, and non-Latino White American students. In R. G. Rumbaut & W. A. Cornelius (Eds.), *California's immigrant children: Theory, research, and implications for educational policy* (pp. 161–190). San Diego: Center for U.S.-Mexican Studies, University of California, San Diego.

Suichu, E. H., & Willms, J. D. (1996). Effects of parental involvement on eighth-grade achievement. *Sociology of Education, 69,* 126–141.

Swanson, C. B., & Schneider, B. (1999). Students on the move: Residential and educational mobility in America's schools. *Sociology of Education, 72,* 54–67.

Teachman, J. D., Paasch, K., & Carver, K. (1996). School capital and dropping out of school. *Journal of Marriage and the Family, 58,* 773–783.

Texas Education Agency. (1998). *1996–97 report on grade level retention.* Austin: Texas Education Agency.

Tyler, J. H., Murnane, R. J., & Willett, J. B. (2000). Estimating the labor market signaling value of the GED. *The Quarterly Journal of Economics, 115,* 431–468.

U.S. Bureau of the Census. (1992). *Workers with low earnings.* Washington, DC: U.S. Government Printing Office.

U.S. Bureau of the Census. (1999). *School enrollment—Social and economic characteristics of students: October 1998.* Washington, DC: U.S. Government Printing Office.

U.S. Department of Education. (1990). *National goals for education.* Washington, DC: U.S. Department of Education.

U.S. Department of Education. (1998). *Goals 2000: Reforming education to improve student achievement.* Washington, DC: U.S. Department of Education.

U.S. Department of Education, National Center for Education Statistics. (2000a). *Dropout rates in the United States: 1999* (NCES 2001-022), by Phillip Kaufman, Jin Y. Kwon, Steve Klein, and Christopher D. Chapman. Washington, DC: U.S. Department of Education.

U.S. Department of Education, National Center for Education Statistics. (2000b). *Digest of education statistics, 1999.* Washington, DC: U.S. Government Printing Office.

U.S. Department of Health, Education, and Welfare. (1964). *The 1963 dropout campaign.* Washington, DC: U.S. Department of Health, Education, and Welfare.

van Heusden Hale, S. (2000). *Comprehensive school reform: Research-based strategies to achieve high standards.* San Francisco: WestEd.

Velez, W. (1989). High school attrition among Hispanic and Non-Hispanic white youths. *Sociology of Education, 62,* 119–133.

Wehlage, G. G., & Rutter, R. A. (1986). Dropping out: How much do schools contribute to the problem? *Teachers College Record, 87,* 374–392.

Wehlage, G. G., Rutter, R. A., Smith, G. A., Lesko, N., & Fernandez, R. R. (1989). *Reducing the risk: Schools as communities of support.* New York: Falmer Press.

Wehlage, G., Smith, G., & Lipman, P. (1992). Restructuring urban schools: The New Futures experience. *American Educational Research Journal, 29,* 51–93.

White, J. A., & Wehlage, G. (1995). Community collaboration: If it is such a good idea, why is it so hard to do? *Educational Evaluation and Policy Analysis, 17,* 23–38.

Wilson, W. J. (1987). *The truly disadvantaged: The inner city, the underclass, and public policy.* Chicago: The University of Chicago Press.

CHAPTER 15

PREVENTION AND TREATMENT OF ADOLESCENT DRUG ABUSE

KENNETH W. GRIFFIN
Cornell University

GILBERT J. BOTVIN
Cornell University

Adolescent substance abuse is a widespread problem that affects young people from all walks of life. Many youth begin to experiment with alcohol, tobacco, or other drugs during the early teenage years, and rates of use typically escalate over the course of adolescence. In addition to more frequent and heavier levels of use with age, this escalation can involve a progression to new and more dangerous classes of substances. Children and adolescents typically begin to experiment with substances that are readily available and legal for adults (i.e., cigarettes and alcohol). A subset of youth who experiment with tobacco and alcohol will become regular or heavy users, and some will eventually use illicit drugs, including marijuana, cocaine, hallucinogens, and narcotics. By the end of secondary school, prevalence rates are often remarkably high for alcohol, tobacco, and marijuana use. These are often referred to as *gateway* substances because their use typically precedes more serious levels of illicit drug involvement (Kandel, 2002).

Two ongoing national school-based surveys provide a great deal of information on the epidemiology of adolescent substance use and abuse. The *Monitoring the Future* study (MTF; Johnston, O'Malley, & Bachman, 2001) administers annual surveys on drug use behavior and attitudes among eighth-, tenth-, and twelfth-grade students and provides detailed data on the use of specific illicit drugs among our nation's youth. The *Youth Risk Behavior Survey* (YRBS; Kann et al., 2000) is administered by the Center for Disease Control and Prevention every two years among ninth- through twelfth-grade students and has a broader focus on several categories of risk behaviors (tobacco use, alcohol and other drug use, risky sexual behaviors, unhealthy dietary behaviors, and physical inactivity). Both of these surveys demonstrate that that alcohol, tobacco, and marijuana are the most widely used substances among adolescents in the United States. The most recent data from these studies demonstrate that, when asked about substance use in the past month, at least one in three twelfth-graders report having been drunk or engaging in binge drinking (i.e., five or more drinks in a single occasion), one in three report smoking cigarettes, and one in four report using marijuana. Furthermore, in both the MTF and YRBS surveys, over half of twelfth-graders reported using marijuana in their lifetimes, making marijuana the most commonly used illicit drug among youth.

In addition to the problem of gateway drug use, there has been growing concern about the use of Ecstasy (MDMA), other "club drugs," and increasingly potent forms of certain illicit drugs among teenagers. Ecstasy, a synthetic compound with mildly halluci- nogenic and stimulant effects, is now used by more American teenagers than cocaine. In fact, Ecstasy has shown the sharpest increase in use of any illicit drug over the past several years. In 1996, approximately 6 percent of U.S. teenagers reported ever having used Ec- stasy; this rate increased to 11 percent in 2000, according to MTF data. In addition, other drugs such as methamphetamines, cocaine (including crack cocaine), rohypnol, LSD, GHB, and heroin have seen increased use among adolescents in the past decade. Some of these drugs can be obtained in purer concentrations and in a greater number of geographic locations (e.g., suburbs and rural areas as well as cities) than in the past. Furthermore, the perceived risk of harm from substance use has been falling among teens in recent years (Johnston, O'Malley, & Bachman, 2001). Taken together, higher potency and availability of drugs combined with lower perceived risk of use indicate that drug abuse and depen- dence is a serious threat among youth. Although national data on prevalence of adolescent substance use disorder are not available, it appears to be a substantial problem. One large- scale study of approximately 75,000 Minnesota youth found that 16 percent of high school seniors met criteria for substance use disorder and 7 percent had substance dependence (Harrison, Fulkerson, & Beebe, 1998).

SUBSTANCE USE AMONG SUBGROUPS OF YOUTH

The adolescent population in the United States, like the population at large, is becoming in- creasingly diverse. Currently, approximately two-thirds of adolescents in the United States are non-Hispanic whites and one-third are of other racial and ethnic backgrounds; however by the year 2050, projections indicate that Hispanic, black, American Indian, and Asian ado- lescents will together constitute more than half (56 percent) of the adolescent population in the United States (MacKay, Fingerhut, & Duran, 2000). Despite the changing demographic makeup of American teens, much of the existing knowledge base on the etiology, prevention, and treatment of adolescent drug use and abuse is based on research conducted with middle- class white youth. Fortunately, this has been changing in recent years with an increasing number of studies examining risk and protective factors, patterns of drug and alcohol use, and the effectiveness of prevention and treatment approaches among diverse samples of youth (e.g., Botvin, Griffin, Diaz, & Ifill-Williams, 2001; Griffin, Scheier, Botvin, & Diaz, 2000; Gottfredson & Koper, 1996; Vega, Zimmerman, Warheit, Apospori, & Gil, 1993).

Epidemiological studies have shown that there are notable differences in alcohol, to- bacco, and other drug use among adolescents according to age, gender, race/ethnicity, and sexual orientation. In addition to the tendency of substance use involvement to increase with age during adolescence, some of the more consistent subgroup differences have been observed by gender. National surveys have shown that male teenagers tend to drink alcohol more frequently and in greater quantities than female teenagers (e.g., Johnston, O'Malley, & Bachman, 2001; Windle, 1991), and this gender difference has been observed across racial/ethnic groups (Kann et al., 2000). The fact that adolescent girls tend to drink less than boys may be a reflection of biological differences (e.g., lower body weight) as well as differences in the social acceptability of drinking, which tends to be higher for males. In terms of cigarette smoking, rates of use have been higher historically among male youth relative to female youth, but this gap has narrowed greatly in the past three decades. Indeed, recent national data from the MTF study indicate that smoking rates for adolescent girls now equal those for boys. The increased rate of smoking among girls, combined with the fact that most adolescents who smoke continue to do so as adults, may explain the fact that lung cancer has surpassed breast cancer as the leading cause of cancer deaths in women in the United States (Office of Research on Women's Health, 1992). Finally, males have considerably higher prevalence rates for most other categories of illicit drugs relative to females, particularly for heavy levels of use during the latter part of adolescence. *Monitoring the Future* data show that the annual prevalence rates in the twelfth grade tend to be at least 1.5 to 2 times as high among males relative to females for hallucinogens, cocaine, crack, and steroids, and that males account for an even greater share of the frequent or heavy users of these drugs (Johnston, O'Malley, & Bachman, 2001).

In terms of race/ethnicity, most national and regional surveys indicate that black youth report lower levels of alcohol, tobacco, and other drug use compared to Hispanic and white youth (Barnes & Welte, 1986; Johnston, O'Malley, & Bachman, 2001; Kann et al., 2000). However, the gap in use between black youth and others has narrowed in recent years, particularly in terms of teen smoking (Office on Smoking and Health, 1998). In the early 1990s, teen smoking began to rise among virtually all segments of youth, including black youth, reducing the racial/ethnic subgroup disparities. In addition, black youth frequently report less alcohol use compared to other groups, although they have been found to report higher levels of alcohol-related problems or negative consequences of drinking in some studies (Barnes & Welte, 1986). Both national school-based surveys indicate that Hispanic youth have rates of drug use that more closely resemble or in some cases exceed that of white youth. In fact, the YRBS study found that Hispanics in the eighth grade have the highest rates of nearly all classes of drugs, but that these rates decrease for most drug categories by the twelfth grade (Kann et al., 2000). This leveling may reflect the high rates of school dropout among Hispanic youth, which would result in fewer high-risk Hispanic youth completing the school-based survey in the later grades of high school. Nevertheless, there is evidence that Hispanic youth are more likely to use some of the most dangerous substances in the later grades of high school. In the MTF study, white youth in the twelfth grade report the highest rates of a number of drugs, including inhalants, hallucinogens, amphetamines, barbiturates, alcohol, and cigarettes; Hispanic twelfth-graders have the highest usage rates for heroin, cocaine, and crack. Although the national surveys report rates of substance use only for white, black, and Hispanic youth, other studies have reported that Asian American youth report lower rates of alcohol and drug use relative to other racial/ethnic groups (Grunbaum, Lowry, Kann, & Pateman, 2000).

Recently, there has been an increased focus on alcohol, tobacco, and other drug use among gay and lesbian youth. Less is known on this topic because the national surveys do not partition the data by sexual orientation and because the few existing studies on this topic have tended to use small, nonrepresentative samples. Nevertheless, the existing evidence suggests that rates of substance use and abuse among gay and lesbian youth are higher than rates for heterosexual youth. A recent review article concluded that heavy drinking and the use of drugs other than alcohol is common among gay and lesbian youth, despite the fact that drug and alcohol use among gay and lesbian adults appears to have declined over the past two decades (Hughes & Eliason, 2002). Other researchers have found that gay and lesbian youth report high levels of illicit drug use (Orenstein, 2001; Rosario, Hunter, & Gwadz, 1997) and it has been suggested that this may represent attempts to cope with the societal stigma of homosexuality (Rosario, Hunter, & Gwadz, 1997).

Further work is needed not only in documenting epidemiological patterns of substance use among subgroups of youth, but also in understanding similarities and differences in the etiology of drug use and abuse among subgroups of youth. A variety of factors may contribute to different substance use rates among youth from different backgrounds. For example, differences by race/ethnicity are likely to reflect different cultural norms and traditions that can occur both across and within a particular racial/ethnic group. In fact, variation within an ethnic group can in some cases be as large as differences across groups. Among Hispanics, for example, those of Caribbean origin are less prone to heavy drinking than other Hispanic groups (Dawson, 1998), and Dominican youth have been found to engage in more alcohol use than Puerto Rican adolescents (Epstein, Botvin, & Diaz, 2001).

OVERVIEW OF RISK AND PROTECTIVE FACTORS

A variety of theoretical models have been developed or applied to the phenomenon of adolescent substance use. These explanatory models suggest that a large number of psychosocial risk and protective factors contribute to the etiology of substance use and abuse among youth (reviewed in Petraitis, Flay, & Miller, 1995). For example, social learning and social influence theories describe the importance of substance-using role models such as parents, siblings, relatives, and friends (e.g., Akers, Krohn, Lanza-Kaduce, & Radosevich, 1979). In addition to the direct modeling of drug use behavior outlined in social learning models, various social attachment and conventional commitment theories—such as the social development model (Hawkins & Weis, 1985)—describe the processes by which youth withdraw from parents or school and begin to associate with peer groups that encourage drug use and other antisocial behavior. Cognitively oriented theories, such as the health belief model (Becker, 1974) and the theory of planned behavior (Ajzen, 1991), emphasize the importance of an individual's perception of risks, benefits, norms, and personal vulnerability regarding substance use, and how these factors play a role in decision-making processes. Personality and affective theories, such as the self-medication hypothesis (Khanzian, 1997), highlight the roles of individual psychological vulnerabilities and affective characteristics that can lead to drug use and abuse. Broader social psychological theories, such as problem behavior theory (PBT; Jessor & Jessor, 1977), attempt to integrate multiple determinants of adolescent substance use. Problem behavior theory proposes that drug use and other problem behaviors have similar etiologies and therefore tend to occur in the same individuals. Furthermore, according to the theory, drug use may serve a functional purpose from the perspective of the adolescent because it can help young people achieve social or personal goals that they don't believe they can achieve in more adaptive ways.

Individual Characteristics

A variety of individual-level factors have been found to be associated with adolescent substance use and abuse. Adolescents who hold favorable attitudes or expectancies regarding substance use or believe that it is normative or highly prevalent tend to engage in greater levels of use (Chen, Grube, & Madden, 1994; Simons-Morton et al., 1999). Also, a young person's propensity for rebelliousness, sensation seeking, and risk taking is an important risk factor for substance use (Wills, Vaccaro, & McNamara, 1994). Conversely, social and personal competence skills have been shown to play a key protective role in youth development in general (Gullotta, Adams, & Monetmayor, 1990; Zins, Elias, Greenberg, & Weissberg, 2000), and adolescent substance use in particular (Griffin, Epstein, Botvin, & Spoth, 2001; Pentz, 1983). Social competence is a broad construct encompassing a variety of social skills and aptitudes, including the ability to use a variety of interpersonal negotiation strategies and to communicate clearly and assertively. Youth with these skills may be well equipped to meet the social, academic, and vocational challenges of adolescence (Brion-Meisels & Selman, 1984; Zins et al., 2000). Personal competence skills, a construct representing various cognitive and behavioral self-management strategies such as decision making, self-regulation, and self-control, have also been shown be important in the etiology of youth substance use. Youth with poor social and personal competence skills may feel that they lack the skills needed to gain the acceptance and approval of peers and adults. These youth may view substance use as a way to attract attention or impress others, or alternatively, as a way to alleviate feelings of distress, meaninglessness, or failure. Indeed, several studies have shown that poor social and personal competence skills play an important role in the etiology of adolescent smoking (Epstein, Griffin, & Botvin, 2000a) as well as alcohol and other drug use (Epstein, Griffin, & Botvin, 2000b; Griffin, Botvin, Epstein, Doyle, & Diaz, 2000; Griffin, Botvin, Scheier, & Nichols, 2002). For example, youth with good competence skills appear to experience a sense of psychological well-being that serves a protective role in terms of substance use, and this protective mechanism has been observed in samples of suburban, white youth (Griffin, Scheier, Botvin, & Diaz, 2001) and urban, minority youth (Griffin, Botvin, Scheier, Epstein, & Doyle, 2002).

Finally, an important risk factor for the development of heavier levels of substance use, abuse, and dependence during late adolescence and adulthood is early age of onset of use (Anthony & Petronis, 1995; Griffin, Botvin, Doyle, Diaz, & Epstein, 1999). The younger an individual is when first beginning to use a substance, the greater the likelihood that the individual will use the substance with increasing frequency and in greater quantity as he or she gets older. Early initiation of substance use also increases the chances of other risk behaviors and adjustment problems (Durant, Smith, Kreiter, & Krowchuk, 1999). One study found that adolescents who had tried alcohol by age 12 were more likely to abuse alcohol later in adolescence and were also more likely to engage in alcohol-related violence, injuries, drinking and driving, and using other drugs during late adolescence (Gruber, DiClimente, Anderson, & Lodico, 1996).

Peer Influences

The peer group is another important social influence factor that is related to substance use and other problem behaviors in adolescents (Snyder, Dishion, & Patterson, 1986). Several studies have demonstrated the importance of peers in the etiology of adolescent smoking and alcohol use (Reifman, Barnes, Dintcheff, Farrell, & Uhteg, 1998; Stanton & Silva, 1992). Through social learning processes, associating with peers who engage in substance use is likely to foster attitudes and beliefs that promote drug use, as well as provide opportunities to learn and practice these new behaviors (Akers et al., 1979). In addition to the direct modeling of substance use behavior, exposure to deviant peer groups can establish a norm of antisocial behavior that can manifest itself not only in substance use but also in a variety of undesirable problem behaviors such as aggression, early sexual activity, and school failure. Peers are also believed to play a role in substance use in ways beyond mere social influences. For example, self-derogation theory (Kaplan, 1980) proposes that adolescents who are negatively evaluated by conventional others or feel deficient in socially desirable attributes will experience low self-esteem, which is in turn a central motivational factor leading to rebellious behavior against conventional standards, including drug use.

One issue in the literature has been the question of whether the substance use of peers tends to influence one's own behavior (peer influence) or whether young people seek out friends whose substance use behavior is similar to their own (peer selection). Although both factors are likely to occur, several studies suggest that similarity among adolescent friendship groups is more related to peer influence rather than peer selection (e.g., Sieving, Perry, & Williams, 1999). A recent study used latent growth analyses to compare peer influence and peer selection processes in adolescent substance use (Wills & Cleary, 1999). Findings indicated that initial levels of peer substance use were positively associated with rate of change in adolescent use, supporting the peer influence mechanism. Conversely, the study found little evidence for a peer selection mechanism and concluded that peer influence is the primary mechanism during middle adolescence.

Family Influences

Research and theory on the etiology of adolescent substance abuse and other problem behaviors often focus on the role of the family in the development of these behaviors (e.g., Jessor & Jessor, 1977; Steinberg, Fletcher, & Darling, 1994). Although there are many ways that family factors may be relevant, two areas have been shown to be important in the development of adolescent substance use: (1) the attitudes and behaviors of parents and siblings in regard to substance use and (2) the quantity and quality of parenting practices such as monitoring, communication, and involvement. Adolescents whose parents hold favorable attitudes about or who engage in substance use are more likely to smoke, drink, or use other drugs themselves. In terms of smoking, some studies suggest that maternal use is particularly influential. Kandel and Wu (1995) examined intergenerational transmission of cigarette smoking between parents and young adolescents and found a dose-related association between maternal smoking and children's smoking (especially daughters), but no link between paternal and child smoking. Additional studies reveal that parents' use of alcohol, marijuana, and other illicit drugs, and parental attitudes that are not explicitly against use, often translate into higher levels of use among children and adolescents (e.g., Windle, 1996).

Parenting practices have been found to be important in terms of a variety of youth outcomes and are believed to influence youth behavior through several mechanisms (Griffin, Botvin, Scheier, Diaz, & Miller, 2000). For example, parents who attend to, support, and communicate well with their children may instill appropriate values and norms regarding conventional behavior and may model appropriate coping skills and self-management strategies. Conversely, poor parent-child communication and support have been found to be frequently associated with greater youth substance use (Anderson & Henry, 1994; Selnow, 1987; Wills & Cleary, 1996). One study found that infrequent communication between parent and child and low amounts of time spent together were associated with higher rates of alcohol and tobacco use onset in fifth- to seventh-graders (Cohen, Richardson, & La Bree, 1994). Finally, parents who monitor the whereabouts of their children may help them avoid involvement with substance use and other forms of delinquency, whereas poor parental monitoring can lead to higher rates of substance use and initiation of use at earlier ages (Chilcoat & Anthony, 1996; Steinberg, Fletcher, & Darling, 1994). Additional studies have shown that other parenting variables, such as poor discipline practices, play an important role in the development of adolescent antisocial behavior (Gorman-Smith, Tolan, Zelli, & Huesmann, 1996).

Other Influences

Environmental factors such as neighborhood disorganization, poverty, and criminal activity have been shown to play a role in the etiology of adolescent problem behavior, including substance use (e.g., Simcha-Fagan & Schwartz, 1986; Wills, Pierce, & Evans, 1996). Low socioeconomic status (SES) neighborhoods are often characterized by high adult unemployment, high rates of mobility, and a lack of informal social networks and controls, and these factors together may have a negative effect on adolescent development and contribute to delinquency (Elliott et al., 1996; Yoshikawa, 1994). A study of inner-city minority youth found that substance use could be predicted by a young person's perceptions of neighborhood risk, as indicated by beliefs about the prevalence of drug-using, gang-involved peers and the availability of drugs in one's neighborhood (Blount & Dembo, 1984). A variety of other environmental factors can influence substance use and abuse, including media advertisements, television and movie portrayals that glamorize substance use, the availability and cost of drugs, and legal and policy initiatives against drug use (e.g., Wills et al., 1996). For example, states with more extensive tobacco control policies have been found to have lower rates of youth smoking (Luke, Stamatakis, & Brownson, 2000).

SUBGROUP DIFFERENCES IN RISK AND PROTECTIVE PROCESSES

Most psychosocial theories assume that the etiologic factors that lead to alcohol and drug use are applicable to youth in general, independent of ethnicity, gender, or other subgroup differences. However, as reviewed earlier, rates of substance use differ across these categories, and research shows that certain risk and protective factors are of particular importance for specific racial/ethnic groups (e.g., Maddahian, Newcomb, & Bentler, 1988). Ethnic groups often have unique traditions or culture-specific norms regarding alcohol and drug use, and there seem to be important cultural differences in drinking socialization patterns, culturally sanctioned drinking behaviors, and the meaning of drug and alcohol use (Strunin, 1999). Furthermore, among Hispanic, Asian, and other immigrant youth, levels of acculturation and acculturative stress have been found to play a role in adolescent substance use. Generally, as youth from immigrant families become more integrated into U.S. society, their drug use behavior becomes more similar to U.S. norms. In addition, when youth become acculturated at a faster rate than adults, this can contribute to deterioration of family traditions, increase acculturative stress, and ultimately increase levels of drug and alcohol use among youth (Gil, Wagner, & Vega, 2000). Similarly, certain risk and protective factors appear to be more prominent for boys or girls due to gender role socialization and other processes. For example, male adolescents often must contend with greater peer pressure to engage in substance use relative to female adolescents (Rienzi et al., 1996). In addition, gender differences in socialization processes within ethnic groups may influence substance use patterns. In many Hispanic subcultures, for example, it is normative for males to drink more alcohol than women; men drink a great deal, whereas women usually abstain from drinking due to cultural norms that discourage alcohol and drug use among Hispanic women (Canino, 1994). Thus, although there is undoubtedly substantial overlap in many of the risk and protective factors for alcohol and drug use across racial, ethnic, and gender categories, there are often important factors unique to specific subgroups of youth that should be considered.

Risk Mechanisms by Race/Ethnicity

Differences in risk and protective factors and differences in rates of substance use have been observed among subgroups of youth according to race/ethnicity, but an important question is whether the fundamental mechanisms that lead to substance use differ. A recent study examined overall levels of psychosocial risk, protection, and alcohol use among black, Hispanic, and white middle school youth and found that prevalence rates for alcohol use and risk/protection varied widely across ethnic groups (Griffin, Scheier, Botvin, & Diaz, 2000); for example, white youth reported the most risk factors and highest levels of alcohol use. Despite these observed differences, a series of structural equation models indicated that a psychosocial vulnerability latent factor consisting of cumulative risk, protection, and their interaction significantly predicted subsequent alcohol use for each ethnic and gender subgroup. This finding suggests that the fundamental mechanisms by which individual vulnerability leads to alcohol use do not depend on an individual's gender or race/ethnicity. Furthermore, some researchers have argued that demographic factors do not play a fundamental role in adolescent drug use and other risk behaviors. In a secondary analysis of data from the National Longitudinal Study of Adolescent Health, Blum and colleagues (2000) found that race/ethnicity, family income, and family structure together explained no more than 7 to 10 percent of variance in adolescent risk behaviors, and therefore "provide only limited understanding of adolescent risk behaviors." The idea that risk processes are largely similar across racial/ethnic groups may seem incompatible with research showing that some risk factors affect specific subgroups of youth. However, these findings can be reconciled when one considers that certain etiological factors are so central to the development of drug use that they affect all subgroups of youth, such as the important role of peer social influences. At the same time, there are certain etiologic factors that are specific to certain subgroups of youth (e.g., acculturation stress among youth from immigrant Hispanic families) that also exert a powerful influence on drug use behavior above and beyond the larger processes that affect all youth. This notion suggests that proven theoretically based programs that address the most central risk and protective factors for drug use are likely to be effective for a variety of youth, although additional tailoring to a specific subgroup of youth may be an effective way to address subgroup-specific risk factors.

PROMISING INTERVENTIONS

Prevention Strategies

Over the past three decades, several approaches to drug and alcohol abuse prevention have been implemented and evaluated. Traditionally, drug and alcohol abuse education has involved the dissemination of information about drug abuse and the negative health, social, and legal consequences of abuse. However, meta-analytic studies of informational approaches have shown that these programs fail to show any impact on drug use behavior or intentions to use drugs in the future (Tobler & Stratton, 1997).

Contemporary approaches to prevention include social resistance and competence enhancement programs that focus on interactive skills training techniques, and less so on didactic instruction. The majority of preventive interventions are provided to students in school settings during middle school (grades 6 to 8) or junior high school (grades 7 to 9)—an age when many youth begin to experiment with substance use. The most promising contemporary approaches are those that are grounded in psychological theories of human behavior and have been shown to be effective in rigorous evaluation studies that use appropriate research designs and statistical methods. Contemporary programs are typically categorized into one of three types: universal programs that focus on the general population, such as all students in a particular school; selective programs that target high-risk groups, such as poor school achievers; and indicated programs that are designed for youth already experimenting with drugs or engaging in other high-risk behaviors.

Social Resistance Approaches.   Contemporary approaches to prevention recognize that social and psychological factors play a central role in the initiation of cigarette smoking and drug and alcohol abuse among youth. The social resistance approach conceptualizes adolescent drug abuse as a result of pro-drug social influences from peers, persuasive advertising appeals and media portrayals that encourage drug use, and exposure to drug-using role models. The social influence prevention programs therefore focus on teaching students how to recognize and deal with social influences (from peers and the media) to use drugs by focusing on skills training to increase students' resistance to negative social influences to engage in drug use, particularly peer pressure. The goal of resistance skills training approaches is to have students learn ways to avoid high-risk situations where they are likely to experience peer pressure to smoke, drink, or use drugs, and/or acquire the knowledge, confidence, and skills needed to handle peer pressure in these and other situations. These programs frequently include a component that makes students aware of pro-smoking influences from the media, with an emphasis on the techniques used by advertisers to influence consumer behavior. Also, because adolescents tend to overestimate the prevalence of tobacco, alcohol, and drug use, social resistance programs often attempt to correct normative expectations that nearly everybody smokes, drinks alcohol, or uses drugs.

Resistance skills programs as a whole have generally been effective. A comprehensive review of resistance skills studies published from 1980 to 1990 reported that the majority of prevention studies (63 percent) had positive effects on drug use behavior, with fewer studies having neutral (26 percent) or negative effects on behavior (11 percent)—with several in the neutral category having inadequate statistical power to detect program effects (Hansen, 1992). Several follow-up studies of resistance skills interventions have reported positive behavioral effects lasting for up to three years (Luepker, Johnson, Murray, & Pechacek, 1983; McAlister, Perry, Killen, Slinkard, & Maccoby, 1980; Telch, Killen, McAlister, Perry, & Maccoby, 1982). However, data from several longer-term follow-up studies have shown that these effects gradually decay over time (Murray, Davis-Hearn, Goldman, Pirie, & Luepker, 1988; Flay et al., 1989), suggesting the need for ongoing intervention or booster sessions.

Competence Enhancement Approaches.   According to the competence enhancement approach, drug use behavior is learned through a process of modeling, imitation, and reinforcement and is influenced by an adolescent's pro-drug cognitions, attitudes, and beliefs (Botvin, 2000). These factors, in combination with poor personal and social skills, are believed to increase an adolescent's susceptibility to social influences in favor of drug use. A weakness of the social influence approach is that it assumes young people do not want to use drugs but lack the social skills or confidence to refuse drug offers. Conversely, the competence enhancement approach recognizes that for some youth, using drugs may have instrumental value and may, for example, help them deal with anxiety, low self-esteem, or a lack of comfort in social situations. Thus, the competence enhancement approach to prevention emphasizes the teaching of generic personal self-management skills and social coping skills in addition to resistance skills training (Botvin, 2000). Over the years, a number of evaluation studies have been conducted testing the efficacy of competence enhancement approaches to drug abuse prevention. These studies have consistently demonstrated behavioral effects as well as effects on hypothesized mediating variables. Notably, the magnitude of reported effects of these approaches has been relatively large, with studies typically reporting reductions in drug use behavior in the range of 40 to 80 percent. In summary, drug abuse prevention programs that emphasize resistance skills and general life skills (i.e., competence enhancement approaches) appear to show the most promise of all school-based prevention approaches.

Programs for Elementary School Students.   Most drug prevention programs are provided to middle school students, but some experts have suggested that the later elementary school years may be a critical time to begin prevention programming for tobacco and alcohol use (Sarvela, Monge, Shannon, & Nawrot, 1999). Some elementary school students begin to experiment with tobacco or alcohol. For example, Elder and colleagues (1996) found that nearly 5 percent of fifth-graders reported smoking cigarettes. Furthermore, many of the same etiologic factors that promote teen substance use appear to play a role in substance use onset among younger populations (O'Loughlin, Paradis, Renaud, & Sanchez, 1998). The type of approaches that have been developed for elementary school students have included smoke-free school policies (Elder et al., 1996), broad-based health promotion efforts (O'Loughlin, Paradis, Renaud, & Sanchez, 1998), and school-based approaches teaching resistance skills and knowledge of immediate negative effects (Shope, Dielman, Butcchart, Campanelli, & Kloska, 1992). Few of these approaches have produced an impact on smoking or alcohol use behavior, although some have had a positive impact on drug knowledge and intentions (Price, Beach, Everett, Tellijohann, & Lewis, 1998). Contemporary approaches adapted for elementary school have shown a limited amount of success. For example, a randomized trial with 5,000 fifth- and sixth-graders tested a prevention program emphasizing resistance skills training for peer pressure, knowledge regarding immediate effects of alcohol, and risks of alcohol misuse and found significant prevention effects on alcohol misuse (Shope, Dielman, Butchart, Campanelli, & Kloska, 1992). Therefore, it may be useful to begin drug abuse prevention programs in the elementary school years and continue them into the middle school years.

Treatment Strategies

Among adolescents, differentiating between substance *use* and *abuse* is complicated by the fact that many parents, teachers, and other adults view any level of substance use among minors to be of concern. Nevertheless, some youth clearly become heavy drug users, develop substance use problems, and/or become dependent on drugs. Heavy or chronic drug abuse during adolescence can impair psychosocial functioning and lead to a variety of serious short- and long-term consequences. For example, drug and alcohol abuse during adolescence may be associated with some delay in normal cognitive, social, and emotional development. Furthermore, chronic alcohol use during adolescence has been shown to be related to greater levels of alcohol problems, aggression, theft, and suicide ideation in young adulthood among both males and females (Duncan, Alpert, Duncan, & Hops, 1997). Other research has shown that adolescent drug or alcohol involvement serious enough to warrant treatment leads to more cumulative health problems during early adulthood (Aarons et al., 1999). To reduce the negative effects of adolescent drug abuse and addiction, effective treatment programs are of utmost importance.

Treatment programs for adolescent drug abuse should be tailored to youth along a continuum, depending on the severity of the substance use problem, from minimal outpatient visits to long-term residential treatment. Early intervention, such as brief outpatient therapy, should be used for less intense drug abuse problems, where the goal is to provide guidance and support for a young person who is able to function in a nonstructured setting; for more severe and intense drug problems, intensive outpatient treatment, partial hospitalization, or medically monitored inpatient or residential treatment may be needed (Center for Substance Abuse Treatment, 1999). Three of the most common and distinctive types of treatments or therapies for adolescents with drug problems in the United States are (1) 12-Step–based support groups, (2) family therapy, and (3) residential therapeutic communities

(Winters, 1999). These approaches may be appropriate for a particular youth, depending on a variety of factors, including the degree of physical and psychological dependence, the levels of social support available within and outside the family, and the degree of comorbidity with conduct disorder, learning problems, and other risk behaviors.

12-Step Approaches. Substance abuse 12-Step programs, such as Alcoholics Anonymous or Narcotics Anonymous, are essentially self-help group meetings in which participants are encouraged to share their experiences with others who have suffered similar problems with substance abuse. According to this approach, drug abuse is a disease and abstinence is the goal of therapy. Most 12-Step programs focus on the first 5 steps during the primary treatment phase, and the remaining steps are addressed during a period of aftercare. These initial phases of therapy encourage the adolescent to share details about his or her problem with drugs and the negative consequences experienced; to interact with others, including those who have been successful in the program; to be open to assistance from others in dealing with their problem; and to accept and be accepted by others in spite of past difficulties. An important goal of this approach is to help the adolescent learn to focus on the present by taking one day at a time without drugs.

Family Therapy. Because most adolescents live at home with their families and, as noted earlier, many family or parenting factors can influence youth substance use and related behaviors, the young person within his or her family context is often an appropriate target of intervention for adolescents with substance use problems. Contemporary family therapy approaches recognize that the way that family members interact with each other is important in the healthy development of young people, and that decreasing family conflicts and improving the effectiveness of communication can be helpful in preventing substance use and other problem behaviors. Family therapy also typically aims to provide parents with the skills and resources to raise their adolescent successfully by providing instruction in parental monitoring skills, appropriate discipline practices, and other parenting skills (Center for Substance Abuse Treatment, 1999).

Therapeutic Communities. Therapeutic communities are highly structured, residential treatment programs that are typically used to treat youth with the most severe substance abuse problems. Daily activities are structured around group activities, seminars, formal and informal interactions with peers and staff, chores, and meals (Center for Substance Abuse Treatment, 1999). The regimented structure of activities and various task responsibilities given to youth for maintaining the community are seen as mechanisms to teach self-development. With time, young members of a therapeutic community typically take on increasing responsibility, and in turn enjoy greater privileges.

The outcome studies examining adolescent substance abuse treatment are few, and most tend to be methodologically weak. A recent comparative review of treatment outcomes found that successful outcomes could be predicted by treatment completion, low pretreatment substance use, and peer/parent social support and parental nonuse of substances (Williams & Chang, 2000). Furthermore, effective treatment programs for adolescents are often not readily available, and more work is needed in identifying what works and how to disseminate these effective approaches.

TWO APPROACHES TO SCHOOL-BASED
DRUG PREVENTION

This section compares two approaches to school-based drug abuse prevention: Project DARE (Drug Abuse Resistance Education) and Life Skills Training (LST).

Drug Abuse Resistance Education (DARE)

The most popular school-based drug education program based on the social influence model is Drug Abuse Resistance Education, or Project DARE. The core DARE curriculum is typically provided to children in the fifth or sixth grades, and contains elements of information dissemination and social influence approaches to drug abuse prevention. Project DARE uses trained, uniformed police officers in the classroom to teach the drug prevention curriculum. The fact that police departments throughout the country have embraced it has provided a natural dissemination system unparalleled by other prevention programs. Being a prevention program that is implemented by police officers and supported by law-enforcement agencies around the country makes DARE unique and has no doubt contributed to its adoption by a large number of schools. According to news accounts, DARE is said to be used in approximately 60 percent of the elementary school classrooms in the United States.

Yet, despite its acknowledged success in promoting awareness of drug abuse and gaining adoption by more schools across the country than any other program, DARE has been plagued by disappointing evaluation results and a surprising amount of negative news coverage. According to a major meta-analysis of studies evaluating the DARE program, it is less effective than other social influence approaches and has produced only minimal effects on drug use behavior (Ennett, Tobler, Ringwalt, & Flewelling, 1994). Recent evaluation studies of Project DARE using scientifically rigorous designs (i.e., large samples, random assignment, and longitudinal follow-up) have shown that project DARE has little or no impact on drug use behaviors, particularly beyond the initial posttest assessment (Rosenbaum & Hanson, 1998).

Because DARE has much in common with other prevention approaches based on the social influence model, its poor evaluation results are difficult to explain. In view of the fact that the main difference between similar programs showing reductions in drug use and DARE is the program provider, a logical conclusion is that the absence of strong prevention effects may be related more to the program provider than the program itself. DARE and other prevention programs are provided during a developmental period when individuals, particularly those who are at greatest risk for engaging in deviant behaviors, are increasingly likely to rebel against authority figures. Because a police officer is the ultimate symbol of authority in our society, it is reasonable to expect them to have lower credibility with high-risk children and adolescents and, correspondingly, to be less effective as a drug abuse prevention program provider. Still, the effectiveness of police officers as program providers has not been directly tested, so it remains an open question in need of empirical clarification.

Life Skills Training (LST)

The Life Skills Training program is a universal prevention program intended to prevent the early stages of drug abuse by addressing risk factors associated with drug use, particularly occasional or experimental use. The LST program is typically implemented in middle schools over the course of 15 class periods in the first year, 10 booster sessions in the second year, and 5 in the third year. Typically, the intervention is started with seventh-graders, and booster sessions (when included) are provided in the eighth and ninth grades. Curriculum materials have been developed to increase the standardization of implementing the LST program and increase its exportability, and these materials consist of a *Teacher's Manual* and a *Student Guide* for each year of the program (for further information, see www. lifeskillstraining.com).

The LST program was designed to promote the development of personal self-management skills and general social skills while also influencing drug-related knowledge, attitudes, and norms, and teaching skills for resisting social influences to use drugs. The personal skills component of the LST program contains material to (1) foster the development of decision making and problem solving, (2) provide students with self-control skills for coping with anxiety and anger/frustration, and (3) provide students with the basic principles of personal behavior change and self-improvement. The social skills component contains material designed to help students improve general interpersonal skills. This material emphasizes the teaching of (1) communication skills; (2) general social skills, such as the ability to initiate social interactions, carry on a conversation, compliment others, and overcome shyness; (3) skills related to personal relationships; and (4) both verbal and nonverbal assertive skills.

The drug-related information and skills component is designed to impact on knowledge and attitudes concerning drug use, normative expectations, and skills for resisting drug use influences from the media and peers. The material contained in this component is similar to that contained in many psychosocial drug abuse prevention programs—such as the consequences of drug use and the immediate physiological effects of cigarette smoking; information to correct normative expectations about drug use; material concerning media pressures to smoke, drink, or use drugs; and techniques for resisting direct peer pressure to smoke, drink, or use illicit drugs.

A variety of intervention methods are used to teach the content of the LST program, including the use of traditional didactic teaching methods, facilitation/group discussion, classroom demonstrations, and cognitive-behavioral skills training. Most of the material can best be taught by facilitating group discussion and through extensive skills training exercises. The LST program has been successfully implemented by several different types of intervention providers, including health professionals, older peer leaders, and regular classroom teachers. Of course, there are several advantages in being able to use a classroom teacher as the program provider. Teachers are readily available and generally have more extensive classroom management skills and teaching experience compared to other potential providers.

The results of our own work suggest that prevention effects from the LST program are relatively long lasting. Results from a large-scale, randomized field trial involving nearly 6,000 seventh-graders from 56 public schools found long-term reductions in smoking, alcohol, and marijuana use at the end of the twelfth grade (Botvin, Baker, Dusenbury, Botvin, & Diaz, 1995). In this study, schools were randomly assigned to prevention and control conditions, and students in the intervention condition received the LST program beginning in the seventh grade through the ninth grade. Students were over 90 percent white, 52 percent male, and over 80 percent lived in two-parent families in suburban or rural areas of New York state. According to the results, the prevalence of cigarette smoking, alcohol use, and marijuana use for the students in the prevention condition was as much as 44 percent lower than for controls in the twelfth grade, and rate of multiple drug use was 66 percent lower for students who received the program relative to controls. Another study examined the long-term impact of the LST program on illicit drug use among an anonymous subsample of students (mean age = 19), and findings indicated that there were significantly lower levels of illicit drug use among the LST students relative to controls on several outcomes, including overall illicit drug use and illicit drug use other than marijuana, hallucinogens, heroin, and other narcotics (Botvin et al., 2000).

More recent work has tested the same underlying prevention strategy with different populations in order to determine its potential effectiveness and generalizability. During the course of this work, some modifications were made, where warranted, to maximize generalizability, cultural sensitivity, relevance, and acceptability to predominantly African American and Hispanic inner-city youth. None of the modifications in prevention materials and methods involved any fundamental changes to the underlying prevention strategy. A recent randomized controlled trial of the LST program among inner-city minority youth tested the effectiveness of the prevention intervention in a sample of predominantly minority students ($n = 3,621$) in 29 New York City schools (Botvin, Griffin, Diaz, & Ifill-Williams, 2001a). Results indicated that those who received the program ($n = 2,144$) reported less smoking, drinking, drunkenness, inhalant use, and polydrug use relative to controls ($n = 1,477$). The program also had a direct positive effect on several cognitive, attitudinal, and personality variables believed to play a role in adolescent substance use. Mediational analyses showed that prevention effects on some drug use outcomes were mediated in part by risk taking, behavioral intentions, and peer normative expectations regarding drug use. The findings from this study show that a drug abuse prevention program originally designed for white middle-class adolescent populations is effective in a sample of minority, economically disadvantaged, inner-city adolescents. Another recent study showed that the prevention program had protective effects in terms of binge drinking at the one-year (eighth-grade) and two-year (ninth-grade) follow-up assessments; the proportion of binge drinkers was over 50 percent lower in the intervention group relative to the control group at the follow-up assessments (Botvin, Griffin, Diaz, & Ifill-Williams, 2001b). Taken as a whole, these studies provide evidence that the same prevention approach with relatively modest modifications is effective with white, African American, and Hispanic youth.

A new version of the Life Skills Training program has been recently developed for elementary school students in grades 3 through 6. The middle school version was adapted and revised to make it developmentally appropriate for younger children. Recently, the impact of the prevention program was tested with respect to early-stage tobacco and alcohol use as well as several hypothesized mediating variables (Botvin, Griffin, Paul, & Macauley, in press). Rates of substance use behavior, attitudes, knowledge, normative expectations, and related variables were examined among students ($n = 1,090$) from 20 schools that were randomly assigned to either receive the prevention program (9 schools, $n = 426$) or serve as a control group (11 schools, $n = 664$). School-level analyses showed that the annual prevalence rate was 61 percent lower for smoking and 25 percent lower for alcohol use at the posttest assessment in schools that received the prevention program when compared with control schools. In addition, mean self-esteem scores were higher in intervention schools at the posttest assessment relative to control schools. Findings indicate that a school-based substance abuse prevention approach previously found to be effective among middle school students is also effective for elementary school students.

SUMMARY

Adolescent substance use and abuse are widespread problems that affect many types of youth. A variety of factors may contribute to patterns of substance use among subgroups of adolescents, such as different cultural norms, traditions, and gender socialization processes. Similarly, several theoretical models suggest that a variety of factors contribute to the etiology of alcohol and drug use among youth, and these theories outline the role of cognitive, social learning, personality, and social attachment factors in the development of drug use and related problem behaviors among youth. Individual characteristics, peer influences, family factors, parenting practices, and a variety of other environmental influences can serve as risk and protective factors for adolescent drug use and abuse.

Substantial progress has been made in drug abuse prevention and treatment programs over the past several years. It has become clear that some of the most widely used prevention approaches, such as those that rely on the provision of information concerning the adverse consequences of drug abuse, are either ineffective or of unproven effectiveness. Prevention approaches that focus on psychosocial factors associated with drug abuse and that emphasize the teaching of social resistance, personal self-management, and social skills are the most promising, and have been found to be capable of reducing drug use for up to several years, including until the end of high school. A variety of treatment options are available for adolescents with drug use disorders or dependence, and these range along a continuum, ranging from outpatient office visits to residential therapy. However, effective prevention and treatment programs are unlikely to have a large public health impact because they are still not widely utilized. An important goal of future research is to identify and overcome the barriers against the dissemination and adoption of proven programs.

DISCUSSION QUESTIONS

1. What factors might help explain the finding that young people increasingly perceive the risk of harm from substance use to be low?

2. What reasons, aside from biological factors and differences in the social acceptability of drinking, might contribute to higher levels of alcohol use among adolescent boys relative to girls?

3. What are the relationships among peer drug use, parental drug use, and a young person's decision to try drugs? Are the effects of peer use and parental use simply additive or are they synergistic in their influence on experimentation?

4. Should drug abuse prevention and treatment programs focus on abstinence only? Why or why not?

5. At what point is treatment for adolescent substance use indicated?

SUGGESTED READINGS

Ammerman, R. T., Ott, P. J., & Tarter, R. E. (Eds.). (1999). Prevention and societal impact of drug and alcohol abuse. Mahwah, NJ: Erlbaum.

Hawkins, J. D., Catalano, R. F., & Miller, J. Y. (1992). Risk and protective factors for alcohol and other drug problems in adolescence and early adulthood: Implications for substance abuse prevention. *Psychological Bulletin, 112,* 64–105.

Kandel, D. B. (2002). *Examining the gateway hypothesis: Stages and pathways of drug involvement.* New York: Cambridge University Press.

Newcomb, M. D., & Bentler, P. M. (1988). *Consequences of adolescent drug use: Impact on the lives of young adults.* New York: Sage.

Preventing Drug Use Among Children and Adolescents: A Research-Based Guide. National Institute on Drug Abuse; National Institute of Health. (Available online at http://www.nida.nih.gov/Prevention/PREVOPEN.html)

REFERENCES

Aarons, G. A., Brown, S. A., Coe, M. T., Myers, M. G., Garland, A. F., Ezzet-Lofstram, R., Hazen, A. L., & Hough, R. L. (1999). Adolescent alcohol and drug abuse and health. *Journal of Adolescent Health, 24,* 412–421.

Ajzen, I. (1991). The theory of planned behavior. *Organizational Behavior and Human Decision Processes, 50,* 179–211.

Akers, R. L., Krohn, M. D., Lanza-Kaduce, L., & Radosevich, M. (1979). Social learning and deviant behavior: A specific test of a general theory. *American Sociological Review, 44,* 636–655.

Anderson, A. R., & Henry, C. S. (1994). Family system characteristics and parental behaviors as predictors of adolescent substance use. *Adolescence, 29,* 405–420.

Anthony, J. C., & Petronis, K. R. (1995). Early-onset drug use and risk of later drug problems. *Drug & Alcohol Dependence, 40,* 9–15.

Barnes, G. M., & Welte, J. W. (1986). Adolescent alcohol abuse: Subgroup differences and relationships to other problem behaviors. *Journal of Research on Adolescence, 1,* 79–94.

Becker, M. H. (1974). *The health belief model and personal health behavior.* Thorofare, NJ: Slack.

Blount, W. R., & Dembo, R. (1984). The effect of perceived neighborhood setting on self-reported tobacco, alcohol, and marijuana use among inner-city minority junior high school youth. *International Journal of the Addictions, 19,* 175–198.

Blum, R. W., Beuhring, T., Shew, M. L., Bearinger, L. H., Sieving, R. E., & Resnick, M. D. (2000). The effects of race/ethnicity, income, and family structure on adolescent risk behaviors. *American Journal of Public Health, 90,* 1879–1884.

Botvin, G. J. (2000). Preventing drug abuse in schools: Social and competence enhancement approaches targeting individual-level etiological factors. *Addictive Behaviors, 25,* 887–897.

Botvin, G. J., Baker, E., Dusenbury, L., Botvin, E. M., & Diaz, T. (1995). Long-term follow-up results of a randomized drug abuse prevention trial in a White middle-class population. *Journal of the American Medical Association, 273,* 1106–1112.

Botvin, G. J., Griffin, K. W., Diaz, T., & Ifill-Williams, M. (2001a). Drug abuse prevention among minority adolescents: One-year follow-up of a school-based preventive intervention. *Prevention Science, 2,* 1–13.

Botvin, G. J., Griffin, K. W., Diaz, T., & Ifill-Williams, M. (2001b). Preventing binge drinking during early adolescence: One- and two-year follow-up of a school-based preventive intervention. *Psychology of Addictive Behaviors, 15,* 360–365.

Botvin, G. J., Griffin, K. W., Diaz, T., Scheier, L. M., Williams, C., & Epstein, J. A. (2000). Preventing illicit drug use in adolescents: Long-term follow-up data from a randomized control trial of a school population. *Addictive Behaviors, 5,* 769–774.

Botvin, G. J., Griffin, K. W., Paul, E., & Macauley, A. P. (in press). Preventing tobacco and alcohol use among elementary school students through Life Skills Training. *Journal of Child & Adolescent Substance Abuse.*

Brion-Meisels, S., & Selman, R. L. (1984). Early adolescent development of new interpersonal strategies: Understanding and intervention. *School Psychology Review, 13,* 278–291.

Canino, G. (1994). Alcohol use and misuse among Hispanic women: Selected factors, processes, and studies. *International Journal of the Addictions, 29,* 1083–1100.

Center for Substance Abuse Treatment. (1999). *Treatment of adolescents with substance use disorders.* Treatment Improvement Protocol (TIP) Series 32 (DHHS Publication No. (SMA) 99–3283). Rockville, MD: Substance Abuse and Mental Health Services Administration.

Chen, M., Grube, J. W., & Madden, P. A. (1994). Alcohol expectancies and adolescent drinking: Differential prediction of frequency, quantity, and intoxication. *Addictive Behaviors, 19,* 521–529.

Chilcoat, H. D., & Anthony, J. C. (1996). Impact of parental monitoring on initiation of drug use through late childhood. *Journal of the American Academy of Child & Adolescent Psychiatry, 35,* 91–100.

Cohen, D. A., Richardson, J., & La Bree, L. (1994). Parenting behaviors and the onset of smoking and alcohol use: A longitudinal study. *Pediatrics, 94,* 368–375.

Dawson, D. A. (1998). Beyond black, white, and Hispanic: Race, ethnic origin, and drinking patterns in the United States. *Journal of Substance Abuse, 10,* 321–339.

Donaldson, S. I., Sussman, S., MacKinnon, D. P., Severson, H. H., Glynn, T., Murray, D. M., & Stone, E. J. (1996). Drug abuse prevention programming: Do we know what content works? *American Behavioral Scientist, 39,* 868–883.

Duncan, S. C., Alpert, A., Duncan, T. E., & Hops, H. (1997). Adolescent alcohol use development and young adult outcomes. *Drug & Alcohol Dependence, 49,* 39–48.

Durant, R. H., Smith, J. A., Kreiter, S. R., & Krowchuk, D. P. (1999). The relationship between early age of onset of initial substance use and engaging in multiple health risk behaviors among young adolescents. *Archives of Pediatric & Adolescent Medicine, 153,* 286–291.

Elder, J. P., Perry, C. L., Stone, E. J., Johnson, C. C., Yang, M., Edmundson, E. W., Smyth, M. H., Galati, T., Feldman, H., Cribb, P., & Parcel, G. S. (1996). Tobacco use measurement, prediction, and intervention in elementary schools in four states: The CATCH study. *Preventive Medicine, 25,* 486–494.

Elliott, D. S., Wilson, W. J., Huizinga, D., Sampson, R. J., et al. (1996). The effects of neighborhood disadvantage on adolescent development. *Journal of Research in Crime & Delinquency, 33,* 389–426.

Ennett, S. T., Tobler, N. S., Ringwalt, C. L., & Flewelling, R. L. (1994). How effective is Drug Abuse Resistance Education? A meta-analysis of Project D. A. R. E. outcome evaluations. *American Journal of Public Health, 84,* 1394–1401.

Epstein, J. A., Botvin, G. J., & Diaz, T. (2001). Alcohol use among Dominican and Puerto Rican adolescents residing in New York City: Role of Hispanic group and gender. *Journal of Developmental & Behavioral Pediatrics, 2,* 1–6.

Epstein, J. A., Griffin, K. W., & Botvin, G. J. (2000a). A model of smoking among inner-city adolescents: The role of personal competence and perceived social benefits of smoking. *Preventive Medicine, 31,* 107–114.

Epstein, J. A., Griffin, K. W., & Botvin, G. J. (2000b). Role of general and specific competence skills in alcohol use among inner-city adolescents. *Journal of Studies on Alcohol, 61,* 379–386.

Flay, B. R., Keopke, D., Thomson, S. J., Santi, S., Best, J. A., & Brown, K. S. (1989). Long-term follow-up of the first Waterloo smoking prevention trial. *American Journal of Public Health, 79,* 1371–1376.

Gil, A. G., Wagner, E. F., & Vega, W. A. (2000). Acculturation, familism, and alcohol use among Latino adolescent males: Longitudinal relations. *Journal of Community Psychology, 28,* 443–458.

Gorman-Smith, D., Tolan, P. H., Zelli, A., & Huesmann, L. R. (1996). The relation of family functioning to violence among inner-city minority youths. *Journal of Family Psychology, 10,* 115–129.

Gottfredson, D. C., & Koper, C. S. (1996). Race and sex differences in the prediction of drug use. *Journal of Consulting & Clinical Psychology, 64,* 305–313.

Griffin, K. W., Botvin, G. J., Doyle, M. M., Diaz, T., & Epstein, J. A. (1999). A six-year follow-up study of determinants of heavy cigarette smoking among high school seniors. *Journal of Behavioral Medicine, 22,* 271–284.

Griffin, K. W., Botvin, G. J., Epstein, J. A., Doyle, M. M., & Diaz, T. (2000). Psychosocial and behavioral factors in early adolescence as predictors of heavy drinking among high school seniors. *Journal of Studies on Alcohol, 61,* 603–607.

Griffin, K. W., Botvin, G. J., Scheier, L. M., Diaz, T., & Miller, N. (2000). Parenting practices as predictors of substance use, delinquency, and aggression among urban minority youth: Moderating effects of family structure and gender. *Psychology of Addictive Behaviors, 14,* 174–184.

Griffin, K. W., Botvin, G. J., Scheier, L. M., Epstein, J. A., & Diaz, T. (2002). Personal competence skills, distress, and well-being as determinants of substance use in a predominantly minority urban adolescent sample. *Prevention Science, 3,* 23–33.

Griffin, K. W., Botvin, G. J., Scheier, L. M., & Nichols, T. R. (2002). Factors associated with regular marijuana use among high school students: A long-term follow-up study. *Substance Use & Misuse, 37,* 225–238.

Griffin, K. W., Epstein, J. A., Botvin, G. J., & Spoth, R. L. (2001). Social competence and substance use among rural youth: Mediating role of social benefit expectancies of use. *Journal of Youth & Adolescence, 30,* 485–498.

Griffin, K. W., Scheier, L. M., Botvin, G. J., & Diaz, T. (2000). Ethnic and gender differences in psychosocial risk, protection, and adolescent alcohol use. *Prevention Science, 1,* 199–212.

Griffin, K. W., Scheier, L. M., Botvin, G. J., & Diaz, T. (2001). The protective role of personal competence skills in adolescent substance use: Psychological well-being as a mediating factor. *Psychology of Addictive Behaviors, 15,* 194–203.

Gruber, E., DiClimente, R. J., Anderson, M. M., & Lodico, M. (1996). Early drinking onset and its association with alcohol use and problem behavior in late adolescence. *Preventive Medicine, 25,* 293–300.

Grunbaum, J. A., Lowry, R., Kann, L., & Pateman, B. (2000). Prevalence of health risk behaviors among Asian-American/Pacific Islander high school students. *Journal of Adolescent Health, 27,* 322–330.

Gullotta, T. P., Adams, G. R., & Monetmayor, R. (1990). *Developing social competency in adolescence.* Newbury Park, CA: Sage Publications.

Hansen, W. B. (1992). School-based substance abuse prevention: A review of the state of the art in curriculum, 1980–1990. *Health Education Research: Theory & Practice, 7,* 403–430.

Harrison, P. A., Fulkerson, J. A., & Beebe, T. J. (1998). DSM-IV substance use disorder criteria for adolescents: A critical examination based on a statewide school survey. *American Journal of Psychiatry, 155,* 486–492.

Hawkins, J. D., & Weis, J. G. (1985). The social development model: An integrated approach to delinquency prevention. *Journal of Primary Prevention, 6,* 73–97.

Hughes, T. L., & Eliason, M. (2002). Substance use and abuse in lesbian, gay, bisexual and transgender populations. *Journal of Primary Prevention, 22,* 263–298.

Jessor, R., & Jessor, S. L. (1977). *Problem behavior and psychosocial development: A longitudinal study of youth.* San Diego, CA: Academic Press.

Johnston, L. D., O'Malley, P. M., & Bachman, J. G. (2001). *Monitoring the future national survey results on drug use, 1975–2000. Volume I: Secondary school students* (NIH Publication No. 01–4924). Bethesda, MD: National Institute on Drug Abuse.

Kandel, D. B. (2002). *Examining the gateway hypothesis: Stages and pathways of drug involvement.* New York: Cambridge University Press.

Kandel, D. B., & Wu, P. (1995). The contributions of mothers and fathers to the intergenerational transmission of cigarette smoking in adolescence. *Journal of Research on Adolescence, 5,* 225–252.

Kann, L., Kinchen, S. A., Williams, B. I., Ross, J. G., Lowry, R., Grunbaum, J., Kolbe, L. J., & State and Local YRBSS Coordinators. (2000). Youth Risk Behavior Surveillance—United States, 1999. *Morbidity & Mortality Weekly Report, 49* (No. SS-5), 1–95.

Kaplan, H. B. (1980). *Deviant behavior in defense of self.* New York: Academic Press.

Khantzian, E. J. (1997). The self-medication hypothesis of substance use disorders: A reconsideration and recent applications. *Harvard Review of Psychiatry, 4,* 231–244.

Luepker, R. V., Johnson, C. A., Murray, D. M., & Pechacek, T. F. (1983). Prevention of cigarette smoking: Three year follow up of educational programs for youth. *Journal of Behavioral Medicine, 6,* 53–61.

Luke, D. A., Stamatakis, K. A., & Brownson, R. C. (2000). State youth-access tobacco control policies and youth smoking behavior in the United States. *American Journal of Preventive Medicine, 19,* 180–187.

MacKay, A. P., Fingerhut, L. A., & Duran, C. R. (2000). *Adolescent health chartbook. Health, United States, 2000.* Hyattsville, MD: National Center for Health Statistics.

Maddahian, E., Newcomb, M. D., & Bentler, P. M. (1988). Risk factors for substance use: Ethnic differences among adolescents. *Journal of Substance Abuse, 1,* 11–23.

McAlister, A., Perry, C. L., Killen, J., Slinkard, L. A., & Maccoby, N. (1980). Pilot study of smoking, alcohol, and drug abuse prevention. *American Journal of Public Health, 70,* 719–721.

Murray, D. M., Davis-Hearn, M., Goldman, A. I., Pirie, P., & Luepker, R. V. (1988). Four and five year follow-up results from four seventh-grade smoking prevention strategies. *Journal of Behavioral Medicine, 11,* 395–405.

Office of Research on Women's Health. (1992). Report of the National Institutes of Health. *Opportunities for research on women's health.* Hunt Valley, MD: U.S. Department of Health and Human Services, National Institutes of Health, NIH Publication No. 92–3457.

Office on Smoking and Health. (1998). *Tobacco use among US racial-ethnic minority groups: A report of the surgeon general.* Atlanta, GA: U.S. Department of Health and Human Services, Centers for Disease Control and Prevention.

O'Loughlin, J., Paradis, G., Renaud, L., & Sanchez, G. L. (1998). One-year predictors of smoking initiation and of continued smoking among elementary schoolchildren in multi-ethnic, low-income, inner-city neighborhoods. *Tobacco Control, 3,* 268–275.

Orenstein, A. (2001). Substance use among gay and lesbian adolescents. *Journal of Homosexuality, 41,* 1–15.

Pentz, M. A. (1983). Prevention of adolescent substance abuse through social skill development. *National Institute on Drug Abuse Research Monograph, 47,* 195–232.

Petraitis, J., Flay, B. R., & Miller, T. Q. (1995). Reviewing theories of adolescent substance use: Organizing pieces in the puzzle. *Psychological Bulletin, 117,* 67–86.

Price, J. H., Beach, P., Everett, S., Tellijohann, S. K., & Lewis, L. (1998). Evaluation of a three year urban elementary school prevention program. *Journal of School Health, 68,* 26–31.

Reifman, A., Barnes, G. M., Dintcheff, B. A., Farrell, M. P., & Uhteg, L. (1998). Parental and peer influences on the onset of heavier drinking among adolescents. *Journal of Studies on Alcohol, 59,* 311–317.

Rienzi, B. M., McMillin, J. D., Dickson, C. L., Crauthers, D., McNeill, K. F., Pesnia, M. D., & Mann, E. (1996). Gender differences regarding peer influence and attitude toward substance use. *Journal of Drug Education, 26,* 339–347.

Rosario, M., Hunter, J., & Gwadz, M. (1997). Exploration of substance use among lesbian, gay, and bisexual youth: Prevalence and correlates. *Journal of Adolescent Research, 12,* 454–476.

Rosenbaum, D. P., & Hanson, G. S. (1998). Assessing the effects of school-based drug education: A six-year multilevel analysis of Project D. A. R. E. *Journal of Research in Crime & Delinquency, 35,* 381–412.

Sarvela, P. D, Monge, E. A., Shannon, D. V., & Nawrot, R. (1999). Age at first use of cigarettes among rural and small town elementary school children in Illinois. *Journal of School Health, 69,* 398–402.

Scheier, L. M., Botvin, G. J., Diaz, T., & Griffin, K. W. (1999). Social skills, competence, and drug refusal efficacy as predictors of adolescent alcohol use. *Journal of Drug Education, 29,* 251–278.

Selnow, G. W. (1987). Parent-child relationships and single and two parent families: Implications for substance usage. *Journal of Drug Education, 17,* 315–326.

Shope, J. T., Dielman, T. E., Butchart, A., Campanelli, P. C., & Kloska, D. D. (1992). An elementary school-based alcohol misuse prevention program follow-up evaluation. *Journal of Studies on Alcohol, 53,* 106–121.

Sieving, R. E., Perry, C. L., & Williams, C. L. (2000). Do friendships change behaviors, or do behaviors change friendships? Examining paths of influence in young adolescents' alcohol use. *Journal of Adolescent Health, 26,* 27–35.

Simcha-Fagan, O., & Schwartz, J. E. (1986). Neighborhood and delinquency: An assessment of contextual effects. *Criminology, 24,* 667–703.

Simons-Morton, B., Haynie, D. L., Crump, A. D., Saylor, K. E., Eitel, P., & Yu, K. (1999). Expectancies and other psychosocial factors associated with alcohol use among early adolescent boys and girls. *Addictive Behaviors, 24,* 229–238.

Snyder, J., Dishion, T. J., & Patterson, G. R. (1986). Determinants and consequences of associating with deviant peers during preadolescence and adolescence. *Journal of Early Adolescence, 6,* 29–43.

Stanton, W. R., & Silva, P. A. (1992). A longitudinal study of the influence of parents and friends on children's initiation of smoking. *Journal of Applied Developmental Psychology, 13,* 423–434.

Steinberg, L., Fletcher, A., & Darling, N. (1994). Parental monitoring and peer influences on adolescent substance use. *Pediatrics, 93,* 1060–1064.

Strunin, L. (1999). Drinking perceptions and drinking behaviors among black urban adolescents. *Journal of Adolescent Health, 25,* 264–275.

Telch, M. J., Killen, J. D., McAlister, A. L., Perry, C. L., & Maccoby, N. (1982). Long-term follow-up of a pilot project on smoking prevention with adolescents. *Journal of Behavioral Medicine, 5,* 1–8.

Tobler, N. S., & Stratton, H. H. (1997). Effectiveness of school-based drug prevention programs: A meta-analysis of the research. *Journal of Primary Prevention, 18,* 71–128.

Vega, W. A., Zimmerman, R. S., Warheit, G. J., Apospori, E., & Gil, A. G. (1993). Risk factors for early adolescent drug use in four ethnic and racial groups. *American Journal of Public Health, 83,* 185–189.

Williams, R. J., & Chang, S. Y. (2000). A comprehensive and comparative review of adolescent substance abuse treatment outcome. *Clinical Psychology Science & Practice, 7,* 138–166.

Wills, T. A., & Cleary, S. D. (1999). Peer and adolescent substance use among 6th–9th graders: Latent growth analyses of influence versus selection mechanisms. *Health Psychology, 18,* 453–463.

Wills, T. A., Pierce, J. P., & Evans, R. I. (1996). Large-scale environmental risk factors for substance use. *American Behavioral Scientist, 39,* 808–822.

Wills, T. A., Vaccaro, D., & McNamara, G. (1994). Novelty seeking, risk taking, and related constructs as predictors of adolescent substance use: An application of Cloninger's theory. *Journal of Substance Abuse, 6,* 1–20.

Windle, M. (1991). Alcohol use and abuse: Some findings from the National Adolescent Student Health Survey. *Alcohol Health & Research World, 15,* 5–10.

Windle, M. (1996). Effects of parental drinking on adolescents. *Alcohol Health & Research World, 20,* 187–190.

Winters, K. C. (1999). Treating adolescents with substance use disorders: An overview of practice issues and treatment outcomes. *Substance Abuse, 20,* 203–225.

Yoshikawa, H. (1994). Prevention as cumulative protection: Effects of early family support and education on chronic delinquency and its risks. *Psychological Bulletin, 115,* 28–54.

Zins, J. E., Elias, M. J., Greenberg, M. T., & Weissberg, R. P. (2000). Promoting social and emotional competence in children. In K. Minke & G. Bear (Eds.), *Preventing school problems—Promoting school success: Strategies and programs that work* (pp. 71–99). Bethesda, MD: National Association of School Psychologists.

CHAPTER 16

AIDS/STD PREVENTION FOR U.S. ADOLESCENTS

MARY ROGERS GILLMORE

University of Washington

The face of acquired immune deficiency syndrome (AIDS) has shifted dramatically since its emergence in the United States in the early 1980s. Initially concentrated primarily among gay and bisexual men, the disease subsequently spread to intravenous drug users among whom it is transmitted very efficiently, resulting in a second wave of the epidemic. In the 1990s, the largest proportional increase in AIDS cases occurred among heterosexuals, with women and persons of color—especially those living in inner cities—disproportionately affected (Centers for Disease Control, 1999). Although adolescents make up only about 1 percent of the AIDS cases nationally, the Office of National AIDS Policy (ONAP, 2000) reported that half of all new HIV infections are thought to occur among persons under age 25—representing some 20,000 new HIV infections each year. Young women, especially women of color, and young men who have sex with men have been hardest hit. Some 63 percent of the HIV infections reported among teenagers in 1999 occurred among young women, and at least half the cases reported among teenaged men occurred among those who had sex with men (ONAP, 2000). Although African Americans and Latinos each represent only about 15 percent of U.S. teenagers, they account for 49 percent and 20 percent, respectively, of the AIDS cases to date among those of ages 13 to 19 (ONAP, 2000).

In 1996, alarmed at the growing rate of HIV infection among our nation's youth, the Office of National AIDS Policy declared them a "generation at risk" (ONAP, 2000, p. iv) and issued a call for a national response to the problem. Four years later, Director Sandra Thurman remarked that although progress has been made, "it is deeply distressing that the number of young people becoming infected has remained constant year after year" (ONAP, 2000, p. vii). Urging renewed commitment in the fight against AIDS, she noted, "Young people are our most valued resource—our best hope for the future" (p. vii).

The human immunodeficiency virus (HIV) among young people is primarily contracted through sexual transmission (ONAP, 2000). Because over half of the teenaged population in the United States is sexually experienced (Gates & Sonenstein, 2000; Henshaw & Feivelson, 2000), the potential for disease transmission is high. However, there is evidence that today's teenagers are sexually more cautious than their predecessors. Teenage pregnancy rates have been declining since the early 1990s. Henshaw and Feivelstein (2000) argued that this trend is not due to increased abstinence because the proportion of sexually active teens has remained fairly stable over time, but rather due to increased use of, or use of more effective, contraception. Nevertheless, our teenage pregnancy rate still remains higher than that of any other developed nation except Russia (Henshaw & Feivelstein, 2000), indicating that many teens continue to engage in unprotected sex. Although condom use has also increased, rates of sexually transmitted diseases (STDs)—such as chlamydia, gonorrhea, human papilloma virus, and herpes—remain higher among teenagers than any other age group (Berman & Hein, 1999). Some national studies have shown a trend toward fewer sexual partners among adolescent men, which is encouraging because the number of partners is associated with increased risk, but, unfortunately, this trend is not evident among women (Santelli, Lindberg, Abma, McNeely, & Resnick, 2000a). Thus, although there is evidence of progress in our efforts to prevent AIDS among our nation's youth, much remains to be done.

REVIEW OF RESEARCH

Common Theoretical Approaches

Three theoretical perspectives have dominated the research on adolescents' risk of acquiring HIV: the theory of reasoned action (TRA), the health belief model (HBM), and social cognitive theory (SCT). The *theory of reasoned action* (Fishbein & Ajzen, 1975) posits that the best predictor of a behavior (e.g., using a condom) is a person's intention to perform the behavior. Intention, in turn, is hypothesized to be a function of the individual's perceptions of social norms regarding the behavior and his or her attitude toward the behavior. Attitudes are formed on the basis of beliefs about the consequences or outcomes of performing the behavior (e.g., condoms reduce pleasure). These beliefs have two components: how likely the outcome is believed to be and how good/bad the outcome is thought to be. Perceived norm is based on the set of normative beliefs one holds—these reflect beliefs about how specific others (e.g., peers, boyfriends, parents) are thought to feel about the behavior and how motivated one is to comply with the wishes of these persons. All other factors (e.g., gender, age) that influence a behavior are presumed to operate through the TRA variables, rather than directly affecting the behavior. A body of research, some of which is reported in this chapter, has provided considerable empirical support for this theory in a wide variety of health applications (see Carter, 1990), including adolescent's decisions to have sexual intercourse and to use condoms.

Ajzen (1985) suggested a modification of the TRA called the *theory of planned behavior.* Trying to understand why, despite the best of intentions, people sometimes fail to follow through with an intended behavior, Ajzen hypothesized that perceived control over the behavior is important to consider. Perceived control over sexual behavior may be especially relevant for understanding young women's sexual behaviors, because often their male partners have greater control over these behaviors. For example, a woman can ask her boyfriend to use condoms, but the boyfriend ultimately controls this behavior. (See Madden, Ellen, & Ajzen, 1992, for a comparison of these two theories.)

The *health belief model* (Rosenstock, Strecher, & Becker, 1994) was developed to explain compliance with health directives. The HBM posits that the decision to engage in a behavior (e.g., using condoms) is a function of five factors: (1) perceived susceptibility to an adverse health outcome (e.g., how likely am I to get AIDS?); (2) perceived severity of the adverse health outcome (e.g., how bad is AIDS?); (3) barriers to the specific preventive behavior being considered (e.g., condoms reduce pleasure); (4) benefits of engaging in the behavior (e.g., condoms reduce the risk of AIDS); and (5) cues to action (e.g., Magic Johnson's announcement that he is HIV positive). Studies have shown support for parts of this model, but perceived susceptibility and perceived severity have not been found consistently related to sexual risk taking, although Rosenstock and colleagues (1994) noted that perceived severity has not been well measured in most studies. Moreover, the cues to action have been rarely investigated, so we know very little about its utility in explaining sexual behaviors.

Bandura's *social learning and social cognitive theories* (Bandura, 1977, 1986) have been particularly influential with regard to intervention research, because the former specifies methods (e.g., modeling, role playing, reinforcement) to influence people to learn new behaviors. Bandura posited that behavior is a function of three general factors: prior experience, social and other environmental contingencies in the immediate environment, and beliefs and attitudes. Although these are very broad factors, the key constructs are self-efficacy (i.e., one's confidence in one's ability to perform a specific behavior in a given setting), outcome expectations (i.e., one's beliefs about the consequences of engaging in a behavior), and goal setting (i.e., an end one wants to achieve).

These theories share several similarities. All assume that behavior is volitional and therefore are not applicable to forced sex. Whether adolescents' sexual behavior is entirely volitional is a matter of some disagreement, but empirical tests of these theories suggest that such an assumption is not unwarranted. All are "expectancy" theories; that is, they are based on the idea that people make decisions about engaging in behaviors based on expected outcomes. All of the theories suggest that environmental factors are mediated by cognitions. Although different labels are used, several of the theories' constructs are very similar. For example, Bandura's construct "outcome expectations" is very similar to the TRA's construct "outcome beliefs," and to the HBM's construct "perceived barriers and benefits of performing the behavior." Similarly, Bandura's construct of "goal setting" is a very similar to that of "intentions" in the TRA. Recently, Fishbein (1998) has integrated features of all three theories into a single integrated model, but to my knowledge this model has not been empirically tested. None of the theories address the emotional aspects of sexual behavior, which may be important to consider. Moreover, all focus on individual decision making in an attempt to explain behaviors like having sex that are fundamentally dyadic. Nevertheless, they have proven to be useful in helping us understand many important aspects of adolescent sexual behavior that are relevant for the prevention of AIDS and STDs.

Correlates of Sexual Behaviors That Place
Teenagers at Risk of Contracting AIDS/STDs

Sociodemographic Factors.   Sociodemographic factors have been found to be related to risky sexual behaviors.

Race/Ethnicity. Consistent differences in sexual behaviors by race and ethnicity have been documented in a large number of studies. Relative to non-Latino European Americans, a larger proportion of African American and Latino teens are sexually experienced, and they tend to initiate sex at a younger age (Abma, Chandra, Mosher, Peterson, & Piccinino, 1997; CDC, 1998; Gates & Sonenstein, 2000; Henshaw & Feivelstein, 2000; Santelli et al., 2000a; Santelli, Lowry, Brener, & Robin, 2000b). Data from a recent national survey of adolescent men showed that rates of anal sex are higher among African Americans and Latinos (Gates & Sonnenstein, 2000). Marin (personal communication) speculated that some Latinas may engage in anal sex in order to remain a technical virgin in a culture that places a strong value on virginity at marriage. Recent studies also show that African American youth report more condom use than European Americans, but the latter report higher rates of oral contraceptive use (Warren et al., 1998). (Data are generally not available for other racial/ethnic groups.) These differences are mirrored in teenage pregnancy rates, which, although declining in every group, remain higher among African Americans and Latinas than among European Americans (Henshaw & Fievelstein, 2000). Rates of STDs, including the most deadly STD—AIDS—are also higher among youth of color (Santelli et al., 2000b).

Gender. Studies generally show that more teenage boys than girls have ever had sex, and that boys report having had more total sexual partners (Blum et al., 2000; Santelli et al., 2000a). Among sexually experienced teens, however, teenage girls are more likely than boys to report having had sex recently, with the single exception of African American teens, among whom slightly more boys report recent sex (Henshaw & Feivelstein, 2000). This difference may simply reflect opportunity—a young woman who wishes to be sexually active may find a willing partner more easily than can a young man. Boys are more likely to report that they use condoms than girls are to report that their partners use condoms and, conversely, girls are more likely to report using oral contraceptives compared to boys' reports of their sexual partners' use (Santelli et al., 2000a; Sheeran, Abraham, & Orbell, 1999). Although adolescent girls appear somewhat sexually more conservative than boys, they experience higher rates of STDs (Berman & Hein, 1999). A young woman's anatomy and immature sexual organs may be the reason for her greater risk. Gender differences in patterns of sexual behavior have been variously attributed to biological (genetic and hormonal), cultural (e.g., gender role socialization), and structural differences (e.g., the more powerful positions of males in society). Although biology may play a role in the sexual behaviors of males and females, the tremendous variations in such behaviors that have been observed cross-culturally (Ford & Beach, 1951) demonstrate the power of culture in shaping these behaviors.

Socioeconomic Status. Although studies have shown relationships between socioeconomic status and teenage sexual behavior, there are inconsistencies in the findings. Studies have consistently shown a relationship between adolescent births and poverty (Santelli et al., 2000b). Consistent with earlier findings (Moore, Miller, Glei, & Morrison, 1995), Santelli and colleagues (2000b) found an inverse relationship between parental educational level and sexual initiation in a recent national study, even after controlling for possible confounding variables. However, this relationship did not hold for African American boys or for Latinas. They also found that parental educational level was positively related to condom use among girls, but no such relationship existed for boys. Socioeconomic status was not related to recent sex, use of contraceptives, or multiple partners. Income was not related to any of the sexual behaviors measured. In contrast, Ku, Sonenstein, and Pleck (1993) found that income was positively related to the number of sexual partners and the frequency of intercourse among adolescent males, but not to contraceptive use. And Blum and colleagues (2000) found that teens from families with higher incomes were less likely to have had sex than those from lower-income families, even when controlling for race/ethnicity and family structure. Clearly, more research is needed to clarify the relationship between socioeconomic status and adolescent sexual behaviors.

Age.   Age is strongly related to sexual initiation—the older an adolescent, the more likely she or he has had sex, and those teens who initiate sex at an older age are more likely to use contraception (Morrison, 1985). A recent meta-analysis of condom use among heterosexuals found that younger persons are more likely than older ones to use condoms (Sheeran et al., 1999), a finding also obtained by Guttmacher and associates (1997) in a multiethnic sample of urban adolescents. Given the rise in condom use over time, this finding may reflect a history effect—condom use messages have been targeted at younger persons, and condoms are more accessible than was true in the past. In a recent study of African American and Latino adolescents, Miller, Forehand, and Kotchick (1999) did not find a significant association between age at first intercourse and consistency of condom use, although there was a positive association with number of sexual partners. The latter is not surprising, since over the course of the twentieth century, age at first intercourse has decreased while age at first marriage has increased, leaving more years to be sexually active before marriage than once was the case. Given that teens tend to engage in "serial monogamy," and that teen relationships tend to be rather short lived, it is not surprising that the older a teen is, the more sexual partners she or he has had. Additionally, Mansergh and Marks (1998) found in a review of the empirical literature that the incidence of unprotected anal intercourse was higher among younger than older men who have sex with men, suggesting that adolescent gay and bisexual youth may be at especially high risk of acquiring HIV, given the prevalence of HIV in the gay/bisexual population.

Biological Factors.   Some time ago, Ford and Beach (1951) extensively studied cross-cultural and cross-species variations in sexual behaviors. They concluded that human sexual behavior is far less influenced by hormones than that of many other mammals. For example, sexual intercourse among humans occurs throughout the monthly cycle, not solely during the period of ovulation, as is the case with most other mammals. Moreover, Ford and Beach observed few universals and wide variations in human sexual behavior that suggest the importance of culture in shaping these behaviors. Among the universals they observed are that (1) all children engage in sexual exploration and sex play prior to puberty; (2) self-stimulation (masturbation) is observed in all cultures; (3) although heterosexual coitus is the most common form of sexual behavior in human societies, homosexual behavior occurs in virtually all societies; (4) humans in virtually all societies engage in some form of nongenital stimulation prior to and during sexual intercourse, although the forms of such behaviors very widely from culture to culture (e.g., kissing is not a part of foreplay in all cultures); and (5) incest taboos that forbid sexual relations between parents and children, and typically between siblings, exist in all societies. They suggested that these behaviors are biologically driven not only because they are found universally in human societies but also because they are found in nonhuman primates as well.

Hormonal Influences on Sexual Behaviors.   More recently, Udry and his colleagues have been studying the effects of hormones on adolescent sexual behaviors. In their early work, they found that pubertal development, which is hormonally driven, was related to sexual initiation among both African American and European American girls, and European American boys (Udry & Billy, 1987). (African American boys have not been included in these analyses because a large proportion were sexually active prior to puberty.) They also found that relative to girls who reach menarche later, girls who reach menarche earlier are more likely to have sex in early or middle adolescence (Halpern & Udry, 1999), a finding that might explain some of the differences between African American and European American girls' age at first intercourse, because the former reach puberty earlier, on average, than the latter. This early work suggests that hormones might have an indirect effect on sexual activity, but Udry and colleagues were most interested in learning whether hormones have a direct effect on sexual behaviors. Thus, in later work, they employed longitudinal research designs and measured hormone levels directly. Results of these studies showed that even when controlling for pubertal development, testosterone levels were related to the transition to first sex among both European American boys (Halpern, Udry, Campbell, & Suchindran, 1994) and African American and European American girls (Halpern, Udry, & Suchindran, 1997). The researchers also showed that increases in testosterone levels were associated with increased sexual activity and decreases were associated with decreased sexual activity (Halpern & Udry, 1999).

These findings provide compelling evidence of a direct link between hormones (testosterone) and sexual activity. However, the amount of variance in sexual behavior explained by testosterone level has been quite small (5 to 10 percent), and a number of inconsistencies have yet to be resolved (Halpern & Udry, 1999). Moreover, models that contained both biological and social factors were the most powerful, underscoring the value of biosocial models for understanding sexual behaviors. For example, they found that religious service attendance moderated the effect of testosterone on the sexual behaviors of European American boys and girls, but not African American girls. Halpern and Udry (1999) remarked that the "ultimate goal...should not be to quantify the relative importance of biological versus social factors, but rather to understand *how* these processes contribute to behavioral outcomes" (p. 155).

Genetic Influences on Sexual Behaviors.   Studies of the genetic influences on human sexual behavior are in their infancy, and Dawood and Bailey (2000) warned us that "to date not a single molecular finding concerning behavior has been widely accepted as valid by the scientific community, and several highly publicized findings have failed to replicate" (p. 247). Nonetheless, based on twin studies, Dawood and Bailey reported evidence of "moderate" heritability for sexual orientation, but pointed out that no one has isolated a gene that would provide definitive evidence of a genetic link. Studies of male twins from a veterans' registry suggest that the tendency to maintain a stable relationship with one partner (pair bonding or monogamy) versus having several partners over the life span also may have a genetic component (Trumbetta & Gottesman, 2000). Other evidence suggests that genes may play a role in age at menarche (Doughty & Rodgers, 2000; MacMurray et al., 2000). Doughty and Rodgers (2000) imply that because age at menarche has been found in some studies to be related to age at first intercourse, there may be a genetic component to age at first intercourse.

Although it is well known that extreme stress (e.g., malnutrition, extreme physical activity) can delay menarche, there is considerable controversy over what has come to be called the *Belsky hypothesis*. Studies have shown that girls raised in single-parent families, or in families in which there is considerable conflict, experience earlier pubertal development and an earlier age at menarche than girls raised in two-parent, less conflicted families (Belsky, 2000). Belsky, Steinberg, and Draper (1991) invoked evolutionary theory to explain this finding by arguing that under difficult and unstable environmental conditions, it is costly to delay childbearing because conditions may worsen, making childbearing difficult or impossible, whereas under favorable conditions it makes sense to delay childbearing and invest in finding a good partner. Rowe (2000) offered an alternative explanation for this finding, arguing that mothers may pass on their genes for timing of puberty and mothers who themselves experienced early puberty may have entered into more unstable and conflicted relationships, given their immaturity. So far, no study has provided a definitive test of these two explanations, and it may be, as Udry and his colleagues have argued, that the most powerful models of adolescent sexual behavior will be models in which both biological and psychosocial factors are included.

Individual Factors.   Individual factors have been found to be related to risky sexual behaviors.

Sexual Orientation.   Most studies of adolescent sexual behaviors have not reported results separately for gay and straight youth, and most studies of gay men have not separated adolescents from adults. Recently reported, however, are the results of a CDC-sponsored multisite survey of gay youth between the ages of 15 and 22 (Valleroy, MacKellar, Duncan, et al., 2000). Forty-one percent of the young gay men surveyed reported having engaged in unprotected anal sex in the prior six months. The overall prevalence of HIV was 7 percent—much higher than that found in heterosexual populations. HIV prevalence was higher among African American, Latino, and those reporting mixed or other races, compared to that for European American and Asian American young men. For example, African American gay youth had an HIV infection rate of 16.9 percent—more than twice the overall rate of HIV.

Relative to straight youth, gay and bisexual youth engaged in much higher rates of anal intercourse, which is thought to be the most efficient route of sexual transmission of HIV. Coupled with the higher rates of HIV in this population, these young men are at very high risk, yet few intervention studies have targeted this population. For some groups of gay and bisexual adolescents, this may be especially challenging. Many Latinos, for example, have strong antihomosexual attitudes, and do not necessarily identify themselves as gay or bisexual if they have sex with other men (Marin, 1988), which may make it difficult to identify and recruit such youth into interventions. Lesbians have been largely neglected in studies of STDs because they were believed to be at very low risk. However, recent data suggest that this may not be the case, in that many lesbians have had sex with men, and bisexual women, particularly, are at higher risk for STDs than women who have sex exclusively with women (Doll & Ostrow, 1999).

Intentions.   Several studies have shown that youth who intend to use condoms are more likely to use condoms than those who do not (see DiClemente's review, 1992, and Sheeran et al.'s meta-analysis, 1999). In our own research with high-risk youth, we have consistently found intentions to be related to condom use among African American and European American boys and girls (e.g., Morrison, Baker, & Gillmore, 1998). We also have found in a sample of urban public school youth (Gillmore et al., 2002) that intentions predict the likelihood that both sexually inexperienced and sexually experienced youth will have sex.

Attitudes and Beliefs.   A growing body of research indicates that teenagers' attitudes and beliefs toward condoms are related to their use of condoms and their intentions to use condoms. DiClemente (1992) reported findings from several studies he reviewed that show that teens who perceive condoms more favorably and associate lower costs with using them are more likely to use them. Similarly findings were reported by Sheeran and colleagues (1999) in their meta-analysis of condom use among heterosexuals. Our findings (Gillmore, Morrison, Lowery, & Baker, 1994; Morrison, et al., 1998) also showed that attitudes and beliefs are related to condom use among both African American and European American girls and boys. Consistent with the TRA, we found that the effects of attitudes and beliefs on condom use were indirect, mediated by intentions to use condoms. Both overall attitude toward condom use, as well as the specific beliefs about the expected consequences, both good and bad, of using condoms have been found to be important predictors of condom use (Gillmore et al., 1994; Jemmott & Jemmott, 1991; Levinson, Jaccard, & Beamer, 1995; Morrison et al., 1998). We have also found that attitudes and beliefs predicted intentions to have sex, among both sexually experienced and sexually inexperienced youth, and, as noted earlier, intentions are related to reports of having had intercourse (Gillmore et al., 2002). The results of these and other studies are consistent with the three theories described above.

Perceived Norms.   Perceived norms about condom use have been found to be related to condom use in a number of studies (DiClemente, 1992). When youths perceive peer norms favorable to condom use, they are more likely to use them. Our work showed that a general perceived norm indirectly predicts condom use through its effects on intentions to use condoms, consistent with the TRA (Morrison et al., 1998). This effect was independent of the effect of attitude, and held for both African American and European American boys and girls. In that study, we also obtained qualitative data regarding whose opinion about condom use mattered to the youth. The youth consistently named five referents: sexual partners, close friends, doctors or health care providers, mothers, and other family members. Jemmott and colleagues (Jemmott, 2001) found very similar referents named by the African American youth they have studied, except that these youth also named their church as a referent. Kinsman, Romer, Furstenberg, and Schwarz (1998) investigated which components of peer norms influence sexual behavior in a sample of sixth-grade students. They found that those who had initiated sex were more likely than those who had not to believe that most of their friends were having sex, that the normative age for having sex was younger than it actually is, and that sexually experienced boys gained respect if they had had sex. In contrast, those who had not initiated sex felt that boys who were having sex would be more likely than those who were not to lose respect. There were no differences between sexually experienced and inexperienced girls on the finding regarding respect. Jaccard, Dittus, and Gordon (1996) found that youth who perceived that their mothers disapproved of sex were less likely to engage in sex and more likely to use contraceptives if they did engage in sex. Parental norms were important predictors of general perceived norms in our study of adolescent sexual decision making (Gillmore et al., 2002), a finding that suggests that parents remain an important source of influence even among teenagers.

Self-Efficacy.   Bandura (1977) suggested that self-efficacy is an important determinant of behavior, and several investigators have investigated its utility for predicting condom use. Both DiClemente's (1992) review and Sheeran and colleagues' (1999) meta-analysis of predictors of condom use concluded that self-efficacy with regard to using condoms is associated with greater condom use. In our study of condom use among higher-risk African American and European American youth, we found that self-efficacy was indirectly associated with condom use through its effects on intentions to use condoms, controlling for the effects of attitudes and norms (Morrison et al., 1998), but only with steady partners. With casual partners, there was no effect of self-efficacy. Because relationships with steady partners carry with them the expectation of monogamy and sexual safety, introducing condom use in a steady relationship is likely to be more challenging than with casual relationships. We suspect this is the reason self-efficacy mattered with steady, but not casual, partners.

Substance Use.   Countless studies have reported that substance use is positively associated with risky sexual behaviors, so much so that the phrase *high = high risk* has become common parlance. The problem with such studies is that typically they have not been designed to determine whether substance use *causes* youth to engage in riskier sex. Most studies have relied on correlational analyses in which it has not been ascertained that the substance use and risky sex occurred on the same occasion, and that the substance use directly preceded the risky sex, which are necessary (but not sufficient) conditions for drawing causal inferences (see Leigh & Stall, 1993, for a cogent methodological critique of this literature). Some studies have examined specific events (e.g., the most recent sexual intercourse) in which the contiguity and temporal ordering of the behaviors is controlled. However, these studies have not controlled for third-variable explanations—it may be that some variable, such as a propensity toward risk taking, causes one to engage in risky sex *and* use substances. In fact, cigarette smoking, which is not known to impair judgment, also has been shown to be related to sexual risk taking (e.g., Biglan et al., 1990), giving greater credibility to the possibility that some third variable(s) may account for the observed relationship between substance use and risky sexual behaviors.

There are few studies in which behavior at the event level has been repeatedly assessed, which not only ensures temporal ordering and contiguity of behaviors, but also controls for several third-variable explanations since a within-subject design controls for personality characteristics such as impulsivity. Using such a design, Fortenberry, Orr, Katz, Brizendine, and Blythe (1997) found no relationship between substance use and risky sexual behaviors in a clinical sample of adolescent young women. In our own research currently underway using a daily event repeated measures design, we have found no evidence of a relationship between drinking and condom use in either a college student sample (Leigh et al., 2002) or a community-based sample (Morrison et al., 2002) of adolescents; this was true for both young men and women. These findings suggest that the "jury is still out" regarding the relationship between substance use and risky sex, despite strongly held beliefs by laypersons and professionals alike.

Family Factors.   Family factors have been found to be related to risky sexual behaviors.

Family Structure.   Family structure (typically defined as one- vs. two-parent families) has been the most frequently examined family factor with regard to adolescent sexual behavior. Relative to living with both parents, adolescents raised in single-parent families are more likely to have had sex, even when controlling for race/ethnicity and income (Blum et al., 2000; Santelli et al., 2000b). However, Santelli and associates (2000b) did not find associations between family structure and other sexual behaviors, such as recent sexual activity, condom use among males, oral contraceptive use, or having multiple sexual partners, and not all studies have found family structure related to sexual initiation (e.g., Kinsman et al., 1998). Based on findings from their study, Miller and colleagues (1999) suggested that family processes (e.g., communication, monitoring, etc.), rather than family structure per se, may be more important in influencing adolescent sexual behaviors.

Parent-Child Communication.   Many adolescents indicate that they would like to talk with their parents about sexuality issues, but feel reluctant because they think that the parents would not understand or that they are too busy to talk (Goodstein & Connelly, 1998). Parents, on the other hand, often feel unprepared to discuss sexuality with their children (Holtzman & Rubinson, 1995). Yet, studies suggest that when parents communicate with their children in a supportive way about sexual behaviors and AIDS, it helps to increase adolescents' knowledge about sex and generally reduces their sexual risk taking (Baumeister, Flores, & Van Oss-Marin, 1995; Adolph, Ramos, Linton, & Grimes, 1995; Jaccard et al., 1996; Holtzman & Rubinson, 1995; Pick & Palos, 1995; Sigelman, Derenowski, Mullaney, & Siders, 1993). This finding seems to hold across a wide variety of racial and ethnic groups. Miller and associates (1999) found that greater general communication between mothers and adolescents was related to less frequent sex and fewer partners—a finding that held for both genders and across racial/ethnic groups (African American and Latino). General communication, rather than communication specifically about sex, seemed to be the more important predictor, perhaps because it conveys something about the quality of the parent-child relationship. Jaccard, Dittus, and Litardo (1998) argued that much of the literature on parent-child communication about sex employs an overly simplistic conceptualization of such communication, typically whether or not the pair have talked about sex, and argued for more complete conceptualization of the construct. Moreover, little is known about why these associations exist, as most of the studies have been based on correlational evidence; thus, it is not possible to determine whether the communication caused the behavior, or the reverse, or whether some third variable might have caused both.

Parental Monitoring.   Parental monitoring and/or supervision has been consistently related to later sexual initiation and less risky sexual behaviors among those who have initiated sex (Capaldi, Crosby, & Stoolmiller, 1996; Luster & Small, 1994; Metzler, Noell,

Biglan, Ary, & Smolkowski, 1994; Paikoff, Parfenoff, Williams, & McCormick, 1997; Romer et al., 1994), although its role with regard to other sexual risk-reducing behaviors has not been well studied. In a recent exception, Miller and colleagues (1999) found that parental monitoring was associated with fewer sex partners, less frequent sex, and greater condom use among adolescents. This finding held across gender and race/ethnic groups (African American and Latino), as well as in a multivariate analysis.

Community Factors.   Community factors have been found to be related to risky sexual behaviors.

Condom Availability.   Very few community factors have been systematically studied with regard to their relationship to sexual behaviors that place adolescents at risk of contracting HIV. One recent study, however, examined the impact of condom availability in schools on condom use and sexual activities (Guttmacher et al., 1997). Comparing New York schools in which condom availability was mandated with a matched sample of Chicago schools in which condoms were not available, Guttmacher and colleagues found that among continuing (as opposed to new) students, New York students were more likely to have used a condom at last intercourse than Chicago students, even when controlling for several possible confounding variables. Condom availability had no effect on the number of partners or ever having had sex. Importantly, there was no evidence, as some have feared, that condom availability increased sexual activities.

Race/Ethnicity and Gender Differences in Risk Factors for AIDS/STDs: A Summary

In summary, it is clear that youth from some racial/ethnic groups are at greater risk than others for contracting AIDS/STD. This is evident in the higher rates of teenage pregnancies and STDs, including AIDS, among African Americans and Latinos relative to European American youth (other racial/ethnic groups have rarely been studied). What is not well understood is why these differences exist. As noted earlier, we know that relative to European Americans, African Americans and Latinos, on average, initiate sex at a younger age, and, hence, a larger proportion are sexually experienced, although these differences have been declining over time. We also know that age of sexual initiation and contraceptive use are positively correlated. It could be that younger adolescents are not developmentally ready to undertake effective precautions against unintended pregnancies and STDs. However, recent studies have shown that overall rates of contraceptive use are similar among African American and European American youth, but they tend to use different types of contraceptives (Santelli et al., 2000b), so maturity does not seem a likely explanation for the differences. Data from a recent study indicated that relative to European American adolescent young men, African American and Latino young men reported higher rates of anal intercourse (Gates & Sonnenstein, 2000). Because anal sex is more efficient for transmitting HIV than other types of sex, this may help explain some of the differences in STD rates, but we do not know why such differences in sexual activities exist, and there is evidence that African American young men have a higher rate of condom use than European American youth, perhaps in response to their higher rates of AIDS. Socioeconomic status differences can be mistaken for racial/ethnic differences because adolescents of color are disporportionately poor and many studies fail to control for SES when examining race/ethnic differences. Yet, Blum and colleagues (2000) found a higher prevalence of intercourse among African Americans relative to European Americans even after controlling for SES. Given the latest evidence from the human genome project, we can be reasonably certain that racial/ethnic differences in adolescent sexual behaviors are not due to genetic differences, because the "races" are virtually genetically indistinguishable. This suggests that social and cultural factors are responsible for such differences.

At the same time, research has documented similarities among youth from differing racial/ethnic backgrounds in factors related to their sexual behaviors. Results of our tests of the theory of reasoned action (cited earlier) suggested that the *relationships* among the TRA variables are similar for both African American and European American youth. Studies of mother-child communication and parental monitoring have suggested that these are protective factors for African American and Latino youth, as well as European American youth. Clearly, more research is needed to understand the underlying reasons for the race/ethnic differences in risk for STD/AIDS. We need to move beyond solely documenting such differences toward a better understanding of the mechanisms responsible for them. Additionally, we need to take into account the fact that there will be large within-group differences, almost surely greater than between-group differences, that need to be understood if we are to build effective interventions.

Gender differences in rates of sexual behavior tend to be predictable, as suggested by the studies reviewed earlier, but these differences, too, have been declining over time. Relative to girls, boys, on average, initiate sex at a young age and report more sex partners and greater use of condoms, but young women bear the costs of unprotected sex to a far greater extent. They become pregnant and bear children, and they experience higher rates of STDs. Like racial/ethnic differences in risk for AIDS/STDs, there is considerable documentation of gender differences, but insufficient understanding of why such differences exist. Studies based on the TRA and studies of maternal communication and parental monitoring suggest that these variables operate in the same way for both genders, but the role of SES seems to differ by gender. Although we have been documenting gender differences in sexual behavior for a long time, there remains little agreement among researchers as to the mechanisms responsible for the differences observed.

INTERVENTIONS: WHAT WORKS, WHAT DOESN'T

School-Based Sexuality Education

Many believe that sexuality education is the key to preventing and/or reducing adolescent risky sexual behaviors, and schools have been the locus of most formal sexuality education. Some time ago, Douglas Kirby (1985) evaluated the effects of sexuality education and concluded that although sexuality education increased knowledge somewhat, it had no effect on behavior. Kirby speculated that the reasons are twofold: First, adolescents were reasonably knowledgeable about sexuality before being exposed to such education, thus the gains in their knowledge could only be minimal. Second, in empirical studies knowledge generally has not been found to be related to behavior change. Since that time, innumerable studies have shown that knowledge alone is not sufficient to change adolescents' sexual risk behaviors, and researchers have concluded that knowledge is a necessary, but not sufficient, condition for behavioral change.

However, Kirby and DiClemente (1994) pointed out that sexuality education in schools has changed considerably over time. They noted that more recent programs are based on theories that have been found useful in other health areas, that newer programs have taken advantage of cumulating knowledge about what works and what does not, and that they tend to be more carefully evaluated. In a review of 11 studies evaluating such programs, about half of which were successful in reducing sexual risk taking, Kirby and DiClemente found several common elements in the successful programs, including: (1) social learning theory, or a variant (e.g., social cognitive theory) was the foundation for the program; (2) the focus was narrow and specifically related to reducing sexual risk taking, and did not include broader topics such as dating; (3) active learning methods that engaged students were used; (4) social and media influences to have sex were addressed; (5) the programs emphasized and reinforced clear values against unprotected sex; the latter were tailored for the developmental level of the students; and (6) all programs included skill development with modeling and practice. It appears that when done well, school-based sexual education program have the potential to positively influence adolescents' sexual behaviors, but the question remains as to whether the community (parents and school administrators) will permit it.

Abstinence-Only Interventions

Although the jury is still out regarding the effectiveness of abstinence-only interventions (i.e., interventions that emphasize that abstinence is the only way to prevent AIDS/STDs), the limited extant evidence suggests that such programs may not be as effective as programs that contain both abstinence and safer-sex content. In a review of the effectiveness of 40 adolescent AIDS risk-reduction interventions, Kim, Stanton, Li, Dickersin, and Galbraith (1997) concluded that intervention effects for abstinence were not encouraging. Others note that abstinence-only programs have produced mixed effects, and that when gains have occurred, they have not been maintained (Haignere, Gold, & McDanel 1999). Lieberman, Gray, Wier, Fiorentino, and Maloney (2000) evaluated the effectiveness of an abstinence program implemented in New York City schools. They found some changes in attitudes toward teen sex, but no differences in intentions to have sex or in actual behaviors. They noted that "positive outcomes were especially limited among students who were already sexually active...a finding that emphasizes the difficulties of reaching adolescents who are already at high risk for pregnancy" (p. 237). In one of the few randomized control studies to directly compare an abstinence-only intervention with a safer-sex intervention, Jemmott, Jemmott, and Fong (1998) found that the abstinence-only intervention produced some short-term gains (described below), but these were not maintained over time. In contrast, the safer-sex intervention produced positive effects that were maintained over a 12-month follow-up. Haignere and associates (1999) stated,

> Despite the lack of evidence supporting the efficacy of abstinence-only education, enthusiasm for abstinence-only education has increased at the local, state, and federal levels....

Misinformation and misuse of the existing research related to abstinence-only education abounds.... The lack of evidence supporting [these programs] is of particular concern given the extent to which these curricula are currently advocated. (p. 49)

Multifaceted Interventions

Be Proud, Be Responsible. John and Loretta Jemmott and colleagues have tested the efficacy of an AIDS prevention intervention targeting African American adolescents in a series of well-designed studies that also have addressed a number of important practical questions. Their intervention, "Be Proud, Be Responsible" is one of a small set of AIDS prevention interventions recommended by the Centers for Disease Control as effective; the curriculum is available through the CDC (http://www.cdc.gov/nccdphp/dash/rtc/curric1.htm). The interventions are based on the theory of reasoned action and social cognitive theory.

The first study (Jemmott, Jemmott, & Fong, 1992) focused on inner-city African American adolescent young men and included a five-hour intervention implemented by trained facilitators and delivered to small groups of participants. The intervention was designed to be developmentally and culturally appropriate, and focused on increasing knowledge, reducing problematic beliefs and attitudes about safer sex, and increasing safer sex negotiation skills. It included skills training and use of culturally appropriate videotapes, games, and exercises. Compared to the controls, immediately following the intervention, those in the AIDS prevention intervention were more knowledgeable about AIDS, more negative about engaging in risky sex, and had lower intentions to engage in risky sex. Most of these differences were maintained through a three-month follow-up. Most encouraging, three months following intervention, those in the intervention had reduced their sexual risk taking relative to those in the control condition.

Their next study (described in Jemmott & Jemmott, 1994) focused on both African American adolescent young women and men, and also determined whether the facilitator's race (African American or white) or gender, or the gender of participants in the small groups influenced the results. The results showed that youths in the intervention condition had stronger intentions to use condoms, had more favorable beliefs about condoms, had greater perceived self-efficacy to use condoms, and were more knowledgeable immediately after intervention, compared to the controls. Most of these effects were maintained six months following intervention. Although there were no differences between the intervention and control groups in mean amounts of unprotected sex at the three-month follow-up, those in the intervention reported more days during which they used condoms than the controls. The intervention effects were the same, regardless of facilitator race or gender, or the gender composition of the small groups, suggesting that the intervention has considerable generalizability.

More recently, Jemmott and colleagues (1998) compared the effects of abstinence and safer-sex AIDS prevention interventions consisting of eight one-hour sessions each. The design also included a no-treatment control group (i.e., it was a three-group design). The abstinence intervention taught that condoms can reduce risks, but emphasized abstinence, whereas the safer-sex intervention acknowledged that abstinence is the best choice, but emphasized the use of condoms. Both programs contained the elements described above. Three months after intervention, youth in the abstinence program reported engaging in less sexual intercourse than those in the control group, but youth in the safer-sex program were more likely to report consistent condom use than either the control group or the abstinence group. The safer-sex group also reported a higher frequency of condom use than the controls. At both 6 and 12 months following the intervention, the effects of the abstinence group intervention had disappeared, but the effects of the safer-sex intervention were maintained. These findings suggest, as noted earlier, that abstinence-only interventions may be of limited utility.

Jemmott, Jemmott, Fong, and McCaffree (1999) again replicated the effects of their AIDS prevention intervention with a new sample of African American adolescents. Although there were no significant differences in sexual behaviors between control and intervention groups at the three-month follow-up, by six months after intervention those who received the AIDS prevention intervention engaged in less unprotected sex, engaged in less anal intercourse, and had fewer sex partners than the controls. This finding speaks to the importance of longer-term follow-ups when studying the efficacy of an intervention. The researchers also found, as before, that the effects of the intervention were the same regardless of the gender of the group facilitators, the gender of the participants, and the gender composition of the groups, providing further evidence that the intervention is quite generalizable. The researchers suggested that neither facilitator race or gender nor group gender composition mattered, because the intervention was designed to be culturally appropriate, the activities were highly structured and facilitator training emphasized the importance of adhering to the study protocol, and the facilitators were trained together, which may have influenced them to behave similarly.

Focus on Kids.   Stanton and colleagues (1995) have taken a somewhat different approach to AIDS risk reduction among African American adolescents. They targeted their intervention to naturally occurring friendship groups of adolescents. Because peer groups have been found to exert a strong influence on their members, the researchers sought to capitalize on this naturally occurring phenomenon to try to maximize the intervention's effectiveness and also to help increase attendance. Their intervention is based on Protection Motivation Theory (PMT), a variant of the health belief model, and was delivered in eight weekly sessions, one of which was a day-long retreat. The sessions focused on one or more of the PMT constructs (intrinsic and extrinsic rewards, severity of and personal vulnerability to the threat of AIDS, response efficacy, self-efficacy, and response cost) and used a variety of formats (e.g., discussions, lectures, videos, games, role playing, storytelling, acting, and arts and crafts) to deliver the content. Condom use was the main focus, but abstinence and substance use were also addressed. Like Jemmott and colleagues' interventions, this intervention was designed to be culturally and developmentally appropriate (see Galbraith et al., 1996, for details). Compared to the control group, youth in the intervention group were significantly more likely to intend to use condoms, to evaluate them more positively, and to use condoms 6 months after intervention, but these differences disappeared by 12 months (Stanton, Ricardo, Galbraith, Feigelman, & Kaljee, 1996).

In a follow-up, Stanton and colleagues (personal communication) added six booster sessions between 15 and 27 months following the initial intervention. Results indicated that following the booster sessions, condom use was higher among youth in the intervention group than among the controls, but again the effect dissipated by 24 months postintervention. Over a three-year follow-up, however, cumulative effects were found in which intervention youth reported greater condoms use and lower rates of substance use than the controls. This intervention also has been endorsed by the CDC, and the curriculum is available through the CDC (http://www.cdc.gov/nccdphp/dash/rtc/curric5.htm).

Take 5.   Based on the theory of reasoned action and social cognitive theory, my colleagues and I designed and compared three AIDS risk reduction interventions for heterosexually active higher-risk African American and European American youths (Balassone, Baker, Gillmore, Morrison, & Dickstein, 1993; Richey, Gillmore, Balassone, Gutierrez, & Hartway, 1997). We called the study the "Take 5 Project" to reinforce the idea of taking time out to think ahead about whether one is willing to have sex and, if so, how to negotiate condom use. The interventions, designed to be culturally sensitive and gender appropriate, included a comic book, a video, and group skills training, each of which was specifically designed for the project. Participants in one condition read the comic book only, another read the comic book and viewed the videotape, and those in the third condition read the comic book, viewed the video, and participated in two four-hour group skills training sessions. The comic book presented basic information, included vignettes that attempted to change problematic beliefs about condoms, and presented four steps for negotiating condom use. The videotape modeled skills to negotiate condom use and reinforced some of the messages in the comic book. The skills training consisted of two four-hour sessions delivered in small mixed-gender groups of 6 to 12 youth co-led by a trained adult facilitator and 1 or 2 peer tutors. The training focused primarily on presentation of basic AIDS prevention information, modeling, role play, and rehearsal of condom negotiation skills. Study participants were youth sampled from a public health STD clinic and a juvenile detention facility. (Great care was taken to ensure that the rights of these vulnerable youth were protected.)

Despite the fact that the interventions contained most of the elements that have been defined as essential for effective interventions, and evidence that the participants rated the quality of the intervention materials and methods highly regardless of race or gender, there were very few differences among the interventions at either the three- or six-month follow-up (Gillmore et al., 1997). This is a particularly perplexing result because the intervention content was not unlike that used in Jemmott and colleagues' studies in which positive effects were found. Although we do not know the answer with certainty, we suspect that a brief intervention with these very high-risk youth may be inadequate. The successful interventions described earlier focused on community samples of youth living in higher-risk urban areas, but who were not chosen for participation on the basis of their risk; in fact, not all participants in those studies were even sexually active. Additionally, although generally interventions that are narrowly, as opposed to more broadly, focused have had better outcomes, we suspect that effective interventions with these especially high-risk youth may require greater attention to other pressing issues in their lives, such as substance abuse and mental health. We also think it would have been wise to include more content on values and value clarification.

Elements of Effective Interventions.   Scholars reviewing the literature on AIDS risk reduction interventions for adolescents have characterized successful interventions as having several common elements. Kirby (1995) described these as: behavioral specificity, experiential, skill-based, theory-based, a minimum of five hours in length, sufficient training for facilitators, values and norms stressed, accurate information provided, and pressures to have sex are addressed. Based on their review of adolescent AIDS prevention intervention studies, Kim et al., (1997) recommended a similar set of factors to increase the chances of success of AIDS prevention interventions: that interventions be based on theory, incorporate community and/or cultural aspects of the target population, include skills training, and carefully consider the length of intervention (longer interventions tended to be more effective).

SUMMARY AND CONCLUSIONS

A large number of studies have investigated factors related to the initiation of sexual intercourse among teenagers, contraceptive use, and condom use (although condoms are also contraceptives, studies since the advent of the AIDS epidemic in the United States have tended to focus on their value for preventing transmission of HIV). Earlier studies tended to focus on sociodemographic characteristics such as gender, age, and race/ethnicity, and were primarily concerned with teenage pregnancy. Since the advent of the AIDS epidemic, studies have been inclined to focus on behaviors that place adolescents at risk of acquiring HIV, primarily use (or nonuse) of condoms. More recent studies have tended to be theory driven, and many have been longitudinal rather than cross-sectional. Such studies are especially useful for building a cumulative body of knowledge upon which interventions can be based. Although there are many programs across the country that try to induce teenagers to change their sexual behaviors in order to reduce their risk of unintended pregnancies and acquisition of STDs, the vast majority of these programs have not been evaluated or have been evaluated with less than rigorous research designs. Nonetheless, there are some well-designed studies of interventions that have shown some efficacy, such as the examples described in this chapter, and these have provided extremely useful information. What is now needed are more carefully designed studies to test theory-based interventions for more diverse groups of adolescents, attention to the inherently dyadic nature of sexual intercourse, and studies of how successful interventions can be implemented and sustained in communities.

DISCUSSION QUESTIONS

1. *How should the effective interventions be tailored for other groups?* Because fewer studies have been conducted with Latino youth, and almost none with Asian American or American Indian youth, we know little about effective intervention with these groups, although there is some research in progress with some of these understudied groups. Although many interventions have been tested with adult gay and bisexual men, very few studies have targeted gay youth, despite their high risk, and lesbians have been completely ignored in such studies because they are presumed, erroneously, to have no risk for STDs.

2. *How can families deliver effective AIDS prevention interventions to their children?* To date, most AIDS prevention interventions have focused on the individual adolescent. Although adolescence is a developmental period when youth struggle for some independence from their families, studies suggest that families still play a major role in the lives of these young people. Families are a relatively untapped resource for intervention delivery. Although

some studies are in progress, more information is needed about how best to tap this underutilized asset.

3. *What are the critical components of successful intervention?* The successful interventions that have been tested in carefully controlled studies are multifaceted. We know very little about which components of these interventions are essential to produce the effects and which are not. This is important cost-effectiveness information to guide future intervention efforts.

4. *How can successful interventions be transferred to the community and retain their effectiveness?* Randomized control trials are an appropriate and important first step to determine whether interventions are efficacious. But once an intervention is found to be efficacious, will it retain its effectiveness in less tightly controlled environments? Are practitioners willing and able to adopt the intervention for use in practice? Questions about feasibility, cost, and sustainability have not been adequately addressed and will need to be in order to bridge the gap between science and practice.

SUGGESTED READINGS

DiClemente, R. J., Hansen, W. B., & Pontonm, L. E. (1996). *Handbook of adolescent health risk behavior.* New York: Plenum Press.

Fischhoff, B. (1992). *Risk taking: A developmental perspective.* In J. F. Yates (Ed.), *Risk-taking behavior.* New York: Wiley.

Fishbein, M., Guinan, M., Holtgrave, D. R., & Leviton, L. C. (1996). Special issue: Behavioral sciences in HIV prevention. *Public Health Reports, 111* (Suppl. 1).

Kirby, D. (2001). Understanding what works and what doesn't in reducing adolescent sexual risk-taking. *Family Planning Perspectives, 33,* 276–281.

Panchaud, C., Singh, S., Feivelson, D., & Darroch, J. E. (2000). Sexually transmitted diseases among adolescents in developed countries. *Family Planning Perspectives, 32,* 24–32, 45.

Rodgers, J. L., Rowe, D. C., & Miller, W. B. (2000). *Genetic influences on human fertility and sexuality: Theoretical and empirical contributions from the biological and behavioral sciences.* Boston: Kluwer.

REFERENCES

Abma, J. C., Chandra, A., Mosher, M. D., Peterson, L. S., & Piccinino, L. J. (1997). Fertility, family planning, and women's health: New data from the 1995 National Survey of Family Growth. *Vital Health Statistics, 23,* 1–114.

Adolph, C., Ramos, D., Linton, K., & Grimes, D. (1995). Pregnancy among Hispanic teenagers: Is good parental communication a deterrent? *Contraception, 51,* 303–306.

Ajzen, I. (1985). From intentions to actions: A theory of planned behavior. In J. Kuhl & J. Beckmann (Eds.), *Action control from cognition to behavior* (pp. 11–39). New York: Springer Verlag.

Alan Guttmacher Institute. (1999). Facts in brief. Retrieved January 20, 2001 from http://www.agi-usa.org/pubsfb_teen_sex.html.

Balassone, M. L., Baker, S., Gillmore, M. R., Morrison, D., & Dickstein, D. (1993). Interventions to decrease the risk of HIV/AIDS and other sexually transmitted diseases among high-risk heterosexual adolescents. *Children and Youth Services Review, 15,* 475–488.

Bandura, A. (1977). Self-efficacy: Toward a unifying theory of behavioral change. *Psychological Review, 84,* 191–215.

Bandura, A. (1986). *Social foundations of thought and action: A social cognitive theory.* Englewood Cliffs, NJ: Prentice-Hall.

Baumeister, L. M., Flores, E., & Van Oss-Marin, B. (1995). Sex information given to Latina adolescents by parents. *Health Education Research, 10,* 233–239.

Belsky, J. (2000). Conditional and alternative reproductive strategies: Individual differences in susceptibility to rearing experiences. In J. L. Rodgers, D. C. Rowe, & W. B. Miller (Eds.), *Genetic influences on human fertility and sexuality: Theoretical and empirical contributions from the biological and behavioral sciences* (pp. 127–146). Boston: Kluwer.

Belsky, J., Steinberg, L., & Draper, P. (1991). Childhood experience, interpersonal development, and reproductive strategy: An evolutionary theory of socialization. *Child Development, 62,* 647–670.

Berman, S. M., & Hein, K. (1999). Adolescents and STDs. In K. K. Holmes, P. F. Sparling, P.-A. Mardh, S. M. Lemon, W. E. Stamm, P. Piot, & J. N. Wasserheit (Eds), *Sexually transmitted diseases* (3rd ed., pp. 129–142). New York: McGraw-Hill.

Biglan, A., Metzler, C. W., Wirt, R., Ary, D., Noell, J., Ochs, L., French, C., & Hood, D. (1990). Social and behavioral factors associated with high-risk sexual behavior among adolescents. *Journal of Behavioral Medicine, 13,* 245–261.

Blum, R. W., Beuhring, R., Shew, M. L., Bearing, L. H., Sieving, R. E., & Resnick, M. D. (2000). The effects of race/ethnicity, income, and family structure on adolescent risk behaviors. *American Journal of Public Health, 90,* 1879–1884.

Capaldi, D. M., Crosby, L., & Stoolmiller, M. (1996). Predicting the timing of first sexual intercourse for at-risk adolescent males. *Child Development, 67,* 344–359.

Carter, W. B. (1990). Health behavior as a rational process: Theory of reasoned action and multi-attribute utility theory. In K. Glanz, F. M. Lewis, & B. K. Rimer (Eds.), *Health behavior and health education: Theory, research, and practice* (pp. 63–91). San Francisco: Jossey-Bass.

Centers for Disease Control and Prevention. (1999). *HIV/AIDS Surveillance Report, 11* (No. 2), 2–45.

Centers for Disease Control and Prevention. (1998). Youth risk behavior surveillance—United States, 1997. *Morbidity and Mortality Weekly Report, 47*(SS-3), 1–89.

Dawood, K., & Bailey, J. M. (2000). The genetics of human sexual orientation. In J. L. Rodgers, D. C. Rowe, & W. B. Miller (Eds.), *Genetic influences on human fertility and sexuality: Theoretical and empirical contributions from the biological and behavioral sciences* (pp. 237–252). Boston: Kluwer.

DiClemente, R. J. (1992). Psychosocial determinants of condom use among adolescents. In R. J. DiClemente (Ed.), *Adolescents and AIDS: A generation in jeopardy* (pp. 34–51). Newbury Park, CA: Sage.

Doll, L. S., & Ostrow, D. G. (1999). Homosexual and bisexual behavior. In K. K. Holmes, P. F. Sparling, P.-A. Mardh, S. M. Lemon, W. E. Stamm, P. Piot, & J. N. Wasserheit (Eds.), *Sexually transmitted diseases* (3rd ed., pp. 151–162). New York: McGraw-Hill.

Doughty, D., & Rodgers, J. L. (2000). Behavior genetic modeling of menarche in U.S. females. In J. L. Rodgers, D. C. Rowe, & W. B. Miller (Eds.), *Genetic influences on human fertility and sexuality sexuality: Theoretical and empirical contributions from the biological and behavioral sciences* (pp. 169–181). Boston: Kluwer.

Fishbein, M. (1998). Changing behavior to prevent STDs/AIDS. *International Journal of Gynecology & Obstetrics, 63,* S175–S181.

Fishbein, M., & Ajzen, I. (1975). *Belief, attitude, intention and behavior: An introduction to theory and research.* Reading, MA: Addison-Wesley.

Ford, C. S., & Beach, F. A. (1951). *Patterns of sexual behavior.* New York: Harper.

Fortenberry, J. D., Orr, D. P., Katz, B. P., Brizendine, E. J., & Blyth, M. J. (1997). Sex under the influence: A diary self-report study of substance use and sexual behavior among adolescent women. *Sexually Transmitted Diseases, 24,* 313–319.

Galbraith, J., Ricardo, I., Stanton, B., Black, M., Feigelman, S., & Kaljee, L. (1996). Challenges and rewards of involving community in research: An overview of the "Focus on Kids" HIV risk reduction program. *Health Education Quarterly, 23,* 383–394.

Gates, G. J., & Sonenstein, F. L. (2000). Heterosexual genital sexual activity among adolescent males: 1988 and 1995. *Family Planning Perspectives, 32,* 295–297.

Gillmore, M. R., Archibald, M. E., Morrison, D. M., Wilsdon, A., Wells, E. A., Hoppe, J. J., Nahom, D., & Murowchick, E. (2002). Teen sexual behavior: Applicability of the theory of reasoned action. *Journal of Marriage and Family, 64,* 885–897.

Gillmore, M. R., Morrison, D. M., Lowery, C., & Baker, S. A. (1994). Beliefs about condoms and their association with intentions to use condoms among youths in detention. *Journal of Adolescent Health, 15,* 228–237.

Gillmore, M. R., Morrison, D. M., Richey, C. A., Balassone, M. L., Gutierrez, L., & Farris, M. (1997). Effects of a skill-based intervention to encourage condom use among high risk heterosexually active adolescents. *AIDS Education and Prevention, 9,* 22–43.

Goodstein, L., & Connelly, M. (1998, April). Teenage poll finds a turn to the traditional. *New York Times.*

Guttmacher, S., Liberman, L., Ward, D., Freudenberg, N., Radosh, A., & Des Jarlais, D. (1997). Condom availability in New York City public high schools: Relationship to condom use and sexual behavior. *American Journal of Public Health, 87,* 1427–1433.

Haignere, C. S., Gold, R., & McDanel, H. J. (1999). Adolescent abstinence and condom use: Are we sure we are really teaching what is safe? *Health Education and Behavior, 26,* 43–54.

Halpern, C. T., & Udry, J. R. (1999). Pubertal changes in testosterone and implications for adolescent sexuality. In L. Severy & W. Miller (Eds.), *Advances in population: Psychosocial perspectives, Vol. 3* (pp. 127–162). London: Jessica Kingsley Publishers.

Halpern, C. T., Udry, J. R., Campbell, B., & Suchindran, C. (1993). Testosterone and pubertal development as predictors of sexual activity: A panel analysis of adolescent males. *Psychosomatic Medicine, 55,* 436–447.

Halpern, C. T., Udry, J. R., & Suchindran, C. (1997). Testosterone predicts initiation of coitus in adolescent females. *Psychosomatic Medicine, 59,* 161–171.

Henshaw, S. K., & Feivelson, D. J. (2000). Teenage abortion and pregnancy statistics by state, 1996. *Family Planning Perspectives, 32,* 272–280.

Holtzman, D., & Rubinson, R. (1995). Parent and peer communication effects on AIDS-related behavior among U.S. high school students. *Family Planning Perspectives, 27,* 235–240, 268.

Jaccard, J., Dittus, P. J., & Gordon, V. V. (1996). Maternal correlates of adolescent sexual and contraceptive behavior. *Family Planning Perspectives, 28,* 159–165.

Jaccard, J., Dittus, P. J., & Litardo, H. A. (1998). Parent-adolescent communication about sex and birth control: Implications for parent based interventions to reduce unintended adolescent pregnancy. In W. Miller & L. Severy (Eds.), *Advances in population: Psychological perspectives* (pp. 222–246). London: Kingsley Publishers.

Jemmott III, J. B., & Jemmott, L. S. (1994). Interventions for adolescents in community settings. In R. J. DiClemente & J. L. Peterson (Eds.), *Preventing AIDS: Theories and methods of behavioral intervention* (pp. 141–174). New York: Plenum.

Jemmott III, J. B., Jemmott, L. S., & Fong, G. T. (1992). Reductions in HIV risk-associated sexual behaviors among black male adolescents: Effects of an AIDS prevention intervention. *American Journal of Public Health, 82,* 372–377.

Jemmott III, J. B., Jemmott, L. S., & Fong, G. T. (1998). Abstinence and safer sex HIV risk-reduction interventions for African American adolescents: A randomized controlled trial. *Journal of the American Medical Association, 279,* 1529–1536.

Jemmott III, J. B., Jemmott, L. S., Fong, G. T., & McCaffree, K. (1999). Reducing HIV risk-associated sexual behavior among African American adolescents: Testing the generality of intervention effects. *American Journal of Community Psychology, 27,* 161–187.

Jemmott, L. (2001). *Reducing HIV risk-related behavior among African American adolescents: From research to practice to policy.* The Elizabeth Sterling Soule Lecture, University of Washington, Seattle, April 5th.

Jemmott, L. S., & Jemmott, J. B. (1991). Applying the theory of reasoned action to AIDS risk behavior: Condom use among black women. *Nursing Research, 40,* 228–234.

Kim, N., Stanton, B., Li, X, Dickersin, K., & Galbraith, J. (1997). Effectiveness of the 40 adolescent AIDS-risk reduction interventions: A quantitative review. *Journal of Adolescent Health, 20,* 204–215.

Kinsman, S. B., Romer, D., Furstenberg, F., & Schwarz, D. F. (1998). Early sexual initiation: The role of peer norms. *Pediatrics, 102,* 1185–1192.

Kirby, D. (1985). Sexuality education: A more realistic view of its effects. *Journal of School Heath, 55,* 421–424.

Kirby, D. (1995). *School programs to reduce sexual risk taking.* Paper presented at the annual meetings of the Psychosocial Workshop, San Francisco, April.

Kirby, D., & DiClemente, R. J. (1994). School-based interventions to prevent unprotected sex and HIV among adolescents. In R. J. DiClemente & J. L. Peterson (Eds.), *Preventing AIDS: Theories and methods of behavioral interventions* (pp. 117–139). New York: Plenum.

Ku, L., Sonenstein, F. L., & Pleck, J. H. (1993). Neighborhood, family, and work: Influences on the premarital behaviors of adolescent males. *Social Forces, 72,* 479–503.

Leigh, B. C., & Stall, R. (1993). Substance use and risky sexual behavior for exposure to HIV: Issues in methodology, interpretation, and prevention. *American Psychologist, 48,* 1035–1045.

Leigh, B. L., Gaylord, J., Hoppe, M. J., Rainey, D. T., Morrison, D. M., & Gillmore, M. R. (2002). *Drinking and condom use: Results from an event-based daily diary.* Unpublished manuscript, University of Washington.

Levinson, R. A., Jaccard, J., & Beamer, L. (1995). Older adolescents' engagement in casual sex: Impact of risk perception and psychological motivations. *Journal of Youth and Adolescence, 24,* 349–364.

Lieberman, L. D., Gray, H., Wier, M., Fiorentino, R., & Maloney, P. (2000). Long-term outcomes of an abstinence-based small-group pregnancy prevention program in New York City schools. *Family Planning Perspectives, 32,* 237–245.

Luster, T., & Small, S. A. (1994). Factors associated with sexual risk-taking behaviors among adolescents. *Journal of Marriage and the Family, 56,* 622–632.

MacMurray, J., Kovacs, B., McGue, M., Johnson, J. P., Blake, H., & Comings, D. E. (2000). Associations between the endothelial nitric oxide synthase gene (NOS3), reproductive behaviors and twinning. In J. L. Rodgers, D. C. Rowe, & W. B. Miller (Eds.), *Genetic influences on human fertility and sexuality sexuality: Theoretical and empirical contributions from the biological and behavioral sciences* (pp. 303–316). Boston: Kluwer.

Madden, T. J., Ellen, P. S., & Ajzen, I. (1992). A comparison of the theory of planned behavior and the theory of reasoned action. *Personality and Social Psychology Bulletin, 18,* 3–9.

Mansergh, G., & Marks, G. (1998). Age and risk of HIV infection in men who have sex with men. *AIDS, 12,* 1119–1128.

Marin, G. (1988). AIDS prevention among Hispanics: Needs, risk behaviors, and cultural values. *Public Health Reports, 104,* 411–415.

Metzler, C. W., Noell, J., Biglan, A., Ary, D., & Smolkowski, K. (1994). The social context for risky sexual behavior among adolescents. *Journal of Behavioral Medicine, 17,* 419–438.

Miller, K. S., Forehand, R., & Kotchick, B. A. (1999). Adolescent sexual behavior in two ethnic minority samples: The role of family variables. *Journal of Marriage and the Family, 61,* 85–98.

Moore, K. A., Miller, B. C., Glei, D., & Morrison, D. R. (1995). *Adolescent sex, contraception, and childbearing: A review of recent research.* Washington, DC: Child Trends Inc.

Morrison, D. M. (1985). Adolescent contraceptive behavior: A review. *Psychological Bulletin, 98,* 538–568.

Morrison, D. M., Baker, S. A., & Gillmore, M. R. (1998). Condom use among high-risk heterosexual teens: A longitudinal analysis using the theory of reasoned action. *Psychology and Health, 13,* 207–222.

Morrison, D. M., Gillmore, M. R., Hoppe, M. J., Gaylord, J., Leigh, B. L., & Rainey, D. (2002). *Adolescent drinking and sex: Findings from a daily diary study.* Unpublished manuscript, University of Washington.

Office of National AIDS Policy. (2000). *Youth and HIV/AIDS 2000: A new American agenda.* Washington, DC: The White House.

Paikoff, R., Parfenoff, S. H., Williams, S. A., & McCormick, A. (1997). Parenting, parent-child relationships, and sexual possibility situations among urban African American preadolescents: Preliminary findings and implications for HIV prevention. *Journal of Family Psychology, 11,* 11–22.

Pick, S., & Palos, P. A. (1995). Impact of the family on the sex lives of adolescents. *Adolescence, 30,* 667–675.

Richey, C. A., Gillmore, M. R., Balassone, M. L., Gutierrez, L., & Hartway, J. (1997). Developing and implementing a group skill training intervention to reduce HIV/AIDS risk among sexually active adolescents in detention. *Journal of HIV/AIDS Prevention & Education for Adolescents & Children, 1,* 71–103.

Romer, D., Black, M., Ricardo, I., Feigelman, S., Kaljee, L., Galbraith, J., Nesbit, R., Hornik, R. C., & Stanton, B. (1994). Social influences on the sexual behavior of youth at risk for HIV exposure. *American Journal of Public Health, 84,* 977–985.

Rosenstock, I. M., Strecher, V. J., & Becker, M. H. (1994). The health belief model and HIV risk behavior change. In R. J. DiClemente & J. L. Peterson (Eds.), *Preventing AIDS: Theories and methods of behavioral interventions* (pp. 5–24). New York: Plenum.

Rowe, D. C. (2000). Environmental and genetic influences on pubertal development: Evolutionary life history traits? In J. L. Rodgers, D. C. Rowe, & W. B. Miller (Eds.), *Genetic influences on human fertility and sexuality: Theoretical and empirical contributions from the biological and behavioral sciences* (pp. 147–168). Boston: Kluwer.

Santelli, J. S., Lindberg, L. D., Abma, J., McNeely, C. S., & Resnick, M. (2000a). Adolescent sexual behavior: Estimates and trends from four nationally representative surveys. *Family Planning Perspectives, 32,* 156–165, 194.

Santelli, J. S., Lowry, R., Brener, N. D., & Robin, L. (2000b). The association of sexual behaviors with socioeconomic status, family structure, and race/ethnicity among U.S. adolescents. *American Journal of Public Health, 90,* 1582–1588.

Sheeran, P., Abraham, C., & Orbell, S. (1999). Psychosocial correlates of heterosexual condom use—A meta-analysis. *Psychological Bulletin, 125,* 90–132.

Sigelman, C. K., Derenowski, E. B., Mullaney, H. A., & Siders, A. T. (1993). Parents' contributions to knowledge and attitudes regarding AIDS. *Journal of Pediatric Psychology, 18,* 221–235.

Stanton, B., Black, M., Feigelman, S., Ricardo, I., Galbraith, J., Li, X., Kaljee, L., Keane, V., & Nesbitt, R. (1995). Development of a culturally, theoretically and developmentally based survey instrument for assessing risk behaviors among African-American early adolescents living in urban low-income neighborhoods. *AIDS Education and Prevention, 7,* 160–177.

Stanton, B. F., Li, X., Ricardo, I., Galbraith, J., Feigelman, S., & Kaljee, L. (1996). A randomized, controlled effectiveness trial of an AIDS prevention program for low-income African-American youths. *Archives of Pediatric & Adolescent Medicine, 150,* 363–372.

Trumbetta, S. L., & Gottesman, I. I. (2000). Endophenotypes for marital status in the NAS-NRC twin registry. In J. L. Rodgers, D. C. Rowe, & W. B. Miller (Eds.), *Genetic influences on human fertility and sexuality: Theoretical and empirical contributions from the biological and behavioral science* (pp. 253–269). Boston: Kluwer,

Udry, J. R., & Billy, J. O. G. (1987). Initiation of coitus in early adolescence. *American Sociological Review, 52,* 841–855.

Valleroy, L. A., MacKellar, D. A., Karon, J. M., Rosen, D. H., McFarland, W., Shehan, D. A., Stoyanoff, S. R., LaLota, M., Celentano, D. D., Koblin, B. A., Thiede, H., Katz, M. H., Torian, L. V., & Janssen, R. S. (2000). HIV prevalence and associated risks in young men who have sex with men. *Journal of the American Medical Association, 284,* 198–204.

Warren, C. W., Santelli, J. S., Everett, S. A., Kann, L., Collins, J. L., Cassell, C., Morris, L., & Kolbe, L. J. (1998). Sexual behavior among U.S. high school students, 1990–1995. *Family Planning Perspectives, 30,* 170–172.

CHAPTER 17

LOST CHILDHOODS

Risk and Resiliency among Runaway and Homeless Adolescents

KIMBERLY A. TYLER

University of Nebraska–Lincoln

LES B. WHITBECK

University of Nebraska–Lincoln

Homelessness is a dynamic situation. It is a continuum of at-risk and marginal living situations ranging from doubling-up or temporary housing arrangements to life in public places. A leading researcher on homelessness has pointed out, "Homelessness is not and cannot be a precisely defined condition" (Wright, 1991, p. 19). Defining homelessness for adults is difficult, but defining it for adolescents and estimating their numbers poses even greater challenges. Many "homeless" adolescents have homes they can return to, either the one they left or that of a relative or a friend. The majority drift in and out of housed situations, living with family members, with foster parents, at group homes, with families of friends, in transitional living programs, and in shared apartments on their own. A significant proportion cannot or will not return home and have no one who will take them in. However, even these children may have institutional options, such as group homes and transitional living programs, that they have left or chosen not to participate in. As with homeless adults, being homeless for young people does not designate a single situation. Rather, homelessness ranges on a continuum from running away for a night to living independently in the open.

A unique difficulty in defining homelessness for children and adolescents is the distinction between being unhoused and unsupervised. For a minor, being away from home overnight and unsupervised constitutes homelessness, even though he or she may be staying with friends or unrelated adults. A tradition has emerged in the literature on homeless youth

Note: This work was supported by the National Institute of Mental Health (MH57110). Address correspondence to Kimberly A. Tyler, University of Nebraska–Lincoln, Department of Sociology, 717 Oldfather Hall, Lincoln, NE 68588-0324. Email: ktyler2@unl.edu.

that distinguishes between runaways, throwaways, and street youth. *Runaway* typically refers to a child or adolescent who is away from home at least overnight without parental consent or knowledge (National Network of Runaway and Youth Services, 1991, p. 3). Some researchers make a distinction between *runaways* and *chronic runaways,* which usually refers to children that have run away three or more times (e.g., Pennbridge, Yates, David, & Mackenzie, 1990). *Throwaway* refers to a child who has been told that he or she may not return home or one that has been kicked out or locked out of the parents' house. Throwaways cannot go home or must meet stringent conditions before being accepted back into the home. *Street youth* is a hazier category that refers to unsupervised youth that may or may not be housed. Some street youth may have homes to go to at night, but lack supervision and structure and are largely on their own (Shane, 1996). The Government Accounting Office has defined *homeless youth* as someone 18 years or younger who cannot return home or has chosen never to return home and who has no permanent residence (GAO, 1989).

ESTIMATING THE NUMBER OF HOMELESS AND RUNAWAY CHILDREN IN THE UNITED STATES

Most national estimates of the number of homeless and runaway youth have become severely dated. Estimates from the 1980s indicate that about 1.3 million youth ran away in 1984 and about 500,000 of these met criteria for homelessness (House Committee on Education and Labor, Subcommittee on Human Resources, 1984). Reliable recent estimates from any source are scarce (Committee on Health Care for Homeless People, 1988) and can vary widely. According to a review article, "There have been no comprehensive studies of the number of homeless youth in the United States" (Rotheram-Borus, Parra, Cantwell, Gwadz, & Murphy, 1996, p. 370). The Office of Juvenile Justice Delinquency Prevention (OJJDP) reported that there were 446,700 "broad scope" runaways in 1988 (OJJDP, 1990). *Broad scope* includes short-term (left home without permission overnight), more long-term, as well as chronic runaways. A survey of 30 U.S. cities indicated that in 1998, children accounted for 25 percent of the urban homeless population and unaccompanied minors (runaway and homeless children) and 3 percent of the urban homeless population (U.S. Conference of Mayors, 1998).

Because of the lack of a national database, the racial and ethnic backgrounds of homeless and runaway children are even more difficult to approximate than are general population estimates. Most survey research that provides racial and ethnic backgrounds has been based on regional samples or samples from single magnet cities such as New York, Los Angeles, New Orleans, and San Francisco. The Government Accounting Office (1989) estimates that 1.3 million young people under the age of 18 years were homeless or had run away. Of these, they classified 21 percent as homeless and 79 percent as runaways. The majority of those categorized as runaways were female; the majority of those considered homeless were male. The GAO estimated the ethnicity of homeless youth as 60 percent European American, 25 percent African American, and 8 percent Hispanic and other ethnic or racial group. Among runaways, 70 percent were estimated to be European American, 17 percent African American, and 3 percent Hispanic and other ethnic or racial group. A large midwestern study of nonmagnet and smaller urban areas ($n = 602$, aged 12 to 22 years) found similar proportions of ethnic and racial backgrounds (Whitbeck & Hoyt, 1999). Sixty-one percent of this sample were European American, 25 percent were African American, with the remaining 14 percent listing themselves as of Hispanic, Native American, Asian, and "other" origin.

In summary, enumerating homeless and runaway adolescents is difficult and imprecise because of the fluidity of their situations. To further complicate the matter, there are age-related definitional issues regarding what constitutes a homeless "youth." Many studies have age ranges from early to very late adolescence (e.g., 12 through 23 years). The circumstances of early adolescents versus late adolescents vary greatly, as do the risks of harm and behaviors when on the streets.

RISK AND RESILIENCY AMONG HOMELESS AND RUNAWAY CHILDREN AND ADOLESCENTS

Risk for Becoming Homeless

Although there are no longitudinal studies available from which to predict likelihood of an adolescent becoming homeless, a great deal of agreement exists across studies based on retrospective reports of runaway children and their parents. General consensus is that young people are running *from* something rather than *to* something. The children are "drifting out" of disorganized, unsupervised family situations or leaving coercive/abusive or potentially abusive families. Contemporary early independence is not about "seeking one's fortune"; it is about troubles within the family.

A persuasive number of studies now indicate high rates of physical and sexual abuse among runaway children. The rates of reported maltreatment vary widely by study, but about 75 to 50 percent of runaways report physical abuse, sexual abuse, or both (Janus, Burgess, & McCormack, 1987; Feital, Margetson, Chamas, & Lipman, 1992; Saltonstall, 1984; Warren, Gary, & Moorehead, 1994). Based on a subsample of 201 matched adolescent and parent/caregiver reports, Whitbeck, Hoyt, and Ackley (1997) found evidence of mutual violence in the families of runaways. Parent/caregiver reports indicated that about 45 percent had been pushed or shoved in anger by the target adolescent, 19 percent had been slapped, 12 percent had been beaten up, and 10 percent threatened with a weapon. Target adolescents told a similar story: 84 percent said that they had been pushed or shoved in anger by a parent/caregiver, 73 percent had been slapped, 34 percent had been beaten up, and 18 percent had been threatened with a weapon. Although parent/caregivers reported lower levels of abusive behaviors than did target adolescents, the picture that emerges is one of high levels of family violence.

There is also considerable evidence that children leave homes where there is less effective parenting (e.g., monitoring, warmth, support). Schweitzer and colleagues (Schweitzer, Hier, & Terry, 1994) reported that homeless adolescents scored higher than housed children on measures of deprivation on the Parental Bonding Inventory (Parker, Tupling, & Brown, 1979) and the Family Environment Scale (Moos & Moos, 1981). Control group studies have indicated that runaways report lower levels of parental care than housed children (Daddis, Braddock, Cuers, Elliott, & Kelly, 1993). Housed children of the same socioeconomic background reported feelings of more parental love, more family cohesion, and less overall family conflict than did homeless children interviewed in youth shelters (Wolfe, Toro, & McCaskill, 1999). A matched subsample of parent/caregiver and runaway adolescents found that both reported higher levels of parental rejection and lower levels of monitoring and warmth and supportiveness than did nonrunaway single- and two-parent families from the same geographical region (Whitbeck et al., 1997).

Retrospective reports from runaways indicate that children tend to run earlier from disorganized families (e.g., multiple changes in family structure and multiple geographic moves) than more stable families. One of the best predictors of running away is having already done so. Those who run at an earlier age are also more likely to become chronic runaways and more likely to spend time living on the streets than those that leave home in later adolescence. The trajectory of multiple "child-initiated transitions" (moves the child makes on his or her own) is one of increasing distance from parental and adult influence and increasing involvement of institutional authority (Whitbeck & Hoyt, 1999).

Characteristics of family members also contribute to risks for running away (Ring-walt, Greene, & Robertson, 1998). Family members' alcohol and drug abuse and histories of legal problems contribute to family instability. For example, 65 percent of the 602 runaway and homeless adolescents in a midwestern study reported that they had lived with at least one parent or step-parent who had an alcohol problem, 23 percent had lived with at least one parent who had a problem with marijuana, and 44 percent had lived with a parent or step-parent who had a problem with hard drugs (Whitbeck & Hoyt, 1999).

Two myths regarding homeless and runaway adolescents persist regardless of overwhelming data to the contrary. The first is that the children are running due to "wanderlust" and the need to travel and "seek one's fortune." Although this may be the case for a very few of the adolescents, the overwhelming majority are running *from* something, typically troubles within the family. The second myth is that these are "problem children" of so-called normal, often frustrated parents who have done their best to control their unruly adolescents. Again, this may be true for a very small minority of the children on the streets. However, when both parents/caregivers and runaway children are interviewed, both report problems in parenting and family violence (Whitbeck et al., 1997).

The following case studies illustrate the numerous transitions that homeless youth experience early on. They move between home, foster care, group homes, detention centers, and treatment centers. Rather than "seeking one's fortune" by running away, these youth often leave troubled family situations or are "pushed out" because parents don't want them. With very few resources and little support, these adolescents do what they have to do to get by. Having to survive on the streets often puts homeless adolescents and runaways in compromised situations, which can result in physical assault and/or rape as the lives of these two females illustrate.

■ ■ ■ ■ ■

CASE STUDY
MICHELLE

Michelle is a 19-year-old who first ran away at age 16. Her father is in the state penitentiary and her mother didn't want her or her brother, so the children went to live with their grandparents. Michelle recalls the next-door neighbor accusing their grandfather of hitting them, so they were taken by the state and placed in foster care. Michelle didn't get along very well with her foster parents and reports being physically abused while in their care. One such incident occurred when one of her foster siblings picked her up by the neck and hit her against the wall when she was 9 years old.

After being in foster care for a period of time, Michelle was placed in a series of group homes, where she contemplated suicide and, on several occasions, used safety pins and needles to scratch her wrists in addition to burning herself with cigarettes. She says that making herself bleed made her feel better. It was her way of dealing with the anger and depression she felt from the time she and her brother went to court and her mom said she didn't want them anymore. Michelle was kicked out of a home because of her aggressiveness and ran away from another group home five or six times. While on her own, she slept on the streets, stayed with friends, and slept in an abandoned building with other street youth. Since being on the street, Michelle has been sexually assaulted four times and reported dating a man who violently beat her up. Michelle smoked weed almost daily and has used crank and coke a couple of times. She was arrested once but has never gone to jail.

Currently, Michelle is living on her own with her 2-month-old daughter, where she is dependent on the state for rent and food. Michelle's goal is to go to Beauty College and raise her daughter better than she was raised. She insists that after what her mom did to her, she would never give up her daughter for anything. In summary, she says that life on the street "sucks" and a lot of things can happen to you, such as getting hurt, raped, or beaten up and robbed. She says that she was able to escape *some* of this because she and her friends hung out together and never walked anywhere by themselves. "We were smart."

CASE STUDY
STEPHANIE

Stephanie ran away for the first time when she was 12 years old and was gone for a month. She had threatened to run away and her mom told her to go ahead. Stephanie describes a very troubled family background. Her father is in prison and her mom was an alcoholic and drug addict who went out to the bars and would bring home men while Stephanie would sit up crying waiting for her mom to return. Stephanie's mom blamed her for scaring away the men with her excessive crying. At this time, Stephanie was approximately 8 or 9 years of age.

Stephanie took care of her little brother, her sister took care of her, and their mom would sell drugs. They felt as if they were always in the way. Stephanie says she was born to be nothing. She recalls smoking pot with her mom for the first time when she was 8 years old. She did drugs with her mom's best friend while her mom was present in the room. The second time she left home, Stephanie was 13 years old and had a 32-year-old boyfriend who sold drugs. She had sex for the first time at age 13, got pregnant, and then had an abortion. Stephanie, her brother, and her mom were on medication (although Stephanie says she never took hers), and one day she tried to commit suicide by overdosing on all of their pills. Her mother and grandmother were unable to "wake her up," so she was rushed to the emergency room and later checked into a treatment hospital. She was told afterwards that she had been in a coma-like state. She was a ward of the state from ages 13 to 17 years because of a violent crime she committed. "Fighting has always been an issue with me." Upon her release, no one wanted her (i.e., her mom or family) and she has been homeless ever since.

LOST CHILDHOODS

383

While on the street, Stephanie was involved with gangs and used drugs frequently, including shooting drugs. She secured shelter with various men, ages 16 to 28 years, with the understanding that she would trade sex and "look pretty" for them. Day-to-day life is a struggle for her trying to find shelter, buy food, and get transportation. Stephanie lived in an abandoned apartment for a period of time and sometimes gets food from street outreach or from friends who work at fast-food restaurants. She has been raped while taking a ride from a stranger and recalls her aunt telling her it was okay because she wasn't pregnant and since she wasn't a virgin anyway, she would survive. She admits having sex on numerous occasions without using protection and has had an STD.

Currently, Stephanie is in an abusive relationship but admits that she dishes it out too, referring to the fact that her boyfriend has had plenty of black eyes. She has no friends she can rely on except this boyfriend. Stephanie and her boyfriend had a baby about a year ago, who was taken from her and put into foster care when she had to go to jail for an outstanding warrant. Her goal right now is to get her son back, to get a house, and be financially secure with or without her current boyfriend (the father of her child). She has been trying to get a job but has no skills or experience. She has little to look forward to and has no idea what her life will be like in the next year. Stephanie is currently 20 years of age.

RISKS ASSOCIATED WITH EARLY INDEPENDENCE

Health Risks

We know surprisingly little about the health effects of running away and homelessness among children and adolescents. Because these children often leave highly disorganized, neglecting, and abusive families, it is safe to assume that many of their early health needs have gone unmet. Moreover, there is slight reason to presume that care, other than on an emergency basis, will be available to them on the streets. One 1992 study of sheltered and street youth indicated that about one-half of the street youth and over one-third of the sheltered youth had no regular source of health care (Klein et al., 2000). In the same report, 25 percent of the street youth indicated that they had had serious health problems in the past year. Health treatment is complicated by the fact that runaways have no guardian or parent to turn to for necessary permissions, unless they have come under institutional supervision and care. Also, injuries or illnesses (e.g., drug overdose) may be the result of illegal activities, so that adolescents may be reluctant to seek care. Even if the reasons for seeking care are not due to illegal behaviors, status as a runaway and issues of confidentiality and mandatory reporting may pose barriers to services (DeRosa et al., 1999; Geber, 1997). Issues of nutrition among homeless adolescents, an ongoing problem with adolescents in general, remain uninvestigated.

Adolescence is known as a time of risk-taking behaviors and perceived invulnerability. It is also a time of experimentation with adult activities, such as alcohol, tobacco, drug use, and sexual activity. In normal development, this experimentation takes place in the context of adult monitoring, limitations, rules, and consequences that may moderate and constrain the degree of experimentation. Among runaway and homeless adolescents, however, there are no such moderating factors. Indeed, risk taking is exacerbated by the act of separation from adult authority and the absence of supervision.

Injuries

The leading causes of death among adolescents (ages 15 to 24 years) are unintentional injuries (e.g., motor vehicle accidents) and intentional injuries (homicide and suicide). In urban settings, the primary causes of adolescent morbidity are unintentional injuries, intentional injuries, substance abuse, sexually transmitted diseases (including HIV infection), and unintentional pregnancy (Ensign, 1998, p. 165).

Homeless and runaway adolescents are at great risk for each of these health conditions, but they are especially at risk for intentional injury from victimization when on the streets. In a Los Angeles study, 51 percent of the runaway adolescents interviewed had been beaten up since being on their own, 45 percent had been chased, and 26 percent had been shot at. In addition, 19 percent reported they had been stabbed, 15 percent sexually assaulted, and 7 percent wounded by gunshot (Kipke, Simon, Montgomery, Unger, & Iverson, 1997). A New York City study indicated that in the three months prior to seeking shelter where they were interviewed, 20 percent had experienced physical assault, 20 percent had been sexually assaulted, and 20 percent had been robbed (Rotheram-Borus, Rosario, & Koopman, 1991). A multisite report of more than 970 runaways from the Midwest and Seattle found that almost one-half of the males (47 percent) and one-third of the females (31 percent) had been beaten up, and 50 percent of the males and 36 percent of the females had been robbed. More than one-half of the males (54 percent) and one-third of the females had been threatened with a weapon, and 30 percent of the males and 13 percent of the females reported they had been assaulted with a weapon. Some 23 percent of the females and 7 percent of the males had been sexually assaulted while on their own (Whitbeck, Hoyt, Yoder, Cauce, & Paradise, 2001).

Young women are more vulnerable to sexual assault, and young men are more likely to be involved in physical fights involving weapons (Whitbeck & Hoyt, 1999). The strongest predictor of physical or sexual victimization when on the streets is association with deviant peers. For males, engaging in victimizing behaviors is strongly associated with physical victimization (Hoyt, Ryan, & Cauce, 1999; Whitbeck et al., 2001). For females, and gay males, participating in survival sex is a strong predictor of sexual victimization (Whitbeck et al., 2001). Among females, interviewer ratings of attractiveness, being well groomed, and being well dressed were also associated with sexual assault (Tyler, Hoyt, Whitbeck, & Cauce, 2001). Having been sexually abused prior to running away is related to later sexual victimization among runaway females (Tyler, Hoyt, & Whitbeck, 2000).

Homeless and runaway adolescents are also at risk for intentional self-injury via suicide attempts and completions. In the very few studies that have addressed suicide among homeless and runaway adolescents, self-reported attempts and ideation are extremely high. In an early study of New York street youth, Shaffer and Caton (1984) reported that 33 percent of the females and 16 percent of the males interviewed during a two-week survey had attempted suicide. In her New York City study, Rotheram-Borus (1993) reported that 37 percent of the runaways surveyed in shelters had attempted suicide in the past. Of these, more than half had attempted more than once. In a study of 291 adolescents in homeless shelters in St. Louis, 30 percent had attempted suicide at some point in their lives (Stiffman, 1989). Also, 24 percent of the runaway and homeless adolescents in a midwestern multistate sample had attempted suicide (Yoder, 1999). Yates and colleagues' (1988) health study ($n = 110$) of homeless youth treated in an outpatient setting in Los Angeles reported an 18 percent attempt rate, more than four times that of nonhomeless outpatient adolescents.

Sexually Transmitted Disease

The lifestyles of runaway and homeless adolescents place them at particular risk for sexually transmitted disease (STD). Indeed, street clinics report that gynecologic problems (e.g., pregnancy tests, STD) account for a major proportion of evaluations (Reuler, 1991). Many runaways engage in various related health-compromising behaviors, such as substance abuse, survival sex, hanging out in areas where infection rates are high, and engaging in IV drug use (Johnson, Aschkenasy, Herbers, & Gillenwater, 1996; Kipke, O'Conner, Palmer, & Mackenzie, 1995; Tyler, Whitbeck, Hoyt, & Yoder, 2000; Yates, MacKenzie, Pennbridge, & Cohen, 1988). Self-reported rates of condom use among sexually active homeless and runaway adolescents range from 18 percent for females and 14 percent for males (Rotheram-Borus et al., 1992) to 32% for females and 41% for males (Whitbeck & Hoyt, 1999). Rates vary by context (e.g., shelter vs. street intercepts) and geographical location (e.g., large magnet cities vs. smaller nonmagnet cities).

Estimates of sexually transmitted disease among street youth have been as high as 50 to 71 percent infection rates (Shalwitz, Coulart, Dunnigan, & Flannary, 1990, cited in Rotheram-Borus et al., 1996). In a Los Angeles sample of clinic contacts, Yates and colleagues (1988) reported an 18 percent diagnostic rate for STDs among runaway patients. Self-reported rates from a midwestern multisite sample for lifetime prevalence of STD were 23 percent for females and 12 percent for males (Whitbeck & Hoyt, 1999). A large clinic-based study of 1,403 patient charts from Seattle street youth clinic indicated a 16 percent rate for STD treated over a five-year period (Deisher & Rogers, 1991).

Because of high-risk sexual behaviors and drug use, runaway and homeless adolescents are thought to be especially susceptible to HIV infection. Regional estimates range from 5.3 percent in New York to a high of 12 percent in San Francisco (Rotheram-Borus, Koopman, & Ehrhardt, 1991). Although only about 4 percent of street youth were estimated to be HIV positive in the early 1990s (Rotheram-Borus et al., 1996), a larger number of exposed runaway and homeless adolescents were expected to emerge in the latter part of the decade. The most recent Centers for Disease Control surveillance studies tend to confirm the expected trend. Among 13- to 24-year-olds, the rate of HIV infection continues to increase: "At least half of all new HIV infections in the United States are among people under 25, and the majority are infected sexually" (CDC, 2001). Among the highest risk groups cited by the CDC are "out-of-school" children, particularly homeless and runaway youth.

MENTAL HEALTH RISKS

The primary mental health risk associated with running away is the experience of homelessness itself. Goodman and colleagues have pointed out that vulnerabilities and losses associated with homelessness are extremely traumatic for adults (Goodman, Saxe, & Harvey, 1991). The trauma associated with becoming homeless is magnified when it is experienced during a developmental period when young people need and expect protection, support, and guidance from caregiving adults. Hypervigilence, anxiety, fear, and sense of vulnerability are normal responses to the perceived and real threats associated with being without a familiar or safe place. A study of street youth in Hollywood indicated that approximately 50 percent feared being shot, stabbed, sexually assaulted, or beaten up since they had been on the streets (Kipke et al., 1997). These responses occur in addition to and simultaneous with symptoms of distress the child may already be experiencing as a result of living in a chaotic or abusive environment and the need or the necessity of leaving. Stress associated with leaving home may exacerbate preexisting symptoms or eventuate new ones (Whitbeck & Hoyt, 1999).

Because of a lack of longitudinal studies on this hard to access population, it is difficult to separate emotional distress and behavioral problems that existed prior to running away from the potentially additive effects of stress experienced from precocious independence. Among runaways, the degree of stress experienced may range from being away from home in a shelter with strangers to traumatic witnessed or experienced violence when living directly on the streets. Research has documented strong psychological effects (e.g., depressive symptoms and symptoms of posttraumatic stress) as a result of victimization when on the streets, even when violence or abuse experienced in the home prior to running away are controlled (Whitbeck, Hoyt, & Bao, 2000; Whitbeck & Hoyt, 1999). In addition, longitudinal research has shown that depressive symptoms, suicidal ideation, and anxiety increase among runaways as a consequence of victimization when they are on their own (Whitbeck, Hoyt, Johnson, Whiteford, & Cauce, under review).

During the past decade, there has been an increasing number of research reports regarding the mental health of this marginal group of adolescents. Control group comparisons indicate that homeless and runaway adolescents typically score higher on symptom measures of behavioral and emotional disorders than do nonrunaway adolescents. For example, Schweitzer and Hier (1993) found that more than one-half (54 percent) of their sample of homeless adolescents in Australia scored within the clinical range of the Youth Self-Report (Achenbach, 1991), compared to about 5 percent of the control group of nonrunaway adolescents. Most studies find high rates of behavior problems, alcohol and drug use, depression, and suicidal behavior.

Diagnostic studies of this population are sparse. Accurate diagnosis is problematic with homeless adults and adolescents because it is difficult to separate normal responses to the stresses of street life from more enduring psychological symptoms. This is especially an issue with diagnosing conduct disorder in runaway adolescents in that running away is a key diagnostic element from Diagnostic Interview Schedule for Children-Revised (DISC-R) and may result in overdiagnosing conduct disorder among this group. Also, most diagnostic studies have been done at a single shelter or, at best, a single city, which reduces the generalizeability of the findings. Feital and colleagues (1992) found that 59 percent of 150 shelter adolescents met criteria for conduct disorder based on DISC-R interviews. Cauce and colleagues (2000) reported that 53 percent of her Seattle sample ($n = 362$) met criteria for conduct disorder or oppositional defiant disorder (DISC-R). McCaskill, Toro, and Wolfe (1998), using a "matched" sample of 118 shelter youth and 118 housed youth, found that the shelter youth were more likely to meet criteria on the DISC-R for disruptive disorders (46 vs. 20 percent) and alcohol use disorders (25 vs. 9 percent) than did the housed youth. No differences between the two groups were found for drug abuse or affective disorders.

Drug and alcohol use is common among homeless and runaway adolescents. Robertson (1989) found that runaways were 5 times more likely to meet criteria for drug abuse than their housed counterparts. In their sample of street clinic outpatients, Los Angeles runaways were 4 times more likely to be treated for drug abuse than nonrunaways (Yates et al., 1988). A more recent study of Los Angeles street youth reports that 93 percent had used marijuana, 66 percent speed, 61 percent LSD, and 50 percent crack cocaine (Kipke, Montgomery, & MacKenzie, 1997). A study based on the National Longitudinal Survey of Youth reported that drug use by repeat runaways was 7 to 12 times that of nonrunaways or those who had run on only one occasion (Windle, 1989). Among New York City runaways, 19 percent had reported using crack cocaine and 43 percent marijuana. About one-half had at least one symptom of alcohol abuse (Koopman, Rosario, & Rotheram-Borus, 1994). Drug use was somewhat lower in the midwestern multisite sample for hard drug use, though this could be an artifact of sampling differences. Some 15 percent reported having used crack cocaine, 26 percent amphetamines, 15 percent cocaine, 26 percent hallucinogens, and 17 percent inhalants (Whitbeck & Hoyt, 1999).

Because of the wide involvement of homeless and runaway adolescents in deviant behaviors (Hagen & McCarthy, 1997), there has been a tendency to overlook internalizing symptoms. Depressive symptoms, symptoms of anxiety, and posttraumatic stress disorder (PTSD) are commonly reported by runaways (Mundy, Robertson, Robertson, & Greenblatt, 1990; Smart & Walsh, 1993; Yates et al., 1988). Fietel and colleagues (1992) found that 49 percent of 150 sheltered runaway adolescents met DISC-R criteria for major depression, 37 percent met criteria for dysthymic disorder, and 32 percent met criteria for PTSD. Based on clinical interviews with 97 street youth in Los Angeles, Mundy and associates (1990) reported that 20 percent met criteria for a clinical level of mood disturbance. DISC-R evaluations of 364 homeless and runaway adolescents in the Seattle area indicated that 21 percent met criteria for major depression, and 12 percent met criteria for PTSD (Cauce et al., 2000). Screening for PTSD in a midwestern multisite sample resulted in 38 percent meeting criteria. Of those who reported experiencing a traumatic event when on their own, 46 percent met criteria (Whitbeck & Hoyt, 1999).

RESILIENT RUNAWAYS

Very little has been written about resiliency among runaway and homeless adolescents. One of the reasons for this is that *resiliency* is difficult to define for this population. What may be adaptive to successful living on the streets is often maladaptive for later adult developmental expectations. Resilience is typically viewed as the ability to overcome serious and cumulative developmental risks so that negative outcomes—such as legal problems, psychological disorders, and occupational difficulties—are avoided (Rak & Patterson, 1996). For runaways, resiliency may mean getting by on the streets, where successful adaptation involves daily survival and avoiding harm. Any street worker can provide stories of amazing ingenuity and survival among these young people. However, successful street life usually involves skills and knowledge that are incongruent with successful adult development. Often, the skills for street adaptation run counter to the interpersonal skills necessary for success in conventional educational settings, conventional employment, healthy interpersonal relationships, and establishing permanent housing.

A second way to view resiliency is avoidance of psychological symptoms. However, some research shows that psychologically healthy young people experience more symptoms of internalization when faced with the stresses of homelessness than the less psychologically healthy. Stefanidis and colleagues (1992) found that homeless adolescents who manifested internalization symptoms were more responsive to treatment and more successful in transitional living programs than those who had fewer symptoms of internalization (Stefanidis, Pennbridge, Mackenzie, & Pottharst, 1992). Although it is far from established, it may be that more psychologically healthy adolescents respond more dramatically to the trauma of homelessness (e.g., Goodman et al., 1991).

There is general agreement among researchers regarding the basic factors that mitigate developmental risk. Protective factors typically fall into three domains: the child's personality characteristics, family characteristics, and the community environment (Garmezy, 1983; Hauser, Vieyra, Jacobson, & Wertlieb, 1985). Personality characteristics that serve as protective factors include self-efficacy, social skills, internal locus of control, and temperament. Family characteristics encompass warmth and supportive parents and parental harmony. Finally, community environment or extrafamilial support factors include successful school experiences and supportive networks with peers and/or grandparents (Emery & Forehand, 1994).

Runaways are usually disadvantaged in all three domains. As noted, many are already experiencing psychological and behavioral problems before they run away. Experiences on the street exacerbate existing symptoms and contribute to new ones. Most are leaving families that are disorganized, coercive, and often abusive. Available family support is more often from extended family members than from biological parents or stepparents (Whitbeck & Hoyt, 1999). The environments in which runaways find themselves are dangerous by location (Hoyt et al., 1999) and by associations (Kipke et al., 1997; Whitbeck et al., 2001). By separating themselves from the sphere of adult controls and asserting precocious adulthood, runaway and homeless adolescents also may have cut themselves off from adult protections and support.

A cluster analysis focusing on resiliency factors (e.g., self-efficacy, school attendance, employment, low externalization scores) of runaway and homeless adolescents in the Midwest indicated that males were more likely to be resilient according to these criteria than were females. Coming from families where there was a history of serious criminal behavior on the part of parents reduced resiliency for females, but had little effect on males. Deviant peer affiliations had stronger negative effects on resiliency among runaway males than for females. Participating in victimizing behaviors reduced the likelihood of inclusion in the resiliency cluster by nearly 50 percent, indicating, perhaps, that the least resilient runaways are those who engage in aggressive behaviors (Whitbeck & Hoyt, 1999).

In summary, we know very little about resiliency among this high-risk population of young people. Certainly, the cumulative risk factors most have experienced create serious impediments that must be overcome (Fergusson, Horwood, & Lynskey, 1994; Rutter, 1985). The crucial indicator of resiliency will be successful transition to adulthood, and, to date, there have been no studies that document this process. No one knows what happens to these adolescents as they grow into early adulthood. Some will no doubt remain on society's margins all of their lives. Many, however, will make more or less successful transitions, become housed and self-supporting. Longitudinal studies and studies of homeless people in early adulthood (e.g., 18 to 25 years) are crucial for understanding the developmental trajectories of these high-risk adolescents.

INTERVENING WITH
HARD-TO-REACH ADOLESCENTS

The most at-risk children and adolescents in our society are also the most difficult to access and the most difficult to treat. The fundamental problem is that many, usually those most in need of intervention, are already adults in a system that is mandated to treat them as children. To maintain their "too early" adult status, runaway and homeless adolescents may avoid traditional social services agencies and, particularly, the criminal justice system. Even nontraditional street agencies may be viewed with suspicion until personal relationships are established.

Intervention Programs

According to the Mayor's Office (New York City Government Home Page, 2001), four types of programs are available for homeless youth in New York City. *Runaway shelters* are group residences of 20 beds or fewer for the purpose of providing a safe place for young people on a 24-hour basis. A small number of *host homes* are available that provide temporary foster care (30 to 60 days) for adolescents up to age 18 years. *Transitional living programs* are available to provide older homeless youth (16 to 21 years) training and skills for independent living for up to one year. Finally, *nonresidential outreach programs* target street youth and provide information and referral services along with crisis intervention and supportive services. Most agencies that serve runaway and homeless adolescents provide one or more components of these four approaches.

Targeted Interventions

There have been several published studies of targeted interventions with homeless and runaway adolescents in the past decade. Many of these have responded to national concern regarding HIV infection among this high-risk population. Typically, these programs have focused on HIV testing and reducing risk factors. Few have sophisticated methodologies, most merely document risk factors among the group and report prevalence rates, and very few have measurable outcomes (Clements, Gleghorn, Garcia, Katz, & Marx, 1997; Goulart & Madover, 1991; Stricof, Kennedy, Nattell, Weisfuse, & Novick, 1991). Prevention efforts typically are education based, often through outreach programs (Booth, Zhang, & Kwiatkowski, 1999; Podschun, 1993). Treatment programs most often are clinic based and involve medical interventions along with support groups (Goulart & Madover, 1991). Very few reported integrated services based on intensive case management to address all aspects of life for HIV-positive youth (Tenner, Trevithick, Wagner, & Burch, 1998). There is some concern that those who are at greatest risk are not participating in clinic testing programs. In fact, one study reported a negative association between risk factors and the likelihood of HIV testing (Goodman et al., 1999).

Other targeted interventions include efforts to provide health care to this underserved population by outreach (Reuler, 1991) and in shelters (Steele & O'Keefe, 2001). Peer counseling education-based programs targeted at reducing drug abuse among runaway and homeless adolescents have been found to be more successful than adult-led and nonintervention groups (Fors & Jarvis, 1995).

Community Intervention Efforts

There are published reports on two citywide initiatives to address care for runaways and homeless youth. Both are in magnet cities for runaways. Seattle has had a Policy Plan for Children and Youth since 1981 that makes city government efforts on behalf of runaways a priority. The plan focuses on broad policy issues, including coordination of services, support of culturally sensitive outreach and shelter programs, and the development of a "unified advocacy agenda" (Smart, 1991). The Division of Adolescent Medicine at the Children's Hospital of Los Angeles has developed a plan for comprehensive care for homeless and runaway youth in Los Angeles County based on five components. These include consolidation of services and better communication between service providers, outreach programs, short-term crisis centers, availability of comprehensive medical care and counseling services, and long-term care and transitional services (Yates, Pennbridge, Swofford, & Mackenzie, 1991). These community efforts could provide models for other cities in identifying the scope of the problem and proposing strategies to address it.

Although we could locate very few methodologically sophisticated outcome studies of intervention programs for homeless and runaway adolescents, many existing programs claim success via early and innovative interventions. For example, the annual report of Youth Care, a Seattle-based organization, points out that the first 72 hours for the runaway is a crucial period for intervention. The agency employs "nonauthority" figures as street workers, including peer counselors. The program has an intensive outreach program that offers shelter, food, clothing, and health care; a drop-in center; a transitional living program; and a teen parent program (Annual Report, Youth Care, 2001).

This agency and many like it in large and small cities throughout the country represent the state-of-the-art interventions for runaways and homeless youth. The genuine knowledge of our nation's street youth resides at the street agency level, and most of this knowledge is passed on through meetings, reports, and conferences attended by street workers. The people who are doing the real work with homeless and runaway youth and developing innovative intervention approaches aren't apt to publish in scholarly journals and are more interested in finding what works in response to urgent needs than in running carefully controlled intervention studies.

To better grasp the peculiar situations in which runaway and homeless adolescent find themselves, we asked their impressions of what sorts of interventions would work best. First and most important was easily available shelter and "safe places." One 15-year-old female told us that she had trouble locating shelters in two different cities. She saw a need for well-advertised, easily accessible "safe places": "I think like Quik Trip, you know, how they put a safe place in there...do something like that, put more safe places around, like everywhere because that way a child knows that they have somebody to turn to" (Whitbeck & Hoyt, 1999, p. 167). Other adolescents pointed out the need for shelters that are welcoming. As one 16-year-old male put it: "I've been to three shelters, stayed at two but been to three where people were so cold-hearted that, I mean, I would rather be alone on the streets and cold" (Whitbeck & Hoyt, 1999, p. 167).

Many of these "too early" adults have severed ties to adult caregivers. Others have multiple reasons for not trusting adults. Most have a social support system largely made up of similarly aged peers. They told us that they relate to and are more comfortable with street outreach workers who are younger. Several cited the need to have someone to talk to, but, as a 15-year-old female put it, it should be someone "just like a friend, usually kids don't like counselors or anything like that. They like to talk to a friend and it gets them like a load off their chest" (Whitbeck & Hoyt, 1999, p. 167).

In summary, all the runaway and homeless adolescents we interviewed regarding interventions that would work cited nontraditional approaches that (1) made safe shelter available unconditionally, (2) made safe shelter welcoming, and (3) staffed shelters with people like themselves in age and experiences. Successful street outreach programs like the agencies with which we worked were aware of these special needs.

LOST CHILDHOODS

Most of the developmental research suggests a difficult life course for chronic runaway and homeless adolescents. Chances for prosocial outcomes diminish as opportunities are missed or delayed. Prosocial adult influences may be reduced by marginal school attendance or by dropping out. Drug and alcohol use may begin to take a toll. Arrests or criminal involvement may close doors as time passes, making employment more difficult. Behavioral problems may be exacerbated by associations with deviant peers on the streets or by engaging in deviant subsistence strategies (Hagen & McCarthy, 1997; Whitbeck & Hoyt, 1999). The transitions brought about by "too early adulthood" close doors so that there is little chance of going back to childhood.

THEORETICAL PERSPECTIVE

Life course developmental theory (Elder, 1997) and *social interaction theory* (Patterson, 1982) are useful for explaining how the early life histories of homeless adolescents affect later developmental outcomes. Patterson has argued that coercive families provide "basic training" for antisocial behaviors (Patterson, Dishion, & Bank, 1984). This first or basic training is the result of continuous failure on the part of the parents to use effective discipline techniques in controlling coercive exchanges between family members. Through this training, the child learns to control other members of the family by means of coercion, and these interaction styles are generalized into other contexts. These coercive and abusive behaviors become coping styles that are carried with the adolescent into peer interactions, which results in rejection by normal friend groups (Patterson et al., 1984; Patterson, DeBaryshe, & Ramsey, 1989). Children who learn to expect rejection may withdraw from future interactions, thereby ruling out opportunities to affiliate with prosocial peers; therefore, they never have the opportunity to practice conventional social skills (Moffitt, 1993).

Moreover, negative interaction styles learned in the family become self-reinforcing, resulting in the selection and creation of environments that are familiar and congruent with these interaction styles. These persistent behavioral patterns are continually reinforced in interactions with others, a process Caspi and colleagues have termed "cumulative continuity" (Caspi, Bem, & Elder, 1987). Therefore, adolescents who grow up in families that display aggressive and antisocial behavior are likely to become part of social groups that display similar characteristics. As adolescents leave or are "pushed out" of their troubled families, interaction patterns learned at home are carried into early independence. The "basic training" for antisocial behavior in the family becomes "advanced training" on the street (Whitbeck et al., 1999). The effects of antisocial behavior, coercive/aggressive exchanges, and early maltreatment in the home gains momentum as the youth becomes more and more separated from adult influences. There is also a cumulative psychological toll. Existing symptoms may be magnified by experiences on the street or new symptoms may emerge (Whitbeck et al., under review).

HOMELESS FAMILIES AND CHILDREN

Homeless families and children is another substantive area in the homeless literature, albeit separate from homeless and runaway adolescents. Homelessness is devastating for families, disrupting every aspect of family life and negatively impacting children's health and development. The fastest growing segment of the homeless population is families with children—constituting 40 percent of all people who become homeless (Shinn & Weitzman, 1996). It is estimated that between 50 and 65 percent of homeless children in shelters are below the age of 6 (Bassuk & Rubin, 1987; National Coalition for the Homeless, 1999).

The causes of family homelessness include poverty, lack of affordable housing, and, more recently, domestic violence. In a study of homeless families with children between the ages of 2 and 16 years, Cumella and colleagues (1998) found that escaping partner violence was the most frequently cited reason for becoming homeless (Cumella, Grattan, & Vostanis, 1998). Additionally, the U.S. Conference of Mayors (1998), cited in the National Coalition for the Homeless (1999), revealed that domestic violence was the primary cause of homelessness in 46 percent of the cities they surveyed.

The negative consequences of homelessness for children are numerous, including high rates of mental health problems such as anxiety, depression, and behavioral problems; developmental delays; learning difficulties and lower levels of education; and poor health (Bassuk & Rubin, 1987; Cumella et al., 1998; Shinn & Weitzman, 1996). Experiencing mental and physical health problems at an early age is likely to have long-term consequences for many of these children. Parents themselves also experience numerous mental health problems, and many mothers report having experienced sexual and or physical abuse during their own childhood (c.f. Bassuk & Rubin, 1987; Cumella et al., 1998). Children who are homeless are not simply at risk but experience physical, psychological, and emotional damage due to the circumstances of their families being homeless (Molnar, Rath, & Klein, 1990).

FUTURE DIRECTIONS

Even though there has been a significant increase in studies pertaining to homeless and runaway adolescents during the past decade, we are still at the stage of documenting risk factors and prevalence. The next generation of research should focus on developmental outcomes. There is little need for more studies documenting risk. However, there is a critical need for new studies in three areas. First, no one knows about the life trajectories of these high-risk adolescents. We don't have information about who is able to leave the streets, become housed, employed, and enter into conventional relationships. Further, we don't know how many remain on society's margins in their adult lives.

Second, we don't have good information about what "works" in intervening with homeless and runaway adolescents. There is some information that indicates that comprehensive services programs are effective (Tenner et al., 1998), but we need sophisticated control group studies that evaluate intervention strategies with this high-risk population. Current social policy has moved more in the direction of a criminal justice response to homeless and runaway adolescents than toward treatment. This criminal justice approach essentially revictimizes the children and reinforces life-long patterns of punitive and coercive responses by authority figures. Because these precocious adults do not fit typical treatment systems available to children and adolescents, their needs are not being addressed. Instead of developing interventions that take into account that precocious adulthood is irreversible, these adolescents are too often viewed as "treatment failures" because they don't respond to interventions aimed at children.

Finally, research is needed that focuses on remediating the psychological harm done by the experience of homelessness. Housing is necessary and immediate protection is a priority for these young people. However, the long-term effects of experiencing homelessness at such critical developmental periods are not yet understood. Certainly, these are among the most traumatized children in our society. Transitional living programs and employment training may prove insufficient for many of these multiply victimized young people. They will need ongoing treatment for the psychological consequences of their early experiences. We need to know the extent and longevity of the damage that has been done and to evaluate effective treatment modalities.

The topic of homeless and runaway adolescents comes and goes as a "hot" media topic. There is classroom interest in their plights and the risks they take. However, it is time to move beyond documenting their situations and begin to focus on their futures. We now have plenty of information that addresses risk. We know that there are populations of runaways and homeless adolescents in small, nonmagnet, middle-American cities. The next generation of researchers and practitioners need to address developmental outcomes and intervention strategies that move the children forward into successful adulthood.

DISCUSSION QUESTIONS

1. What are some of the primary barriers to health care for homeless and runaway youth?

2. Do you agree with the authors of this article? Is it really possible for these children to return to childhood? Must they be viewed and treated as "precocious adults"? Support your answers.

3. Discuss the concept of *resiliency* among this population. What different forms does it take? How would you choose to measure it?

4. Why do "myths" pertaining to reasons for running away persist in our society?

5. Discuss the psychological effects of experiencing homelessness on a person under 18 years of age. What do you suppose it feels like?

6. Any kind of personal victimization creates an emotional response. Now envision victimization when you have no private place in which to retreat. What effects do you think homelessness has on responses to personal victimization among young people?

SUGGESTED READINGS

Hagen, J., & McCarthy, B. (1997). *Mean streets: Youth crime and homelessness.* New York: Cambridge University Press.

Tedeschi, R. G., Park, C. L., & Calhoun, L. G. (1998). *Posttraumatic growth: Positive changes in the aftermath of crisis.* Mahwah, NJ: Lawrence Erlbaum.

Van der Ploeg, J., & Scholte, E. (1997). *Homeless youth.* Thousand Oaks, CA: Sage.

Wright, J. D., Rubin, B. A., & Devine, J. A. (1998). *Beside the golden door: Policy, politics, and the homeless.* New York: Aldine de Gruyter.

REFERENCES

Achenbach, T. (1991). *Manual of the youth self-report and 1991 profile.* Burlington: University of Vermont.

Bassuk, E., & Rubin, L. (1987). Homeless children: A neglected population. *American Journal of Orthopsychiatry, 57,* 279–286.

Booth, R., Zhang, Y., & Kwiatkowski, C. (1999). The challenge of changing drug and sex risk behaviors of runaway and homeless adolescents. *Child Abuse & Neglect, 23,* 1295–1306.

Caspi, A., Bem, D. J., & Elder, G. H. (1987). Moving against the world: Life-course patterns of explosive children. *Developmental Psychology, 23,* 308–313.

Cauce, A. M., Paradise, M., Embry, L., Ginzler, J. A., Morgan, C., Lohr, Y., & Wagner, V. (2000). The characteristics and mental health of homeless adolescents: Age and gender differences. *Journal of Emotional and Behavioral Disorders, 8,* 230–239.

Centers for Disease Control & Prevention, Division of HIV/AIDS Prevention. (2001). *Young people at risk: HIV/AIDS among America's youth.* Atlanta, GA: Author.

Clements, K., Gleghorn, A., Garcia, D., Katz, M., & Marx, R. (1997). A risk profile of street youth in northern California: Implications for gender-specific human immunodeficiency virus prevention. *Journal of Adolescent Health, 20,* 343–353.

Committee on Health Care for Homeless People. (1988). *Health and human needs.* Washington, DC: National Academy Press.

Cumella, S., Gratten, E., & Vostanis, P. (1998). The mental health of children in homeless families and their contact with health, education, and social services. *Health and Social Care in the Community, 6,* 331–342.

Daddis, M., Braddock, D., Cuers, S., Elliott, A., & Kelly, A. (1993). Personal and family distress in homeless adolescents. *Community Mental Health Journal, 29,* 413–422.

Deisher, R., & Rogers, W. (1991). The medical care of street youth. *Journal of Adolescent Health, 12,* 500–503.

DeRosa, C., Montgomery, S., Kipke, M., Iverson, E., Ma, J., & Unger, J. (1999). Service utilization among homeless and runaway youth in Los Angeles, California: Rates and reasons. *Journal of Adolescent Health, 24,* 449–458.

Elder, G. (1997). Life course and human development. In R. Lerner (Ed.), *Handbook of child psychology, volume 1: Theoretical models of human development* (pp. 939–991). New York: Wiley.

Emery, R. E., & Forehand, R. (1994). Parental divorce and children's well-being: A focus on resilience. In R. J. Haggerty, L. R. Sherrod, N. Garmezy, & M. Rutter (Eds.), *Stress, risk, and resilience in children and adolescents* (pp. 64–99). New York: Cambridge University Press.

Ensign, J. (1998). Health issues of homeless youth. *Journal of Social Distress and the Homeless, 7,* 159–174.

Feital, B., Margetson, N., Chamas, J., & Lipman, C. (1992). Psychosocial background and behavioral and emotional disorders of homeless and runaway youth. *Hospital and Community Psychiatry, 43,* 153–163.

Fergusson, D., Horwood, L., & Lynskey, M. (1994). The childhoods of multiple problem adolescents: A 15 year longitudinal study. *Journal of Child Psychology and Psychiatry, 32,* 1123–1140.

Fors, S., & Jarvis, S. (1995). Evaluation of a peer-led drug abuse risk reduction project for runaway and homeless youths. *Journal of Drug Education, 25,* 321–333.

GAO. (1989). *Homeless and runaway youth receiving services at federally funded shelters.* Report HRD-90-45. Washington, DC: Author.

Garmezy, N. (1983). Stressors of childhood. In N. Garmezy & M. Rutter (Eds.), *Stress, coping, and development in children* (pp. 43–84). New York: McGraw-Hill.

Geber, G. (1997). Barriers to health care for street youth. *Journal of Adolescent Health, 21,* 287–290.

Goodman, E., Samples, C., Keenan, P., Fox, D., Melchiono, M., & Woods, E. (1999). Evaluation of a targeted HIV testing program for at-risk youth. *Journal of Health Care for the Poor and Underserved, 10,* 430–442.

Goodman, L., Saxe, L., & Harvey, M. (1991). Homelessness as psychological trauma. *American Psychologist, 46,* 1219–1225.

Goulart, M., & Madover, S. (1991). An AIDS prevention program for homeless youth. *Journal of Adolescent Health, 12,* 573–575.

Hagen, J., & McCarthy, B. (1997). *Mean streets: Youth crime and homelessness.* New York: Cambridge University Press.

Hauser, S., Vieyra, M., Jacobson, A., & Wertlieb, D. (1985). Vulnerability and resilience in adolescence: Views from the family. *Journal of Early Adolescence, 5,* 81–100.

House Committee on Education and Labor, Subcommittee on Human Resources. (1984). *Juvenile Justice, Runaway Youth, and Missing Children's Act,* amendments, 98th Congress, 2nd session, 7 March, Y4, E8, 1:j98/15.

Hoyt, D., Ryan, K., & Cauce, A. (1999). Personal victimization in a high-risk environment: Evaluating the relative effects of exposure, attractiveness, and guardianship. *Journal of Research in Crime and Delinquency, 36,* 371–392.

Janus, M., Burgess, A., & McCormack, A. (1987). Histories of sexual abuse in adolescent male runaways. *Adolescence, 22,* 405–417.

Johnson, T., Aschkenasy, J., Herbers, M., & Gillenwater, S. (1996). Self-reported risk factors for AIDS among homeless youth. *AIDS Education and Prevention, 8,* 308–322.

Kipke, M., Montgomery, S., & Mackenzie, R. (1997). Substance abuse among youth seen at a community based clinic. *Journal of Adolescent Health, 20,* 360–367.

Kipke, M., O'Conner, S., Palmer, R., & Mackenzie, R. (1995). Street youth in Los Angeles: Profile of a group at high risk for human immunodeficiency virus infection. *Archives of Pediatrics & Adolescent Medicine, 149,* 513–519.

Kipke, M., Simon, T., Montgomery, S., Unger, J., & Iverson, E. (1997). Homeless youth and their exposure to and involvement in violence while living on the streets. *Journal of Adolescent Health, 20,* 360–367.

Klein, J., Woods, A., Wilson, K., Porspero, M., Greene, J., & Ringwalt, C. (2000). Homeless and runaway youths' access to health care. *Journal of Adolescent Health, 27,* 331–339.

Koopman, C., Rosario, M., & Rotheram-Borus, M. (1994). Alcohol and drug use and sexual behaviors placing runaways at risk for HIV infection. *Addictive Behaviors, 19,* 95–103.

McCaskill, P., Toro, P., & Wolfe, S. (1998). Homeless and matched housed adolescents: A comparative study of psychopathology. *Journal of Clinical Child Psychology, 27,* 306–319.

Moffitt, T. E. (1993). Adolescence-limited and life-course-persistent antisocial behavior: A developmental taxonomy. *Psychological Review, 100,* 674–701.

Molnar, J. M., Rath, W. R., & Klein, T. P. (1990). Constantly compromised: The impact of homelessness on children. *Journal of Social Issues, 46,* 109–124.

Moos, R., & Moos, B. (1981). *Family environment scale manual.* Palo Alto, CA: Consulting Psychology Press.

Mundy, P., Robertson, M., Robertson, J., & Greenblatt, M. (1990). The prevalence of psychotic symptoms in homeless adolescents. *Journal of the American Academy of Child/Adolescent Psychiatry, 29,* 724–731.

National Coalition for the Homeless. (1999). Homeless families with children. NCH Fact Sheet #7. Washington, DC: Author.

National Network of Runaway and Youth Services. (1991). *To whom do they belong? Runaway, homeless, and other youth in high-risk situations in the 1990s.* Washington, DC: Author.

New York City Government Home Page. 2001.

Office of Juvenile Justice Delinquency Prevention. (1990). *Missing, abducted, runaway and thrownaway children in America, first report: Numbers and characteristics, national incidence studies.* Washington, DC: OJJDP, U.S. Department of Justice.

Parker, G., Tupling, H., & Brown, L. (1979). A parental bonding instrument. *British Journal of Medical Psychology, 53,* 1–10.

Patterson, G. R. (1982). *Coercive family processes.* Eugene, OR: Castilia.

Patterson, G. R., DeBaryshe, B. D., & Ramsey, E. (1989). A developmental perspective on antisocial behavior. *American Psychologist, 44,* 329–335.

Patterson, G. R., Dishion, T. J., & Bank, L. (1984). Family interaction: A process model of deviancy training. *Aggressive Behavior, 10,* 253–267.

Pennbridge, J., Yates, G., David, T., & Mackenzie, R. (1990). Runaway and homeless youth in Los Angeles County. *Journal of Adolescent Health Care, 11,* 159–165.

Podschun, G. (1993). Teen peer outreach-street work project: HIV prevention education for runaway and homeless youth. *Public Health Reports, 108,* 150–155.

Rak, C., & Patterson, L. (1996). Promoting resilience in at-risk children. *Journal of Counseling and Development, 74,* 368–373.

Reuler, J. (1991). Outreach health services for street youth. *Journal of Adolescent Health, 12,* 561–566.

Ringwalt, C., Greene, J., & Robertson, M. (1998). Familial backgrounds and risk behaviors of youth with thrown away experiences. *Journal of Adolescence, 21,* 241–252.

Robertson, M. (1989). *Homeless youth in Hollywood: Patterns of alcohol use.* National Institute on Alcohol Abuse and Alcoholism. Berkeley, CA: Alcohol Research Group.

Rotheram-Borus, M. (1993). Suicidal behavior and risk factors among runaway youths. *American Journal of Psychiatry, 150,* 103–107.

Rotheram-Borus, M., Koopman, C., & Ehrhardt, A. (1991). Homeless youths and HIV infection. *American Psychologist, 46,* 1188–1197.

Rotheram-Borus, M., Meyer-Bahlburg, H., Koopman, C., Rosario, M., Exner, T., Henderson, R., Matthieu, M., & Gruen, R. (1992). Lifetime sexual behaviors among runaway males and females. *The Journal of Sex Research, 29,* 15–29.

Rotheram-Borus, M., Parra, M., Cantwell, C., Gwadz, M., & Murphy, D. (1996). *Runaway and homeless youths.* In R. DiClemente, W. Hansen, & L. Ponstoro (Eds.), *Handbook of adolescent risk behavior* (pp. 369–392). New York: Plenum.

Rotheram-Borus, M., Rosario, M., & Koopman, C. (1991). Minority youth at high-risk: Gay males and runaways. In S. Gore & M. Colton, (Eds.), *Adolescent stress: Courses and consequences* (pp. 181–200). New York: Aldine de Gruyter.

Rutter, M. (1985). Resilience in the face of adversity: Protective factors and resistance to psychiatric disorders. *British Journal of Psychiatry, 147,* 598–611.

Saltonstall, M. (1984). *Street youth and runaways on the streets of Boston: One agency's response.* Boston: The Bridge.

Schaffer, D., & Caton, C. (1984). *Runaway and homeless youth in New York City: A report to the Ittleson Foundation.* New York: Division of Child Psychiatry, New York State Psychiatric Institute and Columbia University College of Physicians and Surgeons.

Schweitzer, R., & Hier, S. (1993). Psychological maladjustment among homeless adolescents. *Australian & New Zealand Journal of Psychiatry, 147,* 598–611.

Schweitzer, R., Hier, S., & Terry, D. (1994). Parental bonding, family systems, and environmental predictors of adolescent homelessness. *Journal of Emotional and Behavioral Disorders, 2,* 39–45.

Shalwitz, J., Goulart, M., Dunnigan, K., & Flannery, D. (1990). *Prevalence of sexually transmitted diseases (STD) and HIV in a homeless youth medical clinic in San Francisco.* Presentation at the Sixth Annual International Conference on AIDS. San Francisco.

Shane, P. (1996). *What about America's homeless children?* Thousand Oaks, CA: Sage.

Shinn, M., & Weitzman, B. (1996). Homeless families are different. In J. Baumohl (Ed.), for the National Coalition for the Homeless, *Homelessness in America*. Phoenix, AZ: Oryx Press.

Smart, D. (1991). Homeless youth in Seattle. *Journal of Adolescent Health, 12*, 519–527.

Smart, R., & Walsh, G. (1993). Predictors of depression in street youth. *Adolescence, 28*, 41–53.

Steele, R., & O'Keefe, M. (2001). A program description of health care interventions for homeless teenagers. *Clinical Pediatrics, 40*, 259–263.

Stefanidis, N., Pennbridge, J., Mackenzie, R., & Pottharst, K. (1992). Runaway and homeless youth: The effects of attachment history on stabilization. *American Journal of Orthopsychiatry, 62*, 442–446.

Stiffman, A. R. (1989). Physical and sexual abuse in runaway youth. *Child Abuse & Neglect, 13*, 417–426.

Stricof, R., Kennedy, J., Nattell, T., Weisfuse, I., & Novick, L. (1991). HIV seroprevalence in a facility for runaway and homeless adolescents. *American Journal of Public Health, 81*, 50–53.

Tenner, A., Trevithick, L., Wagner, V., & Burch, R. (1998). Seattle Youth Care's prevention, intervention, and education program. *Journal of Adolescent Health, 235*, 96–106.

Tyler, K., Hoyt, D., & Whitbeck, L. (2000). The effects of early sexual abuse on later sexual victimization among female homeless and runaway adolescents. *Journal of Interpersonal Violence, 15*, 235–250.

Tyler, K., Hoyt, D., Whitbeck, L., & Cauce, A. (2001). The effects of a high-risk environment on the sexual victimization of homeless and runaway youth. *Violence & Victims, 16*, 441–455.

Tyler, K., Whitbeck, L., Hoyt, D., & Yoder, K. (2000). Predictors of self-reported sexually transmitted diseases among homeless and runaway adolescents. *The Journal of Sex Research, 37*, 369–377.

U.S. Conference of Mayors. *A status report on hunger and homelessness in America's cities: 1998*. Washington, DC: U.S. Conference of Mayors.

Warren, J., Gary, F., & Moorhead, J. (1994). Self-reported experiences of physical and sexual abuse among runaway youths. *Perspectives in Psychiatric Care, 30*, 23–28.

Whitbeck, L., & Hoyt, D. (1999). *Nowhere to grow: Homeless and runaway adolescents and their families*. New York: Aldine de Gruyter.

Whitbeck, L., Hoyt, D., & Ackley, K. (1997). Families of homeless and runaway adolescents: A comparison of parent/caretaker and adolescent perspectives on parenting, family violence, and adolescent conduct. *Child Abuse & Neglect, 21*, 517–528.

Whitbeck, L., Hoyt, D., & Bao, W. (2000). Depressive symptoms and co-occurring depressive symptoms, substance abuse, and conduct problems among runaway and homeless adolescents. *Child Development, 71*, 721–732.

Whitbeck, L., Hoyt, D. R., Johnson, K. D., Whiteford, S. W., & Cauce, A. M. (under review). A longitudinal study of the effects of street victimization on symptoms of internalization among homeless and runaway adolescents. *Journal of Interpersonal Violence*.

Whitbeck, L., Hoyt, D., Yoder, K., Cauce, A., & Paradise, M. (2001). Deviant behavior and victimization among homeless and runaway adolescents. *Journal of Interpersonal Violence, 16*, 1175–2104.

Windle, M. (1989). Substance use and abuse among adolescent runaways: A four year follow-up study. *Journal of Youth and Adolescence, 18*, 331–334.

Wolfe, S., Toro, P., & McCaskill, P. (1999). A comparison of homeless and matched housed adolescents on family environment variables. *Journal of Research on Adolescence, 9*, 53–56.

Wright, J. (1991). Health and the homeless teenager: Evidence from the National Health Care for the Homeless Program. *Journal of Health and Social Policy, 2*, 15–36.

Yates, G., Mackenzie, R., Pennbridge, J., & Cohen, E. (1988). A risk profile comparison of runaway and non-runaway youth. *American Journal of Public Health, 78*, 820–821.

Yates, G., Pennbridge, J., Swofford, A., & Mackenzie, R. (1991). The Los Angeles system of care for runaway/homeless youth. *Journal of Adolescent Health, 12*, 555–560.

Yoder, K. (1999). Comparing suicide attempters, suicide ideators, and nonsuicidal homeless and runaway adolescents. *Suicide and Life-Threatening Behavior, 29*, 25–36.

Youth Care. (2001). *Annual report*. Seattle: Author.

CHAPTER 18

ADOLESCENT PREGNANCY AND PARENTING

A Bio-Psychosocial Framework

JACQUELINE CORCORAN

Virginia Commonwealth University

CYNTHIA FRANKLIN

University of Texas at Austin

This chapter will apply a bio-psychosocial perspective to adolescent pregnancy. Risk and protective factors will be identified, along with discussion of risks to particular groups, specifically those of Hispanic and African American origin and teens younger than age 15. Evidence-based interventions to reduce risk and bolster key protections will be discussed.

PREVALENCE

The past decade has brought a national decline in adolescent pregnancy rates. According to the U.S. General Accounting Office (1998), birth rates for adolescents in the United States decreased nationally by 18 percent between 1991 and 1998. Even though these statistics represent advancement on resolving the social problems associated with adolescent pregnancy, rates for births to unmarried adolescents still remain higher in the United States than in other developing countries (Henshaw & Feivelson, 2000). Henshaw and Feivelson (2000) report that 10 percent of women aged 15 to 19 in the United States became pregnant and had a birth, abortion, or miscarriage. (Risks to particular populations will be discussed later.) Adolescent males were the fathers of teenage pregnancies in an estimated two-thirds of cases (Lindberg, Sonentein, Ku, & Martinez, 1997). More recent data from Child Trends, Inc. (2001) indicates that 494,456 births occurred to teenagers in 1998. The major-

Note: Grateful acknowledgment to Sara Ballon for assistance in the preparation of this chapter.

ity (79 percent) of these births occurred outside of marriage. Alarmingly, 22 percent of childbearing involved repeat births.

REVIEW OF RESEARCH RELATED TO THE PROBLEM

In this section, empirically identified risk and protective factors at the three different bio-psychosocial levels—the individual level, the immediate social environment, and the broad social environment—will be described for both the primary and secondary prevention of pregnancy. Most researchers who investigate the etiologies and outcomes of adolescent pregnancy do not identify risk and resilience as their underlying framework, with the notable exceptions of Kalil and Kunz (1999) and Smith (1994). However, the risk and resilience, bio-psychosocial framework organizes the substantial amount of research conducted on adolescent pregnancy in a way that targets the system of impact. Moreover, it provides a framework for identifying risks to be ameliorated and protective factors to be enhanced.[1]

Risk and Protective Factors for Adolescent Pregnancy

The following discussion will address the continuum of risk and protection at the three system levels that influence teenage pregnancy. See Table 18.1 for case examples for teens with different levels of risk and protective factors.

Individual Factors.   Individual factors do not explain adolescent pregnancy and parenting as well as environmental factors. For instance, self-esteem and other psychological factors do not clearly discriminate between those who are pregnant and parenting and those who are not (Gohel, Diamond, & Chambers, 1997). Indeed, the only individual risk factor identified consistently is use of alcohol, which generally occurs in a peer context.

Substance Use.   Numerous studies link substance use and sexual activity (Elliott & Morse, 1989; Mott & Haurin, 1988; Perkins, Luster, Villarruel, & Small, 1998; Zabin, Hardy, Edward, Smith, & Hirsch, 1986). The CDC (2002) reports in their 1999 national survey that almost one-quarter (24.8 percent) of youth reported using alcohol or drugs before last intercourse. The risk factor of substance use is also associated with one-third of unplanned teen pregnancies (Flanigan, Mclean, Hall, & Propp, 1990). Substance use contributes to pregnancy by increasing teen susceptibility to acting on sexual impulses without consideration to possible consequences, poor choice of partners, lack of use of contraceptives, and not being able to recall sexual experiences (Franklin, Corcoran, & Ayers-Lopez, 1997).

Immediate Social Environment.   The immediate social environment comprises the teen's family environment, school, peer group, neighborhood, and involvement in church.

---

1. Sexual activity, although clearly a precursor to adolescent pregnancy, will not be a focus of the literature review given the amount of research accumulated on pregnancy. Please see Corcoran (1998) for a review of the literature on sexual activity.

TABLE 18.1   Case Studies of Risk and Protective Factors for the Occurrence of Teenage Pregnancy

RISK AND PROTECTIVE FACTORS	YOLANDA, AGE 16, AVOIDED PREGNANCY	REGINA, AGE 16, BECAME PREGNANT AS TEENAGER
SES	Father works as construction worker; mother cleans hotels	Family is supported by public assistance; father is not involved with family's support
RACE	African American	African American
POLICIES ON SEX EDUCATION IN SCHOOLS	Received an abstinence-based sex education program in school	Received an abstinence-based sex education program in school
FAMILY STRUCTURE	Two parents, one sibling	One parent, four siblings
FAMILY FUNCTIONING	Supervision and monitoring for Yolanda	Lack of rules and supervision
RELIGION	Committed to Baptist Church, attends services weekly	Belongs to Baptist Church; does not attend services
NEIGHBORHOOD	Working-class homes (Yolanda's parents rent their home) near urban area	Housing project in urban area with high ratio of teenage pregnancies
SCHOOL	Maintains a B average and plans to attend college	Failing classes
PEERS	Friends are involved in school activities and sports	Friends are alienated from the school setting, with low grades in school and lack of involvement in school activities
SUBSTANCE USE	Doesn't drink mainly because of religious reasons	Uses alcohol, smokes cigarettes, and uses marijuana

Maltreatment.   Sexual abuse by parents puts a teen at risk for early sexual activity (Perkins et al., 1998) and pregnancy (Luster & Small, 1997). Large-scale surveys indicate that teens who have been sexually abused have had sex by age 15 (Raj, Silverman, & Amaro, 2000; Stock et al., 1997), have had more partners (Luster & Small, 1997; Raj et al., 2000; Stock et al., 1997), failed to use birth control at last intercourse (Stock et al., 1997), and were more likely to have been pregnant or caused a pregnancy (Raj et al., 2000) when compared to their nonsexually abused peers. Dietz and colleagues (1999) also found that women with a history of sexual abuse have a higher rate of unintended pregnancies as adults. A history of sexual abuse may predispose a young woman to a pattern of victimization and sexual risk taking.

Education.   A positive school experience may act as a protective factor. Teens who are performing well in school may be motivated to prevent pregnancy so as not to compromise their future education and income opportunities. Indeed, career and academic development have been linked to the prevention of pregnancy (Kirby, 2001).

Conversely, adolescents with poor school performance and failure are at risk for early sexual experience and childbearing (Abrahamse, Morrison, & White, 1988; Beutel, 2000; Hofferth, 1987; Perkins et al., 1998; Robbins, Kaplan, & Martin, 1985; Santelli & Beilenson, 1992) and may see early parenting as a viable alternative to education and a career (DeBolt, Pasley, & Kreutzer, 1990). In the case studies provided in Table 18.1, the reader will note that Yolanda and Regina, both 16 years of age and African American, have very different experiences of school. Yolanda maintains a solid grade-point average, whereas Regina receives failing grades. Yolanda is motivated to avoid pregnancy so that she does not compromise her plans to finish high school and attend college. Regina may not feel she has much to lose by having a child at a young age.

Peers.   The teen's peer group may act as a protective or a risk factor. As a protective factor, nonsexually active and contraceptive-using peers, both same-sex friends and sexual partners, can positively influence a teen's abstinence or the consistency of contraceptive use. Risks include peer group behaviors, such as drug and alcohol usage, which, as noted, is also associated with early sexual activity (Billy & Udry, 1985; DiBlassio & Benda, 1990; Perkins et al., 1998; Billy, Rodgers, & Udry, 1984). Peers of both genders also impact an adolescent's decision to become sexually active. According to a recent summary of a survey released by the National Campaign to Prevent Teen Pregnancy (1997), a large majority of girls say they received pressure from boys and other girls to be sexually active. Many girls reported being afraid of losing their boyfriends if they refused sex.

Peer group attitudes and behaviors further influence a teen's likelihood of parenting at a young age. A best friend who has been pregnant is implicated in repeat pregnancies (Gillmore, Lewis, Lohr, Spencer, & White, 1997). Male teens who believed their peers viewed early childbearing as favorable were more likely to be fathers (Gohel et al., 1997).

In the case examples from Table 18.1, Yolanda, who avoided pregnancy, is in a group of friends who value school performance and are involved in sports and school clubs, whereas Regina's peers use substances and do not participate in school-related activities.

Household Composition.   Protective factors for pregnancy include living in a two-parent home and one in which there are fewer than two siblings. In these type of family situations, there are more financial resources and two parents are available for monitoring and support. On the risk dimension, adolescents from single-parent homes are sexually active at earlier ages than are those from two-parent families (see Corcoran, 2000, for a review) and are at increased risk for pregnancy and parenting (Gohel et al., 1997; Kalil & Kunz, 1999; Robbins et al., 1985). Several mechanisms may affect this process. First, single-parent status tends to be confounded with low SES (McAnarney & Hendee, 1989), a chief variable associated with both early sexual activity and childbearing (see Socioeconomic Status later in chapter). A role modeling effect may also take place in which single parents may date and be sexually active themselves. Whereas in two-parent families two adults can provide financial security, guidance, and emotional support (Young, Jensen, Olsen, & Cundick, 1991), single parents are more likely to work full time and therefore are not as available for supervision, monitoring, or time spent with the child (Newcomer & Udry, 1987).

Another family structure factor involves living in a household with three or more siblings (Kalil & Kunz, 1999). Perhaps in families with a lot of children, fertility is valued, as well as modeled, and the risk of childbearing at a young age is increased. In addition, larger families have fewer resources, both financial and emotional, available to each child. The risks presented by the lack of resources may also increase the likelihood of early sexual activity and premature childbearing.

The case examples from Table 18.1 illustrate the differential impact of household composition. Yolanda lives in a home where two parents work to provide for the family and monitor Yolanda and her sister's activities. Regina's mother is raising her five children as a single parent. She is overwhelmed by the stressors of poverty and has difficulty organizing the household and keeping track of Regina and her siblings. Lack of monitoring increased the likelihood of Regina's participation in sexual risk taking and her subsequent pregnancy.

Family Functioning.   Family functioning, though measured in different ways—family conflict (Barth, Schinke, & Maxwell, 1983), stress (Robbins et al., 1985), family strengths (Barnett, Papini, & Gbur, 1991), problems with family, problem solving, communication, roles, affective responsiveness, affective involvement, behavior control (Corcoran, Franklin, & Bennett, 2000), adaptability, and cohesion (Barnett et al., 1991)—can act as either a protective or a risk factor against teenage pregnancy. Parental supervision and monitoring over dating assumes a protective function (Hanson, Myers, & Ginsburg, 1987; Perkins et al., 1998; Santelli & Beilenson, 1992), as does explicit disapproval of sexual activity from parents (McAnarney & Hendee, 1989), especially when it occurs in the context of a close mother-daughter relationship (Jaccard, Dittus, & Gordon, 1996). Parental communication about sexuality that occurs in an open and skilled manner also serves as a protective factor against early pregnancies and increases condom use (Whitaker, Miller, May, & Levin, 1999).

Conversely, lack of parental monitoring and general family dysfunction may lead a teenager to get involved with an older partner, which may, in turn, put a young woman at risk of pregnancy. Compared with teenagers whose first partners were roughly their age, adolescents with first partners at least three years older were younger at first intercourse (13.8 vs. 14.6 years), less likely to use a condom both at first and most recent intercourse, used condoms less consistently, and were more likely to become pregnant (38 vs. 12 percent) (Miller, Clark, & Moore, 1997). Another study found that adolescent girls who have sex with partners at least six years older than themselves have pregnancy rates 3.7 times as high as the rate among those whose partner was no more than two years older (Darroch, Landry, & Oslak, 1999). Women with younger partners were 70 percent less likely to have an unintended pregnancy and 21 percent less likely to terminate an unintended pregnancy. Further, Lindberg, Sonentein, Ku, and Martinez (1997) reported that among teens aged 15 to 17 who gave birth in 1988, almost one-third (27 percent) had a partner five years or older than themselves. Therefore, the data seem to indicate that dating older men puts a teenager at risk for becoming pregnant.

Neighborhood.   Neighborhood factors may contribute to protection or risk. Living in rural or suburban areas in which many two-parent families reside is a protective factor, whereas living in an urban area and one with a high percentage of female-headed households clevates risk (Kalil & Kunz, 1999). In the latter type of communities, sanctions against early childbearing may be lacking, and more acceptable alternatives are unavailable.

Neighborhood factors may have contributed to Regina's pregnancy. She lives in an urban housing project where many single-parent families live and where many teen pregnancies take place. Her pregnancy in such a context is not viewed as an unusual occurrence. In contrast, Yolanda's parents are able to earn enough together to afford to rent a house in a working-class neighborhood, where teenage pregnancies are much less accepted.

Religious Attendance. Most of the research indicates that participation in a religion acts as a protective factor against early sexual activity (e.g., Bingham, Miller, & Adams, 1990; DiBlassio & Benda, 1990; Flewelling & Bauman, 1990; Forste & Heaton, 1988; Thornton & Camburn, 1989). On the other hand, religious teens are less likely to use contraceptives when sexually active, which may result in greater pregnancy risk (Studer & Thornton, 1987). Although Regina considers herself "Baptist" in religion, she does not participate formally, whereas Yolanda and her parents are actively involved in a local church. Indeed, one of the reasons Yolanda does not use alcohol is her religious beliefs, and she has friends at her church who support this decision.

Broad Societal Factors. Broad societal factors include the teen's socioeconomic status and public policies such as sex education and access to abortion and other family planning services.

Socioeconomic Status. High socioeconomic status is a protective factor against early childbearing rates. For higher-income youth, the costs associated with adolescent parenting—truncated educational achievement and potential lost income—can be very high, and adolescent parenting is seen as a state to be avoided. On the converse, low socioeconomic status has long been established as a risk factor for premature pregnancy and childbearing (Abrahamse et al., 1988; Barnett et al., 1991; Corcoran et al., 2000; Hanson et al., 1987; Kalil & Kunz, 1999; Mayfield-Brown, 1989; Robbins et al., 1985; Shah & Zelnik, 1981). With low-income teens, future opportunities may not appear available, and childbearing may seem a viable way to achieve fulfillment and identity (Luker, 1996). For instance, a survey of 42 adolescent fathers compared to demographically similar young men who were not parents found that fathers believed that parenthood would not interfere with their future. Fathers were also less likely to have developed a concrete five-year plan (Gohel et al., 1997). (For discussion of the interaction between race and poverty, see Particular Risk Populations later in the chapter.)

Public Policies. On the protective side, societal recognition of the costs of teenage pregnancy has brought policies and funding for pregnancy prevention programs. Indeed, sex education in schools is widespread—in two of three districts, according to a 1999 survey of public school district superintendents (Wilson, 2000). However, programs and policies developed in schools may achieve little in the way of bolstering protective factors and ameliorating risk. The 1999 survey reported that only 14 percent of districts have a comprehensive policy that includes both abstinence-based and contraceptive-building tenets (Wilson, 2000). Half of the districts (51 percent) have abstinence as the preferred option for instruction, where contraception is also discussed, and a little over a third (35 percent) have abstinence as the only basis for instruction with discussion of contraception forbidden. Districts in the South are far more likely than those in the Northeast to have an abstinence-only policy (Wilson, 2000). These findings are confirmed by a 1999 national survey of teachers in secondary public schools. Schools are less focused on contraceptive information than abstinence-based curriculums and prevention of HIV and AIDS, even prior to the 1996 passage of the federal Welfare Reform Act, with its funding provisions for abstinence-based programs (Darroch, Landry, & Singh, 2000). As an example, both Yolanda and Regina received an abstinence-based program through their school system.

As well as sex education, access to abortion and other family planning services may also influence birth rates. Birth rates are lower when there is access to family planning and abortion services. The presence of such services act as a protective factor. Conversely, risk for birth rates is elevated when access to obstetrician-gynecologists and family planning services is reduced (Matthews, Ribar, & Wilhelm, 1997). In addition, decreased access to abortion services may have accounted for about one-quarter of the 5 percent decline in abortion rates between 1988 and 1992 (Matthews, Ribar, & Wilhelm, 1997). Between 1992 and 1996, abortion rates fell even further; the number of abortions dropped from 1,529,000 to 1,266,000, and the rate decreased from 26 to 23 per 1,000 women aged 15 to 44 (Henshaw, 1998). During this time period, fewer providers were available for abortion services, with a drop of 14 percent to a total number of 2,042. Henshaw (1998) further reported that 86 percent of counties claimed no known abortion provider, with almost a third of women (32 percent) living in these counties.

Specifically examining teenage access to abortion, during the 1980s, many states, in response to high teenage pregnancy rates, enacted parental involvement abortion laws. Parental involvement laws require minors (less than 18 years of age) to notify or get the consent of one or both parents in order to obtain an abortion. The effect of parental involvement laws depends on a variety of factors (Medoff, 1999). First, the laws vary widely in their restrictiveness. Some states require notification by physicians before they can perform teenage abortions; some states allow grandparents, clergy, or other responsible adults to give their permission. Second, the level of state enforcement of these laws varies considerably. For example, many states permit minors to bypass parental involvement by appearing before a judge. Some judges routinely approve the procedure; others rarely do so. Third, most teenagers routinely involve a parent anyway. Henshaw and Kost (as cited in Medoff, 1999) related that 61 percent of unmarried teenagers said that at least one parent was aware of the abortion. Medoff (1999) further examined state-pooled data from 1980 to 1992 and found that neither parental involvement laws nor educational attainment impacted the level of teenage abortions. Abortion demand was found to relate instead to a state's abortion attitudes (abortion is lower when a state is less condoning of abortion) and to the level of AFDC benefits (abortion is lower when benefits are lower).

Risk and Protective Factors
for Adolescent Childbearers

Individual Factors.   Adolescent pregnancy culminates in an emotional and developmental crisis for young girls (Martin, Hill, Kelly, & Welsh, 1998; Osofsky, Osofsky, & Diamond, 1988; Pines, 1988; Trad, 1994), and the demands of parenting create considerable distress and psychological turmoil for parenting teens (Corcoran et al., 2000). While the young woman is trying to develop autonomy and self-identity, for example, she is thrust into a premature parental role, requiring problem solving, parenting skills, and socioeconomic roles and other adult competencies that she has not yet acquired (de Anda, Darroch, Davidson, Gilly, Javidi, Jefford, Komorowski, & Morejon-Schrobsdorf, 1992). The result is risk for numerous role conflicts, psychosocial stressors, initial depression, and turmoil over the unexpected life transitions that accompany pregnancy and parenting (Sandfort & Hill, 1996; Stern & Alvarez, 1992). (Refer to Table 18.2 for case examples for teens with differential levels of risk and protection.)

Immediate Social Environment. Factors at the immediate social environment involve school achievement, single-parent status, family size, and other social support.

School Achievement. School dropout and poverty are strongly associated with early childbearing (Burdell, 1998; U.S. General Accounting Office, 1998; Rudd, McHenry, & Nah, 1990; Turner, Grindstaff, & Phillips, 1990) and persist over time. A 17-year longitudinal study found high school graduation rates for teen childbearers were half that of their nonchildbearing counterparts (Furstenberg, Brooks-Gunn, & Morgan, 1987). By the time they reach their late 20s, only 32 percent have graduated from high school, compared to 75 percent of mothers who delayed childbearing until ages 20 to 21, controlling for factors such as parental educational level, single-parent status, and income (Maynard, 1996).

TABLE 18.2   Case Studies of Risk and Protective Factors for Adolescent Childbearers

RISK AND PROTECTIVE FACTORS	GRACE, AGE 17	TERESA, AGE 17
SES	Receives public assistance	Receives public assistance
RACE	Hispanic	Hispanic
SCHOOL	Still attending school	Dropped out of school
FAMILY STRUCTURE	Involved with the father of the child; has remained nonpregnant	One parent; father of the child has little involvement with child; Teresa is currently pregnant with second child
SOCIAL SUPPORT	Mother and grandmother are financially and emotionally supportive	Conflictual relationship with her mother; little extended family involvement
MENTAL HEALTH	Copes adequately with multiple stressors	Suffers from clinical depression
PROGRAMS	Receives regular nurse home visits with an emphasis on infant development	Receives regular check-up services at local health clinic

These low educational levels translate into reduced employment and income opportunities (Rudd et al., 1990).

A protective factor is therefore more education attained before the pregnancy and after the childbirth. A 20-year longitudinal study found that more schooling prior to the pregnancy and school attendance 26 months post-partum without being pregnant with another child was associated with greater long-term adjustment (Horwitz et al., 1991). Other research suggests that adolescent mothers who are attending school do better in adolescent pregnancy programs and have more successful long-term outcomes (Seitz & Apfel, 1999). Mothers who stay in school and complete high school also tend to earn more and be less dependent on welfare than mothers who drop out (Harris, 1991). In the case studies provided in Table 18.2, Grace and Teresa are described as 17 years of age, Hispanic, and parenting as teenagers. However, Grace demonstrates more potential for resilience, since she has remained in school, whereas Teresa dropped out during her pregnancy.

Single-Parent Status.   Adolescent childbearers are at increased risk for single-parent status into adulthood. One-third of adolescent mothers are still single 13 years later, compared to only 7 percent of their later childbearing counterparts (Maynard, 1996). In the Furstenberg and colleagues' (1987) longitudinal study, teen mothers who married or lived with a partner were less likely to remain on welfare when they worked than were single-parent mothers. Marriage is a protective factor for the teen mother, but unfortunately adolescent couples also have high rates of separation and divorce (e.g., Furstenberg et al., 1987).

Family Size.   One of the main reasons teenage mothers have a tendency to stay on welfare longer is that they have larger families than women who start childbearing in their 20s (Granger & Cryton, 1999). Teenage childbearers are at much greater risk for larger families as adults than women who start the families at a later period in life. Adolescent childbearers have 2.6 versus 2 children by the age of 30 (Maynard, 1996), which adds to the teen parent's financial burden and makes it more difficult to provide emotional support, supervision, and monitoring to children (Hofferth, 1987).

Conversely, a protective factor involves a teen parent limiting her fertility. A 20-year follow-up of 121 African American adolescent parents found that success, which was defined as either employed or supported by a spouse and a high school education, was associated with having only one or two children after the first (Horwitz et al., 1991). Preventing rapid, repeat childbearing is an important protective factor for both teenage mothers and their children. Mothers who only had one child at five years had children who were better adjusted, more prepared for school, and showed better behavior than families with more children (Furstenberg et al., 1987). In young adulthood, firstborns who had had two or more siblings by age 5 had significantly lower literacy skills than did those whose mothers had spaced their childbirths more widely (Baydar, Brooks-Gunn, & Furstenberg, 1993). Seitz and Apfel (1999) reported in their review that mothers who postponed childbearing were less likely to maintain long-term welfare dependency and were more likely to complete their education and to have children with higher achievement. Experimental studies have indicated that brief pre- and postnatal interventions and prolonging contacts and education with mothers after childbirth had substantive impacts on rapid, repeat childbearing (Seitz & Apfel, 1999). Interventions, such as nurse visitation in the home and ongoing educational classes, for example, were found effective for decreasing rapid, repeat childbearing (Seitz & Apfel, 1999). Referring to the case examples in Table 18.2, Grace receives nurse home visits that began when Grace was pregnant and will continue until her child is 2 years old. As well as focusing on maternal and child health, the nurse monitors Grace's contraceptive use and discusses infant stimulation and parenting behaviors. So far, Grace has managed to avoid a subsequent pregnancy, whereas Teresa, who receives only routine services at the local health clinic, is already pregnant with another child.

Social Support.   Social support, although defined in different ways, acts as a protective factor for many aspects of teen pregnancy and childbearing, such as birth weight (Oakley, 1985), maternal adjustment (Barth & Schinke, 1983; Causby, Nixon, & Bright, 1991; Rhodes & Wood, 1995; Schilmoeller, Baranowski, & Higgins, 1991; Unger & Wandersman, 1988), parenting behavior (Colletta & Lee, 1983; Reis & Herz, 1987; Schilmoeller & Baranowski, 1985), child development knowledge (Schilmoeller & Baranowski, 1985), infant health outcomes (Turner, Grindstaff, & Phillips, 1990), family relationships (Causby, Nixon, & Bright, 1991), and maternal satisfaction with pregnancy and prenatal and postpartum health-care seeking (Giblin, Poland, & Sachs, 1987). Social support confers benefits both at the time of the birth and at long-term follow-up (Horwitz et al., 1991). Cohen and Wills (1985) indicate the possible protective mechanisms underlying social support: "Support may reduce stress by altering appraisal of stressors, by changing coping patterns, or by affecting self-perceptions. For example, support may serve a buffering function through direct effects on self-esteem, enhancement of self-efficacy (leading to increased persistence at coping efforts), or direct changes in problem-solving behaviors" (p. 351).

Grace has social support in that her parents provide financial and emotional resources to her and her baby. She is still involved with the father of her child, and his parents offer child care and gifts. In contrast, Teresa and her mother do not get along well, Teresa's father is not part of her life, and she has little extended family involvement. The father of Teresa's child is also not part of her child's care.

Broad Societal Factors.   At the broad societal level, socioeconomic status will be a focus.

Socioeconomic Status.   Low educational levels, child-care demands, and limited employment experience constrain the economic prospects of young parents (Furstenberg et al., 1987) and persist into adulthood. A substantial proportion (40 percent) live in poverty by age 27 (Moore, Myers, Morrison, Nord, Brown, & Edmonston, 1993). The majority (80 percent) have received public assistance, almost half (44 percent) for more than a five-year time frame (Maynard, 1996). A protective factor, gleaned from longitudinal data, is that initial dependence on public assistance may serve benefits for the adolescent parent so she can graduate from high school (Harris, 1991). A high school diploma is preferable to dropping out and getting a low-skilled, low-paying job.

In the case example, although both teens rely on public assistance, Grace remains in school, whereas Teresa has dropped out. Grace's high school diploma will hopefully provide a foundation for her ability to gain sufficient employment to support herself and her child. For Teresa, the lack of a high school diploma may translate into persistent dependence on public assistance.

PARTICULAR RISK POPULATIONS

Younger Age at Childbearing

According to Child Trends, Inc. (2001), a nonprofit, nonpartisan research organization that studies child and adolescent outcomes, in 1998, the number of births to teens 15 years and younger was 9,481 in the United States. When younger teens become pregnant, they are at risk for poor outcomes for both medical and psychosocial reasons. A chief problem is the tendency of young pregnant teens to deny and/or conceal their condition, thus delaying optimal prenatal care (Brooks-Gunn & Furstenberg, 1986). Younger age at first pregnancy also seems to make it more difficult for adolescents to get off welfare (Harris, 1991; Rudd et al., 1990).

Results of a meta-analysis on pregnancy prevention programs indicate that older adolescents (15 to 19 years old) perform better on contraceptive use measures than women age 14 and younger (Franklin, Grant, Corcoran, O'Dell, & Bultman, 1997). In addition, younger females employ less effective methods (e.g., condoms and withdrawal) and use contraception less consistently (Alan Guttmacher Institute, 1996).

African American Teens

African American teens tend to initiate sexual activity at younger ages and have more partners (CDC, 2002), which translates into higher pregnancy risk. African American students reported being pregnant or getting someone pregnant at least once at a 13.4 percent rate compared to Hispanics (6.4 percent) and whites (4.3 percent) (CDC, 2002). Further, African American teen females have a rate of 91.4 births per 1,000 (Guttmacher Report, 1998). In comparison, white non-Hispanic adolescent females have a birth rate of 48.1 per 1,000. African American teens are at particular risk because of high poverty rates and high proportions of single-parent households (Children's Defense Fund, 1997), which, in turn, present substantial risk factors for early childbearing.

When African American teens become childbearers, they are at increased risk for welfare dependence and for longer duration than their white counterparts, mainly because they are more likely to remain single parents (Rudd et al., 1990). At 10 years after teenage pregnancy, 50 percent of African American mothers are living in poverty and two-thirds are welfare dependent (Maynard, 1996). There are also particular risks to the children of African American childbearers in terms of cognitive deficits first appearing during the preschool years (Brooks-Gunn & Furstenberg, 1986). (For more discussion of risks to the children of teen childbearers, see Corcoran, 1998.)

Hispanic Teens

Adolescent females of Hispanic ethnicity now have the highest teen birthrate with a rate of 101.8 per 1,000 adolescents in 1996 (Guttmacher Report, 1998). Little attention has been paid to the particular risk and protective factors for this ethnic group despite these high prevalence rates. Hispanics are, however, overrepresented in lower socioeconomic stratas (Children's Defense Fund, 1997), with a commensurate risk for limited resources and access to health care and reproductive services. Cultural determinants may also be operating, such as the traditional value and status of marriage and motherhood for individuals of Hispanic race, which may contribute to high fertility rates for teenagers (Balassone, 1991).

On the protective side, Hispanic teens seem to outperform white and African American teens in their use of contraceptives after primary prevention program efforts (Franklin, Grant et al., 1997). Apparently, Hispanic teens might be responsive to interventions concentrating on contraceptive knowledge building and distribution.

REVIEW OF PROMISING INTERVENTIONS

This section is organized according to whether interventions involve primary prevention (efforts to avoid pregnancy before it has occurred) or secondary prevention (working to avoid additional pregnancies for the parenting teen and improving outcomes for teen mothers and their children).

Practice Guidelines for Primary Prevention

A recent review by Kirby (2001) reported several promising interventions for the primary prevention of adolescent pregnancy. A stringent set of criteria was used in identification of effective interventions. Kirby's review, for example, included only experimental and quasi-experimental studies with 100 or more participants. Findings showed that there are a number of promising interventions, including sex and HIV curricula, youth development and service learning programs, and comprehensive programs targeting both sexuality and youth development activities. For girls, Kirby (2001) recommends the Children's Aid Society Carrera Program, which was shown to reduce pregnancies for as long as three years. Carrera is a comprehensive program that includes several components: (1) family life and sex education, (2) individual academic assessment and preparation for standardized tests and college prep exams, (3) tutoring, (4) self-expression activities through the use of the arts, and (5) comprehensive health and mental health care. Certain other types of service learning programs that require youth to volunteer in the community and to participate in journaling, group reflections, and discussions also show a great deal of promise for interventions of a nonsexual nature.

Five effective sex and HIV curricula, endorsed by the Centers for Disease Control, were identified in the Kirby (2001) review. These curricula include (1) Safer Choices, (2) Becoming a Responsible Teen, (3) A Safer Sex Approach to STD, Teen Pregnancy, and HIV AIDS, (4) Making a Difference: An Abstinence Approach to STD, and (5) Teen Pregnancy and HIV, AIDS Prevention. In general, effective curricula have common types of components (Kirby, 2001). First, they target one or more sexual risk behaviors that lead to pregnancy and deliverance and deliver a clear, consistent message about risk and how to avoid it. Second, curricula have a strong theoretical base that addresses antecedents of teen pregnancy, most commonly either the health beliefs model or cognitive-behavioral skills-building. Third, they include activities that teach how to avoid and cope with social pressures that influence sexual behaviors of adolescents and provide practice with communication, negotiation, and refusal skills. Fourth, a youth's age, development, and culture are considered in the delivery of the curricula. In addition, effective curricula are of sufficient duration to produce a sustained effect. They are not just brief, one-hour presentations, for example. Finally, teachers are selected carefully, have training provided, and have faith in the curricula used. (See Figure 18.1 for other curricula organized by program type according to Kirby's review.)

Another suggestion for primary prevention is that sex education classes should be combined with alcohol and drug abuse prevention curriculums, given that these health risks seem to co-occur (Elliott & Morse, 1989; Mott & Haurin, 1988; Perkins, Luster, Villarruel, & Small, 1998; Zabin, Hardy, Edward, Smith, & Hirsch, 1986). As much as possible, interventions should not be fragmented (i.e., separate treatments for depression, stress, substance use, etc.) but rather broad-based skills building should be presented, which includes training for social skills, problem solving, communication, assertiveness, and coping skills (Garland & Zigler, 1993; Peterson, Compas, Brooks-Gunn, Stemmler, Ey, & Grant, 1993).

A meta-analysis of 32 primary pregnancy prevention outcome studies (Franklin, Grant, Corcoran, O'Dell, & Bultman, 1997) showed that the programs in existence up until that point had almost no impact on the sexual activity rates of teenagers. For example, a large evaluation project of Postponing Sexual Involvement, with a large-scale sample of

FIGURE 18.1 Programs with Strong Evidence of Success

Programs with a Focus on Sexual Antecedents	Sex Education (covering both pregnancy and STDs/HIV)	*Reducing the Risk*
		Safer Choices
	HIV Education	*Becoming a Responsible Teen: An HIV Risk Reduction Intervention for African-American Adolescents*
		Making a Difference: An Abstinence Approach to STD, Pregnancy, and HIV/AIDS Prevention
		Making a Difference: A Safer Sex Approach to STD, Teen Pregnancy, and HIV/AIDS Prevention
Programs with a Focus on Nonsexual Antecedents	Service Learning	*Teen Outreach Program*
		Reach for Health Community Youth Service Learning
Programs with a Focus on Sexual and Nonsexual Antecedents	Multicomponent Programs (sexuality and youth development)	*Children's Aid Society—Carrera Program*

Source: Adapted from Kirby (2001).

10,600 youth found that the treatment produced no statistically significant differences from no intervention on sexual activity, pregnancy, or sexually transmitted diseases (Kirby, Korpi, Barth, & Cagampang, 1997).

According to the meta-analysis, programs were most effective in increasing contraceptive use and, to a lesser extent, on reducing pregnancy rates (Franklin, Grant, et al., 1997). Overall, it appears that contraceptive knowledge building and distribution is the most effective primary prevention effort. In a qualitative study, surveying 105 teens' opinions about effective pregnancy prevention programs, this finding was seconded by the teens themselves (Corcoran, Franklin, Grant, & Bell, 1997). When asked, "If you could design a program for teens who might be at risk of becoming pregnant and pregnant/parenting teens, what kind of services would it contain?" the main issue seemed to be obtaining birth control, including condoms, and having birth control available in schools. Results of the meta-analysis further indicate that community-based clinics are more effective than other types of pregnancy prevention efforts, although school-based clinics did affect contraceptive use more effectively than other school-related sex education programs (Franklin, Grant, et al., 1997).

Practice Guidelines for Secondary Prevention

When childbearing has already occurred, comprehensive programs for pregnant and parenting teens offering health, educational, vocational, and counseling services, as well as life skills training, yield long-term (5 to 20 years) positive outcomes (Furstenberg et al., 1987; Horwitz et al., 1991; Polit, 1989). Financial incentives have also been used as a protective factor. In one program, 65 teen parents were given a $1 for every day that they didn't have another pregnancy (Brown, Saunders, & Dick, 1998). After five years of program operation, only 15 percent became pregnant, compared to national statistics of 50 percent to 70 percent repeat pregnancy rates. In another study, 107 teenagers were given $7 a week for attending peer-support meetings about pregnancy prevention (Stevens-Simon, Dolgan, Kelly, & Singer, 1997). Financial incentives seemed to increase meeting attendance, but not pregnancy prevention when making a comparison to 24 young women who did not get financial incentives. It seems, therefore, that financial incentives are directly linked to pregnancy prevention.

According to a thorough review by Seitz and Apfel (1999), the more successful programs for adolescent mothers have certain components. Successful programs had goals compatible with what motivated the adolescent—her own health and well-being and that of her child—rather than goals to address deficits, such as welfare dependency. Effective programs provided knowledge and skills to help adolescent mothers prepare themselves for the challenges of childbirth, child development, life management, parenting, and job training. Therefore, the more successful programs are voluntarily selected by the teen mother as opposed to mandated programs. More successful programs are offered when mothers are first pregnant and parenting and while still in school (and delivered in the school), rather than being offered later when they had dropped out. Apparently, a critical period exists when adolescents are more receptive to help and specific information that addresses their concerns. This critical period might extend until 24 months post-partum (Coard, Nitz, & Felice, 2000). For instance, in comparison group studies, nurse home visiting extended from seven weeks to three years post-partum is particularly effective in terms of preventing repeat childbearing and child maltreatment, thereby reducing welfare dependence and criminal activity (see Seitz & Apfel, 1999).

Impacting outcomes for teen parents and their children is challenging and expensive; therefore, attention to the aforementioned guidelines for program development and implementation is crucial for the achievement of desired benefits. Because of these challenges, preventing pregnancy should be a first line of services with empirically validated programs disseminated on a widespread basis, especially to those communities in which the risk of pregnancy is high.

DISCUSSION QUESTIONS

1. How can empirically validated programs be accepted and implemented on a widespread basis?

2. What are the costs associated with the implementation of various secondary prevention programs, and what are their benefits in terms of improved outcomes for adolescents and their offspring?

3. How can ecologically sensitive programs be designed for both the primary and secondary prevention of teenage pregnancy now that the bio-psychosocial risk and protective factors have been identified?

4. Because sexual risk taking and pregnancy co-occur with other problem behaviors, such as substance abuse and child abuse, with some of the same underlying risk factors (i.e., lack of support and monitoring in the home), how can interventions best address broad-based risk factors rather than programs being fragmented into separate problem areas?

SUGGESTED READINGS

Franklin, C., Grant, D., Corcoran, J., O'Dell, P., & Bultman, L. (1997). Effectiveness of prevention programs for adolescent pregnancy: A meta-analysis. *Journal of Marriage and the Family, 59*(3), 551–567.

Furstenberg, F. F., Brooks-Gunn, J., & Morgan, S. P. (1987). *Adolescent mothers in later life.* Cambridge: Cambridge University Press.

Kirby, D. (2001). *Emerging answers: Research findings on programs to reduce teenage pregnancies.* Washington, DC: The National Campaign to Prevent Teenage Pregnancy.

Maynard, R. (Ed.). (1996). *Kids having kids: A Robin Hood Foundation special report on the costs of adolescent childbearing.* New York: Robin Hood Foundation.

Seitz, V., & Apfel, N. H. (1999). Effective interventions for adolescent mothers. *Clinical Psychology: Science and Practice, 6,* 50–66.

REFERENCES

Abrahamse, A. F., Morrison, P. A., & Waite, L. J. (1988). Teenagers willing to consider single parenthood: Who is at greatest risk? *Family Planning Perspectives, 20,* 13–18.

Alan Guttmacher Institute. (1996). *Facts in brief: Teen sex and pregnancy.* Washington, DC: Author.

Balassone, M. L. (1991). A social learning model of adolescent contraceptive behavior. *Journal of Youth and Adolescence, 20,* 593–615.

Barnett, J. K., Papini, D. R., & Gbur, E. (1991). Familial correlates of sexually active pregnant and non-pregnant adolescents. *Adolescence, 26,* 457–472.

Barth, R. P., & Schinke, S. P. (1983). Coping with daily strain among pregnant and parenting adolescents. *Journal of Social Service Research, 7,* 51–63.

Barth, R. P., Schinke, S. P., & Maxwell, J. S. (1983). Psychological correlates of teenage motherhood. *Journal of Youth and Adolescence, 12,* 471–487.

Baydar, N., Brooks-Gunn, J., & Furstenberg, F. (1993). Early warning signs of functional illiteracy: Predictors in childhood and adolescence. *Child Development, 64,* 815–829.

Beutel, A. M. (2000). The relationship between adolescent nonmarital childbearing and educational expectations: A cohort and period comparison. *The Sociological Quarterly, 41*(2), 297–314.

Billy, J., Rodgers, J. L., & Udry, J. R. (1984). Adolescent sexual behavior and friendship choice. *Social Forces, 62,* 653–678.

Billy, J., & Udry, J. R. (1985). The influence of male and female best friends on adolescent sexual behavior. *Adolescence, 20,* 21–32.

Bingham, C. R., Miller, B. C., & Adams, G. R. (1990). Correlates of age at first intercourse in a national sample of young women. *Journal of Adolescent Research, 5,* 18–33.

Brooks-Gunn, J., & Furstenberg, F. F., Jr. (1986). The children of adolescent mothers: Physical, academic, and psychological outcomes. *Developmental Review, 6,* 224–251.

Brown, H. N., Saunders, R. B., & Dick, M. J. (1999). Preventing secondary pregnancy in adolescents: A model program. *Health Care for Women International, 20*(1), 5–16.

Burdell, P. (1998). Young mothers as high school students: Moving toward a new century. *Education and Urban Society, 30*(2), 202–223.

Causby, V., Nixon, C., & Bright, J. M. (1991). Influences on adolescent mother-infant interactions. *Adolescence, 26,* 619–630.

Center for Disease Control (CDC). (2002). Youth risk behavior surveillance system, 1999 National Survey. Retrieved April 2, 2002, from http://apps.nccd.cdc.gov/YRBSS.

Center for Disease Control and Prevention (CDC). (2000). Programs that work. Retrieved July 31, 2002, from http://www.cdc.gov/nccdphp/dash/rtc/curriculum.htm.

Child Trends, Inc. (2001). Facts at a glance, 12/99 overview. Retrieved July 31, 2002, from http://www.childtrends.org/.8.

Children's Defense Fund. (1997). *The state of America's children: Yearbook 1997.* Washington, DC: Author.

Coard, S. I., Nitz, K., & Felice, M. F. (2000). Repeat pregnancy among urban adolescents: Sociodemographic, family, and health factors. *Adolescence, 35*(137), 193–202.

Cohen, S., & Wills, T. A. (1985). Stress, social support, and the buffering hypothesis. *Psychological Bulletin, 98,* 310–357.

Colletta, N. D., & Lee, D. (1983). The impact of support for black adolescent mothers. *Journal of Family Issues, 4,* 127–143.

Corcoran, J. (1998). Consequences of adolescent pregnancy/parenting: A review of the literature. *Social Work in Health Care, 27,* 49–67.

Corcoran, J. (2000). Ecological factors associated with adolescent sexual activity. *Social Work in Health Care, 30,* 547–588.

Corcoran, J., Franklin, C., & Bennett, P. (2000). Ecological factors associated with adolescent pregnancy and parenting. *Social Work Research, 24,* 29–39.

Corcoran, J., Franklin, C., Grant, D., & Bell, H. (1997). Pregnancy prevention from the teen perspective. *Child and Adolescent Social Work Journal, 14,* 365–382.

Darroch, J., Landry, D., & Oslak, S. (1999). Age differences between sexual partners in the United States. *Family Planning Perspectives, 31*(4), 160–167.

Darroch, J., Landry, D., & Singh, S. (2000). Changing emphases in sexuality education in U.S. public secondary schools, 1988–1999. *Family Planning Perspectives, 32,* 204–211, 265.

de Anda, D., Darroch, P., Davidson, M., Gilly, J., Javidi, M., Jefford, S., Komorowski, R., & Morejon-Schrobsdorf, A. (1992). Stress and coping among pregnant adolescents. *Journal of Adolescent Research, 7*(1), 94–100.

DeBolt, M. E., Pasley, B. K., & Kreutzer, J. (1990). Factors affecting the probability of school dropout: A study of pregnant and parenting adolescent females. *Journal of Adolescent Research, 5,* 190–205.

DiBlassio, F. A., & Benda, B. B. (1990). Adolescent sexual behavior: Multivariate analysis of a social learning model. *Journal of Adolescent Research, 5,* 449–466.

Dietz, P., Spitz, A. M., Anda, R. F., Williamson, D. F., McMahon, P. M., Santelli, J. S., Nordenberg, D. F., Felitti, V. J., & Kendrick, J. S. (1999). Unintended pregnancy among adult women exposed to abuse or household dysfunction during their childhood. *Journal of the American Medical Association, 282*(14), 1359–1364.

Elliott, D. S., & Morse, B. J. (1989). Delinquency and drug use as risk factors in teenage sexual activity. *Youth & Society, 21,* 32–60.

Flanigan, B., Mclean, A., Hall, C., & Propp, V. (1990). Alcohol use as a situational influence on young women's pregnancy risk-taking behaviors. *Adolescence, 25,* 205–214.

Flewelling, R. L., & Bauman, K. E. (1990). Family structure as a predictor of initial substance use and sexual intercourse in early adolescence. *Journal of Marriage and the Family, 52,* 171–180.

Forste, R. T., & Heaton, T. B. (1988). Initiation of sexual activity among female adolescents. *Youth & Society, 19,* 250–268.

Franklin, C., & Corcoran, J. (1999). Preventing adolescent pregnancy: A review of programs and practices. *Social Work, 45*(1), 40–52.

Franklin, C., Corcoran, J., & Ayers-Lopez, S. (1997). Adolescent pregnancy prevention. In M. W. Fraser (Ed.), *Risk and resilience in childhood: An ecological perspective* (pp. 195–219). Washington, DC: NASW Press.

Franklin, C., Grant, D., Corcoran, J., O'Dell, P., & Bultman, L. (1997). Effectiveness of prevention programs for adolescent pregnancy: A meta-analysis. *Journal of Marriage and the Family, 59*(3), 551–567.

Furstenberg, F. F., Brooks-Gunn, J., & Morgan, S. P. (1987). *Adolescent mothers in later life.* Cambridge: Cambridge University Press.

Garland, A., & Zigler, E. (1993). Adolescent suicide prevention: Current research and social policy implications. *American Psychologist, 48,* 169–182.

Giblin, P. T., Poland, M. L., & Sachs, B. A. (1987). Effects of social supports on attitudes and health behaviors of pregnant adolescents. *Journal of Adolescent Health Care, 8,* 273–279.

Gillmore, M. R., Lewis, S. M., Lohr, M. J., Spencer, M. S., & White, R. D. (1997). Repeat pregnancies among adolescent mothers. *Journal of Marriage and the Family, 59*(3), 536–550.

Gohel, M., Diamond, J. J., & Chambers, C. V. (1997). Attitudes toward sexual responsibility and parenting: An exploratory study of young urban males. *Family Planning Perspectives, 29*(6), 280–283.

Granger, R. C., & Cytron, R. (1999). Teenage parent programs: A synthesis of the long-term effects of the new chance demonstration, Ohio's learning, earning, and parenting program, and the teenage parent demonstration. *Evaluation Review, 23*(2), 107–145.

Guttmacher Report. (1998, October). Falling teenage pregnancy, birthrates: What's behind the declines? *The Guttmacher Report on Public Policy, 1*(5), 6–9. Retrieved February 8, 1999, from the World Wide Web: http://206.215.210.5/pubs/journals/gr010506.html.

Hanson, S. L., Myers, D. E., & Ginsburg, A. L. (1987). The role of responsibility and knowledge in reducing teenage out-of-wedlock childbearing. *Journal of Marriage and the Family, 49,* 241–256.

Harris, K. M. (1991). Teenage mothers and welfare dependency: Working off welfare. *Journal of Family Issues, 12,* 492–518.

Harris, M. B., & Franklin, C. (manuscript under review). Effects of a cognitive-behavioral, school-based, group intervention with Mexican-American pregnant and parenting mothers.

Henshaw, S. K. (1998). Abortion incidence and services in the United States, 1995–1996. *Family Planning Perspectives, 30*(6), 263–270, 287.

Henshaw, S. K., & Feivelson, D. (2000). Teenage abortion and pregnancy statistics by state, 1996. *Family Planning Perspectives, 32*(6), 272–280.

Hofferth, S. L. (1987). Social and economic consequences of teenage childbearing. In S. L. Hofferth & C. D. Hayes (Eds.), *Risking the future* (pp. 123–144). Washington, DC: National Academy Press.

Horwitz, S. M., Klerman, L. V., Sung Kuo, H., & Jekel, J. F. (1991). School-age mothers: Predictors of long-term educational and economic outcomes. *Pediatrics, 87*(6), 862–868.

Jaccard, J., Dittus, P., & Gordon, V. (1996). Maternal correlates of adolescent sexual and contraceptive behavior. *Family Planning Perspectives, 28,* 159–165.

Kalil, A., & Kunz, J. (1999). First births among adolescent girls: Risk and protective factors. *Social Work Research, 23*(3), 197–208.

Kirby, D. (2001). *Emerging answers: Research findings on programs to reduce teenage pregnancies.* Washington, DC: The National Campaign to Prevent Teenage Pregnancy.

Kirby, D., Korpi, M., Barth, R. P., & Cagampang, H. H. (1997). The impact of the postponing sexual involvement curriculum among youths in California. *Family Planning Perspectives, 29*(3), 100–108.

Lindberg, L. D., Sonenstein, F. L., Ku, L., & Martinez, G. (1997). Age differences between minors who give birth and their adult partners. *Family Planning Perspectives, 29*(2), 61–66.

Luker, K. (1996). *Dubious conceptions: The politics of teenage pregnancy.* Cambridge, MA: Harvard University Press.

Luster, T., & Small, S. (1997). Sexual abuse history and number of sex partners among female adolescents. *Family Planning Perspectives, 29,* 204–211.

Martin, C. A., Hill, K. K., & Welch, R. (1998). Adolescent pregnancy, a stressful life event: Cause and consequence. In T. Miller (Ed.), *Children of trauma: Stressful life events and their effects on children and adolescents* (pp. 21–23). Madison, CT: International Universities Press.

Matthews, S., Ribar, D., & Wilhelm, M. (1997). The effects of economic conditions and access to reproductive health services on state abortion rates and birthrates. *Family Planning Perspectives, 29*(2), 52–60.

Mayfield-Brown, L. (1989). Family status of low-income adolescent mothers. *Journal of Adolescent Research, 4,* 202–213.

Maynard, R. (Ed.). (1996). *Kids having kids: A Robin Hood Foundation special report on the costs of adolescent childbearing.* New York: Robin Hood Foundation.

McAnarney, E. R., & Hendee, W. R. (1989). Adolescent pregnancy and its consequences. *Journal of the American Medical Association, 262,* 74–77.

Medoff, M. H. (1999). An estimate of teenage abortion demand. *Journal of Socio-Economics, 28*(2), 175–186.

Miller, K., Clark, L., & Moore, J. (1997). Sexual initiation with older male partners and subsequent HIV risk behavior among female adolescents. *Family Planning Perspectives, 29,* 212–214.

Moore, K. A. Myers, D. E., Morrison, D. R., Nord, C. W., Brown, B. V., & Edmonston, B. (1993). Age of first childbirth and later poverty. *Journal of Research on Adolescence, 3*(4), 393–422.

Mott, F. L., & Haurin, R. J. (1988). Linkages between sexual activity and alcohol and drug use among American adolescents. *Family Planning Perspectives, 20,* 128–136.

The National Campaign to Prevent Teenage Pregnancy. (April, 1997). *What the polling data tell us: A summary of past surveys.* Retrieved March 22, 2002, from http://www.teenpregnancy.org/resources/data/polling97.asp.

Newcomer, S., & Udry, J. (1985). Parent-child communication and adolescent sexual behavior. *Family Planning Perspectives, 17,* 169–174.

Oakley, A. (1985). Social support and the outcome in pregnancy: The soft way to increase birth weight? *Social Science and Medicine, 21,* 1259–1268.

Osofsky, J. D., Osofsky, H. J., & Diamond, M. O. (1988). The transition to parenthood: Special tasks and risk factors for adolescent parents. In G. Y. Michaels & W. A. Goldberg (Eds.), *The transition to parenthood: Current theory and research* (pp. 209–232). New York: Cambridge University Press.

Perkins, D. F., Luster, T., Villarruel, F. A., & Small, S. (1998). An ecological, risk-factor examination of adolescents' sexual activity in three ethnic groups. *Journal of Marriage and the Family, 60,* 660–673.

Peterson, A., Compas, B., Brooks-Gunn, J., Stemmler, M., Ey, S., & Grant, K. (1993). Depression in adolescence. *American Psychologist, 48,* 155–168.

Pines, D. (1988). Adolescent pregnancy and motherhood: A psychoanalytical perspective. *Psychoanalytic Inquiry, 8*(2), 234–251.

Polit, D. (1989). Effects of a comprehensive program for teenage parents: Five years after Project Redirection. *Family Planning Perspectives, 21,* 164–187.

Raj, A., Silverman, J. G., & Amaro, H. (2000). The relationship between sexual abuse and sexual risk among high school students: Findings from the 1997 Massachusetts Youth Risk Behavior Survey. *Maternal and Child Health Journal, 4*(2), 125–134.

Reis, J. S., & Herz, E. J. (1987). Correlates of adolescent parenting. *Adolescence, 22,* 599–609.

Rhodes, J. E., & Woods, M. (1995). Comfort and conflict in the relationships of pregnant, minority adolescents: Social support as a moderator of social strain. *Journal of Community Psychology, 23,* 74–84.

Robbins, C., Kaplan, H. B., & Martin, S. S. (1985). Antecedents of pregnancy among unmarried adolescents. *Journal of Marriage and the Family, 43,* 339–348.

Rudd, N. M., McKenry, P. C., & Nah, M. (1990). Welfare recipient among black and white adolescent mothers: A longitudinal perspective. *Journal of Family Issues, 11,* 334–352.

Sandfort, J. R., & Hill, M. S. (1996). Assisting young unmarried mothers to become self-sufficient. The effects of different types of early economic support. *Journal of Marriage and the Family, 58*(2), 311–326.

Santelli, J. S., & Beilenson, P. (1992). Risk factors for adolescent sexual behavior, fertility, and sexually transmitted diseases. *Journal of School Health, 62,* 271–279.

Schilmoeller, G. L., & Baranowski, M. D. (1985). Child rearing of firstborns by adolescent and older mothers. *Adolescence, 20,* 805–822.

Schilmoeller, G. L., Baranowski, M. D., & Higgins, B. S. (1991). Long-term support and personal adjustment of adolescent and older mothers. *Adolescence, 26,* 787–797.

Seitz, V., & Apfel, N. H. (1999). Effective interventions for adolescent mothers. *Clinical Psychology: Science and Practice, 6,* 50–66.

Shah, F., & Zelnik, M. (1981). Parent and peer influence on sexual behavior, contraceptive use, and pregnancy experience of young women. *Journal of Marriage and the Family, 43,* 339–348.

Smith, T. (1994). Adolescent pregnancy. In R. J. Simeonsson (Ed.), *Risk, resilience and prevention: Promoting the well being of all children* (pp. 125–149). Baltimore, MD: Brookes Publishing.

Stern, M., & Alvarez, A. (1992). Pregnant and parenting adolescents: A comparative analysis of coping response and psychosocial adjustment. *Journal of Adolescent Research, 7*(4), 469–493.

Stevens-Simon, C., Dolgan, J. I., Kelly, L., & Singer, D. (1997). The effect of monetary incentives and peer support groups on repeat adolescent pregnancies: A randomized trial of the dollar-a-day program. *Journal of the American Medical Association, 277,* 977–982.

Stock, J. L., Bell, M. A., Boyer, D. K., & Connell, F. A. (1997). Adolescent pregnancy and sexual risk-taking among sexually abused girls. *Family Planning Perspectives, 29*(4), 200–203, 227.

Studer, M., & Thornton, A. (1987). Adolescent religiosity and contraceptive use. *Journal of Marriage and the Family, 49,* 117–128.

Thornton, A., & Camburn, D. (1989). Religious participation and adolescent sexual behavior and attitudes. *Journal of Marriage and the Family, 51,* 641–652.

Trad, P. V. (1994). Adolescent pregnancy: An intervention challenge. *Child Psychiatry & Human Development, 24*(2), 99–113.

Turner, R. J., Grindstaff, C. F., & Phillips, N. (1990). Social support and outcome in teenage pregnancy. *Journal of Health and Social Behavior, 31,* 43–57.

Unger, D. G., & Wandersman, L. P. (1988). The relation of family and partner support to the adjustment of adolescent mothers. *Child Development, 59,* 1056–1060.

U.S. General Accounting Office. (June 6, 1998). *Teen mothers: Selected socio-demographic characteristics and risk factors.* Retrieved March 22, 2002, from http://www.teenpregnancy.org/resources/data/polling97.asp.

Whitaker, D., Miller, K., May, D., & Levin, M. (1999). Teenage partners' communication about sexual risk and condom use: The importance of parent-teenager discussions. *Family Planning Perspectives, 31,* 117–121.

Wilson, S. (2000). Sexuality education: Our current status, and an agenda for 2010. *Family Planning Perspectives, 32*(5), 252–254.

Yamaguchi, K., & Kandel, D. (1987). Drug use and other determinants of premarital pregnancy and its outcome: A dynamic analysis of competing life events. *Journal of Marriage and the Family, 49,* 257–270.

Young, E. W., Jensen, L. C., Olsen, J. A., & Cundick, B. P. (1991). The effects of family structure on the sexual behavior of adolescents. *Adolescence, 26,* 977–986.

Zabin, L. S., Hardy, J. B., Smith, E. A., & Hirsh, M. B. (1986). Substance use and its relation to sexual activity among inner-city adolescents. *Journal of Adolescent Health Care, 7,* 320–331.

CHAPTER 19

BULLYING AND PEER VICTIMIZATION IN SCHOOLS

RON AVI ASTOR

University of Southern California

RAMI BENBENISHTY

Hebrew University

RONALD O. PITNER

Washington University

HEATHER ANN MEYER

Wells College

One time, all the second-graders were on the yard playing basketball and a fifth-grader named Joe just walks up to me and says that all the stinky second-graders need to get off the basketball court because we want to play. I went to the teacher on the playground but she didn't really do anything because there wasn't a fight, we just had words with each other and he lied and said that the fifth-graders were there first when they weren't. When Joe found out that I told on him and tried to get him in trouble, he got a bunch of other fifth-grade boys, I think seven of them, to beat me up after school. They waited for me after school and jumped me and I got kicked and punched and slapped and stuff like that for a long time. My little brother was walking with me and ran back to the principal's office to tell but only the secretary was there and nothing really happened. All the first-, second-, and third-graders are afraid of Joe because he's really big and mean. He always picks on me now after school. I don't think the fifth-graders really like him because they pick fights with him also all the time. I think one day somebody's dad is really going to whoop him for being a mean old bully.—8-year-old male, Michigan

Studies in developmental psychology suggest that one of the most familiar and lasting memories many students, adolescents, and even adults have of their school years is the school bully (e.g., Olweus, Limber, & Mihalic, 1999; Turiel, 1987). The phenomenon of the bully appears to be cross-cultural and international (Bosworth, Espelage, & Simon, 1999; Olweus, 1993; Olweus, et al., 1999; Rigby, 1994; Benbenishty & Astor, in press; Smith et al., 1999). Based on the frequent references and accounts in historical and fictional literature, it is likely that bullying behaviors among children have existed for much of modern human history. The image of the school bully also has been portrayed extensively in modern fictional literature, movies, television programs, and other forms of mass media. Hence, most individuals have experienced school bullying in real life and are familiar with the phenomenon in fictional situations.

The empirical and intervention literature related to bullying on school grounds is extensive and is perhaps the most developed of the school violence literatures (e.g., school fighting, sexual harassment in schools, corporal punishment, school shootings, school vandalism, crisis intervention). For more than three decades, researchers in psychology, sociology, and education have been exploring (1) epidemiological rates of bullies and victims at different ages, (2) risk factors associated with bullying and victimization, (3) individual child characteristics of bullies and victims, (4) parenting styles that increase or decrease a child's chance of being a bully or victim, (5) school setting characteristics associated with bullying/victim behaviors, and (6) intervention strategies and programs that reduce the rates of bullying and victimization. This research has been conducted in multiple countries, including but not limited to Norway, Sweden, Australia, New Zealand, Great Britain, Israel, Japan, Spain, Canada, and, to a much lesser extent, the United States. The most comprehensive and ongoing studies on school bullying have been conducted in Scandinavia, Great Britain, and Australia. Consequently, a central goal of this chapter is to review key findings regarding school bullying and victimization from an international and cross-cultural perspective (e.g., Olweus et al., 1999; Pellegrini & Bartini, 2000; Smith et al., 1999).

This chapter will also highlight some remarkably successful anti-bullying intervention programs in Great Britain, Scandinavia, and Australia. The authors of this chapter advocate for data-based strategies to adapt bully/victim intervention programs at the school and school district level. This chapter will provide case examples and methods to assess bully/victim problems in schools.

WHAT IS BULLYING? DEFINITIONS, LIMITATIONS, CONCEPTUAL ISSUES

Most researchers cite the definition of bullying originally put forth by Olweus (see Olweus, 1993; Olweus et al., 1999; Nansel et al., 2001; Smith & Sharp, 1994; Smith, et al., 1999; Sullivan, 2000, for discussions of definitions). *Bullying* is most often defined as a subtype of aggressive behavior that is characterized by (1) the *intention* to harm another person, (2) the perpetration of harmful acts to the same or similar victim targets that occur repeatedly and over time, and (3) an imbalance of power between the bully and the victim—where the more powerful bully asserts physical or psychological power over the weaker victim.

Bullying behaviors can take many forms. Actions can be physical, such as behaviors that cause visible harm (often termed *direct bullying*), or they could be psychological (often termed *indirect bullying*). Indirect bullying is more subtle and complex than direct bullying. Psychological bullying can be either verbal or nonverbal (Sullivan, 2000). Most commonly, indirect aggression centers around disrupting, damaging, or manipulating relationships or friendships (e.g., Olweus, 1991, 1993; Ross, 1996). According to Ross, this kind of bullying is often referred to as *relational aggression.* For example, a bully may try to get the peer group to dislike a student through scapegoating (e.g., Ahmad & Smith, 1994; Olweus, 1993). Other common forms of indirect aggression center around gossiping or spreading rumors about a certain person. This can and often does include intentional sexual rumors or gossip (Nansel et al., 2001), slandering someone, and/or spreading rumors with the intent of causing someone distress (Olweus, 1993, 1994).

This definition of bullying has some components that are not used commonly by the media, public, or even by some school violence researchers when they refer casually to bullying. There are also some conceptual limitations with aspects of this definition. For example, the component of the definition referring to *an imbalance of power between the bully and the victim—where the more powerful bully asserts physical or psychological power over the weaker victim* is fraught with potential conceptual problems. Using this component, researchers would not be allowed to define a younger or physically weaker child as a bully, even if that child continually perpetrates harmful psychological or physical acts on an older or stronger child. Another problematic example is a child who continually targets another child who is physically of the *same strength* or *size,* but would not be defined as a bully even if the victim, other children, or teachers perceive him or her as one.

From a conceptual stance, the emphasis on power imbalance is problematic and may not fit most people's common use of the term *bullying.* Although an imbalance of power could increase the potential harm incurred by the victim, it is highly plausible that some children normally seen as bullies (by teachers and students) also pick on children their own size and sometimes they may pick on children larger then themselves. This possibility is even more salient when we consider psychological forms of bullying behaviors. Given this rather strict definition, a younger sibling who is continually harming an older sibling, or a smaller girl causing severe psychological harm to a same-sized girl or a larger boy, would not be considered bullies.

Another problematic component in definitions of bullying is the idea that bullying is usually repetitive and occurs over time within an ongoing interpersonal relationship (Olweus, 1999). Hence, an incident in which a student violently attacks a group of students with whom he or she did not have direct interaction before the incident will not be called bullying. Olweus suggests that the term *bullying* should not be used interchangeably with *school violence.* As Olweus (1999) emphasizes, bullying is a form of aggression and violent behavior, with specific characteristics (such as repetitive behaviors and imbalance of power) that overlap other forms of violent behavior in school only partially.

Discussions concerning the relationships between bullying behaviors and some *Diagnostic Statistical Manual (DSM)* disorders are absent in the research or practice literatures. It could be argued that chronic bullies involved in physical/direct bullying would in almost all cases fit the criteria for conduct disorders or oppositional defiant disorder in *DSM.* However, the concurrence of these categorical labels is not entirely clear, especially when indirect bullying is considered. This is particularly true when comparing bullying by gender. Many girls who might easily fit the formal definition of *bully* may not fit the criteria of conduct disorder or oppositional defiant disorder if most of their actions are exclusionary, only verbal, or indirect forms of bullying.

PSYCHOLOGICAL AND SOCIAL CONSEQUENCES OF BULLYING

Bullying has numerous documented negative consequences for victims, and certain detrimental effects on bullies, as well. Smith and colleagues (1999) review the available evidence and conclude that continuous or severe bullying impacts the psychological and physical health of the victims. Victims reported being afraid to go to school, feeling unhappy and stressed, and having physical symptoms (e.g., stomach aches and headaches), sleep disturbances, and difficulties concentrating on academics in school. There are indications that victimization from bullying behaviors leads to lower self-esteem and problems with the development of close interpersonal relationships. For example, Rigby and Slee (1999) report that high school students who have been victimized also reported a relatively high incidence of physical health complaints. Among girls, there were many significant correlations between victimization and negative mental health outcomes.

There have been numerous reports in the media about victims who committed suicide because they were unable to cope with continuous and malicious bullying (see examples from countries such as Norway, England, Ireland, and Japan in Smith et al., 1999). Rigby and Slee (1999) report that there are indications that suicidal ideation and attempts at self-harm were significantly associated with self and peer reports of bullying and victimization.

Research indicates that being a bully also can also have negative social and psychological consequences on the bully. If bullies are "successful," they learn maladaptive behaviors (Sharp & Smith, 1994). Over time, bullies appear to acquire interpersonal interaction patterns that lead to antisocial behaviors later in life. Longitudinal research (Olweus, 1991) indicates that students who were bullies in adolescence were four to five times more likely than others to be involved in antisocial behaviors as young adults.

Situating Bullying as a Behavior within School Violence Issues in the United States

Bullying as One Form of School Violence.   The recent focus in the United States on bullying is associated with burgeoning public concerns regarding a much wider array of school violence behaviors that include murder (Bragg, 1997; Hays, 1998), the presence of weapons (Pittel, 1998), sexual harassment (Stein, 1999), school fighting (Boulton, 1993; Schafer & Smith, 1996), corporal punishment (Youssef, Attia, & Kamel, 1998), gang violence (Kodluboy, 1997; Parks, 1995), rape (Page, 1997), hate crimes (Berrill, 1990), vandalism (Goldstein, 1996), and dating violence (Burcky, Reuterman, & Kopsky, 1988; Cano, Avery-Leaf, Cascardi, & O'Leary, 1998).

Therefore, it is important to understand that the current focus on bullying in the United States falls within the context of the broader umbrella of school violence. With this in mind, throughout the 1990s the public's concern has increased dramatically not only about bullying but also about school safety issues broadly defined. In fact, dozens of public opinion polls and surveys have suggested that school safety has been the top concern regarding U.S. education for at least eight years (e.g., Elam & Rose, 1995; Elam, Rose, & Gallup, 1994, 1996; Kaufman et al., 2000; Morrison, Furlong, & Morrison, 1997; Rose &

Gallup, 1999; Rose & Gallup, 2000; Rose, Gallup, & Elam, 1997; U.S Departments of Education and Justice, 2000). It is important to note that public concern about school safety precedes the highly publicized multiple school shootings. Nevertheless, these shootings, combined with the intense media coverage following the shootings, have only magnified the public's already high concern about school violence (see Astor, Benbenishty, Pitner, & Meyer, in press).*

Growing Awareness and Changing Public Norms. Because the interest in bullying as a form of school violence is only very recent in the United States, researchers do not have comparable national epidemiological data regarding the increase or decrease of bullying in the United States during the last decade. Later in this chapter, we will report results from the only nationally representative studies conducted on bullying in the United States (Nansel et al., 2001). It is possible that the general public's concern is higher regarding school violence because societal norms regarding the acceptability of aggressive behaviors have been changing during this period. This heightened sensitivity may make the public less tolerant of many forms of school violence (including lower-level violence, such as verbal teasing or harassment) and therefore could be contributing to a belief that school violence is more frequent today then it has been in the past.

This hypothesis of changed norms is supported by the multitude of new laws and national/local school zero tolerance policies that focus on school violence behaviors that in

---

*Although concern from the general public has been increasing, the empirical data documenting national trends of different kinds of school violence presents a different temporal portrait of school violence in the United States than what is portrayed currently in the general media and believed by the public. Multiple national surveys from credible government organizations (for discussions, see Kann et al., 2000; Kaufman et al., 2000; U.S Departments of Education and Justice, 2000) indicate that most forms of school violence (including lethal events) have decreased dramatically over the past eight years. For example, government data and independent research indicate that violent deaths on school grounds existed at comparable or higher rates before the intense media coverage of the late 1990s. Kachur and colleagues (1996) reported in the *Journal of the American Medical Association* that there were 105 violent deaths on school grounds in 1992–1993 (these numbers include suicide, manslaughter, student, and nonstudent deaths). However, in 1997–1998 (the year of the Columbine shootings), there were 60 violent deaths on school grounds. In 1998–1999 there were 50 violent deaths on school grounds. If the number of fatal events is examined (not number of people who died but events that had fatalities), government data show that the actual number of events has also decreased in recent years (e.g., 49 events in 1995–1996 to 34 events in 1998–1999). Given these data, how can we explain the rising public concern over lethal violence on school grounds? One could argue that we now have a greater awareness about school deaths and will not tolerate even 50 deaths (we support such a position). However, a greater sensitivity and awareness regarding lethal events should not negate the fact that U.S. schools may have had more than a 50 percent reduction in violent deaths on school grounds since 1992–1993.

As another exemplar of declining trends, between 1993 and 1999, the Department of Education reported that the percentage of students in grades 9 through 12 who reported bringing a gun on school grounds during the 30 days preceding the survey dropped from 12 to 7 percent. If accurate, this would be is an astonishing 42 percent reduction in the number of students who report bringing weapons on to school grounds. Very few in the general public are aware of these data. There are many other remarkable reductions in rates of school violence behaviors that are beyond the scope of this chapter (see Astor, Benbenishty, Pitner, & Meyer, in press, for a more detailed review on reductions for other forms of school violence). Although the U.S. government has published many documents detailing these trends, the national media have not reported them extensively and many in the general public still believe that school violence rates have increased rather than decreased (with some forms of violence like school fights the rates have remained stable over the past 20 years) during the past decade.

the past were not included as part of a definition for *violence* (e.g., bullying, sexual harassment, school fights, stalking, verbal threats; see Hyman & Snook, 2000, for an interesting review on zero tolerance and punitive measure for these behaviors). Hence, in addition to the recent school shootings in the United States, the public and media are concerned about forms of school violence that may have existed in the past at high rates but were most likely not considered a problem 20 years ago.

Given this background, it is important to note that until the late 1990s, very little research on bullying was conducted in the United States. Also, as recently as the late 1990s, few schools nationwide had instituted anti-bullying programs. In one national survey, Astor, Behre, Wallace, and Fravil (1998) reported that only 14 percent of U.S. school social workers had anti-bullying programs in their schools and only 9 percent were involved in their implementation. During this period, very few graduate programs in social work, school psychology, school counseling, or teacher/administrator education included any formal training or content on bullying in their curricula (Astor et al., 1998).

Bullying and Mass Homicides in the United States.   In the late 1990s, the mass media began suggesting that many of the perpetrators of school homicides were retaliating for years of being victimized by bullies on school grounds (Bragg, 1997; Hays, 1998; Gegax, Adler, & Peterson, 1998). Although this was not true in all cases (Vossekuil, Reddy, Fein, Borum & Modzeleski, 2000), this theme has appeared repeatedly in media reports for all the school shootings that followed the Columbine massacre. In response to this widespread belief about the relationship between being a victim of bullying and mass homicides in schools, many federal agencies began discussing the necessity for anti-bully programs in schools (Kaufman et al., 2000). Currently, some states (such as Michigan and Washington) are in the process of passing legislation that requires schools to develop specific policies and discipline codes that address bullying (Franklin, 2001). Likewise, many school districts across the country have begun instituting and promoting anti-bullying programs directed at young children.

However, empirical studies or theoretical conceptualizations have not explored carefully the relationships between bullying victimization and committing lethal acts of violence in schools (Pellegrini & Bartini, 2000; Vossekuil et al., 2000). Some federal agencies, such as the Secret Service and Federal Bureau of Investigation (FBI), have nonetheless suggested that being a victim of bullying played some role in the recent rash of school homicides. However, they also suggest that bullying was either nonexistent, not severe, or not as prolonged as the mass media has been suggesting (Vossekuil et al., 2000).

For the vast majority of students categorized both as victims and bullies, there does not appear to be a developmental progression from victimization to lethal revenge. In general, the empirical relationships between personal victimization and bullying (in the same child) are not well understood. Studies show that a sizable number of chronic bullies are also chronic victims of bullying (Nansel et al., 2001; Olweus, 1993; Sullivan, 2000). However, researchers are not certain why such a relatively large proportion of students are both chronic bullies and victims while others fit solely into one category. It is possible that the risk factors and protective factors for these groups are different over time. The patterns are sufficiently complex to warrant more research on the relationships between victimization and bullying.

Prevalence of Bullies and Victims of Bullying

Overall Rates in the International Context.   Rates of bullying and bully victimization vary widely from country to country. Representative samples conducted in different nations report bully/victim rates that range from 15 to 70 percent depending on the country (Nansel et al., 2001). For instance, in Norway, 15 percent of students were involved in bullying either as victims or bullies—9 percent as victims, 7 percent as bullies, and 1.6 percent as both bullies and victims (Olweus, 1999, reporting on a survey of 130,000 students). In England, Whitney and Smith (1993) found that 27 percent of primary school students reported being bullied "sometimes" or more frequently, and 12 percent reported bullying others. In Ireland, Byrne (1999) reports that 5.3 percent of the students were bullies and 5.1 percent reported being victims.

The World Health Organization (WHO) also has been conducting health surveys among school children for the last decade. The Health Behavior of School-Aged Children (HBSC) survey includes a handful of questions on bullying and victimization. This cross-national study showed large differences among the various countries. For instance, the percentage of youth reporting on being bullied at least once during the academic year ranged from 77.3 percent for 11-year-old males in Greenland and 76.7 percent in French Belgium to 29.9 percent in Scotland and 20.4 percent in Sweden.

Bully/Victim Rates in the United States.   Recently, the United States has participated in a cross-national research project coordinated by the WHO, and supported in the United States by the National Institute of Child Health and Human Development. This first U.S. representative sample consisted of 15,686 students in grades 6 to 10. Nansel and colleagues (2001) found that 10.6 percent of the sample reported bullying others sometimes (moderate), and 8.8 percent admitted to bullying others frequently (once a week or more). Reports on victimization were slightly lower—8.5 percent of students reporting being bullied sometimes and 8.4 percent once a week or more. About 30 percent of the sample reported being involved in school bullying, either moderately or frequently, as bullies (13.0 percent), victims (10.6 percent), or both as victims and bullies (6.3 percent).

Characteristics of Bullies and Victims

Bullies.   Stephenson and Smith (1989) suggested that there are three distinct types of bullies: the confident bully, the anxious bully, and the bully who is also a chronic victim. *Confident bullies* tend to be strong physically (usually stronger than their victims), fairly confident, popular among certain groups, and appear to enjoy acting aggressively. *Anxious bullies* tend not to be as popular as confident bullies; they have poor academic performance and poor concentration. *Bullies who are also victims* tend to go back and forth between a victim profile and a bully profile. Compared to the other types of bullies, they tend to be very unpopular (Stephenson & Smith, 1989). Nansel and colleagues (2001) reported that bullies who are also victims exhibit the lowest levels of psychosocial skills. Several researchers suggest that bullies from all three categories tend to gravitate toward children who share similar social status and beliefs about bullying and victimization.

Victims.   Based on a large body of international research, Olweus (1993) suggests that there are two types of victims of bullies: the passive victim and the provocative victim. *Passive victims* are the most common type, and tend to be anxious, insecure, sensitive, cautious, and have low self-esteem (Olweus, 1993; Olweus et al., 1999; Sullivan, 2000). *Provocative victims,* on the other hand, are less common and tend to exhibit both anxious and aggressive behavior. In fact, their behaviors may be confused with hyperactivity. The provocative victim's behavior tends to provoke anger among others, which leads them to being victimized and bullied more frequently at school.

Stability of Bullying Behaviors over Time.   Longitudinal research suggests that bullying behaviors tend to be remarkably stable over time. That is, a child who is seen as a bully at a young age by peers and teachers has a high likelihood of remaining a bully 10 and 15 years later if no intervention is provided to deal with these behaviors (Olweus, 1991; Pepler & Rubin, 1991). This finding is similar to many other longitudinal studies conducted in diverse countries (Smith et al., 1999). This finding could be interpreted as evidence that bullying is a personality-like trait that is stable over time. However, we caution the reader not to attribute the stability to the child alone. The "stability" of bullying over time may also reflect the bully's social status in the class and school that remains stable over time. Most likely, it is a combination of these two factors. One important implication from these stability patterns is that in the absence of interventions, early bullying behavior is a strong predictor of later bullying behaviors. The findings from longitudinal studies point to the importance of early intervention to break these very stable relational patterns (Olweus, 1991).

Risk Factors Associated with Bullying and Victimization

Factors Associated with the Individual.   Generally, certain characteristics are indicative of bullies and victims.

Age.   Findings from the United States and international studies suggest that there is an inverse relationship between age and bullying victimization (Olweus et al., 1999; Smith et al., 1999; Sullivan, 2000). The chances of becoming a victim of bullying are much higher in the early elementary school grades and then drops significantly every year as a child grows older (Olweus, 1993). Internationally, bullying victimization is lower in high schools than in middle or elementary schools, and middle schools have lower rates than elementary schools (e.g., Smith et al., 1999). In the United States, we have little epidemiological data, but these trends conform to international patterns (Olweus, 1986, 1993; Olweus et al., 1999; Nansel et al., 2001; Sullivan, 2000; Whitney & Smith, 1993). In the United States and some other countries (Sullivan, 2000), there is a slight increase in bullying behaviors in grades 6 through 8, with a slight decrease in bullying in high school.*

---

*For example, in the United States, 18.8% of sixth-graders, 19.6% of seventh-graders, 24.1% of eighth-graders, 18.6% of ninth-graders, and 15.5% of tenth-graders reported frequent bullying of others (Nansel et al., 2001).

Gender. Overall, the international body of research suggests that compared with girls, boys are more frequently victims of bullies and engaged in bullying behaviors. Boys also tend to report higher rates of chronic victimization in the international literature on bullies. In a recent national study in the United States, 25.9 percent of boys and 13.7 percent of girls in grades 6 through 10 reported being frequent victims of bullying (Nansel et al., 2001).

Overall, boys tend to be victimized more often by direct forms of bullying (e.g., hitting, slapping) and girls are victimized more often by indirect forms of bullying (e.g., rumors, exclusion from groups) (e.g., Nansel et al., 2001; Olweus et al., 1999; Smith & Sharp, 1994; Sullivan, 2000). However, recent U.S. data show that both boys and girls report similar rates of indirect bullying, whereas boys have much higher rates of direct bullying (Nansel et al., 2001). In the United States, boys are almost twice as likely as girls to report being bullies (Nansel et al., 2001). Some theories point to the differences in the friendship patterns of boys and girls as the underlying reason for these distinctive forms of bullying (e.g., Owens, Slee, & Shute, 2000; Owens & McMullin, 1995). Since girls tend to have closer-knit groups of friends based on intimacy and belonging, bullying based on exclusion and/or social isolation would have the most significant impact on girls. During the teenage years, boys tend to form bigger and more amorphous friendship groups, where indirect forms of bullying would not be as effective as direct methods of aggression (Owens & Mac-Mullin, 1995).

Direct forms of aggression (hitting, punching, physical intimidation) are much more overt and easy to identify and punish than the more indirect forms of bullying that girls appear to use more often than boys. Olweus (1993) reported that in his research studies, female bullies "typically use less visible, and more sneaky means of harassment" (p. 59). This brings up interesting questions surrounding the reporting of indirect forms of aggression by other classmates and/or teachers. The nature of indirect aggression often allows it to be missed easily by teachers, parents, or even other students (Owens & MacMullin, 1995). However, despite being a more covert form of aggression, studies have found that indirect forms of aggression can have a lasting negative impact on victims (Owens, et al., 2000; Owens & MacMullin, 1995). Some of the negative psychological effects that girls who were victims reported included "embarrassment, anger, worry, fear, humiliation, loneliness, self-consciousness, betrayal, and sadness" (Owens & MacMullin, 1995, p. 367). In addition, Owens and colleagues (2000) found that victims did not receive the support they needed from teachers, parents, and school staff—often because these acts of bullying were so invisible. Overall, these findings suggest that both genders are vulnerable to different kinds of bullying victimization.

Ethnic Background. In the United States, bullying rates also vary slightly by the child's ethnic background and community setting. Hispanic youth report marginally higher involvement in moderate (12 percent) to frequent (10.4 percent) bullying compared with African American youth (10.2 percent and 8.3 percent for moderate and frequent bullying, respectively) and with white youth (10.5 percent and 8.5 percent for moderate and frequent bullying, respectively). Interestingly, contrary to popular belief, there are no differences in bullying victimization rates between urban, suburban, town, or rural settings. There are very marginal differences in the rates that students report that they bully others, with rural students only slightly (3 to 5 percent) more likely to report bullying others than students in suburban and urban settings (Nansel et al., 2001). Moreover, these results seem to be similar in many other countries (Olweus, 1993; Smith et al., 1999; Sullivan, 2000).

Physical Characteristics and Group Stereotypes.   Research from Europe suggests that some popular notions associated with victimization may be more myth than reality (Olweus et al., 1999). For example, it is assumed commonly that children who are physically different from other children along several dimensions (e.g., obesity, hair color, unusual dialect or foreign language, or unusual clothing/glasses) may be picked on and bullied more by other school children. Research in Scandinavian countries, however, suggests that these kinds of factors do not distinguish between those who are chronic victims and those who are not (Olweus, 1991, 1993).

The only common physical factor shown to make a difference in the bullying literature so far is the child's size and physical strength. Victims tended to be physically smaller and weaker than average children their age. Bullies, on the other hand, tended to be physically larger and stronger than other children their age (see Olweus, 1993, for a detailed description of these studies). In fact, Olweus contends that what characterizes victims of bullying is a combination of their anxious behavior and physical weakness. Bullies, on the other hand, are characterized by a combination of their aggressive behavior and physical strength.

In the United States, some researchers have noted that gender, racial background, ethnic affiliations, and sexual orientation may be risk factors for bully victimization (see Klipp, 2001, for a review of this issue). The literature on lesbian, gay, bisexual, transsexual, or queer (LGBT-Q) youth suggests that bullying in schools is a serious problem for students who are openly LGBT-Q. Moreover, this literature suggests that bully victimization is a serious problem for any student who is viewed as LGBT-Q (Klipp, 2001). Often, these students are teased, bullied, and harassed because of stereotypes based on their physical appearance, speech or motor patterns, or gendered social preferences. Students may be harassed only because they are deemed by the peer group to be LGBT-Q. Anti-LGBT-Q pejorative comments are commonly heard in the hallways and playgrounds of many U.S. schools (see Klipp, 2001). For boys, this appears to include the appearance of physical weakness or stereotypical "feminine" characteristics. For girls, these stereotypes seem to surround "male" characteristics (looking like a male, talking like a male; Klipp, 2001). Problems of LGBT-Q youth have not been addressed directly in bullying studies. Future studies should explore bullying that may be targeting other specific vulnerable groups surrounding gender, race, ethnic affiliations, religious practice, and physical disabilities. Most studies have not included these variables as possible risk factors or contributors to bully/victim behaviors.

Risk Factors Associated with Parenting Styles

Parenting of Bullies and Victims.   Researchers suggest that certain parenting styles increase the chances of a child becoming a bully. For example, a lack of emotional support for the child and a lack of overall parental involvement with the child tend to increase bullying behaviors (Batsche & Knoff, 1994; Bowers et al., 1994; Olweus, 1980, 1993; Rigby, 1994; Sullivan, 2000). Summarizing the research literature on parenting and bullying, Olweus (1993) suggests that there are four parenting factors that contribute to bullying behavior. Foremost among these is that parenting that is not characterized by warmth or direct involvement in the child's daily life increases the risk that the child will act out, often aggressively. Second, parents who do not set clear ground rules about what behavior is acceptable and unacceptable, or who are tolerant of their child's aggressive behavior, will likely increase the risk that the child will become a bully. This includes parents who use "power assertive" methods such as physical punishments on a frequent basis. Third, parents who model aggressive behavior in their daily interactions with others will likely increase the risk that the child will become a bully. This is the typical "violence begets violence" argument, which suggests that children learn violence through their exposure to it. Many other researchers support this perspective (e.g., Batsche & Knoff, 1994; Farrington, 1993). The fourth and final factor is that bullies tend to be born with a predisposition toward irritable temperaments. Olweus hypothesizes that parents of bullies may be less likely to know how to raise a child with a difficult temperament and thus the child's behavior is not addressed by the parents in a consistent manner. However, Olweus warns that this last factor has been shown to be relatively weak in empirical studies when compared with the first three parenting factors (Olweus, 1993).

Research suggests that victims of bullies tend to come from *overprotective* families. Thus, these children tend not to develop the assertive skills that make them less vulnerable to bullying (Bowers et al., 1994; Nansel et al., 2000; Sullivan, 2000). An important research finding regarding parenting practices of both victims and bullies is that parents have poor and deteriorating relationships with the school over time. Research indicates that parents of victims and of bullies are rarely aware of the bullying and victimization on a day-to-day basis (Olweus, 1993). Furthermore, parents rarely respond in any concrete way when they find out about bullying at school. Schools, on the other hand, tend not to contact parents of either victims or bullies on a regular basis unless the bullying results in severe physical injury (Olweus, 1991, 1993). Finally, over time, parents of victims and bullies develop negative views toward the school and the school toward these parents. This tends to create an atmosphere of noncooperation and a lack of contact between the home and school. Several researchers speculate that this dynamic prevents the problem of victimization and bullying from being addressed at home and at school.

Risk Factors Associated with School Characteristics

A great deal of research has been devoted to school characteristics that contribute to high rates of bullying behaviors. First, studies have identified school contexts as being the primary location where bullying occurs. Neighborhoods, communities, and home settings have far fewer bullying events than schools (Olweus, 1993). Nevertheless, even within the same communities there appears to be sizable variation in the bullying and victimization rates between different schools. Some studies (see Olweus, 1993, for a review) have shown that the risk of being victimized or becoming a bully is four to five times greater depending on the school. These consistent findings suggest that factors within the school have the capacity to increase or reduce levels of bullying and victimization.

School Size. It is commonly believed that the size of a school or a classroom is related to bullying in schools. However, studies indicate that the ratios of bullies and victims tend to be similar whether a school has a large or small student population. Educators frequently believe larger schools contribute to bullying because they actually have a larger absolute number of bullies and victims; however, the proportion is similar in most settings, despite school size (Olweus, 1993).

Location and Time. As with other forms of school violence, studies show that bullying and victimization mainly occur in specific locations and times in each school (Astor & Meyer, 1999, 2000; Astor, Meyer, & Behre, 1999; Astor, Meyer, & Pitner, 2001). Most commonly, playgrounds during recess and before/after school have high rates of bullying. The cafeteria and territories immediately outside of school grounds are also areas with high rates of bullying. Each school may have specific locations and times that tend to have clusters of bullying/victim rates by age, gender, ethnic group, or other variables. Elementary, middle schools, and high schools tend to have different organizational structures, and daily patterns that affect where, when, and with whom violent and bullying events occur (Astor et al., in press; Astor, Meyer, & Pitner, 2001). Lack of adult supervision in locations with many students tend to be highly associated with bullying behaviors, as they are with other forms of school violence such as fighting, sexual harassment, and verbal aggression.

In terms of the location of bullying, some interesting gender differences exist (see Astor & Meyer, 1999, for a discussion). The American Association of University Woman report (AAUW, 2001) shows that bullying and harassment happen primarily in schools. At the middle school level, the playground was the most common place that bullying was reported for both boys and girls (Ahmad & Smith, 1994). At the high school level, boys still reported the playground as the place where they were most commonly bullied; however, girls reported the classroom as the place they were most likely to be bullied.

School Climate, Awareness, and Policies. Negative school climate has also been implicated as a contributing risk factor for bullying. Schools that have a larger-than-average bullying problem tend to be characterized by an overall negative social climate (Rigby, 1996). In general, these schools tend to be less focused academically, students at these schools feel less satisfied with school life, and the teachers are less clear on what procedures to follow or their role/responsibility surrounding bullying events (Olweus et al., 1999; Sullivan, 2000).

The attitudes and behaviors of the school staff, particularly the teachers and the principal, play the most vital role in contributing to or decreasing bullying behaviors (Olweus et al., 1999). International studies suggest that what teachers and school staff do surrounding a bullying event makes a big difference in outcomes for both the bully and the victim as well as other students in the class (Smith et al., 1999). Early bullying studies suggested that on the whole, without specific training or an awareness of bullying patterns and their long-term effects, school staff tended to do "nothing" in response to persistent bullying (Olweus, 1993). Olweus also found that students were aware and critical of their teachers for their lack of response. For example, the vast majority of junior high and high school students reported that teachers almost never talked about bullying to individuals or their classes. Over 85 percent of secondary students said that their teachers did not respond or rarely responded to bullying events (Olweus, 1993). Recent studies on school violence in the United States and Israel report similar findings regarding students and their views of teachers who do not respond to violent situations at school (Astor, Meyer, & Behre, 1999; Benbenishty, Zeira, & Astor, 2000).

Studies have shown that the response of the peer group to bullying behaviors and their support of victims is essential to reduce bullying levels (Olweus, 1993). A crowd of students encouraging and cheering acts of bullying can have a very different effect than when the bully is confronted by multiple peers or older students who respond negatively to the bully or attempt to intervene (Besag, 1989; Olweus, 1993). Lack of a response by the peer group, by parents/caregivers, and by school staff has been identified as a risk factor for the perpetuation of bullying behaviors.

Olweus (1991, 1993; Olweus et al., 1999; see also Smith & Sharp, 1994; Smith et al., 1999, for a similar perspective) states that without schoolwide awareness of the problem, many of the methods recommended will not be effective. The lack of an overarching vision or ideology could also put schools at risk for bullying behaviors. Creating an ongoing awareness of the problem based on accurate data are key elements to prevention. He also states that the schools' approaches to dealing with bullying and victimization should emerge from a democratic principle rather than psychological theories alone. He believes that the schools' responses should mirror how people in a democratic society are expected to treat each other. This perspective moves the view of bully/victim problems from psychological theory to a more community/ecological oriented perspective that requires the mobilization of the entire school community. Olweus (1993) states:

> Bully/victim problems...concern some of our fundamental democratic principles: Every individual should have the right to be spared oppression and repeated, intentional humiliation, in school as in society at large. No student should have to be afraid of going to school for fear of being harassed or degraded and no parent should need to worry about such things happening to his or her child. (p. 48)

Based on this kind of philosophy, Olweus designed the first national (Norway) anti-bullying program. The following section will describe major components of the program.

Examples of Effective School-Based Bully/Victim Intervention Programs

Bullying Prevention Program, Norway. A comprehensive, nationwide anti-bullying program was first conducted in Norway (see Olweus, 1993, for details). This was the world's largest bullying intervention program, and other countries subsequently modeled or modified their programs based on this one. Norway's initial readiness to implement a national program came after some highly publicized suicides that were attributed to bully victimization on school grounds.* In an effort to reduce bully and victim problems, Olweus, along with the Norwegian government, developed a nationwide program for children in grades 1 through 9.

---

*Smith and colleagues (1999) comment that it is common for national bullying campaigns to begin after a highly publicized event such as a suicide or homicide that captures the public's attention. This kind of sequence was the beginning of bullying programs in Japan, Australia, Great Britain, and other countries. The United States is in a similar situation and this may be a good time to implement statewide or national programs.

The program has a clustering of simple interventions aimed at different school constituents, such as students, teachers, and parents. It also targets different levels of intervention, such as the entire school, whole classrooms, and specific individuals. Findings from 42 schools that participated in the program showed a *50 percent reduction in rates of bullying and victimization.* Furthermore, the positive effects of the program appeared to *increase over time* and there was an increase in student satisfaction with school life (Olweus, 1993).

Similar anti-bullying programs have been developed in Great Britain (see Sharp & Smith, 1994, and Smith & Sharp, 1994, for empirical evaluations and detailed practical procedures for educators) and Australia (Rigby, 1996). Evaluations of those programs also show significant reductions in aggressive behaviors and increases in student satisfaction with school life (especially during lunch and recess). We will review and describe programs from Norway, the United Kingdom, and Australia, as they have been implemented on a large scale and have empirical evidence to suggest strong reductions in bullying and aggression.

To date, large-scale anti-bullying programs have not yet been conducted in the United States. Nevertheless, Gottfredson (1997) reports positive effects from U.S.-based "capacity building programs" that focus on school improvement, staff development, and policy creation around issues of crime, violence, and discipline (e.g., Projects Pathe, Basis, and Status) but not bullying/victimization per se. These programs appear to have many of the school, classroom, and individual components developed in the Norwegian program. Specifically, these programs attempt to (1) increase the clarity of rules; (2) promote consistency of rule enforcement; (3) increase student and staff sense of responsibility and involvement around discipline issues; (4) create a sense of ownership to solve the school's violence problem; (5) focus on the entire school; (6) involve all school staff and students in owning their rules and consequences; (7) change the overall norms about school violence; and (8) target many levels (i.e., student, teacher, parent, administrator, classroom, individual school) of the school system with the interventions.

What is remarkable about this genre of Olweus's anti-bullying programs is that they reduced both the prevalence and incidence of bullying and victimization. The term *prevalence* refers to the number of cases or children in a given country that would fit the category of *bully. Incidence* refers to the number of new cases or chronic bullies or victims that emerge in a given year. In this situation, the program reduced the number of children who would have become chronic bullies. A reduction of incidence rates is a true hallmark of a successful primary prevention program—what that means in practical terms is that if a group of students had multiple risk factors that predisposed them to become bullies or victims, they may never actually develop into a bully or victim. Furthermore, the program's effects appear to be cumulative and increase over time (rather than decrease, as is usually the case with many current interventions in the United States). One reason for this increase in effect size could be related to the fact that school staff felt ownership over the program and the interventions were easy to implement.

Table 19.1 represents a schematic overview of Olweus's program. As can be seen in the table, there are multiple components at the school, classroom, and individual student level (Olweus, 1993). Those components considered "core" are marked by a ++. Those components considered highly desirable are marked by a + (as defined by Olweus et al., 1999). However, it should be noted that these separate interventions are more powerful

TABLE 19.1   Overview of the Olweus Anti-Bully Intervention Program

MEASURES AT SCHOOL LEVEL	MEASURES AT CLASS LEVEL	MEASURES AT THE INDIVIDUAL LEVEL
GENERAL PREREQUISITES: AWARENESS AND INVOLVEMENT ++		
■ Questionnaire survey ++	■ Class rules against bullying: clarification, praise, and sanctions ++	■ Serious talks with bullies and victims ++
■ School conference day on bully/victim problems ++	■ Regular class meetings ++	■ Serious talks with parents of involved students ++
■ Better supervision during recess and lunch time ++	■ Role-playing, literature	■ Teacher and parent use of imagination
■ More attractive school playground	■ Cooperative learning	■ Help from "neutral" students +
■ Contact telephone +	■ Common positive class activities	■ Help and support for parents
■ Meeting staff and parents +	■ Class meeting teacher/parents/children ++	■ Discussion groups for parents of bullies and victims
■ Teacher groups for the development of the social milieu of the school		■ Change of class or school
■ Parent circles		

Note: A ++ sign indicates components that appear to be core to the program's success. A + sign is not core but considered highly desirable by Olweus and other bullying researchers.

Source: Adapted from Olweus (1993, p. 64). See Olweus (1993) for further explanation.

when they are all implemented together. These components are implemented across the entire social system of the school rather than targeting bullies or one segment of the school social system alone. This way, bus drivers, children in all classes, parents, teachers, yard monitors, and others in the school community are all part of any specific strategy developed by the school. We will elaborate on only select components of this approach.

At the school level, creating an atmosphere of awareness, involvement, and urgency among the staff and students are the most important underlying components. There are several ways this can be accomplished. Having students, school staff, and parents conduct a comprehensive schoolwide survey is considered a requirement. With survey results, each group has the opportunity to respond to the data generated by other school constituencies. The compilation and analysis of survey results can suggest specific areas for intervention that were not evident to the school before conducting the survey. Having a school conference day is also suggested as a core component. When a school has committed itself to addressing the bullying problem, it is important to bring together teachers, school staff, pupil personnel staff, and selected parents and representatives of the student population to develop a short- and long-term action plan. This may include a set of principles surrounding the school's policy and approach to bullying and victims. It may also include the creation of ongoing programs and structures (e.g., committees or coordinating groups) that could deal with bullying. The main objective of the day-long conference is to create a collective commitment and responsibility for running the anti-bullying program.

Another school-level component of a successful anti-bullying approach is to create effective supervision plans during recess, lunch, and before/after school. School maps and surveys can be used to identify other bullying-prone locations that may require further supervision. A focus on bullying-prone locations and times is often neglected by schools in their planning, and this component is believed to be a major contributor for the overall reduction of bullying. (More examples of this will be discussed later in the chapter.)

Notifying parents of both bullies and victims immediately after bullying events is an intervention that stems directly from the research literature on parents' lack of awareness regarding school bullying events. Calling parents after each bullying/victim event raises the awareness of the parent/guardian and serves as an additional constraint for bullies and as a potential support for victims. In these phone conversations, parents/guardians are simply informed about what happened and what disciplinary measures the school took. Parents would, of course, need to be prepared before a school institutes such a phone call policy. If the bully/victim problem persists over a short period of time, the parents may be called in to problem solve and generate joint school/home solutions to the problem.

At the classroom level, clearly defining rules and consequences for bullying is essential. Rewarding and encouraging peers to help victims or discourage bullies is also an effective approach. Another effective approach is to schedule regular meetings where students can discuss the topic of bullying openly. In these class meetings, students could bring up class or personal issues they are having with bullying or victimization. These kinds of meetings make bullying visible to the entire class as well as to the teacher. Meetings elevate the importance of dealing with bullying problems, as well as allowing students to generate ideas surrounding interpersonal and schoolwide solutions to bullying problems. Integrating themes of bullying into the regular literature curriculum is also a widely used method. Sometimes it is easier for students to talk about fictional characters before talking about similar situations at their school. Integrating bullying themes into the literature curricula offers a unique opportunity to have class discussions about bullies/victims and the school's role.

At the individual level, making sure every bullying and victim event is taken seriously with formal student and parent talks regarding the incident appears to be important in reducing the incidence level. The use of imagination to engage individual students in the process is also an important component. For example, the students and teacher could develop ways through the arts that help students express or deal with their feelings surrounding bullying and victimization. Finding creative means to help bullies and victims could entail writing poetry, the visual arts, creative writing, drama, video construction, or an array of self-generated interventions. The primary focus should be centered on using every means available to stop the cycle at the individual level.

U.K. Sheffield Anti-Bullying Project, Great Britain.   Smith and Sharp (1994) adapted an Olweus-type model in Great Britain. Compared with Olweus, Smith and Sharp provide a greater level of detail and empirical evidence surrounding components of the model. This project involved 23 schools in Sheffield, England (16 primary and 7 secondary schools).

The program emphasized two main components: developing a whole-school policy on bullying and offering a series of optional interventions.

Developing a Policy on Bullying. Bullying is understood as a problem of the school system rather than of particular bullies and victims. Hence, the cornerstone of the program is efforts to change the school climate and organization and create a "bully-proof" environment. The whole-school policy is "a statement of intent which guides actions and organization within the school" (Sharp & Smith, 1994, p. 23). Both the process leading to the anti-bullying policy and its content involve the whole school—principals, teaching and nonteaching staff, students, and parents. It helps to bring all these groups to shared commitments and goals surrounding the program.

In this program, most of the school policies include the rationale of the policy that clearly indicates that the school identifies bullying as a serious problem that should not be tolerated. The policy should state that the goal is the reduction or elimination of bullying behaviors. Most policy statements also include a set of rules and guidelines that explicate clearly what behaviors are considered bullying, what is to be done to prevent bullying, what should be done and documented when bullying occurs, and what the consequences are for the students involved. These policies clarify who is responsible for performing each task, and what organizational units (such as committees and student councils) should be operating as part of the policy (for examples of school policies, see Sullivan, 2000).

Optional Interventions. All schools that participated in the project implemented a *whole-school policy* as their main intervention. In addition, a range of optional interventions were offered to the schools. These interventions can be grouped as follows:

■ *Curriculum-based strategies.* These educational activities and materials are used within the curriculum to enhance awareness and understanding of the problem and teach coping skills. These interventions include *quality circles* of students meeting to solve problems of bullying; video for classroom discussion; a video presentation of a play about bullying; drama and role-play; the use of relevant children's literature; and creative writing.

■ *Direct work with students.* These activities are designed to get all students involved in efforts to prevent and address bullying and work with victims and bullies. These interventions include assertiveness training for victims, school tribunals (or bully "courts") to deal with complaints and reports about bullying, and peer counseling. The interventions also include *Pika's Method of Shared Concern*, which is particularly appropriate in situations that involve a group bullying one or more students (see details in Sullivan, 2000, Chapter 16). A similar approach is called the *No Blame Approach* (Maines & Robinson, 1992, 1998).

■ *Changes to playgrounds and lunch breaks.* These interventions are aimed at changing organizational and physical aspects of school environment, which include training lunchtime supervisors and redesigning playground environments. Boulton (1994) describes in detail the training provided to supervisors (similar to hall monitors) to improve their abilities to identify bullying, collaborate with teaching staff to respond appropriately to aggression, resolve conflicts, encourage positive behavior, and use sanctions effectively. Higgins (1994) provides detailed information on ways in which playgrounds may be improved in order to reduce bullying. Her work addresses issues of boredom, crowding, marginalization of younger or minority students who are excluded from playing areas, and "hard to supervise areas." She proposes engaging students in helping to redesign the organizational and physical aspects of the playgrounds. These may include planting trees, improving structures and surfaces (e.g., planting grass), and adding activities. Changes may also include creating and enforcing a schedule that allocates time and space fairly among the various age groups in the school.

Smith and Sharp (1994) report that in a pre-post design, they found that in primary schools they could see appreciable reduction in numbers of victims, averaging 15 percent across all schools and in some schools up to 80 percent. These changes were much more modest in most secondary schools. Most schools participating in the project show reductions in the number of students reporting that they bullied others. These authors also report indications that the intensity of involvement in the project was correlated with many of the outcomes that these schools achieved. It is interesting to note that the authors suggest that schools that are more active in their efforts to reduce bullying may not show the full extent of their improvements because they simultaneously increase the students' awareness of bullying, who tend to report more than students in other schools (for a similar point, see Rigby & Slee, 1999, p. 335).

P.E.A.C.E., Australia.   Slee (in cooperation with Rigby) developed a program called P.E.A.C.E., which includes a booklet and series of worksheets containing ideas and details on workshops. The acronym describes the steps in this program:

P. *Preparation.* Provide information on bullying and its effects to all school constituents, to form a basis for involvement and policy development.

E. *Education.* Gather information about the school policies and the status of bullying in school, including carrying out student surveys.

A. *Action.* Identify what actions can be taken and in what ways the school system can be accessed.

C. *Coping.* Implement interventions in school that target attitudes regarding bullying, behavioral strategies to change responses to bullying, and curriculum development.

E. *Evaluation.* Assess to what extent things have changed and what should be done in the future.

Rigby and Slee (1999) conclude that results have been supportive of the use of the program, with reports of 25 percent reductions in bullying.

The Process of Developing and Implementing Anti-Bullying Programs

The review of the literature strongly suggests that anti-bully programs should be developed and implemented in a process that would ensure their relevance and applicability to each specific site. In our assessment, one reason for the promising results of bullying programs in Europe and Australia has to do with the implementation process and underlying philosophical approaches of the programs. Important assumptions of the bullying programs center on (1) the belief that the efforts to "fit" a program to a school involves *grass-roots* participation, (2) a belief that students and teachers in the school need to be *empowered* to deal with the problem, (3) a belief that *democracy* is the core of a good bullying program, and (4) a belief that schools should demonstrate a *proactive vision* surrounding the bullying problem in their school. The implementation of interventions or components of the program are slightly different for each school site. These beliefs enable each school to adapt the program or general principles to their unique demographic, philosophical, and organizational needs. This is a very different process than many "skills oriented" curricular approaches used in the United States.

One other major difference exists between the bullying programs cited here and the anti-violence programs in the United States: Bullying programs begin with an overriding belief that *data* are necessary for the successful adaptation of the bullying program to each school. Hence, an important element of successful bullying programs is the use of data in an ongoing and interactive manner. Figure 19.1 represents our interpretation of the cycle of monitoring and how data should be used to maintain successful anti-bullying programs.

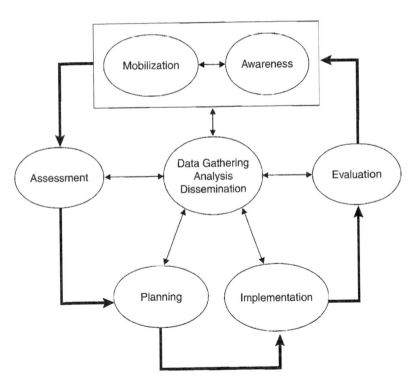

FIGURE 19.1   The Role of Data in the Development and Implementation of Interventions

This perspective proposes that the continuous and ongoing analysis and interpretation of data is an essential part of the intervention process. Data are used to create awareness, mobilize different school constituents, assess the extent of the problem, plan interventions, and serve as the basis for implementation and evaluation. Information is provided continually to different groups in each step of the intervention process. By contrast, many U.S. schools purchase evidence-based programs but do not actually collect any data about their own district or school. Schools in the United States rarely use data to inform the process described in Figure 19.1.

For example, we argue that the process of introducing data allows each school to identify its specific needs, limitations, strengths, and resources so that choices can be made regarding which specific interventions and components to implement. Moreover, the process of building and implementing anti-bullying programs is continuous and cyclical, always changing to respond to new circumstances and emerging needs. Hence, the evaluation of the progress after programs are implemented becomes a reassessment of the situation, leading to a new cycle of awareness building, planning, the implementation of modified programs, evaluation of their success, and so on. Not having site-specific and comparative data at the school site level could be a significant obstacle in (1) assessing whether that specific school has a bully/victim problem, (2) adapting an anti-bullying program, and (3) evaluating the implementation process and outcomes of the program over time.

Olweus and other researchers on bullying do not provide detailed information on how schools or practitioners should collect accurate and usable data to establish the extent of bullying within their schools. Given how important this step is for the success of the project, we believe this warrants further elaboration. Also, the reader should note that there is no mention in the bullying literature about the creation of a school *district-level* policy or *district data* on bullying or victimization. Most of the intervention literature remains primarily at the school-site level. Most often, it is the school district that has the expendable resources to implement districtwide interventions such as the anti-bullying program. In the next portion of this chapter, we present two *schoolwide/data-based* approaches surrounding bully/victim programs that depart from an individual/student orientation. The following sections on monitoring and school mapping are presented as quantitative and qualitative processes that help create a "whole-school response" and that help the school identify, create, and/or adapt programs to the site.

Monitoring at the School-District Level: Examples from the Hertzelia School District, Israel. Two authors of this chapter (Benbenishty and Astor) conducted a multiyear project examining the uses of data (as shown in Figure 19.1) for an entire school district in Israel.* The district annually surveyed all of their students. Therefore, each school had comparative data for specific types of perpetration and victimization involved with bullying. The school violence and bullying data were then provided to each of 29 schools in the district to inform assessment, planning, and evaluation of grass-roots projects developed by the teachers and students in each school. Schools in this project were able to compare

*Funded by the Kellogg Foundation, the University of Michigan School of Social Work's Global Youth Initiative, Hebrew University, and the Hertzelia School District.

themselves by grades, by gender groups, and between other schools in their district. We will highlight the advantages of such an approach for bully/victim interventions.

Comparing a School Site to District Student Victimization Norms. One school wanted to know how it compared with other schools in its district on specific kinds of bullying/ victim behaviors. The local media were suggesting that this specific school had problems with sexual harassment bullying behaviors. Prior to monitoring, the school staff was not sure if their school was similar or higher than the school district norms. Consequently, the information from Figure 19.2 was helpful because it showed that the school was lower than the district average on every sexual harassment item. This information helped teachers, parents, and the media situate the extent of the school problem within their district and counter harmful media stereotypes about this school with regard to sexual harassment. The data also raised awareness in the school as to which types of behaviors were most prevalent in the school (e.g., unwanted sexual touching, unwanted removal of parts of clothing). The issues presented in the data were brought to the teachers, students, and principal in forums where they could discuss what could/should be done to address the issue. The school then focused on developing interventions around these data. After several months of interventions, these behaviors were measured again to see if the new policies

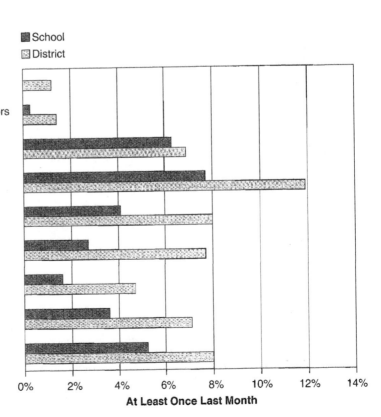

FIGURE 19.2 Sexual Harassment: A Comparison between the School and the District

and grass-roots interventions reduced the prevalence of sexual harassment behaviors in their school.

Assessment: Identifying Target Groups.   Identifying specific target groups for interventions is another way data can/should be used. District administrators were particularly interested in knowing if students in their district who were victimized were also perpetrators. Students who were both bullies and victims may require different types of interventions. Some of this concern came from the numerous U.S. school shootings that received media attention.

Figure 19.3 shows the percent of students in this district that reported being both *victims and perpetrators* by grade and by gender. It showed two distinct patterns for boys and girls who fit the criteria of high victimization and perpetration in their district. It suggested that far more boys fit the dual criteria than girls. Girls who were both victims and perpetrators had relatively stable rates throughout the grade span. Boys who fit the criteria had greater variability from a low of 15 percent in twelfth grade to a high of 30 percent in seventh grade. This suggested that there may be a need to have a dual gender-oriented strategy when targeting students who were both victims and perpetrators. It also suggested that prevention programs should begin at least by the fourth grade. This information was extremely helpful for the district in addressing its particular concerns surrounding students who were both bullies and victims. For this group of students, teachers and parents decided

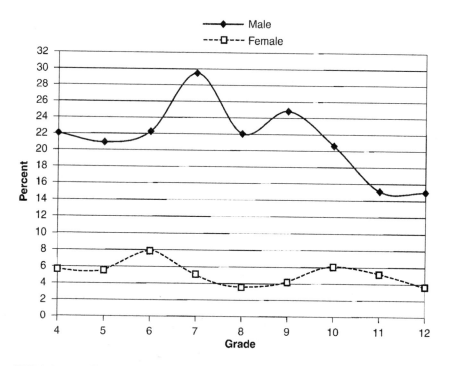

FIGURE 19.3   Percent of Students in District Who Report High Victimization and Perpetration by Grade and Gender

to develop policies and procedures focused on the process of provocation and retribution. They also had forums where teachers and students could address ways to help students who were both bullies and victims. Students revealed that this group was an easy target because they already had a reputation as a bully and teachers would not believe them when there was an altercation. This information made teachers more responsive to situations where children (who were bullies) suggested that other students were also bullying them.

Evaluation: Assessing Change Following Interventions. A school that uses this monitoring system to identify particular problem areas could then track progress in reducing bullying in this location over time. For example, one junior high school wanted to know where violence most often occurred in its school. Using the process outlined in Figure 19.1, it used the data to develop specific interventions generated by teachers and students around certain locations (e.g., increased monitoring, school beautification projects, alterations to the schedule so not too many students are in the hallways at the same time). They then monitored progress in specific areas in their school over time. Figure 19.4 represents a comparison between the 1999–2000 and 2000–2001 academic years in a school that implemented intervention programs during 2000–2001. Figure 19.4 suggests that the students' perceptions of danger decreased in all the targeted areas when compared to the prior

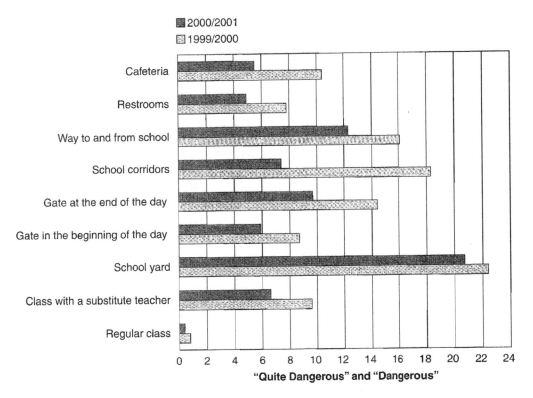

FIGURE 19.4 Specific Places Perceived by Students to Be Dangerous in a School, by School Year

year, before the intervention was initiated. This was not readily evident by data collected from focus groups. The figure represented the views of the entire student body.

Each of the 29 school sites in the district used this flexible monitoring system in different ways depending on its specific kinds of bully/victim problems. The programs adopted by schools were quite diverse but included school beatification projects (murals, planting grass/plants, targeting violence-prone locations), increasing student/staff ratios in key times and locations, efforts to improve staff and school morale, traditional bully/victim programs, creation of policies and procedures surrounding bullying, and community interventions that targeted locations where students felt unsafe walking to and from schools due to bullies.

A Qualitative Data Process: Mapping Violence within the School.   This procedure is designed to involve school constituents in revealing how bully/victim issues and other forms of violence within a school building interact with locations, patterns of the school day, and social organizational variables (e.g., teacher and student relationships, teachers' professional roles, and the school's organizational response to violence; for more detail, see Astor et al., 1999; Astor & Meyer, 1999; Astor et al., 2001). An important goal of this procedure is to *allow students and teachers to convey their personal theories* about why specific locations and times in their schools are more dangerous. This approach assumes that students, teachers, school staff, and administrators have important information that should be the foundation for *setting specific* interventions. Usually, interventions emerge from the information presented by the students, teachers, staff, and administrators in each school. Most successful bullying interventions involve a spatial and temporal analysis because many of the interventions are centered around specific bullying/victim prone locations.

Mapping, Interviews, and Interventions.   The first step in this assessment procedure is obtaining a map of the school. Ideally, the map should contain all internal school territory, including the areas surrounding the school and playground facilities. In some communities where the routes to and from school are dangerous, a simple map of the surrounding neighborhood may be added to the assessment process (see Meyer & Astor, in press, for a description of this process). The school maps are an essential part of the interviewing process. They help to anchor discussions to places and times in ways that interviews about "issues" alone cannot. The focus groups should begin with the facilitator distributing two sets of identical school maps to each individual.

Maps A and B.   Two photocopied maps of the school are needed for each student and teacher. A first map should be used to determine what students and teachers believe to be the location of the greatest number of bully events in or around the school building. Participants should be asked to identify the locations (on the maps) of up to three of the most violent events that occurred within the past academic year. Next to each marked event on the map, participants are asked to write the following information: (1) the general time frame of the event (e.g., before school, after school, morning period, afternoon period, evening sports event, between classes, etc.); (2) the grade and gender of those involved in the violence; and (3) their knowledge of any organizational response to the event (e.g., sent to principal's office, suspended, sent to peer counselor, nothing, etc.). On the second map, members should be asked to circle *areas* or *territories* that they perceive to be unsafe or potentially dangerous. This second map provides information about areas within the school that participants avoid or fear, even though they may not possess knowledge of a particular event.

Discussion of Violent Events and Areas. The first part of the group discussion should center on the specific bully events and the areas marked as unsafe or dangerous on the participants' personal maps. We have asked questions such as, "Are there times when those places you've marked on the maps are less safe?"; "Is there a particular group of students that is more likely to get hurt there?"; and "Why do you think that area has so many incidents involving bully/victim events?" The overall purpose of the group interviews is to explore why bullying or victimization occurs at those specific times. Consequently, the interviews should also focus on gathering information regarding the organizational response to the event (e.g., "What happened to the two students after the event?"; "Did the hall monitors intervene when they saw what happened?"), procedures (e.g., "What happens when the students are sent to the office after a fight?"; "Did anyone call the parents of the bully or victim?"), follow-up (e.g., "Do the teachers, hall monitors, and/or administrators follow-up on any consequences given to the students?"; "Did anyone check on the welfare of the victim?"), and clarity of procedures (e.g., "Does it matter who stops the bullying?" [e.g., a volunteer, security guard, teacher, or principal]).

Interviewers should also explore participants' ideas for solutions to the specific bully problems (e.g., "Can you think of ways to avoid bullying or victimization in that place?"; "If you were the principal what would you do to make that place safer?"). In addition, the interviewer should explore any obstacles participants foresee with implementation (e.g., "Do you think that type of plan is realistic?"; "Has that been tried before? What happened?"; or "Do you think that plan would work?"). Such obstacles could range from issues related to roles (e.g., "It's not my job to monitor students during lunch"), to discipline policy and issues of personal safety (e.g., "I don't want to intervene because I may get hurt").

In schools that already have programs designed to address school violence, specific questions should be asked about the effectiveness of those interventions, why they work or do not work, and what could be done to make the current measures more effective. We recommend that the interviewer ask both subjective questions (e.g., "Do you think the anti-bullying program is working? Why do you think it works or why does it not work?") as well as specific questions related to the reduction of bullying/victimization (e.g., "Do you believe the anti-bully program has reduced the number of bullying events on the playground? Why or why not?").

Transferring all of the reported events onto one large map of the school enables students and staff to locate specific "hot spots" for violence and dangerous time periods within each individual school. The combined data are presented to all school constituents and they are asked to once again discuss and interpret the maps. Teachers and students use the maps and interviews to suggest ways to improve the settings. For example, in one school, events were clustered by time, age, gender, and location. In the case of older students (eleventh- and twelfth-graders), events were clustered in the parking lot outside of the auxiliary gym immediately after school, whereas for younger students (ninth- and tenth-graders), events were reported in the lunchroom and hallways during transition periods. For this school, the map suggested that interventions be geared specifically toward older students, directly after school, by the main entrance, and in the school parking lot. Students and teachers agreed that increasing the visible presence of school staff in and around the parking lot for the 20 minutes after school had great potential for reducing many violent events. Younger students were experiencing violence mainly before, during, and after lunch, near the cafeteria. Many students expressed feelings of being unsafe between classes in the hallways.

Compiling all the interview suggestions into themes is an important second step in creating context relevant interventions. Students, teachers, and administrators may have differing viewpoints regarding the organizational response of the school when victimization happened. Relaying the diversity of responses to students, teachers, and administrators can provide an opportunity for reflection and may generate ways to remedy the bully/victim problem in certain situations. When the data are presented to students, teachers, and administrators, they can focus their discussions on why those areas are dangerous and what kinds of interventions can be done to make the location safer. The data are collected and used in different stages of the process outlined in Figure 19.1. Both the monitoring and mapping methods provide data-based approaches to gathering information about bullying/victimization in schools. Moreover, they provide specific information, which makes it easier for schools to address these problems.

CONCLUSION

Bullying in schools existed long before researchers began to explore the phenomenon. Fortunately, there is a large and rich international research and intervention literature that suggests it is possible to reduce dramatically the levels of both victimization and perpetration by bullies. These bully intervention programs have been replicated in many different countries and cultures (Smith et al., 1999). Therefore, these kinds of interventions, if implemented in the United States, could also show some positive effects. One major difference between the international programs and ones in the United States are that the international programs are based on school site data. Therefore, all interventions are (1) created and adapted to fit the school site and (2) involve the entire school setting. This requires a high degree of commitment and awareness of school staff to change the organizational response of the school to bullying. Many of the currently popular U.S. anti-school violence programs are curricular based and geared at improving students' social skills. Few U.S. violence prevention programs are focused on altering the whole-school climate, policy, and procedures. Moreover, few U.S. programs involve the principal and the entire teaching staff during the adaptation and implementation phase (for an example of a U.S. risk behavior program that does includes some components of school-level system changes, see Hawkins, Catalano, Kosterman, Abbott, & Hill, 1999).

Programs that focus on the entire school community have a greater likelihood of being sustained over time and showing strong reductions in victimization. In the Norwegian intervention study, Olweus (1993) reported a 50 percent reduction in bully/victim problems after the implementation of the program. On the U.S. national scale, this would translate into millions of bullying and victimization acts that could be prevented. Given such a strong and successful intervention strategy, it is no longer a question of how we reduce bully and victim problems, but rather a question of our willingness as a country to engage in what has already been shown to be effective.

DISCUSSION QUESTIONS

Please read the following comments about bullying made by different students.

STUDENT 1

I think the girls are bullies too, it's not just the boys with fighting and stuff. I mean the girls do stuff that really hurts your feelings and you'll remember for the rest of your life. Like, there is one girl named Mary that got lots of the other girls to ditch me at our final school trip to a roller coaster park.... She knew I'd be left alone and I cried for a long time. She seemed happy when she heard I was upset. But she keeps on picking on me for no reason and getting the other kids to do nasty things to me. Like she found a way to keep me out of a talent show by having all the rehearsals at her house and not telling me about them. At school she said they were not rehearsing. Then the day of the talent show she told me that she didn't want me to dance in the show because I would ruin the dance because I'm a bad dancer, which isn't true—I've always been one of the best dancers in my school. She wanted to hurt my feelings again—she even told some of the other girls she hated me. She started to spread rumors and lies about me and another boy. She told some of my friends that she did not like me and thought I was a nerd. She's never said it to me to my face but my friends say she's telling everyone lies about me. She does this to other girls, too. —12-year-old female middle school student

1. Is this situation a form of bullying or do you think that these kinds of situations are a part of normal adolescent development? Explain.

2. How do you distinguish between normal adolescent friendship patterns and bullying behaviors?

3. Is this student a victim of bullying? Why or why not?

4. How should these kinds of situations be dealt with in schools?

5. Do you think boys and girls need separate kinds of interventions surrounding bullying and victimization? Why or why not?

STUDENT 2

There are different cliques in my school, some are more popular than other ones. Like the jocks are like the school heroes but some of the football and basketball team players are mean bullies that pick on immigrant students all the time. They tease the nerdy kids too and try to humiliate them in front of everyone else. Lots of students think it's funny when they trip or push someone who is different from them. One boy is only in sixth grade and they call him "Mr. Penis Head" because he wears a turban on his head because of his religion. They've been picking on him all year. I thought that was so mean because it was his religion and culture and he can't do anything about it. They would slap him from behind on his head or try and pull at his turban, make fun of his religion, and get other kids to be mean to him on the bus and at lunch. One day when I told them to stop, they started picking on me too. I went to the principal and told on them—I waited a long time to tell on them and I did not want anyone to know that I was the one who told on them. They called them in to talk with the principal and they [the jocks] haven't done anything to that boy since I told on them. The bus driver also chewed them out one day in front of everyone. So I know the principal talked to her too. I don't think they know that I was the one who told on them. —11-year-old female middle school student

1. Compare this situation described by Student 2 with the situation described by Student 1. In what ways are the situations similar and in what ways are they different?

2. Should witness students be encouraged to tell adults when they see bullying behaviors? Why or why not? Should they be allowed to tell anonymously? Why or why not?

3. What are the roles and responsibilities of the "bystander" witnessing bullying?

4. Should witnesses who encourage the bully be held responsible as well as the bully? Why or why not?

5. Should the school have separate responses to different kinds of bullying? Explain.

6. In this instance, the student was bullied because of his ethnic and religious practice. Is this form of bullying different from bullying for other reasons? Or are the final outcomes essentially the same for the victim of bullying? Why or why not?

SUGGESTED READINGS

Nansel, T., Overpeck, M., Pilla, R., Ruan, W., Simons-Morton, B., & Scheidt, P. (2001). Bullying behaviors among U.S. youth: Prevalence and association with psychosocial adjustment. *Journal of the American Medical Association, 285,* 2094–2100.

Olweus, D. (1993). *Bullying at school.* Cambridge, MA: Blackwell Publishers.

Sharp, S., & Smith, P. (1994). *Tackling bullying in your school: A practical handbook for teachers.* London, England: Routledge.

Smith, P., Morita, Y., Junger-Tas, J., Olweus, D., Catalano, R., & Slee, P. (1999). *The nature of school bullying: A cross-national perspective.* New York: Routledge.

Sullivan, K. (2000). *The anti-bullying handbook.* Auckland, NZ: Oxford University Press.

INTERNATIONAL RESOURCES

http://www.luckyduck.co.uk   This website features videos, books, and training materials published by Lucky Duck. The publications are listed in the following categories: bullying; self-esteem; circle time materials; special needs; social skills; equal opportunities; secondary emotional literacy; and writing and movement.

Australian bullying site: http://www.education.unisa.edu.au/bullying/   This website provides information that helps people understand more about bullying in schools and how it can be stopped. It presents several Internet sources and various related articles on bullying and harassment, and the current suggestions that are being made to overcome this problem.

Sample questionnaire: http://www.education.unisa.edu.au/bullying/questdescrip.htm   This website provides information on the Peer Relations Questionnaire (PRQ), the Peer Relations Assessment Questionnaire, and the computer-based questionnaire known as the Relations Assessment Package (SRAP).

Canadian bullying site: http://www.crime-prevention.org/english/main.html   This website provides information by the National Crime Prevention Center, which is responsible for implementing the National Strategy on Community Safety and Crime Prevention.

Scotland bullying site: http://www.scre.ac.uk/bully   On this website, the Scottish Council for Research in Education (SCRE) provides extensive information about bullying and what can be done to help the problem.

RESOURCES

Colorado Center for the Prevention of Violence   http://www.Colorado.EDU/cspv   This website features extensive violence prevention information produced by the Center for the Study and Prevention of Violence (CSPV). CSPV has a threefold mission: (1) collecting research literature and resources on the causes and prevention of violence; (2) offering technical assistance for the evaluation and development of violence prevention programs; and (3) maintaining a basic research component on the causes of violence and the effectiveness of prevention/ intervention programs.

National School Safety Center   http://www.NSSC1.org/   This website is devoted to providing information that helps combat school safety problems. Provided in this website are books, resource papers, films, and workshops on school safety-related topics.

National Center for Educational Statistics   http://nces.ed.gov   This website provides data from several National Center for Educational Statistics (NCES) sources, including the Condition of Education, the Digest of Education Statistics, and the Projections of Education Statistics.

Department of Justice   http://www.ojp.usdoj.gov/bjs/   This website provides data from the Bureau of Justice Statistics. Statistics are provided in the following categories: crime and victims; criminal offenders; special topics; law enforcement; prosecution; federal justice system; courts and sentencing; corrections; expenditures and employment; and criminal record systems.

National Resource Center for Safe Schools   http://www.safetyzone.org   This website provides information for schools, communities, and state and local education agencies in hopes to create safe learning environments and prevent school violence.

REFERENCES

Ahmad, Y., & Smith, P. K. (1994). Bullying in schools and the issue of sex differences. In J. Archer (Ed.), *Male violence* (pp. 70–83). New York: Routlege.

American Association of University Women. (2001). *Hostile hallways: Bullying, teasing, and sexual harassment.* Washington, DC: Author.

Astor, R., Behre, W., Wallace, J., & Fravil, K. (1998). School social workers and school violence: Personal safety, violence programs and training. *Social Work, 43,* 223–232.

Astor, R., Benbenishty, R., Pitner, R., & Meyer, H. A. (in press). Monitoring and mapping school violence. In L. A. Rapp-Paglicci, A. Roberts, & J. Wodarski (Eds.), *Handbook of violence.* New York: Wiley.

Astor, R., & Meyer, H. (1999). Where girls and women won't go: Female students', teachers', and school social workers' views of school safety. *Social Work in Education, 21,* 201–219.

Astor, R. A., & Meyer, H. (2001). The conceptualization of violence prone school sub-contexts: Is the sum of the parts greater than the whole? *Urban Education, 36,* 374–399.

Astor, R., Meyer, H., & Behre, W. (1999). Unowned places and times: Maps and interviews about violence in high schools. *American Educational Research Journal, 36,* 3–42.

Astor, R., Meyer, H., & Pitner, R. (2001). Elementary and middle school students' perceptions of violence-prone school subcontexts. *The Elementary School Journal, 101,* 511–528.

Batsche, G., & Knoff, H. (1994). Bullies and their victims: Understanding a pervasive problem in schools. *School Psychology Review, 23,* 165–174.

Benbenishty, R., & Astor, R. A. (in press). Cultural specific and cross-cultural bully/ victim patterns. In P. K. Smith, (Ed.), *Violence in schools: The response in Europe*. London: Routledge Falmer.

Benbenishty, R., Zeira, A., & Astor, R. A. (2000). *A national study of school violence in Israel—Wave II: Fall 1999*. Israeli Ministry of Education, Jerusalem.

Berrill, K. (1990). Anti-gay violence and victimization in the U.S.: An overview. *Journal of Interpersonal Violence: Special Issue, 5*, 274–294.

Besag, V. (1989). *Bullies and victims in schools: A guide to understanding and management*. Philadelphia: Open University Press.

Bosworth, K., Espelage, D., & Simon, T. (1999). Factors associated with bullying behavior in middle school students. *Journal of Early Adolescence, 19*, 341–362.

Boulton, M. (1993). Aggressive fighting in British middle school children. *Educational Studies, 19*, 19–39.

Bowers, L., Smith, P., & Binney, V. (1994). Perceived family relationships of bullies, victims and bully/ victims in middle childhood. *Journal of Social and Personal Relationships, 11*, 215–232.

Bragg, R. (1997, December 3). Forgiveness, after 3 die in Kentucky shooting; M. Carneal opens fire on fellow students at Heath High School in West Paducah. *New York Times*, p. A16.

Burcky, W., Reuterman, N., & Kopsky, S. (1988). Dating violence among high school students. *School Counselor, 35*, 353–358.

Byrne, B. (1999). Ireland. In P. K. Smith et al. (Eds.), *The nature of school bullying: A cross-national perspective*. London & New York: Routledge.

Cano, A., Avery-Leaf, S., Cascardi, M., & O'Leary, K. (1998). Dating violence in two high school samples: Discriminating variables. *Journal of Primary Prevention, 18*, 431–446.

Elam, S., Rose, L., & Gallup, A. (1996). The 28th annual Phi Delta Kappa/Gallup poll of the public's attitudes toward the public schools. *Phi Delta Kappan, 78*, 41–59.

Franklin, A. (2001, May 28). Law would address school policies on bullying. *Associated Press Article*.

Gegax, T., Adler, J., & Pedersen, D. (1998, April 6). The boys behind the ambush. *Newsweek, 131*, 21–24.

Goldstein, A. (1996). *The psychology of vandalism*. New York: Plenum Press.

Gottfredson, D. (1997). School based crime prevention. In L. Sherman, D. Gottfredson, D. MacKenzie, J. Eck, P. Reuter, & S. Bushway (Eds.), *Preventing crime: What works, what doesn't, what's promising: A report to the United States Congress*. Washington, DC: Department of Justice. http://www.ncjrs.org/works/chapter5.htm.

Hawkins, J. D., Catalano, R. F., Kosterman, R., Abbott, R., & Hill, K. G. (1999). Preventing adolescent health-risk behaviors by strengthening protection during childhood. *Archives of Pediatric and Adolescent Medicine, 153*, 226–234.

Hays, K. (1998, April 26). Boy held in teacher's killing. *The Detroit News & Free Press*, p. 5A.

Higgins, C. (1994). Improving the school ground environment as an anti-bullying intervention. In P. K. Smith & S. Sharp (Eds.), *School bullying* (pp. 160–192). London: Routledge.

Hyman I. A., & Snook P. A. (2000). Dangerous schools and what you can do about them. *Phi Delta Kappan, 81*, 7, 488–501.

Kachur, P., Stennies, G., Powell, K., Modzeleski, W., Stephens, R., Murphy, R., Kresnow, M., Sleet, D., & Lowry, R. (1996). School-associated violent deaths in the United States, 1992 to 1994. *Journal of the American Medical Association, 275*, 1729–1733.

Kaufman, P., Chen, X., Choy, S., Ruddy, S., Miller, A., Fleury, J., Chandler, K., Rand, M., Klause, P., & Planty, M. (2000) *Indicators of school crime and safety, 2000*. U.S. Departments of Education and Justice. NCES 2001-017/NCJ-184176.

Klipp, G. (2001). *Resallying quids: Resilience of queer youth in school*. Unpublished doctoral dissertation, University of Michigan, Ann Arbor.

Kodluboy, D. (1997). Gang-oriented interventions. In A. Goldstein (Ed.), *School violence intervention: A practical handbook* (pp. 189–214). New York: Guilford.

Maines, B., & Robinson, G. (1992). *Michel's story: The no blame approach*. Bristol: Lame Duck Publishing (video and booklet).

Maines, B., & Robinson, G. (1998). The no blame approach to bullying. In D. Shorrock-Taylor (Ed.), *Directions in educational psychology* (pp. 281–295). London: Whurr Publishers.

Meyer, H. A., & Astor, R. A. (in press). Child and parent perspectives on routes to and from school in high crime neighborhoods. *Journal of School Violence*.

Morrison, G., Furlong, M., & Morrison, R. (1997). In A. Goldstein & J. Conoley (Eds.), *School violence intervention: A practical handbook* (pp. 236–264). New York: Guilford.

Nansel, T., Overpeck, M., Pilla, R., Ruan, W., Simons-Morton, B., & Scheidt, P. (2001). Bullying behaviors among US youth: Prevalence and association with psychosocial adjustment. *Journal of the American Medical Association, 285,* 2094–2100.

Olweus, D. (1980). Familial and temperamental determinants of aggressive behavior in adolescent boys: A causal analysis. *Developmental Psychology, 16,* 644–660.

Olweus, D. (1991). Bully/victim problems among schoolchildren: Basic facts and effects of a school based intervention program. In D. Pepler & K. Rubin (Eds.), *The development and treatment of childhood aggression* (pp. 441–448). Hillsdale, NJ: Erlbaum.

Olweus, D. (1993). *Bullying at school.* Cambridge, MA: Blackwell Publishers.

Olweus, D. (1994). Annotation: Bullying at school: Basic facts and effects of a school based intervention program. *Journal of Child Psychiatry, 35,* 1171–1190.

Olweus, D. (1996). Bully/victim problems at school: Facts and effective intervention. *Reclaiming Children and Youth: Journal of Emotional and Behavioral Problems, 5,* 15–22.

Olweus, D., Limber, S., & Mihalic, S. (1999). *Blueprints for violence prevention, Book Nine: Bullying prevention program.* Boulder, CO: Center for the Study and Prevention of Violence.

Owens, L., & MacMullin, C. (1995). Gender differences in aggression in children and adolescents in South Australian schools. *International Journal of Adolescence and Youth, 6,* 21–35.

Owens, L., Slee, P., & Shute, R. (2000). 'It hurts a hell of a lot...': The effects of indirect aggression on teenage girls. *School Psychology International, 21,* 359–376.

Page, R. (1997). Helping adolescents avoid date rape: The role of secondary education. *High School Journal, 80,* 75–80.

Parks, C. (1995). Gang behavior in the schools: Reality or myth? *Educational Psychology Review, 7,* 41–68.

Pellegrini, A., & Bartini, M. (2000). A longitudinal study of bullying, victimization, and peer affiliation during the transition from primary school to middle school. *American Educational Research Journal, 37,* 699–725.

Pepler, D., & Rubin, K. (1991). *The development and treatment of childhood aggression.* Hillsdale, NJ: Erlbaum.

Pittel, E. (1998). How to take a weapons history: Interviewing children at risk for violence at school. *Journal of the American Academy of Child & Adolescent Psychiatry, 37,* 1100–1102.

Rigby, K. (1994). Psychosocial functioning in families of Australian adolescent schoolchildren involved in bully/victim problems. *Journal of Family Therapy, 16,* 173–187.

Rigby, K. (1996). *Bullying in schools: And what to do about it.* Melbourne: Australian Council for Educational Research.

Rigby, K., & Slee, P. (1999). Australia. In P. K. Smith et al. (Eds.), *The nature of school bullying: A cross-national perspective.* London & New York: Routledge.

Rose, L., & Gallup, A. (1999). The 31st annual Phi Delta Kappa/Gallup poll of the public's attitudes toward the public schools. *Phi Delta Kappan, 81,* 41–56.

Rose, L., & Gallup, A. (2000). The 32nd annual Phi Delta Kappa/Gallup poll of the public's attitudes toward the public schools. *Phi Delta Kappan, 82,* 41–66.

Rose, L., Gallup, A., & Elam, S. (1997). The 29th annual Phi Delta Kappa/Gallup poll of the public's attitudes toward the public schools. *Phi Delta Kappan, 79,* 41–56.

Ross, C. (1996). Conflict at school: The use of an art therapy approach to support children who are bullied. *Art Approaches to Conflict, 389,* 131–151.

Schafer, M., & Smith, P. (1996). Teacher's perceptions of play fighting and real fighting in primary school. *Educational Research, 38,* 173–181.

Sharp, S., & Smith, P. (1994). *Tackling bullying in your school: A practical handbook for teachers.* London: Routledge.

Smith, P., Morita, Y., Junger-Tas, J., Olweus, D., Catalano, R., & Slee, P. (1999). *The nature of school bullying: A cross-national perspective.* New York: Routledge.

Smith, P., & Sharp, S. (1994). *School bullying: Insights and perspectives.* New York: Routledge.

Stein, N. (1999). *Classrooms and courtrooms: Facing sexual harassment in K–12 schools.* New York: Teachers College Press.

Stephenson, P., & Smith, D. (1989). Bullying in the junior school. In D. Tattum & D. Lane (Eds.), *Bullying in schools*. Stoke-on-Trent: Trentham Books.

Sullivan, K. (2000). *The anti-bullying handbook*. Auckland, NY: Oxford University Press.

Turiel, E. (1987). Potential relationships between the development of social reasoning and childhood aggression. In D. H. Crowell, I. M. Evens, & C. R. O'Donnell (Eds.), *Childhood aggression and violence: Sources of influence, prevention and control* (pp. 95–114). New York: Plenum Press.

U.S. Departments of Education and Justice. (2000). *2000 annual report on school safety*. Washington, DC: Author.

Vossekuil, B., Reddy, M., Fein, R., Borum, R., & Modzeleski, W. (2000). *U.S.S.S. Safe School Initiative: An interim report on the prevention of targeted violence in schools*. Washington, DC: U.S. Secret Service, National Threat Assessment Center.

Whitney, I., & Smith, P. (1993). A survey of the nature and extent of bullying in junior/middle and secondary schools. *Educational Research, 35,* 3–25.

Youssef, R., Attia, M., & Kamel, M. (1998). Children experiencing violence II: Prevalence and determinants of corporal punishment in schools. *Child Abuse & Neglect, 22,* 975–985.

CHAPTER 20

REVIEW OF RESEARCH ON PREDICTORS OF YOUTH VIOLENCE AND SCHOOL-BASED AND COMMUNITY-BASED PREVENTION APPROACHES

TODD I. HERRENKOHL
University of Washington

ICK-JOONG CHUNG
Duksung Women's University (Seoul, Korea)

RICHARD F. CATALANO
University of Washington

Recent media reports of school shootings have increased concern about youth violence. Although such reports might give the impression that serious violent crime among juveniles is on the rise, official record estimates of youth violence show a decline (Snyder, 2000). Rates of juvenile arrests for very serious violent crimes (such as murder and rape) are well below their peaks recorded in the early- to mid-1990s (Snyder, 2000). Less serious violent crimes (such as aggravated and simple assault) have also shown moderate declines or have remained nearly constant since the mid-1990s (Snyder, 2000). Nonetheless, violence continues to claim the lives of many youths in the United States, and leaves countless others seriously injured. Due to an increase in the youth population, there is reason to believe that juvenile arrests will rise again if swift action is not taken now to develop programs that can address possible causes of violent behavior (Blumstein & Rosenfeld, 1998; Kelley, Huizinga, Thornberry, & Loeber, 1997).

This chapter reviews current research on risk and protective factors for youth violence and examines gender and ethnic differences in the developmental etiology of violence. It also summarizes evidence on empirically based preventive interventions that have sought to reduce risks and enhance protection among children of elementary school age and older. We focus here on school-based and community-based programs. Attention is given to those interventions that target high-risk children and youths, as well as those that seek to change larger systems to support children's cognitive, social, and emotional development. The chapter includes a brief discussion of programs focused on reducing recidivism among court-involved and violent youths, and it concludes with a discussion about areas for further research and the role of social work professionals in prevention practice.

RISK AND PROTECTIVE FACTORS
FOR YOUTH VIOLENCE

There is a growing consensus that youth violence and other problem behaviors can be prevented by identifying predictors of such problems and then seeking to modify those predictors in the developmental experiences of children and youths (Hawkins, Herrenkohl, et al., 1998; Howell, 1997; Mrazek & Haggerty, 1994). The term *predictor* describes both risk factors and protective factors. As defined by Coie and colleagues (1993, p. 1013), "Risk factors are variables associated with a high probability of onset, greater severity, and longer duration" of problems such as violence, delinquency, or substance use. Protective factors generally act to decrease the probability of onset or continuation of these problems by reducing the impact of risk exposure through mediation or moderation (Farrington, 1998).

Risk factors for youth violence and delinquency have been summarized in several comprehensive reviews (Farrington, 1998; Hawkins, Herrenkohl, et al., 1998; Lipsey & Derzon, 1998; Reiss & Roth, 1993). Results from empirical studies indicate that risk factors are related to the socialization of children in families, schools, peer groups, and communities (see related discussion by Sameroff and Gutman in Chapter 2 of this book). Risk for violence also is associated with the skills, temperament, and behavior of individual children.

Some risk factors are linked only to a single developmental period (Brewer, Hawkins, Catalano, & Neckerman, 1995; Hawkins, Herrenkohl, et al., 1998), whereas others remain salient across developmental periods (Herrenkohl et al., 2000). Herrenkohl and colleagues found that child hyperactivity, low academic performance, involvement with delinquent peers, and drug availability predicted later violence (at age 18) among boys and girls from elementary school, middle school, and high school. Other factors, such as poor family management, family conflict, and low school commitment were only predictive of violence when measured in middle school and high school.

There is evidence that certain risk factors increase the likelihood of violence perpetration more so than do others, and that children exposed to multiple risk factors at any point in development are much more likely to engage in violence (Herrenkohl et al., 2000). Sameroff and Gutman (this volume) refer to this dynamic as it relates to developmental outcomes other than violence for children and youths. Table 20.1 summarizes the most empirically supported risk factors for youth violence and delinquency across socialization units and developmental periods.

Hypotheses about the relations between risk factors and youth violence are specified in criminological theories, such as differential association theory (Sutherland, 1947; Sutherland & Cressey, 1970); social learning theory (Akers, 1985; Bandura, 1977); social control theory (Hirschi, 1969); and social disorganization theory (Sampson & Lauritsen, 1994;

TABLE 20.1 Well-Established Risk Factors for Delinquency and Youth Violence Grouped by Domain of Influence

INDIVIDUAL	FAMILY	SCHOOL	PEER	COMMUNITY
Male Gender	Poverty/Low SES	Low Academic Performance	Peer Rejection	Neighborhood Disadvantage
Early Aggressiveness/Antisocial Behavior/Defiance	Poor Family Management/Child Maltreatment	Low School Commitment/Low Educational Aspirations	Involvement with Delinquent (Antisocial) Peers/Gang Membership	Residential Mobility
Hyperactivity/Attention Deficit	Family and Marital Conflict	Poorly Defined Rules and Expectations for Behavior		Neighborhood Laws and Norms Favorable to Crime
Risk Taking	Parent Criminality	Inadequate Enforcement of Rules Against Antisocial Behavior		Availability of Firearms/Drugs
Impulsivity	Parental Attitudes Favorable to Violence/Antisocial Behavior			Media Portrayals of Violence
Substance Use	Family Breakup/Parent-Child Separation			
Attitudes Favorable to Offending Low IQ				

Source: T. I. Herrenkohl, J. D. Hawkins, I.-J. Chung, K. G. Hill, and S. R. Battin-Pearson, "School and Community Risk Factors and Interventions" (pp. 211–246), in R. Loeber and D. P. Farrington (Eds.), *Child Delinquents: Development, Intervention, and Service Needs*. Copyright © 2000 by Sage Publications. Reprinted by permission of Sage Publications, Inc.

Sampson, Raudenbush, & Earls, 1997; Shaw & McKay, 1942). Several more recent integrative theories—for example, the social development model (Catalano & Hawkins, 1996), Elliott's integrated theory on delinquent behavior (Elliott, Ageton, & Canter, 1979; Elliott & Huizinga, 1985), Moffitt's theory of life course persistent offending (Moffitt, 1993), and Patterson's theory of coercive family process (Patterson, 1982; Patterson, DeBaryshe, & Ramsey, 1989; Patterson & Dishion, 1985)—combine hypotheses from these other theories so as to better capture the complex etiology of antisocial behavior. Many integrative theories have acquired empirical support, although few have been tested in their full forms. The social development model (Catalano & Hawkins, 1996) guides our work on the developmental etiology of youth violence. Tests of that model have shown its ability to predict delinquency, youth violence, and substance use among adolescents (Catalano, Oxford, Harachi, Abbott, & Haggerty, 1999; Herrenkohl, Huang, et al., 2001; Huang, Kosterman, Catalano, Hawkins, & Abbott, 2001; Lonczak et al., 2001).

In this chapter we do not review the details of any one theory, but we do refer to hypotheses derived from these theories in our review of literature on etiology and promising prevention programs.

Resilience and Protection from Risk Exposure

Fortunately, not all children exposed to one or more risk factors engage in violence (Farrington, 1994; Herrenkohl et al., 2000). In fact, errors in prediction about who will and will not engage in violence on the basis of risk exposure alone are quite common (Farrington, 1995; Herrenkohl et al., 2000). This suggests that some children encounter protective influences that reduce the impact of risk exposure on their later development (Cowan, Cowan, & Schulz, 1996; Garmezy, 1983; Rutter, 1979, 1985; Sameroff & Gutman, Chapter 2 of this volume; Smith & Carlson, 1997; Werner & Smith, 1992). It appears that even children exposed to multiple risk factors can avoid later involvement in antisocial behavior if they are adequately protected against those risks (Catalano, Arthur, Hawkins, Berglund, & Olson, 1998; Chung, Hill, Hawkins, Gilchrist, & Nagin, 2002; Herrenkohl et al., under review; Smith & Carlson, 1997). Like risk factors, protective factors are linked to socialization units—family, school, peer groups, and the community—and to individuals themselves (Brewer et al., 1995). A resilient temperament and high intelligence, for example, can be protective for some children (Sameroff & Gutman, Chapter 2 of this volume; Smith & Carlson, 1997; Werner & Smith, 1992). Strong bonds of attachment to prosocial adults also have been shown to reduce violence risk (Catalano & Hawkins, 1996; Hirschi, 1969; Smith & Carlson, 1997; Werner & Smith, 1992). Finally, research suggests that healthy beliefs and clear standards for behavior in families and in schools also have protective effects (Catalano et al., 1998; Catalano & Hawkins, 1996; Pollard, Catalano, Hawkins, & Arthur, 1997).

Although it is clear that protection from violence is possible, several recent studies have shown that with exposure to a greater number of risks, concurrent or later exposure to a greater number of protective factors is needed to lessen the probability of youth violence (Herrenkohl et al., under review; Pollard, Hawkins, & Arthur, 1999). In one of our recent studies from the Seattle Social Development Project that examined protective factors against the continuation of childhood aggression to later violence, we found that aggressive children at highest risk for violence because of exposure to multiple risk factors (three or more) during adolescence were not as likely as were those at lower levels of risk during adolescence to encounter enough protective influences to counteract the effect of earlier risk exposure. In other words, our data showed that it is difficult to develop levels of protection in the face of high levels of risk exposure. Other studies that have examined the co-occurrence of risk and protective factors for antisocial behavior have reported similar results (Pollard et al., 1999). The implication of this finding for intervention is that programs directed to high-risk youths must seek not only to enhance protection but also to reduce risk factors directly (Fraser & Richman, 2001; Herrenkohl, Hawkins, Chung, Hill, & Battin-Pearson, 2001).

CONTINUITY IN ANTISOCIAL BEHAVIOR FROM CHILDHOOD THROUGH ADOLESCENCE

The importance of early prevention as a tool for combating youth violence is underscored by empirical research that has linked childhood conduct problems (e.g., hyperactivity, aggression, and oppositionality) to later violence and delinquency (Farrington, 1998; Hawkins, Herrenkohl, et al., 1998; Nagin & Tremblay, 1999) For many youths who engage in the most serious forms of violence during adolescence and early adulthood, there appears to be a continuity in antisocial behavior that begins very early in life (Elliott, 1994; Farrington, 1998; Farrington & Loeber, 1999; Hawkins, Herrenkohl, et al., 1998; Herrenkohl et al., 2000; Loeber, 1990, 1996; Loeber & Farrington, 2001; Loeber & Hay, 1997; Loeber & Stouthamer-Loeber, 1998; Moffitt, 1993). This pattern in behavior might extend from underlying personality traits and temperament that predispose children to poor conduct over time (Moffitt, 1993). It might also be that poor conduct in childhood sets in motion negative socialization experiences that strengthen antisocial behavior over the course of development (Catalano & Hawkins, 1996; Patterson, 1982; Patterson et al., 1989; Patterson & Dishion, 1985).

Several theories offer hypotheses about how the socialization of children works to maintain antisocial behavior. For example, Patterson's theory of coercive family process (Patterson, 1982; Patterson et al., 1989; Patterson & Dishion, 1985), which is based on social learning theory, suggests that children learn violent behavior through coercive exchanges with parents. Parents, although not so intending, reinforce poor conduct by giving into a child's demands and aggressive outbursts. Such conduct eventually spills over into school, thereby affecting the child's social interactions and academic progress. Research suggests that children who enter school without being able to control aggressive impulses are more likely to be rejected by their prosocial peers (Dishion, McCord, & Poulin, 1999). Social isolation and school failure can lead some youths into delinquent peer groups and gangs, within which violence is further reinforced (Battin, Hill, Abbott, Catalano, & Hawkins, 1998; Dishion et al., 1999; Patterson et al., 1989).

The social development model (SDM; Catalano & Hawkins, 1996) offers a related perspective. The SDM combines hypotheses of social control theory, social learning theory, and differential association theory. It suggests that children who are poorly bonded to their families, as well as to prosocial peers and school, are most vulnerable to negative peer influences and are at highest risk for antisocial behavior. Frequent involvement with delinquent peers supports the continuation of antisocial behavior as children proceed through adolescence. In the same way that bonds to prosocial individuals and institutions can reduce risk for youth violence (Huang et al., 2001; Resnick et al., 1997), bonds to antisocial others can increase violence risk.

Adolescent Initiators

Although children who exhibit antisocial behavior at a young age are more likely than are other children to engage in later violence, evidence suggests that not just early initiators engage in violence (Loeber & Stouthamer-Loeber, 1998; Moffitt, 1993). Some children appear to initiate various forms of antisocial behavior later, during adolescence, for the first time (Moffitt, 1993). According to Moffitt's (1993) theory of life-course-persistent and adolescent-limited youth offending, antisocial behavior can be initiated by youths in adolescence and continue briefly as negative peer influences intensify. Moffitt hypothesizes that unlike life-course-persistent offenders who continue to be antisocial (violent) into their adult years, adolescent initiators will give up violent behaviors as they near adulthood. This hypothesis is supported by research evidence that shows transitions into adult roles for many individuals (spouse, parent, worker) encourage positive behavior (Moffitt, 1993; Sampson & Laub, 1993). In the same way that strong bonds of attachment to prosocial others can act to reduce antisocial behavior in children (control theory; SDM), prosocial bonds in early adulthood appear also to be important.

Moffitt's distinction between various offending trajectories has received some empirical support. In one study, Moffit and Caspi (2001), reported that not only do differing offending trajectories exist but they also relate to differing profiles of risk in children. Youths who showed an early onset pattern of antisocial behavior in their study (the Dunedin longitudinal study) were found to have had childhoods characterized by poor parenting, neurocognitive problems, and temperament and behavior problems. In contrast, adolescent-limited offenders were not found to have had these risks. Males and females in each category had similar risk profiles.

Studies done elsewhere are less clearly in support of Moffitt's taxonomic theory (Fergusson, Horwood, & Nagin, 2000; Nagin, Farrington, & Moffitt, 1995). In fact, several studies on the etiology and consequences of adolescent onset offending call into question the strength of Moffitt's hypothesis that adolescent onset offending has a short duration (Fergusson et al., 2000; Nagin et al., 1995). According to a study by Nagin and colleagues (1995), it appears that although adolescent offenders show improvements during early adulthood in some domains of activity (employment and marital relationships), they continue to exhibit antisocial behavior. Nagin and colleagues found that adolescent offenders, during early adulthood, were involved in property crime, theft, alcohol and drug use, and fighting. Thus, although Moffitt's theory is useful from the standpoint of demarcating distinct offending trajectories, it is not clear that the full theory is supported.

GENDER AND RACE DIFFERENCES
IN YOUTH VIOLENCE

Gender Differences in Violence

Research has shown that males engage in higher rates of aggression and more serious forms of physical violence than do females (Chesney Lind, 1989; Giordano & Cernkovich, 1997; Loeber & Hay, 1997; Tolan & Loeber, 1993). Level differences in violence are most evident after school entry when social interactions among children from diverse backgrounds are more regular.

Early research on gender differences in violence focused on biological/constitutional factors. Females were seen as "different" from males because of their physiological makeup. More recently, research has increasingly focused on social developmental explanations. Some research suggests that boys are strongly socialized to be independent and confrontational, whereas girls are socialized to be relationship oriented (Loeber & Hay, 1997). The hypothesis is that girls are less overtly physical but use indirect and verbal forms of aggression, such as alienation, ostracism, and character defamation (Loeber & Stouthamer-Loeber, 1998). Another explanation is that boys and girls use physical violence equally but that girls underreport their negative behavior (Loeber & Hay, 1997). This latter explanation would not account for differences between males and females in official record counts of violent crimes.

Another area of research on the gender difference in violence focuses on social control. Some research suggests parents tend to be more restrictive with girls than with boys (Block, 1984; Bursik, Merten, & Schwartz, 1985). Girls are expected to stay closer to home and to arrive home earlier at night from social activities. Girls also are more likely than are boys to be disciplined for disobeying curfew (Belknap, 1996; Gilligan, Ward, Taylor, & Bardige, 1988). In short, less violence from girls could reflect the fact that girls are more closely supervised and are allowed less independence than are boys (Hagan, Simpson, & Gillis, 1988; Oxford, Harachi, Catalano, Haggerty, & Abbott, 2000). Closer supervision would restrict opportunities for girls to interact with antisocial peers and to engage in violence (Siegel & Senna, 1994).

Violence and Race

Official crime statistics indicate that African American youths, males in particular, are overrepresented as both perpetrators and victims of the most serious forms of violence (Hawkins, Laub, & Lauritsen, 1998; Snyder, 2000). However, as noted by Hawkins and associates (Hawkins, Laub, et al., 1998), higher arrest and conviction rates for African American youths might not reflect true level differences in violence perpetration. Rather, they could reflect that African Americans are singled out for arrest by police and then are treated differently from others during court processing.

Self-report data on youth violence should, theoretically, provide more accurate statistics on violence and race (Hawkins, Laub, et al., 1998). However, such data can be biased by under- or overreporting. More problematic is that crime is difficult to study in general population samples because analyses will not capture the most serious forms of violence, thereby limiting the extent to which race comparisons in violent crime perpetration could be made. Elliott's (1994) study of self-reported violence among youths in the National Youth Survey (NYS), however, calls into question the extent to which general population surveys are limited in this way. He found very high prevalences for index offenses (such as aggravated assault, robbery, and rape) reported by youths in that sample. Elliott argued that those offenses measured in the NYS involve levels of weapon use and injury that are comparable to the most serious crimes recorded in official records.

To understand race differences in crime, it is important to consider data from multiple sources, recognizing the limitations associated with each. Evidence across sources does appear to suggest that African Americans are victimized at a higher rate than are youths of other races. African American youths also appear to commit more serious acts of violence

(Nettle & Pleck, 1996), which suggests they are exposed to a greater number and more severe social and environmental risk factors (Hawkins, Laub, et al., 1998). Research has shown that African American youths tend to reside in some of the most disadvantaged communities (Hawkins, Laub, et al., 1998). Such communities are characterized by poverty, drug selling, and high residential turnover (Sampson & Laub, 1993; Sampson & Lauritsen, 1994; Sampson & Wilson, 1995). Sampson and colleagues have shown that disadvantaged communities experience a breakdown in networks of informal social control that, if present, would work to inhibit crime (Sampson et al., 1997). Residents within disadvantaged communities tend to remain distant from one another and are removed from neighborhood upkeep and maintenance. Absent resident involvement and collective action to uphold the law, youth activity goes unmonitored and violent crime unnoticed. Youths within disadvanged communities witness violence more often than do others and are exposed to norms that support antisocial behavior. These findings are consistent with hypotheses from social disorganization theory and differential association theory, both of which were mentioned earlier. Large-scale studies of neighborhood patterns that support and deter opportunities for violent crime are ongoing (Sampson et al., 1997). Knowledge gained from these studies should provide further evidence of the factors that increase risk for violence among African American youths.

PROMISING PREVENTION APPROACHES

Scholars have suggested that programs aimed at preventing youth violence should seek to foster protection against risk exposure while directly reducing risks (Brewer et al., 1995; Catalano & Hawkins, 1996; Coie et al., 1993; Hawkins, Catalano, & Miller, 1992; Mrazek & Haggerty, 1994). Programs that have shown the most promise for preventing youth violence focus on several risk and protective factors in combination (Brewer et al., 1995; Hawkins, Catalano, Kosterman, Abbott, & Hill, 1999; Hawkins, Herrenkohl, et al., 1998; Hawkins & Herrenkohl, in press; Herrenkohl, Hawkins, et al., 2001; Wasserman & Miller, 1998). Effective programs tend to have a strong empirical base and to have clear implementation and evaluation goals (Wasserman & Miller, 1998). The duration and the intensity of an intervention also can affect whether a program achieves success in preventing or reducing violence (Hawkins & Herrenkohl, in press; Mrazek & Haggerty, 1994).

Many federal and state agencies, as well as individual researchers, have called for the use of prevention approaches that have been shown to be effective. Prevention scholars have tended to rely on differing criteria in their determination of which programs to support and replicate. For this reason, it is important to assess the standard of evidence used to qualify a given program as effective. At a minimum, we advocate that at least one rigorous outcome study be completed before a program is offered as exemplary. The most rigorous research involves an experimental design. Experimental studies use random assignment of participants to intervention and control conditions to achieve comparable samples. Quasi-experimental studies with adequate investigation into selection bias also are rigorous, as are those that use multiple baseline designs. Only programs that have been rigorously evaluated will be discussed here.

In the pages that follow, we summarize several intervention approaches and exemplary programs. We discuss programs directed to children of elementary school age, as well as those directed to older children and adolescents. Reviews of programs for children younger than elementary school age are provided elsewhere (Hawkins & Weis, 1985; Wasserman & Miller, 1998; Yoshikawa, 1994). In some cases, the same approaches have been used with children of differing ages. That is so noted in the text. This is a selective review that is meant to introduce the reader to the several prevention strategies that have recently been tested or are currently in their testing phase. We do not describe in full detail the components of each program, sampling method, or evaluation procedure. More comprehensive reviews of most programs are available in our earlier publications (see Catalano et al., 1998; Hawkins, Catalano, & Miller, 1992; Hawkins, Herrenkohl, et al., 1998; Herrenkohl, Hawkins, et al., 2001). Loeber and Farrington's (1998, 2001) and Howell and colleagues' (1995) edited books from the Office of Juvenile Justice and Delinquency Prevention Study Group and Elliott's (1998) Blueprint series on violence prevention (http://www.colorado.edu/cspv/blueprints/) also are good sources for information on promising violence prevention programs. We focus in our review on school-based and community-based efforts due to our research and practice interests in these areas.

PREVENTION PROGRAMS FOR CHILDREN OF ELEMENTARY SCHOOL AGE

Elementary school interventions are likely to reach the largest number of children, including those at particularly high risk for youth violence. Effective prevention approaches for elementary children include, but are not limited to, classroom behavior management programs, social competence and violence prevention curricula, and comprehensive classroom-based interventions.

Children who do poorly in school are at higher risk than are others for antisocial behavior, as are those who have low educational aspirations and weak bonds to school (Hawkins, Herrenkohl, et al., 1998; Maguin & Loeber, 1996). Some programs seek to enhance the competency of individual children through academic tutoring and one-on-one counseling. Others seek to positively influence student learning by enhancing teaching practices and classroom management. Still others focus on broader school policies and norms against antisocial behavior. Ultimately, most school-based programs aim to create a school environment conducive to learning and positive social interaction among children (Dryfoos, 1990, 1996).

Behavior Management Programs

Not only must classroom teachers deliver subject material effectively to children with different learning styles but they also must manage behavior and discipline appropriately. Intervention studies have shown that the use of proactive behavior management practices by teachers can produce less student misbehavior and more on-task, academically focused behavior in the classroom (Evertson, 1985; Evertson, Emmer, Sanford, & Clements, 1983; Kellam & Rebok, 1992). Kellam and Rebok's (1992) and Kellam, Rebok, Ialongo, and Mayer's (1994) evaluations of the Good Behavior Game illustrate a basic, yet effective, behavior management approach. Their evaluations have shown that a token reward system (checkmarks to designate good behavior followed by positive rewards for cooperation) with first-grade students in an urban area can lower misbehavior in the classroom, even among the most poorly behaved, aggressive children. In the program, students were assigned to groups, which each included an equal number of aggressive and disruptive children. While the Good Behavior game was in progress, teachers monitored the behavior of students in each group. Misbehavior of any student in a group resulted in a checkmark being placed on the chalkboard for that group. At the end of the session, groups with fewer than five checkmarks received a reward.

In the beginning of the program, game sessions were announced and tangible rewards (e.g., stickers) were given immediately following the session. As the program became more familiar to students, sessions started unannounced and less tangible rewards were used (e.g., extended recess). Also, the time between sessions and the granting of rewards was extended. The program lasted for two years in the first and second grades. An experimental longitudinal study of the students revealed that a positive influence on children's behavior was maintained after the program had ended. Positive effects of the program were most evident in children rated as mostly highly aggressive when the program began.

Behavior management programs also have been implemented at the school level. Such interventions seek to increase school safety and improve student behavior by defining and enforcing rules for appropriate conduct and by fairly and consistently disciplining students in and outside of the classroom. Several behavior management programs have been evaluated, mostly in secondary schools. Therefore, we will turn to this approach later in another section that discusses programs for older children and adolescents.

Social Competence and Violence Prevention Curricula

Many children who engage in aggressive behavior lack positive social interaction and effective problems-solving skills. Such children tend to approve of the use of violence to address interpersonal conflict (Slaby & Guerra, 1988). Social competence and violence prevention curricula seek to promote the development of norms against the use of violence in conflict situations and to improve students' skills in resolving conflict prosocially. Several programs have shown that early aggressive and violent behavior among elementary school children can be reduced when skills are taught in a clear and consistent manner at a level appropriate for children of a given age (Hawkins & Herrenkohl, in press). We discuss here two programs that are implemented in elementary school settings: the PATHS curriculum (Greenberg & Kusche, 1993, 1997) and the Committee on Children's Second Step curriculum (Grossman, Neckerman, & Rivara, 1997), both of which have shown success in preventing or reducing aggressive behavior.

The Promoting Alternative Thinking Strategies (PATHS) curriculum, used with elementary school students, was designed to enhance children's self-control of behavior by strengthening their awareness and understanding of emotions and by building interpersonal and problem-solving skills. Structured lessons to enhance social competence are taught with the use of drawings and photographs, dialoguing, role-playing, and modeling by teachers and peers. The PATHS curriculum has been used in schools in the United States and in other countries with demonstrated success in standard classrooms, in classrooms for children with behavior and learning disorders, and in classrooms for deaf children. Children in grades 1 through 6 have shown gains in self-control and emotional awareness, and the use of positive conflict-resolution strategies. Reductions in levels of aggression and depression after the intervention also have been found (Greenberg & Kusche, 1993).

Grossman and colleagues' (1997) experimental evaluation of the Committee on Children's Second Step curriculum provides another useful illustration. The Second Step curriculum teaches elementary students skills for anger management, impulse control, and empathy. Photographs that reflect different social scenarios are used to generate discussion among children and to guide role-play activities. Children are taught to identify and understand their own feelings and to relate to the feelings of others. They also are taught to take others' perspectives in conflict situations, and control impulses when provoked. Teachers model skills through role-plays and provide feedback to students during group activities. A randomized controlled trial of the Second Steps curriculum showed that children who received the intervention were less aggressive as rated by observers in the lunchroom and on the playground. Children in the experimental condition also were more empathetic and had better interpersonal problem solving, anger management, and behavioral social skills than controls.

Comprehensive Classroom-Based Programs

Perhaps the most intuitively appealing of all school-based interventions for elementary school children are those that combine social competence enhancement, behavior management training for teachers and parents, and some method to enhance student achievement. Such interventions have strong appeal because they address multiple risk and protective factors within the school and family domains.

We illustrate a comprehensive classroom-based approach with three programs: the Fast Track intervention (Conduct Problems Prevention Research Group, 1999a, 1999b; Greenberg, 1998), the Child Development Project (Battistich, Schaps, Watson, & Solomon, 1996; Battistich, Solomon, Watson, & Schaps, 1997), and the Seattle Social Development Project (Hawkins et al., 1999; Hawkins et al., 1992; Hawkins, Von Cleve, & Catalano, 1991; O'Donnell, Hawkins, Catalano, Abbott, & Day, 1995).

The Fast Track intervention is being tested in a multisite randomized trial directed to children in kindergarten through grade 8 (Conduct Problems Prevention Research Group, 1999a, 1999b). Fast Track includes a universal social competence curriculum (PATHS, described earlier) as well as selective prevention elements for children who already have begun to manifest conduct problems at school entry.

The selective prevention elements include (1) parent-training groups designed to promote the development of positive family/school relationships and to teach parents behavior management skills, (2) home visits, (3) child social skill training groups, (4) child tutoring in reading, and (5) child friendship enhancement in the classroom (called *peer pairing*).

An evaluation of the full Fast Track intervention showed that at the end of the first grade (when children in the intervention had completed one year of the intervention), children exposed to the intervention had better social cognitive skills than comparison children and were more able to interact in positive ways with peers (Conduct Problems Prevention

Research Group, 1999a, 1999b; Greenberg, 1998). Children also exhibited less aggressive and hyperactive behavior. Children with high baseline rates of problem behavior exhibited lower levels of disruptive-oppositional behavior at the end of first grade as compared to controls (Conduct Problems Prevention Research Group, 1999a, 1999b).

The Child Development Project, another example of a comprehensive classroom-based program, responds to a growing consensus among prevention scholars and educators that schools must integrate the teaching of academic and socioemotional skills in the classroom (Battistich et al., 1996; Dryfoos, 1996). The Child Development Project uses cooperative learning and proactive classroom management methods to foster responsibility, establish prosocial norms, and strengthen conflict resolution skills among elementary children. The program, which spans a three-year period, also offers classroom and schoolwide community building activities, activities for students and parents to do at home together, and a reading and multicultural language arts program that emphasizes students' critical thinking about relevant social and ethical issues.

A longitudinal, multisite test of the Child Development Project showed that one year after the intervention, children in grades 5 and 6 were more strongly attached and committed to school than were those in a comparison condition (Battistich et al., 1996; Battistich et al., 1997). Reductions in weapon carrying, interpersonal aggression, and vehicle theft among intervention children also were noted for those in a high implementation subgroup.

Evidence for the effectiveness of comprehensive school-based programs also comes from *the Seattle Social Development Project (SSDP).* The SSDP was a multicomponent intervention designed specifically to prevent antisocial behavior by promoting academic achievement and commitment to schooling among children in the elementary grades. The intervention employed a package of classroom management and instruction methods for teachers, including proactive classroom management, interactive teaching, and cooperative learning, as well as an interpersonal skills training curriculum for elementary school-aged children. In addition, the program included a parenting component that provided behavior management and academic support skills training for adult caregivers in three developmentally adjusted programs (Hawkins, Catalano, Morrison, et al., 1992; O'Donnell et al., 1995).

The SSDP involved three intervention conditions: a full intervention condition in which children received the intervention in first through sixth grades, a late intervention condition in which children received the intervention in fifth and sixth grades only, and a control condition in which no intervention was used. The intervention was tested with a multiethnic urban sample. Positive effects of the full intervention on behavior were found early. By the end of grade 2, boys in the full intervention classrooms were rated by teachers as significantly less aggressive than boys in control classrooms, and girls were less likely to engage in self-harm (Hawkins et al., 1991). By the beginning of grade 5, full intervention students were significantly less likely to have initiated delinquent behavior and alcohol use than controls (Hawkins, Catalano, Morrison, et al., 1992). By the end of grade 6, full intervention boys from low-income families had significantly greater academic achievement, better teacher-rated behavior, and lower rates of delinquency initiation than did control boys from low-income families (O'Donnell et al., 1995). A six-year follow up at age 18 found significantly higher achievement and lower rates of lifetime violent delinquent behavior among children exposed to the full intervention compared with controls (Hawkins et al., 1999).

PROGRAMS DIRECTED TO OLDER CHILDREN AND ADOLESCENTS

Violence prevention programs directed to older children and adolescents vary in approach and form (Wasserman & Miller, 1998). Whereas prevention programs directed to elementary school children have tended to reflect a broader focus on risk and protective factors within schools or families, many programs directed to adolescents are narrower in scope. Often, programs at this age seek to intervene with youths directly by strengthening problem-solving and communication skills, promoting good work habits and responsible decision making, and increasing awareness about the consequences of violent behavior. There are, however, examples of programs that seek to change social influence and context factors associated with schools and communities (Catalano et al., 1998; Dryfoos, 1990, 1996; Wasserman & Miller, 1998). Unfortunately, several programs that have been tried with adolescents are ineffective or have not been rigorously studied (e.g., peer mediation and counseling, job and vocational training).

In our following summary of programs, we highlight social competence enhancement and anger management programs, bullying prevention, mentoring programs, gang prevention, school organization programs, and, finally, larger community efforts. We conclude with a brief note on a program directed to youths involved in the juvenile justice system. That program seeks to prevent the recurrence of violent crime among youths at high risk for recidivism.

Social Competence Enhancement and Anger Management Programs for Adolescents

As with programs for younger children, there is evidence that skills-focused programs can benefit adolescents (Catalano et al., 1998; Dryfoos, 1990, 1996; Wasserman & Miller, 1998). Social competence enhancement programs for adolescents focus on preventing various forms of antisocial behavior, or a single form, such as violence (Brewer et al., 1995). Those that address violence directly do so through anger management training and empathy building (Brewer et al., 1995).

The Social-Competence Promotion Program for Young Adolescents (Weissberg, Barton, & Shriver, 1997; Weissberg & Caplan, under review; Weissberg & Greenberg, 1998) is one example of a social competence enhancement program that is relevant to many outcome behaviors. This program teaches cognitive, behavioral, and affective skills to middle school students through classroom instruction (Weissberg et al., 1997; Weissberg & Caplan, under review). Youths are taught to respond to various problem situations when they arise. Visual displays in the classroom and throughout the school remind youths of the skills they are taught and encourage their use of those skills. Evaluations of the program have shown positive results. Several evaluations indicate that after completing the program, youths are more skilled in solving problems, managing stress, resolving conflicts constructively, and controlling impulses. Antisocial behavior among youths also has been reduced (Weissberg & Greenberg, 1998).

An example of a skills-focused curriculum that is more specific to anger management and violence prevention is the Positive Adolescents Choices Training (PACT) program. The

PACT program was developed for African American middle/junior high students. Trained doctoral-level facilitators lead group instruction that focuses on receiving and giving positive and negative feedback to others, resisting peer pressure, problem solving, and negotiation. Skills are taught with vignettes that feature youths in various social scenarios. Students role-play their responses and then review their effectiveness in using the skills they have been taught. A randomized controlled trial of the program showed that youths who participated in the intervention were less likely than controls to be referred to juvenile court charged with a violent offense (Hammond & Yung, 1993).

Bullying Prevention

Astor and colleagues (Chapter 19 of this book) summarize research on bullying in schools. As they explain, one of the most important evaluations of a school-based antibullying program was done in Bergen, Norway, by Olweus (1991). We review the program here because of its relevance to youth violence prevention. A more detailed summary of the program is provided by Astor and colleagues. Although the program involved children in grades 1 through 6 (and is therefore relevant for elementary school children), we review it in this section because findings have been reported for youths ages 12 to 15.

The Olweus antibullying program sought to increase awareness and knowledge of bullying by distributing (to teachers, parents, and students) booklets on what is known about bullying and how it can be alleviated. Teachers were encouraged to develop explicit rules on bullying (e.g., bullying will not be tolerated, tell someone when bullying happens, try to help victims) and to discuss with students the effects of bullying using a video and role-playing exercises. In addition, teachers were encouraged to improve their monitoring and supervision of children during recreation periods. Following the intervention, bullying and victimization were reduced, as was delinquent behavior (vandalism, theft, and truancy).

A replication of the Olweus antibullying program took place in Sheffield, England, from 1991 to 1993 (Eslea & Smith, 1998). Results of that program (one year after it was completed) showed that schools with strong program implementation experienced reductions in bullying behaviors among male students. Program effects were less consistent for females (Eslea & Smith, 1998).

Mentoring

Mentoring programs typically involve nonprofessional volunteers who spend time with youths in a supportive, nonjudgmental manner, while acting as role models. Mentoring has become a popular approach, although the evidence of its effectiveness is mixed (see Brewer et al., 1995). One example of a mentoring program that has shown positive results is Big Brothers/Big Sisters. Tierney, Grossman, and Resch (1995) evaluated the effect of the Big Brothers/Big Sisters program in a study of 10- to 15-year-old boys and girls (55 percent nonwhite). Youths were randomly assigned to treatment and control conditions. Those in the treatment condition were paired with an adult mentor who was matched on several characteristics (including background and preferences) and geographic proximity. Those in the control condition were placed on a waiting list for future assignment. The average length of a mentoring match before evaluation was 12 months. The majority of youths met with their mentors at least three times per month during that period. Tierney and associates (1995) reported that youths matched to a mentor were significantly less likely to initiate illegal drug use and alcohol use during the study period. Those in the treatment condition also were less likely to have reported "hitting someone." No significant differences were found on other outcomes, such as stealing or damaging property, being sent to the principal's office, engaging in risky behaviors, fighting, cheating, or using tobacco. Differences in some prosocial outcomes for Caucasian youths and youths of color were found. For example, male children of color showed stronger gains following the mentoring relationship in peer emotional support.

Gang Prevention Programs

A number of strategies have been proposed to reduce gang activity (Howell & Hawkins, 1998). The effectiveness of many of these approaches has not yet been assessed. However, there are a few examples of promising programs. One such program is Gang Resistance and Education Training (G.R.E.A.T.). The G.R.E.A.T. program is a school-based intervention that uses uniformed law-enforcement officers to teach a nine-week curriculum to middle school students (seventh-graders). Weekly sessions address, among other topics, the consequences of crimes for victims, schools, and neighborhoods; cultural sensitivity and prejudice; conflict resolution; and drug use.

A preliminary study of the program showed that youths who received the intervention were less likely than were nonparticipants (or noncompleters) to report being affiliated with a gang; those youths also reported less delinquency than nonparticipants. Participants also reported more positive attitudes to the police, more negative attitudes about gangs, more commitment to school, stronger attachment to parents, and fewer friends involved in delinquent activity.

School Organization Efforts

As noted earlier, research continues to highlight the importance of school context in the etiology of youth violence (Gottfredson, 2001). Poorly functioning, disorganized schools promote, rather than deter, antisocial norms and opportunities for negative peer involvement. Moreover, when students fear for their safety, they may take action to protect themselves by carrying a weapon or by bullying others. Recent school reform efforts are intended to reduce student misbehavior, strengthen the academic culture of schools, and increase student safety and involvement.

Several school reorganization efforts have shown effects on student antisocial behavior. For example, Gottfredson (1986) evaluated Project PATHE (Positive Action Through Holistic Education), a comprehensive school intervention for secondary schools in low-income, predominantly African American areas in Charleston County, South Carolina. The six main components were (1) teams composed of teachers, other school staff, students, parents, and community members that designed, planned, and implemented school improvement programs, with the assistance of two full-time project staff; (2) curriculum and discipline policy review and revision, including student participation in the development of school and classroom rules, and ongoing in-service training for teachers in instructional and classroom management practices; (3) schoolwide academic innovations, including study skills programs and cooperative learning methods; (4) schoolwide climate innovations, including expanded extracurricular activities, peer counseling, and a school pride campaign intended to improve the overall image of the school; (5) career-oriented innovations, including a job-seeking skills program and a career exploration program; and (6) special academic and counseling services for low-achieving and disruptive students.

The evaluation showed that low-achieving and disruptive students in intervention schools who received special academic and counseling services scored significantly better on standardized tests of basic academic skills and were significantly less likely to report drug involvement than were controls. High school seniors who were part of the intervention were significantly more likely to graduate (76 percent) than were seniors in the corresponding control group (42 percent). However, there were no significant differences between students who received special services and their controls on delinquency, court contacts, or other educational or behavioral measures.

Another example of a school reorganization effort is from the work of Robert Felner and colleagues (1993). Felner's School Transitional Environment Project (STEP) sought to ease the transition to high school among students from disadvantaged low-income backgrounds. Students entering ninth grade were assigned to units of 65 to 100 students in a "school within a school." Homeroom and academic classes were composed only of students in the same unit, and classrooms for the same unit were located in close proximity to each other. Academic subject teachers also served as homeroom teachers and as the main administrative and counseling link between the students, their parents, and the rest of the school. Homeroom teachers contacted parents before the school year and also held brief individual check-in sessions with each homeroom student once a month.

Participating students had significantly more positive perceptions of school, teachers, and other school personnel than did comparison students at the end of the one-year intervention. Intervention students also showed a significantly smaller drop in academic performance and attendance during the transition between junior and senior high school. Overall, intervention students had a significantly lower school dropout rate (24 percent) than did comparison students (43 percent).

Community Interventions

Catalano and associates (1998) reviewed research evidence on community interventions to address risk and protective factors for youth violence and delinquency. Such programs include community mobilization (such as neighborhood block watch and citizen patrols); situational prevention efforts (surveillance techniques and target removal); comprehensive community interventions; policing strategies; policy change (to address drug, alcohol, and gun sales and to strengthen laws for felonies that involve firearms); and mass media interventions. They found limited to strong support for the promise of most of these approaches. However, they call for more rigorous research to examine program process and impact, as well as for replication studies.

Those who support the use of comprehensive community interventions to address youth violence argue that to be effective, such interventions must be tailored to individual communities. Communities are likely to have different profiles of risk and protection. Thus, an approach that might be suited to one community might not be suited to another. Prevention programs should address the highest priority risk factors within a given community, as well as build on the strengths of that community. Consistent with principles of community practice in social work (Wiel & Gamble, 1995), such efforts require that community leaders and residents take ownership of the efforts that are developed and later implemented. Absent strong support and participation among key members of a community, even the most well-planned and carefully implemented efforts can fail (Catalano et al., 1998).

Howell and Hawkins (1998) note several other lessons learned from research on community prevention efforts: (1) leaders and residents must have a shared understanding of the risk- and protection-focused approach to prevention; (2) service providers, whether professionals or paraprofessionals, must be given thorough training in the preventive methods they are expected to implement; (3) regular in-service training for program staff, supportive supervision, and sufficient compensation are necessary to provide quality programs; (4) special prevention-oriented training and technical assistance might be needed to facilitate necessary changes in a community's service delivery system; and (5) expectations about the magnitude of intervention effects should be realistic, given available resources. As with prevention efforts based in other settings, community interventions should include a combination of programs to decrease salient risks and enhance protection across developmental stages and domains of influence.

Unfortunately, there are very few tests of community prevention efforts to address youth violence. Increasing interest in the area of community prevention, however, should lead to more research on such programs. In the absence of strong empirical evidence on any one program, we offer here an introduction to a model that informs our work in community research and practice: Communities That Care (CTC) (Hawkins, Catalano, & Associates, 1992). Studies of CTC are ongoing.

Communities That Care. The CTC model informs comprehensive community interventions to reduce risk and enhance protection based on the social development model (SDM, previously mentioned). The CTC strategy consists of five phases. In the first phase, readiness of the community to take on a comprehensive community intervention is assessed in the diverse sectors and populations existing in the community. The history of collaboration, view of prevention, and definition of the problems faced in the community are assessed in each of these diverse groups. In the second phase, key community leaders—which include the mayor, superintendent of schools, chief law-enforcement officer, judges, and business and other community leaders—are provided a half-day orientation to the project. If they commit to implementing it, they decide as a group to become the oversight body for the project and to appoint a prevention board of diverse members of their community. During the third phase, the community prevention board is constituted to include a broad crosssection of the community including those connected to multiple sectors and diverse community groups. This group is trained to conduct a community risk and resource assessment. Over a six-month period, the board gathers survey data from students in grades 6, 8, 10, and 12 supplemented by archival indicators on the risk and protective factors, and relevant problem behaviors. During the fourth phase, the board prioritizes risk and protective factors for preventive action. The board then designs its prevention strategy to address targeted risk factors and to enhance protective factors, selecting preventive interventions from a menu of programs and strategies that have shown positive effects in controlled studies. In the fifth phase, the board implements and evaluates the combined effects of the selected preventive strategies, using task forces composed of community members with a stake in the outcome and expertise in the particular intervention component. Baseline risk assessment data are compared to data collected in reassessments every two to three years in order to judge community progress in risk reduction in subsequent years.

Several implementation tests of the CTC approach have revealed the importance of ongoing training and proactive technical assistance during the first few years of the community mobilization process to ensure the institutionalization of risk and protection focused prevention. These tests have indicated the importance of developing epidemiological methods for assessing risk and protective factors in the community, guiding the prioritization of targets for preventive intervention (Harachi Manger, Hawkins, Haggerty, & Catalano, 1992). Through the Six State Consortium project (PI: J. D. Hawkins, funded by the Center for Substance Abuse Prevention), we have developed and validated a standardized risk and protective factor assessment system that incorporates and integrates archival and student survey data on risk and protective factors and prevalence of antisocial behavior (Arthur, Hawkins, Catalano, Pollard, & Howze, 1997; Pollard, et al., 1997). These standardized data allow local communities to plot their own unique profiles and trends in risk and protective factors relative to state and national averages and in relation to other communities. Process evaluations have demonstrated that CTC is flexible to meet community profiles of needs (GAO, 1995), that effective prevention strategies are selected (Jenson, Hartman, & Smith, 1997), and that the approach is more effective than another risk and protection approach at sustaining efforts and in planning tested programs (Arthur, Ayers, Graham, & Hawkins, in press). Outcomes from pre-post uncontrolled studies have also found reduction in risk and protective factors, delinquency, and violence (Jenson, et al., 1997; Office of Juvenile Justice and Delinquency Prevention, 1996).

PROGRAMS TO REDUCE RECIDIVISM AMONG VIOLENT YOUTHS

Our final category focuses on programs to reduce recidivism among court-involved and violent youths. In recent years, there has been growing interest in such programs as alternatives to youth detention and standard probation. We mention one program here: Multisystemic Therapy (Henggeler, 1997; Henggeler & Borduin, 1990) because of its strong ecological focus and its effectiveness in addressing youth violence.

Multisystemic Therapy (MST) is a well-studied treatment for juvenile offenders (Henggeler, Schoenwald, Borduin, Rowland, & Cunningham, 1998). The MST program posits that antisocial behavior stems from multiple factors associated with all primary socializing units—family, peer group, school, and community. The full intervention is designed to enhance parenting practices and family relations, build family-school connections, and empower youths to avoid involvement with antisocial peers. Intervention strategies include strategic family therapy, structural family therapy, behavioral parent training, and cognitive behavior therapies. Multisystemic Therapy is brief, yet intensive; the typical duration of a MST intervention is approximately four months. Within that short time, well-trained therapists work with each family to reduce family conflict, enhance parent/child communication, and strengthen relational bonds. Attention also is directed to the individual youth. Work outside the family (i.e. with peers and schools) occurs on an as-needed basis. Such work is tailored to the risk profile of that youth. Research has shown that MST is more effective than standard juvenile justice programs and community treatment in reducing recidivism. Moreover, several evaluations have documented improvements in familial and peer relations (Borduin et al., 1995; Henggeler et al., 1986). Youths who receive the MST intervention also are less likely than are others to be placed outside the home (Henggeler, Melton, Brondino, Scherer, & Hanley, 1997; Henggeler, Melton, Smith, Schoenwald, & Hanley, 1993). Studies suggest that the positive effects of the intervention are maintained over time (Borduin, Henggeler, Blaske, & Stein, 1990; Henggeler et al., 1997; Schoenwald, Ward, Henggeler, Pickrel, & Patel, 1996).

IMPLICATIONS FOR PRACTICE AND SUGGESTIONS FOR FURTHER RESEARCH

Longitudinal studies have identified risk and protective factors for youth violence. If modifiable, these precursors of violence are potential foci for preventive intervention. If not modifiable, precursors can be used to target populations for intervention. Research has shown that many foci for prevention programs exist and that most are tied to the socialization of children in families, schools, peer groups, and in their communities. In addition, risk and protective factors are associated with children themselves (skills, temperament, beliefs, etc.). Further, there is evidence that comprehensive prevention approaches can significantly reduce antisocial behavior among youths, while also strengthening protection. This chapter summarized several prevention programs that have reduced youth violence or have reduced risk factors or enhanced protective factors related to that outcome. Several of the programs have shown enduring effects on behavior.

As was noted earlier, more is currently known about risk factors for youth violence than about protective or resiliency factors (Farrington, 1994). To support strengths-based models of prevention practice, more research on protective factors is needed. Knowing about those factors that buffer the effects of risk factors on violent behavior will strengthen our collective ability to develop programs for youths who are exposed to the most toxic, but less directly changeable, environmental conditions and influences (Brewer et al., 1995; Catalano & Hawkins, 1996; Herrenkohl, Guo, et al., 2001).

We examined in this chapter prevention approaches for children of elementary school age and older. Promising programs for children and adolescents include classroom behavior management programs, social competence and violence prevention curricula, and multicomponent classroom-based programs. Other approaches for adolescents include bullying and gang prevention programs, mentoring, and school reorganization efforts.

Replication of promising programs is needed. Few of the programs referred to in this chapter have been studied across geographic areas or with differing youth populations. For those that have been replicated, larger-scale effectiveness trials could be initiated, perhaps at the community, state, or even national level. There is evidence that programs can be effective if they address risk and protective factors and are based on strong empirical intervention theory, and if they are well implemented and monitored. The most compelling findings are from multisite programs that use rigorous evaluation designs. To advance knowledge of programs that work and those that do not, systematic efforts must be made to study processes and outcomes of programs over extended periods. Findings should then be disseminated to wide audiences that include policymakers and practitioners. The importance of longitudinal follow-up studies is supported by intervention research that has shown delayed or lagged effects on targeted outcomes.

Although it appears inconsistent with reports on the recent school shootings, rates of the most serious violent crimes among youths have dropped in the past several years (Snyder, 2000). Some have attributed this drop to changes in drug markets and weapon carrying among youths involved with drugs, increases in police action to reduce weapon carrying, and stronger employment opportunities in a healthy economy (Blumstein & Rosenfeld, 1998). It also is conceivable that prevention efforts across the nation have begun to take effect. In order to stave off future upswings in rates of violent crime arrests that might occur with changes in the U.S. population, it is necessary to commit additional resources now to efficacious prevention programs.

Currently, 94 percent of the resources used to combat violent offending are used after violent offenses have occurred. A study completed by the RAND Corporation (Greenwood, Model, Rydell, & Chiesa, 1998) has demonstrated that effective prevention programming can be cost effective. Greenwood and colleagues examined the costs and effects of the three strikes legislation in California and compared them to the costs and effects of prevention. They estimated that the three strikes program costs the state of California 5 billion dollars per year and reduces crime by 21 percent. By investing one-fifth of that money in a combination of parenting programs and graduation incentives, the researchers estimated an equal amount of crime could be prevented. Thus, prevention programs could have the same effect on crime for 20 percent of the cost.

Social work professionals, and those in related human service fields, can play an important role in prevention practice. To do so, practitioners will have to develop knowledge of the etiology of youth violence and the local epidemiology of risk and protective factors and violence. They also must become familiar with prevention principles and the practices used in effective prevention approaches. Moreover, a continued dialogue between researchers and social work practitioners is necessary to facilitate a stronger integration of tested programs in routine policy and practice.

Perhaps an additional contribution that social work researchers could make is in the area of gender and culturally sensitive practice. Research consistently has shown that intervention programs are more effective when they are tailored to the groups they target. To date, knowledge about cultural differences in levels and strength of risk and protection is limited, as is knowledge of cultural similarities and differences in the effectiveness of practice applications. Also needed is further study of gender differences in violence and methods of intervention for girls. To date, most of the research on violent behavior and interventions has been done on males. In some prevention programs directed to boys and girls both, differential effects on targeted outcomes have been shown (Wasserman & Miller, 1998). Although it is the case that boys more often than girls perpetrate the most serious acts of physical violence (as documented by police and court records), the use of violence among girls cannot be ignored. As a starting point, more attention should be devoted to understanding whether the developmental etiology of violence differs for girls and also whether girls manifest other forms of violence that require different interventions (Loeber & Stouthamer-Loeber, 1998; Wasserman & Miller, 1998).

DISCUSSION QUESTIONS

1. Compare and contrast concepts of risk and protection. Should interventions focus on risk factors, protective factors, or both? Why?

2. Early explanations for gender and race differences in violence focused on biological or constitutional factors. More recent explanations focus on contextual, social structural, or experiential factors. What have researchers found to explain gender and race differences in violence? What combination of factors would you explore to explain these observed differences?

3. Several theories exist that try to explain the multivariate nature of the predictors of youth violence. Which theories or combination of theories match your practice experience?

4. The growing trend toward the use of evidence-based practice in social work interventions has created some buzz. Discuss how the term *evidence-based practice* has been used at your practice site. Discuss the implications of the different definitions for the profession as well as for the field of prevention.

5. A number of prevention programs have demonstrated reductions in violence and its predictors. Effective programs exist for families, schools, communities, and individuals. If you were the director of the state agency responsible for children and family services, how would you use this information to choose which program(s) to implement? Does one size fit all? How can you encourage informed decision making regarding program development and implementation at the local level?

6. Examine needs assessment instruments used at your practice site. These often are part of routine intake interviews. Do these instruments assess risk and protective factors? Ask your supervisor why these instruments include or don't include such factors. Bring your findings to class to discuss with your classmates.

7. Most resources are provided to those programs that support treatment over prevention. Discuss this fact from a social justice perspective, from a cost-effectiveness perspective, and from a continuum of care perspective. Should the current allocation of resources be changed? Why or why not.

8. Choose one effective preventive approach from those described in this chapter that you want to learn more about. Locate and read research articles that describe the program and its effects. Critically review these articles with an eye for strengths and weaknesses in practice strategy, as well as research design and methodology. Report back to your classmates on what you have found.

SUGGESTED READINGS

Catalano, R. F., & Hawkins, J. D. (1996). The social development model: A theory of antisocial behavior. In J. D. Hawkins (Ed.), *Delinquency and crime: Current theories* (pp. 149–197). New York: Cambridge University Press.

Elliott, D. S. (1998). *Blueprints for violence prevention.* Boulder, CO: Center for the Study and Prevention of Violence, Institute of Behavioral Science, University of Colorado at Boulder.

Hawkins, J. D. (1999). Preventing crime and violence through communities that care. *European Journal of Criminal Policy and Research, 7,* 443–458.

Hawkins, J. D., Herrenkohl, T., Farrington, D. P., Brewer, D., Catalano, R. F., & Harachi, T. W. (1998). A review of predictors of youth violence. In R. Loeber & D. P. Farrington (Eds.), *Serious and violent juvenile offenders: Risk factors and successful interventions* (pp. 106–146). Thousand Oaks, CA: Sage.

Lipsey, M. W., & Derzon, J. (1998). Predictors of violence and serious delinquency in adolescence and early adulthood: A synthesis of longitudinal research. In R. Loeber & D. P. Farrington (Eds.), *Serious and violent juvenile offenders: Risk factors and successful interventions* (pp. 86–105). Thousand Oaks, CA: Sage.

REFERENCES

Akers, R. L. (1985). *Deviant behavior: A social learning approach* (3rd ed.). Belmont, CA: Wadsworth.

Arthur, M. W., Ayers, C. D., Graham, K. A., & Hawkins, J. D. (in press). Mobilizing communities to reduce risks for drug abuse: A comparison of two strategies. In W. J. Bukoski & Z. Sloboda (Eds.), *Handbook of drug abuse theory, science and practice.* New York: Plenum Press.

Arthur, M. W., Hawkins, J. D., Catalano, R. F., Pollard, J. A., & Howze, T. H. (1997). *Six State Consortium for Prevention Needs Assessments Studies Project: Measurement validation results. Final report submitted to the Kansas Department of Social and Rehabilitation Services, Alcohol and Drug Abuse Service.* Seattle: Social Development Research Group, University of Washington.

Bandura, A. (1977). *Social learning theory.* Englewood Cliffs, NJ: Prentice-Hall.

Battin, S. R., Hill, K. G., Abbott, R. D., Catalano, R. F., & Hawkins, J. D. (1998). The contribution of gang membership to delinquency beyond delinquent friends. *Criminology, 36,* 93–115.

Battistich, V., Schaps, E., Watson, M., & Solomon, D. (1996). Prevention effects of the Child Development Project: Early findings from an ongoing multisite demonstration trial. *Journal of Adolescent Research, 11,* 12–35.

Battistich, V., Solomon, D., Watson, M., & Schaps, E. (1997). Caring school communities. *Educational Psychologist, 32,* 137–151.

Belknap, J. (1996). *The invisible woman: Gender, crime and justice.* San Francisco: Jossey-Bass.

Block, J. (1984). *Sex role identity and ego development.* San Francisco: Jossey-Bass.

Blumstein, A., & Rosenfeld, R. (1998, October). Assessing the recent ups and downs in U.S. homicide rates. *National Institute of Justice Journal,* 9–11, 237.

Borduin, C. M., Henggeler, S. W., Blaske, D. M., & Stein, R. J. (1990). Multisystemic treatment of adolescent sexual offenders. *International Journal of Offender Therapy and Comparative Criminology, 34,* 105–113.

Borduin, C. M., Mann, B. J., Cone, L. T., Henggeler, S. W., Fucci, R. B., Blaske, D. M., & Williams, R. A. (1995). Multisystemic treatment of serious juvenile offenders: Long-term prevention of criminality and violence. *Journal of Consulting and Clinical Psychology, 63,* 569–578.

Brewer, D. D., Hawkins, J. D., Catalano, R. F., & Neckerman, H. J. (1995). Preventing serious, violent, and chronic juvenile offending: A review of evaluations of selected strategies in childhood, adolescence, and the community. In J. C. Howell, B. Krisberg, J. D. Hawkins, & J. J. Wilson (Eds.), *A sourcebook: Serious, violent, and chronic juvenile offenders* (pp. 61–141). Thousand Oaks, CA: Sage.

Bursik, R. J., Jr., Merten, D., & Schwartz, G. (1985). Appropriate age-related behavior for male and female adolescents: Adult perceptions. *Youth and Society, 17,* 115–130.

Catalano, R. F., Arthur, M. W., Hawkins, J. D., Berglund, L., & Olson, J. J. (1998). Comprehensive community and school based interventions to prevent antisocial behavior. In R. Loeber & D. P. Farrington (Eds.), *Serious and violent juvenile offenders: Risk factors and successful interventions* (pp. 248–283). Thousand Oaks, CA: Sage.

Catalano, R. F., & Hawkins, J. D. (1996). The social development model: A theory of antisocial behavior. In J. D. Hawkins (Ed.), *Delinquency and crime: Current theories* (pp. 149–197). New York: Cambridge University Press.

Catalano, R. F., Oxford, M. L., Harachi, T. W., Abbott, R. D., & Haggerty, K. P. (1999). A test of the social development model to predict problem behaviour during the elementary school period. *Criminal Behaviour and Mental Health, 9,* 39–56.

Chesney Lind, M. (1989). Girls' crime and woman's place: Toward a feminist model of female delinquency. *Crime and Delinquency, 35,* 5–29.

Chung, I.-J., Hill, K. G., Hawkins, J. D., Gilchrist, L. D., & Nagin, D. (2002). Childhood predictors of offense trajectories. *Journal of Research in Crime and Delinquency, 39,* 60–90.

Coie, J. D., Watt, N. F., West, S. G., Hawkins, J. D., Asarnow, J. R., Markman, H. J., Ramey, S. L., Shure, M. B., & Long, B. (1993). The science of prevention. A conceptual framework and some directions for a national research program. *American Psychologist, 48,* 1013–1022.

Conduct Problems Prevention Research Group. (1999a). Initial impact of the Fast Track Prevention Trial for Conduct Problems: I. The high-risk sample. *Journal of Consulting and Clinical Psychology, 67,* 631–647.

Conduct Problems Prevention Research Group. (1999b). Initial impact of the Fast Track Prevention Trial for Conduct Problems: II. Classroom effects. *Journal of Consulting and Clinical Psychology, 67,* 648–657.

Cowan, P. A., Cowan, C. P., & Schulz, M. S. (1996). Thinking about risk and resilience in families. In E. M. Hetherington & E. A. Blechman (Eds.), *Stress, coping, and resiliency in children and families. Family research consortium: Advances in family research* (pp. 1–38). Mahwah, NJ: Erlbaum.

Dishion, T. J., McCord, J., & Poulin, F. (1999). When interventions harm: Peer groups and problem behavior. *American Psychologist, 54,* 755–764.

Dryfoos, J. G. (1990). *Adolescents at risk: Prevalence and prevention.* New York: Oxford University Press.

Dryfoos, J. G. (1996). *Adolescents-at-risk revisited: Continuity, evaluation, and replication of prevention programs.* (Unpublished manuscript).

Elliott, D. S. (1994). Serious violent offenders: Onset, developmental course, and termination. The American Society of Criminology 1993 Presidential Address. *Criminology, 32,* 1–22.

Elliott, D. S. (1998). *Blueprints for violence prevention.* Boulder, CO: Center for the Study and Prevention of Violence, Institute of Behavioral Science, University of Colorado at Boulder.

Elliott, D. S., Ageton, S. S., & Canter, R. J. (1979). An integrated theoretical perspective on delinquent behavior. *Journal of Research in Crime and Delinquency, 16,* 3–27.

Elliott, D. S., & Huizinga, D. (1985). *The relationship between delinquent behavior and ADM problems.* Paper presented at the ADAMHA/OJJDP State of the Art Research Conference on Juvenile Offenders with Serious Drug, Alcohol, & Mental Health Problems, Behavioral Research Institute, Boulder, CO.

Eslea, M., & Smith, P. K. (1998). The long-term effectiveness of anti-bullying work in primary schools. *Educational Research, 40,* 203–218.

Evertson, C. M. (1985). Training teachers in classroom management: An experimental study in secondary school classroom. *Journal of Educational Research, 79,* 51–58.

Evertson, C. M., Emmer, E. T., Sanford, J. P., & Clements, B. S. (1983). Improving classroom management: An experiment in elementary school classrooms. *Elementary School Journal, 84,* 173–188.

Farrington, D. (1998). Predictors, causes, and correlates of male youth violence. In M. Tonry & M. H. Moore (Eds.), *Crime and justice: A review of research* (Vol. 24, pp. 421–475). Chicago: University of Chicago Press.

Farrington, D. P. (1994, June). *Protective factors in the development of juvenile delinquency and adult crime.* Paper presented at the Sixth scientific meeting of the Society for Research in Child and Adolescent Psychopathology, London.

Farrington, D. P. (1995). The development of offending and antisocial behavior from childhood: Key findings from the Cambridge study in delinquent development. *Journal of Child Psychology and Psychiatry, 36,* 929–964.

Farrington, D. P., & Loeber, R. (1999). Transatlantic replicability of risk factors in the development of delinquency. In P. Cohen, C. Slomkowski, & L. N. Robbins (Eds.), *Historical and geographical influences on psychopathology* (pp. 299–329). Mahwah, NJ: Erlbaum.

Felner, R. D., Brand, S., Adan, A. M., Mulhall, P. F., Flowers, N., Sartain, B., & Dubois, D. L. (1993). Restructuring the ecology of the school as an approach to prevention during school transitions: Longitudinal follow-ups and extensions of the School Transitional Environment Project (STEP). *Prevention in Human Services, 10,* 103–136.

Fergusson, D. M., Horwood, L. J., & Nagin, D. S. (2000). Offending trajectories in a New Zealand birth cohort. *Criminology, 38,* 525–551.

Fraser, M. W., & Richman, J. M. (2001). Resilience: Implications for evidence-based practice. In M. W. Fraser & J. M. Richman (Eds.), *The context of youth violence: Resilience, risk and protection* (pp. 187–198). Westport, CT: Praeger.

Garmezy, N. (1983). Stressors of childhood. In N. Garmezy & M. Rutter (Eds.), *Stress, coping, and development in children* (pp. 43–84). Baltimore: Johns Hopkins University Press.

Gilligan, C., Ward, J. V., Taylor, J. M., & Bardige, B. (1988). *Mapping the moral domain: A contribution of women's thinking to psychological theory and education.* Cambridge, MA: Harvard University Press.

Giordano, P. C., & Cernkovich, S. A. (1997). Gender and antisocial behavior. In D. M. Stoff, J. Breiling, & J. D. Maser (Eds.), *Handbook of antisocial behavior* (pp. 496–510). New York: Wiley.

Gottfredson, D. C. (1986). An empirical test of school-based environmental and individual interventions to reduce the risk of delinquent behavior. *Criminology, 24,* 705–731.

Gottfredson, D. C. (2001). *Schools and delinquency.* Cambridge: Cambridge University Press.

Greenberg, M. T. (1998, August). *Testing developmental theory of antisocial behavior with outcomes from the Fast Track Prevention Project.* Paper presented at the Annual Meeting of the American Psychological Association, Chicago.

Greenberg, M. T., & Kusche, C. A. (1993). *Promoting social and emotional development in deaf children: The PATHS project.* Seattle: University of Washington Press.

Greenberg, M. T., & Kusche, C. A. (1997, April). *Improving children's emotion regulation and social competence: The effects of the PATHS curriculum.* Paper presented at the Annual Meeting of the Society for Research in Child Development, Washington, DC.

Greenwood, P. W., Model, K. E., Rydell, C. P., & Chiesa, J. (1998). *Diverting children from a life of crime: Measuring costs and benefits.* Santa Monica, CA: Rand Corporation.

Grossman, D. C., Neckerman, H. J., & Rivara, F. P. (1997). Effectiveness of a violence prevention curriculum among children in elementary school: A randomized controlled trial. *JAMA: The Journal of the American Medical Association, 277,* 1605–1611.

Hagan, J., Simpson, J., & Gillis, A. R. (1988). Feminist scholarship, relational and instrumental control, and a power-control theory of gender and delinquency. *British Journal of Sociology, 39,* 301–336.

Hammond, W. R., & Yung, B. R. (1993). *Evaluation and activity report: Positive Adolescents Choices Training (PACT) program.* (Grant No. 92-DG-B01–7138). (Ohio Governor's Office of Criminal Justice Services). Dayton, OH: Wright State University, School of Professional Psychology.

Harachi Manger, T. H., Hawkins, J. D., Haggerty, K. P., & Catalano, R. F. (1992). Mobilizing communities to reduce risks for drug abuse: Lessons on using research to guide prevention practice. *Journal of Primary Prevention, 13,* 3–22.

Hawkins, D. F., Laub, J. H., & Lauritsen, J. L. (1998). Race, ethnicity, and serious juvenile offending. In R. Loeber & D. P. Farrington (Eds.), *Serious and violent juvenile offenders: Risk factors and successful interventions* (pp. 30–46). Thousand Oaks, CA: Sage.

Hawkins, J. D., Catalano, R. F., & Associates. (1992). *Communities That Care: Action for drug abuse prevention* (1st ed.). San Francisco: Jossey-Bass.

Hawkins, J. D., Catalano, R. F., Kosterman, R., Abbott, R., & Hill, K. G. (1999). Preventing adolescent health-risk behaviors by strengthening protection during childhood. *Archives of Pediatrics and Adolescent Medicine, 153,* 226–234.

Hawkins, J. D., Catalano, R. F., & Miller, J. Y. (1992). Risk and protective factors for alcohol and other drug problems in adolescence and early adulthood: Implications for substance abuse prevention. *Psychological Bulletin, 112,* 64–105.

Hawkins, J. D., Catalano, R. F., Morrison, D. M., O'Donnell, J., Abbott, R. D., & Day, L. E. (1992). The Seattle Social Development Project: Effects of the first four years on protective factors and problem behaviors. In J. McCord & R. E. Tremblay (Eds.), *Preventing antisocial behavior: Interventions from birth through adolescence* (pp. 139–161). New York: Guilford Press.

Hawkins, J. D., & Herrenkohl, T. I. (in press). Prevention in the school years. In D. P. Farrington & J. W. Coid (Eds.), *Early prevention of anti-social behavior.* Cambridge: Cambridge University Press.

Hawkins, J. D., Herrenkohl, T., Farrington, D. P., Brewer, D., Catalano, R. F., & Harachi, T. W. (1998). A review of predictors of youth violence. In R. Loeber & D. P. Farrington (Eds.), *Serious and violent juvenile offenders: Risk factors and successful interventions* (pp. 106–146). Thousand Oaks, CA: Sage.

Hawkins, J. D., Von Cleve, E., & Catalano, R. F., Jr. (1991). Reducing early childhood aggression: Results of a primary prevention program. *Journal of the American Academy of Child and Adolescent Psychiatry, 30,* 208–217.

Hawkins, J. D., & Weis, J. G. (1985). The social development model: An integrated approach to delinquency prevention. *Journal of Primary Prevention, 6,* 73–97.

Henggeler, S. W. (1997, May). Treating serious antisocial behavior in youth: The MST approach. *OJJDP Juvenile Justice Bulletin,* 1–7.

Henggeler, S. W., & Borduin, C. M. (1990). *Family therapy and beyond: A multisystematic approach to treating the behavior of children and adolescents.* Pacific Grove, CA: Brooks/Cole.

Henggeler, S. W., Melton, G. B., Brondino, M. J., Scherer, D. G., & Hanley, J. H. (1997). Multisystemic therapy with violent and chronic juvenile offenders and their families: The role of treatment fidelity in successful dissemination. *Journal of Consulting and Clinical Psychology, 65,* 821–833.

Henggeler, S. W., Melton, G. B., Smith, L. A., Schoenwald, S. K., & Hanley, J. H. (1993). Family preservation using multisystemic treatment: Long-term follow-up to a clinical trial with serious juvenile offenders. *Journal of Child and Family Studies, 2,* 283–293.

Henggeler, S. W., Rodick, J. D., Borduin, C. M., Hanson, C. L., Watson, S. M., & Urey, J. R. (1986). Multisystemic treatment of juvenile offenders: Effects on adolescent behavior and family interaction. *Developmental Psychology, 22,* 132–141.

Henggeler, S. W., Rowland, M. D., Pickrel, S. G., Miller, S. L., Cunningham, P. B., Santos, A. B., Schoenwald, S. K., Randall, J., & Edwards, J. E. (1997). Investigating family-based alternatives to institution-based mental health services for youth: Lessons learned from the pilot study of a randomized field trial. *Journal of Clinical Child Psychology, 26,* 226–233.

Henggeler, S. W., Schoenwald, S. K., Borduin, C. M., Rowland, M. D., & Cunningham, P. B. (1998). *Multisystemic treatment of antisocial behavior in children and adolescents.* New York: Guilford Press.

Herrenkohl, T., Huang, B., Kosterman, R., Hawkins, J. D., Catalano, R. F., & Smith, B. (2001). A comparison of the social development processes leading to violent behavior in late adolescence for childhood initiators and adolescent initiators of violence. *Journal of Research in Crime and Delinquency, 38,* 45–63.

Herrenkohl, T. I., Guo, J., Kosterman, R., Hawkins, J. D., Catalano, R. F., & Smith, B. H. (2001). Early adolescent predictors of youth violence as mediators of childhood risks. *Journal of Early Adolescence, 21,* 447–469.

Herrenkohl, T. I., Hawkins, J. D., Chung, I.-J., Hill, K. G., & Battin-Pearson, S. R. (2001). School and community risk factors and interventions. In R. Loeber & D. P. Farrington (Eds.), *Child delinquents: Development, intervention, and service needs* (pp. 211–246). Thousand Oaks, CA: Sage.

Herrenkohl, T. I., Hill, K. G., Chung, I.-J., Guo, J., Abbott, R. D., & Hawkins, J. D. (under review). *Protective factors against serious violent behavior in adolescence: A prospective study of aggressive children.*

Herrenkohl, T. I., Maguin, E., Hill, K. G., Hawkins, J. D., Abbott, R. D., & Catalano, R. F. (2000). Developmental risk factors for youth violence. *Journal of Adolescent Health, 26,* 176–186.

Hirschi, T. (1969). *Causes of delinquency.* Berkeley: University of California Press.

Howell, J. C. (1997). *Juvenile justice and youth violence.* Thousand Oaks, CA: Sage.

Howell, J. C., & Hawkins, J. D. (1998). Prevention of youth violence. In M. Tonry & M. H. Moore (Series Eds.), *Crime and justice: A review of research* (Vol. 24, pp. 263–315). Chicago: University of Chicago Press.

Howell, J. C., Krisberg, B., Hawkins, J. D., & Wilson, J. J. (Eds.). (1995). *A sourcebook: Serious, violent, and chronic juvenile offenders.* Thousand Oaks, CA: Sage.

Huang, B., Kosterman, R., Catalano, R. F., Hawkins, J. D., & Abbott, R. D. (2001). Modeling mediation in the etiology of violent behavior in adolescence: A test of the social development model. *Criminology, 39,* 75–107.

Jenson, J., Hartman, H., & Smith, J. (1997). *Evaluation of Iowa's Juvenile Crime Prevention Community Grant Fund Program.* Iowa City: University of Iowa, School of Social Work.

Kellam, S. G., & Rebok, G. W. (1992). Building developmental and etiological theory through epidemiologically based preventive intervention trials. In J. McCord & R. E. Tremblay (Eds.), *Preventing antisocial behavior: Interventions from birth through adolescence* (pp. 162–195). New York: Guilford Press.

Kellam, S. G., Rebok, G. W., Ialongo, N. S., & Mayer, L. S. (1994). The course and malleability of aggressive behavior from early first grade into middle school: Results of a developmental epidemiology-based preventive trial. *Journal of Child Psychology and Psychiatry and Allied Disciplines, 35,* 259–281.

Kelley, B. T., Huizinga, D., Thornberry, T. P., & Loeber, R. (1997, June). Epidemiology of serious violence. *Office of Juvenile Justice and Delinquency Prevention: Juvenile Justice Bulletin, 11.*

Lipsey, M. W., & Derzon, J. H. (1998). Predictors of violent or serious delinquency in adolescence and early adulthood: A synthesis of longitudinal research. In R. Loeber & D. P. Farrington (Eds.), *Serious and violent juvenile offenders: Risk factors and successful interventions* (pp. 86–105). Thousand Oaks, CA: Sage.

Loeber, R. (1990). Development and risk factors of juvenile antisocial behavior and delinquency. *Clinical Psychology Review, 10,* 1–41.

Loeber, R. (1996). Developmental continuity, change, and pathways in male juvenile problem behaviors and delinquency. In J. D. Hawkins (Ed.), *Delinquency and crime: Current theories* (pp. 1–27). New York: Cambridge University Press.

Loeber, R., & Farrington, D. P. (1998). *Serious and violent juvenile offenders: Risk factors and successful interventions.* Thousand Oaks, CA: Sage.

Loeber, R., & Farrington, D. P. (2001). The significance of child delinquency. In R. Loeber & D. P. Farrington (Eds.), *Child delinquents: Development, intervention, and service needs* (pp. 1–22). Thousand Oaks, CA: Sage.

Loeber, R., & Hay, D. (1997). Key issues in the development of aggression and violence from childhood to early adulthood. *Annual Review of Psychology, 48,* 371–410.

Loeber, R., & Stouthamer-Loeber, M. (1998). Development of juvenile aggression and violence. Some common misconceptions and controversies. *American Psychologist, 53,* 242–259.

Lonczak, H. S., Huang, B., Catalano, R. F., Hawkins, J. D., Hill, K. G., Abbott, R. D., Ryan, J. A. M., & Kosterman, R. (2001). The social predictors of adolescent alcohol misuse: A test of the Social Development Model. *Journal of Studies on Alcohol, 62,* 179–189.

Maguin, E., & Loeber, R. (1996). Academic performance and delinquency. *Crime and Justice: A Review of the Research, 20,* 145–264.

Moffitt, T. E. (1993). Adolescence-limited and life-course-persistent antisocial behavior: A developmental taxonomy. *Psychological Review, 100,* 674–701.

Moffitt, T. E., & Caspi, A. (2001). Childhood predictors differentiate life-course persistent and adolescence-limited antisocial pathways among males and females. *Development and Psychopathology, 13,* 355–375.

Mrazek, P. J., & Haggerty, R. J. (1994). *Reducing risks for mental disorders: Frontiers for prevention intervention research.* Washington, DC: National Academy Press.

Nagin, D., & Tremblay, R. E. (1999). Trajectories of boys' physical aggression, opposition, and hyperactivity on the path to physically violent and nonviolent juvenile delinquency. *Child Development, 70,* 1181–1196.

Nagin, D. S., Farrington, D. P., & Moffitt, T. E. (1995). Life-course trajectories of different types of offenders. *Criminology, 33,* 111–139.

Nettle, S. M., & Pleck, J. H. (1996). Risk, resilience, and development: The multiple ecologies of black adolescents in the United States. In R. J. Haggerty, L. R. Sherrod, N. Garmezy, & M. Rutter (Eds.), *Stress, risk, and resilience in children and adolescents: Processes, mechanisms, and interventions* (pp. 147–181). New York: Cambridge University Press.

O'Donnell, J., Hawkins, J. D., Catalano, R. F., Abbott, R. D., & Day, L. E. (1995). Preventing school failure, drug use, and delinquency among low-income children: Long-term intervention in elementary schools. *American Journal of Orthopsychiatry, 65,* 87–100.

Office of Juvenile Justice and Delinquency Prevention. (1996). *1996 report to Congress. Title V incentive grants for local delinquency prevention programs.* Washington DC: Author.

Olweus, D. (1991). Bully/victim problems among schoolchildren: Basic facts and effects of a school based intervention program. In D. J. Pepler & K. H. Rubin (Eds.), *The development and treatment of childhood aggression* (pp. 411–448). Hillsdale, NJ: Erlbaum.

Oxford, M. L., Harachi, T. W., Catalano, R. F., Haggerty, K. P., & Abbott, R. D. (2000). Early elementary school-aged child attachment to parents: A test of theory and implications for intervention. *Prevention Science, 1,* 61–70.

Patterson, G. R. (1982). *A social learning approach: Vol. 3. Coercive family process.* Eugene, OR: Castalia.

Patterson, G. R., DeBaryshe, B. D., & Ramsey, E. (1989). A developmental perspective on antisocial behavior. *American Psychologist, 44,* 329–335.

Patterson, G. R., & Dishion, T. J. (1985). Contributions of families and peers to delinquency. *Criminology, 23,* 63–79.

Pollard, J., Catalano, R. F., Hawkins, J. D., & Arthur, M. W. (1997). *Development of a school-based survey measuring risk and protective factors predictive of substance abuse, delinquency, and other problem behaviors in adolescent populations.* Seattle: Unpublished manuscript. Social Development Research Group, University of Washington.

Pollard, J. A., Hawkins, J. D., & Arthur, M. W. (1999). Risk and protection: Are both necessary to understand diverse behavioral outcomes in adolescence? *Social Work Research, 23,* 145–158.

Reiss, A. J., Jr., & Roth, J. A. (1993). *Understanding and preventing violence, Vol. 1.* Washington, DC: National Academy Press.

Resnick, M. D., Bearman, P. S., Blum, R. W., Bauman, K. E., Harris, K. M., Jones, J., Tabor, J., Beuhring, T., Sieving, R. E., Shew, M., Ireland, M., Bearinger, L. H., & Udry, J. R. (1997). Protecting adolescents from harm: Findings from the National Longitudinal Study on Adolescent Health. *JAMA: The Journal of the American Medical Association, 278,* 823–832.

Rutter, M. (1979). Protective factors in children's responses to stress and disadvantage. In M. W. Kent & J. E. Rolf (Eds.), *Primary prevention of psychopathology: Vol. 3. Social competence in children* (pp. 49–74). Hanover, NH: University Press of New England.

Rutter, M. (1985). Resilience in the face of adversity: Protective factors and resistance to psychiatric disorder. *British Journal of Psychiatry, 147,* 598–611.

Sampson, R. J., & Laub, J. H. (1993). *Crime in the making: Pathways and turning points through life.* Cambridge, MA: Harvard University Press.

Sampson, R. J., & Lauritsen, J. L. (1994). Violent victimization and offending: Individual-, situational-, and community-level risk factors. In A. J. Reiss & J. A. Roth (Eds.), *Understanding and preventing violence, Vol. 3: Social influences* (pp. 1–114). Washington, DC: National Academy Press.

Sampson, R. J., Raudenbush, S. W., & Earls, F. (1997). Neighborhoods and violent crime: A multilevel study of collective efficacy. *Science, 277,* 918–924.

Sampson, R. J., & Wilson, W. J. (1995). Toward a theory of race, crime, and urban inequality. In J. Hagan & R. D. Peterson (Eds.), *Crime and inequality* (pp. 37–54). Stanford, CA: Stanford University Press.

Schoenwald, S. K., Ward, D. M., Henggeler, S. W., Pickrel, S. G., & Patel, H. (1996). Multisystemic therapy treatment of substance abusing or dependent adolescent offenders: Costs of reducing incarceration, inpatient, and residential placement. *Journal of Child and Family Studies, 5,* 431–444.

Shaw, C. R., & McKay, H. D. (1942). *Juvenile delinquency in urban areas.* Chicago: University of Chicago Press.

Siegel, L. J., & Senna, J. J. (1994). *Juvenile delinquency: The theory, practice, and law* (5th ed.). St. Paul, MN: West Publishing.

Slaby, R. G., & Guerra, N. G. (1988). Cognitive mediators of aggression in adolescent offenders: I. Assessment. *Developmental Psychology, 24,* 580–588.

Smith, C., & Carlson, B. E. (1997). Stress, coping, and resilience in children and youth. *Social Service Review, 71,* 231–256.

Snyder, H. N. (2000, December). Juvenile arrests 1999. *OJJDP Juvenile Justice Bulletin.*

Sutherland, E. H. (1947). *Principles of criminology* (4th ed.). Philadelphia: J. B. Lippincott.

Sutherland, E. H., & Cressey, D. R. (1970). *Criminology.* New York: Lippincott.

Tierney, J. P., Grossman, J. B., & Resch, N. L. (1995). *Making a difference: An impact study of Big Brothers/Big Sisters.* Philadelphia, PA: Public/Private Ventures.

Tolan, P. H., & Loeber, R. (1993). Antisocial behavior. In P. H. Tolan & B. J. Cohler (Eds.), *Handbook of clinical research and practice with adolescents. Wiley series on personality processes* (pp. 307–331). New York: Wiley.

Wasserman, G. A., & Miller, L. S. (1998). The prevention of serious and violent juvenile offending. In R. Loeber & D. P. Farrington (Eds.), *Serious and violent juvenile offenders: Risk factors and successful interventions* (pp. 197–247). Thousand Oaks, CA: Sage.

Weissberg, R. P., Barton, H. A., & Shriver, T. P. (1997). The Social-Competence Promotion Program for Young Adolescents. In G. W. Albee & T. P. Gullotta (Eds.), *Primary prevention works. Issues in children's and families' lives* (Vol. 6, pp. 268–290). Thousand Oaks, CA: Sage.

Weissberg, R. P., & Caplan, M. (under review). *Promoting social competence and preventing antisocial behavior in young urban adolescents.* Chicago: University of Illinois at Chicago.

Weissberg, R. P., & Greenberg, M. T. (1998). School and community competence-enhancement and prevention programs. In W. Damon, I. E. Sigel, & K. A. Renninger (Eds.), *Handbook of child psychology: Vol. 4. Child psychology in practice* (5th ed., pp. 877–954). New York: John Wiley & Sons.

Werner, E. E., & Smith, R. S. (1992). *Overcoming the odds: High risk children from birth to adulthood.* Ithaca, NY: Cornell University Press.

Wiel, M., & Gamble, D. (1995). Community practice models. In R. L. Edwards (Ed.), *Encyclopedia of social work* (19th ed., Vol. 1, pp. 577–593). Washington, DC: NASW Press.

Yoshikawa, H. (1994). Prevention as cumulative protection: Effects of early family support and education on chronic delinquency and its risks. *Psychological Bulletin, 115,* 28–54.

CHAPTER 21

ADOLESCENT SEX OFFENDERS
Characteristics, Prevention, and Treatment

WILLIAM D. MURPHY
University of Tennessee Health Science Center

I. JACQUELINE PAGE
University of Tennessee Health Science Center

MELISSA L. HOFFMANN
University of Tennessee Health Science Center

Adolescent sex offenders are a diverse group, and legal and clinical definitions of sexual offending vary substantially (Murphy, Haynes, & Page, 1992). Ryan (1991) identified three factors that determine whether sexual behaviors constitute sexual offending: (1) equality, (2) consent, and (3) coercion. Murphy and colleagues (1992), in a similar vein, suggested six factors: (1) age difference between the victim and offender, (2) use of force, (3) power differences between the offender and victim, (4) developmental differences, (5) differences in emotional stability, and (6) compulsive sexual behavior. Clinical definitions such as these include offensive behavior that may not meet legal definitions of a sexual offense but that nonetheless is exploitive.

Adolescents account for a significant proportion of sexual offenses, especially offenses against children. Barbaree, Hudson, and Seto (1993) and Weinrott (1996) found that adolescents are responsible for 30 to 50 percent of child molestations and for 15 to 20 percent of rapes. It is also well recognized that many adult offenders began their offending or deviant sexual interest during adolescence (Abel & Rouleau, 1990; Marshall, Barbaree, & Eccles, 1991). Although juveniles account for a significant proportion of sexual offenses, especially those against children, and many adult offenders began their deviant sexual interest in adolescence, it also appears that many adolescents desist from their behavior. In an extensive review of recidivism research, the vast majority of studies found a sexual reoffense rate of 12 percent or less (Weinrott, 1996).

Although sex offending is primarily a male crime, a recent review found that 2.6 to 20 percent of adolescent offenders were female (Hilsop, 2001). Unfortunately, little data exist to contrast male and female adolescent offenders. Adolescent female offenders do appear to have much more extensive histories of sexual abuse and physical abuse in their backgrounds (Mathews, Hunter, & Vuz, 1997). The higher rates of abuse among female offenders and what in general appear to be more severe psychological disturbances have led some (e.g., Mathews et al., 1997) to recommend that treatment for female offenders needs to be different and more specific to gender issues. For example, such treatment may need to focus more on victimization/trauma, including issues such as female identity development, self-esteem, establishing appropriate boundaries, and understanding healthy relationships.

Data related to other individual differences are not available. There are no reliable data or rates of sexual offending in different ethnic/racial groups or for gay/lesbian groups.

FACTORS ASSOCIATED WITH ADOLESCENT SEXUAL OFFENDING

There have been a number of factors proposed as risk factors for sexual offending (see Table 21.1). Unfortunately, few studies examine protective factors. What information there is on protective factors will be covered in the text as we discuss relevant risk factors.

Individual Factors

Studies have attempted to identify factors within the adolescent offender that have possible etiological significance, such as delinquency, social competence, and sexual victimization

TABLE 21.1   Potential Risk Factors for Adolescent Sexual Offending

GENERAL AREAS OF RISK	SPECIFIC RISK FACTORS
INDIVIDUAL FACTORS	Biological (neurological, testosterone)
	Generalized delinquency
	Social competence and anger management
	Sexual victimization
	Deviant sexual interest
	Cognitive distortions
	Comorbid psychiatric disorders
FAMILY FACTORS	Family instability
	Violence
	Parental loss/separation
	Marital discord
	Parental rejection
SOCIAL/CULTURAL FACTORS	Cultural factors influencing male socialization
	Gender inequality
	Acceptance of rape-supportive attitudes
	Subordination of women/Hostility toward women
	Sexual scripts
	Pornography

(see Table 21.1). Initial studies of these factors were often demographic, without adequate control groups and without reliable and valid measures. As will be seen, adolescent sex offenders many times do not differ from other populations, such as psychiatric samples or individuals in juvenile corrections. In addition, adolescent sex offenders are a very heterogeneous group; currently, we have inadequate systems for classifying offenders into more homogenous groups.

Little evidence exists to support biological factors as risk factors for sex offending per se. Neuropsychological studies have produced inconsistent results (Lewis, Shanok, & Pincus, 1981; Tarter, Hegedus, Alterman, & Katz-Garris, 1983). One study has looked at testosterone levels (Brooks & Reddon, 1996) in groups of 15- to 17-year-olds. Testosterone levels were found to be highest in violent offenders, with no difference between nonviolent nonsexual offenders and the sex offender group (Brooks & Reddon, 1996). Such findings indicate that biological factors may be more related to general violence than sex offending specifically.

Evidence is mixed regarding differences between sex offenders and general delinquents, as well as whether sex offenders demonstrate specific deficits in social competence (e.g., social inadequacy, anger management, or general emotional management) when compared to other clinical or criminal groups (Weinrott, 1996). Initially, the approach to adolescent sex offenders was to assume that they differed and had different needs than youth engaging in generalized delinquent behavior. However, as evidence accumulates this assumption has been challenged (Milloy, 1998). Some of the mixed findings are related to the populations studied. Offenders against children alone appear to have fewer previous criminal charges than offenders against peers/adults (Richardson, Kelly, Bhate, & Graham, 1997). Courtship-disordered groups (i.e., exhibitionists, obscene phone callers, and toucherism) appear to have the lowest levels of criminality (Awad & Saunders, 1991; Saunders, Awad, & White, 1986).

In terms of social competence, adolescent child molesters have been found to be socially anxious, be threatened by heterosexual interactions, and perceive themselves as socially inadequate and socially isolated (Katz, 1990). Adolescent rapists have been shown to display significantly more problems with anger management than general delinquents in a residential program (Van Ness, 1984).

A recent study by Worling (2001) sheds some light on these issues. Using cluster analysis, four groups were identified: Antisocial/Impulsive, Unusual/Isolated, Overly Controlled and Reserved, Competent/Aggressive (Worling, 2001). These groups differed in their recidivism rates as well as their level of social competence. As might be expected, the Unusual/Isolated and Overly Controlled groups tended to have poorer social skills than the Antisocial and Aggressive groups. These groupings appear to explain some of the discrepancies found in studies of social competence.

One of the most widely held beliefs is that being a victim of sexual abuse causes sex offending behavior. Data related to this question have been reviewed in a number of places (see Murphy, Haynes, & Page, 1992; Righthand & Welch, 2001; Weinrott, 1996). Approximately 40 percent of juvenile sex offenders appear to have experienced sexual abuse, although the estimates vary widely across studies. Studies have found that offenders of male victims report much higher rates of personal abuse than offenders of female victims (Worling, 1995b), and offenders of children show much higher rates of personal sexual abuse than offenders of peers or adults (Awad & Saunders, 1991; O'Brien, 1991).

It is clear that at least some subsets of adolescent sex offenders have higher rates of sexual abuse than the general population. It is also clear that given the high rates of abuse in the general population, most young boys who are sexually abused do not go on to become sex offenders. A direct link between being a victim and becoming an offender has not been established. When adult male sex offenders who had been abused were compared to adult male survivors who were not offenders, the victims who were not offenders were found to have had more peer support and family support during childhood and adolescence (Lambie, Seymour, Lee, & Adams, 2002). These may be seen as protective factors.

Within the adult offender area, deviant sexual arousal measured physiologically has been a major assessment and treatment target (Murphy & Barbaree, 1994). In addition, physiologically measured sexual arousal of children has been shown to be the single best predictor of recidivism (Hanson & Bussière, 1998). However, few studies have investigated actual erectile responses in adolescent sex offenders. A summary of findings to date indicate that those adolescent offenders who abuse young males tend to show the highest levels of deviant sexual arousal (Becker, Hunter, Stein, & Kaplan, 1989; Hunter, Goodwin, & Becker, 1994; Murphy, DiLillo, Haynes, & Steele, 2001; Seto, Lalumière, & Blanchard, 2000).

Evidence linking physiological sexual responding to recidivism is somewhat limited. Evidence from therapist ratings (Schram, Milloy, & Rowe, 1991) and offender self-report (Worling & Curwen, 2000) suggests that deviant sexual interest is related to recidivism. However, the only study using physiological measures with adolescents found that deviant sexual arousal was not related to sexual recidivism (Gretton, McBride, Hare, O'Shaughnessy, & Kumka, 2001).

Another primary sex offender specific individual factor within the adult offender area has been the role of cognitive distortions in the etiology and/or maintenance of sexual offending (Murphy & Carich, 2001). Cognitive distortions include self-statements such as:

- The abuse did not hurt the victim.
- She was asking for it.
- I was just providing sex education.
- I only touched her, I only did it once.
- I was abused.

Addressing these types of cognitive processes has become a major component of the treatment of both adult and adolescent sexual offenders. However, within the adolescent literature, very few studies have actually investigated these factors. In one study reporting on the development of an adolescent cognition scale, cognitions did not discriminate between groups of juvenile sex offenders and a nondelinquent community control group (Hunter, Becker, Kaplan, & Goodwin, 1991).

Questions regarding psychological disturbances as a factor in adolescent sex offending have been reviewed in a number of sources (Righthand & Welch, 2001; Weinrott, 1996). These studies suggest that adolescent sex offenders evidence a variety of psychological problems and often show little differences from other groups. Identified psychological problems include a range of symptoms such as depression, anxiety, shyness, impulsivity, and delinquency. Rather than looking at individual symptoms, there have also been attempts to look at psychiatric disorders. In one of the few studies to use structured diagnostic interviews, 19 percent of adolescent sex offenders had no diagnosable psychiatric disorder. The most frequent diagnosis was conduct disorder (48 percent). Type of diagnosis was related to type of offense, with 70 percent of rapists having conduct disorders and only 25 percent of nonrapists meeting criteria for conduct disorder (Kavoussi, Kaplan, & Becker, 1988).

Family Factors

A significant number of adolescent sexual offenders come from homes in which some type of family dysfunction is present (Graves, 1993 [as cited in Weinrott, 1996]; Righthand & Welch, 2001). This dysfunction may include family instability, disorganization, violence, and parental loss or separation. However, when comparison groups are used (Weinrott, 1996), the families of adolescent sex offenders do not appear different from families of other groups. In fact, some studies (e.g., Blaske, Borduin, Henggeler, & Mann, 1989) found that the families of sexual offenders more closely approximate families of nondelinquent adolescents than families of nonsexual delinquent offenders in terms of family bonding and adaptability. Although family dysfunction may not clearly differentiate sexual offenders from nondelinquents, it may differentiate different types of adolescent offenders from one another. Higher levels of marital discord, parental rejection, physical discipline, negativism, and overall family dissatisfaction have been found among sibling incest offenders as compared to nonfamilial offenders (Worling, 1995a).

The following two cases represent the heterogeneity of the adolescent sex offender.

■ ■ ■ ■ ■ ▬▬▬▬▬▬▬▬▬▬▬▬▬▬▬▬▬▬▬▬▬▬▬▬▬▬▬▬▬▬▬▬▬

CASE STUDY
KEVIN AND KEITH

Kevin and Keith are 14-year-old identical twins of Hispanic origin. Both are quite small for their age. Their adoptive parents sought evaluation and treatment for them due to their sexual abuse of their 3-year-old adoptive sister on multiple occasions. The offenses occurred independently of each other, although each knew that the other was abusing. Early childhood history is positive for significant physical and emotional neglect as well as physical and sexual abuse. Their biological mother had psychiatric problems related to depression and also abused alcohol and drugs. The biological father did not have contact with the children and information about him was not available. Both boys were in this dysfunctional environment until approximately 5 or 6 years of age when they were placed at a group home. Upon placement, both were reported to have significant developmental and language delays. Highly sexualized behaviors were present, as was a preoccupation with violence and danger. The boys required constant supervision. Their biological mother and grandmother maintained sporadic contact with them while they were at the group home.

The twins' current adoptive parents became involved with them when their biological maternal grandmother approached them through the church about helping with the boys. Both Kevin and Keith went to live with their adoptive parents at age 7. At the time of their adoption, Kevin and Keith were the only children in the home. The adoptive parents now have two female biological children, ages 3 years and 1 year, and are expecting a male child. The adoptive parents have provided an overall stable home environment, although the father has had some incidents of being overly physical when disciplining them. Both Kevin and Keith have demonstrated significant developmental improvement since their placement with their adoptive parents. However, both boys have continued to engage in sexualized behavior, including frequent masturbation. They also engaged in sexual contact with each other during their initial time in the adoptive home. Behaviors consistent with trichotillomania and some obsessive traits were present. There has been a severe degree of oppositional behavior, with this usually being directed towards the adoptive mother. Both boys engage in lying and destructive behaviors.

Over the years, Kevin and Keith have received a variety of psychiatric diagnoses, including attention deficit hyperactivity disorder, obsessive compulsive disorder, trichotillomania, sexual abuse of a child, post-traumatic stress disorder, reactive attachment disorder, and learning problem. They have each been on medication related to ADHD and obsessive-compulsive behaviors.

CASE STUDY
LARRY

Larry is a 13-year-old Caucasian male who was referred for evaluation due to his fondling, on one occasion, of a 5-year-old female neighbor. His family life has been stable and Larry lives with his mother, stepfather, and 9-year-old sister. His stepfather has been in the home since Larry was 5 or 6 years old. He has a 19-year-old sister who lives with her husband and baby in the same town, and the two families often have contact. Larry has not seen his biological father since age 4, and it is reported that he has been in jail for DUI and stealing.

Both Larry and his mother report a positive relationship. The relationship with his stepfather is not as positive, but in general is described as "good." Recently, Larry has been standoffish with his stepfather and describes his offense as occurring when he was angry at him. The family engages in family activities together. Larry is in the eighth grade and is a B student. He has no history of behavioral problems as a child. He has had one suspension for fighting, when he was in an altercation that another student allegedly started. Larry has been involved in community activities, playing in a youth basketball league, and is interested in playing football as a ninth-grader. He has friends, including some close friends, and overall has adequate social skills. Except for masturbation, the sexual abuse of the 5-year-old is the only sexual experience Larry has had.

Social/Cultural Factors

To this point, we have focused on individual-level factors and family-level factors in terms of the etiology and maintenance of sexually aggressive behavior in adolescents. However, individuals function in a larger social environment, and thus are likely to be influenced by social/cultural factors. Two such factors are cultural values influencing male socialization and pornography. Little data exist to assess the impact of other media on adolescent sex offenders. No data link sexual offending to other social/cultural factors such as racial discrimination or neighborhood status.

The influence of cultural values and male socialization on sexual offending have been reviewed both empirically and theoretically by White and Koss (1993). Much of this literature has focused on more normative populations, often using samples of college students, and considers a continuum of sexually coercive behaviors with significant focus on coercion of peers. Very few of the studies have actually focused on adolescents, and therefore one has to be careful in generalizing to this age group. A number of issues related to male socialization have received modest support in the literature (White & Koss, 1993). These include issues around gender inequality, the subordination of women, and the acceptance of rape-supportive attitudes, as well as sexual scripts such as males being socialized to see themselves as the sexual aggressor. A large literature suggests that these variables may be related to sexually aggressive behavior in college students (White & Koss, 1993), although one study failed to find such attitudes to be related to sexual aggression in an adolescent population (Ageton, 1983).

In their confluence model of sexual aggression, Malamuth and colleagues (Malamuth, Sockloskie, Koss, & Tanaka, 1991; Malamuth, Linz, Heavey, Barnes, & Acker, 1995) identify two factors, Social Promiscuity/Impersonal Sex and Hostile Masculinity, which account for a significant proportion of the variance for coercion against women. Sexual promiscuity was shown to be influenced by delinquency, which is in turn influenced by parental violence and child abuse, especially child sexual abuse. Hostile masculinity is influenced by negative attitudes toward women, which are somewhat weakly influenced by delinquent behavior.

This model, at least for sexual offenses against peers or adults, clearly indicates that a number of the individual factors outlined earlier tend to have indirect effects on sexual abuse and interact with factors that are probably part of male socialization. Such factors include negative attitudes toward women, acceptance of rape myths, hostility toward women, and a tendency toward impersonal sex. Unfortunately, there is no similarly derived model for child sexual abuse with empirical support. For child sexual abuse, Finkelhor (1984) has described a theoretical model that includes social/cultural influences, labeled the *four preconditions model*. This model proposes that factors such as erotic portrayals of children in advertising, a masculine requirement to be dominant in sexual relationships, child pornography, and a male tendency to sexualize all emotional needs could relate to child sexual abuse. However, none of these factors has been clearly tested in offender populations of any type, including adolescent offender populations.

One social factor that is frequently proposed as being related to sexual offending is exposure to pornography. It appears that the vast majority (over 90 percent) of adolescents have viewed pornography (Bryant, 1985, as cited in Malamuth & Impett, 2001). In the adolescent sex offender literature, there is mixed evidence of whether adolescent sex offenders use pornography more than nonoffenders (Righthand & Welch, 2001; Weinrott, 1996), and whether they underestimate usage (Weinrott, 1996). There is, however, a large, well-reviewed literature that looks at the impact of pornography in nonclinical populations on a variety of measures (Malamuth, Addison, & Koss, 2000; Malamuth, 1993; Malamuth & Impett, 2001). In general, the literature shows that viewing violent sexual pornography, especially violent sexual pornography that shows a positive outcome (e.g., a woman enjoying it), is associated with negative attitudes toward women, acceptance of rape myths, a more callous attitude toward rape victims, and increased aggression against women in a laboratory setting. Such material tends to desensitize subjects to sexually violent behavior (Linz, Donnerstein, & Penrod, 1998). However, the literature is also clear that pornography does not impact all subjects similarly and that individual differences moderate the effects of exposure to pornographic media (Malamuth, Addison, & Koss, 2000; Malamuth & Impett, 2001). Some factors that have been found to moderate the influence of pornography include positive family environment and family communication. In general, violent pornography appears to have the greatest impact on those individuals who are already accepting of sexual aggression. Overall, whether the use of pornography influences sexually aggressive behavior or is a byproduct of sexually aggressive behavior has not been established.

PREVENTION

Foshee, Bauman, Greene, Koch, Linder, and MacDougall (2000) and McMahon and Puett (1999) have outlined a need to increase efforts toward prevention of abuse rather than focusing on intervention after the abuse has occurred. Prevention approaches involve primary, secondary, and tertiary prevention.

Primary prevention programs include child sexual abuse prevention education programs designed for elementary-age children and rape prevention/safe dating programs aimed primarily for adolescents and college students. Of 2,000 children aged 10 to 16 involved in a national survey, two-thirds had participated in at least one sex abuse prevention program in their school (Finkelhor & Dziuba-Leatherman, 1995). These programs tend to focus on teaching "good touch–bad touch," saying "no," escaping the situation, and telling someone. Evidence does suggest that children learn the concepts being taught but long-term follow-up studies of retention of information are lacking, as are studies of whether these program actually prevent abuse (Daro, 1994; Wurtele, 1998). A recent study by Gibson and Leitenberg (2000), comparing college women who did or did not participate in a school-based child sexual abuse prevention program, reported promising findings. The groups did not differ in terms of age, race, or socioeconomic level. Rates of abuse for those participating ($n = 499$) in a prevention program were 8 percent versus 14 percent for those who had not participated ($n = 312$) in such a program—a significant difference. Whether these results will generalize to other populations is unknown.

A second prominent type of prevention intervention is rape prevention programs found on the campuses of most colleges/universities and in some high schools. These programs have a primary prevention focus on potential victims protecting themselves and a secondary prevention focus through attempting to alter rape-supportive attitudes of males. In a meta-analysis of rape prevention programs for college students, Brecklin and Forde (2001) found that such programs do alter rape-supportive attitudes, at least over the short term (changes tended to decline over time). Foshee and colleagues (2000) and Lanier (2001) found similar results for high school programs. These studies compared a group receiving a rape education program to a matched group not receiving such a program and included baseline and one-year follow-up measures. Some evidence suggests caution in applying these types of programs. Those at risk for sexual aggression may develop even more negative attitudes after intervention (see Malamuth, 1993, for a review). The reasons for this are not clear. Although no data are available, it may occur if the content in these programs is delivered in an overly confrontational style and where the focus is viewed as attacking males in general.

As noted, some of the preceding interventions may target at-risk groups, but the field generally lacks secondary prevention approaches. The major hindrance to such programs is a lack of knowledge in defining at-risk groups, especially those at risk for perpetration. A potential risk group could include children who have been sexually abused. However, most children who are sexually abused do not go on to offend, and one must be careful in labeling and stigmatizing these youth (Daro, 1994). Lambie and colleagues' 2002 study provides some direction in identifying victims that might be at higher risk for offending. However, further research is necessary before clear risk factors can be determined.

TREATMENT

The major goal for the treatment of sexual offenders is to reduce victimization. Because of this, treatment of the adolescent sex offender has both a therapeutic component and a supervisory component. Most treatment providers work closely with juvenile court, probation and parole, and child protective services to ensure that there is an external component to monitoring in addition to strengthening internal controls through therapeutic approaches. External monitoring can include frequent home visits, "house arrest," and, for some sexual offenders, electronic monitoring.

The most frequent approach to the treatment of sexual offenders is cognitive behavioral therapy within a relapse prevention context, usually delivered in a group format. Treatment focuses on a number of issues felt to be related to recidivism. These issues include denial, justification, identifying factors that trigger offending, developing adequate skills to cope with these factors, and developing victim empathy. Programs also focus, when appropriate, on assisting the adolescent in managing deviant sexual arousal. This approach to treatment has basically been borrowed from the adult sex offender literature where there is currently meta-analytic support (Hanson, Gordon, Harris, et al., in press) that cognitive behavioral approaches do reduce recidivism in adult sex offenders.

This section will provide basic information about the main phases of sex offender treatment, and should not be considered to be inclusive of all phases and components. Although sexual offending may be the identified problem, other issues may be present and should be addressed as well. The two cases presented earlier are clear examples of this. The twins in the first case study will need extensive sex offender-oriented treatment but will also need a number of other interventions. They will need medication evaluations for ADHD and their compulsive behavior. Psychotherapy will need to address issues around their own neglect and abuse and their difficulties bonding. They will need to work on developing more appropriate peer interaction skills, and the family will need assistance in learning behavioral management skills. The second case study should need a much more limited intervention. Treatment for that child would basically focus on sex offender issues such as cognitive distortions and recognizing the impact of this behavior.

The initial phase of treatment addresses issues related to denial and also focuses on the offender understanding basics about sex abuse. Motivational interviewing techniques (Miller

& Rollnick, 1991) are especially beneficial in assisting the offender in developing internal recognition that his or her behavior(s) were abusive. Motivational interviewing is a nonconfrontational approach that assists individuals in resolving ambivalence about changing, and helps them move along the path of change (Miller & Rollnick, 1991). A confrontational approach can result in the adolescent becoming resistant. Offenders in denial can benefit from assignments that focus on the process of denial rather than the specific content of their denial. For example, having the adolescent and group focus on reasons offenders deny, what they feel are consequences for admitting, and reasons to be truthful is generally more helpful than direct confrontation. This approach is based on the five general principles of motivational interviewing, which are "express empathy, develop discrepancy, avoid argumentation, roll with resistance, and support self-efficacy" (Miller & Rollnick, 1991, p. 55).

As the adolescent becomes more honest, treatment shifts to focus on cognitive distortions and attitudes supportive of offending. Many times distortions and attitudes supportive of offending are identified as the offender provides an offending history. The therapist's role is to identify these distortions and assist the adolescent in recognizing how these beliefs are false. The adolescent needs to be able to challenge his or her distortions, and the group format can enhance this process. Offenders are typically able to recognize their peers' distortions, and then are able to apply this knowledge to their own distorted thinking.

A major phase of treatment involves recognizing factors that place the adolescent at risk to reoffend, and developing strategies for dealing with the risk of reoffending. This phase is generally referred to as *relapse prevention*. There are a number of approaches (see Suggested Readings) to relapse prevention with adolescent sex offenders. However, the basic approach is for the adolescent to recognize that there are choices he or she makes that can increase or decrease the risk to reoffend and to recognize that there are connections between situations, thoughts, feelings, and behaviors. In general, the adolescent is asked to analyze life events that precede the abuse. These include two sets of factors. First is identifying events that directly preceded the offending where one generally identifies the grooming process—that is, how the offender set up the situation and got the victim to "go along." However, treatment also tries to identify more general life events or feelings that may trigger offending. These can include factors such as family conflict, peer rejection, and so on.

It is important in doing relapse prevention that treatment does not just focus on what the offender needs to avoid or give up, but that it also focuses on developing positive replacement behaviors. Haaven and Coleman (2000) have described this as developing the "New Me." Current relapse prevention approaches recognize that treatment will be more successful if one has approach goals and not just avoidance goals (Mann & Thornton, 2000).

As the adolescent begins to identify risk, he or she must also develop coping skills to deal with such risk. Most programs include more traditional skills building components, such as basic social skills training for more inhibited offenders, anger and emotional management, and skills for developing healthy relationships. As part of developing healthy relationships, many programs also include modules on healthy sexuality.

For those adolescents who appear to have deviant sexual arousal or sexual preoccupation, some programs teach procedures in managing sexual urges. These can include relatively simple techniques, such as using distraction or thought stopping. For those offenders who have significant difficulties controlling deviant urges, this may involve specific behavioral procedures, such as covert sensitization. More recently, there has been increased use of selective serotonin reuptake inhibitors to manage more sexually compulsive offenders (Bradford, 1993).

Victim empathy is also a component of many sex offender programs. This component overlaps with interventions designed to address cognitive distortions, as it is more difficult to justify offending behavior when one recognizes the impact of his or her behavior on others. Victim empathy training can also motivate the offender to implement his or her relapse prevention plan. Programs frequently utilize victim specific readings and commercial videotapes that focus on victim experiences in addition to education and discussion regarding the impact of sexual abuse.

For the adolescent who has been victimized, these issues will need to be taken into consideration. Adolescent sex offenders who have been sexually abused show similar symptoms to other sexual abuse victims. These may take the form of internalizing disorders but often are seen as more externalizing disorders. A specific issue for male victims is that abuse is usually by a male, and at times the victim will get an erection during the abuse. This leads to questions of sexual orientation and increases the self-blame that is many times seen in victims. However, the timing of when to address these issues is important, and the treatment provider needs to ensure that the offender does not utilize his or her own abuse as a justification. The first case study serves as a good example of the need to address these types of issues while balancing the offender's responsibility for his own actions. For these twins who suffered severe abuse and neglect, some primary victimization issues were related to attachment and the use of sexuality as a coping mechanism. At the same time, these youth, and to some extent their family, justified their sexually abusive behavior because of their early childhood experience. It is clear that these experiences had a significant negative impact. Although these experiences need to be addressed, the therapist must consistently reinforce the message that being abused does not give one the right to abuse others.

In addition to the sex offender specific components of treatment, family involvement is also an important focus. This involves not only the family being educated about offending issues, including relapse prevention plans and supervision, but also includes a focus on the family functioning overall. In the absence of a biological family, the treatment provider can involve the adolescent's support system.

Because of the high rate of delinquent recidivism with adolescent sex offenders, it has been suggested that treatment approaches for more generalized delinquent behavior might be more appropriate than more traditional sex offender approaches (Milloy, 1998). One such approach, Multisystemic Therapy (MST; Henggeler & Borduin, 1990), is a well-validated treatment approach for juvenile offending and has been recommended as a treatment for adolescent sex offenders. Basically, MST is an intensive case management approach with in-home services that attempts to target family relationships and interpersonal relationships, and that works closely with a variety of social support agencies in the juvenile's life. Two clinical trials, one with 16 subjects and a three-year follow-up (Borduin, Henggeler, Blaske, & Stein, 1990) and one with 48 subjects with an eight-year follow-up (Borduin & Schaeffer, in press) have shown MST to be superior to individual therapy and usual services (undefined) in reducing sexual recidivism and general recidivism. To date, however, there are no studies comparing MST to sex offender specific therapy.

Related to most of this discussion is the fact that we currently lack adequate risk assessment instruments for adolescent sex offenders so that our populations can be more clearly defined. Although instruments are under investigation (Prentky, Harris, Frizzell, & Righthand, 2000; Worling & Curwen, 2000), there is at this time no validated instrument to assess static risk factors or, more importantly, to assess dynamic risk factors. *Static risk factors* are those that cannot change, such as previous sex offenses, previous general criminal offenses, and so on; whereas *dynamic factors* are those that are changeable, such as cognitive distortions, social competence, and the like. Based on the literature and clinical experience, adolescent sex offenders vary on a number of dimensions. Important dimensions appear to be deviant sexual arousal/preoccupation, delinquency, social competence, and family support. The ability to adequately and reliably assess these dimensions would allow a more rational approach to treatment planning. We also lack, in the literature and the field, adequate data to inform treatment decisions for either special populations (offenders with mental retardation, female offenders, those with major psychiatric disorders) or for defining treatments that are appropriate for various ethnic or socioeconomic groups.

SUMMARY

Adolescent sexual offenders are a diverse, heterogeneous group who account for a significant proportion of sex offenses. Offenders are predominantly male but can also be female. They come from a variety of backgrounds. Some are similar to adolescents with general criminal histories, whereas others have markedly low levels of criminality or antisocial behavior. Adolescent sex offenders appear to have poor peer relations, but generally, few factors have been shown to describe all, or even most, offenders. Thus, adolescent sex offenders must be considered from a multifactor view, taking into account a combination of individual, family, and social factors. The study of adolescent sex offenders is young, but work in this field is steadily increasing. Studies demonstrate the effectiveness of cognitive behavioral treatment in adults, and this treatment has been replicated with adolescents. Unfortunately, randomized studies have not yet been conducted with adolescents, but there are some general guidelines accepted by the field:

- Treatment of the adolescent sex offender should include a focus on sex offender-specific factors and general psychosocial issues based on a comprehensive assessment of the individual.
- Sex offender specific issues include such factors as denial, cognitive distortions, victim empathy, developing relapse prevention plans and, for a subset, deviant sexual arousal.
- General psychosocial issues include such factors as impulsivity/delinquency, poor coping/social skills, family dysfunction, educational deficits, and personal victimization issues.
- Appropriate management of the adolescent sex offender involves a number of systems, including juvenile courts, child protective services, and mental health services.

Adolescent sex offenders present challenges to the clinician. They have a variety of sexual and psychological problems and many times enter treatment with poor motivation and a denial of problems. However, this population also presents to the clinician the opportunity to prevent future victimization. Future work can only improve the understanding, prediction, prevention, and treatment of adolescent sex offenders.

DISCUSSION QUESTIONS

1. Sexually aggressive behavior occurs much more frequently in males as compared to females. What factors may contribute to this gender difference?

2. What are some factors that argue for and against an early history of sexual victimization being a cause of sexual offending?

3. Discuss whether pornography use contributes to sexual aggression or is a byproduct of an individual's interest in sexual aggression.

4. Based on our current knowledge of adolescent sex offenders, discuss what seem to be the most promising treatment targets.

5. Given our knowledge of adolescent sex offenders, how might one design a prevention program that is directed at potential offenders rather than potential victims?

SUGGESTED READINGS

Association for the Treatment of Sexual Abusers. (2001). *Practice standards and guidelines for members of the Association for the Treatment of Sexual Abusers.* Beaverton, OR: Author.

Gray, A. S., & Wallace, R. (1992). *Adolescent sex offender assessment packet.* Brandon, VT: Safer Society Press.

Haaven, J., Little, R., & Petre-Miller, D. (1990). *Treating intellectually disabled sex offenders: A model residential program.* Brandon, VT: Safer Society Press.

Kahn, T. J. (1990). *Pathways: Guide for parents of youth beginning treatment* (rev. ed.). Brandon, VT: Safer Society Press.

Kahn, T. J. (2001). *Pathways: A guided workbook for youth beginning treatment* (3rd ed.). Brandon, VT: Safer Society Press.

Steen, C. (1993). *The relapse prevention workbook for youth in treatment.* Brandon, VT: Safer Society Press.

REFERENCES

Abel, G. G., & Rouleau, J. L. (1990). The nature and extent of sexual abuse. In W. L. Marshall, D. R. Laws, & H. E. Barbaree (Eds.), *Handbook of sexual assault: Issues, theories, and treatment of the offender* (pp. 9–21). New York: Plenum.

Ageton, S. (1983). *Sexual assault among adolescents.* Lexington, MA: Lexington Books.

Awad, G. S., & Saunders, E. B. (1991). Male adolescent sexual assaulters: Clinical observations. *Journal of Interpersonal Violence, 6,* 46–460.

Barbaree, H. E., Hudson, S. M., & Seto, M. C. (1993). Sexual assault in society: The role of the juvenile offender. In H. E. Barbaree, W. L. Marshall, & S. M. Hudson (Eds.), *The juvenile sex offender* (pp. 1–24). New York: Guilford.

Becker, J. V., Hunter, J., Stein, R., & Kaplan, M. S. (1989). Factors associated with erection in adolescent sex offenders. *Journal of Psychopathology and Behavioral Assessment, 11,* 353–362.

Blaske, D. M., Borduin, C. M., Henggeler, S. W., & Mann, B. J. (1989). Individual, family and peer characteristics of adolescent sex offenders and assaultive offenders. *Developmental Psychology, 25,*
846–855.

Borduin, C. M., Henggeler, S. W., Blaske, D. M., & Stein, R. J. (1990). Multisystemic treatment of adolescent sexual offenders. *International Journal of Offender Therapy and Comparative Criminology,
34,* 105–113.

Borduin, C. M., & Schaeffer, C. M. (in press). Multisystemic treatment of juvenile sexual offenders: A
progress report. *Journal of Psychology and Human Sexuality.*

Bradford, J. M. W. (1993). The pharmacological treatment of the adolescent sex offender. In H. E. Barbaree, W. L. Marshall, & S. M. Hudson (Eds.), *The juvenile sex offender* (pp. 278–288). New York:
Guilford.

Brecklin, L. R., & Forde, D. R. (2001). A meta-analysis of rape education programs. *Violence and Victims,
16,* 303–321.

Brooks, J. H., & Reddon, J. R. (1996). Serum testosterone in violent and nonviolent young offenders. *Journal of Clinical Psychology, 52,* 475–483.

Bryant, J. (1985). Frequency of exposure, age of initial exposure, and reactions to initial exposure to por-
nography [Report presented to the Attorney General's Commission on Pornography, Houston, TX].
In D. Zillmann & J. Bryant (Eds.), *Pornography: Research advances and policy considerations.*
Hillsdale, NJ: Erlbaum.

Daro, D. A. (1994). Prevention of child sexual abuse. *Sexual Abuse of Children, 4,* 198–223.

Finkelhor, D. (1984). *Child sexual abuse: New theory and research.* New York: Free Press.

Finkelhor, D., & Dziuba-Leatherman, J. (1995). Victimization prevention programs: A national survey of
children's exposure and reactions. *Child Abuse & Neglect, 19,* 129–139.

Foshee, V. A., Bauman, K. E., Greene, W. F., Koch, G. G., Linder, G. F., & MacDougall, J. E. (2000). The
safe dates program: 1-year follow-up results. *American Journal of Public Health, 90,* 1619–1622.

Gibson, L. E., & Leitenberg, H. (2000). Child sexual abuse prevention programs: Do they decrease the occurrence of child sexual abuse? *Child Abuse & Neglect, 24,* 1115–1125.

Graves, R. E. (1993). *Conceptualizing the youthful male sex offender: A meta-analytic examination of offender characteristics by offense type.* Unpublished dissertation at Utah State University.

Gretton, H. M., McBride, M., Hare, R. D., O'Shaughnessy, R., & Kumka, G. (2001). Psychopathy and recidivism in adolescent sex offenders. *Criminal Justice and Behavior, 28,* 427–449.

Haaven, J. L., & Coleman, E. M. (2000). Treatment of the developmentally disabled sex offender. In D. R.
Laws, S. M. Hudson, & T. Ward (Eds.), *Remaking relapse prevention with sex offenders: A sourcebook* (pp. 369–388). Thousand Oaks, CA: Sage.

Hanson, R. K., & Bussière. M. T. (1998). Predicting relapse: A meta-analysis of sexual offender recidivism studies. *Journal of Consulting and Clinical Psychology, 66,* 348–362.

Hanson, R. K., Gordon, A., Harris, A. J. R., Marques, J. K., Murphy, W. D., Quinsey, V. L., & Seto, M. C.
(in press). First report of the collaborative outcome data project on the effectiveness of treatment for
sex offenders. *Sexual Abuse: A Journal of Research and Treatment.*

Henggeler, S. W., & Borduin, C. M. (1990). *Family therapy and beyond: A multisystemic approach to
treating the behavior problem of children and adolescents.* Pacific Grove, CA: Brooks/Cole.

Hilsop, J. (2001). *Female sex offenders: What therapists, law enforcement and child protective services
need to know.* Ravensworth, WA: Issues Press.

Hunter, J. A., Becker, J. V., Kaplan, M. S., & Goodwin, D. W. (1991). Reliability and discriminative utility of
the Adolescent Cognitions Scale for juvenile sexual offenders. *Annals of Sex Research, 4,* 281–286.

Hunter, J. A., Goodwin, D. W., & Becker, J. V. (1994). The relationship between phallometrically measured deviant sexual arousal and clinical characteristics in juvenile sexual offenders. *Behaviour Research and Therapy, 32,* 533–538.

Katz, R. C. (1990). Psychosocial adjustment in adolescent child molesters. *Child Abuse & Neglect, 14,*
567–575.

Kavoussi, R. J., Kaplan, M. S., & Becker, J. V. (1988). Psychiatric diagnoses in adolescent sex offenders.
Journal of the American Academy of Child and Adolescent Psychiatry, 27, 241–243.

Lambie, I., Seymour, F., Lee, A., & Adams, P. (2002). Resiliency in the victim-offender cycle in male
sexual abuse. *Sexual Abuse: A Journal of Research and Treatment, 14,* 31–48.

Lanier, C. A. (2001). Rape-accepting attitudes. *Violence Against Women, 7,* 876–885.

Lewis, D. O., Shanok, S. S., & Pincus, J. H. (1981). Juvenile male sexual assaulters: Psychiatric, neurological, psychoeducational, and abuse factors. In D. O. Lewis (Ed.), *Vulnerabilities to delinquency* (pp. 89–105). Jamaica, NY: Spectrum.

Linz, D. G., Donnerstein, E., & Penrod, S. (1988). Effects of long-term exposure to violent and sexually degrading depictions of women. *Journal of Personality and Social Psychology, 55,* 758–768.

Malamuth, N. M. (1993). Pornography's impact on male adolescents. *Adolescent Medicine: State of the Art Reviews, 4,* 563–576.

Malamuth, N. M., Addison, T., & Koss, M. (2000). Pornography and sexual aggression: Are there reliable effects and can we understand them? *Annual Review of Sex Research, 11,* 26–91.

Malamuth, N. M., & Impett, E. A. (2001). Research on sex in the media. In D. G. Singer & J. L. Singer (Eds.), *Handbook of children and the media* (pp. 269–287). Thousand Oaks, CA: Sage.

Malamuth, N. M., Linz, D., Heavey, C. L., Barnes, G., & Acker, M. (1995). Using the confluence model of sexual aggression to predict men's conflict with women: A 10-year follow-up study. *Journal of Personality and Social Psychology, 69,* 353–369.

Malamuth, N. M., Sockloskie, R. J., Koss, M. P., & Tanaka, J. S. (1991). Characteristics of aggressors against women testing a model using a national sample of college students. *Journal of Consulting and Clinical Psychology, 59,* 670–681.

Mann, R. E., & Thornton, D. (2000). An evidence-based relapse prevention program. In D. R. Laws, S. M. Hudson, & T. Ward (Eds.), *Remaking relapse prevention with sex offenders: A sourcebook* (pp. 341–350). Thousand Oaks, CA: Sage.

Marshall, W. L., Barbaree, H. E., & Eccles, A. (1991). Early onset and deviant sexuality in child molesters. *Journal of Interpersonal Violence, 6,* 323–335.

Mathews, R., Hunter, J. A., & Vuz, J. (1997). Juvenile female sexual offenders: Clinical characteristics and treatment issues. *Sexual Abuse: A Journal of Research and Treatment, 9,* 187–199.

McMahon, P. M., & Puett, R. C. (1999). Child sexual abuse as a public health issue: Recommendations of an expert panel. *Sexual Abuse: A Journal of Research and Treatment, 11,* 257–266.

Miller, W. R., & Rollnick, S. (Eds.). (1991). *Motivational interviewing: Preparing people to change addictive behavior.* New York: Guilford.

Milloy, C. D. (1998). Specialized treatment for juvenile sex offenders: A closer look. *Journal of Interpersonal Violence, 13,* 653–656.

Murphy, W. D., & Barbaree, H. E. (1994). *Assessments of sex offenders by measures of erectile response: Psychometric properties and decision making.* Brandon, VT: Safer Society Press.

Murphy, W. D., & Carich, M. S. (2001). Cognitive distortions and restructuring in sexual abuser treatment. In M. S. Carich & S. E. Mussack (Eds.), *Handbook for sexual abuser assessment and treatment* (pp. 65–76). Brandon, VT: Safer Society Press.

Murphy, W. D., DiLillo, D., Haynes, M. R., & Steere, E. (2001). An exploration of factors related to deviant sexual arousal among juvenile sex offenders. *Sexual Abuse: A Journal of Research and Treatment, 13,* 91–103.

Murphy, W. D., Haynes, M. R., & Page, I. J. (1992). Adolescent sex offenders. In W. O'Donohue & J. H. Geer (Eds.), *The sexual abuse of children: Clinical issues* (Vol. 2, pp. 394–429). Hillsdale, NJ: Erlbaum.

O'Brien, M. J. (1991). Taking sibling incest seriously. In M. Q. Patton (Ed.), *Family sexual abuse: Frontline research and evaluation* (pp. 75–92). Newbury Park, CA: Sage.

Prentky, R., Harris, B., Frizzell, K., & Righthand, S. (2000). An actuarial procedure for assessing risk in juvenile sex offenders. *Sexual Abuse: A Journal of Research and Treatment, 12,* 71–93.

Richardson, G., Kelly, T. P., Bhate, S. R., & Graham, F. (1997). Group differences in abuser and abuse characteristics in a British sample of sexually abusive adolescents. *Sexual Abuse: A Journal of Research and Treatment, 9,* 239–257.

Righthand, S., & Welch, C. (2001). *Juveniles who have sexually offended: A review of the professional literature.* Washington, DC: Office of Juvenile Justice and Delinquency Prevention.

Ryan, G. (1991). Juvenile sex offenders: Defining the population. In G. D. Ryan & S. L. Lane (Eds.), *Juvenile sexual offending: Causes, consequences, and correction* (pp. 3–8). Lexington, MA: Lexington Books.

Saunders, E., Awad, G. A., & White, G. (1986). Male adolescent sexual offenders: The offender and the offense. *Canadian Journal of Psychiatry, 31,* 542–548.

Schram, D. D., Milloy, C. D., & Rowe, W. E. (1991). *Juvenile sex offenders: A follow-up study of reoffense behavior.* Seattle: Washington State Institute for Public Policy.

Seto, M. C., Lalumière, M. L., & Blanchard, R. (2000). The discriminative validity of a phallometric test for pedophilic interests among adolescent sex offenders against children. *Psychological Assessment, 12,* 319–327.

Tarter, R. E., Hegedus, A. M., Alterman, A. I., & Katz-Garris, L. (1983). Cognitive capacities of juvenile violent, nonviolent, and sexual offenders. *The Journal of Nervous and Mental Disease, 171,* 564–567.

Van Ness, S. R. (1984). Rape as instrumental violence: A study of youth offenders. *Journal of Offender Counselling, Services and Rehabilitation, 9,* 161–170.

Weinrott, M. R. (1996). *Juvenile sexual aggression: A critical review.* Boulder, CO: Center for the Study and Prevention of Violence.

White, J. W., & Koss, M. P. (1993). Adolescent sexual aggression within heterosexual relationships: Prevalence, characteristics, and causes. In H. E. Barbaree, W. L. Marshall, & S. M. Hudson (Eds.), *The juvenile sex offender* (pp. 182–202). New York: Guilford.

Worling, J. R. (1995a). Adolescent sibling-incest offenders: Differences in family and individual functioning when compared to adolescent nonsibling offenders. *Child Abuse & Neglect, 19,* 633–643.

Worling, J. R. (1995b). Sexual abuse histories of adolescent male sex offenders: Differences on the basis of the age and gender of their victims. *Journal of Abnormal Psychology, 104,* 610–613.

Worling, J. R. (2001). Personality-based typology of adolescent male sexual offenders: Differences in recidivism rates, victim-selection characteristics, and personal victimization histories. *Sexual Abuse: A Journal of Research and Treatment, 13,* 149–166.

Worling, J. R., & Curwen, T. (2000). Adolescent sexual offender recidivism: Success of specialized treatment and implications for risk prediction. *Child Abuse & Neglect, 24,* 965–982.

Wurtele, S. K. (1998). School-based child sexual abuse prevention programs: Questions, answers and more questions. In J. R. Lutzker (Ed.), *Handbook of child abuse research and treatment* (pp. 501–516). New York: Plenum.

CHAPTER 22

YOUTH GANGS

Prevention and Intervention

JAMES C. HOWELL

Adjunct Researcher, National Youth Gang Center

Research on risk and protective factors for gang membership in the United States is reviewed in this chapter. The social development processes by which risk and protective factors operate to produce gang membership is described. Finally, a comprehensive framework for integrating a continuum of program interventions is presented. First, though, definitions central to a risk-protection framework are provided, followed by empirical data on the prevalence of youth gang membership and demographic characteristics of youth gang members.

Youth gangs are a serious problem in the United States. This country has seen a rapid proliferation of youth gangs since the early 1980s. The number of cities with gang problems increased from an estimated 286 jurisdictions with more than 2,000 gangs and nearly 100,000 gang members in 1980 (Miller, 1992) to about 3,330 localities with more than 24,500 gangs and 772,500 gang members in 2000 (Egley & Arjunan, 2002). In the 1970s, only about 25 percent of the urban population in all cities were affected by gang problems. This proportion rose to about 60 percent of the population of all cities in the late 1990s (W. B. Miller, 2001). The proportion of cities with populations over 100,000 reporting gang problems increased by 58 percent from the 1970s to the 1990s (p. 38). Since 1996, the number of localities with youth gangs has been gradually decreasing; however, the number of gang members in larger cities has increased recently (Egley, 2002). Equally important, all cities with a population of more than 250,000 reported persistent gang activity from 1996 to 2000 (Egley, 2002). The percentage of students reporting gang presence at school nearly doubled between 1989 and 1995 (Howell & Lynch, 2000).

Have youth gang violence trends followed the decreasing level of adolescent violence? This does not appear to be the case. Nationwide data on violent gang crimes are not available in the sources traditionally used to gauge national violence trends—the FBI Uniform Crime Reports and the National Crime Victim Survey. Thus, trend data on gang homicides is the best indicator of changes in levels of gang violence. In the first part of the 1990s, the overall drop in gang homicides was noticeably smaller than the decrease in the total number of homicides among 14- to 24-year-olds (Maxson, Curry, & Howell, 2002).

Thus, to the extent that gang homicides serve as a good indicator of overall gang violence, it does not appear that gang violence is decreasing as rapidly as overall youth violence (see Howell, 2003).

PREVALENCE AND DEMOGRAPHIC CHARACTERISTICS OF GANG MEMBERS

Prevalence

Only one national survey has measured the percentage of all youngsters that belong to gangs—the 1997 National Longitudinal Survey of Youth (Bureau of Labor Statistics, 1998). It found that only 5 percent of adolescents between the ages of 12 and 16 have "ever" belonged to a gang, and 2 percent currently claim to be gang members (Snyder & Sickmund, 1999, pp. 58–59). These percents are higher in cities known to have gang problems. An 11-city survey of eighth-graders in such localities found that 9 percent were currently gang members, and 17 percent said they had belonged to a gang at some point in their young lives (Esbensen & Osgood, 1997). Membership is yet higher among representative samples of high-risk youth in large cities, ranging from 14 to 30 percent in Denver (Colorado), Seattle (Washington), and Rochester (New York) (Thornberry, 1998).

Age

The peak age for active membership for girls is age 14, whereas the peak for boys is age 16 (Gottfredson & Gottfredson, 2001). Youth gang members reported by law-enforcement agencies in the National Youth Gang Survey (NYGS) are much older. Also called *street gangs*—to emphasize the location of their activity—the majority of the members of gangs recognized by law-enforcement agencies are young adults. In 1999, nearly two-thirds (63 percent) of the gang members reported in the NYGS were estimated to be young adults, and slightly more than one-third (37 percent) were juveniles (Egley, 2002). Naturally, the question arises as to how gangs reported by law enforcement agencies could be so much older than the members of gangs revealed in student surveys. There are three main reasons. First, student surveys cover a restricted age range; young adults are not included. Second, law-enforcement officers are more likely to notice young adult members—whose crimes are more serious and violent than those of young adolescents. Third, law-enforcement agencies may not regularly purge inactive gang members from their gang intelligence systems (Howell, Moore, & Egley, 2002).

Gender

The prevalence of youth gang membership among girls is much more common than in the past (Bjerregaard & Smith, 1993; Curry, 1998; Esbensen & Deschenes, 1998; Moore & Hagedorn, 2001). The male-to-female ratio, previously estimated to be about 10 to 1, is now 2 to 1 (6 percent vs. 3 percent) among those who had ever belonged to a gang, and 3 to 1 (3 percent vs. 1 percent) among current members (Bureau of Labor Statistics, 1998).

In the 11-site survey of eighth-graders in known gang problem localities (Esbensen & De-schenes, 1998), about 14 percent of the boys and 8 percent of the girls were gang members; and 38 percent of the students who said they were gang members were females (Esbensen & Osgood, 1997). The proportion of females in older youth gangs observed by law-enforcement agencies is much lower—about 6 percent in 2002 (Egley, 2002). Girls appear to be most predominant among very young gang members (Bjerregaard & Smith, 1993), in part because they tend to leave gangs earlier than boys (Thornberry, Krohn, Lizotte, Smith & Tobin, 2003). This fact, together with lower serious crime rates among girls in gangs, in large part explains the lower proportion of females in older youth gangs reported by law-enforcement agencies.

Racial/Ethnic Composition

The racial/ethnic composition of youth gangs tends to reflect the racial/ethnic makeup of the locality. This principle applies nationwide. Early in U.S. history, large proportions of gang members were Caucasian, composed of youth of various European backgrounds (Sante, 1991; Spergel, 1995). By the late 1990s—after enormous growth in minority populations and concomitant social and economic disadvantage—African American and Hispanic youngsters made up nearly 80 percent of all gang members reported by law enforcement (Egley, 2002). However, these minority youngsters have no special predisposition to gang involvement. They happen to be overrepresented in low socioeconomic areas that most give rise to gang activity (Bursik & Grasmick, 1993).

REVIEW OF RESEARCH RELATED
TO GANG INVOLVEMENT

This section reviews research related to gang involvement using a risk-protection framework. This framework, popularly referred to as the *public health model*, is first explained. A "developmental" theoretical perspective is used to examine the process by which risk and protective factors operate to influence individuals' gang involvement.

The Risk-Protection Framework

Risk factors are "individual or environmental hazards that increase an individual's vulnerability to negative developmental outcomes" (Small & Luster, 1994, p. 182). Put another way, *risk factors* are conditions in the individual or environment that predict an increased likelihood of developing a problem such as violent behavior (Catalano & Hawkins, 1996). Some risk factors are causally related to negative outcomes, whereas others are "correlates" of potential negative outcomes (Kirby & Fraser, 1997). Male gender is an example of a delinquency correlate for other risk factors that cause or increase the risk of delinquency.

Protective factors are any influences that decrease the probability of a more serious problem condition (Kirby & Fraser, 1997, pp. 10–11). Kirby and Fraser (1997, p. 16) define *protective factors* as "both the internal and external forces that help children resist or ameliorate risk." *Resilience* is the term used to describe children who achieve positive outcomes in the face of risk. "Only about one-third of any population of at-risk children experiences a negative outcome; two-thirds appear to survive risk experiences without major developmental disruptions" (Kirby & Fraser, 1997, pp. 13–14).

Risk and protective factors predict increased or decreased probability of developing problem behaviors. Put simply, a *risk factor*—or predictor—is anything that increases the probability that a person will suffer harm, and a *protective factor* is something that decreases the potential harmful effect of a risk factor. Problem behaviors normally develop in individuals who have a preponderance of risk factors over protective factors (Browning & Huizinga, 1999; Smith, Lizotte, Thornberry, & Krohn, 1995; Thornberry, Huizinga, & Loeber, 1995, pp. 230–232).

Predictors of delinquency and violence typically are organized in five major risk factor domains: individual, family, school, peer group, and community contexts (Hawkins, Herrenkohl, Farrington, et al., 1998; Hawkins, Arthur, & Catalano, 1995; Hawkins, Catalano, & Miller, 1992; Herrenkohl, Chung, & Catalano, Chapter 20 of this volume; Lipsey & Derzon, 1998; Sameroff & Gutman, Chapter 2 of this volume). Gang involvement is also predicted by the same risk factors—because this is the main context in which serious and violent delinquency occurs. However, research has not clearly distinguished risk factors for gang involvement versus general forms of delinquency or violence. More research is needed that distinguishes factors predictive of offending in general versus factors predictive of gang involvement and offending in the context of the gang. Organizing risk factors into a causal chain also is problematic because theories and research disagree in this area (Kirby & Fraser, 1997). Nevertheless, as noted by Kirby and Fraser, we can say with certainty that some risk factors are more important than others at different points as the developmental process from childhood to adolescence unfolds.

Indeed, studies of risk factors for general delinquency and violence show that early in childhood, individual characteristics and family risk factors are most important, followed in a few years by school factors (Lipsey & Derzon, 1998). Later—in the adolescent period—the peer group becomes important. Community risk factors appear to have a ubiquitous influence throughout the developmental process.

A Developmental Perspective of Gang Membership and Gang Careers

Youth gang involvement is integrally linked with delinquency and other problem behaviors. Gang studies show that individual, family, school, peer group, and community risk factors operate in a developmental fashion over the childhood and adolescent periods. Their sequencing is similar to the way they operate in producing general delinquency and violence (Hill, Howell, Hawkins, & Battin-Pearson, 1999; Lahey, Gordon, Loeber, Stouthamer-Loeber, & Farrington, 1999; Thornberry et al., 2003).

Youths who join gangs typically are socially dysfunctional children when compared to other children in the community (Hill et al., 1999; Lahey et al., 1999; Thornberry et al., 2002). Moreover, they are on a trajectory of worsening antisocial behavior (Esbensen & Huizinga, 1993; Hill et al., 1999; Lahey et al., 1999). There is some evidence that early gang participation (i.e., during the latter part of the childhood period) is a result of dysfunctional characteristics, whereas later gang participation (i.e., during adolescence) is influenced by gang-involved peers (Lahey et al., 1999). This empirical reality contradicts the romanticized notion that youths join gangs mainly because of lack of access to legitimate means of achieving societal goals (Cloward & Ohlin, 1960).

During childhood, conduct problems, elementary school failure, and involvement in delinquency are stepping stones to gang membership (Esbensen & Huizinga, 1993; Hill et al., 1999; Lahey et al., 1999; Thornberry et al., 1993). Child delinquents are at risk for gang membership (Hill et al., 1999; Krohn, Thornberry, Rivera, & LeBlanc, 2001); that is, they are more likely than youths who begin to engage in delinquency at an older age to become gang members (Hill et al., 1999). Studies suggest that child delinquents are more likely to later become involved in crimes of a more serious and violent nature, including gang fights (Thornberry et al., 2003). In this sense, gang entry might be thought of as the next developmental step in escalating antisocial behavior (Esbensen & Huizinga, 1993; Lahey et al., 1999). Gang participation dramatically increases the likelihood of becoming a serious, violent, chronic juvenile offender in the adolescent period (Thornberry et al., 2003). Membership in youth gangs may be one of the more important environments for explaining adolescent delinquency (Thornberry et al., 2003, p. 121). For example, "gang membership appears to have a more consistent and powerful impact on general delinquency and on violence than on either drug sales or drug use" (p. 112).

Risk Factors for Gang Membership

Risk factors for gang membership span all major risk factor domains that research has shown to be related significantly to a variety of adolescent problem behaviors: individual characteristics, family features, school performance, peer group influences, and the community context (Hill et al., 1999; Thornberry et al., 2003). Youths who experience multiple risk factors in multiple domains are at an elevated risk of gang participation (Thornberry et al., 2003). Figure 22.1 shows risk factors for gang membership from longitudinal studies of representative samples. The level of proof is higher in these kinds of studies, mainly because longitudinal research designs permit measurement of the risk factors at an earlier point in time than the outcome variable—gang membership. Thus, longitudinal research designs are stronger than cross-sectional studies for determining causal relationships between risk factors and gang membership. Because cross-sectional studies measure both risk factors and outcomes at the same point in time, the causal order cannot be determined using this type of research design. What appears to be predictor could well be an outcome of gang involvement.

Major Risk Factors for Gang Involvement

Community or Neighborhood Risk Factors. As seen in Figure 22.1, several community or neighborhood risk factors predict gang membership. Gangs tend to cluster in high-crime, socially disorganized neighborhoods where firearms are readily available, where gangs are present (possibly, a normal fixture in the community), where many youths are in trouble, and where youths feel unsafe (Curry & Spergel, 1988; Hill et al., 1999; Kosterman, Hawkins, Hill, et al., 1996). Illegal firearm ownership, or illegal gun carrying, is a key predictor of gang membership (Lizotte, Tesoriero, Thornberry, & Krohn, 1994). Gangs

FIGURE 22.1   **Risk Factors for Gang Membership**

COMMUNITY/NEIGHBORHOOD RISK FACTORS

Availability of drugs (Hill et al., 1999; Thornberry, 1998)
Neighborhood youth in trouble (Hill et al., 1999)
High-crime neighborhood (Lahey et al., 1999; Thornberry et al., 2003)
Feeling unsafe in the neighborhood (Kosterman et al., 1996)
Low neighborhood attachment (Hill et al., 1999)
Low neighborhood integration (Thornberry, 1998)
Neighborhood residents in poverty or family poverty (Hill et al., 1999; Thornberry et al., 2003)
Availability of firearms (Bjerregaard & Lizotte, 1995; Lizotte et al., 2000)
Disorganized neighborhoods (Thornberry et al., 2003)

FAMILY RISK FACTORS

Family structure (Hill et al., 1999; Thornberry, 1998)
Family poverty (Hill et al., 1999; Thornberry, 1998)
Sibling antisocial behavior (Hill et al., 1999)
Poor family management (Hill et al., 1999)
Child abuse/neglect and incest (Thornberry et al., 2003)
Low parent education level (Thornberry et al., 2003)
Parent pro-violent attitudes (Hill et al., 1999)
Low parent involvement and attachment to child (Thornberry, 1998)
Low parent supervision/control/monitoring (Thornberry, 1998; Walker-Barnes & Mason, 2001)

SCHOOL RISK FACTORS

Low achievement in elementary school (Hill et al., 1999)
Negative labeling by teachers (Esbensen et al., 1993)
Low academic aspirations (Hill et al., 1999; Thornberry, 1998)
Low school attachment (Hill et al., 1999)
Low attachment to teachers (Thornberry, 1998; Thornberry et al., 2003)
Low parent expectations for schooling (Bjerregaard & Smith, 1993; Thornberry, 1998)
Low degree of commitment to school (Thornberry, 1998; Thornberry et al., 2003)
Low math score (Thornberry et al., 2003)
Identified as learning disabled (Hill et al., 1999)

PEER GROUP RISK FACTORS

Association with peers who engage in delinquency (Bjerregaard & Smith, 1993; Bjerregaard & Lizotte, 1995; Esbensen et al., 1993; Hill et al., 1999; Lahey et al., 1999; Thornberry, 1998)
High commitment to delinquent peers (Esbensen et al., 1993)
Low commitment to prosocial peers (Esbensen et al., 1993)
Association with aggressive peers (Lahey et al., 1999)
Unsupervised time spent with friends (Thornberry, 1998)

INDIVIDUAL RISK FACTORS

Violence or aggression tendencies (Hill et al., 1999; Thornberry et al., 2003)
Conduct disorders[1] (Lahey et al., 1999)
General delinquency involvement (Hill et al., 1999; Thornberry et al., 2003; Esbensen & Huizinga, 1993)

(continued)

FIGURE 22.1   CONTINUED

INDIVIDUAL RISK FACTORS

Illegal gun ownership/carrying (Bjerregaard & Lizotte, 1995; Lizotte et al., 2000; Lizotte, Tesoriero, Thornberry, & Krohn, 1994)

Early dating (Thornberry et al., 2003)

Precocious sexual activity (Bjerregaard & Smith, 1993; Thornberry et al., 2003)

Antisocial/delinquent beliefs (Hill et al., 1999; Thornberry et al., 2003)

Poor social integration (alienation) (Esbensen et al., 1993)

Externalizing behaviors (disruptive, antisocial, conduct disorders) (Hill et al., 1999; Lahey et al., 1999; Thornberry et al., 2003)

Hyperactive (Hill et al., 1999)

Poor refusal skills (Hill et al., 1999)

Alcohol/drug use (Hill et al., 1999; Thornberry et al., 2003; Bjerregaard & Smith, 1993; Thornberry, Krohn, Lizotte, & Chard-Wierschem, 1993)

Depression (Thornberry, 1998; Thornberry et al., 2003)

Negative/stressful life events[2] (Thornberry, 1998; Thornberry et al., 2002)

Pro-drug use attitudes (Thornberry, 1998)

Low self-esteem (Thornberry, 1998)

Poor social and interpersonal skills (Hill et al., 1999)

[1]As measured in this study, conduct disorder symptoms include bullying, fighting, lying, cruelty toward animals, attacking people, running away from home, firesetting, theft, truancy, and vandalism. Most of these behaviors are illegal, and, when detected, may result in a "delinquent" label.

[2]These consist of failing a course at school, being suspended or expelled from school, breaking up with a boyfriend/girlfriend, having a big fight or problem with a friend, and the death of someone close.

are more likely to recruit adolescents who own illegal firearms, and gang members are more than twice as likely as nongang members to own a gun for protection, more likely to have peers who own guns for protection, and more likely to carry their guns outside the home (Bjerregaard & Lizotte, 1995). Gang membership also significantly increases the probability of gun carrying (Lizotte, Krohn, Howell, Tobin, & Howard, 2000). Interestingly, up to about age 16, gang membership was found to be the strongest predictor of hidden gun carrying in a Rochester (New York) study (Lizotte et al., 2000). After this age, the importance of gang membership as a predictor of hidden gun carrying diminished, and involvement in drug trafficking, especially high amounts of drug selling, became the strongest predictor.

Family Risk Factors.   Gang members tend to grow up in broken homes or in families with high levels of conflict. Whether they are living with one or both parents, their parents tend to have pro-violent attitudes and poor family management practices. The brothers and sisters of future gang members often are involved in antisocial behavior and they also may be gang members, along with friends. The gang serves as a sanctuary for troubled youth from troubled families (Fleisher, 1998). For girls, in particular, finding solace from a violent family life and personal protection are major motivations for gang joining (J. A. Miller, 2001; Moore, 1978). Gangs provide street socialization where the family leaves off, or when social service agencies fail youths. There often is a discontinuity between the actual problems in future or current gang-affiliated adolescents' lives and the remedies offered by social service and law-enforcement agencies (Fleisher, 1998). These agencies don't give future or current gang members "what they need…when they need it" (p. 211). Moreover, the challenge of intervening effectively in transgenerational family problems proves too difficult for most agencies.

School Risk Factors. Low achievement in elementary school and having learning problems are among the strongest school-related predictors of gang membership. Lack of success in the school environment leaves youths extremely vulnerable to gang influences. Related risk factors include low academic aspirations, low school attachment, low attachment to teachers, low parent expectations for their children's schooling, low commitment to school, and general academic failure. Feeling unsafe at school also proved to be a strong predictor of gang membership in a cross-sectional study (Gottfredson & Gottfredson, 2001). Thus, youths may seek protection from the gang. Although the impact of school suspension and dropout have not been researched, these events are likely to have the unintended effect of increasing youths' exposure to the influence of gangs on the streets.

Peer Group Risk Factors. Delinquent peers have a very strong impact on later gang membership. Associating with delinquent friends and unsupervised "hanging around" with friends is a potent combination (Hill et al., 1999; Thornberry, 1998). Two gang studies suggest that youngsters generally learn about the gang at age 12, start hanging out with gang members at ages 12 to 13, and join the gang about six months later at ages 13 to 14 (Decker, 1996; Huff, 1996).

Aggression often underlies the friendships of gang members (Decker & Van Winkle, 1996; Lahey et al., 1999; Miller, Geertz, & Cutter, 1962; Short & Strodtbeck, 1965). But gang violence takes on many forms. The following examples come from an observational study of the Fremont Hustlers gang in Kansas City, Missouri (Fleisher, 1998, p. 49):

> Violence is difficult to explain in the context of daily Fremont social life. Generally speaking, there is gang violence, or violence perpetrated by the Fremont Hustlers to protect their collective resources (marijuana and cocaine sales), and nongang violence, or violence perpetrated by individual Fremont kids, each acting on his or her own behalf…. Personal violence originates in verbal insults and challenges, envy, public humiliation, and most often in fights over suitors…Fremont girls, more so than boys, are troublemakers…. Intergang violence is a different matter. [It could be] about something a Fremont boy said about a Northeast or Southside boy, and before long, a drugged boy wields a handgun or rifle and a drive-by shooting occurs.

Individual Risk Factors. As seen in the introduction to this chapter, specific demographic characteristics put some youngsters at greater risk than others for gang involvement. For example, African American and Hispanic/Latino youths are at greater risk than Caucasian youngsters. However, the latter group is about at equal risk in localities where gang problems first developed in the last 10 to 15 years of the past century (Howell, Egley,

& Gleason, 2002). For example, in localities where gang problems first developed in 1995 or 1996, a slightly larger proportion of gang members are Caucasians (35 percent) than African Americans (31 percent) or Hispanic/Latino (27 percent). Additionally, these later onset localities have a far higher proportion of younger gang members, females, and middle-class youngsters than localities in which onset of gang problems occurred earlier. The main explanation for these changes is the faddish attraction of gangs that developed in the late 1980s and early 1990s.

The individual risk factors of future gang members begin to play out at a very early age. Increasing levels of conduct disorders—measured thus far as early as the first grade—predict initial gang entry (Lahey et al., 1999). Youngsters who use drugs *and* are involved in delinquency—violent delinquency, in particular—are more likely to become gang members than are youths who are less involved in delinquency and drug use (Thornberry et al., 2003).

Mental health problems as risk factors for gang membership have not been well researched. However, as seen in Figure 22.2, several indicators of mental health problems have been shown to predict gang involvement, including hyperactivity, internalizing (e.g., depression, anxiety), and externalizing behaviors (e.g., conduct disorders and oppositional behavior). Cognitive behavioral problems also may lead to school failure, which is a predictor of gang membership (Hill et. al., 1999). Child abuse and neglect are relatively strong predictors of gang involvement (Thornberry et al., 2003). Other negative or stressful life events also elevate youths' risk of gang involvement (Thornberry et al., 2003).

Protective Factors

Research on protective factors has been slower to develop than risk factor studies, in part because of the absence of a standard for determining what constitutes protection, and also because little research has been done in this area. A related concern is confusion about whether protective factors are distinct from risk factors as developmental predictors of youth violence and gang involvement. The polar opposites of a single risk factor element can be considered to increase risk or provide protection. Family conflict is an example. Viewed along a continuum, high family conflict is seen as a risk factor, whereas low family conflict is considered a protective factor (Kirby & Fraser, 1997, p. 17). Early academic achievement, the antithesis of low school performance, can be expected to protect children from gang involvement. However, protective factors are not simply the opposite extreme of risk factors (Stouthamer-Loeber, Loeber, Farrington, et al., 1993). Other protective factors (Dodge, Bates, & Pettit, 1990) may reside in mental (e.g., cognitive ability) and social processes (e.g., self-improvement or self-efficacy initiatives) that are not linked to risk factors (Rutter, Giller, & Hagell, 1998, p. 211).

It is important to recognize that protection against delinquency involvement also serves to insulate youths from gang involvement—because gangs tend to recruit youths who already are delinquent (Hill et al., 1999; Thornberry et al., 1993). Longitudinal studies in Rochester (Smith et al., 1995) and Denver (Browning & Huizinga, 1999) have identified key protective factors against delinquency. The latter study shows that the chances of a successful adolescence are not good until the number of protective factors far exceeds the number of risk factors.

FIGURE 22.2   Protective Factors Against Gang Participation

COMMUNITY

Provide clear and consistent social norms.
Institute effective social policies.
Reduce gang presence and influence in the neighborhood/community.
Improve community social and economic advantages.
Provide a healthy start for infants in public housing projects.
Decrease neighborhood crime.
Provide sanctuaries from gang life.
Reduce availability of firearms.
Reduce perceptions of police unfairness.

FAMILY

Cultivate good parent/child relationships.
Increase family stability.
Improve family management practices, especially child/adolescent supervision.
Increase attachment to parents.
Reduce criminal involvement.
Reduce family conflict and violence (child abuse, spouse abuse).

SCHOOL

Develop high-quality schools.
Improve early academic success and attitudes about school.
Increase school attendance and reduce truancy and dropout.
Remediate learning disabilities (improve screening and identification of problems).
Provide structured after-school programs with adult supervision.
Increase teacher supervision of playgrounds.
Increase commitment to school.
Increase aspirations and expectations to go to college.
Increase the feeling of safety at school.

PEER GROUP

Provide positive peer modeling.
Increase attachments to conventional (nondelinquent) peers.
Facilitate association of antisocial youths with prosocial youths.
Increase attachments to peers approved by parents.
Increase adult supervision of adolescents.
Prevent/reduce bullying.

INDIVIDUAL

Enhance personal and social skills.
Promote self-efficacy.
Increase bonding to prosocial others.
Instill healthy beliefs and clear standards for behavior.
Improve mental health.
Provide positive expectations for the future.
Provide job training and gainful employment for gang members.
Increase self-control (against impulses and risk taking or sensation seeking).

(continued)

FIGURE 22.2   CONTINUED

INDIVIDUAL

Provide counseling for youths who experience multiple stressful events.
Dispel perception that gangs are beneficial to their members.
Improve conflict-resolution skills.
Prevent child/adolescent victimization.
Prevent early delinquency and drug use.
Prevent/reduce illegal gun ownership and carrying.
Enhance life skills (communication skills, problem-solving techniques, and decision-making abilities).
Increase cognitive, social, and emotional competence.

Figure 22.2 contains suggested protective factors that might insulate youths from gang participation (both joining and active involvement). Although research has not established the main protective factors that buffer risk factors for gang involvement, many of them are suggested in the gang literature (see especially Bjerregaard & Smith, 1993; Esbensen, Huizinga, & Weiher, 1993; Hill et al., 1999; Maxon & Whitlock, 2002; Thornberry et al., 2003; Walker-Barnes & Mason, 2001; Wyrick, 2000). All of these protective factors need to be tested in experimental studies. Several of these protective factors were identified in a comprehensive review of common risk and protective factors in successful prevention programs (Durlak, 1998). Other protective factors in Figure 22.2 can be inferred from the well-documented risk factors for gang membership (Figure 22.1).

Social support is a key protective factor that can occur in all of the protective factor domains (Durlak, 1998). Children and adolescents can be supported directly or indirectly by parents, peers, teachers, and other helpful persons in their daily lives. This form of protective support also has been called *lifelines* (Cairns & Cairns, 1994). Readers should keep in mind that some of these protective factors may be effective only in preventing child and adolescent involvement in delinquency and violence; however, these behaviors are risk factors for gang membership.

A COMPREHENSIVE STRATEGY FOR GANG PREVENTION AND INTERVENTION

A continuum of interventions is needed to interrupt youth gang involvement and the development of gang problems. This conceptual framework comes from the Comprehensive Strategy for Serious, Violent, and Chronic Juvenile Offenders (Wilson & Howell, 1993; Howell, 1995). The Comprehensive Strategy is a two-tiered system for responding proactively to juvenile delinquency and crime. In the first tier, delinquency prevention and early intervention programs are relied on to prevent and reduce the onset of delinquency. If these efforts fail, then the juvenile justice system, in the second tier, needs to make proactive responses to juvenile delinquency by addressing the risk factors for recidivism and associated treatment needs of delinquents, particularly those with a high likelihood of becoming serious, violent, chronic juvenile offenders. A continuum of sanctions and services is needed for them that reduce this likelihood.

The Comprehensive Strategy framework consists of three principal components:

1. Preventing youths from becoming delinquent by empowering communities to conduct risk- and protection-focused prevention and select needed prevention programs from a menu of effective program options
2. Early intervention in problem families in high-risk communities and delinquent careers, especially potentially serious and violent offenders
3. A system of graduated sanctions and a parallel continuum of treatment alternatives that include immediate intervention, intermediate sanctions, intensive supervision, community-based correctional programs, secure corrections, and aftercare*

The Comprehensive Strategy integrates a balanced approach of prevention, early intervention, and graduated sanctions in a continuum of sanctions and treatment program options. This framework helps communities organize effective interventions in each of these areas in a continuum of care, thus producing a much more comprehensive and cost-effective system of interventions (Howell, 2003).

Theoretical Foundations
of the Comprehensive Strategy

Developmental Criminology and the Public Health Model are overarching theoretical models in the Comprehensive Strategy. The Public Health Model (Institute of Medicine, 1994) is used to translate the research base on risk and protective factors and offender careers in the three Comprehensive Strategy components. Application of the Public Health Model in prevention programming involves preventing delinquency by reducing risk factors and increasing protective factors. The Communities That Care approach (Hawkins, Catalano, & Associates, 1992) is an operating system for engaging communities in risk- and protective-focused prevention (see Herrenkohl et al., Chapter 20 of this volume). It is guided theoretically by the Social Development Model (Catalano & Hawkins, 1996), which integrates learning theory (Akers, Krohn, Lanza-Kaduce, & Radosevich, 1979; Bandura, 1999) and control theory (Hirschi, 1969). The Social Development Model (Catalano & Hawkins, 1996) hypothesizes that youths commit offenses across developmental periods because they encounter antisocial influences in the family, peer group, school, and community domains that reinforce (learning) offending. Conversely, they resist or desist from offending if they encounter pro-social influences that inhibit (control) offending.

Developmental Criminology (Loeber & Le Blanc, 1990; Le Blanc & Loeber, 1998) provides the research base of risk and causal factors for development of delinquent behav-

---

*A system of "graduated" sanctions applies increasingly restrictive sanctions for progressively more serious and dangerous offenders. An "intermediate" sanction, for example, might be placement in a secure community-based facility instead of court probation (a less restrictive sanction) or confinement in a juvenile reformatory (a more restrictive sanction).

ior over the child and adolescent periods. This theoretical framework focuses attention on the development of offender careers—from childhood disorders to involvement in serious, violent, and chronic delinquency. The graduated sanctions component integrates "positivist criminology" (efficacy of rehabilitation) and "classical criminology" (use of sanctions to control offenders) in a balanced approach to recidivism reduction. Sanctions should be viewed as providing only the setting for service delivery; it is the intervention within the setting that has the actual power to produce change in offenders (Andrews & Bonta, 1998). There is considerable evidence of the effectiveness of graduated sanctions systems when combined with a continuum of program options (Howell, 2003).

It is useful for youth gang prevention and intervention purposes to view gang involvement from a developmental perspective. Parallel types of interventions would be appropriate, given youngsters' progression along the pathway to gang involvement and subsequent more serious delinquency involvement. A continuum of program options—including prevention, early intervention, and sanctions (including suppression)—combined with treatment is likely to have a much larger impact on the local gang problem than individual interventions. This is because of the greater effect of multiple-level interventions that are implemented simultaneously.

A community's efforts to prevent and intervene in gang problems can be integrated within its overall Comprehensive Strategy for Serious, Violent, and Chronic Juvenile Offenders (see Howell, 1995, 1998, for an illustration of this process). A Comprehensive Community-Wide Approach to Gang Prevention, Intervention, and Suppression has been developed (Burch & Kane, 1999) for targeting youth gangs. The theoretical foundations of the two approaches are compatible. Both frameworks call for a continuum of integrated interventions. There are only two differences between the two models. The first model targets chronic serious offenders in general; the other one targets the subgroup of gang members. The first model targets individuals; the second one targets gangs as a distinct group—particularly with police suppression (control) activities.

Implementation of the Comprehensive Community-Wide Approach to Gang Prevention, Intervention, and Suppression has produced positive results in a number of sites (National Youth Gang Center, 2001b). A gang problem assessment protocol is available that any community can use (National Youth Gang Center, 2001a). A planning guide has also been prepared to assist communities in developing a comprehensive plan to implement this gang intervention framework (National Youth Gang Center, 2001b). Integration of the two strategies should produce a much more effective approach to dealing with serious, violent, and chronic juvenile offenders, because of the overlap between these offenders and gang members.

EFFECTIVE AND PROMISING GANG PROGRAMS

This section discusses promising and effective gang programs in three strategies: prevention, early intervention, and treatment and control. The treatment and control strategy corresponds with the suppression strategy in the comprehensive gang model (Burch & Kane, 1999).

This is not intended to be an exhaustive review of all promising and effective gang intervention programs (see Howell, 2000, for a comprehensive review). Programs that prevent and reduce delinquency and violence are discussed in Herrenkohl and colleagues' Chapter 20 of this book. Herrenkohl and colleagues discuss programs that are implemented in elementary school settings that have shown success in preventing or reducing aggressive behavior. In addition, they discuss comprehensive school-based programs, notably the Seattle Social Development Project, which has proved effective in preventing lifetime violent behavior among children (Hawkins, Catalano, Kosterman, et al., 1999). Readers' attention also is called to the violence reduction programs Herrenkohl and colleagues discuss, particularly the very effective Multisystemic Therapy (Henggeler, 1997) program. The MST strategy has been demonstrated as an effective family-centered treatment for multiple problems of serious and violent juvenile offenders in different settings (Borduin, Mann, Cone, Henggeler, et al., 1995; Henggeler, Cunningham, Pickrel, Schoenwald, & Brondino, 1996; Henggeler, Melton, & Smith, 1992; Henggeler, Melton, Smith, et al., 1993).

Gang Prevention Programs

The Gang Resistance Education and Training (G.R.E.A.T.) program is a very promising school-based gang prevention program for girls and boys. This curriculum is taught in entire classrooms of mainly middle school students by uniformed law-enforcement officers in a 13-week course (Esbensen & Osgood, 1999; Esbensen, Osgood, Taylor, Peterson, & Freng, 2001). In addition to educating students about the dangers of gang involvement, the lesson content places considerable emphasis on cognitive behavioral training, social skills development, refusal skills development, and conflict resolution. Thus, the curriculum aims to reduce risk factors and increase protective factors—where stronger emphasis is placed. The G.R.E.A.T. curriculum has shown positive long-term effects (Esbensen et al., 2001). Although the reductions in gang membership and delinquency involvement were not statistically significant, the curriculum had a "small but systematic beneficial" program effect (p. 102), particularly on victimization, negative views about gangs, attitudes toward police, pro-social peers, and risk seeking. It should be noted that Esbensen and colleagues evaluated an earlier version of the G.R.E.A.T. curriculum. The improved curriculum described here may well produce larger positive effects.

Early Intervention Programs

Early intervention programs that use graduated sanctions in tandem with treatment programs can forestall progression of young delinquents' careers into serious, violent, chronic juvenile offenders (Howell, 2003). As seen earlier in this chapter, this progression is likely to be accelerated via gang involvement. The 8% Early Intervention Program in Orange County, California, is a successful intervention for potentially serious and violent juvenile offenders that appears to be effective for gang members as well (Schumacher & Kurz, 2000). It is based on an analysis of Orange County court referrals showing that 8 percent of referred adolescents account for more than half of all repeat offenses among juveniles on probation. Potential 8% cases are identified during screening at court intake using a comprehensive risk assessment instrument (Howell, 2001). Gang involvement is one of the risk factors in this instrument.

A continuum of graduated sanctions and services is provided to potential 8% cases in a "wraparound"* model consisting of prevention, intervention (treatment), secure corrections, and transitional aftercare components (Howell, 2003). Services are literally wrapped around the youngster and his or her family through a Youth and Family Resource Center. These services target the major protection/risk domains. Potential 8% cases are placed in the Center's Repeat Offender Prevention Program that provides intensive services with graduated sanctions levels. Evaluation results to date show that recidivism has been reduced by about one-third (Orange County Probation Department, 2000). This program demonstrates how a comprehensive approach with multiple rehabilitation and control interventions—for family members as well as the offender—is very effective. A key factor is that the program provides protection while reducing risk. However, the impact of the program specifically for gang members has not yet been evaluated.

Treatment and Control (Suppression)

Two approaches to gang member rehabilitation and one gang suppression model have shown positive results. Interpersonal skills training is a promising intervention for improving social skills and reducing anger and, possibly, violence among street gang youths in institutionalized populations (Goldstein, 1993). The Aggression Replacement Training (ART) model teaches gang members anger control and other interpersonal skills and has produced impressive results with gang members both inside and outside of correctional facilities (Gibbs, Potter, & Goldstein, 1999; Goldstein & Glick, 1994; Goldstein, Glick, & Gibbs, 1998). The ART model also has proved to be cost effective (Aos, Phipps, Barnoski, & Lieb, 2001). Presently, ART is being implemented in probation departments and detention centers in 28 counties throughout the state of Washington, in a number of juvenile institutions in the state of New York, and in the Texas Department of Youth (corrections).

The Lifeskills '95 program, in San Bernadino and Riverside County, California, is an aftercare treatment program for youthful offenders released from the California Youth Authority. The reintegration approach was based on six principles of programmatic action that address risk and protective factors for delinquency and gang involvement (Josi & Sechrest, 1999):

1. Improve the basic socialization skills necessary for successful reintegration into the community.
2. Significantly reduce criminal activity in terms of amount and seriousness.
3. Alleviate the need for, or dependence on, alcohol or illicit drugs.

---

*Wraparound is "a philosophy of care that includes a definable planning process involving the child and family and results in a unique set of community services and natural supports that are individualized for the child and family to achieve a positive set of outcomes" (Burns, Schoenwald, Burchard, et al., 2000, p. 295).

4. Improve overall lifestyle choices (i.e., social, education, job training, and employment).
5. Reduce the individual's need for gang participation and affiliation as a support mechanism.
6. Reduce the high rate of short-term parole revocations.

The treatment regimen consists of 13 counseling modules, each of which represents a three-hour program of lecture and group discussion. Participants are exposed to a series of lifestyle choices designed to restore self-control of their lives and initiate a positive decision-making process geared toward success (Degnan, 1994). An outcome comparison (Josi & Sechrest, 1999) of experimental (Lifeskills '95 program) and control group (similar parolees from a California Youth Authority reformatory who lived outside the project area), all of whom were high-risk, chronic juvenile offenders, showed considerable program success. Individuals assigned to the control group were about twice as likely as experimental group members to have been arrested and to have abused drugs and/or alcohol frequently since release. In addition, only 8 percent of the Lifeskills '95 youths associated frequently with former gang associates, versus 27 percent of the control group members.

The Tri-Agency Resource Gang Enforcement Team (TARGET) is a multiagency approach for targeting current gang members with suppression measures while also targeting entire gangs with police suppression. Each TARGET team consists of gang investigators, a probation officer, a deputy district attorney, and a district attorney investigator (Capizzi, Cook, & Schumacher, 1995). The program aims to reduce gang crime in a three-pronged strategy: (1) selectively incarcerating the most violent and repeat older gang offenders in the most violent gangs, (2) enforcing probation controls on younger less violent gang offenders, and (3) arresting gang leaders in "hotspots" of gang activity (Rackauckas, 1999). Although recidivism of gang members has not been evaluated, the TARGET program has succeeded in producing a sharp increase in incarceration of gang members and a cumulative 47 percent decrease in gang crime over a seven-year period (Kent, Donaldson, Wyrick, & Smith, 2000), and in reducing the overall level of gang crime in a targeted hotspot to near zero (Wiebe, 1998).

Integration of all of these interventions in a single community is quite likely to produce a much larger impact than implementation of a single intervention. If programs that prevent youths from joining gangs are effective, then fewer youths would require early intervention programming. Resources would then be reserved for treatment and control (graduated sanctions and police suppression) efforts that target the more intractable gangs and gang members who persist in gang careers. Such a continuum of care and sanctions will help communities more effectively address gang problems.

CONCLUSION AND ONGOING ISSUES

This chapter raises several important practical issues with respect to gang interventions. First, few studies have addressed protective (resilience) factors that buffer children and adolescents from gang involvement. For example, the role of service providers such as youth workers and social workers in enhancing resilience for future and current gang members needs to be better understood. Practitioners need to work with program evaluators to measure possible effects.

Second, the effects of prior violent victimization as a risk factor for gang membership needs to be better understood. Only one form of pre-gang violent victimization of individuals has been researched: child abuse and neglect. The impact of other forms of pre-gang violent victimization, such as a climate of violence in the home, has not been systematically examined.

Third, the prevention of gang member recruiting and gang violence in the school context needs more program attention. The development of gang interventions in the school context should be a top priority. Equally important, these interventions must be well implemented. Most school-based gang programs are not implemented well according to plan (Gottfredson & Gottfredson, 2001).

Fourth, practitioners need to consider how the services their agency provides can be integrated in a seamless continuum of services with those of other service agencies. The most appropriate intervention point for integrating services is a key issue—that is, in prevention, in early intervention, or in treatment/control strategies. This is a challenge because it appears as if the juvenile justice system, schools, and social services agencies work in grain silos (VanDenBerg, 1999). They exist and function in a vertical sphere and seldom mix services with each other even when children and families they serve have needs that cut across the boundaries of each service category.

DISCUSSION QUESTIONS

1. What firsthand knowledge do you have of youth gangs? Were they present in your high school or community? If so, how would you describe their characteristics?

2. Have you ever known any youth gang members? If so, how would you characterize them in terms of risk and protective factors in their lives?

3. How can good social work practices help prevent or reduce child or adolescent gang involvement? How can these practices be integrated with the efforts of other human service agencies?

SUGGESTED READINGS

Fremon, C. (1995). *Father Greg and the homeboys*. New York: Hyperion. This book focuses on the daily street lives of gang boys in Los Angeles that Father Greg Boyle attempts to rescue from gang life.

Klein, M. W. (1995). *The American street gang*. New York: Oxford University Press. This is an outstanding overview of youth gangs and characteristics of gang members.

Kotlowitz, A. (1992). *There are no children here: The story of two boys growing up in the other America*. New York: Anchor Books. This is the story of two young boys growing up in a housing project in Chicago. It depicts the strength of risk factors in their everyday lives—of which gang involvement is but one of many.

REFERENCES

Akers, R. L., Krohn, M. D., Lanza-Kaduce, L., & Radosevich, M. (1979). Social learning and deviant behavior: A specific test of a general theory. *American Sociological Review*, 44, 636–655.

Andrews, D. A., & Bonta, J. (1998). *The psychology of criminal conduct* (2nd ed.). Cincinnati, OH: Anderson.

Aos, S., Phipps, P., Barnoski, R., & Lieb, R. (2001). *The comparative costs and benefits of programs to reduce crime*. Olympia: Washington State Institute for Public Policy. (www.wsipp.wa.gov/crime/costben.html).

Bandura, A. (1999). Social learning and aggression. In F. T. Cullen and R. Agnew (Eds.), *Criminological theory: Past to present* (pp. 21–32). Los Angeles: Roxbury.

Bjerregaard, B., & Lizotte, A. J. (1995). Gun ownership and gang membership. *The Journal of Criminal Law and Criminology*, 86, 37–58.

Bjerregaard, B., & Smith, C. (1993). Gender differences in gang participation, delinquency, and substance use. *Journal of Quantitative Criminology*, 9(4), 329–355.

Bordiun, C. M., Mann, B. J., Cone, L. T., Henggeler, S. W., Fucci, B. R., Blaske, D. M., & Williams, R. A. (1995). Multisystemic treatment of serious juvenile offenders: Long-term prevention of criminality and violence. *Journal of Consulting and Clinical Psychology*, 63, 569–578.

Browning, K., & Huizinga, D. (1999). Highlights of findings from the Denver Youth Survey. *Fact Sheet* (#106). Washington, DC: U.S. Department of Justice, Office of Juvenile Justice and Delinquency Prevention.

Burch, J., & Kane, C. (1999). Implementing the OJJDP comprehensive gang model. *Fact Sheet* (#122). Washington, DC: U.S. Department of Justice, Office of Justice Programs, Office of Juvenile Justice and Delinquency Prevention.

Bureau of Labor Statistics. (1998). *The National Longitudinal Survey of Youth 1997, version 1.0* [machine readable data file]. Washington, DC: U.S. Department of Labor.

Burns, B. J., Schoenwald, S. K., Burchard, J. D., Faw, L. F., & Santos, A. B. (2000). Comprehensive community-based interventions for youth with severe emotional disorders: Multisystemic Therapy and the wraparound process. *Journal of Child and Family Studies*, 9(3), 282–314.

Bursik, R. J., Jr., & Grasmick, H. G. (1993). *Neighborhoods and crime: The dimensions of effective community control*. New York: Lexington Books.

Cairns, R. B., & Cairns, B. D. (1994). *Lifelines and risks: Pathways of youth in our time*. New York: Cambridge University Press.

Capizzi, M., Cook, J. I., & Schumacher, M. (1995, March/April). The TARGET model: A new approach to the prosecution of gang cases. *The Prosecutor*, 18–21.

Catalano, R. F., & Hawkins, J. D. (1996). The Social Development Model: A theory of antisocial behavior. In J. D. Hawkins (Ed.), *Delinquency and crime: Current theories* (pp. 149–197). New York: Cambridge University.

Cloward, R. A., & Ohlin, L. E. (1960). *Delinquency and opportunity: A theory of delinquent gangs*. New York: The Free Press.

Curry, G. D. (1998). Female gang involvement. *Journal of Research on Crime and Delinquency*, 35(1), 100–118.

Curry, G. D., & Spergel, I. A. (1988). Gang homicide, delinquency and community. *Criminology*, 26(3), 381–405.

Decker, S. H. (1996). Collective and normative features of gang violence. *Justice Quarterly*, 13(2), 243–264.

Decker, S. H., & Van Winkle, B. (1996). *Life in the gang: Family, friends, and violence*. New York: Cambridge University Press.

Degnan W. (1994). *Lifeskills post-parole treatment program*. Sanger, CA: Operation New Hope.

Dodge, K. A., Bates, J. E., & Pettit, G. S. (1990). Mechanisms in the cycle of violence. *Science*, 250, 1678–1683.

Durlak, J. A. (1998). Common risk and protective factors in successful prevention programs. *American Journal of Orthopsychiatry*, 68(4), 512–520.

Egley, A., Jr. (2000). Highlights of the 1999 National Youth Gang Survey. *Fact Sheet* (#2000-20). Washington, DC: U.S. Department of Justice, Office of Juvenile Justice and Delinquency Prevention.

Egley, A., Jr. (2002). National Youth Gang Survey Trends from 1996 to 2000. *Fact Sheet* (#2002-03). Washington, DC: U.S. Department of Justice, Office of Juvenile Justice and Delinquency Prevention.

Egley, A., Jr., & Arjunan, M. (2002). Highlights of the 2000 National Youth Gang Survey. *Fact Sheet* (#2002-04). Washington, DC: U.S. Department of Justice, Office of Juvenile Justice and Delinquency Prevention.

Esbensen, F., & Deschenes, E. P. (1998). A multi-site examination of gang membership: Does gender matter? *Criminology,* 36(4), 799–827.

Esbensen, F., & Huizinga, D. (1993). Gangs, drugs, and delinquency in a survey of urban youth. *Criminology,* 31(4), 565–589.

Esbensen, F., Huizinga, D., & Weiher, A. W. (1993). Gang and non-gang youth: Differences in explanatory variables. *Journal of Contemporary Criminal Justice,* 9(1), 94–116.

Esbensen, F., & Osgood, D. W. (1997). National evaluation of G.R.E.A.T. *Research in brief.* Washington, DC: U.S. Department of Justice, National Institute of Justice.

Esbensen, F., & Osgood, D. W. (1999). Gang Resistance Education and Training (G.R.E.A.T.): Results from the National Evaluation. *Journal of Research in Crime and Delinquency,* 36(2), 194–225.

Esbensen, F., Osgood, D. W., Taylor, T. J., Peterson, D., & Freng, A. (2001). How great is G.R.E.A.T.? Results from a longitudinal quasi-experimental design. *Criminology and Public Policy,* 1(1), 87–117.

Fleisher, M. S. (1998). *Dead end kids: Gang girls and the boys they know.* Madison: University of Wisconsin.

Gibbs, J. C. (1993). Moral-cognitive interventions. In A. Goldstein & C. R. Huff (Eds.), *The gang intervention handbook* (pp. 159–185). Champaign, IL: Research Press.

Gibbs, J. C., Potter, G., & Goldstein, A. P. (1999). *EQUIP: Equipping youth to help one another.* Champaign, IL: Research Press.

Goldstein, A. P. (1993). Interpersonal skills training interventions. In A. Goldstein & C. R. Huff (Eds.), *The gang intervention handbook* (pp. 159–185). Champaign, IL: Research Press.

Goldstein, A. P., & Glick, B. (1994). *The prosocial gang: Implementing aggression replacement training.* Thousand Oaks, CA: Sage.

Goldstein, A. P., Glick, B., & Gibbs, J. C. (1998). *Aggression Replacement Training: A comprehensive intervention for aggressive youth* (rev. ed.). Champaign, IL: Research Press.

Gottfredson, G. D., & Gottfredson, D. C. (2001). *Gang problems and gang programs in a national sample of schools.* Ellicott City, MD: Gottfredson Associates.

Hawkins, J. D., Arthur, M. W., & Catalano, R. F. (1995). Preventing substance abuse. In M. Tonry, & D. P. Farrington (Eds.), *Building a safer society: Strategic approaches to crime prevention* (Vol. 19, pp. 343–428). Chicago: University of Chicago Press.

Hawkins, J. D., Catalano, R. F., & Associates. (1992). *Communities that care.* San Francisco: Jossey-Bass.

Hawkins, J. D., Catalano, R. F., Kosterman, R., Abbott, R. D., & Hill, K. G. (1999). Preventing adolescent health-risk behavior by strengthening protection during childhood. *Archives of Pediatric Adolescent Medicine,* 153, 226–234.

Hawkins, J. D., Catalano, R. F., & Miller, J. Y. (1992). Risk and protective factors for alcohol and other drug problems in adolescence and early adulthood: Implications for substance abuse prevention. *Psychological Bulletin,* 112, 64–105.

Hawkins, J. D., Herrenkohl, T. I., Farrington, D. P., Brewer, D., Catalano, R. F., & Harachi, T. W. (1998). A review of predictors of youth violence. In R. Loeber & D. P. Farrington (Eds.), *Serious and violent juvenile offenders: Risk factors and successful interventions* (pp. 106–146). Thousand Oaks, CA: Sage.

Henggeler, S. W. (1997). Treating serious anti-social behavior in youth: The MST approach. *Juvenile Justice Bulletin.* Washington, DC: U.S. Department of Justice, Office of Juvenile Justice and Delinquency Prevention.

Henggeler, S. W., Cunningham, P. B., Pickrel, S. G., Schoenwald, S. K., & Brondino, M. J. (1996). Multisystemic therapy: An effective violence prevention approach for serious juvenile offenders. *Journal of Adolescence,* 19, 47–61.

Henggeler, S. W., Melton, G. B., & Smith, L. A. (1992). Family preservation using multisystem therapy: An effective alternative to incarcerating serious juvenile offenders. *Journal of Consulting and Clinical Psychology,* 60, 953–961.

Henggeler, S. W., Melton, G. B., Smith, G. B., Schoenwald, L. A., & Hanley, J. H. (1993). Family preservation using multisystem treatment: Long-term follow-up to a clinical trial with serious juvenile offenders. *Journal of Child and Family Studies,* 2, 283–293.

Hill, K. G., Howell, J. C., Hawkins, J. D., & Battin-Pearson, S. R. (1999). Childhood risk factors for adolescent gang membership: Results from the Seattle Social Development Project. *Journal of Research in Crime and Delinquency,* 36(3), 300–322.

Hirschi, T. (1969). *Causes of delinquency.* Newbury Park, CA: Sage.

Howell, J. C. (Ed.). (1995). *Guide for implementing the comprehensive strategy for serious, violent, and chronic juvenile offenders.* Washington, DC: U.S. Department of Justice, Office of Juvenile Justice and Delinquency Prevention.

Howell, J. C. (1998). Promising programs for youth gang violence prevention and intervention. In R. Loeber & D. P. Farrington (Eds.), *Serious and violent juvenile offenders: Risk factors and successful interventions* (pp. 284–312). Thousand Oaks, CA: Sage.

Howell, J. C. (2000). *Young gang programs and strategies.* Washington, DC: U.S. Department of Justice, Office of Juvenile Justice and Delinquency Prevention.

Howell, J. C. (2001). Risk-needs assessments and screening devices. In R. Loeber & D. P. Farrington (Eds.), *Child delinquents: Development, interventions, and service needs* (pp. 395–404). Thousand Oaks, CA: Sage.

Howell, J. C. (2003). *Preventing and reducing juvenile delinquency: A comprehensive framework.* Thousand Oaks, CA: Sage.

Howell, J. C., Egley, A., Jr., & Gleason, D. K. (2002). Modern day youth gangs. *Juvenile Justice Bulletin.* Youth Gang Series. Washington, DC: U.S. Department of Justice, Office of Juvenile Justice and Delinquency Prevention.

Howell, J. C., & Lynch, J. (2000). Youth gangs in schools. *Juvenile Justice Bulletin.* Youth Gang Series. Washington, DC: U.S. Department of Justice, Office of Justice Programs, Office of Juvenile Justice and Delinquency Prevention.

Howell, J. C., Moore, J. P., & Egley, A., Jr. (2002). The changing boundaries of youth gangs. In C. R. Huff (Ed.), *Gangs in America* (3rd ed., pp. 3–18). Thousands Oaks, CA: Sage.

Huff, C. R. (1996). The criminal behavior of gang members and non-gang at-risk youth. In C. R. Huff (Ed.), *Gangs in America* (2nd ed., pp. 75–102). Thousand Oaks, CA: Sage.

Institute of Medicine. (1994). *Reducing risks for mental disorders: Frontier for preventive intervention research.* Washington, DC: National Academy Press.

Josi, D., & Sechrest, D. K. (1999). A pragmatic approach to parole aftercare: Evaluation of a community reintegration program for high-risk youthful offenders. *Justice Quarterly,* 16(1), 51–80.

Kent, D. R., Donaldson, S. I., Wyrick, P. A., & Smith, P. J. (2000). Evaluating criminal justice programs designed to reduce crime by targeting repeat gang offenders. *Evaluation and Program Planning,* 23, 115–124.

Kirby, L. D., & Fraser, M. W. (1997). Risk and resilience in childhood. In M. W. Fraser (Ed.), *Risk and resilience in childhood* (pp. 10–33). Washington, DC: National Association of Social Workers.

Kosterman, M. D., Hawkins, J. D., Hill, K. G., Abbott, R. D. Catalano, R. F., & Guo, J. (1996). *The developmental dynamics of gang initiation: When and why young people join gangs.* Paper presented at the annual meeting of the American Society of Criminology, Chicago, November.

Krohn, M. D., Thornberry, T. P., Rivera, C., & Le Blanc, M. (2001). Later careers of very young offenders. In R. Loeber & D. P. Farrington (Eds.), *Child delinquents: Development, interventions, and service needs* (pp. 67–94). Thousand Oaks, CA: Sage.

Lahey, B. B., Gordon, R. A., Loeber, R., Stouthamer-Loeber, M., & Farrington, D. P. (1999). Boys who join gangs: A prospective study of predictors of first gang entry. *Journal of Abnormal Child Psychology,* 27(4), 261–276.

Le Blanc, M., & Loeber, R. (1998). Developmental criminology updated. In M. Tonry (Ed.), *Crime and Justice: A review of research* (pp. 115–198). Chicago: University of Chicago Press.

Lipsey, M. W., & Derzon, J. H. (1998). Predictors of violent or serious delinquency in adolescence and early adulthood: A synthesis of longitudinal research. In R. Loeber & D. P. Farrington (Eds.), *Serious and violent juvenile offenders: Risk factors and successful interventions* (pp. 86–105). Thousand Oaks, CA: Sage.

Lizotte, A. J., Krohn, M. D., Howell, J. C., Tobin, K., & Howard, G. J. (2000). Factors influencing gun carrying among young urban males over the Adolescent–Young Adult Life Course. *Criminology,* 38(3), 811–834.

Lizotte, A. J., Tesoriero, J. M., Thornberry, T. P., & Krohn, M. D. (1994). Patterns of adolescent firearms ownership and use. *Justice Quarterly,* 11, 51–73.

Loeber, R., & Le Blanc, M. (1990). Toward a developmental criminology. In M. Tonry & N. Morris (Eds.), *Crime and justice: A review of research* (pp. 375–473). Chicago: University of Chicago Press.

Maxson, C. L., Curry, G. D., & Howell, J. C. (2002). Youth gang homicides in the United States in the 1990's. In S. Decker & W. Reed (Eds.), *Responses to gangs: Evaluation and research.* Washington, DC: U.S. Department of Justice, National Institute of Justice.

Maxson, C. L., & Whitlock, M. L. (2002). Joining the gang: Gender differences in risk factors for gang membership. In C. R. Huff (Ed.), *Gangs in America III* (pp. 19–35). Thousand Oaks, CA: Sage.

Miller, J. A. (2001). *One of the guys: Girls, gangs and gender.* New York: Oxford University Press.

Miller, W. B. (1992). *Crime by youth gangs and groups in the United States.* Washington, DC: U.S. Department of Justice, Office of Juvenile Justice and Delinquency Prevention.

Miller, W. B. (2001). *The growth of youth gang problems in the United States: 1970–1998.* Washington, DC: U.S. Department of Justice, Office of Juvenile Justice and Delinquency Prevention.

Miller, W. B., Geertz, H., & Cutter, H. S. G. (1962). Aggression in a boys' street-corner group. *Psychiatry,* 24, 283–298.

Moore, J. W. (1978). *Homeboys: Gangs, drugs and prison in the barrios of Los Angeles.* Philadelphia, PA: Temple University Press.

Moore, J. W., & Hagedorn, J. M. (2001). Female gangs. *Juvenile Justice Bulletin.* Youth Gang Series. Washington, DC: U.S. Department of Justice, Office of Juvenile Justice and Delinquency Prevention.

National Youth Gang Center. (2001a). *Assessing your community's youth gang problem.* Washington, DC: U.S. Department of Justice, Office of Juvenile Justice and Delinquency Prevention.

National Youth Gang Center. (2001b). *Planning for implementation of the OJJDP comprehensive gang model.* Washington, DC: U.S. Department of Justice, Office of Juvenile Justice and Delinquency Prevention.

Orange County Probation Department. (2000). *The 8% Solution: A collaborative approach to prevent chronic juvenile crime.* Santa Ana, CA: Orange County Probation Department.

Rackauckas, T. (1999). *1998 Annual report, Gang Unit and Tri-Agency Resource, Gang Enforcement Teams (TARGET).* Santa Ana, CA: Orange County District Attorney's Office.

Rutter, M., Giller, H., & Hagell, A. (1998). *Antisocial behavior by young people.* New York: Cambridge University Press.

Sante, L. (1991). *Low life: Lures and snares of old New York.* New York: Vintage Books.

Schumacher, M., & Kurz, G. (2000). *The 8% Solution: Preventing serious, repeat juvenile crime.* Thousand Oaks, CA: Sage.

Short, J. F., Jr., & Strodtbeck, F. L. (1965). *Group process and gang delinquency.* Chicago: University of Chicago Press.

Small, S. A., & Luster, T. (1994). Adolescent sexual activity: An ecological risk-factor approach. *Journal of Marriage and the Family,* 56, 181–192.

Smith, C., Lizotte, A. J., Thornberry, T. P., & Krohn, M. D. (1995). Resilient youth: Identifying factors that prevent high-risk youth from engaging in delinquency and drug use. In J. Hagan (Ed.), *Delinquency in the life course* (pp. 217–247). Greenwich, CT: JAI.

Snyder, H. N., & Sickmund, M. (1999). *Juvenile offenders and victims: 1999 national report.* Washington, DC: U.S. Department of Justice, Office of Juvenile Justice and Delinquency Prevention.

Spergel, I. A. (1995). *The youth gang problem.* New York: Oxford University Press.

Stouthamer-Loeber, M., Loeber, R., Farrington, D. P., Zhang, Q., Van Kammen, W., & Maguin, E. (1993). The double edge of protective and risk factors for delinquency: Interactions and developmental patterns. *Development and Psychology,* 5, 683–701.

Thornberry, T. P. (1998). Membership in youth gangs and involvement in serious and violent offending. In R. Loeber & D. P. Farrington (Eds.), *Serious and violent juvenile offenders: Risk factors and successful interventions* (pp. 147–166). Thousand Oaks, CA: Sage.

Thornberry, T. P., Huizinga, D., & Loeber, R. (1995). The prevention of serious delinquency and violence: Implications from the program of research on the causes and correlates of delinquency. In J. C. Howell, B. Krisberg, J. D. Hawkins, & J. J. Wilson (Eds.), *Sourcebook on serious, violent, and chronic juvenile offenders* (pp. 213–237). Thousand Oaks, CA: Sage.

Thornberry, T. P., Krohn, M. D., Lizotte, A. J., & Chard-Wierschem, D. (1993). The role of juvenile gangs in facilitating delinquent behavior. *Journal of Research in Crime and Delinquency, 30*(1), 55–87.

Thornberry, T. P., Krohn, M. D., Lizotte, A. J., Smith, C. A., & Tobin, K. (2003). *Gangs and delinquency in developmental perspective.* New York: Cambridge University Press.

VanDenBerg, J. (1999). History of the wraparound process. In B. J. Burns & S. K. Goldman (Eds.), *Promising practices in wraparound for children with serious emotional disturbances and their families. Systems of care: Promising practices in children's mental health, 1998 Series* (Vol. 4, pp. 1–16). Washington, DC: Center for Effective Collaboration and Practice, American Institutes for Research.

Walker-Barnes, C. J., & Mason, C. A. (2001). Ethnic differences in the effect of parenting on gang involvement and gang delinquency: A longitudinal, hierarchial linear modeling perspective. *Child Development, 72*(6), 1814–1831.

Wiebe, D. J. (1998, November). *Targeting and gang crime: Assessing the impacts of a multi-agency suppression strategy in Orange County, California.* Paper presented at the annual meeting of the American Society of Criminology, Washington, DC.

Wilson, J. J., & Howell, J. C. (1993). *A comprehensive strategy for serious, violent and chronic juvenile offenders.* Washington, DC: U.S. Department of Justice, Office of Juvenile Justice and Delinquency Prevention.

Wyrick, P. A. (2000). Vietnamese youth gang involvement. *Fact Sheet* (#2000-01). Washington, DC: U.S. Department of Justice, Office of Juvenile Justice and Delinquency Prevention.

CHAPTER 23

EATING DISORDERS

Prevention and Intervention Strategies with Children and Adolescents

ROSLYN B. BINFORD
The University of Chicago and University of Minnesota

MELISSA PEDERSON MUSSELL
University of Minnesota and the University of St. Thomas

LISA ROGERS
The Emily Program

JOY L. JOHNSON-LIND
University of Minnesota

KATHRYN B. MILLER
University of Minnesota

Eating disorders are serious, potentially life-threatening conditions that if left untreated have the potential to be chronic and refractory. They negatively impact the medical, emotional, social, and familial functioning of the child. However, if properly diagnosed and expeditiously treated, the prognosis is much more favorable (Lask & Bryant-Waugh, 1993). Because of this, early detection and swift treatment of disordered eating is vital.

This chapter addresses a number of issues related to eating disorder prevention and intervention in children and adolescents and includes (1) an overview of clinical features, demographic variables, and reported risk factors; (2) prevention efforts and intervention approaches that have been recognized as efficacious; and (3) two case studies illustrating the primary forms of psychotherapy outlined.

DIAGNOSTIC CONSIDERATIONS

Anorexia nervosa (AN), according to the *Diagnostic and Statistical Manual of Mental Disorders (DSM-IV;* American Psychiatric Association [APA], 1994), is characterized by a refusal to maintain a minimally normal body weight or, in physically developing children, a failure to achieve an expected weight gain. Fundamental to the diagnosis of AN is a striking fear of weight gain, despite being underweight. In AN, at least one of the following is prominent: body image disturbance, self-evaluation "unduly influenced" by shape or weight, or denial of the seriousness of maintaining a low body weight. *Amenorrhea,* defined as the absence of menstrual periods for at least three consecutive months, is an additional diagnostic criterion.

Bulimia nervosa (BN) is marked by recurrent binge eating episodes that are typified by eating an objectively large amount of food in a circumscribed period of time and experiencing a sense of loss of control while binge eating. Recurrent compensatory mechanisms—including self-induced vomiting; misuse of laxatives, diuretics, or enemas; strict fasting; and excessive exercise—are employed to offset effects of binge eating and prevent weight gain. A central feature of BN is the influence of shape and weight as a main aspect of self-evaluation (*DSM-IV;* APA, 1994).

The modal age of onset for anorexia nervosa and bulimia nervosa occurs during adolescence (APA, 1994), with most cases developing prior to age 25 (see Smolak & Levine, 1996). The sex ratio is less pronounced in pre-pubertal children and adolescents than in post-pubertal adolescents and adults. For example, males comprised 19 percent of a childhood AN sample in one study (Hawley, 1985).

It has been argued that children with disordered eating do not fall as neatly into existing diagnostic categories as adults. As reported by Bryant-Waugh and Lask (1995), only half of children referred to an early onset eating disorders treatment facility met stringent diagnostic criteria for AN or BN. This discontinuity may reflect the fact that extant criteria sets were formed on the basis of observations of adults; certain features that are salient for adults may not be germane to children or young adolescents given their developmental level. For example, the significance of shape and weight to their self-concept may be largely absent in children because they have not reached the level of cognitive development necessary to think and reason abstractly (Bryant-Waugh & Lask, 1995).

Comorbid psychopathology is common in individuals with eating disorders. Frequently seen comorbid conditions include depressive, anxiety (particularly obsessive-compulsive disorder), and substance use disorders (see review by Steiner & Lock, 1998).

EPIDEMIOLOGY

Epidemiological studies exclusively examining eating disorders in children are lacking (Lask & Bryant-Waugh, 1993). The prevalence rate of anorexia nervosa in females is reported to range from 0.10 to 1.0 percent (see Walters & Kendler, 1995), whereas prevalence rates for bulimia nervosa are usually estimated to be between 1 to 3 percent of females (APA, 1994). In adolescent females, partial syndrome eating disorders are two to five times more common than diagnosable eating disorders (Dancyger & Garfinkel, 1995; Johnson-Sabine, Wood, Patton, Mann, & Wakeling, 1988), affecting 4 to 16 percent of the population (Killen et al., 1994; Shisslak, Crago, & Neal, 1987).

Eating disorders are more prevalent in westernized countries and have been most frequently reported in affluent Caucasian females. However, this may be an artifact of middle-class Caucasians presenting for treatment more frequently than individuals from different social classes or ethnic backgrounds. Although large-scale epidemiological studies with more ethnically diverse samples of children and adolescents are warranted, there is some indication that eating disorders among youth are not limited to middle/upper-class Caucasians youth (Lacey & Dolan, 1988; Lask & Bryant-Waugh, 1993; Pumariega, 1986).

CASE STUDY
KELLEY

Kelley, a 12-year-old sixth-grader, has early stage anorexia nervosa. She is five feet, two inches tall and weighs 90 pounds. Kelley began dieting last year after her gymnastics coach told her she needed to be in the best shape possible to enhance performance. These comments coincided with her growing frustration over recent normal changes in her body shape and weight as a result of puberty. She began to attribute her less-than-perfect performance during the last season to these physical changes and decided that she needed to lose weight. She became increasingly restrictive of food, eliminating certain foods entirely. Her menstrual periods ceased a couple months after she began dieting.

Kelley lives with her parents and older sister in a middle-class suburban area. She describes her mother as a "perpetual dieter" who openly expresses dissatisfaction with her own body. Her father, a self-proclaimed "workaholic," has always expected high achievement in multiple domains from his daughters. Growing up, both Kelley and her sister were strongly encouraged to succeed in school and extracurricular activities.

CASE STUDY
CARMEN

Carmen, a 15-year-old high school freshman, has bulimia nervosa. She is five feet, five inches tall and weighs 130 pounds. She reports a pattern of binge eating accompanied by self-induced vomiting and laxative abuse. Carmen experienced the transition to high school as stressful. In particular, she was teased by male peers and siblings regarding physical changes associated with pubertal maturation. In response to this, Carmen began to restrict her food intake. She stopped eating breakfast altogether and ate only yogurt for lunch. She developed a pattern of overeating "forbidden" foods whenever she felt depressed or anxious. For instance, she would plan to eat only one cookie or one handful of potato chips, but when she ate more, she would think, "I've already blown it, so I might as well eat the whole bag." After binge eating, she would feel guilty and disgusted with herself, and she feared gaining an inordinate amount of weight from the calories she had consumed. Consequently, she induced vomiting and took laxatives to compensate for the binge eating episodes.

Carmen is the middle child in a family of five. Her mother passed away when Carmen was only 10 years old. Her father is the sole proprietor of a restaurant, which consumes most of his time. Her father was ill-equipped financially and emotionally to handle the demands of single parenting following his wife's death. Consequently, Carmen and her siblings were left at home, unsupervised, much of the time.

RISK FACTORS

A number of factors are involved in the development of eating disorders. Although the case studies highlighted a few of them, see Figure 23.1 and Mussell, Binford, and Fulkerson (2000) for a more extensive list.

FIGURE 23.1   Risk Factors

SOCIOCULTURAL FACTORS

Media influences: Unrealistic ideals of thinness, societal acceptance of nonattainable messages for girls

Industrialized societies' high premium on beauty

Peer teasing

Preoccupation with shape and weight, high drives for thinness, weight concerns and dieting

DEVELOPMENTAL STAGES/LIFE TRANSITIONS

Onset of puberty

Early menarche

Academic demands

Geographic moves and relationship changes

PERSONALITY FACTORS

Negative self-evaluation

Perfectionism

Perceived ineffectiveness

Low self-esteem

Negative emotionality and body dissatisfaction

Negative affect and dietary restraint

ATHLETIC FACTORS*

Participation in specific competitive sports (e.g., gymnastics, running, figure skating) that emphasize leanness

TRAUMA FACTORS

Sexual abuse

Physical abuse and parental discord

FAMILIAL FACTORS

Familial enmeshment and maternal overprotectiveness

Mothers' dieting and weight concerns as well as fathers' preference for thinness

Direct parental comments regarding shape and weight

Family history of an eating disorder

GENETIC FACTORS/BIOLOGICAL FACTORS

Serotonergic abnormalities

*It is important to point out that, in general, sports do not heighten the risk for developing disordered eating. Involvement in sports may act as a protective factor in that it enhances psychological well-being.

EXISTING EATING DISORDER PREVENTION PROGRAMS

Approximately a dozen controlled research studies (i.e., using a no-treatment or minimal-treatment control condition) have been published evaluating the efficacy of school-based eating disorder prevention curricula (see review by Mussell et al., 2000). Program components include the following goals:

1. Provide psychoeducation (i.e., negative consequences of unhealthy weight control practices; natural changes in body composition associated with physical maturation).
2. Develop healthy eating and exercise patterns.
3. Encourage the development of a positive body image.
4. Facilitate knowledge of, and resistance to, negative media images about eating and body image.
5. Establish coping skills to resist sociocultural pressures for thinness and dieting.

Unfortunately, the results of most eating disorder prevention programs have been somewhat disappointing. Although increased knowledge about eating disorders or improvements in eating disorder-related attitudes have been demonstrated by some studies, the majority of programs have not been able to demonstrate improvements in, or prevention of, eating disorder behavior. Particularly concerning is the fact that two recently published prevention studies (Carter et al., 1997; Mann et al., 1997) suggest the potential iatrogenic effect of such interventions after observing an increase in eating disorder behavior.

A number of methodological limitations (e.g., insufficient assessment instruments, lack of control groups, inadequate sample sizes) may help to explain these unexpected and inconsistent research results. However, even large-scale studies using sophisticated designs (e.g., Killen et al., 1993) have been unable to show favorable findings. It is possible that the assessment period for the studies has not been long enough to capture whether a participant in the program may have developed resiliency against developing an eating disorder that otherwise might have emerged in the future. Most importantly, the inability to detect beneficial prevention outcomes may be because the programs are implemented to students after eating disorder symptoms have already emerged. In order to demonstrate efficacy, primary prevention programs may need to begin as early as elementary school before the onset of the targeted symptoms.

New Directions in Prevention Research

Some authors argue that the disappointing findings of most primary prevention programs are due to the "disease-specific approach" upon which most of the programs are premised (Striegel-Moore & Steiner-Adair, 1998). Without modifying the social and political environment in which eating disorders emerge, it may be that insufficient attention is devoted to assisting girls in developing resilience to larger sociocultural influences. Increasingly, eating disorder experts are calling for efforts to modify the systemic context in which eating disorders develop (e.g., Striegel-Moore & Steiner-Adair, 1998).

A number of other authors have provided suggestions for improving outcome (see review by Mussell et al., 2000). One important factor is to target the prevention program to the developmental age of the audience. For instance, when delivering programs to elementary school children, using experiential components such as poems, stories, humor, and games has been found to be beneficial (Kater, Rohwer, & Levine, 2000). Prevention programs aimed at older children have encouraged participants to actively work toward finding solutions. These programs have included elements involving media awareness, activism, feminist work groups (Levine, Piran, & Stoddard, 2000), and actively challenging the thin ideal (Stice, Mazotti, Weibel, & Agras, 2000). In addition, Paxton (2000) suggests that for adolescents, modifying the peer group is important. Paxton advocates reinforcing healthy eating practices and attitudes about body image within peer groups so that members can approach one another with concerns and label detrimental "fat talk" (p. 139). Future prevention programs will benefit from taking the larger sociocultural context into account as well as adapting programs to specific developmental stages.

TREATMENT

Treatment of eating disorders for children and adolescents is best approached as a multidisciplinary endeavor, often requiring concomitant use of psychotherapy, nutritional counseling, family intervention, and medical management. In addition, more intensive treatment such as inpatient hospitalization is sometimes required for weight restoration and medical stabilization.

Cognitive Behavioral Therapy

Extensive research has empirically established cognitive behavioral therapy (CBT) as the "gold standard" "treatment of choice" for bulimia nervosa (see review by Wilson & Fairburn, 1998). Cognitive behavioral therapy also has been adapted and recommended to treat those with anorexia nervosa (Garner, Vitousek, & Pike, 1997), although the number of studies for these indications is limited to date. Cognitive behavioral therapy for BN has been associated with reductions in binge eating and purging behaviors, dietary restraint, as well as improvements in body image and attitudes regarding shape and weight (see review by Wilson & Fairburn, 1998).

There are certain modifications that may need to be made to CBT when working with children and adolescents. First, CBT treatment models suppose a certain level of motivation for completion of homework and therapeutic tasks. Many adolescents, particularly those with AN, approach treatment with ambivalence, reluctance, or even disdain. Thus, early stages may need to focus on increasing motivation and reinforcing the need for treatment. Second, CBT requires a certain level of cognitive sophistication. The therapist may need to tailor CBT tasks and cognitive work to a developmentally appropriate level. Modifications for how to make CBT more applicable to children are described in Lask & Bryant-Waugh (2000) and a few techniques are highlighted here.

The fundamental goal of cognitive behavioral therapy for BN is to eliminate eating disorder symptoms by modifying dysfunctional attitudes and thoughts about eating, shape, and weight. Information is provided to help the client understand the cyclical relationship between dieting, binge eating, and compensatory measures, as well as the relationship between self-esteem and shape/weight concerns and the behavioral symptoms they help to engender and maintain. Cognitive behavioral therapy specifically targets the risk factor of dieting early in treatment by replacing dietary restriction with a regular pattern of eating in order to reduce physiological and psychological deprivation. Consultation with a nutritionist is often used to assist in this goal.

Food monitoring logs are used throughout the course of treatment to obtain a clear picture of eating patterns and antecedents of core behaviors. However, these often require a level of motivation and organization not common for children and adolescents. Thought diary cartoons (Young & Faneslow-Brown, 1996) in which the child records his or her thoughts and feelings in cartoon bubbles rather than more adult self-monitoring logs may be useful for children and adolescents with eating disorders.

Problem-solving skills and coping strategies are strengthened by identifying interpersonal, psychological, and contextual cues for binge eating. Clients are instructed how to identify and alter perfectionistic thinking, cognitive distortions, and problematic assumptions about shape and weight via cognitive restructuring. This cognitive work can be employed in children through a technique proposed by Binnay and Wright (1997) termed the "bag of feelings" task. This activity gives children the opportunity to externalize their inner worries and concerns by having them draw their worries in the outline of an empty bag drawn on a piece of paper. For example, a child draws "no one will play with me if I am overweight" in the worry bag. Next, the child is told to record the names of people she played with at school and bring it to the next therapy session. In a collaborative process, the therapist helps the child see that the "no one will play with me if I am overweight" worry is not justified given her list of playmates. The child is then instructed to throw the worry into the trash. Role-playing techniques can also be employed to make the content of CBT more explicit.

Dietary restriction is further targeted through the gradual exposure of previously avoided foods and increasing the overall amount of food eaten. With the "growing a flower" technique (Christie, 2000), a child is instructed to experiment with sampling small portions of novel foods. The child is told to record how the food tastes and whether he or she likes the taste (e.g., with a smiley- or frown-face). Then, the list of foods the child likes are transposed onto colorful petal shaped pieces of paper and stuck onto the center of a flower without petals. The last stage of CBT, relapse prevention planning, needs to be done in collaboration with parents.

INTERPERSONAL PSYCHOTHERAPY

In contrast to CBT, which focuses specifically and directly on disordered eating behaviors and cognitions, the goal of Interpersonal Psychotherapy (IPT; Klerman, Weissman, Rounsaville, & Chevron, 1984) as adapted for bulimia nervosa (Fairburn, 1994; Fairburn et al.,

1991; Fairburn, Jones, Peveler, Hope, & O'Connor, 1993) is to reduce or eradicate eating disorder symptoms by targeting changes in the individual's interpersonal relationships rather than eating disorder symptoms. Originally designed for the treatment of adults with depression, the IPT approach has been modified for use with depressed adolescents (Mufson, Woreau, Weissman, & Klerman, 1993). Although found to be efficacious in studies of adults with BN (Fairburn et al., 1991), it has not been investigated with adolescent eating disorder samples.

Derived from psychodynamically oriented therapies, the present-focused, time-limited approach of IPT involves three phases over the course of approximately 12 weeks. In the early stage of therapy, the client is encouraged to view her or his eating disorder symptoms as stemming from interpersonal difficulties. The goal of the first three to four sessions of therapy is to conduct a thorough assessment of the individual's interpersonal relationships in an attempt to identify the extent to which the individual has difficulty with one or more of the following issues: (1) grief reactions, (2) interpersonal role disputes, (3) role transitions, (4) interpersonal deficits, and (5) single-parent family (an additional category included for adolescent clients). After developing a therapeutic contract to address one or more of these issues, therapy is devoted to working in a focused but nondirective manner to identify strategies to overcome these interpersonal problem areas. Clients are encouraged to look for opportunities to make changes in the way they relate to others. Toward the end of the course of therapy, the client is encouraged to continue positive changes independent from treatment.

Carmen was willing to meet with a nutritionist and readily responded to the reintroduction of a regular eating plan; however, she was still binge eating and purging in response to interpersonal stressors. Based on her history, it appeared that the binge eating was functionally related to emotional regulation, especially as it pertained to interpersonal issues, and dieting was used to counter effects of the binge eating. Therefore, the therapist thought that Carmen would be ideally suited for interpersonal therapy.

Carmen and her therapist spent the first few sessions reviewing important events in Carmen's life, paying special attention to her significant relationships. During these conversations, it became clear that Carmen's profound sadness and loneliness began shortly after her mother died. Through a tearful discussion, Carmen revealed that her father displayed anger and disapproval whenever her mother's name was mentioned, probably because he, too, had difficulty dealing with the enormity of the loss. Consequently, Carmen had never had the opportunity to talk about the depth of her pain from losing her mother. Further review of Carmen's history indicated that her binge eating began shortly after her mother's death and that the intense dieting and purging behaviors began recently in response to teasing at her new school.

The sessions focused on Carmen's accounts of how she missed her mother and wished that she could be present to help guide her through this time in her life. Without offering specific suggestions, her therapist encouraged her to look for opportunities to honor her mother's memory and cherish the love that she had shared with Carmen. Sessions also focused on the daily challenges Carmen encountered as a freshman at a new school. As Carmen experienced bulimic episodes, her therapist encouraged her to reflect on the social obstacles she had encountered that week that might have prompted the bulimic behavior. She was gently encouraged to take risks and to keep herself open to opportunities to form relationships with peers and trusted adults at her new school. As therapy progressed,

Carmen began to become more actively involved with her peers and to feel less depressed and to substantially reduce any disordered eating.

FAMILY THERAPY

Although there may be debate among practitioners and researchers regarding the most effective treatments for adolescents and children with eating disorders, there is fairly strong consensus regarding the importance of family involvement (Lock, Le Grange, Agras, & Dare, 2001; Robin, Gilroy, & Dennis, 1998; Steiner & Lock, 1998). Adolescents, particularly younger adolescents, are embedded in a family system. To work for the significant level of change that is required during treatment for an eating disorder, without any concomitant change in the familial environment, is difficult. In addition, the stress an eating disorder exacts on a family can be enormous; many families require support in order to cope with the stress. Therefore, most family therapy models for the treatment of eating disorders have included a component placing the parent in an active and involved role.

Minuchin (1974) was one of the first authors to write about family therapy for eating disorders. He described an approach aimed at increasing parents' concerns about the symptoms, placing them in charge of recovery, and using "lunch sessions" where parents were instructed to "make her eat" (p. 244). He also addressed a range of behavioral strategies and worked to change roles and relationships within the family.

Pieces of this approach were further developed and expanded by a group of researchers at the Maudsley Hospital in England who have completed a series of controlled trials (e.g., Eisler et al., 1997; Eisler et al., 2000; Le Grange, Eisler, Dare, & Russell, 1992; Russell, Szmukler, Dare, & Eisler, 1987). The first study (Russell et al., 1987) investigated whether family therapy or individual therapy was more effective in treating 80 weight-restored anorexia nervosa patients posthospital. They demonstrated that for patients 18 years old or younger with a short duration (< 3 years) of illness, family therapy was more effective than individual therapy, whereas the converse was true for patients over age 18 with a longer duration of illness. This difference continued to be significant at one year (Russell et al., 1987) and five years posttreatment (Eisler et al., 1997).

Given the success of these initial studies, a well-defined model was established and described in a recently published treatment manual (Lock, Le Grange, Agras, & Dare, 2000). One of the initial goals of this treatment is to heighten the parents' awareness that AN is a dangerous illness of which they must take control if their child is to improve. During the initial stages of treatment until the child is reasonably weight restored, the parents (with some therapist guidance) take primary responsibility for making decisions about what, when, and how much the child or adolescent needs to eat. If necessary, it is suggested that parents take a leave from work to focus the level of time and energy needed to monitor the child and implement change. In later stages of therapy, assuming there is appropriate weight gain, the adolescent regains more control over his or her eating and issues related to adolescence and emancipation are addressed. The primary format of this treatment is conjoint family-based therapy. However, two studies have found that high levels of maternal criticism were associated with poor outcome and affected family retention within treatment and may warrant separating the parents and child during therapy (Eisler et al., 2000; Le Grange et al., 1992).

In a randomized trial, Robin and colleagues (1999) compared Behavioral Family Systems Therapy (BFST; Robin, Siegel, Koepke, Move, & Tice, 1994) with Ego-Oriented Individual Therapy (EOIT; Robin et al., 1994) with the addition of collateral family counseling in 37 participants over a 12- to 18-month time span. Similar to the Maudsley Model, parents are placed in the role of the primary treatment providers in BFST; however, the therapy addresses a broader range of more traditional family therapy issues, such as triangulation and enmeshment through strategic interventions. In the last stage of therapy, the work focuses on problem solving and communication within the family. Ego-Oriented Individual Therapy is primarily an individual therapy focused on developing ego strength and on developmental interpersonal issues. The individual therapist meets bimonthly with the parents in a collateral manner in order to provide psychoeducational information regarding adolescent development and to help the family to better accept their daughter's increasing independence and autonomy. In EOIT, the therapist does not establish behavioral goals for the parents or ask them to be involved in implementing change.

Results indicated that although both treatments were efficacious in restoring the health of participants, the BFST group reached some health goals more quickly. By one year posttreatment, any differences between the treatments were negligible. Surprisingly, there were no measured differences in family functioning as a result of these differing levels of family involvement. These researchers suggest that this provides evidence that family involvement is important, but that the level of involvement can vary with similar results.

There has been far less research on the treatment of BN and family therapy. This may be, in part, due to the older average age at time of presentation. In addition, individuals with bulimia nervosa often are secretive about their symptoms, which may be difficult for parents to detect if the individual's weight remains relatively stable. Dodge, Hodes, Eisler, and Dare (1995) provide preliminary support for the use of a similar form of family therapy that is a promising treatment approach for adolescent AN and for adolescent BN. However, it is important to note that this was not a randomized trial and was limited by a small sample size. Currently, two outpatient psychotherapy trials for adolescents with BN are ongoing: one by LeGrange at The University of Chicago and the other by Schmidt at the Institute of Psychiatry in London.

The parameters about when and how much to involve family are not rigid. The level of involvement will be guided by the level of severity of the eating disorder, the age and maturity level of the client, the preexisting dynamics of the family, available resources, and the family's willingness to be involved. A seriously underweight 12-year-old who is minimizing the seriousness of her symptoms dictates a different level of family involvement than a 17-year-old college freshman who purges two or three times a week, but presents for treatment independently and is motivated to make changes. However, most authors writing on the subject of children and adolescents with eating disorders agree that some degree of parent involvement is essential.

Family therapy was recommended in Kelley's case and initial stages of therapy focused on stabilizing her weight to a medically healthy level by reintroducing previously avoided foods. Involving parents is often a complicated task. Despite encouragement from the treatment team and presentation of research indicating the importance of parental involvement, Kelley's father stopped attending sessions, because he felt that his wife could fill him in on Kelley's progress. The therapist reiterated that AN is a very serious, potentially fatal condition that demands their full time and attention and encouraged them to take a more active, directive role with Kelley regarding food issues.

The culture created at home was revealed in therapy. The negative impact of disparaging remarks about eating, shape, and weight by both of Kelley's parents as well as her mother's dietary restriction on their daughters was stressed. Mixed messages communicated by Kelley's mother, such as, "No, you eat. I can't eat. I'm on a diet," as well as comments made regarding achievement, including, "We love you unconditionally, but look at all those As!" were highlighted in therapy. Ways in which her parents communicated their high expectations for both girls, in particular her mother's hopes for Kelley to surpass her own gymnastics achievements, were targeted. Kelley's sister corroborated the high level of achievement expected from her and her sister when their parents claimed during the session that they just wanted their daughters to be happy and did not care what they achieved. Over time, her parents began to see the amount of pressure they unknowingly placed on their daughters. Later stages of therapy supported Kelley's goal of more autonomously making her own decisions, including making some of her own meal choices.

The treatment team collaborated with the school in facilitating Kelley's recovery. The school counselor acted as an informant of Kelley's social interaction at school. One of the therapeutic goals was to have Kelley eat meals in the lunchroom instead of alone in the library. The therapist and Kelley also developed a plan to employ her friends to help her feel supported and adhere to the principles learned in therapy, such as having her friends remind her to eat a snack before practice, if Kelley forgot. Although Kelley was very eager to return to gymnastics, the treatment team insisted that gymnastics was a privilege she would have to earn. As therapy progressed, Kelley started to work on going out with her friends and trying new things. Therapy was broadened to include issues beyond the eating disorder.

OTHER FORMS OF TREATMENT

Other forms of treatment that have been written about or used with children and adolescents include, among others, group therapy, play therapy, and art therapy. These forms of therapy have not been well studied but are often mentioned (Lask & Bryant-Waugh, 2000; Natenshon, 1999).

Groups are almost always provided as part of inpatient or partial hospitalization programs and are often part of outpatient therapy as well (see review by Polivy & Federoff, 1997). These may be very focused educational groups that are time limited or open ended supportive groups. Manley and Needham (1995) wrote about an "Anti-Bulimia" group designed for adolescents in the early stages of treatment. This group helped members mobilize against societal pressures for thinness and rigid female roles. Other adolescent groups have focused on helping members cope with developmental tasks and stressors without using eating disorder symptoms as coping mechanisms (Cramer-Azima, 1992). Although open-ended supportive or interpersonally focused groups appear to be widely used treatment modalities for adolescents, we found no research investigating their efficacy, either in reducing symptoms or in improving overall functioning.

Play therapy encompasses many theoretical models of therapy; it can be based in psychodynamic theory, family systems theory, or cognitive behavioral theory among others. The common element is the use of play as a method of interacting with the client. Play can be used to elicit communication from a child or adolescent or to communicate ideas or teach a client new ideas or ways of looking at something (Schaeffer & O'Connor, 1994).

In psychodynamic therapy, a child may be given a sketchbook to draw in during sessions and then the progression of drawings are interpreted. Within a cognitive behavioral framework, play therapy may translate a researched therapy technique, such as addressing food hierarchies, into an art project. Or, instead of talking about cognition and feelings related to one's body, an adolescent may draw a picture of the body with different colors for different feelings. These kinds of techniques are written about by authors drawing on traditional research and trying to apply the principles to young clients (Christie, 2000). In addition, play therapy techniques that are designed for other populations may be appropriate for children with eating disorders. For example, many techniques help children identify and learn to express feelings directly. These are relevant skills for young clients with eating disorders. Two sources for further reading on this subject are Schaefer and O'Connor (1994) and Timberlake and Cutler (2000).

PHARMACOTHERAPY

Although the primary focus of this review is psychotherapeutic treatments of eating disorders, it would be remiss not to include psychoactive medication. Clinical trials have shown therapeutic responses to a range of antidepressant medications for adults with BN, with selective serotonin reuptake inhibitors being the most effective. However, no studies have investigated the use of these medications specifically with children or adolescents for eating disorders. For a complete review of research on medication and issues related to medication with children and adolescents, Mitchell (2001) and Lask and Bryant-Waugh (2000) are recommended, respectively.

CONCLUSIONS AND DIRECTIONS FOR FURTHER RESEARCH

To date, there has been interesting and innovative research conducted with children and adolescents with eating disorders. However, more research is needed to better understand how to prevent and effectively treat these devastating conditions. Existing prevention programs have been implemented in schools with disappointing findings regarding their effectiveness at preventing eating disorders. Future studies may benefit from targeting elementary-aged children prior to the onset of eating disorder symptoms, and making efforts to modify the larger environmental context in which eating disorders develop. In addition, issues of diversity need to be considered, with increased attention paid to studying heterogeneous samples.

Families, peers, and school systems play important roles in the prevention and treatment of eating disorders. For instance, Kelley's parents were the primary agents of therapeutic change in the refeeding process, and the involvement of her school and peers was important in her recovery. More research involving systemic interventions—including family, peers, and school systems—needs to be undertaken.

The treatment of eating disorders has been more extensively researched in adults than children or adolescents. In particular, CBT and IPT are known to be efficacious treatments for adults with bulimia nervosa. Additional research is needed to determine whether these results are also applicable to eating disorder children and adolescents like Carmen. The promising findings regarding the effectiveness of family therapy, particularly the manualized Maudsley Model, in treating individuals with early onset AN need to be replicated and expanded. Furthermore, it would be beneficial to have a better understanding of what general therapeutic techniques used with children and adolescents (e.g., play therapy, art therapy, etc.) are efficacious in ameliorating eating disorder symptoms. By broadening our understanding of the development and maintenance of eating disorders in children and adolescents, hopefully we can design more comprehensive and effective prevention and treatment programs.

DISCUSSION QUESTIONS

1. How can we most effectively modify the larger sociocultural environment that contributes to the development and maintenance of eating disorders?

2. What are the most helpful strategies to employ the potential benefits of peers as protective factors in eating disorder prevention?

3. What is the most effective way to increase knowledge and awareness about the early warning signs of eating disorders among professionals (e.g., school social workers, guidance counselors, teachers, coaches) and parents in order to facilitate intervention?

4. What additional interventions may prove efficacious with younger populations?

SUGGESTED READINGS

Bryant-Waugh, R., & Lask, B. (1999). *Eating disorders: A parent's guide.* London: Penguin.

Fairburn, C. G., & Wilson, G. T. (1993). *Binge eating: Nature, assessment and treatment.* New York: Guilford Press.

Garner, D. M., & Garfinkel, P. E. (1997). *Handbook of treatment for eating disorders* (2nd ed.). New York: Guilford Press.

Kater, K., Rohwer, J., & Levine, M. P. (2000). An elementary school project for developing healthy body image and reducing risk factors for unhealthy and disordered eating. *Eating Disorders: The Journal of Treatment and Prevention, 8,* 3–16.

Kearney-Cooke, A. (2000). *Helping girls become strong women.* New York: Columbia University Press.

Lask, B., & Bryant-Waugh, R. (2000). *Anorexia nervosa and related eating disorders in childhood and adolescence* (2nd ed.). East Sussex: Psychology Press.

Lock, J., Le Grange, D., Agras, W. S., & Dare, C. (2001). *Treatment manual for anorexia nervosa: A family-based approach.* New York: Guilford Press.

Mitchell, J. E. (Ed.). (2001). *The treatment of eating disorders: A guide for dieticians, therapists and physicians.* Minneapolis: University of Minnesota Press.

Natenshon, A. H. (1999). *When your child has an eating disorder: A step-by-step manual for parents and other caregivers.* San Francisco: Jossey-Bass.

Neumark-Sztainer, D., Butler, R., & Palti, H. (1995). Eating disturbances among adolescent girls: Evaluation of a school-based primary prevention program. *Journal of Nutrition Education, 27,* 24–31.

RESOURCES

AABA   American Anorexia/Bulimia Association
165 West 46th Street, #1108
New York, NY 10036
(212) 575-6200
http://members.aolcom/AmanBU

AED   Academy for Eating Disorders
6728 Old McLean Village Dr.
McLean, VA 22101
(703) 556-9222
www.acadeatdis.org

AHELP   Association for the Health Enrichment for Large People
P.O. Drawer C
Radford, VA 24143
(703) 731-1778

ANAD   National Association of Anorexia Nervosa and Associated Disorders
P.O. Box 7
Highland Park, IL 60035
(847) 831-3438
www.healthtouch.com/level1/leaflets/anad/anad001.html

ANRED   Anorexia Nervosa and Related Eating Disorders Inc.
P.O. Box 5102
Eugene, OR 97401
(541) 344-1144
www.anred.com

Council on Size & Weight Discrimination, Inc.
P.O. Box 305
Mt. Marion, NY 12456
(914) 679-1209; fax: (914) 679-1206

EDAP   Eating Disorders Awareness and Prevention Inc.
603 Stewart St., Suite 803
Seattle, WA 98101
(800) 931-2237; (206) 382-3587; fax: (206) 829-8501
www.edap.org

Eating Disorder Referral and Information Center
2923 Sandy Pointe, Suite 6
Del Mar, CA 92014-2052
(858) 792-7463
www.edreferral.com

LAEDP   International Association of Eating Disorders Professionals
123 NW 13th St., #206
Boca Raton, FL 33432-1618
(800) 800-8126; fax: (407) 338-9913

Largesse: The Network for Size Esteem
P.O. Box 9404
New Haven, CT 06534
(203) 787-1624

NAAFA   National Association to Advance Fat Acceptance, Inc.
P.O. Box 188620
Sacramento, CA 95818
(916) 558-6880
www.naafa.org

NEDO   National Eating Disorders Organization
        (affiliated with Laureate Eating Disorders Program)
        6655 S. Yale Ave.
        Tulsa, OK 74136
        (918) 481-4044
        www.laureate.com

NEDSP   The National Eating Disorders Screening Program
        One Washington Street, Suite 304
        Wellesley Hills, MA 02181
        (781) 239-0071
        www.nmisp.org

OA   Overeaters Anonymous Headquarters
        P.O. Box 44020
        Rio Rancho, NM 87174-4020
        (505) 891-2664
        www.overeatersanonymous.org

REFERENCES

American Psychiatric Association. (1994). *Diagnostic and statistical manual of mental disorders* (4th ed.). Washington, DC: Author.

Binnay, V., & Wright, J. C. (1997). The bag of feelings: An ideographic technique for the assessment and exploration of feelings in children and adolescents. *Clinical Child Psychology and Psychiatry, 2,* 449–462.

Bryant-Waugh, R., & Lask, B. (1995). Annotation: Eating disorders in children. *Journal of Child Psychology and Psychiatry, 36,* 191–202.

Carter, J. C., Stewart, D. A., Dunn, V. J., & Fairburn, C. G. (1997). Primary prevention of eating disorders: Might it do more harm than good? *International Journal of Eating Disorders, 22,* 167–172.

Christie, D. (2000). Cognitive-behavioural therapeutic techniques for children with eating disorders. In B. Lask & R. Bryant-Waugh, R. (Eds.), *Anorexia nervosa and related eating disorders in childhood and adolescence* (2nd ed., pp. 205–226). East Sussex: Psychology Press.

Cramer-Azima, F. J. (1992). Adolescent group treatment. In H. Harper-Giuffre & K. R. MacKenzi (Eds.), *Group psychotherapy for eating disorders.* Washington, DC: American Psychiatric Press.

Dancyger, I. F., & Garfinkel, P. E. (1995). The relationship of partial syndrome eating disorders to anorexia nervosa and bulimia nervosa. *Psychological Medicine, 25,* 1019–1025.

Dodge, E., Hodes, M., Eisler, I., & Dare, C. (1995). Family therapy for bulimia nervosa in adolescents: An exploratory study. *Journal of Family Therapy, 17,* 59–77.

Eisler, I., Dare, C., Hodes, M., Russell, G., Dodge, E., Le Grange, D. (2000). Family therapy for adolescent anorexia nervosa: The results of a controlled comparison of two family interventions. *Journal of Child Psychology & Psychiatry & Allied Disciplines, 41,* 727–736.

Eisler, I., Dare, C., Russell, G. F., Szmukler, G., Le Grange, D., & Dodge, E. (1997). Family and individual therapy in anorexia nervosa. A 5-year follow-up. *Archives of General Psychiatry, 54,* 1025–1030.

Fairburn, C. G. (1994). Interpersonal psychotherapy for bulimia nervosa. In G. L. Klerman & M. M. Weissman (Eds.), *New application of interpersonal psychotherapy* (pp. 353–378). New York: Guilford.

Fairburn, C. G., Jones, R., Peveler, R. C., Carr, S. J., Solomon, R. A., O'Connor, M. E., Burton, J., & Hope, R. A. (1991). Three psychological treatments for bulimia nervosa: A comparative trial. *Archives of General Psychiatry, 48,* 463–469.

Fairburn, C. G., Jones, R., Peveler, R. C., Hope, R. A., & O'Connor, M. E. (1993). Psychotherapy and bulimia nervosa: The longer-term effects of interpersonal psychotherapy, behavior therapy and cognitive-behavioral therapy. *Archives of General Psychiatry, 50,* 419–428.

Garner, D. M., Vitousek, K. M., & Pike, K. M. (1997). Cognitive-behavioral therapy for anorexia nervosa. In D. M. Garner & P. E. Garfinkel (Eds.), *Handbook of treatment for eating disorders* (2nd ed., pp. 95–144). New York: Guilford.

Hawley, R. M. (1985). The outcome of anorexia nervosa in younger subjects. *British Journal of Psychiatry, 146*, 657–660.

Johnson-Sabine, E., Wood, K., Patton, G., Mann, A., & Wakeling, A. (1988). Abnormal eating attitudes in London schoolgirls—A prospective epidemiological study: Factors associated with abnormal response on screening questionnaires. *Psychological Medicine, 18*, 615–622.

Kater, K., Rohwer, J., & Levine, M. P. (2000). An elementary school project for developing healthy body image and reducing risk factors for unhealthy and disordered eating. *Eating Disorders: The Journal of Treatment and Prevention, 8*, 3–16.

Killen, J. D., Taylor, C. B., Hammer, L. D., Litt, I., Wilson, D. M., Hayward, C., Simmonds, B., Kraemer, H., & Varady, A. (1993). An attempt to modify unhealthful eating attitudes and weight regulation practices of young adolescent girls. *International Journal of Eating Disorders, 13*, 369–384.

Killen, J. D., Taylor, C. B., Hayward, C., Wilson, D. M., Haydel, K. F., Robinson, T. N., Litt, I., Simmonds, B. A., Varady, A., & Kraemer, H. (1994). Pursuit of thinness and onset of eating disorder symptoms in a community sample of adolescent girls: A three-year prospective analysis. *International Journal of Eating Disorders, 16*, 227–238.

Klerman, G. L., Weissman, M. M., Rounsaville, B. J., & Chevron, E. S. (1984). *Interpersonal psychotherapy for depression.* New York: Basic Books.

Lacey, H., & Dolan, B. (1988). Bulimia in British blacks and Asians. *British Journal of Psychiatry, 152*, 73–79.

Lask, B., & Bryant-Waugh, R. (Eds.). (1993). *Childhood onset anorexia and related eating disorders.* Hillsdale, NJ: Erlbaum.

Lask, B., & Bryant-Waugh, R. (2000). *Anorexia nervosa and related eating disorders in childhood and adolescence* (2nd ed.). East Sussex: Psychology Press.

Le Grange, D., Eisler, I., Dare, C., & Russell, G. F. M. (1992). Evaluation of family therapy in anorexia nervosa: A pilot study. *International Journal of Eating Disorders, 12*, 347–357.

Levine, M. P., Piran, N., & Stoddard, C. (2000). Mission more probably: Media literacy, activism, and advocacy as primary prevention. In N. Piran, M. P. Levine, & C. Steiner-Adair (Eds.), *Preventing eating disorders: A handbook of interventions and specific challenges* (pp. 3–25). Ann Arbor, MI: Burnner/Mazel.

Lock, J., Le Grange, D., Agras, W. S., & Dare, C. (2001). *Treatment manual for anorexia nervosa: A family-based approach.* New York: Guilford.

Manley, R., & Needham, L. (1995). An anti-bulimia group for adolescent girls. *Journal of Child and Adolescent Group Therapy, 5*, 19–33.

Mann, T., Nolen-Hoeksema, S., Huang, K., Burgard, D., Wright, A., & Hanson, K. (1997). Are two interventions worse than none? Joint primary prevention of eating disorders in college females. *Health Psychology, 16*, 215–225.

Minuchin, S. (1974). *Families and family therapy.* Cambridge, MA: Harvard University Press.

Mitchell, J. E. (Ed.). (2001). *The treatment of eating disorders: A guide for dieticians, therapists and physicians.* Minneapolis: University of Minnesota Press.

Mufson, L. H., Woreau, D., Weissman, M. M., & Klerman, G. L. (1993). Interpersonal psychotherapy for adolescent depression. In G. L. Klerman & M. M. Weissman (Eds.), *New applications of interpersonal psychotherapy* (pp. 129–166). Washington, DC: American Psychiatric Press.

Mussell, M. P., Binford, R. B., & Fulkerson, J. A. (2000). Eating disorders: Summary of risk factors, prevention programming, & prevention research. (Special Issue: Prevention in Counseling Psychology). *The Counseling Psychologist, 28*, 764–796.

Natenshon, A. H. (1999). *When your child has an eating disorder: A step-by-step manual for parents and other caregivers.* San Francisco: Jossey-Bass.

Paxton, S. J. (2000). Peer relations, body image, and disordered eating in adolescent girls: Implications for prevention. In N. Piran, M. P. Levine, & C. Steiner-Adair (Eds.), *Preventing eating disorders: A handbook of interventions and specific challenges* (pp. 134–147). Ann Arbor, MI: Burnner/Mazel.

Polivy, J., & Federoff, I. (1997). Group psychotherapy. In D. M. Garner & P. E. Garfinkel (Eds.), *Handbook of treatment for eating disorders* (pp. 462–475). New York: Guilford.

Pumariega, A. (1986). Acculturation and eating attitudes in adolescent girls: A comparative and correlational study. *Journal of the American Academy of Child Psychiatry, 25,* 276–279.

Robin, A., Gilroy, M., & Dennis, A. (1998). Treatment of eating disorders in children and adolescents. *Clinical Psychology Review, 18,* 421–446.

Robin, A. L., Siegel, P. T., Koepke, T., Moye, A. W., & Tice, S. (1994). Family therapy versus individual therapy for adolescent females with anorexia nervosa. *Journal of Developmental and Behavioral Pediatrics, 15,* 111–116.

Robin, A., Siegel, P., Moye, A., Gilroy, M., Dennis, A., & Sikand, A. (1999). A controlled comparison of family versus individual therapy for adolescents with anorexia nervosa. *Journal of American Academy of Child and Adolescent Psychiatry, 38,* 1482–1489.

Russell, G., Szmukler, G., Dare, L., & Eisler, I. (1987). An evaluation of family therapy in anorexia nervosa and bulimia nervosa. *Archives of General Psychiatry, 44,* 1047–1056.

Schaefer, C. E., & O'Connor, K. J. (Eds.). (1994). *Handbook of play therapy: Advances and innovations* (Vol. 2). New York: John Wiley & Sons.

Shisslak, C. M., Crago, M., & Neal, M. E. (1987). Prevention of eating disorders among adolescents. *Journal of Consulting and Clinical Psychology, 55,* 660–667.

Smolak, L., & Levine, M. P. (1996). Adolescent transitions and the development of eating problems. In L. Smolak, M. P. Levine, & R. Striegel-Moore (Eds.), *The developmental psychopathology of eating disorders: Implications for research, prevention and treatment* (pp. 207–234). Mahwah, NJ: Erlbaum.

Spitzer, R. L., Devlin, M., Walsh, B. T., Hasin, D., Wing, R. R., Marcus, M. D., Stunkard, A., Wadden, T., Yanovski, S., Agras, S., Mitchell, J. E., & Nonas, C. (1991). Binge eating disorder: To be or not to be in DSM-IV? *International Journal of Eating Disorders, 10,* 627–629.

Steiner, H., & Lock, J. (1998). Anorexia nervosa and bulimia nervosa in children and adolescents: A review of the past 10 years. *Journal of American Academy of Child and Adolescent Psychiatry, 37,* 352–359.

Stice, E., Mazotti, L., Weibel, D., & Agras, W. S. (2000). Dissonance prevention program decreases thin-ideal internalization, body dissatisfaction, dieting, negative affect, and bulimic symptoms: A preliminary experiment. *International Journal of Eating Disorders, 27,* 206–217.

Striegel-Moore, R. H., & Steiner-Adair, C. (1998). Primary prevention of eating disorders: Further considerations from a feminist perspective. In W. Vandereycken & G. Noordenbos (Eds.), *The prevention of eating disorders* (pp. 1–23). New York: New York University Press.

Timberlake, E. M., & Cutler, M. M. (Eds.). (2000). *Developmental play therapy in clinical social work.* Boston: Allyn and Bacon.

Walters, E. E., & Kendler, K. S. (1995). Anorexia nervosa and anorexic-like syndromes in a population-based female twin sample. *American Journal of Psychiatry, 151,* 64–71.

Wilson, G. T., & Fairburn, C. G. (1998). Treatments for eating disorders. In P. E. Nathan & J. M. Gorman (Eds.), *A guide to treatments that work* (pp. 501–530). New York: Oxford University Press.

Young, J., & Faneslow-Brown, P. (1996). Cognitive behaviour therapy for anxiety: Practical tips for using it with children. *Clinical Psychology Forum, 91,* 19–21.

CHAPTER 24

INTERVENTION WITH CHILDREN AND ADOLESCENTS

New Hope and Enduring Challenges

MARK W. FRASER

University of North Carolina at Chapel Hill

PAULA ALLEN-MEARES

University of Michigan

In the past 20 years, the findings from hundreds of studies allow us to be more sanguine about the effectiveness of programs for children and adolescents. Based on this research, the purpose of this book has been to summarize the latest findings on the prevalence, etiology, prevention, and treatment of major social problems in childhood and adolescence. One indicator of the growing hopefulness characterizing intervention for children and youth is the growing number of what might be called *model program* electronic resources, where organizations such as the Cochrane Collaboration in medicine or the Campbell Collaboration in social science have scanned the literature and developed searchable websites with systematic literature reviews and descriptions of empirically-supported programs. Shown in Table 24.1, these resources are exemplified by the Blueprints Series of the federal Office of Juvenile Justice and Delinquency Prevention (which describes promising programs to prevent violence) and the Promising Practices programs of the RAND Corporation (which describes model programs indexed to various "benchmarks" of child development).

Several commonalities emerge across these program reviews, the chapters in this book, and reviews published in the literature (see, e.g., U.S. Department of Health and Human Services, 2001). First, there is growing agreement on the standards of evidence for rating programs. Programs must be thoroughly evaluated, and they must produce positive findings related to significant social problems or factors that lead to social problems. Moreover, it is the pattern of findings and not a single finding that elicits a rating of "promising," "exemplary," or "model." These emerging standards or criteria involve at least one controlled trial (with random assignment to experimental and control groups), follow-up of at least 12 months, and (usually) independent replication. Most reviews also require measures of the

TABLE 24.1 Web-Based Sources of Information on Effective Programs

NAME AND SPONSOR	LOCATION (URL)	TYPES OF PROGRAMS
Blueprints Series *Source:* Office of Juvenile Justice and Delinquency Prevention, U.S. Department of Justice	http://www.colorado.edu/cspv/blueprints	Individual, family, peer, school, and neighborhood programs designed to prevent violence.
Campbell Collaboration *Sources:* various	http://www.campbellcollaboration.org/ (home page) http://www.aic.gov.au/campbellcj/ (justice group)	Searchable database of systematic reviews and literature related to social, behavior, and educational interventions. Special review groups for education, crime and justice, and social welfare.
Cochrane Collaboration *Sources (USA center):* National Library of Medicine, Milbank Memorial Fund, National Eye Institute, and others	http://www.cochrane.org/ (home site in United Kingdom) http://www.cochrane.us/index.htm (USA site)	Searchable database of systematic reviews of health-care interventions, including a variety of mental health disorders, substance abuse, sexually transmitted diseases, and other health problems (*Note:* requires subscription to obtain full reviews).
Model Programs *Source:* Center for Substance Abuse Prevention, U.S. Department of Health and Human Services	http://www.samhsa.gov/centers/csap/modelprograms	Individual, family, peer, school, and neighborhood programs designed to decrease substance abuse and other high-risk behaviors in children and adolescents.
Model Programs *Source:* Safe and Drug Free Schools, U.S. Department of Education	http://www.ed.gov/offices/OESE/SDFS/model_programs.html	School-based programs designed to promote healthy students and safe, disciplined, and drug-free schools.
Promising Practices Network *Source:* Rand Corporation and others	http://www.promisingpractices.net/	Individual, family, peer, school, and neighborhood programs designed to improve developmental outcomes for children, youth, and families.

strength of treatment (e.g., effect sizes on the order of .2 or .3) and indicators of treatment fidelity (e.g., use of treatment manuals and measures suggesting that the program can be delivered faithfully in a real-world setting). Some practice electronic resources—for example, the Model Programs resource developed by the Center for Substance Abuse Prevention of the U.S. Department of Health and Human Services and the Safe and Drug Free Schools resource developed by the U.S. Department of Education—use a panel review process for identifying and scoring programs. Experts from across the country review programs and the research supporting them. Then they determine which programs obtain the highest ratings.

Second, the same programs pop up on different resources, and these programs—many of which are discussed by chapter authors in this book—appear to have similar elements. They attempt to address a variety of risk factors related to targeted social or health problems. To address these risk factors, they provide several different kinds of services. Typically, these services include behavioral child management training for parents and teachers (or others who have child-care responsibilities), where principles such as providing contingencies of rewards for desired behaviors are taught and then applied with supervision in vivo. Most also include training for children or adolescents in problem solving, communications, anger management, impulse or arousal control, and other forms of self-regulation. And most also include some type of restructuring of the environment—creating new learning opportunities by changing the size or character of the classroom or after-school environment, altering the peers with whom a child interacts via group work or mentoring, or devising means for parents and teachers to communicate more readily by establishing home-school note systems or telecommunications.

Third, although they produce positive effects on targeted outcomes, many of the programs that appear in these reviews and in this book have a wide variety of effects. This is perhaps the most intriguing finding. These programs appear to produce unexpectedly diverse positive outcomes. Cited in chapters on youth violence, drug abuse, and gangs, a recent longitudinal follow-up of 329 children ($n = 144$ intervention; $n = 205$ control) who participated in a first- through sixth-grade drug abuse prevention program called Project SOAR (Skills, Opportunities, and Rewards, formerly the Seattle Social Development Project) exemplifies this serendipity.

The SOAR program was a complex intervention. It consisted of teacher training in classroom instruction and management of classroom behavior, child social and emotional skill development (problem-solving and drug-refusal skills), and parent training (behavior management skills, academic support, and skills to reduce risks for drug use). Research has shown that SOAR reduced drug use and delinquency (Hawkins, Catalano, Kosterman, Abbott, & Hill, 1999). But in a follow-up of participants at age 21, former-children-now-adults who received the intervention reported significantly fewer sexual partners. Females in the intervention group were less likely to have become pregnant and experienced birthing. Moreover, after controlling for socioeconomic status, African American participants had a significantly lower risk of contracting a sexually transmitted disease (Lonczak, Abbott, Hawkins, Kosterman, & Catalano, 2002). In itself, this is good news, but what is intriguing is that this project was rooted in research on substance abuse and delinquency. It was not designed to prevent adolescent pregnancy or to reduce HIV risk.

So is the finding just dumb luck? We don't think so. According to the Social Development Model, a risk-based framework that was developed concomitantly by the researchers who conceived of SOAR, the factors that produce delinquency and drug abuse are sufficiently similar to those that produce adolescent pregnancy that—in retrospect—an effect on adolescent pregnancy should have been anticipated (for a review of the Social Development Model, see Lonczak, Huang, Catalano, Hawkins, Hill, Abbott, Ryan, & Kosterman, 2001). Programs such as SOAR and others discussed in chapters throughout this book may have positive collateral results because risk factors for delinquency, drug use, academic failure, sexual activity, and other social problems are highly correlated (for a review, see Reid, Patterson, & Snyder, 2002).

Today, we have an increasingly complex understanding of risk factors, and we have a growing number of programs with SOAR-like findings. When Metzler, Taylor, and Eddy (2002, p. 1) analyzed programs listed on exemplary programs websites and in recent literature reviews, they concluded, "Many of the 'best' programs are being identified as the best approaches to address a wide variety of social problems, including preventing and treating mental health problems, drug abuse, delinquency, violence, and physical child abuse." In short, these programs appear to be effective in addressing factors that affect the quality of home life, parent-classroom partnerships, and the behavior management skills of parents, teachers, and children. When programs are effective in addressing these factors, they interrupt negative developmental trajectories associated with many different social and health problems.

DEVELOPING PRACTICE STRATEGIES

Developing effective interventions is a fundamental goal of practice and practice research. What else might we say about the interventions described in this book? If we look globally at the patterns in the research across various types of social and health problems, five simple but compelling conclusions can be drawn. On balance, recent research shows that

1. There are identifiable risk factors for social and health problems.
2. These risk factors range from constitutional to environmental influences.
3. Cumulative risk is generally more important than any single risk factor.
4. Some risk factors are malleable (i.e., responsive to specific change strategies).
5. When malleable risk factors are changed, developmental trajectories change.

Given this, we think that intervention should serve two general goals: (1) it should reduce risk and (2) it should promote protection. Of course, this is not easy. Developing a practice strategy starts with developing an understanding of risk factors, and then it requires a change strategy that is effective in changing risk or protective factors. That is, knowledge of risk and protective factors informs the designation of intervention goals, and activities within the intervention are selected because they reduce specific risk factors or they promote protection.

Addressing Cumulative and Problem-Specific Risk

The value of the risk and protective factor perspective is that it provides a multidisciplinary, cross-problem conceptual framework for intervention. Regardless of our professional training or the problem that confronts us, it helps us keep both individual and contextual issues foremost in our thinking. Developing an understanding of risk requires understanding the impact of cumulative risk and of problem-specific risk. In Chapter 2, Sameroff and Gutman showed that cumulative risk—the sheer number of risk factors—accounts for a variety of poor developmental outcomes in childhood and adolescence. But clearly some risk factors have more problem relevance than others.

The fact that cumulative risk is more important than single risk factors does not imply that the same risk factors affect all social and health problems. The cumulative effect of risk can include the effect of highly specific, problem-related risk factors. In Chapter 23 on eating disorders, Binford and colleagues identify one of these problem-specific risk factors as frequent maternal dieting or concern about body shape and weight. It is an important risk for eating disorders, but it is not much of a risk factor for other problems, such as gang violence and serious mental illness. By itself, is it a sufficient risk for eating disorders? Probably not. Its effect becomes important in the context of other risk factors. Like many problem-specific risks (including those with biological bases), its effect is triggered in the context of other risk factors. Acknowledging that there are some highly influential risk factors (e.g., the sudden death of both parents usually has an immediate impact on child development, having parents or siblings who are gang members has a strong effect on gang involvement, etc.), it is more the *number* of risk factors—their cumulation—than the *nature* of risk factors that produces poor developmental outcomes. To be sure, one has to understand the problem in term of its full risk "structure"—both risk factors that have high problem specificity (e.g., genetic risks for specific disorders) and those that have high common variation across problems (e.g., poverty or early academic failure). An understanding of the principal individual (both constitutional and learned), family, peer, school, neighborhood, and societal factors that give rise to social and health problems provides critical clues in devising more effective interventive strategies. Both cumulative and problem-specific factors are foundational in assessing risk.

Promotive and Protective Factors

In the same vein, an understanding of factors that suppress or moderate problems and that promote positive developmental outcomes in the face of risk also provides clues for devising more effective interventive strategies. We know far less about this. Sameroff and Gutman (Chapter 2) defined *promotive* factors as those influences that directly produce positive outcomes. Promotive factors can be conceptualized as the opposite of risk factors. Dimensionally, protection and risk are seen from this perspective as polar opposites. Lack of a strong parent/child bond of attachment, for example, can be considered a risk factor. Conversely, the presence of a strong parent/child bond can be considered a factor that "promotes" positive developmental outcomes. Sameroff and Gutman use the term *promotive* to contrast the risk end of a dimensional influence such as parent/child attachment.

In contrast to promotive factors, *protective* factors operate via risk. That is, they moderate risk and operate more strongly in the presence of adversity. A strong parent/child bond might have a protective effect on the relationship between neighborhood violence (high adversity) and gang membership. In neighborhoods where violence is high and where there are many opportunities to join gangs, parents who maintain strong bonds of attachment with their children may be more likely to structure after-school and weekend activities so that children have less exposure to gangs and the enticements associated with gang membership. As a promotive factor, parent/child bonds of attachment promote positive outcomes for children regardless of risk. A promotive effect can be thought of as an effect that elevates the odds of a positive developmental outcome in general. However, bonds of attachment add also an *extra increment of protection in the face of adversity*, such as high neighborhood violence. They seem to suppress risk or buffer children from risk. You may have heard protective factors described as having a "buffering effect" on risk factors. This idea is based in the concept of moderation—a protective factor moderates or buffers the effect of a risk factor. Sometimes it is thought of as a nonlinearity. It is interactive, operating more strongly at higher levels of risk.

Unfortunately, this distinction between promotive and protective factors is not yet widely accepted, and the term *protective* factor is often used to describe both promotive and protective effects. The authors of the Surgeon General's Report on Youth Violence (U.S. Department of Health and Human Services, 2001, p. 62) found that this approach "blurs the distinction between risk and protection, making them essentially the same thing." Recently, too, Michael Rutter (2000, p. 658), who has been a leader in the field of resilience, argued, "There is not much to be gained, apart from the introduction of unhelpful confusion, in calling the low risk end of a risk dimension a protective factor."

So, although the idea of promotive versus protective effects makes a useful distinction—particularly in light of the influence of literatures on strengths and assets—it is not clear whether the field will wind up using Sameroff and Gutman's terminology. It is awkward using the term *risk factor* to describe an influence that may at one end have a negative developmental effect and at the other end a positive developmental effect. For that reason, many authors use the term *protective factor* to include both promotive and protective effects. But, as suggested in the Surgeon General's report, this confounds different concepts.

Some scholars have distinguished different types of "protective" effects. Drawing on statistical models for expressing interactions and other types of effects, Luthar, Cicchetti, and Becker (2000) posited six different types of protective effects: (1) direct (main and mediating) protective, (2) protective-stabilizing, (3) protective-enhancing, (4) protective but reactive, (5) vulnerable-stable, and (6) vulnerable-reactive effects. From this perspective, for example, the protective value of an inoculation (say, for smallpox), which is realized only in the presence of a (smallpox) pathogen, is a protective-enhancing effect. It confers enhanced protection at the point of great risk (when inoculation may reduce harm), and it provides little added protection in the absence of risk. Today, there is an increasingly growing agreement that risk and protective factors must inform intervention. But in spite of their appeal, there is less agreement on how various types of moderating and mediating protective effects should be defined and labeled (for a more detailed discussion, see Fraser, Kirby, & Smokowski, 2003).

VARIATION IN RISK AND PROTECTIVE FACTORS

Tailoring Interventions on the Basis of Gender, Ethnicity, Culture, Race, and Sexual Orientation

Understanding the interplay of risk, promotive, and protective factors is complicated because their net influence often varies by gender, ethnicity, culture, race, and sexual orientation. Discussed by Potter (Chapter 4), Barbarin and colleagues (Chapter 3), and Longres and Etnyre (Chapter 5), these factors alter risk factors and, under some circumstances, provide added protection that, if malleable, can be integrated into intervention plans.

Gender. Girls and boys develop at different rates and, whether biological or environmental in origin, they tend to manifest different risk patterns. In Chapter 4, Potter argues that girls

> are much more likely to be victims of sexual assault by strangers, romantic partners, and family members. They are more likely to experience internalizing mental health problems such as depression and anxiety, and they are more likely to attempt suicide than are boys. Girls are more likely to endanger their health by extreme dieting practices and be diagnosed with eating disorders. Their links to some risky behaviors come through relationships.

Gender-based norms affect risk structures and must be considered in the design of interventions. Because girls tend to be more relational, strategies that incorporate verbal problem solving and communication may be more effective. Certainly, programs focused on aggressive behavior and drug abuse should consider relational aggression as a construct. Similarly, programs should incorporate gender-related constructs when they focus on problems where boys and girls clearly have different developmental trajectories or where problems appear to have a gender element. For example, recovery from sexual abuse, prevention of dating violence, and treatment of eating disorders have gendered etiological threads and risk structures that might be addressed—as one element of intervention—in girls-only groups.

Ethnicity, Culture, and Race. In a similar sense, ethnicity, culture, and race affect children and must be considered in the design of programs. According to Barbarin, McCandies, Coleman, and Atkinson (Chapter 3), ethnicity, culture, and race alter developmental outcomes in at least three ways. First, because economic inequality varies by ethnic and racial groupings, ethnicity, culture, and race affect the depth and diversity of resources available to children and the communities in which they live. Second, ethnicity, culture, and race introduce socialization practices that buffer against risk and, if malleable and included in the design of interventions, hold the potential to strengthen outcomes. Third, through stigmatizing social processes related to skin color, language, and other aspects of appearance, they affect opportunities and self-efficacy—the sense of having personal control over a range of possible outcomes in the context of a setting such as the classroom.

Understanding the aspects of ethnicity, culture, and race that promote resilience is an essential element of understanding risk structures. Resilient children do well in spite of exposure to risk (Fraser, 2003). They have internal (e.g., easy temperament) and external (e.g., insistent, involved mother) resources that permit them to prevail over adversity or to sustain a high level of performance in the face of stress. If we can understand why and how resilience works, we may be able to strengthen interventions for children who experience economic disadvantage and stigmatizing social processes. Current studies are beginning to provide some clues. For example, they suggest that having an ethnic or racial identity may promote positive developmental outcomes (Laursen & Williams, 2002; O'Brien-Caughy, Randolph, & O'Campo, 2002). Similarly developing and using culture-based aspects of family life such as *familism* may contribute to the effectiveness of interventions (Vega, Gil, & Wagner, 1998).

Sexual Orientation.   Although less is known about it, sexual orientation also affects both the risks to which children are exposed and the protective resources that may be available to solve developmental problems. In many U.S. cities, gay-affirming social and health services are now available and, in many schools, students who come out find support among teachers. But coming out can be a painful process. Longres and Etnyre (Chapter 5) describe a variety of issues that must be addressed in working with gay, lesbian, and bisexual children. These include such contextual factors as the level of homophobia in the community and such idiographic factors as the end of expectations for heterosexual relations and isolation or harassment from peers. The challenge, they argue, is distinguishing between "basically healthy youth who are experiencing the normal vicissitudes of coming out and those youth whose experiences are mediated by personality and mental disorders rooted in dysfunctional family patterns."

POVERTY AND CONTEXTUAL INFLUENCES

In addition to the effects of gender, ethnicity, culture, race, and sexual orientation, recent research suggests that *the influence of the context has been vastly underestimated.* Environmental factors such as poverty are strongly implicated in the development of social, academic, and health problems in childhood and adolescence. Well-known biological risks—such as exposure to lead, cadmium, and other environmental toxins—directly affect health and behavior. Children's exposure to environmental toxins is context dependent. Poor children live in more hostile environments. Discussed by Linver, Fuligni, Hernandez, and Brooks-Gunn in Chapter 6, children in low-income families are more likely to be exposed to hazardous materials, inadequate schools (with less well-trained teachers), and dangerous neighborhoods.

In the near future, we are likely to develop far more precise understandings of the ways in which the physical and social environment interact with individual risk factors, especially biological risk factors, to influence developmental outcomes. Sequences in which the context affects neurochemistry and which, in turn, neurophysiological factors affect behavior are likely to become part and parcel of understanding human behavior (see, e.g., Evans & English, 2002). We already know, for example, that variation in hypothalamic, pituitary, and adrenal functioning—which relates to the secretion of cortisol, a stress-related hormone—is linked to adaptive capacity (for a review of neurobiological mechanisms, see Vance, 2001).

In addition to biologically mediated influences, the context exerts both direct and indirect social influence. In Chapter 6, Linver and colleagues describe how poverty directly affects children by lowering the quality of their food and shelter, and how it indirectly affects children by placing parents under such constant strain that they find it difficult to respond consistently to a child's needs. Contextual effects often appear to be mediated by, or at least entangled with, family and individual factors (for detailed discussions, see Duncan & Raudenbush, 2001; McLoyd, 1998). The sheer hassle of dealing with hostile neighborhoods and inadequate schools make parenting in low-income communities harder.

It should be no surprise that social problems have high context dependence; however, the contribution of the context is only now beginning to be understood. In a three-year longitudinal study of 425 10-year-old boys from 73 neighborhoods in Pittsburgh, poverty, neighborhood conditions, and impulsivity were related to delinquency (Lynam, Caspi, Moffitt, Wikstrom, Loeber, & Novak, 2000). Controlling for poverty and neighborhood conditions, impulsivity (an individual-level risk factor) was highly predictive of future offending. Consistent with prior research, neighborhood effects (e.g., percentage of families below poverty line, percentage of unemployed men, and percentage of households receiving public assistance) were modestly related to delinquency after controlling for impulsivity and poverty. The cumulative direct effect of neighborhood was weaker than the effect of impulsivity. In the past, this pattern of findings has been interpreted as showing the relatively greater importance of individual over contextual effects. However, Lynam and associates persevered. They found that in neighborhoods where conditions were the worst, the correlation between impulsivity and delinquency was much stronger. In other words, the context potentiated impulsivity—it exacerbated an individual effect. It is not clear why this happened. It could be that poorer communities have lower levels of collective efficacy, both formal and informal social supports and social controls. But the point is that the effect of higher-order contexts such as the neighborhood (versus lower-order or more proximal contexts such as the family) is nonlinear. It is expressed, at least in part, in interactions. An understanding of risk is incomplete if it fails to include Person X Environment interaction. Whether biological or psychological, individual risk factors appear to vary—perhaps nonlinearly—as a function of the context (for an example of Genetic X environment interaction, see Cadoret, Yates, Troughton, Woodworth, & Stewart, 1995).

IS THERE A COMMON RISK MECHANISM THAT INFLUENCES DEVELOPMENTAL TRAJECTORIES?

The fact that interventions that address both contextual and individual risk appear to have a wide range of positive outcomes. And the fact that some family and peer influences (e.g., parental monitoring and association with risk-taking peers) appear to elevate the odds for many different social and health problems suggest that a common mechanism may underlie seemingly dissimilar problems such as unwanted pregnancy, drug use, dropout, sexually transmitted diseases, and delinquency. This is not a new idea (see, e.g., Jessor & Jessor, 1977), but it is receiving new support from a variety of sources. A study designed to prevent smoking tracked 698 adolescents for 18 months. Ary, Duncan, Biglan, Metzler, Noell, and Smolkowski (1999) separately assessed antisocial behavior, sexual activity, academic failure, marijuana use, tobacco use, and alcohol use. Each measure was highly correlated. They were so highly correlated that a composite "problem behavior" index was created.

Ary and colleagues then asked: What are the precursors of scoring highly on this multiproblem index? They wanted to identify the risk factors for what seemed to be a common clustering of interrelated adolescent problems—antisocial behavior, sexual activity, academic failure, marijuana use, tobacco use, and alcohol use. Holding aside the effect of the intervention (which was positive), they identified a three-step risk mechanism that seemed to lead to high problem ratings. At the first step, family conflict led to poor family involvement. At the second step, poor family involvement led to inadequate parental monitoring. Then, in the third step of the risk sequence, inadequate parental monitoring led to both association with substance using peers and high scores on the problem index (Ary, Duncan, Biglan, Metzler, Noell, & Smolkowski, 1999; see also Duncan, Duncan, Biglan, & Ary, 1998). In other words, a common risk mechanism predicted a variety of problems. In more recent research, this model was shown to apply to children and families across three ethnic groups (European American, Mexican American, and American Indian) and with gender (Biglan & Smolkowski, 2002). Moreover, the core elements of the model have been shown to predict delinquency in an entirely separate study involving an urban sample of African American, European American, and Latino adolescents (Henry, Tolan, & Gorman-Smith, 2001). Thus, at least at the family and peer levels, a latent risk sequence involving family interaction and subsequent peer influence appears common across a variety of social and health problems in adolescence (see also Patterson, Dishion, & Yoerger, 2000; Reid, Patterson, & Snyder, 2002). Devising interventions to interrupt this risk sequence is a major challenge.

DO WE KNOW ENOUGH?

We know a lot. In particular, we know so much about family and peer processes that interventions focused on antisocial, aggressive behavior might be considered somewhat strange if they did not attempt to disrupt the risk sequence just described. Both family- and school-based interventions have been shown effective in interrupting this risk sequence. As indicated in chapters of this book on autism, bullying, dropping out, drug use, emotional/behavioral disorders, and youth violence, it is particularly apparent that schools are a key in preventing social and health problems. Their mandate cannot be limited to academic achievement. They are society's central public mechanism for socialization, and recent studies, such as SOAR, suggest that their mission may be too narrowly conceived. When teachers are better trained, when social skills training is infused into core curricula, and when families are involved in parent-classroom partnerships, developmental trajectories that lead to costly social problems can be changed (see, e.g., Ialongo, Poduska, Werthamer, & Kellam, 2001; Lonczak, Abbott, Hawkins, Kosterman, & Catalano, 2002).

CHALLENGES

Although we have learned a great deal about risk sequences and intervention, major challenges endure. First, the effect sizes observed in intervention studies continue to be modest. Statistically significant differences between intervention and control groups have been observed in major studies across a variety of settings. But large numbers of children and their families are not responsive to intervention. They fail to respond to recruitment or, once recruited, they drop out or fail to comply to intervention protocols. For many children and families, intervention occurs too late—after developmental trajectories are so firmly established that only costly out-of-home placement or residential treatment remain as options. We need a flowering of intervention studies to

- Identify innovative ways to recruit children and their families into prevention services (before minor problems exacerbate into major problems).
- Alter negative family and peer processes.

- Infuse school curricula with social developmental content as well as academic content.
- Strengthen protective mechanisms related to culture, religion, and neighborhood.

Second, too little is known about the effects of protection and ways to change it. Much can be learned by studying resilience—the ways children prevail over adversity. If this knowledge can be developed and systematized, it holds the potential to increase the effectiveness of interventions.

Third, because family and peer factors have contextual dependencies, programs and policies that alter contextual risk may be as or more effective than individual- or family-centered interventions. However, the relative influence of contextual risk is only now being teased out of individual and family effects. Moreover, although advances are being made in developing theory related to the effects of disorganized neighborhoods and communities (Sampson, Morenoff, & Earls, 1999), there are almost no rigorous studies of the effectiveness of contextually focused interventions at the neighborhood and community levels.

Fourth, the risk and protective factor perspective and the interventions that are arising from it do not appear to be rapidly penetrating the central systems that serve children, youth, and families. The services provided by child welfare, education, juvenile justice, and mental health systems lag behind the available knowledge (Burns, Landsverk, Kellsher, Faw, Hazen, & Keeler, 2001). In spite of significant gains in knowledge regarding the prevention of social and health problems, principal child and family systems rely on programs where children are removed from normative settings and placed in foster or group care, special education classrooms, residential treatment, hospitals, and other institutions. Some children need and benefit from this type of care. However, as shown throughout this book, a growing number of family-, school-, and community-based prevention and early intervention studies with positive findings suggest that the central systems serving children and families could make reforms that would significantly improve outcomes for many children and adolescents. In a comprehensive review of the services provided by child welfare, education, juvenile justice, and mental health systems, Burns and colleagues (2001) concluded:

> A critical…question is how to transfer efficacious treatment—in-home treatment, parenting training, and other approaches—into service sectors, particularly schools, where children and parents are likely to use and benefit from such services…. To transfer the evidence-based interventions into usual clinical practice constitutes a long-term agenda. (p. 302)

This is perhaps the greatest public policy and practice challenge. In the context of developing further our understanding of the social conditions that both create and suppress risk, and while pressing forward with research to further advance interventive knowledge, we must change practice. It cannot be a long-term agenda. The findings emerging from dozens and dozens of studies hold great promise for children and adolescents. Chronicled throughout this book, this knowledge can transform practice and the lives of many children.

REFERENCES

Ary, D. V., Duncan, T. E., Biglan, A., Metzler, C. W., Noell, J. W., & Smolkowski, K. (1999). Development of adolescent problem behavior. *Journal of Abnormal Child Psychology, 27,* 141–150.

Biglan, A., & Smolkowski, K. (2002). Intervention effects on adolescent drug use and critical influences on the development of problem behavior. In D. B. Kandel (Ed.), *Stages and pathways of drug involvement: Examining the Gateway Hypothesis* (pp. 158–183). New York: Cambridge University Press.

Burns, B. J., Landsverk, J., Kelleher, K., Faw, L., Hazen, A., & Keeler, G. (2001). Mental health, education, child welfare, and juvenile justice service use. In R. Loeber & D. P. Farrington (Eds.), *Child delinquents: Development, intervention, and service needs* (pp. 273–303). Thousand Oaks, CA: Sage.

Cadoret, R. J., Yates, W. R., Troughton, E., Woodworth, G., & Stewart, M. (1995). Genetic-environment interaction in the genesis of aggressivity and conduct disorders. *Archives of General Psychiatry, 52,* 916–924.

Duncan, G. J., & Raudenbush, S. W. (2001). Neighborhoods and adolescent development: How can we determine the links? In A. Booth & A. C. Crouter (Eds.), *Does it take a village?* (pp. 105–136). Mahwah, NJ: Erlbaum.

Duncan, S. C., Duncan, T. E., Biglan, A., & Ary, D. (1998). Contributions of the social context to the development of adolescent substance use: A multivariate latent growth modeling approach. *Drug and Alcohol Dependence, 50,* 57–71.

Evans, G. W., & English, K. (2002). The environment of poverty: Multiple stressor exposure, psychophysiological stress, and socioemotional adjustment. *Child Development, 73*(4), 1238–1248.

Fraser, M. W. (Ed.). (2003). *Risk and resilience in childhood: An ecological perspective* (2nd ed.). Washington, DC: NASW Press.

Fraser, M. W., Kirby, L. D., & Smokowski, P. R. (2003). Risk and resilience in childhood. In M. W. Fraser (Ed.), *Risk and resilience in childhood: An ecological perspective* (2nd ed.). Washington, DC: NASW Press.

Hawkins, J. D., Catalano, R. F., Kosterman, R., Abbott, R., & Hill, K. G. (1999). Preventing adolescent health-risk behaviors by strengthening protection during childhood. *Archives of Pediatric and Adolescent Medicine, 153,* 226–234.

Henry, D. B., Tolan, P. H., & Gorman-Smith, D. (2001). Longitudinal family and peer group effects on violence and nonviolent delinquency. *Journal of Clinical Child Psychology, 30*(1), 172–186.

Jessor, R., & Jessor, S. L. (1977). *Problem behavior and psychosocial development: A longitudinal study of youth.* New York: Academic Press.

Laursen, B., & Williams, V. (2002). The role of ethnic identity in personality development. *Paths to successful development: Personality in the life course* (pp. 203–226). New York: Cambridge University Press.

Lonczak, H. S., Abbott, R. D., Hawkins, J. D., Kosterman, R., & Catalano, R. F. (2002). Effects of the Seattle Social Development Project on sexual behavior, pregnancy, birth, and sexually transmitted disease outcomes by age 21 years. *Archives of Pediatric and Adolescent Medicine, 156,* 438–447.

Lonczak, H. S., Huang, B., Catalano, R. F., Hawkins, J. D., Hill, K. G., Abbott, R. D., Ryan, J. A., & Kosterman, R. (2001). The social predictors of adolescent alcohol misuse: A test of the Social Development Model. *Journal of Studies on Alcohol, 62*(2), 179–189.

Luthar, S. S., Cicchetti, D., & Becker, B. (2000). The construct of resilience: A critical evaluation and guidelines for future work. *Child Development, 71*(3), 543–562.

Lynam, D. R., Caspi, A., Moffitt, T. E., Wikstrom, P. H., Loeber, R., & Novak, S. (2000). The interaction between impulsivity and neighborhood context on offending: The effects of impulsivity are stronger in poorer neighborhoods. *Journal of Abnormal Psychology, 109*(4), 563–574.

McLoyd, V. C. (1998). Socioeconomic disadvantage and child development. *American Psychologist, 53*(2), 185–204.

Metzler, C. W., Taylor, T. K., & Eddy, J. M. (2002, May). *Finding common ground among best practice lists: The evidence base and program elements of top family-focused and school-based programs.* Presentation at the annual meeting of the Society for Prevention Research, Seattle, WA.

O'Brien-Caughy, M., Randolph, S. M., & O'Campo, P. J. (2002). The Afrocentric Home Environment Inventory: An observational measure of the racial socialization features of the home environment for African American preschool children. *Journal of Black Psychology, 28*(1), 37–52.

Patterson, G. R., Dishion, T. J., & Yoerger, K. (2000). Adolescent growth in new forms of problem behavior: Macro- and micro-peer dynamics. *Prevention Science, 1*(1), 3–13.

Reid, J. B., Patterson, G. R., & Snyder, J. (2002). *Antisocial behavior in children and adolescents.* Washington, DC: American Psychological Association.

Rutter, M. (2000). Resilience reconsidered: Conceptual considerations, empirical findings, and policy implications. In J. P. Shonkoff & S. J. Meisels (Eds.), *Handbook of early childhood intervention* (2nd ed., pp. 651–682). New York: Cambridge University Press.

Sampson, R. J., Morenoff, J. D., & Earls, F. (1999). Beyond social capital: Spatial dynamics of collective efficacy for children. *American Sociological Review, 64*, 633–660.

U.S. Department of Health and Human Services. (2001). *Youth violence: A report of the surgeon general.* Rockville, MD: U.S. Department of Health and Human Services, Centers for Disease Control and Prevention, National Center for Injury Prevention and Control; Substance Abuse and Mental Health Services Administration, Center for Mental Health Services; and National Institutes of Health, National Institute of Mental Health.

Vance, J. E. (2001). Neurobiological mechanisms of psychosocial resiliency. In J. M. Richman & M. W. Fraser (Eds.), *The context of youth violence: Resilience, risk, and protection* (pp. 43–81). Westport, CT: Praeger Publishers.

Vega, W. A., Gil, A. G., & Wagner, E. (1998). Cultural adjustments and Latino adolescent drug use. In W. Vega & A. G. Gil (Ed.), *Drug use and ethnicity early adolescence* (pp. 125–148). New York: Plenum Press.

INDEX